12/2009

"A study of burning focus and intimate depth."

— KIRKUS REVIEWS

"Anthony Pitch looks through a wide-angle lens at the assassination in his emotionally wrenching new account . . . Pitch worked on the book for nine years, and his dedication shows in its pitch-perfect level of detail. Quotes from diaries of the time, some of them apparently never published before, portray the nation's post-assassination grief in high relief . . . In perhaps the most revealing parts of the book, Pitch explores the deplorable treatment of the alleged conspirators, their circus trial, and the remarkable escape of conspirator John Surratt, who hid at the Vatican.

Other recent books have covered some of the same ground. But *'They Have Killed Papa Dead!'* provides an excellent overview, bringing thoughtful analysis to one of the most sensational events in American history."

— *The Christian Science Monitor*

"Anthony Pitch's remarkable new book on the Lincoln assassination aches with sadness and pulses with page-turning excitement. The narrative is authoritative, the research impeccable to the last detail, and the style wonderfully, magically evocative of the period. This is a perfect storm of a book — so well done at every level of scholarship and style that one cannot imagine another version of the story at once as tense and heartbreaking. To me, the mark of a superior story-teller comes with the telling of a familiar saga: in Pitch's work, though one knows how the book will end, one is almost compelled to read on, in anticipation of the next scene, the next chapter. I applaud and highly recommend the book."

— HAROLD HOLZER,

co-chair, US Abraham Lincoln Bicentennial Commission

and winner of a Lincoln Prize

"What, another book on the assassination of Abraham Lincoln? What more can be said about the regicide of our greatest President? Actually, Anthony Pitch's beautifully written narrative stands on its own as a splendid contribution to the subject. It is told by an author who has an intimate knowledge of all the sites related to the assassination and the trials that followed."

FRANK J. WILLIAMS,
Chief Justice of the Rhode Island Supreme Court and founding chair of The Lincoln Forum

"So well-written and -researched that it will add greatly to our knowledge of Lincolniana."

DR. WAYNE TEMPLE,
author of many books on Lincoln and deputy director of the Illinois State Archives

"The assassination of Abraham Lincoln is one of the tragic moments in the American experience. The story of that awful night and its aftermath is familiar to most of us, but Anthony Pitch's masterful prose brings it to life with a wealth of compelling detail and a sense of immediacy that makes it seem startlingly new. This is history as it should be told, in an engrossing book that is truly worthy of its subject."

RICHARD MOE, *president,*
National Trust for Historic Preservation

" '*They Have Killed Papa Dead!*' abundantly displays the skills of a master storyteller and a tenacious researcher."

DR. RICHARD BAKER, *historian and author*

"THEY HAVE KILLED PAPA DEAD!"

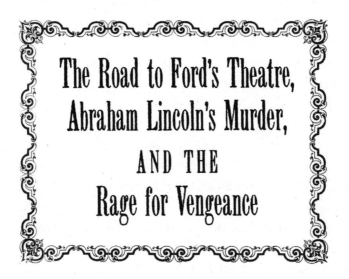

The Road to Ford's Theatre,
Abraham Lincoln's Murder,
AND THE
Rage for Vengeance

ANTHONY S. PITCH

STEERFORTH PRESS
HANOVER, NEW HAMPSHIRE

Copyright © 2008 by Anthony S. Pitch

ALL RIGHTS RESERVED

For information about permission to reproduce
selections from this book, write to:
Steerforth Press L.L.C., 45 Lyme Road, Suite 208,
Hanover, New Hampshire 03755

The Library of Congress has cataloged the hardcover as follows:

Pitch, Anthony.
 They have killed Papa dead! : the road to Ford's Theatre, Abraham Lincoln's
murder, and the rage for vengeance / Anthony S. Pitch. — 1st ed.
  p. cm.
 Includes bibliographical references and index.
 ISBN 978-1-58642-158-8
 1. Lincoln, Abraham, 1809–1865 — Assassination. 2. Lincoln, Abraham, 1809–
1865 — Assassination — Sources. 3. Assassins — United States — History — 19th
century. 4. Prisoners — United States — History — 19th century. 5. Political
culture — United States — History — 19th century. 6. Revenge — Social aspects
— United States — History — 19th century. 7. Revenge — Political aspects —
United States — History — 19th century. I. Title.
 E457.5.P58 2009
 973.7092–dc22
                2008043222

ISBN (paperback): 978-1-58642-162-5

FIRST PAPERBACK EDITION

For my wife, Marion
So much like a wildflower

For my grandchildren, Kayla and Maya
Who will hopefully learn from the past

And in memory of Lucky, our beloved beagle,
Who lay by my side while I wrote
Until the day she died in my arms

CONTENTS

"There are a thousand ways of getting at a man
if it is desired that he should be killed."
ABRAHAM LINCOLN

"When needed most he has been taken from us."
CHARLES MORRELL
Union soldier camped outside Richmond

"I could have jumped upon the shoulders of each as they hung."
BENJAMIN BROWN FRENCH
Commissioner of Public Buildings

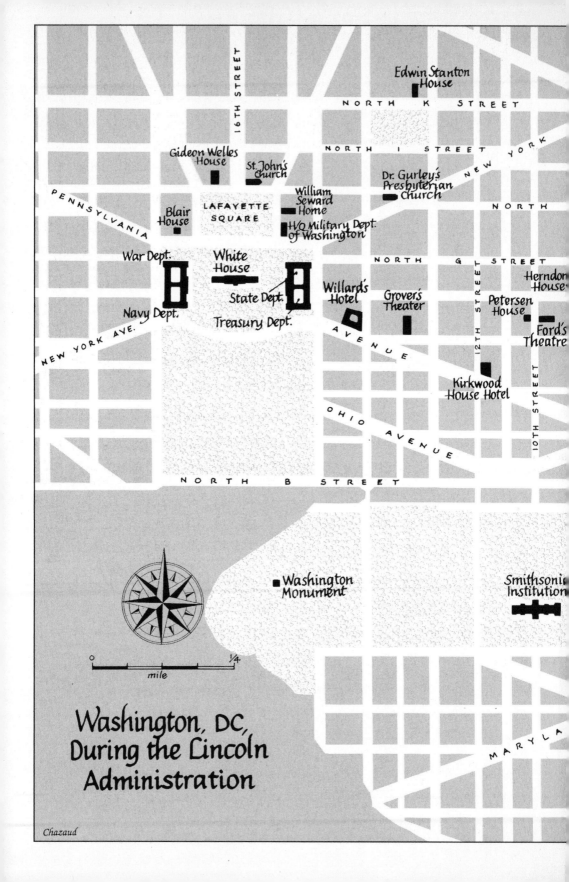

Washington, DC, During the Lincoln Administration

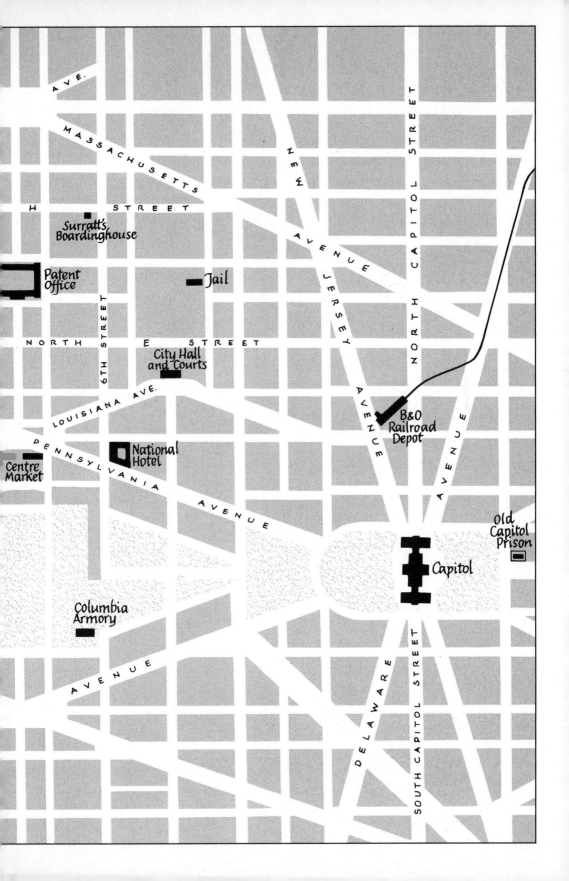

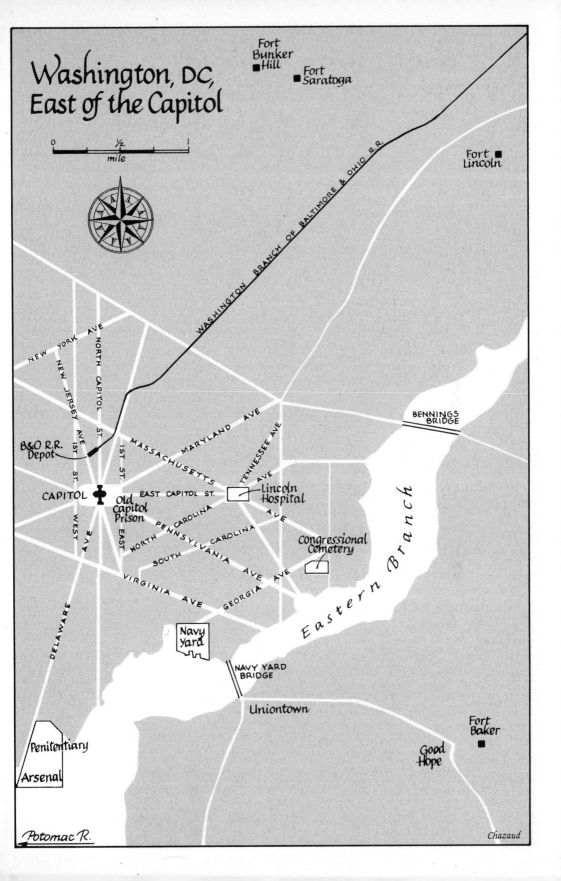

PREFACE

I was unprepared for the derision that came my way soon after I began researching this book. Critics assumed that nothing new could be found to justify publication of yet another volume on the assassination of Abraham Lincoln. I always replied that five hundred artists painting the same landscape would come up with five hundred different canvases, none of which could be stamped as definitive.

Nine years later my tale is told and *"They Have Killed Papa Dead!"* bulges with new finds. It is unlikely they could have been uncovered by anyone living beyond my commuting distance, twenty miles from the Library of Congress and the National Archives. Proximity to these institutions gave me the luxury of searching for primary source material for weeks on end, year after year.

From the outset I worked on the assumption that nineteenth-century Washingtonians would more likely have confided in their daily chronicles and extended families than in officialdom or anyone else. And so I went hunting for private letters, diaries, and journals, the authentic voices of contemporaneous observers. There was no doubt they would provide texture, insight, and color for the era.

I never expected such a sequence of surprises. Many voices began to speak, as if competing to break confidences and disclose impressions. Very early into my research I could not stifle a whistle on finding a letter from Benjamin Brown French, commissioner of public buildings, describing how he forcibly restrained John Wilkes Booth from doing possible harm to President Lincoln in the rotunda of the US Capitol during second inaugural ceremonies, six weeks before the assassination. When I found a later letter by French, his yearning for vengeance was as fresh as the day he wrote of the quartet of conspirators put to death for Lincoln's murder: "I could have jumped upon the shoulders of each as they hung, after the ancient manner of rendering death certain." With oversight of White House expenditures, French

probably knew Mary Todd Lincoln better than any other public official, which gave credence to a confidence he shared in private correspondence after the assassination, of the president's wife purchasing
about one thousand dollars' worth of mourning goods a month
before the murder. "What do you suppose possessed her to do it!
Please keep that fact in your own house."

As testimony in the "everlasting" trial of the conspirators came to
a close, one of the rigidly stern military judges figuratively leapt out
of the courtroom to write his wife, "I feel like a boy out of school."
In another letter to a spouse, the irritable architect of the Capitol,
Thomas Walter, confessed to being unmoved by the obsequies that
had overcome other Washingtonians, regretting instead that Lincoln's
lying in state "stops work another day, which is wholly useless."
One diarist fortunate to enter the White House to view Lincoln's
coffin (tens of thousands were turned away at the gates) came away
with the lasting impression of its being "studded with great numbers
of silver nails." Another chronicler, standing within twenty feet of
the president during the second inaugural address, recalled Lincoln's
"loud, rather shrill, distinct, far-reaching voice."

Tracking the escape of co-conspirator John Surratt to Rome, at a
time when the pope's temporal authority was crumbling in the face
of armed opponents intent on unifying the country, led me to correspondence between the US Minister to the Papal States and the State
Department in Washington. In one extraordinary letter, the American
diplomat reported that several officials in the papal government had
confided to him that "if the Pope felt to abandon Rome he might seek
refuge in the United States." The decline of papal political power and
the Vatican's need for allies may well have influenced the pope to
surrender Surratt into the custody of American officials.

As if to vindicate years in quest of new material, I unearthed an
electrifying letter in the National Archives from one of the convicted
conspirators, Samuel Arnold, to his nemesis, Secretary of War Edwin
Stanton. When I found it just months before finishing this book, I was
probably the only person to have read it since it was filed into virtual
oblivion 143 years earlier. In his distinctively neat, right-sloping

script, Arnold had applied for a job three months *after* enthusiastically signing on to John Wilkes Booth's madcap scheme to kidnap the president. Even Arnold overlooked this letter in the trial that took place six months after he wrote it, for he never mentioned it to solicit belief that he had wavered in support of the conspiracy.

My luckiest find came in a sprawling warehouse filled with antiques from a consortium of dealers in the quaint Pennsylvania town of New Oxford, ten miles east of Gettysburg. I do not recall why I suddenly looked up after exploring rooms full of aging and rusty exhibits, but the framed page of a broadsheet newspaper caught my eye and I had to buzz the reception desk for help in hauling it down. The glass-enclosed front page had columns of print about a credible plot to abduct President Lincoln and carry him off to the Confederate capital of Richmond. Until that moment I had dismissed a crucial prosecution witness, Louis Weichmann, as a perjurer or at best forgetful, for having testified, "I remember seeing in the New York *Tribune* of March 19, the capture of President Lincoln fully discussed . . ." I assumed he meant 1865, the year of the assassination, and had scanned many editions of the *Tribune* on that and surrounding dates, looking for the story, but had always drawn a blank. Only now did I know why it had eluded me. The framed broadsheet happened to be the same edition Weichmann had referred to in his testimony — the New York *Tribune* of March 19, *1864.* Weichmann, it turned out, had told the truth.

I have always believed Lincoln's assassination to be the saddest story in American history. This man of inestimable humanity had risen to the presidency, despite a self-described "defective" education, with no one to give him a leg up in life. Many warmed to his abundance of humor, wisdom, compassion, and judgment. Add to that his enviable gift for profound and melodious expression, and it is easy to understand why his legacy continues to resonate. Less evident is the grief that endures among Lincoln devotees. A contemporary mourner likened the national sorrow to a biblical plague, "as though some Herod had robbed each home of its first-born." The passage of time has in no way diminished the loss; successive generations continue to mourn. I will never forget taking a visitor, the former premier of New South Wales, Australia, on a tour of Lincoln assassination sites in Washington, DC. During the tour, he remarked that he grieves on the anniversary of Abraham Lincoln's death. Surely this was one measure of the sixteenth president's place in history.

———— ✦ ◆ ✦ ————

CHAPTER 1

"Lincoln Shall Not Pass through Baltimore Alive"

As President-elect Abraham Lincoln's train prepared to chug noisily out of the Great Western Railroad Depot in Springfield, Illinois, on a cold, wet February 11, 1861, security officials far to the east worked overtime to prevent his assassination. The exhausting railroad journey would take him across half the country before passing through the slave state of Maryland into neighboring Washington, DC, for the inauguration on March 4. Both the state and the nation's capital teemed with slaveholders and Southern sympathizers impatient for secession and political violence. The most extreme wanted Lincoln dead and his supporters terrorized into silence. A Bostonian visiting Baltimore, who had his head shaved for calling Lincoln a gentleman, wrote the president-elect: "It will be madness for you to attempt to reach Washington at any time."[1] But Lincoln had refused to take special precautions, spurning the offer of a Chicagoan to round up others and accompany him as bodyguards, explaining, "There is no immediate necessity for employing the proffered help."[2] Aware of the tensions that threatened the Union and perhaps his own life, Lincoln told the well-wishers at Springfield, "I now leave not knowing when, or whether ever, I may return, with a task before me greater than that which rested upon [George] Washington."[3]

General Winfield Scott, seventy-four, overseeing military defenses in Washington, let slip to a few insiders that the secessionists hoped to kill the president-elect together with anyone in close line of succession and all prominent members of Lincoln's Republican Party, in the hope of decapitating the Union government and opening the way for rule by Southerners.[4] Scott, who at six foot five was the imposing hero of the

War of 1812 and the Mexican-American War, found a letter on his own desk vowing that Lincoln, President James Buchanan, and the general himself would be killed by Inauguration Day.[5] There was open talk of a coup d'état. Some had threatened to block the tally of presidential electoral votes scheduled to take place inside the US Capitol on February 13. Others vowed to disrupt the inauguration less than three weeks later.[6] The capital itself, with a population of sixty-one thousand,[7] was in imminent danger of seizure by Maryland secessionists, who wanted to reclaim land that had once belonged to their state.[8] A virulently anti-government group, the National Volunteers, had recently evolved from a political association into paramilitary units, their ranks swollen with slaveholders and others angered by the plummeting value of slaves and land since Lincoln's election.[9] Many expected that the organization would take the lead in fomenting violent opposition to the incoming administration. Several hundred members had already stormed the headquarters of the victorious Republican Party in downtown Washington the night Lincoln won the election, firing pistols, ransacking the interior, terrorizing the occupants, and inciting arson before police moved in.[10]

Rumors were rife, and some people feared that mobs might make good on threats to burn the city. Residents looking grave moved about in a state of anxiety, heightened by the sound of military drums, uneasy at the presence of so many men in uniform, and alarmed by the great number of strangers who had arrived. Washingtonians became suspiciously watchful, some taking to sleeping within easy reach of loaded firearms.[11] The sense of peril was palpable. "I am afraid that much is kept from the ears of the timid," one woman wailed in a letter to her uncle farming twenty-five miles south of Washington.[12] Anna Maria Thornton, widow of the first architect of the Capitol, repetitively wrote "gloomy" to register the daily mood in her diary.[13] When a salute of thirty-four guns boomed across the city on January 29 to mark the admission of Kansas into the Union, many mistook it for the outbreak of insurrection.[14]

Even though Scott urged his staff to be vigilant, he cautioned against rash provocation, warning, "We are now in such a state that a dog-fight might cause the gutters of the capital to run with blood."[15]

Scott scrambled to bolster the defenses and protect public property. Five weeks before the inauguration he warned Secretary of War Joseph Holt of grave dangers to the capital unless more troops arrived. "It is not necessary to be an alarmist to believe that the Federal metropolis will be at the next inauguration — nay, on 13 February, and even much earlier — in great peril, and I am obliged to add that without a considerable augmentation of troops I do not feel that I can guarantee its safety during the next five days."[16]

Intelligence from security agents, spies, informants, and loyalists in almost half the states, even from those in rebellion, confirmed the threat of imminent insurrection and assassination. Word from the latest clandestine meeting of the National Volunteers was that as many as two thousand men devoted to the Confederacy could be relied upon to seize the nation's capital.[17]

Scott could not depend on Washington's militia of about four hundred men, because more than half were suspected of being disloyal and probably would defect to the rebels. The remainder were too inexperienced to be of much use.[18] There were only one hundred policemen, with another twenty-eight Capitol police — recently doubled just for the inauguration — whose commander was ready to join the secessionists the moment neighboring Virginia made good on its threat to secede.[19] John Blake, commissioner of public buildings, appealed to the secretary of war to arm them with muskets and ammunition because Colt pistols would be inadequate "if the building should be attacked by a considerable force."[20] Blake had the Capitol police in a state of "unusual vigilance" to guard against "surprise by evil-disposed persons" lying in wait to sneak into the building.[21] Scott had fewer than five hundred artillerymen, infantry, sappers, and miners, and only 240 marines to deploy. They would be spread thin guarding the city armory and other vulnerable points.[22]

It was a combustible mix ready to ignite. Only a huge influx of loyalist forces, it seemed, could protect against assassination and save the capital from falling to the rebels. But Scott was hamstrung by regional rivalries, aware that he could not recruit help randomly from any state. "No regiment or company can be brought here from a distance without producing hurtful jealousies in this vicinity," he wrote the governor of New York. The sole exception, he noted, was the New York Seventh Infantry Regiment, which had become "somewhat national" and highly respected after escorting the remains of President James Monroe from New York to Richmond, Virginia, and for attending the dedication of a statue of George Washington in Washington.[23] He would have called for ten thousand men to protect the capital if he had the authority, but he knew President James Buchanan would never acquiesce, believing it would ignite even more fury among secessionists in Virginia and Maryland.[24] Scott settled for far fewer, pleading with Secretary of War Holt to transfer to Washington "at once" — or at least several days before the presidential ballot count — artillery batteries from West Point and Fort McHenry, infantrymen temporarily in Texas, and seven companies of volunteers offered by the governor of Maryland.[25] A week later he telegraphed a military barracks in Pennsylvania for the immediate dispatch of forty mounted cavalrymen, with the remainder to follow as soon as possible.[26]

Scott acted boldly. Even though he was aged and infirm, and his glory days long gone, he was still an icon, known by the affectionate nickname Old Fuss and Feathers for his delight in wearing colorful military uniforms. He summoned marines for temporary duty in the city, holding them in readiness to shield the area adjacent to the Capitol from violent street rioters.[27] A day before the counting of electoral college ballots in the House of Representatives, Scott fired off orders for the deployment of specific military units to defend the White House, executive departments, and other public buildings. To safeguard against spies, rebels, or anyone else masquerading as officers acting under his authority, he ordered all general staff officers to attach blue scarves over their uniforms from the right shoulder to the left hip, to authenticate their identities to troops.[28]

Fear of disorder was so great that the House of Representatives had set up a Select Committee in January to report whether any secret organization hostile to the US government existed in the nation's capital, and whether any of its members might include Federal employees in the executive and judicial branches, or staff in the local administration. Testimony from twenty-four individuals, including the mayor of Washington, General Scott, and the most outspoken opponents of the Federal government, confirmed a rumble of political rage so intense that open warfare seemed inevitable in the nation's capital. As Lincoln's train repeatedly stopped before curious, hopeful, and cheering onlookers on its slow journey east, the committee published its mixed findings, declaring that insurgents might attack the Capitol or the District of Columbia if "the surrender should be demanded by a State to which they profess a high degree of allegiance."[29]

There was no mistaking the committee's reference to Maryland, the neighboring border state that had become a powder keg of conflicting political passions. The outcome in Maryland would be key to the future of the nation's capital. And Lincoln's train would have to pass through Maryland to reach Washington. For now, the state that surrounded Washington on the north, east, and south was headed by a beleaguered governor, Thomas Hicks, himself an unabashed slaveholder, though as he told the committee, "I am a Union man, and would live and die in the Union."[30]

Hicks used all the authority of his office to fend off pressure from Maryland secessionists wanting to convene the legislature, where they had the numbers to vote the state out of the Union.[31] Delay, he hoped, would give even zealots time to reflect on their "mad crusade." Disunion, the governor predicted, would make Maryland the battleground between North and South, because Unionists would never allow secessionists to overrun the nation's capital.[32] The consequences for Maryland would be catastrophic, with death and destruction, bankruptcies, ruinous taxes, depreciation of property, and worse — the abolition of slavery. Hicks, like Scott, had overwhelming evidence that the ultimate goal of secessionists was to remove Maryland from the Union so that it could absorb the national capital. It would then seek international recognition for the entire Confederacy. "The plan contemplates forcible opposition to Mr. Lincoln's inauguration and consequently civil war upon Maryland soil," the governor warned citizens of his turbulent state.[33] One of his confidential sources, an editor of Washington's *Daily National Intelligencer* newspaper, told him the insurrectionists hoped to triumph before Lincoln's inauguration.[34]

Though Scott's reinforcements trickled in to defend Washington, Marylanders remained a graver threat to Lincoln's life. Several weeks before the president-elect's train pulled out of Springfield, a distinguished woman walked into the Maryland office of Samuel Felton, president of the Philadelphia, Wilmington & Baltimore Railroad. Dorothea Dix, the pioneer advocate for the mentally ill who would soon take charge of all Union nurses, came to pass on word of treason, murder, and sabotage. She made sure the door was closed before disclosing all she knew from travels in the South of a conspiracy to seize Washington and abort the inauguration — failing which, Lincoln was to be assassinated. Over the next hour she confided that insurgents were conducting military exercises along Felton's and other railroad lines. They planned to cut every rail and other communication link north, east, and west of the capital to prevent Union troops from coming to the rescue.

Felton rushed a confidant overnight to Washington to brief Scott, but with no apparent effect. The general seemed exasperated by President Buchanan's failure to prepare for a military showdown and feared Lincoln might have to be inaugurated in the safety of Philadelphia.

A few days later an elderly man walked up to the keeper of the PW&B bridge over the Back River, six miles east of Baltimore. He too knew of secret plans for sabotage and assassination. Respectable and earnest, he insisted on anonymity and on a promise that officials would not put his life at risk by trying to track down his name or residence. Given the assurance, he told the bridge keeper he wanted Felton to know of a plot to burn the bridge just before Lincoln's train approached it "and in the excitement, to assassinate him." These Baltimore plotters also were targeting other PW&B bridges, including those nearly a mile long over the Bush and Gunpowder rivers, to prevent troops from being transported down for the defense of Washington. The informant said the saboteurs had combustible materials ready to set the bridges alight and were to disguise themselves as blacks for the attack on Lincoln's train.[35]

Felton bought a hundred revolvers to arm the conductors on his trains[36] then hurried to Washington to check with sources to help determine whether Baltimore's police chief, Marshal George Kane, could be trusted to investigate. Was he a Union man? Would he keep the sensitive news to himself? Inexplicably, Felton's contact was poorly informed and vouched for Kane, who was in reality so enamored of the Confederate cause that he would soon incite rioters against Union troops passing through Baltimore and be imprisoned before heading South to join the Confederate army.

Acting on the flawed opinion, Felton asked Kane to detail a police force to investigate the threat to the bridges. The police chief brusquely dismissed the conspiracy as rumor without foundation. Only then did the railroad president summon Detective Allan Pinkerton, founder of the Chicago-based Pinkerton National Detective Agency, whom he had hired before for an undisclosed "important matter," which led him to admire the investigator's "great skill and resources."[37]

As Lincoln's train halted for the president-elect to greet crowds and give speeches in cities and towns along the meandering route eastward, Pinkerton and a single female and eight male assistants dispersed undercover to penetrate militant bands in Maryland. Pinkerton himself opened a bogus stock brokerage firm in Baltimore, a city of 212,000 residents,[38] under one of his aliases, John H. Hutchinson. His aides, masquerading as rebellious Southerners from Charleston, New Orleans, and Mobile, infiltrated three companies of paramilitary forces drilling along the railroad lines in the guise of citizens preparing for home defense. The detectives reported by code to Pinkerton that two of the three companies were preparing for rebellion, with plans to burn the bridges and march on Washington. One unsuspecting conspirator talked of "about one thousand men in Baltimore well organized and ready for anything." They hoped Lincoln would speak to crowds outdoors, where they "would not be surprised if they killed him."[39] Another Baltimorean told an undercover detective, "If our company would draw lots to see who would kill Lincoln, and the lot should fall on me, I would do it willingly."[40]

From his own sources, meanwhile, Felton had no doubt that "it was made as certain as strong circumstantial and positive evidence could make it that there was a plot to burn the bridges, destroy the road, and murder Mr. Lincoln on his way to Washington." He employed some two hundred armed men to guard the bridges and practice drills along the line between the Susquehanna River and Baltimore, about thirty miles southwest. There they also worked as railroad laborers, painting the bridges with half a dozen layers of whitewash heavily dosed with salt and alum to make them almost fireproof. Felton even arranged for a train to be on standby to transport all the forces to a single location if need be.[41]

Simultaneously, Pinkerton passed himself off as one of the impassioned regulars drawn to Barnum's Hotel in Baltimore, a majestic, seven-story, red-brick landmark, where the swill of liquor amid the noisy camaraderie of political kin led to careless talk about rebellion and armed resistance. Initially he knew only of a plot to blow up Maryland bridges and ferry boats essential to the railroad that had hired him.[42] Then, having won the trust of the would-be saboteurs, he was introduced to the redoubtable Cypriano Ferrandini, one of the apparent ringleaders. Pinkerton was instantly taken by this "fine-looking, intelligent-appearing," and excitable Italian immigrant barber, who supported the South with such fervor that "his eyes fairly glared and glistened and his whole frame quivered" as they sat in the corner of Barr's saloon on South Street. Even the seasoned investigator felt himself pulled by "the influence of this man's strange power." Ten days earlier Ferrandini had testified uncowed before a select committee of the House of Representatives investigating the possible existence of secret organizations hostile to the government. He had predicted bloodshed if volunteer militiamen from northern states tried to pass through Maryland to defend the capital.[43] Now, thinking Pinkerton was a like-minded subversive, the barber volunteered that Lincoln would never be president. He was willing to sacrifice his own life to rid the nation of the president-elect. "Murder of any kind is justifiable and right to save the rights of the Southern people," he declared. "If I alone must do it, I shall. Lincoln shall die in this city."[44]

The following night while Pinkerton eavesdropped on Marshal Kane at Barnum's Hotel, he heard the police chief discredit the idea of "giving a police escort." Pinkerton felt certain that this "rabid rebel"[45] intended to leave Lincoln exposed to the guns and knives of assassins; he also concluded that he could not expect help from elsewhere, knowing that committed rebels had a lock on local government and the courts.[46]

Other leads confirmed that the conspirators had shifted their locale for assassination from the bridges and trains to a specific Baltimore railroad depot. Pinkerton learned from the superintendent of the PW&B Railroad that the son of a distinguished Marylander had taken an oath with others to kill Lincoln at this transfer point.[47] In this scenario, twenty conspirators, all sworn to secrecy, had drawn lots in a darkened room to determine who would take the life of the president-elect. The assassin was to have drawn a single red ballot, with none of the co-conspirators disclosing the color of their ballots. To make doubly sure the plot succeeded, the leaders had quietly arranged for eight red ballots to be drawn from the hat, so that each of the eight assassins would think he was acting alone. The bloodletting was to take place as Lincoln walked through a narrow vestibule at the Calvert Street Station before boarding a carriage for a change of trains at the Camden Street Station, more than a mile away. The conspirators expected to make their getaway to Virginia in a small chartered steamer, lying in wait in one of the inlets leading into the Chesapeake Bay.[48]

With the VIP train just days away from Maryland, Pinkerton rushed off a warning note to Norman Judd, a member of Lincoln's entourage, who was not only a close friend of the president-elect but also the influential chairman of the Illinois Republican Central Committee.[49] The alert warned of imminent danger, though Judd kept the tip to himself to avoid panic. More details awaited him during a stopover in Buffalo. But he did not get a personal briefing until he checked into the Astor House in New York City, and then it came from a source whom no one would suspect — Mrs. Kate Warne, in her midthirties and head of Pinkerton's Female Detective Agency.[50] She told Judd the threat was so grave that she had come in person rather than trust the mail. She arranged a secret rendezvous for the following night in Philadelphia, when Pinkerton himself would lay out proof of the conspiracy.

When Lincoln arrived in Philadelphia, he was greeted with boisterous enthusiasm. Tumultuous crowds packed the streets and bells pealed as Lincoln, Judd, and others rode in a procession of barouches and other horse-drawn carriages from the train depot to the Continental Hotel. As the four plumed white horses pulling Lincoln's carriage neared the corner of Broad and Chestnut streets, a young man broke through police lines and slipped a note to the unsuspecting Judd. It was brief: "St. Louis Hotel. Ask for J.H. Hutchinson."

Judd did not even pause to hear Lincoln speak from the balcony of the Continental. As fireworks exploded over the festive city, the heavyset lawyer with distinctive flowing gray hair and beard raced over to the St. Louis. For more than two hours Felton and Pinkerton, alias John H. Hutchinson, shared their secrets with Judd. The mood in Baltimore was ugly. The threats and taunts credible. The president-elect's life was in peril. Pinkerton warned of imminent danger from a class of men "who would deem it an honor to become martyrs in their cause"; desperate men determined "that Lincoln shall not pass through Baltimore alive." Some, he cautioned, had even spoken of tossing fireballs or hand grenades.[51]

Judd, who frequently chomped on an unlit cigar,[52] needed no more prodding. He was convinced that Lincoln was headed toward a lethal trap. He agreed that the president-elect should be whisked from the city that night, preferably on the eleven o'clock train for Washington. But Judd knew Lincoln well enough to doubt he would consent. He asked Pinkerton, also a trusted acquaintance of the president-elect, to try to persuade him.[53]

The Continental was jammed with so many well-wishers that Judd and Pinkerton had to sneak in the back door used by servants to reach Lincoln. They told the president-elect everything they knew, then pressed him to take the night train south. But Lincoln was characteristically pensive. He had listened attentively without interruption. Now he calmly asked for more detail. Pinkerton said he thought no more than fifteen or twenty men would be plucky enough to make the attempt on Lincoln's life. But any assassin could easily mix in with a crowd and in the confusion of the moment open fire.[54]

Judd worried about negative political consequences if they had to slip into Washington in the dead of night. But they had their hands tied. They would never win public approval for the dash in the darkness, because they would have to withhold all evidence of a plot to protect Pinkerton's undercover agents. "You will necessarily be subjected to the scoffs and sneers of your enemies," he warned, "and the disapproval of your friends, who cannot be made to believe in the existence of so desperate a plot."[55]

Lincoln was silent and contemplative. Then he said he was prepared to "stand anything that was necessary." However, as he rose from his chair in Judd's room, Lincoln quashed all hope of an immediate flight. "I cannot go tonight," he said. "I have promised to raise the flag over Independence Hall tomorrow morning, and to visit the legislature at Harrisburg."[56] He would agree to any plan — so long as he kept these commitments.

It was an opening Pinkerton had hoped for. He said if Lincoln could leave the state capital of Harrisburg, about ninety miles west of Philadelphia, at dusk the following night, they could arrange a special Pennsylvania Railroad train to take him back from Harrisburg to Philadelphia in time to catch the PW&B train with sleeping cars. Those cars eventually would be coupled to the Baltimore & Ohio Railroad train at Baltimore as it waited to go on to Washington. Lincoln gave a reluctant nod, with the caveat that he would have to bring his wife into the secret plan, and she would probably insist on his being accompanied by his friend and self-styled bodyguard, Ward Hill Lamon.[57] His tone and manner were decisive, and there was no further discussion.[58] Lincoln left the room apparently unafraid, but skeptical of the danger and unconvinced of a plot.[59]

But then to his surprise he was waylaid by Frederick Seward as he passed through swarms of well-wishers on the way back to his room. Seward had come from Washington and immediately handed over two startling notes that instantly changed Lincoln's mind. One, from Seward's father, the designated secretary of state William Seward, urged Lincoln to alter his travel plans on account of alarming news received that morning. "No one here but Gen. Scott, myself, and the bearer is aware of this communication," Seward wrote.[60]

The accompanying note, from Scott, relayed a report from the head of a separate team of New York detectives working clandestinely in Baltimore who knew nothing of Pinkerton's activities. Yet in ominous generalities it mirrored the findings and conclusions of Pinkerton's survey. The detective from New York feared "serious danger of violence to and assassination of Mr. Lincoln" in his passage through Baltimore. He further reported that he had personally heard men declare that if Lincoln was to be assassinated, "they would like to be the men." The detective's findings described the danger as imminent, which local authorities and ordinary residents would be unable to guard against. Like Pinkerton, the other detective recommended avoiding all risk by secretly switching Lincoln's travel arrangements so that he would slip through Baltimore by the night train.[61]

The danger of assassination was stark. The corroborating evidence weighty. Professional rivals who would later squabble in public for the sole credit of whisking the president-elect out of harm's way had simultaneously offered dire warnings. Lincoln was no longer in doubt, though some years would pass before he publicly acknowledged that "I now believed such a plot to be in existence."[62] But he would not cancel appearances in Philadelphia and Harrisburg. His advisers would have to plan around those as he left them and went to bed.

While Lincoln slept, Pinkerton crisscrossed Philadelphia through-out the night to put in place an elaborate scheme of deception in a frantic race to bamboozle any mobs and would-be assassins. He conferred with only a handful of loyal and trusted top executives with authority to reroute trains and sever telegraph lines. Success depended on stealth and clockwork efficiency. If it failed, then the man elected to the presidency might not make it alive to Washington for his inauguration.

Past midnight Pinkerton received an assurance from the superin-tendent of the Pennsylvania Railroad that a special train would pull up half a mile from the Harrisburg depot to speed Lincoln incognito back to Philadelphia.[63]

A top aide to the head of the American Telegraph Company was asleep when Pinkerton's horse-drawn hack pulled up outside his Philadelphia home. Only hours remained before Lincoln was scheduled to speak at Independence Hall. The detective told him of the scheme to smuggle Lincoln out of Harrisburg after sunset. He directed the aide to go very early to the telegraph office, enlist "a practical telegraph climber," and board the president-elect's 9 AM train for Harrisburg. There they would cut the telegraph lines to isolate Harrisburg from the outside world until the following daybreak, and to sever telegraphic communication all the way along the railroad route to Baltimore, so that no one would be able to report Lincoln's movements until he arrived in Washington.[64]

As dawn neared, the weary detective streamlined the ruses and subterfuge that would hopefully outmaneuver Lincoln's enemies. All southbound trains were to be sidelined to clear the track from Harrisburg, so that Lincoln's special unlit carriage, parked half a mile outside the Pennsylvania capital, could soon barrel through the darkness back to Philadelphia. Telegraph lines between both cities would be cut to prevent any instant communication between conspirators monitoring Lincoln's movements. But for everything to fall into place Lincoln would still have to go unnoticed as he boarded his carriage at Harrisburg, and later when he switched trains at Philadelphia. The risk remained of chance recognition by railroad employees or fellow passengers. Saboteurs might also be hidden anywhere along miles of unguarded railroad tracks. To minimize discovery, Lincoln would be accompanied by Pinkerton and only a few others. If all worked well, the man elected to be the sixteenth president would arrive in Washington at dawn the following day, when everyone would still expect him to be in Harrisburg.

At 6 AM on George Washington's birthday, Friday, February 22, 1861, Lincoln made his scheduled appearance at Independence Hall, the historic eighteenth-century red-brick birthplace of the Declaration of Independence and the US Constitution. Despite the early hour, rapturous crowds gave him an ovation. They cheered when he said he would rather be assassinated than surrender the principles of liberty enshrined in the Declaration of Independence. But then, as if regretting that he had spoken of assassination, he said his remarks were unprepared. "I may, therefore, have said something indiscreet, but I have said nothing but what I am willing to live by, and, in the pleasure of Almighty God, die by."[65]

His long, muscular arms, which had served him well as a wrestler in his young manhood, now pulled on the halyards as the Stars and

Stripes rose and flapped in the breeze. The crowd roared as the ensign of the Republic reached the top of the staff, signaling the moment for cannons to boom and a band to strike up "The Star Spangled Banner."[66]

In Baltimore, only ninety miles southwest, flags fluttered conspicuously all over town as military companies paraded and loyal Unionists excitedly prepared for Lincoln's arrival at one o'clock the next day. "There are no palmetto flags in our midst," rejoiced one staunch Republican — he was referring to the flag of South Carolina, which just the previous month had become the first state to secede — "and I hope they never appear in our little state of Maryland." But the observer could not suppress a sense of unease when writing that night to an out-of-towner: "I have no doubt there will be a good deal of pushing and crowding, hissing etc. I hope our new police will be on hand and goodly members, and put down any disturbance that may arise."[67]

Within hours, the president-elect was on a train bound for the state capital at Harrisburg. Judd waited until they were alone before telling Lincoln what they had planned. He wanted permission to brief key members of the traveling entourage, who were already suspicious of something being discussed behind their backs. Lincoln consented, even though he had already resigned himself to the ridicule he knew would be heaped on him. "I reckon they will laugh at us, Judd, but you had better get them together."[68]

Although Lincoln accepted the plan, not everyone in his entourage approved of it. Outraged that anyone would force a detour upon the man elected to the presidency, military aide Colonel Edwin Sumner fumed, "I'll get a squad of cavalry, sir, and *cut* our way to Washington, sir!"

"Probably before that day comes," Judd interjected, "the inauguration day will have passed. It is important that Mr. Lincoln should be in Washington on that day."

There was silence as Judge David Davis, one of Lincoln's closest friends from earlier years in Illinois when they rode the judicial circuit together, asked the president-elect what he thought of the plan.

"Unless there are some other reasons, beside fear of ridicule, I am disposed to carry out Judd's plan," Lincoln said.

"That settles the matter, gentlemen," the judge declared.[69]

Harrisburg was festive and swollen with an influx of thousands of revelers come to witness the military parade with marching bands in honor of George Washington's birthday. A gun salute greeted the arrival of the president-elect in the early afternoon. One of the banners strung across buildings proclaimed PENNSYLVANIA LOYAL TO THE UNION WELCOMES THE PRESIDENT TO THE CAPITAL. Lincoln attended a reception in the domed state legislative building and acknowledged the cheers of thousands gathered for his appearance on a balcony of The Jones House, a hotel brilliantly illuminated with gas lights and decked with flags at every window.[70]

As darkness fell during a late-afternoon dinner with Pennsylvania's Governor Andrew Curtin at The Jones House, Lincoln confided that he was pained and surprised to hear that his life was in danger. But even though concerned about his personal safety and the peace of the country, at no time did he show any sign of fear or alarm.[71]

Shortly before 6 PM a carriage drove up to the side door of the hotel, and Lincoln, on cue, announced he was not feeling well. He went up to his room, changed from a formal dinner suit to traveling clothes, and exited from the back door. Then he put on a soft wool hat of a kind he had never worn before, which had been given to him in New York. Lamon, his tall, bulky friend and bodyguard, joined him in the carriage. So too did two top officials of the Pennsylvania Railroad. As Sumner, the military aide, approached the carriage, Judd gently waylaid him, explaining as he blocked the irate colonel from joining Lincoln's entourage, now limited in number so it would attract less attention: "When we get to Washington Mr. Lincoln shall determine what apology is due to you."[72]

Meanwhile, the telegraphic lineman detailed to deaden the lines in Harrisburg had completed his task. Accompanied by two colleagues, he had carried tools and a coil of copper wire as they walked through parts of the city, tracing the path of the cables while looking for specific lines to sabotage. At a point two miles south of the state capitol, the lineman climbed a pole and placed the fine copper ground wire on the lines, instantly severing the link between Harrisburg and Baltimore. To make sure, he went to the telegraph office in Harrisburg, where he learned of his successful sabotage when an unwitting operator told him the line to Baltimore was out of order.[73] The telegraphic lineman's manager sat in his Philadelphia office as backup throughout the night to ensure that no messages passed over the wires between Harrisburg and Baltimore. The single exception was a coded early-evening confirmation of Lincoln's departure for Philadelphia.[74]

The president-elect and his entourage rode to a crossing just below Harrisburg where the lone passenger car, hitched to a locomotive, waited in the dark to whisk them secretly to Philadelphia. If any outsider wondered why they had been idling on the tracks at the city's perimeter, he was to be told it had been requisitioned to transport railroad officials to Philadelphia. The lamps inside were unlit as the train sliced through the darkened countryside. When they stopped at Downington, a village some twenty miles west of Philadelphia, to take on water, everyone but Lincoln got out to eat. Someone brought him a roll and a cup of tea.[75]

The stumpy train pulled into the West Philadelphia depot of the Pennsylvania Railroad after 10 PM. The group disembarked and boarded a carriage for the PW&B depot to continue their journey to Baltimore. Pinkerton guided Lincoln and Lamon into a carriage, while the superintendent of the PW&B Railroad Company sat beside the driver. They dared not be early because they would be conspicuous waiting for the connecting train, so they passed the time driving slowly through the city, pretending now to be on the lookout for someone.

Shortly before 11 PM the PW&B Railroad official guided the driver into Carpenter Street, and they stepped from the carriage in an unlit area near a yard fence close to the depot. Lincoln wore a muffler around his neck, a soft black Kossuth hat on his head, and an overcoat over the shoulders of his six-foot-four frame, with sleeves dangling free. He carried a traveling bag in one hand and leaned with the other on Pinkerton's arm, stooping to disguise his height as they walked toward the end of the train where the sleeping berths were located. To minimize the chance of the president-elect being recognized as he entered the train and pushed his way through the narrow passageway, a top railroad official had earlier that day followed the plan of Detective Kate Warne to hoodwink the sleeping-car supervisor into thinking Lincoln was an "invalid" who had special permission to board with two assistants.

With Lincoln safely aboard and no sign of trouble, the PW&B official walked toward the conductor carrying a bogus package of newspapers addressed to another of Pinkerton's aliases, E.J. Allen, Willard's Hotel, Washington. The conductor had strict orders not to let the train move out until this package, ostensibly from the president of the railroad company, was handed over in person. At 10:55 PM the conductor took possession and signaled the engineer to pull out. The train was five minutes behind schedule.[76] No one aboard, save for Pinkerton and Lamon, knew of the illustrious man's presence. When the conductor did his rounds taking tickets, Pinkerton gave him one for the curtained-off "sick man."[77]

Throughout the ride to Washington, Pinkerton was alert and watchful. Whenever they came to a bridge he stood on the platform, looking for the telltale white lights from his agents' lanterns, signaling *All's Well*. Each time he returned to give Lincoln a positive report. As they passed through Havre de Grace, about twenty-five miles northeast of Baltimore, the sleepless president-elect remarked to Pinkerton, "We are getting along very well. I think we are on time."[78] Lincoln did not sleep throughout the night, but he never appeared to Pinkerton to be anything but "cool, calm, and collected."[79]

In Baltimore, the conspirators were caught off guard. As the train pulled into the President Street Depot at 3:30 AM, the city was quiet. Men with rage and violence in their hearts now slept as if tranquilized. Later that day rogues would curse and jeer when they learned how they had been cheated and trumped. But for now the depot was all but deserted.

The master machinist of the PW&B Railroad, who had been the first to give Pinkerton inklings of assassination, boarded the sleeping car at his company's depot in Baltimore and whispered to the detective, "All is right."[80] It was welcome news. But the long night's journey was not yet over. It took only a few minutes for the cars to be hauled in the customary manner by horses across deserted Pratt Street, then coupled to the Baltimore & Ohio train at Camden Street

Station.[81] At 4 AM the quiet was broken to the amusement of some by an Irishman banging a club against a wooden booth in a futile attempt to waken the ticket agent inside.

Pinkerton was the only one to leave the car during its thirty-minute stopover in Baltimore. When he returned, Lincoln was still wide awake and began telling jokes, which he always delivered with such verve and delight that listeners recalled them long afterward.[82]

A cabinet secretary would remember decades later one of Lincoln's stories, told on another occasion, about a man so enamored of Revolutionary War relics that when he heard of an old lady who still had the dress she had worn as a young girl in that earlier era, he made a special excursion to ask if he might see it. She obliged by opening a drawer and laying it out before him. Rapturously, he held it up, remarking, "Were you the dress that this young lady, once young and blooming, wore in the time of Washington? No doubt when you came home from the dressmaker she kissed you as I do now." With that, he kissed it heartily. The old lady looked at this foolishness over old clothing and spoke up. "Stranger, if you want to kiss something old you had better kiss my ass. It's sixteen years older than my dress."[83]

As so often in the past, Lincoln's timely jokes provided comic relief from tension, this time as his anxious colleagues hoped for uneventful passage to Washington.

Dawn had already broken when the train came to a final halt inside the long, dreary B&O Railroad Depot in Washington, within sight of the Capitol two blocks south and a little more than a mile east of the White House. Almost immediately Congressman Elihu Washburne of Illinois, Lincoln's longtime friend who had been singled out and briefed by Washington insiders on the closely guarded arrival time, recognized Lincoln standing on the platform. "Abe, you can't play that one on me!" he joked as he came forward with outstretched hand. Pinkerton and Lamon, not recognizing Washburne, rushed to block his path, but Lincoln quickly stopped them. "Don't strike him!" Lincoln ordered. "It is Washburne. Don't you know him?"[84]

Lincoln's carriage arrived at Willard's, the city's most elegant hotel, a mere block from the White House. Its celebrated lobby was invariably lively with hordes of influence peddlers, lobbyists, and office seekers alert for opportunities to move in on the constant presence of notables, public officials, and elected office holders. Lincoln was greeted with transparent relief by William Seward, who had been waiting conspicuously alone in the lobby since before 6 AM, to the astonishment of the few people about at that early hour.[85] Seward was effusively thankful that the president-elect had eluded the danger by taking a "secret passage" to Washington.[86]

Though unprepared for Lincoln's sudden arrival, the hotel management hastily provided him with a suite of five elegant rooms overlooking Pennsylvania Avenue, the broad inaugural parade route along which he hoped to ride in less than two weeks.[87]

While Lincoln rested, then breakfasted privately,[88] Pinkerton hurried off to the telegraph office to send a prearranged coded message to Judd and insiders from the railroad and telegraph companies, reassuring them of Lincoln's arrival by writing *Plums* had delivered *Nuts* safely.[89]

As expected, the president-elect was derided and caricatured in the newspapers and magazines for the manner in which he arrived in the nation's capital. A reporter for the *New York Times* wrote a fanciful account of Lincoln wearing "a Scotch plaid cap and a very long military cloak, so that he was entirely unrecognizable."[90] These wholly imaginative details were a boon to cartoonists. In one drawing Lincoln was portrayed as something of a dim-witted country bumpkin, easing open the doors of a railroad freight car to see if the coast was clear while a cat with arched back hissed at him.[91]

Mrs. Lincoln and their sons, Robert, seventeen, Willie, ten, and Thomas "Tad," seven, arrived with their entourage that evening. A fourth son, Eddie, had died eleven years earlier at age three. Later in a private parlor in the hotel the president-elect asked Margaret Williams, daughter of a prominent Pennsylvania state legislator, to sing for him. When she asked what kind of music he liked, Lincoln replied, "Sing me something sad." The young woman, whom Mrs. Lincoln had invited to join her in the train journey from Harrisburg to Washington, sang "Alone," a ballad with the mournful refrain *Under thy window I sing alone, Alone; ah! love, alone.* As she sang, she thought the president-elect's face was the saddest she had ever seen, until he smiled, and then it was transformed into what she would always remember as "one of the most attractive."[92]

Many more Washingtonians got their first startled glimpse of the president-elect when he took Seward's pew in fashionable St. John's Church opposite the White House the following morning. It put to rest fears that he would not make it to Washington alive. But Lincoln's appearance and demeanor raised doubts about his fitness or ability to hold the highest office in the land during particularly turbulent times. "There was no sign of refinement and education about him," observed White House neighbor and famed explorer Admiral Charles Wilkes. "A tall, ill gainly, awkward individual with no manners or address, a raw-boned Western man with a long, ungainly stride . . . and to all appearances stupid."[93]

However, one office seeker who spoke with the president-elect shortly after his arrival in Washington found him to be "very pleas-ant, full of jokes, and as quick as a mouse."[94] His simple ways would always surprise strangers. An attendee at a White House reception three years later was flabbergasted when Lincoln, with white cotton gloves, shook his hand, saying "How do, sir!"[95] But as the chief exec-utive became better known, few mocked his intelligence based upon his lugubrious appearance. A White House visitor noted Lincoln's "long, thin, and angular" body, then affectionately described him as "the quintescent extract of awkward grace and courteousness."[96] A French visitor to Lincoln's White House office took Europeans to task for expecting "the former Mississippi boatman" to have the manners of a king or a prince. "Slang comes easily to his tongue," noted the Frenchman, who was jolted by the president's awkward posture. "Partly rigid and partly loose-jointed; he doesn't seem to know how to carry his great height."[97] In time, many would warm to his puckish sense of humor, evident from his days as a boy, when he had amused himself with playful verse:

> *Abraham Lincoln*
> *His hand and pen*
> *He will be good*
> *But God knows when.*[98]

It would not be long before skeptics began to reassess Lincoln and admire his talent for relating the topic at hand to anecdotal wisdom or an amusing tale, as when he hailed a notorious lecher who had just returned home from California. "Well, Jim, how was your favorite pursuit out there?" he asked. "I suppose you found it like the boy's ginger bread: he said he never saw anything he liked so much that he got so little of."[99]

While the president-elect paid courtesy calls on congressmen, Supreme Court justices, and other notables, revelers streamed into the muddy capital for the quadrennial pageant. But the tense state of alert held. Sharpshooters looked down from rooftops, and armed units were deployed around city hall and Willard's Hotel. The city was like an armed camp, fortified by many more reliable troops than General Scott had anticipated. The District of Columbia assembled two thousand armed men, supported by additional cavalry, infantry, and artillery from the neighboring municipality of Georgetown.[100] The visibility of so many armed loyalists had apparently saved the capital from being overrun by secessionists. In the opinion of Charles Sumner of Massachusetts, one of the foremost abolitionist senators of the day, Congress would have been forced to convene in the safety of Independence Hall in Philadelphia had it not been for Scott's deployment of massive military manpower.[101]

Yet warnings of assassination continued. An anonymous letter dated February 21 and postmarked Dansville, New York, arrived at the president-elect's hotel warning, "A club of unprincipled wretches, secessionists every one, have held a meeting and sworn to take your life in two weeks by assassination. One of their number left Rochester for Washington Friday last. I do not know the manner, the means, or the time. I have wronged you. I have hated you, but I never was nor can be a murderer. Take every precaution for safety. Be surrounded only by staunch friends on 4th March."[102]

Throughout the succession of alarms, Lincoln's principal private secretary, John Nicolay, was blithely unruffled. Well before Lincoln began the cross-country train ride, Nicolay had dismissed the possibility of an insurrection in Washington as "scarcely well-founded, as yet."[103] Now, from the discomfort of "sorry accommodations"

forced upon him by a fully booked Willard's Hotel, Nicolay wrote to
his fiancée: "There is not the least apprehension about trouble at the
inauguration. That cloud has blown over."[104]

His confidence was not shared by many others. Luther Barnett
Bruen was one of countless arrivals flooding the capital "in a wild
hunt" for jobs from the incoming administration. "I saw a man today
who went to Baltimore to ferret out the conspiracy to assassinate Mr.
Lincoln," he wrote to his wife in Dayton, Ohio, a day before the
inauguration. "He thinks an attempt will be made to take his life
tomorrow. If it is, there will be a lively time. I shall not be surprised
myself if his life is attempted."[105]

But the show of overwhelming force was apparently enough to
abort any uprising. Bruen explained to his wife after the inauguration that nearly everyone was armed "and the Southerners were very
mad. It would not have taken very much to have started a bloody
fight."[106]

On March 4 President Buchanan, delayed at the Capitol signing
last-minute legislation, arrived at Willard's more than an hour behind
schedule. Inauguration Day in Washington was as warm as a summer's
day even though winter was weeks from over.[107] At ten minutes after
noon, Buchanan and his successor, sharing an open carriage, led the
colorful procession of vehicles, horses, and marching dignitaries
past tens of thousands of jubilant spectators jostling along the edges
of Pennsylvania Avenue. The presidential carriage moved within a
protective security bubble — a company of sappers and miners in
front, double files of cavalry on the flanks, and District of Columbia
infantry and riflemen marching behind. Unseen along the length of
the parade route were sharpshooters on the roofs of buildings, with
orders to scan windows on the opposite side and open fire if need
be. Throughout the procession a colonel used his spurs to irritate his
horse and upset the calm of other cavalry so that an assassin would
have difficulty taking aim at Lincoln.[108] All the while other cavalrymen blocked off side streets by moving down the outer edges of the
avenue as the procession progressed. Parade participants, who had
restlessly assembled at city hall for more than three hours, primped
and frolicked along the route without incident.[109] Prominent among

the decorated "cars" was an ornamented vehicle, drawn by six white horses with signs proclaiming UNION. Aboard were thirty-four young girls dressed in white, each representing one of the Union's states and territories.[110] Few among the multitudes could imagine that in just one month the festooned Capitol to which Lincoln was headed would be the living quarters for as many as three thousand Union soldiers, and an oversize pantry for the thirteen thousand barrels of flour required to feed them.[111]

Lincoln took his seat in the dignified chamber of the newly constructed extension to the Senate wing for the formal inauguration of Vice President Hannibal Hamlin. The small wooden desks assigned each legislator were temporarily replaced by plush chairs for Supreme Court justices, senators, diplomats in full court dress, and other dignitaries.

The formal ceremony over, Lincoln walked in slow procession through the rotunda to the outside platform beneath the east portico, where an estimated ten thousand spectators awaited the historic moment.[112] Large numbers of plainclothes policemen mingled with the multitudes, who were held in check at the base of the steps by a loyal battalion of District of Columbia troops in response to a tip that secessionists would blow up the platform. Two riflemen in each window of the House and Senate wings overlooking the platform stood ready to cut down any armed assassin.[113] The sixteenth president, towering above others, raised his right hand and swore to the best of his ability to "preserve, protect, and defend the Constitution of the United States."

His inaugural address focused immediately on the Constitution and the limits imposed on his powers. Reaching out to reassure political foes who would break with the Union, Lincoln vowed to abide by constitutional restraints. He did not have the power to interfere with slavery where it already existed, and he had no intention of doing so. But he insisted that the Union was perpetual, and that the Constitution had been written "to form a *more perfect* union." It could not be rescinded unless all sides agreed.

For the first time Washingtonians at large would hear the rhythm of biblical cadences that became the hallmark of his speeches. Not

s Jefferson had an American president given such clar-
 and sheathed it in such lilting language. "A disruption
l Union, heretofore only menaced, is now formidably
        he continued. "One section of our country believes slav-
ery is right, and ought to be extended, while the other believes it
is wrong, and ought not to be extended. This is the only substantial dispute," he declared. There need be no bloodshed or violence,
and there would be none, he promised, unless forced upon the
national authority. With the wisdom of a self-educated lawyer who
had emerged from rural pennilessness, Lincoln called for reason and
reflection: "Suppose you go to war, you cannot fight always; and
when, after much loss on both sides, and no gain on either, you cease
fighting, the identical old questions, as to terms of intercourse, are
again upon you." He had shown forbearance and understanding.
Now as he neared the end of his speech he would display something
of the determination that would sustain him during the long years of
fratricidal bloodletting. "In your hands, my dissatisfied fellow countrymen, and not in mine, is the momentous issue of civil war. You can
have no conflict without being yourselves the aggressors. You have
no oath registered in heaven to destroy the government, while I shall
have the most solemn one to 'preserve, protect and defend it.'"

It would have been summons enough to bring his countrymen
back from the brink. But Lincoln made one final appeal for his foes
to remember the common heritage and shared legacies that had
made them a people and bequeathed them a nation. "We must not be
enemies. Though passion may have strained, it must not break our
bonds of affection. The mystic chords of memory, stretching from
every battlefield and patriot grave to every living heart and hearth-
stone, all over this broad land, will yet swell the chorus of the Union
when again touched, as surely they will be, by the better angels of
our nature."[114]

It was a bravura performance, giving hope to many that this
new leader might yet rescue the country from a deteriorating feud.
Benjamin Brown French, sixty, chief marshal for the inaugural ceremonies, was delighted, almost euphoric. In the last few days he had
spoken several times with the president-elect and was so taken with

his unassuming manner that he was convinced Lincoln would make "a first-rate president."[115] He was more certain than ever after listening to the president's first address. "It is exactly what we Union men want," he confided to his journal. "It is the right tone and spirit, and is evidence as strong as proof from Holy writ, that the United States of America is no longer to be triumphed over as if it were a coward and dared not protect itself. Some of us will now try to show the South that we have a Union to defend, peaceably if we can and forcibly if we must."[116]

French was so overjoyed that when the parade ended, he took the thirty-four girls from the decorated Union "car" to the White House reception and introduced them to the president. Lincoln first asked permission, then kissed them all.[117] It was a welcome diversion from the inherited burdens of state. Less than three weeks had passed since he had left Springfield, Illinois, telling well-wishers that he did not know whether he would ever return, and that the task before him was greater than that which had rested upon George Washington.[118]

John Nicolay was cheerfully confident as he prepared to be Lincoln's right-hand man in the White House. But in another letter to his fiancée the day after the swearing in, there was an edge of caution: "Mr. Lincoln is inaugurated. *For the present,* you need have no apprehensions of danger to him or those about him."[119]

Others were less confident, and General Scott directed an avowed Lincoln loyalist, Major David Hunter, to take charge of security at the Lincoln White House. During the election campaign Hunter had tipped off Lincoln to subversive talk at a Kansas army base, where he had overheard an officer vowing to block Lincoln's inauguration. The president-elect had subsequently invited Hunter to accompany him to Washington. The officer set up his nightly headquarters in the East Room of the White House for the first six weeks of the new administration, supervising some one hundred volunteer guards.[120]

Their tenure had no sooner ended than an alert went out in anticipation of a rebel attack on the city. Civil war had erupted on April 12 with the Confederate bombardment of Fort Sumter, at Charleston, South Carolina. Lincoln's immediate summons for volunteers to rally to the ranks of the Union army led to Virginia's secession on April 17.

That night some two hundred notables, mostly from western states in Washington on business, were summoned to the concert room in Willard's Hotel, organized into a squad, supplied with breech-loading rifles and twelve rounds of ammunition each, and drilled for several hours in accordance with the army manual. They were ordered to be ready at any time for immediate deployment. The novices waited throughout the night before standing down without incident. Likewise that night, cavalrymen who had recently been stationed in Texas joined hundreds of infantrymen and artillerists at the Long Bridge over the Potomac River to repel any attempt by insurrectionists to invade from Virginia. In the morning about six hundred troops arrived from Harrisburg and immediately took up quarters inside the US Capitol, while the city awaited the entry of an identical number of Rhode Islanders later that day. Meanwhile meals were ordered for almost five hundred more Pennsylvanians and sixty Minnesotans scheduled to arrive by special trains the following day. If, as expected, they were stoned or jeered at on their path through Baltimore, at least one armed volunteer in Washington forecast they would "charge bayonets on their opponents and lay a few of them out cold."[121]

Even though the city stiffened with armed and loyal Unionists, it would be months before a soldier could justifiably write home that "Washington is in no more danger than a dead man coming to life again."[122]

CHAPTER 2

A Presidential Envelope Marked "Assassination"

Assassination could not be ruled out, for Abraham Lincoln was now at the helm of a government despised by millions in open rebellion. The first threatening letters had come in shortly after he won the Republican Party's nomination in 1860. They made him "a little uncomfortable," but after the hate mail became more frequent, the threats no longer alarmed him. He even joked about expecting "a regular installment of this kind of correspondence."[1] But it was never distant from his mind. He kept some of the letters tucked away in his White House desk drawer, in an envelope he had marked "Assassination."[2]

But for all his apparent calm, Lincoln was never able to shake off the vivid memory of a ghostly illusion seen on the day of his election to the presidency in 1860 when, lying on a couch, he had glimpsed the double image of his face in a mirror on his desk. One of his faces was normal, but the other, three inches above, looked faded and much paler. Startled, he had walked over to the mirror for a closer look, whereupon the double image vanished, only to reappear when he lay down again. Even though the haunting image reappeared one more time a few days later, Lincoln's best efforts to re-create the experience had failed. It had left him "with a little pang, as if something uncomfortable had happened." When he described the eerie sight to his wife she was troubled, instantly taking it as a bad omen. She told him it was a sign he would be reelected, but she thought the paler face might be an omen that he would not live through his second term.[3]

In time Lincoln would become a fatalist, resigned to the hazards of office and the risks of the times. He accepted that no amount of vigilance could thwart a determined assassin, reasoning that he "would not be dying all the while."[4] To guard against all menace he would have to shut himself up in an iron box.[5] On numerous occasions during the four years following his first inauguration he tried to make light of it, reassuring confidants that if he was not troubled, they should not be. Once, when shown two anonymous letters threatening his murder, Lincoln laughingly replied, "If they kill me, they will run the risk of getting a worse man."[6]

At times he would throw aside all caution and walk to the theater accompanied only by a friend. Invariably he did this for his own amusement to surprise the theater management, who would only just have received notice of his attendance that night.[7]

Lincoln pressed on with the normalcy of his routines, even in the face of very public pronouncements of grave danger to his person. Three years after the first inauguration a correspondent of the *New York Daily Tribune* reported an elaborate plot to kidnap the president and carry him off to Richmond, capital of the Confederacy, failing which he would be assassinated. The front page report detailed how 150 conspirators were to infiltrate the Union bastions of Washington and adjacent Georgetown as well as the port cities of Baltimore and Alexandria, Virginia. At a date to be determined by their leader, some would seize the president "at a quiet hour" at the White House, or while he was going to or returning from church, "or on some other favorable occasion," then thrust him into a carriage and gallop south. More than two dozen armed horsemen would join them a few miles out of the city, giving way to relays of riders on fresh horses until they reached the settlement of Indian Head on the banks of the Potomac River, about twenty-five miles south of the capital. There Lincoln was to be bundled into a boat and taken across the river to Occoquan, Virginia, then smuggled by night through the woods to Confederate lines. To prevent pursuit, some of the conspirators were detailed to mine the bridges and blow them up once the abductors had crossed over. Heavy trees, almost cut through at their bases, were to be toppled to block the roads at various points along the escape route. The newspaper correspondent quoted a source in Richmond familiar with the kidnapping plot who was so confident of success that he boasted, "You will see Old Abe here in the spring as sure as God."[8]

Eight months after this conspiracy was widely publicized, metropolitan policeman Thomas Pendel began guard duty at the White House and walked a quarter mile with the president to the residence of the secretary of war. As they exited the front door of the executive mansion, Lincoln remarked, "I have received a great many threatening letters, but I have no fear of them."[9] It was obvious that he felt hamstrung and confined when the cavalry guard accompanied him, but at no time did he countermand the orders of their superiors to protect him.[10]

White House security was abysmally inadequate and lax. Lincoln was in the White House almost four years with only two night watchmen and not a single daytime guard. Thieves once took advantage of this by ripping off wallpaper and stealing a lace curtain from a window in the East Room. Others had cut a square yard out of a rich silk damask curtain and even snatched cords, tassels, and half of the gilded shields supporting the curtains at the sides of windows in the elegant Green Room. Congress had for years ignored the exasperated appeals of Benjamin Brown French, commissioner of public buildings, for more guards to "prevent these depradations."[11] He had to make do with a sign that asked visitors to respect the furnishings, which belonged to the government.[12]

Security around the chief executive was at times so offhand that eight groundsmen were regularly ordered for duty as coachmen and house servants after they had finished their regular full day's employment. These same men doubled as nocturnal guards and watchmen when Lincoln stayed at the Soldiers' Home, a presidential retreat several miles north of the White House, during the clammy summer months.[13]

In the winter of 1865 William Crook, twenty-six, a two-year veteran of the Washington police force, arrived at the White House to serve as a self-described personal bodyguard to the president. Late one night in February of that year Crook walked with the president across the western grounds, past the box trees and up the stairs of the imposing War Department building. The walk was a regular ritual for Lincoln, who during the Civil War spent more time at the

War Department than anywhere but the White House. It was the nerve center of the Union's sprawling military machine. Inside, on the second floor overlooking Pennsylvania Avenue and historic Lafayette Square, was the military telegraph office with its cipher machines and the young cryptographers upon whom the president was so dependent for updates on troop movements and battlefields.

Many worried about the president's safety when he walked alone in the open space between his residence and the War Department. His wife was as anxious as others but no more successful in reining him in. "You know you are surrounded with danger," Mary Todd Lincoln would caution. To which he would reply, "All imagination. What does anyone want to harm me for? Don't worry about me, mother, as if I were a little child."[14]

She fretted so often that one night, to quell her anxiety, he took an oak cane with him to the War Department. But he knew it would be ineffective against an assassin. As he walked from the War Department back to the White House with his friend, the eminent journalist Noah Brooks, he remarked, "I long ago made up my mind that if anybody wants to kill me, he will do it. There are a thousand ways of getting at a man if it is desired that he should be killed."[15]

One night Lincoln and a guard were on the steps of the War Department when a suspicious man passed by and glared at the president. Lincoln stared back and said later that the man exactly matched the description of a would-be assassin he had been warned about in a letter received the night before.[16]

He was stalked and targeted without letup. One night in August 1862 a lone gunman almost succeeded when his bullet cut clean through Lincoln's plug hat as the president rode alone near the Soldiers' Home. Lincoln again made light of it, telling his friend Lamon that the gunman may well have been a hunter who had not even targeted him.[17]

More recently Secretary of War Edwin Stanton had tried to prevent him walking along the tree-lined footpath from the back door of the War Department to the White House, but Lincoln had answered, "I don't believe there's any danger there, day or night." Still, Stanton prevailed, and the two men took the secretary of war's carriage along the well-lit stretch of Pennsylvania Avenue back to the adjacent executive mansion.[18]

By the time the city readied for Lincoln's second inaugural the war was nearing its end. Fear of assassination had receded, and security was looser and more relaxed. Lincoln's equestrian generals had the Confederates on the run or hunkered down under siege, and confidence had returned to Washington.

The pulse of the South was feeble. More Southerners would die before long, but the toll already was ghastly. An estimated six hundred thousand, on both sides, had fallen during Lincoln's first term. Fertile fields in the North and the South would lie fallow for generations, becoming sacred and windswept monuments to victors and vanquished alike. In time they would also belong to "the mystic chords of memory."[19]

Lincoln had not expected to win election in November 1864 to a second term, because the war had dragged on for so long without resolution or letup in fatalities. Almost four years had elapsed since the Confederate forces had shown their mettle by routing Union troops at Manassas, Virginia, sending Washingtonian picnickers scampering back to the capital instead of witnessing the anticipated thrashing of their foe and an early end to hostilities. Abler and more daring Southern generals had won epic battles and even savaged Union forces at clashes they had lost. The lexicon of military battlefields with staggering tallies of dead had broadened with the additions of Shiloh, Bull Run, Antietam, Fredericksburg, Murfreesboro, Chancellorsville, Vicksburg, Gettysburg, Chickamauga, the Wilderness, and Spotsylvania. Lincoln had replaced his top generals several times in vain hopes of finding a man bold enough to bring overall victory. Three years had dragged by before he placed Ulysses S. Grant in command, confident that at last he had a champion, both resolute and daring, to defeat the enemy.

However, the summer of 1864 had not brought the victories he needed to give hope to dejected Unionists. Grant had failed to smash Confederate forces under command of the equally able Robert E. Lee, even though Lincoln's top general had been prepared to suffer huge casualties, losing more than fifty thousand Union troops in a month of clashes at the Wilderness, Spotsylvania Court House, and Cold Harbor. Grant's siege of Petersburg, a railroad center south of Richmond, underlined the seemingly endless stalemate as it stretched beyond the summer and fall. Everything seemed bleak as Lincoln prepared for an inglorious end to his presidency.

By contrast, Southerners were so confident that when British prime minister Lord Palmerston asked the unaccredited Confederate commissioner in London that summer what his side would do if they captured Washington, James Mason replied, "It would be destroyed, not vindictively, but to keep the enemy at a distance."[20]

Ten weeks before the election Lincoln gloomily forecast his own political demise. He would not concede that his policies were wrong, nor that an alternative would bring an honorable peace. He could never agree to compromise on slavery, which his Democratic Party opponents were willing to do to stop the casualties and end the war. It would therefore "be my duty," he wrote in a memo to himself, "to so co-operate with the President-elect as to save the Union between the election and the inauguration; as he will have secured his election on such ground that he cannot possibly save it afterwards."[21]

But one week after that note to himself the funereal mood evaporated with General William Sherman's capture of Atlanta, Georgia. It was the victory Lincoln had yearned for, and the exhilarated North responded with political support. The great burden of war was still there, but victory was no longer an illusion. Reinvigorated and galvanized, the loyal states gave Lincoln a landslide victory over his would-be Democratic usurper, General George McClellan, whom Lincoln had dismissed two years earlier for chronic caution and indecisiveness.

Men, women, and children surged into Washington for Lincoln's second inaugural. They came by train and by carriage, in wagons and carts, and even over the Potomac in crowded river craft and light ferries. Many who remembered how difficult it had been to secure accommodation four years before came into Washington by special trains arriving that morning.[22] A carnival mood prevailed. The parade promised to be cheered like none other.

But Washington's appearance did not merit much applause. The city had buckled under four years of war, straining to take the weight of the military and growing slovenly, unwashed, and disfigured. Roads built from stiff, adhesive clay, lightly coated with coarse gravel from creeks and knolls, were never designed to support more than the lightweight traffic of peaceful times. The daily movement of heavily loaded wagons had ground the gravel to dust that, mixed with clay, turned into muddy bogs when it rained. Horses could barely pull carriages free from the cloying mix.[23] So many thoroughfares were battered that they were all but closed to vehicles. Inaugural parade officials had to make last-minute changes to the rendezvous because many streets were impassable.[24]

Lincoln's capital was a far cry from the idyllic vision portrayed in paintings and etchings, which could never convey foul smells nor the constant cacophony of the military. Even before the war, garbage was thrown into carriageways and back alleys; now the open pastures and serene farmlands were overrun by encampments, parade grounds, wagon yards, mule pens, field hospitals, and ammunition dumps.[25] Pigs and cows roamed freely in dirty streets, even in the fashionable area now called Franklin Square, opposite which Secretary of War Stanton had his residence.[26] A nauseous stench pervaded the city, much of it seeping from sewage and muck in the canal that cut across Washington from west to east.[27] Land in the rear of a prison opposite the east front of the US Capitol was in such a "filthy condition" that police cited it as a health hazard to prisoners and neighborhood residents.[28] There was also the strong odor of manure, regularly shoveled from cavalry stables and spread over public grounds.[29] Southeasterly winds carried a particularly loathsome smell from a soap factory into the White House, to the vocal disgust of Mrs. Lincoln.[30] A putrid stench from dead horses being burned every night at a veterinary hospital in the north wafted into the city with sickening regularity.[31]

The White House was a run-down eyesore in dire need of repair. After living in it for four years as Lincoln's secretary, John Nicolay shuddered at the "dilapidated old shanty," which was decidedly "ill-kept, inconvenient, and [a] dirty old rickety concern from top to bottom."[32] With only weeks remaining until Lincoln's second inaugural, the commissioner of public works made several frantic appeals to the financially strapped Congress for eight thousand dollars to spruce up the "shabby condition" with a paint job, inside and out and to the surrounding fences.[33]

Even Willard's, the city's premier hotel, did not measure up to its fabled reputation. One discerning European traveler left the city disgruntled over the hotel's "abominable" service and its skulduggery in providing an elaborate menu while it was "all too evident that they serve left-overs from other people's plates."[34]

Unsightly ruin and decay had also spread half a mile east of the US Capitol to Congressional Cemetery, the final resting place of many prominent Americans, where tombstones and enclosures had fallen down from years of baleful neglect.[35] The Long Bridge, linking Washington and Virginia over the Potomac River, was so dilapidated that when blocks of ice swept parts of it away in a winter storm, a top naval commander rejoiced, declaring it had been "a disgrace to a civilized community."[36]

Outsiders would have to be wary by day and by night during the inaugural celebrations. Robbers and pickpockets abounded, and violent crimes were plentiful. The police superintendent had taken extra precautions to station a force of detectives at the Baltimore & Ohio Railroad Depot, several hundred yards north of the Capitol, to look out for thieves and sleight-of-hand artists who were expected to prey on the deluge of unsuspecting arrivals.[37] There was little hope of protecting the uninitiated who strayed into the isolated grounds around the Smithsonian Institution's red-brick museum on the Mall, packed with stuffed animals, birds, reptiles, and mummies but now partially blackened from an accidental fire six weeks earlier.[38] Tourists risked violent attack, particularly after sunset. Only two watchmen patrolled the Smithsonian's environs of walks and driveways planted with trees and shrubbery. Savvy locals kept clear of the fifty-two-acre site, knowing it was a favored stalking ground for predatory ruffians.[39]

One of the worst of the more than two thousand violent crimes reported in 1865 occurred on the night of the inauguration, when the city recorder, Walter Cox, was savagely beaten by drunks after boarding a streetcar near the White House.[40] Visitors would have to be especially careful of Irish immigrants, who made up one quarter of everyone arrested — a consequence, lamented the Catholic archbishop of Baltimore and metropolitan Washington, of their excessive drinking.[41] Anyone taken into custody and imprisoned during Lincoln's inauguration might suffocate in one of the police precinct cells, notoriously unsafe, unscrubbed, and inhumane.[42] Conditions were no better in the poorly ventilated city jail, built to hold one hundred but now crammed with three hundred inmates.[43] Some of the cells had been sealed with iron to prevent escapees from cutting holes in the walls.[44]

Soldiers on furlough in the city were often drunk and disorderly, and prostitutes were readily available.[45] Reckless troops had destroyed many of the hundred iron settees fixed to the grounds of the Capitol and south of the White House.[46] They vandalized at will, especially for souvenirs, chipping stone from the incomplete, stumpy Washington Monument[47] and cutting strips off the celebrated tree near the front of the White House where a congressman had shot dead his wife's lover.[48]

Freed from the restraints of their distant hometowns, soldiers flocked nightly to the bars and the theaters, especially the Canterbury, an amusement hall on Louisiana Avenue near 6th Street, where they would quickly forget the rigors of military discipline and enjoy the comics and performing dogs, daring tightrope walkers, pantomimes, and strongmen performing awesome feats of physical strength.[49]

On the eve of the second inaugural a storm lashed the city, battering roofs and windowpanes with the staccato sound of hail and buffeting homes with powerful winds. A sudden gust at dawn brought on such a loud crash of hail on the Capitol that weary congressmen, up all night debating last-minute legislation, mistook the bang for an explosion and rushed helter-skelter for the doors. Proceedings came to a halt until the Speaker rose from his chair to report that the noise was "only a storm."[50]

The rain continued to fall in the morning, loosening the gravel and clay into muddied pools and puddles. But the road muck did not deter the exuberant masses who lined Pennsylvania Avenue for hours before the late-morning parade. Only the middle-aged and elderly could remember seeing a president sworn in for a second term, and that was thirty-two years back, when Andrew Jackson took office.[51]

Much had changed in Washington over those three-plus decades — most noticeably the racial mix of the onlookers, half of whom, by one account, were blacks in brightly colored Sunday-best clothes. They had come to rejoice in sight of the author of the Emancipation Proclamation. Many females would go home that day with their hems soiled by ankle-deep mud, but the presence of Lincoln was worth it, even though they would see him only on his return from the Capitol.[52] Few spectators were aware that he had passed by much earlier that day to sign legislation in the Capitol as the congressional session wound down.[53] But there was much to be proud of among the African American contingent as four companies of black troops marched for the first time in inaugural history. There were even black Masons in the long stream of pageant participants.[54]

Gone were the fear and suspicion that marked the tension of Lincoln's first inaugural. Now police marched across the breadth of the avenue simply to clear the route for others. Still more police lined the edge of the sidewalks, keeping energetic crowds in check.[55] Flags fluttered atop buildings, out of windows, on carriages and streetcars, and even from the harnesses of horses.[56]

Bands added much to the merriment even as rain continued falling. Bystanders squeezed tightly at the best vantage points, bunching between the columns of the Treasury, and on the swooping west front of the Capitol.[57] And still the long procession continued, with cavalry and artillery, marines, sailors, veterans, corporate authorities, civic associations, patriotic groups, fire companies with steam engines pulled by powerful bay horses, and — perhaps most popular of all — infantrymen in the familiar rumpled blue uniforms that were now synonymous with glory. There was so much excitement, bustle, and activity along this, the capital's broadest thoroughfare, that a *New York Times* correspondent conceded, "Pennsylvania Avenue, for once, rivaled Broadway in its busiest days."[58]

All the Senate's overhead seating had been set aside for female spectators, with the exception of some space confined to reporters and the diplomatic gallery, reserved for Mrs. Lincoln and other distinguished guests. The moment the doors opened an estimated eighteen hundred women charged in, elbowing one another in a dash for coveted seats. Many did not have mandatory tickets, and some even sat among journalists. Unmindful of the session below, they kept up a noisy chatter, notwithstanding futile attempts by the presiding officer to gavel for quiet and order. Only when dignitaries began taking their seats did the public galleries grow quiet.[59] Diplomats, resplendent in uniforms with sashes and sparkling decorations, grouped behind grave, black-robed Supreme Court justices whom one resident described as "a very sober, serious, sedate looking set of men, more like a synod of high priests than worldly men."[60] The cabinet, senators, representatives, and more notables sat below the dais. Lincoln, dressed in black with a plain frock coat,[61] sat upright in the middle of the front row.

Retiring vice president Hannibal Hamlin of Maine entered arm in arm with his successor, Andrew Johnson of Tennessee.[62] Loyal and faithful, Hamlin had been dumped from the ticket to broaden the appeal of the party when Lincoln looked vulnerable in the summer leading up to the election. Republicans needed a Southern war Democrat to present a veneer of unity in a time of deep geographic division. Former Senator Johnson, a vocal and loyal Unionist, fit the bill. But until Johnson took the oath, Hamlin remained first in the line of succession. It was of insignificant consequence, for nobody expected an assassin could possibly be lurking close by.

Hamlin's speech was brief. When it came time for Johnson to give his address, it was apparent to all that he was intoxicated. Apologists suggested he might have been drinking to prepare for the ordeal, or to overcome fatigue, or even because he did not feel well. But it also could have been the confines of the windowless Senate chamber that made him light-headed, leading onlookers to think he was drunk.[63] Isaac Bassett, the longest-serving Senate official, said Johnson had swallowed very little whiskey in the vice president's office shortly before the ceremony and his demeanor was due to physical exhaustion from travel.[64] But no one could deny the embarrassment and shame.

As Johnson's speech rambled on, he became forgetful, even leaning over to ask a Senate official the first name of the secretary of the navy. He waved his hands, and his voice fluctuated between a boom and a whisper. The former tailor spoke with a slur of pride in his humble roots. "I am a plebeian. I glory in it. The people, yes, the people of the United States, the great people, have made me what I am. And I am a-going for to tell you here today, yes today, in this place, that the people are everything." The correspondent of the London *Times* likened the performance to that of "a vulgar and drunken rowdy," suggesting that had it been played out in the legislature of any other country, it would have resulted in arrest by the sergeant at arms.[65] Mrs. Sue Wallace, wife of a prominent general, squirmed, convinced Johnson was "drunk as a fool." Later she would write to her sister-in-law, "There are certain sounds that make you 'goose flesh' from head to foot. This was my sensation, and it seemed as if he never would stop."[66]

Johnson, a former military governor of Tennessee, ignored Hamlin's tug from behind. He continued on even after Bassett stepped up and whispered, "Mr. Johnson, it is time for the Senate to proceed to the portico to attend the inauguration of Mr. Lincoln." Noah Brooks, the newspaper reporter, scanned the faces of the dignitaries. The secretary of war looked "petrified." The attorney general closed his eyes. The postmaster general's complexion turned red and then white. A Supreme Court associate justice sat stupefied, "his lower jaw being dropped clean down in blank horror." Throughout, Lincoln sat patiently waiting for the end. Finally Johnson turned his back to the spectators and took the oath. He was now first in line to succeed Lincoln. But the mortifying spectacle was not quite over. Clasping the Bible in one hand, he faced the dignitaries and in a loud voice declared, "I kiss this book in the face of my nation of the United States."[67] Mrs. Wallace looked on aghast. "The foreign ministers sat just before him," she regaled her sister-in-law, "and if he had shaken his fist in their faces and said, 'I am as good as you are,' it would have been in as good taste as what he did say."[68]

When word arrived that the weather had cleared and Lincoln would take the oath of office outside as planned, there was a sudden rush for the doors. But all exits had been locked excepting one for the presidential party, and the other through which everyone had arrived, on the east. The surge of the impatient crowd propelled everyone forward. In the tumult women fell down staircases, and some squeezed out the door were pushed flat into the mud. Tempers fla Few saw anything of the ceremony.[69]

The president led the formal procession through the rounded rotunda linking the House and Senate wings. High above, on the inside canopy of the Capitol dome, George Washington peered down from the center of Constantino Brumidi's masterpiece fresco in progress.[70]

Lincoln had just reached the door leading out to the East Portico when a man, who may have gained access by pretending to be a reporter,[71] burst out of the heaving crowd a few feet behind the president-elect. Benjamin Brown French, who on this day was chairman of the inaugural ball committee as well as public buildings commissioner, instinctively reached out to hold back the intruder, an actor named John Wilkes Booth. French put both his hands against the young man's chest, telling him he had to go back. The nearest policeman, John William Westfall, a four-year veteran of the Capitol force,[72] seized the medium-size man by the arm, gripping it tighter when the stranger tried to struggle free and fight back. During the scuffle the slightly built Booth, twenty-six, scowled at French with blazing black eyes under dark eyebrows and jet black hair. He was so fierce and intimidating, so insistent upon his right to be there, that French, sixty-four — who as grand master of the city's Masons had laid the cornerstone of the Washington Monument seventeen years earlier — had second thoughts.[73] Perhaps this zealous young man was a new congressman whom he did not know. Unsure of himself, and perhaps a little unnerved, French ordered Westfall to "let him go."[74] Abraham Lincoln had meanwhile walked outside to the East Portico, blissfully unaware of the commotion behind.

The incident was instantly overtaken by the roar of applause and hurrahs as Lincoln appeared on the makeshift platform built above the portico's steps. In a break with tradition, thousands of blacks, many in military uniforms, looked out from the multiracial crowd.[75]

Lincoln placed his right hand upon the open Bible, almost inaudibly repeating the oath administered by Chief Justice Salmon Chase. As Lincoln kissed the book he had read so often from childhood, the masses again cheered in the giant concourse.

The densely packed audience spilled beyond the wide plaza, across which Lincoln had walked many times as a one-term congressman two decades earlier while boarding at Mrs. Annie Sprigg's house immediately across the road. In those days there was always a hush and a sense of eager anticipation at the communal dining table whenever Lincoln laid down his knife and fork, put his elbows on the table, cupped his face between his hands, and began another of his inimitable tales or jokes with the familiar opening, "That reminds me."[76] Now too the expectant masses grew still and respectful as Lincoln, fifty-six, began to speak beside a table wrought of surplus iron from the new dome above the Capitol.[77]

Many, including Lincoln himself, would see a celestial sign of good omen when the sun burst through the clouds just as he began his address.[78] Corporal Richtmyer Hubbell, twenty-two, serving with a Wisconsin heavy artillery company some twenty miles south of Washington, had sloshed through the mud and stood within twenty feet of Lincoln, whom he idolized. He would never forget the sound of the president's "loud, rather shrill, distinct, far-reaching voice" as he opened with the words, "Fellow Countrymen."[79] Strongly influenced by the measured tones of the Bible, the book he knew best, the president defined the epic struggle in stark, declarative truths. "Both parties deprecated war, but one of them would *make* war rather than let the nation survive, and the other would *accept* war rather than let it perish." No one had been so expressive of the pull on the patriot's heart. His words resonated like the sound of a bugle, or as if the national standard had been unfurled and raised high. The great crowd responded deliriously. They roared with one voice so mighty that Lincoln had to wait until quiet returned before he could add, like the delayed beat on a drum, ". . . And the war came."

He stood with bared head, a tall and commanding figure offering words of reason and compassion, readying for the embrace of what seemed like the imminent return of a prodigal son. "With malice toward none, with charity for all; with firmness in the right, as God gives us to see the right, let us strive on to finish the work we are in; to bind up the nation's wounds; to care for him who shall have borne the battle, and for his widow, and his orphan — to do all which may achieve and cherish a just, and a lasting peace, among ourselves, and with all nations."

The earlier rain and the ankle-deep mud[80] were hardly discomforting in the presence of such a venerated leader. Artillery salvos echoed across the city as marchers and bands prepared to return to the White House.[81] Lincoln stepped into an open barouche drawn by four white horses, and the coachmen prodded them back along the parade route.

Neither French nor Westfall gave any thought to the passing incident in the rotunda. John Wilkes Booth had neither broken the law nor harmed anyone. He had quickly disappeared from sight, and no one thought to question his identity or his motives.

CHAPTER 3

"An Excellent Chance to Kill the President!"

John Wilkes Booth had always craved lasting notoriety. It was a fantasy he had nurtured since childhood. A close school friend remembered a discussion about ambition in which Booth insisted he would do something to make his name live forever.[1] But for now Booth cast himself as Brutus and Lincoln as Julius Caesar. He despised Lincoln with a fury, blaming him for all the misery and suffering in the South. He called him a tyrant.

Booth could never forgive the president for undermining the slave-holding culture of the South and fomenting expectations among blacks. In Booth's eyes blacks were inferior. It was an unquestionable truth. Once he rode to his home in Cockeysville, west of Baltimore, and threw a packet of candies far from the black servants who came out to greet him. "After it, Nigs!" he had cried. "Don't let the dogs get it!"[2] Livid and exasperated on learning that General Robert E. Lee had surrendered to Union forces, Booth complained: "We are all slaves now. If a man were to go out and insult a nigger now, he would be knocked down by the nigger and nothing would be done to the nigger."[3] And after seeing Confederate prisoners brought into Washington under black guards, he railed at "the shame thus to hurt the feelings of the Southern people."[4]

No one had been able to moderate Booth's views or temper his fanaticism. Instead he had gone in search of stimuli to sustain the hate. As an adolescent he attended meetings of the Know-Nothings, the strident bigots and braggarts with their particular nativist loathing for Irish Catholic immigrants who would soon swell the ranks of the Union army. And he had traveled far to Harpers Ferry, then in Virginia, seventeen months before the outbreak of Civil War to witness the public hanging of the fanatical crusader for black freedom, John Brown.[5]

Even his immediate family found him hard to endure. Booth's older brother, Edwin, almost as eminent a Shakespearean actor as their late father, Junius Brutus Booth, had once ejected John Wilkes from his home because of his insufferable secessionist talk.[6] And an inflamed John Wilkes had physically attacked his brother-in-law, John Clarke, for disparaging the South.[7] Booth told his sister, Asia, that he would never have entered Clarke's home again if she were not living there. He also would have stayed away from Edwin's house forever were it not also the residence of their mother.[8]

Only with Asia did he become close and confidential. During their childhood they had idled among the trees and frolicked in the quiet of their rural home near Bel Air, Maryland. With her he was tender, carefree, and gentle, taking his turn to recite poetry as they sat side by side on the swing under the gum trees and hickories. If he digressed into politics, she would give way, delicately suggesting he choose politics or the stage, for they did not go well together, though she thought he was ably suited for either.[9]

Booth always regretted his pledge to his mother that he would not go into battle with the Confederate army, if possible.[10] Still, he believed he was serving the South even more usefully by smuggling in large quantities of quinine, used to treat fever and pain, which he could afford because his most lucrative acting season had earned him the princely sum of more than twenty thousand dollars[11] at a time when an accomplished Washington, DC, lawyer earned about fifteen thousand dollars a year.[12]

Supremely self-confident, Booth was about average height and a slim 160 pounds. Cultured, cultivated, and graceful, he was fascinating in conversation. He was also a fashionable dresser, dapper and conspicuously stylish, sometimes in an elegant dark claret cloth coat with velvet lapels, a pale buff waistcoat, and dove-colored trousers strapped under boots — all topped by his wide-brimmed straw hat with broad black ribbon band.[13] A regular exerciser, he was agile and athletic, on and off stage, and a deft swordsman.[14] Those who knew

Booth well noticed his fine hands, his left showing the initials JWB, which he had marked with indelible india ink when still a child.[15]

Above all Booth was in the eyes of many women as handsome as an Adonis, with wavy black hair, a mustache, and an expression of almost classically stylized perfection. One woman, flattered merely to shake his hand, recalled his "fascinating theatrical air of self-consciousness, as if he were only to be seen to be admired."[16]

But the fine cut of the serene face masked a deep anxiety, recurring intermittently ever since he had paid a Gypsy woman to read his palm when he was no more than a boy. "I've never seen a worse hand, and I wish I hadn't seen it," she told him in the woods near his home. "It's full enough of sorrow. Full of trouble. You'll die young. You're born under an unlucky star. You'll make a bad end." Yet for all her show of supernatural superiority, next to Booth the Gypsy was a mere mortal, a transfixed female who told him she was glad she was not a young woman because, as Booth later said, citing a comment from her, "she'd follow me through the world for my handsome face." The ghastly prophecy was so unsettling that he had penciled it down and read it often enough for the paper to become worn and ragged.[17]

By the summer of 1864 Booth was already obsessed with kidnapping Lincoln and smuggling him south; the president would then be ransomed for untold numbers of Confederate prisoners, desperately needed for the thinning ranks of rebel forces. The single most powerful advantage the North had over the South was manpower, huge reserves that could be tapped to compensate for casualties and those taken captive. Booth, if successful in trading Lincoln for Southern prisoners, might be able to offset some of this imbalance. Perhaps, he began to scheme, the president could be abducted in a Washington theater with which Booth was most familiar, or snatched while riding between the White House and his summer retreat a few miles north at the Soldiers' Home.

There was no shortage of potential co-conspirators in a capital teeming with Southern sympathizers and spies. Booth's contacts extended far beyond the reach of the acting community, within whose ranks he was a formidable colleague and acknowledged star. There was no doubt he would command the absolute loyalty of those he selected, because he had a naturally dominant personality. Just as he effortlessly charmed and bewitched women, so too many men, even untutored and vulgar brutes, became pliant subordinates to this gentleman of impressive bearing. They were honored to be in his company, especially when favored with tickets to see him perform in the lead role at Ford's Theatre.

In August 1864, when Booth was staying at Barnum's Hotel in Baltimore, he made contact with Samuel Arnold, a man he had last seen twelve years earlier when they wore the gray uniforms of artillery cadets at St. Timothy's Hall, an Episcopalian school at nearby Catonsville.[18] Arnold, glad for any respite from his dull, monotonous subsistence in the country, had often been reminded of Booth when the actor's name began appearing in newspapers and on posters as he rose to prominence.[19]

The reunion between the successful sophisticate and the college graduate who had drifted into slothful tedium was anything but awkward. They shared remembrances of youthful escapades and found no differences in the extreme passions of their uncompromising politics. Both were solidly for the South, in whose ranks Arnold had served as a soldier before returning to Baltimore to be with his ailing mother.[20] Arnold was dazzled by Booth's demeanor, his dignified appearance, the sparkling flow of conversation, and the actor's keen intelligence. The mild and timid look of the schoolboy had matured into a mesmerizing presence, an admirable man of the world.[21]

Soon they were joined by Michael O'Laughlin, another of Booth's close friends from childhood, whom Arnold now met for the first time. O'Laughlin's family had lived in Baltimore for many decades; Michael, like Samuel Arnold, had served in the rebel army before crossing into Union lines in 1863 and taking the oath of allegiance as a mere formality to allow him to go home.[22]

The three men drank wine and smoked cigars all afternoon in Booth's hotel room as he spoke in glowing terms of the Confederacy and its purpose. Booth had no doubt he was among friends. They had common links to childhood and now were as one on politics. But the conspiracy was of such magnitude that he made them take an oath of secrecy before tipping his hand. Then he told of his plan to kidnap the president.[23] He lulled them into the conspiracy by the artful ease of his manner, confidently explaining how Lincoln frequently rode unguarded to the Soldiers' Home, and was accompanied only by his carriage driver when crossing the Eastern Branch Bridge to a hospital. In the absence of armed guards, interception would not be difficult for a disciplined and organized team. Booth even detailed how they would stretch ropes across the flight path to trip up the horses of any would-be pursuers.[24] He gave assurances of successful escape, noting that a boat had already been purchased and moored, with a boatman on standby, ready for Booth's signal to ferry the captive president across the Potomac River into the custody of the South. And as an alternative, he told them Lincoln might even be abducted from the theater, which he frequently attended.[25]

Arnold and O'Laughlin willingly agreed to participate. Plucked from obscure anonymity, they could end up as legends. If not bungled or foiled, the abduction could well be considered heroic. At the very least it offered adventure for young men summoned to action in the noble cause of the South.

Booth told them he hoped they could kidnap Lincoln before the presidential election, less than three months away. He would remain in touch, though his immediate plans called for a trip to Canada to arrange for shipment of his possessions to the South.[26] But almost immediately he fell ill with a fever and the painful inflammation of his arm through erysipelas, a streptococcal skin infection.

It would be January before Booth met O'Laughlin and Arnold again, but in a gesture he would repeat with other would-be conspirators he sent them gifts of money to help assure their allegiance. In early September, as Arnold and others were threshing wheat on a neighbor's land, someone brought him a letter. There was a bill of currency inside. An inquisitive bystander, Littleton Newman, could not tell whether it was a twenty-dollar bill or a fifty. But Arnold, down and out and finding it hard to make ends meet, read the letter then said he was flush with money. He gave it to Newman, who could not make sense of the half dozen lines of cryptic language. Newman would later recollect that Arnold then remarked that "something big would take place one of these days, or be seen in the paper."[27]

However, Arnold's commitment was not solid, and the initial rush of enthusiasm to link up with Booth now competed with a longing for a job with regular income. When he learned that the Federal government was opening positions to Confederate soldiers who had deserted or were refugees, he wrote to the quartermaster general's office in Washington applying for a clerkship, but he was told to make application to the secretary of war.[28] Even though he had signed on to Booth's criminal conspiracy to seize the commander in chief, Arnold wasted no time in writing to the formidable Edwin Stanton, telling him he had been without work for eight months. "If there be a vacancy, the duties of which you think I can perform, which you can give me, I will be under obligation to you," he wrote. "I can give testimonials from Baltimore merchants as to honesty."[29] The letter was bounced back to the quartermaster general's office, which passed on the dispiriting news that there were no vacancies at headquarters. Arnold was told to apply to the quartermasters in any one of the separate military districts.[30] It was a runaround that Arnold did not care for, and he apparently abandoned the job hunt.

Still mulling the possibility of seizing the president from Ford's Theatre in Washington, Booth focused on several actors and stagehands familiar with the layout of the building who might be suitable co-conspirators. At the beginning of winter, in late November or early December 1864, Booth traveled to New York to ingratiate himself with Samuel Chester, an actor he had known for half a dozen years[31] and whom he knew to be unhappy in New York City. Booth had offered to try to find him a position in Washington or Baltimore, and had even tried to use his close friendship with John Ford, proprietor of Ford's Theatre, to coax him into hiring Chester; but Ford had demurred, saying it would be dishonorable to lure Chester away from another theater company. Booth had persisted, going so far as to fabricate the statement that Chester had once saved his life. He said he would do anything to make Chester happy, even offering to pay his salary if only Ford would hire him. But Ford refused.[32]

Booth could make these generous offers only because he had dug into capital, borrowed from others, and accepted charitable assistance from the man who managed his investments in Pennsylvania land and oil fields. Only this friend and co-investor, John Simonds, knew that Booth had never profited from any of the oil investments.[33] The drain on his financial resources picked up sharply as his acting career stalled. Once the source of enviable income, it had all but dried up while he obsessed over the inevitable outcome of the war. Neither Chester nor any of those already recruited had any inkling of the reality of Booth's circumstances. To them, as to the general public, he was still the celebrity and a man of commanding presence.

The two actors talked frequently in the early winter, when Booth would suddenly appear alongside Chester on Broadway, in the theater district. Once, as they walked together, Booth spoke cryptically of investments, telling Chester: "They are laughing at me about a speculation. But I have a greater speculation than they know, that they won't laugh at."[34] At their next meeting Booth asked if Chester would like to join him in speculation in farms and lands in Maryland and Virginia. When Chester said he had no money, Booth offered to provide everything that was needed. But Chester backed off, saying he did not know anything about speculation. The dialogue was repeated several times on other occasions, even in letters Booth wrote to Chester.

One Sunday night — the only evening Chester allowed himself a break from his family — he went drinking with Booth in the House of Lords on Houston Street, near Broadway. Booth did not divulge anything until they were back on the street and Chester had said good night.

"Hold on," said Booth, "I want to tell you what the speculation is."

"Yes," said Chester, "I wish you would. You have worried me enough about it."

They walked along Broadway and then up 4th Street. "It is something not public. We want it private," said Booth. "This is the speculation that I am concerned in. There is an immense party connected with it." Chester would later recollect that Booth mentioned fifty or a hundred people. "It is," said Booth, "a conspiracy against the government."

"To do what?"

Booth told him they had been planning for some time to capture Abraham Lincoln and leading figures in the government in Washington and carry them off to Richmond. "It is nearly made up now and we want you in."

"No, John. I can't have anything to do with anything of that kind."

"Why?"

Chester said it would mean a lifetime of harm for himself and his family.

"If it is money you require, I have three or four thousand dollars that I can leave them."

"It is no compensation for my loss."

Unrelenting, Booth said he needed Chester because he was familiar with the theater, and his role would be to hold the back door open as others seized the president. He had tried to recruit others for this task, but no one was prepared to help. Once, he had tried to enroll an actor called Matthews, but the man had shied away, terrified, especially when Booth warned him to keep quiet or risk being implicated through incriminating documents Booth supposedly possessed. Chester, however, would not change his mind.

Convinced that he would not budge, Booth threatened, "You won't betray me because you can't, for I have facts in my possession that will ruin you for life."

Chester pleaded, "It is very wrong, John, because I have always looked upon you as a friend and have never done you any wrong."

But Booth was unmoved and menacing. Just as he would terrify others into silence, Booth told Chester the group had sworn under oath to hunt down for life, if necessary, anyone who betrayed them. With chilling emphasis, he declared, "I carry a Derringer loaded to shoot everyone that betrays us."

Chester again begged out, saying he was astonished Booth would have anything to do with "such a foolish affair."

They said good night and parted.

A week later Booth wrote Chester, imploring him to come to Washington. "We cannot do without you." Again Chester refused.

Booth wrote by return mail, "You *must* come. Enclosed you will find $50 to pay your expenses, and more money when you get here. If you don't come, keep this money."

But Chester would have none of it.

On Booth's next visit to New York, he apologized for the pressure and said Chester need not be concerned any longer. He was being released from all connection with the plot. Booth said he respected Chester, his wife, and his mother, and added that he was sorry he had ever mentioned the conspiracy.

Before going their separate ways, Booth announced he was going to Richmond. "If anything happens to me, I am going to leave something I want you to get, and want you to attend to it. I want you to promise me you will do it."

"I will, John, if it is nothing to do with this affair."

"Oh, no, it is nothing of that kind."[35]

In late January or early February 1865 the two met briefly in the House of Lords. Booth said he had given up the idea and that the affair had fallen through because some people had backed out.

"Thank God, for your sake, John," Chester said. "I always liked you and am glad you are clear of it."

Chester returned the fifty dollars and Booth accepted it, saying he would not have taken it back if he had not been short of funds. The affair had already cost him more than four thousand in horses and other expenses, he added, though he thought he would recoup some of it.[36]

By the time Booth gave up on recruiting Chester he had already made substantial progress in mapping the escape route and signing on other accomplices. For the abduction to succeed, the kidnappers would have to race south and hide out in Charles County, southern Maryland, before crossing the Potomac River into the safety of rebel-held areas of Virginia. Booth would need vital assistance from a trusted few for food and shelter, and perhaps concealment from the inevitable pursuit by Federal cavalrymen.

Charles County had always been a hotbed of Southern sympathizers. Rural and traditionally conservative, it had voted almost unanimously for anyone but Lincoln in the 1860 presidential election. Some of the farmers, who grew tobacco and corn, traced their county

roots back several generations. Days were measured by the slow
crawl of the sun over the lush expanse of rolling farmland. There was
a metronomic certainty to the rhythms of the isolated communities in
Charles County. This lower county of the border state of Maryland
had no quarrel with the people of the South. It was hospitable territory for shadowy couriers and smugglers riding between Richmond
authorities and their agents in the North. There was little fear of
betrayal or arrest.

In October 1864, while Booth was staying at St. Lawrence Hall,[37]
the Montreal hotel favored by Confederate spies, agents, and couriers, he received a letter of introduction from one of them, Patrick
Martin, to two eminent Charles County physicians, Dr. Samuel Mudd
and Dr. William Queen.[38] Both were slaveholding farmers with sentiments rigidly favoring the South. They would be in a position to offer
aid and comfort to Booth during the projected flight from Washington
to Virginia. They also would be useful in widening Booth's circle of
associates by introducing him to other dependable Charles County
residents with like political prejudices.

In early November Booth went down to Charles County under the
pretext of looking for investments in land. He stayed overnight at
Queen's home and the following morning was introduced to Mudd
in front of a Catholic church in Bryantown, a tiny settlement four
miles south of Mudd's farm. That night Booth slept at Mudd's house.
A week before Christmas Booth returned to the church, from where
he rode with Mudd to be introduced to Confederate agent Thomas
Harbin at the Bryantown tavern.[39]

The two retired to a room on the second floor; it is not known
whether Mudd went with them. There the wary actor scouted the
room and surroundings, glancing in the passageways and probing the
entrances and exits. Only then did he make known his purpose —
even though Harbin had a reputation as one of the most active spies,
couriers, and signal officers in the service of the Confederacy, reporting directly to President Jefferson Davis. Fortuitously for Booth, the
thirty-one-year-old former Bryantown postmaster was a native of
Charles County who knew the lower counties of Maryland as well as
would be expected of a top-flight secret operative. Booth sketched the

plan to kidnap Lincoln and hustle him through Prince George's and
Charles counties, across the Potomac, and into Virginia. He needed
help and invited Harbin to join the ranks. It sounded outlandish, but
Harbin offered to cooperate.[40]

Later Booth told Mudd he was interested in buying some horses.
That night he was invited to sleep over at the doctor's farm, planted
with tobacco[41] and other crops, close to the treacherous Zekiah
Swamp. Booth arrived after supper and stayed all night.[42] According
to Mudd, Booth asked if three or four actors headed south would
be able to cross the Potomac in a small boat without getting caught.
His object, he stated, was to act in the South, where he had already
sent his wardrobe. Mudd assured him he would have no difficulty
crossing the river at any time as people were constantly coming and
going over it.[43]

In the morning Mudd took his guest to the adjoining farm of
George Gardiner, where Booth told the seller he needed a horse for
only one year. He paid eighty dollars for a very old dark bay saddle
horse conspicuously blind in the right eye. Mudd knew the horse well
as "a very fine mover" but took no part in the sale. Booth took delivery the next day at the Bryantown tavern. He could now ride back to
Washington at his own pace instead of taking the stage.[44]

Mudd, the son of a large landowner who farmed close by,[45] was
born in the county but looked older than his thirty-one years: A thick
beard almost concealed his mouth, and his thinning red hair had left
him almost bald.[46] He was married with four children, the oldest
only seven years old.[47] Severe and strict with his slaves, even to the
point of allegedly shooting one,[48] Mudd detested Lincoln and the
abolitionist policies of the Federal government.[49]

The physician would regularly host junior army officers who
crossed over the Potomac from Virginia. Slaves familiarized themselves with the same few rebel officers who came dressed in gray coats
trimmed with yellow, and gray breeches with yellow stripes down
the legs. Whenever the officers ate in Mudd's house, he would have
the slaves stand outside on the lookout. If anyone approached, the
visitors would run for cover among the pines of nearby woods, and
Mudd would have slaves carry the food out to them. Occasionally

the officers slept in the house, but at other times in the woods not far from a spring. One of the slaves saw Mudd exchanging letters with the officers, and giving them clothing and socks.

Mudd's most frequent visitor was John Surratt, a slim, light-haired Confederate courier with a pale complexion, sunken eyes, and prominent forehead[50] whom slaves remembered staying over from Saturday night through Monday evening and always being addressed by Mudd and his wife, Sarah, as "Mr. Surratt."[51] By one slave's reckoning he came about a dozen times in the summer of 1864, when he would talk with Mudd in the privacy of an upstairs room, away from other members of the family.[52]

Surratt had grown up in the county at Surrattsville, midway between Mudd's farm and Washington. The speck of a community had been named after his late father, whose frame house still served as a private residence, tavern, hostelry, and post office. From the outbreak of war it had been a popular rendezvous for Southern sympathizers and a convenient mail drop for Confederate dispatch riders. Since November 1864 John had been boarding with his mother, Mary, in the boardinghouse she owned nine blocks east of the White House in Washington, while she rented out her Surrattsville tavern.

One year after the outbreak of war Surratt, eighteen, had dropped out of St. Charles College, a Catholic seminary twenty miles from Baltimore,[53] and become a Confederate dispatch rider, delivering secret mail between Washington spies and Confederate boatmen on the Potomac River. The young man thrilled to the dangers and risks, reveling in the challenge of crossing Union territory with compromising documents tucked into the heels of his boots or stuffed between the planks of a buggy,[54] even though capture would result in death by a bullet or from the grip of a noose. In the winter of 1864–1865 he had playfully thrown his head back and told a friend, "If the Yankees knew what I was doing they would stretch this old neck of mine."[55]

One evening two days before Christmas 1864 John Surratt and his friend, Louis Weichmann, strolled down 7th Street NW in Washington, half a block from his mother's boardinghouse. They had been friends since studying together at the Catholic seminary, and for the past two months had been sharing a room in the boardinghouse. Weichmann had also given up on studying for the priesthood and now worked as a clerk in the War Department building adjacent to the White House. When they were opposite Odd Fellows' Hall someone called out, "Surratt! Surratt!" John turned and saw Dr. Mudd, visiting from his Charles County farm. Surratt introduced him to Weichmann, then Mudd introduced the two young friends to the man standing beside him. His name was John Wilkes Booth.

The actor invited everyone to his room at the National Hotel at 6th and Pennsylvania Avenue, and en route Mudd and Surratt walked arm in arm. The National was Booth's favorite hotel, but even though patronized by many celebrities, it did not have a spotless reputation. The wife of one general had stormed out in disgust, complaining that she was not rugged enough to endure the sickening filth.[56]

Booth ordered wine and cigars all round, but Weichmann was shunted aside as Booth and Mudd huddled outside the room in whispered conversation for about five minutes before they summoned Surratt to join them. When they reentered, both Mudd and Booth apologized for their absence, saying they were unsuccessfully negotiating a price for the sale of Mudd's farm to Booth. But again the three separated themselves from Weichmann, who sat eight feet away. The trio bunched at a table, speaking softly as Booth took an envelope from his pocket and on the back of it drew lines, trying to get Surratt to name Charles County roads and locations where Booth said he had become lost a few days earlier.

Mudd later gave a different account, saying he called Surratt out of the room alone to caution him, thinking Booth was a Union spy. Mudd claimed he had introduced Surratt to Booth earlier only after the actor insisted. Twenty minutes later all four walked over to Mudd's room at the Pennsylvania House, where Surratt and Booth distanced themselves from the others until they all parted before 11 PM.[57] It was Weichmann's first indication that his friendship with John Surratt had limits, that he was an outsider, and that he would never share the secrets of the furtive men who would come and go with increasing regularity at Mary Surratt's narrow brick boardinghouse.

Over time Booth kept pressing Surratt for information on routes and roads leading south from Washington to the Potomac River.

But he did so without revealing any of his plans to kidnap Lincoln. Surratt, wary and frustrated, began balking at Booth's inquisitiveness and his failure to explain the purpose of his questioning. Finally, in exasperation, Surratt scolded Booth, "It is useless for you to seek any information from me at all. I know who you are, and your intentions." Booth, cautious, did not reply immediately, but then he promised to tell all if Surratt would promise secrecy. The younger man seemed offended. "I will do nothing of the kind," he bristled. "You know well I am a Southern man. If you cannot trust me, we will separate."

Booth had no need for further evasion. He was now sure of his man. But before full disclosure he wanted to explain his motivation, so he told of the desperate need to fill the depleted ranks of the Confederate armies. "I have a proposition to submit to you, which I think if we can carry out will bring about the desired exchange," said Booth. To break a long silence that followed, Surratt asked, "Well, sir, what is your proposition?" Booth stood up, looked under the bed, into the wardrobe, out the doorway, and down the passage, then cautioned, "We will have to be careful. Walls have ears." He drew his chair closer to Surratt and whispered, "It is to kidnap President Lincoln and carry him off to Richmond!"

Flabbergasted, Surratt exclaimed, "Kidnap President Lincoln!" It was absurd, foolhardy, a pipe dream. He told Booth it was foolish. But Booth did not blanch; and as he had done with Arnold and O'Laughlin, he described in well-reasoned and specific detail how easy it would be to capture the chief executive during one of his many unguarded rides to the Soldiers' Home. He even gave the precise role to be assigned to each conspirator. It was tempting and daring but outrageously silly. Surratt was at once frightened and exhilarated by the sheer audacity of the plot. He asked for time to consider, but he did not need long. Just two days later he signed on as an eager and ardent collaborator.[58]

Booth now began to call frequently at Mrs. Surratt's gray-painted boardinghouse, where ten people slept in seven bedrooms on three floors and in the attic.[59] Booth and John Surratt would nearly always go upstairs to Surratt's room at the back of the third floor, where they would remain secluded for as long as three hours. If John Surratt was out, Booth would talk out of earshot of others with his widowed mother, a pious convert to Catholicism.[60] She shared Booth's rigid commitment to the lifestyle and cause of the South. She also enjoyed his company, finding him pleasant, handsome, and gentlemanly.

Her daughter, Anna, twenty-two, was either enamored of Booth or so flattered to have such a celebrity visiting the house that she and her friend and fellow boarder Honora Fitzpatrick bought two photographs of the handsome actor from a daguerreotype gallery and brought them back to the house. When her brother, John, saw them he vehemently demanded she tear them up and burn the scraps, or else he would take them away. But Anna could not bring herself to destroy Booth's image. She hid the photograph behind an innocuous picture titled *Morning, Noon, and Night* that stood on the mantelpiece in Mrs. Surratt's bedroom.[61]

The success of Abraham Lincoln's abduction would depend heavily on men with an infinite knowledge of Prince George's and Charles Counties, an intimate feel for the terrain, and familiarity with the creeks and inlets by the ragged banks of the swollen Potomac River. There would be no time to improvise or risk galloping blindly if pursuers closed in quicker than expected. Collaborators experienced in the art of crossing the river would have to be on standby, ready to cast off in a jiffy. John Surratt had covered more or less the same route on his dangerous rides, but his experience was limited. He was a novice when the wiliest of scouts were needed, horsemen who knew the counties as well as avian predators above.

In the fall of 1864 Surratt met George Atzerodt, twenty-nine, a Prussian-born immigrant who spoke with a slight German accent even though he had lived two-thirds of his life in the United States. Atzerodt knew how to build carriages, but for the past seven or eight years he had specialized as a carriage painter at Port Tobacco, a village of about five hundred blacks and whites deep in Charles County, near the waters of the Potomac.[62] He rented premises to work on carriages, but one resident who saw him daily said "his business was about run out. He was a trifling kind of man, not very responsible."[63] Even his peers called him "a country man."[64] Atzerodt had never amounted to anything and had no ambition beyond making ends meet. Though he knew he was looked upon as a fool, he told one acquaintance that he knew how to behave himself in the company of decent people.[65] He was five foot seven, thickly built, scruffy, and surly looking. He had dark brown hair and facial fuzz over his jaw, chin, and upper lip. Even his brother thought he looked "sickly" with his sallow, yellowish complexion. He had an awkward gait, tilting his head to one side and walking with one shoulder higher than the other.[66] A heavy drinker, he was frequently in bars but always backed out of trouble, even when picked upon or insulted by others spoiling for a fight.[67] For some years he had been living with a widowed mother of four, the youngest fathered by Atzerodt.[68]

His usefulness to the conspirators lay in his weak and malleable character and his acquired expertise in the nooks and crannies, paths and trails of Charles and neighboring counties. A loser in urban society, Atzerodt needed neither guidance nor mentor when riding off the beaten track in Maryland's lower counties. Here he was the leader whom others would have to follow to find their way out of the wild. And he knew the shores of the Potomac better than most, having frequently ferried men and supplies across the swift currents in the unqualified service of the Confederacy. He was adept at securing boats and skilled in maneuvering them to the safety of either shore, and he considered himself well paid for the work.[69] His expertise with carriages and rowboats would make him an invaluable ally should those modes of transporting Lincoln be in need of instant repair.

Shortly after Christmas 1864 John Surratt tempted the carriage painter with a vague remark that he, Surratt, was "going to get a great prize" and wanted Atzerodt to accompany him because he knew the area fronting the Potomac so well. Three weeks later, after Surratt had again run the blockade, the two men rode into Washington, where Atzerodt put up at Mary Surratt's boardinghouse. Without divulging names, John Surratt explained that other parties to the undisclosed prize were in New York and Baltimore, so Atzerodt returned home.

A week later Surratt summoned him again. Atzerodt arrived by stage, staying at the hotel he often frequented, the Pennsylvania House on C Street NW, where rooms were shared with strangers. Surratt came for him, took him to his mother's boardinghouse six blocks away, and there introduced him to the celebrated actor. John Wilkes Booth did not disclose anything of consequence, but when he met the carriage painter again at the Pennsylvania House, Booth used the same tack he had employed to ensnare others, asking how Atzerodt would like to go into the oil-leasing business, adding disarmingly, "Don't mind the capital. I have that." But Atzerodt begged off, and nothing came of the offer. Before parting, Booth gently suggested that Atzerodt cut down on his drinking.[70]

Atzerodt, however, was gradually sucked into the conspiracy to abduct Lincoln. He began visiting the boardinghouse more often, even staying overnight at least once.[71] The residents never warmed to his rough-edged personality and vulgar appearance. They nicknamed him Port Tobacco.[72]

David Herold's recruitment as a co-conspirator was almost inevitable. He had been friendly with John Surratt for the past eight or nine years and with Atzerodt for about half that time. He had even met John Wilkes Booth a few years back when the accomplished actor was in Washington playing the lead role for almost two weeks in nine different plays at Ford's Theatre, while the mediocre Herold, though an alumnus of Georgetown College, was a mere clerk in William Thompson's drugstore a block east of the White House. Booth had given him a complimentary ticket to the theater, and Herold was flattered when invited to go backstage. It was a rare honor to meet the star who had drawn the largest Washington audience ever to see *Richard III,* with an overflow of hundreds willing to stand just to see him perform. The *Evening Star*'s critic thought it unfair to make a comparison between Booth and his late father at his best, but raved, "He is a performer of singular promise," and noted that the ovation given Booth proved he "had made his mark."[73] The two young Marylanders, with harmonious political instincts, had met several times a week for many months following, sometimes standing on the sidewalk merely to chat.[74]

Herold, twenty-two, shared with Atzerodt an intuitive feel for the countryside and a yearning to be on horseback away from the clutter of the cities. He had a particular passion for shooting partridges and nearly every fall would spend two or three months indulging this great love. Foxhunting was another of his profoundly gratifying pastimes. He delighted in riding across Maryland's southern counties — which he knew as well as, if not better than, Atzerodt — because he was congenial and had built up a widely dispersed network of friends. He was acquainted with so many rural residents that he would lay claim to knowing "nearly everyone in Maryland" south of Washington in Prince George's County.[75] These dependable contacts would be invaluable to conspirators in need of food and shelter on their flight south from Washington.

Herold was about an inch shorter than Atzerodt and had a habit of partially closing his dark eyes when looking at anyone. One law enforcement official who met him noticed his small, fleshy hands, small feet with very high instep, rather heavy eyebrows on a full face, and a very round body.[76] Considered by many to be boyish, immature, and trivial in conversation, Herold was nevertheless credited with being instinctively quick and smart. A Washingtonian who lived two doors from his widowed mother's home outside the Navy Yard thought Herold somewhat vacuous, "a wild young man [with] very little to do. He kept a horse and rode a great deal."[77] Another observer, the son of a druggist who employed Herold for almost a year, said the muscular young man was not easily provoked, but when angry, would fight. He considered Herold a "blackguard" towards women, who did not like him because "he would, on being merely introduced, take liberties."[78] An only son, Herold lacked all sense of masculine responsibility toward his mother and six sisters, even leaving home for the pleasures of the countryside only days before his ailing father died.[79] One of Herold's sisters noted his lack of common sense, judging him too credulous and "easily made a fool of by anybody."[80]

Atzerodt was equally vulnerable to the influence of others. The two friends, crafty and resourceful in the boondocks, were relative simpletons in the city, spending much of their time together in bars, enjoying the circus, amusing themselves with popular entertainment at the Canterbury, and sharing a room at the Pennsylvania House.[81]

The most likely recruit to the conspiracy was also the most

physically daunting, a muscular brute at times devoid of emotion, an automaton geared for violence, much like a great white shark. Lewis Payne, twenty,[82] was a handsome, commanding presence, about six foot two and 175 pounds.[83] He was a drifter without obligations, accomplishments, or dreams. Payne was born Lewis Thornton Powell in Alabama, the son of a Baptist minister who moved to Florida.[84] The father's religious influence so affected the son that from ages twelve through seventeen he was kindhearted and pious, attending the Young Men's Prayer Meetings and often singing his favorite hymn:

> *Farewell, farewell to all below,*
> *My Savior calls and I must go.*[85]

At the outbreak of war, however, Payne cut loose from his family, defied their pleas, and enlisted in the Confederate army. They would never see him again, learning of his whereabouts only from scraps of information in odd letters home. Payne served in the Army of Northern Virginia, and while he was in Richmond he attended his first play out of curiosity. He was instantly captivated by the voice and appearance of one of the actors, John Wilkes Booth, and stayed behind afterward to introduce himself. Payne was, in the words of his lawyer, "irresistibly drawn to follow a man so wondrously fascinating and intellectual. The actor was pleased to have a follower so powerful in his muscles."[86] They formed a close bond, with Payne deferring to his idol, whom he always called "Captain."[87]

In the summer of 1863 Payne was wounded in the arm, captured, and hospitalized at Gettysburg, where he later served as a nurse, tending the wounded of both armies. According to Margaret Branson, a Baltimore resident who volunteered as a nurse for six weeks at the Gettysburg General Hospital, Payne still went by the name Powell. He wore blue pants and a dark slouch hat, and used the title of *Doctor.*

Eventually he escaped and made his way back to Confederate lines. On New Year's Day 1865 witnesses in Warrenton, Virginia, saw Payne uncharacteristically save the lives of two captive Union soldiers from the wrath of Confederate troops by facing down fellow Southerners, ordering them to back off or risk losing their own lives.[88] Shortly afterward Powell changed his name to Payne, the name of the family he had lived with in Warrenton, apparently to disguise his identity and avoid recapture for escaping from Union custody or deserting from Confederate service. That fall Payne called briefly on young Margaret Branson at her mother's house in Baltimore.

Payne and Margaret Branson must have corresponded, for he returned to her home in Baltimore in mid-January, staying for more than six weeks and often accompanying her to church. He spoke freely about his escapades with John Singleton Mosby's dashing rangers, notorious for wreaking havoc in lightning raids on Union camps and bases in Virginia. He also told her two of his brothers had been killed in the army, but did not say on which side they had served.[89] Payne's normally placid temperament gave way to an explosive outburst one day when goaded by the apparent insolence of a black female servant who refused to clean his room. He struck her on the forehead, threw her to the ground, stomped on her, and threatened to kill her.[90]

John Wilkes Booth appeared for the last time on the New York stage in November 1864 when he and brothers Edwin and Junius Jr. made theatrical history by appearing together in *Julius Caesar*. But even as he won applause from admiring audiences, the plot to kidnap the president was advancing stealthily with the acquisition of a getaway boat. Booth delegated Surratt to secure the craft to carry the trussed-up president across the Potomac. He found "a good, large, and stout boat" owned by Richard Smoot, a farmer living two miles from Port Tobacco who had taken to running the blockade across the river with passengers and goods to compensate for lost income from unprofitable farming during wartime.

Surratt said he might also need two more boats, each able to hold fifteen people. If the sale went through, Surratt insisted on immediate possession because, as Smoot remembered him saying, "It would be the sequence of an event of unprecedented magnitude in the history of the country, which would astound the entire world." Smoot guessed it had something to do with vague rumors circulating of a plan to abduct the president. But he did not ask questions, and Surratt withheld further comment. Having agreed on a sale price of $250, payable in full when the boat was put to use, they met in the Port Tobacco office of a distinguished lawyer, Frederick Stone, a former member of the Maryland legislature, whose family roots in Charles County included a grandfather who was a member of the first Congress; a great-uncle, Thomas Stone, who was one of the signers of the Declaration of Independence; and an earlier ancestor who was deputy colonial governor of Maryland as far back as 1649. Stone took $125 from Surratt to be held in trust for Smoot, with the lawyer standing guarantor for the balance.

The boat was turned over to Atzerodt, who followed Surratt's orders and had a man named George Bateman take it to his farm about ten miles away up Kings Creek, a branch of the Potomac River. Bateman kept it hidden on the waterway, readied for immediate use.[91] But Atzerodt was not as tight-lipped as he should have been. In January, with the river iced over, Atzerodt told a stranger who had paid to be taken across to Virginia that he had bought two boats for Surratt. The stranger, who also met Surratt at the Port Tobacco hotel, left with the impression that Surratt was the manager, with Atzerodt in his employ.[92]

Atzerodt was even more indiscreet among his family. He boasted to his sister that she would "either hear of his being hung or making a good deal of money" — a foolish gloat given that his brother John, a loyal Unionist whom he looked up to, was a detective on the staff of Provost Marshal James McPhail in Baltimore.[93]

Booth lay low for the next few months, even though the principals had been selected and poised for action. John Surratt's indiscreet remark to Smoot, and Samuel Arnold's loose tongue on receiving money in an envelope he opened on a Maryland threshing field, were not the only gaffes from insiders plotting a crime of unprecedented magnitude. Booth himself in early March had told Harry Ford, the treasurer of Ford's Theatre, that something would happen in two weeks that would "astonish the world." He did not elaborate.[94] And in Montreal, a visiting New York lawyer had met with old acquaintances now prominent among resident Confederate leaders and thought they were simply grandstanding when they predicted "something startling was to occur, which might end the war despite Federal successes."[95] Surratt would reflect later that the plotters seldom saw one another that winter "owing to the many rumors afloat that a conspiracy of some kind was being concocted in Washington."[96]

Sometime in January, Booth surprised Arnold and O'Laughlin in Baltimore when he arrived with a heavy trunk concealing carbines, revolvers, knives, belts, cartridge boxes, cartridges, caps, canteens, and even two pairs of handcuffs to restrain the president. Fearful that the weight of the trunk might attract attention, Booth handed over the pistols, knives. and handcuffs, and they were shipped express in a box to Washington.[97] When the trio linked up later in Washington the actor took his charges to Ford's Theatre, where he quietly went over the alternative abduction plan, pointing out the rear exits of the building he knew so well.

Arnold and O'Laughlin, presumably financed by Booth, rented a room in a boardinghouse only a few minutes' walk from Mary Surratt's building. For almost two months they saw Booth regularly, at least three or four times a week, but only for brief periods.[98] Their inquisitive landlady had once seen a pistol in the room and took note when they stayed out all night.[99]

The two unemployed co-conspirators never lacked funds to indulge themselves. They relished the merriment of entertainment halls and the comfort of liquid opiates at bars in the company of friends from Baltimore. Arnold and O'Laughlin fooled their friends, family, and even the landlady with the cover story that they were trading stocks in the oil business.[100]

A week after Lincoln's second inauguration, Booth signaled a readiness to act upon his simmering hatred of the president. Some of the co-conspirators began appearing at the Surratt boardinghouse nine blocks east of the White House. One resident guessed Atzerodt visited at least ten or fifteen times.[101] Payne puzzled the residents from the moment he climbed the steps to the entrance on his initial visit in late February. He came dressed in a rumpled hat, black coat, gray pants, and a worn black overcoat and said his name was Wood. Mrs. Surratt asked Weichmann to take him upstairs to his room and serve him a meal, which Payne ate ravenously, volunteering only that he was a clerk in a Baltimore china store.

A few weeks later Payne returned to the boardinghouse on H Street NW, this time telling the skeptical residents that he was a Baptist preacher named Lewis Payne. He carried only a linen coat and two shirts but stayed three days.[102] Anna Surratt took an instant dislike to him, certain he did not look anything like a preacher, and she was rattled by the look of his eyes. When she confided her feelings to her mother, Mary Surratt replied, "No, I don't admire him myself."[103] Another resident, Eliza Holahan, was equally suspicious, suggesting he did not look as if he would convert many souls.[104]

On March 13 Booth telegraphed a thinly coded message to O'Laughlin in Baltimore: "Don't fear to neglect your business. You had better come at once."[105]

Two days later Weichmann picked up a large, false black mustache lying on his table. Without telling Payne, to whom it apparently belonged, he took it to his office at the Commissary General of Prisoners and clowned with colleagues, wearing it with a pair of glasses.[106] But he never returned it, and when Payne asked if he had seen it, Weichmann feigned ignorance.[107]

The following day Weichmann came back from work, and as he opened the door to the room in the back of the attic John Surratt and Payne, sitting on a bed, scrambled to cover up two long navy-issue revolvers, two bowie knives, and eight spurs.[108] They relaxed when they saw who had entered, but Weichmann went downstairs to confide his unease to Mrs. Surratt. She told him not to worry, that her son needed the weapons for protection when riding in the countryside. Weichmann apparently accepted the explanation; he too knew that her son was running the dangerous blockade.[109]

Booth had chosen the night of March 15 to invite some of the co-conspirators and a few of the boardinghouse female residents to watch a performance of a play at Ford's Theatre even though he was not acting in it. Their presence would give the accomplices an opportunity to see the layout of the theater. John Surratt and Payne accompanied Honora Fitzpatrick and Apollonia Dean, a girl nine years old.[110] They sat in one of the private boxes, and toward the end of the performance Booth came in and whispered to Surratt. They moved to the doorway, talking softly, and were joined by Payne. The interruption lasted no more than a few minutes.[111]

Once the females had been taken back to the boardinghouse, all the conspirators gathered around Booth at Gautier's, a popular saloon not far from the Kirkwood House Hotel, where newly installed vice president Andrew Johnson roomed. It was the first time the motley band of unemployed, reckless young men had come together.

They huddled throughout the night, eating oysters, smoking cigars, drinking, and getting to know one another. But they were careful to lower their voices when Booth began sketching the unthinkable. He was now riveted on snatching Lincoln from Ford's Theatre as the president sat in his box twelve feet above the stage. They would need all the precision and timing of acrobats and trapeze artists to pull it off. There was no room for laggards or the fainthearted. At the precise moment, O'Laughlin and one of the other accomplices were to extinguish the gas lights; Arnold was to burst into the box and seize the president while Booth and Atzerodt handcuffed and lowered him onto the stage, where Payne, the strongest by far, would restrain him until Booth and Atzerodt arrived to help out. Surratt and Herold were to wait on the other side of the Eastern Branch Bridge, less than three miles east, ready to gallop away with the presidential hostage. But Booth was tentative, and soon switched individuals' assignments, delegating Payne to help him grab the president while Atzerodt was to replace Herold on the other side of the bridge.

There were misgivings among the subordinates, and Booth was immediately challenged. Months back he had artfully seduced them into joining forces to kidnap Lincoln as he rode unguarded in the open. Now Booth was advocating an indoor abduction before more than sixteen hundred theatergoers. Arnold thought the concept harebrained, fanciful, insane, and incapable of success. On the off chance that they were able to get as far as the bridge, they would be confronted by a sentinel.

"Shoot the sentinel!" Booth interjected.

But Arnold said that would not help because once the alarm had been sounded, the game was up. He denounced it as "impracticable."[112]

He wanted, at the very least, the possibility of success. O'Laughlin wanted to back up Arnold, but Booth cut in, "You find fault with everything in it." Arnold objected. He merely wanted a chance to pull it off. He said he would defer to Booth as his leader, but not as his executioner. Booth bristled and, in a tone Arnold described as stern and commanding, threatened, "Do you know that you are liable to be shot? Remember your oath."

Arnold would not be cowed. He argued that the original plan had been changed, and an agreement broken by one party voided it for all. If Booth felt inclined to shoot him, he had no farther to go. But Arnold warned he would defend himself. Then he gave an ultimatum. "Gentlemen, if this is not accomplished this week, I forever withdraw from it."[113] However, he qualified the demand by promising, "You have naught to fear from me in the matter as I never would betray you."[114]

John Surratt had reservations of his own and worried that authorities had wind of their group, or information on some kind of plot.

But Booth would not back down. "Well, gentlemen," he said, "If the worst comes to the worst, I shall know what to do."

It touched off a rancorous exchange of threats and curses between Booth and some of those around him. Surratt remembered that four got up to leave, with one of them, perhaps Arnold, declaring, "If I understand you to intimate anything more than the capture of Mr. Lincoln, I for one will bid you goodbye."

Everyone except Booth then got up to leave, some even putting on their hats. Booth could not let it happen. He apologized, saying he "had drank too much champagne." They had conspired throughout the night. Everyone was weary and testy and in no mood for further discussion. According to Surratt, "Everything was amicably arranged." By the time they separated it was already dawn.[115]

The following day Booth was riding down Pennsylvania Avenue when he stopped to talk to Arnold and O'Laughlin. He apologized for the words he had used, saying he thought Arnold must have been drunk. Uncowed, Arnold replied that he had never been more sober and stood by everything he had threatened.[116]

On St. Patrick's Day, March 17, a day celebrated with Mass and much carousing in the city's crowded saloons, Booth got word that President Lincoln would be riding by on the very country road along which he had considered abducting him. The chief executive was expected to attend a matinee performance of the comedy *Still Waters Run Deep* for the benefit of wounded soldiers at the Campbell Hospital several miles north up 7th Street, near the Soldiers' Home.[117]

It seemed that the long wait might now be over. All the conspirators were committed to this plot, and each knew his role. They would strike swiftly, overpower resistors, seize the carriage, speed over Bennings Bridge several miles east, then abandon the vehicle outside the city limits and hurry off with their hostage for the friendly sanctuary of southern Maryland. If all went well, Lincoln would be bundled into a boat, rowed across the Potomac River, whisked deep into Virginia, and brought trussed up in triumph to Richmond.[118]

Booth detailed Herold to ride south to Surrattsville or the nearby village of TB, taking with him the trunk with two carbines, a monkey wrench, ammunition, and four pieces of rope readied weeks earlier. Arnold and O'Laughlin went to their rooming house to arm themselves while Booth corralled Payne, Surratt, and Atzerodt.

Everyone except the absent Herold drank with Booth in a nearby restaurant until the ringleader rode off alone to the hospital for a final check on the president's whereabouts. Only then did he learn that Lincoln had not arrived and was not even expected. Unknown to Booth, the president had accepted an invitation to speak at 4 PM in Washington at the ceremonial presentation to the governor of Indiana of a Confederate garrison flag, captured at Fort Anderson, North Carolina, by volunteers from Indiana. Ironically, the outdoor event before two thousand onlookers and the marine band took place on a balcony of the National Hotel, where Booth was staying. And in words that would have infuriated Booth had he been present, Lincoln derided the rebels for considering the recruitment of slaves for their armed forces, suggesting that any black agreeing to fight for the South deserved to be enslaved, together with whites who promoted human bondage.[119]

The depth of Booth's exasperation can only be imagined as he raced back to abort the assault. Disappointment gave way to fright as the freelance rogues, all novices at high crimes and treason, lost confidence in their own safety. What if the president had changed his plans because the military or law enforcement knew of the plot? Perhaps they were already under surveillance. Whatever the cause of Lincoln's absence, they doubted they could remain undiscovered much longer.[120] Deflated, they sped off independently.

Louis Weichmann, who remained unaware of the conspiracy, was reading in his boardinghouse room when Surratt charged in, wildly animated, irrational, and almost incoherent. He clutched a four-barreled Sharpe's revolver so small, it could be hidden in his vest pocket.

"John, what is the matter? Why are you so much excited?" Weichmann asked.

"I will shoot anyone that comes into this room! My prospect is gone! My hopes are blighted!"

Weichmann told him to settle down.

Ten minutes later Payne rushed into the room, his face flushed, a pistol visible beneath his raised vest. Only a quarter of an hour passed before Booth stormed in grasping a riding whip. He was so distracted, pacing the room, that he noticed only Surratt and Payne until Weichmann spoke up.

Surprised, Booth remarked, "Hello! You here? I did not see you." Instantly the three arrivals disappeared upstairs into Payne's attic room, where they stayed for about half an hour before leaving the building together.[121]

The reckless scheme to grab the president without even cover of darkness seemed in the immediate aftermath to have been sheer lunacy. The conspirators were now disheartened. Some momentarily lost their nerve. But for Booth, it was a mere setback. The plan had been foiled through no fault of their own, and he was characteristically unsubdued. His obsession with striking at the Union's figurehead had festered for months and become a driving force with a relentless momentum. He was no longer open to reason nor even skeptical of his barmy fixation.

Herold had meanwhile hidden the trunk with weaponry at his lodgings in TB, then ridden the five miles back to Mrs. Surratt's tavern at Surrattsville, rented by John Lloyd. He drank whiskey and played cards until about 10 PM, when he declined Lloyd's invitation to sleep over, claiming he had business to attend to in TB.

The next morning John Surratt in a buggy and Atzerodt on horseback pulled up briefly outside the tavern, then set off for TB, returning half an hour later with Herold. When Lloyd was called into the front parlor he saw two carbines, cartridge boxes, rope, and a monkey wrench on the sofa. Surratt told Lloyd to hide them. Surratt, carrying the cartridge boxes, followed by Lloyd clutching the carbines, led the way up to an unfinished attic on the second floor at the back of the dwelling quarters used by Lloyd. There, in an opening to a space between the main building and the unplastered attic where Lloyd said he had never been, Surratt indicated that the carbines could be hidden under the joists between the floor and the ceiling. The monkey wrench and rope were stashed in a storeroom below. Surratt gave no explanation but said he would call for them soon.[122]

That night Surratt, Atzerodt, and Herold presented complimentary tickets given by Booth to see him appear in *The Apostate* at Ford's Theatre. It would be Booth's last theatrical performance, even though he was only twenty-six years old.[123]

After the show, which Booth performed for the benefit of a friend and fellow actor, he traveled to New York again. His departure did not signal any relaxation of his hold over the gang he had courted and cajoled for so long. On March 23 he sent a cryptic telegraph from New York to Weichmann: "Tell John to telegraph number and street at once." Puzzled, Weichmann handed over the message to John Surratt the same day, but when he asked what it was about, his roommate snapped, "Don't be so damned inquisitive."[124]

Booth had wanted the address of the Herndon House, where surreptitious arrangements had been made for a room to be held for Payne, who had signed an oath of allegiance in Baltimore on March 14, agreeing to remain north of Philadelphia during the war.[125] If recognized in Washington, he would be arrested immediately. The boardinghouse stood on the southwest corner of 9th and F streets, at the far end of the same long block housing Ford's Theatre and a stroll away from Mrs.

Surratt's building on H Street. Booth's female intermediary had even arranged for Payne's meals to be sent up to his room, on the pretext that the occupant who would move in was "a delicate gentleman."[126]

Unemployed and clearly without independent means of support, Payne had moved in toward the end of March and was visited shortly afterward by Mrs. Surratt. She slipped in to speak with him for about twenty minutes as she strolled back to her boardinghouse with her daughter and several of her own boarders after attending an evening service at nearby St. Patrick's Church.[127]

O'Laughlin and Arnold had meanwhile lost no time in returning to Baltimore, the latter uncomfortable and uneasy, sensing himself under suspicion even from within his own family. His self-esteem was again low. He was unemployed and felt no better than a vagabond. Arnold retreated for a few days to his brother's home in isolated rural Hookstown, six miles outside the city. On March 25 he returned to the parental residence in Baltimore to find a card from Booth wanting to see him at Barnum's Hotel on urgent business. Nonetheless, prodded by his father, he applied that day for a clerk's position in a storehouse at Old Point Comfort, near Fortress Monroe in Virginia, which guarded the entrance to the James River about 160 miles south of Baltimore.

By the time Arnold arrived at Barnum's Hotel the actor had already checked out and boarded the train for Washington.[128] He had left behind an unwelcome letter for Arnold, calling for one final attempt at abduction the following week. If it failed, Booth pledged to abandon the plot forever.[129]

Already angered at finding Booth gone, Arnold mixed admonition with words of caution in a long response to "Dear John," dated Hookstown, March 27. He wrote that he had come as soon as he could but found Booth had gone to W ——n (Washington). "I called also to see Mike, but learned from his mother he had gone out with you, and had not returned." He scolded Booth for being inconsiderate. "When I left you, you stated we would not meet in a month or so. Therefore, I made application for employment, an answer to which I shall receive during the week. I told my parents I had ceased with you. Can I, then, under existing circumstances, come as you request?" In guarded language he warned that the government was suspicious, making the undertaking more complicated. "Why not, for the present, desist, for various reasons . . . None, no not one, was more in favor of the enterprise than myself, and today would be there, had you not done as you have . . . Time more propitious will arrive yet. Do not act rashly or in haste."

In a cryptic comment he never subsequently explained, hinting at links to Southern authorities, Arnold suggested, "I would prefer your first query, go and see how it will be taken at R———d [Richmond], and ere long I shall be better prepared to again be with you." But loath to split with Booth, Arnold ended, "Do not in anger peruse this. Weigh all I have said, and, as a rational man and a friend, you cannot censure or upbraid my conduct. Write me to Balto [Baltimore] or . . . I will . . . meet you in Baltimore." He signed off "Your friend, Sam."[130]

When O'Laughlin called four days later and asked Arnold to accompany him to Washington to reclaim five hundred dollars he had loaned Booth, the two took the train to the capital. They met briefly with Booth in the actor's room at the National Hotel, where he had registered again on his return from New York. He told them he had jettisoned the abduction plot and was going to return to his acting career. Arnold's letter of March 27 had not yet arrived, and at Sam's suggestion Booth agreed to destroy it. He told the Baltimoreans that Surratt had gone to Richmond, having volunteered to accompany a female courier following the arrest of the man who regularly ferried blockade runners across the Potomac River. This would be the last meeting and the final communication with Booth; before parting, the ringleader told them they could keep the weapons he had bought for them, even sell the arms if they wished.[131]

Arnold returned home to find his job application approved. The following morning he went to the Hookstown farm and gave his brother custody of a revolver and knife, but took a second revolver with him when he sailed that evening for the new clerical job at the bathing resort of Old Point Comfort.[132] The kidnapping plot that would have brought him within point-blank range of the commander in chief and head of state had clearly evaporated. Outspoken at times in questioning Booth's judgment, Arnold now prepared to distance himself from the plotters. At long last he hoped to earn a decent living. But he had mailed Booth incriminating evidence, and it would boomerang, flushing him out of the remote shelter at his new place of employment.

The conspirators' erratic behavior and guarded communications in the Surratt boardinghouse had meanwhile alerted one of the boarders, Louis Weichmann, to the possibility of physical harm to the president. Weichmann had turned a blind eye to Surratt's blockade-running because of their close friendship. But he was suspicious that something more ominous was being hatched after Booth and Payne began to appear more frequently at the boardinghouse. He became sensitive to the whispered huddles between Booth and John Surratt, both of whom often nudged the other to disappear upstairs, where they would remain for two or three hours at a time. Weichmann's curiosity intensified with the appearance of the false mustache during Payne's stopover and the chance sighting of Surratt and Payne handling weapons on a bed. He was even more keenly alert after recalling an article he had read in the *New York Daily Tribune* exactly a year earlier about the likelihood of the president being kidnapped.[133]

One day he confided these misgivings to Captain Gleason, a colleague in the War Department. "Captain, do you think any party could attempt the capture of President Lincoln?" Gleason hooted, dismissing the very idea as ludicrous. But the day after the aborted attempt on the road to Campbell Hospital, Weichmann again told the captain of his suspicions, describing his acquaintances' bizarre behavior and repeating John Surratt's strange outbursts. Whatever they were up to had been a failure, and Weichmann was glad of it. "Captain," he pressed, "let us think it over, and let us think of something it could have been." He suggested blockade-running, delivering dispatches, even plotting a jail break at the Old Capitol Prison, but none of the ideas seemed plausible. Nothing seemed to account for the hints that the men were definitely up to no good. By April, however, Payne and Atzerodt no longer visited, and Weichmann's interest faded.[134]

In the first week of April, Booth was again in Manhattan, drinking once more in the House of Lords with Samuel Chester, the actor he had unsuccessfully pressured to join the kidnap plot. Suddenly Booth struck the table hard, exclaiming spiritedly, "What an excellent chance I had to kill the president, if I had wished, on inauguration day!" He said he was as near to the president that day, five weeks back, as he and Chester were seated next to each other now. When Chester asked what good it would have done to commit such an act, Booth replied with simple candor that he could live in history.[135]

CHAPTER 4

"The Last Speech He Will Ever Make"

At 4:30 PM on Monday, April 3, 1865, fourteen-year-old Willie Kettles was in the telegraph office of the War Department when a dispatch arrived announcing the fall of Richmond. Barely able to contain his excitement, Kettles ran with it to a colleague who opened a window and bellowed to all and sundry, "Richmond has surrendered!"[1]

The cry reverberated throughout the capital as residents relayed the news to anyone within earshot. Washingtonians went giddy with joy. Throughout the long years of war, even during the happiest times of the second inaugural parade, there had been nothing to surpass the ecstasy of this moment. The surrender of the Confederate capital doomed the rebels and gave luminous proof of imminent Union victory. Even the stern and scowling secretary of war, Edwin Stanton, before whom subordinates quaked and cowered, now joined in the general merriment. Lifting the teenage boy to the window to show him to the cheering crowds below, Stanton joyously declared, "My friends! Here is the young man who received the telegram which tells us of the fall of Richmond!"[2]

For two days the city celebrated as never before. In an instant all the horrors of war, the anguish, the suffering, the monotonous news of battles and casualties, the endless gloom, strife, and hardship, dissipated in an extravagant display of gaiety. Residents hoisted the Stars and Stripes above office buildings, shops, and private homes as the most visible expression of common pride. Steam-powered fire engines clanked up and down the streets, piping shrill whistles to the delight of boisterous crowds.[3] Bands appeared spontaneously, and notables offered words of praise to divine providence as they addressed jostling masses in front of government buildings and the poshest of the capital's hotels.

The city rejuvenated in a dizzying swirl of activity. After a Treasury guard band serenaded Secretary of State William Seward at his home on Lafayette Square, he invited well-wishers into his parlor to sip wine, brandy, or gin.[4] There was a palpable feeling of bonhomie, with strangers reaching out to one another in this moment of expansive goodwill. One eyewitness described to his wife in Michigan how he had "waded into the dense sea of humanity, rocking to and fro" in front of the War Department, before running across the White House grounds "on a hen canter" for a choice location outside Willard's Hotel.[5] Others filled saloons resounding with the raucous discord of drunks.[6]

The fall of Richmond had been so sudden that it surprised John Surratt when he rode into Washington that evening. Only days earlier the cocksure Southern press had shown no sign of impending collapse when it continued to mock Lincoln as "the paternal ape."[7] Just two days had passed since Surratt had left Richmond carrying secret dispatches from the Confederate secretary of war, Judah Benjamin, for agents in Canada. As he walked into his mother's boardinghouse parlor, he told Weichmann he had been to Richmond.

"Richmond is evacuated," said Weichmann. "Did you not hear the news?"

"No it is not," said Surratt. "I saw Benjamin and [Jefferson] Davis in Richmond, and they told me it would not be evacuated."[8]

Half an hour later the two men walked down the crowded streets to Pennsylvania Avenue, where they ate oysters. Surratt said he was en route to Montreal. That night he slept at the Metropolitan Hotel, explaining later that a detective had been to his mother's boardinghouse and had asked a servant for his whereabouts.[9]

On the second night of revelry, Washington shimmered with light from countless candles flickering at windowsills in a quiet show of synchronized unity. At the White House flames burned from multiple tiers of candles set on strips of wood nailed to the windows. It was a hazardous undertaking that kept at least one man guarding the curtains against accidental fire.[10] Elsewhere bonfires crackled, lighting up all parts of the city. Government departments vied with one another to showcase their decorated buildings. Gas jets illuminated the word UNION on the front of Willard's Hotel and highlighted banners strung across the pillared Treasury building, one of which showed a facsimile of a ten-dollar Treasury note, while another read U.S. GREENBACKS AND U.S. GRANT — GRANT GIVES THE GREENBACKS A METALLIC RING. The adjacent State Department was strung with another transparency promoting PEACE AND GOODWILL TO ALL NATIONS, BUT NO ENTANGLING ALLIANCES AND NO FOREIGN INTERVENTION. By far the densest crowds stood before the War Department building, its columns of stately pillars wrapped with flags. A band played on the balcony, festooned with a Star Spangled Banner stretched from one end to the other, while flags of every corps and division of the Army of the Potomac flew above. One heady observer, reporting to his family in Philadelphia, was thrilled with a display of light from colored balls resembling campfires lit so brightly on the grounds of the War Department that it was possible to see the color of another person's eyes. Vice President Andrew Johnson spoke to enthusiastic citizens jamming the street in front of the Patent Office. High above the rest of the city, the US Capitol shone with a brilliance under the gleaming dome. A banner fastened across the East Portico, where Lincoln had been inaugurated, proclaimed, THIS IS THE LORD'S DOING; IT IS MARVELLOUS IN OUR EYES.[11] The booming guns, pealing bells, and blaring bands were sure signs to another onlooker of the heartfelt feelings of the multitudes.[12]

That same day, April 4, the president's youngest surviving son, Tad, turned twelve and walked hand in hand with his father on a surprise visit through the streets of Richmond, about ninety miles south of Washington. Many acres of the city blazed from fires set by fleeing Confederate troops. Blown-up boats littered the James River in a tableau of desolation and ruin. Large quantities of torpedoes scooped out of the water by Union naval units lay on the banks of the river. "Richmond is one great mob. There does not appear to be any military control," Provost Marshal General Marsena Patrick wrote in his journal after briefing the president over several days. Earlier he had noted how "happy" Lincoln had been as he "talked freely about many persons in high position, as freely as I would talk of them in my own family."[13]

The breakdown of law and order was immaterial to men and women in the black community, now freed from generations of bondage, who could scarcely believe their deliverer was walking among them. Huge numbers hurried to be in his presence, all eager to see the man they regarded with reverence. One aging black man offered a benediction on behalf of his thankful people as he stooped to kneel and kiss the emancipator's boots. "Bless the Lord. Here is the great Messiah! Glory! Hallelujah!" he cried. Taken aback and embarrassed by the black man's hyperbole, Lincoln, hat in hand, at once acknowledged the dignity of a race so long oppressed. "Don't kneel to me. That is not right. You must kneel to God only, and thank Him for the liberty you will hereafter enjoy."[14] But the masses of joyful black people swelled during the slow procession, blocking his path through the conquered city until the president could no longer move forward. "My poor friends," he said as the great crowd hushed, "you are free — free as air. You can cast off the name of slave and trample upon it. But you must try to deserve this priceless boon. Learn the laws and obey them. Obey God's commandments and thank Him for giving you liberty, for to him you owe all things." Then he urged them to "let me pass on. I want to see the capital, and must return at once to Washington to secure to you that liberty which you seem to prize so highly."[15]

The following afternoon, as the *River Queen* pushed up the Potomac River returning Lincoln to Washington, Secretary of State William Seward went for a ride in his carriage with his son, Frederick, who was the assistant secretary of state, and his youngest child, Fanny, twenty. The carriage door had not been closed tightly and it swung open. The coachman stopped and dismounted, but suddenly the horses bolted. Frederick, hoping to head them off, prepared to get out but was thrown headlong onto the ground as the horses swung around, charging back to the Seward home. The secretary of state rose up, ignored desperate appeals from his daughter to sit down, and reached out for the reins, but the heel of a new shoe caught on the step, and he was flung out, crashing hard onto the road. By now the horses were racing down the street, the reins swinging wildly beyond reach. They galloped past the corner house then turned sharply left into the alley separating another residence from the Seward home. Fanny was preparing to be dashed against a brick wall when suddenly a horse stumbled and fell. But it quickly recovered itself, and they pressed on until an alert soldier headed them off, grabbed the reins, and brought the panting horses to a halt.

Fanny, thin and frail, ran back to look for her father. Bystanders had already picked him up and were carrying the unconscious man toward his house. He looked dead. Frederick, dazed and bruised, told her to run into their home and prepare a bed. A man who looked like a ruffian told Fanny her father had merely cut his nose.

By the time the surgeon general and other doctors arrived, Seward had recovered consciousness. However, his normally guttural, muffled voice[16] had become nothing more than a strained mumble. But he cried out in excruciating pain when they examined his left arm and discovered that it had broken near the shoulder. His fractured jaw ached even more. Seward was barely recognizable, his face disfigured, bloated, and bruised, with blood running from his nose and his eyes all but invisible behind the puffy, discolored flesh.

When Secretary of War Stanton arrived, he sat by the bedside. Fanny watched as the austere man with a reputation for being coldly disciplined, blunt, and impervious to the feelings of others gently wiped blood from the lips of his cabinet colleague. He comforted and consoled with such tenderness that Fanny thought he acted "like a woman in the sick room, much more efficient than I, who did not know what to do."[17]

Seward passed the next few days in and out of delirium, restless in his sleep, sipping only liquids, and watched over by his anxious wife, Frances, and children, all fearful that congestion or inflammation could speed his death. But four days after the accident the facial swelling subsided and he was able to speak more freely. Stanton, who lived several blocks north, called three times that Palm Sunday, April 9.

Once again Fanny was present as her father took Stanton's hand and in a stronger voice said, "God bless you Stanton. I can never tell you half."

"Don't try to speak," Stanton replied, his voice quivering with concern.

"You have made me cry for the first time in my life," said Seward.[18]

Later that afternoon Stanton returned, this time carrying fruit prepared by his wife, Ellen.

In the evening President Lincoln visited Seward.

"You are back from Richmond?" Seward asked, barely audible.

"Yes," Lincoln replied. "I think we are near the end at last."[19]

When Fanny entered the bedroom she saw the president lying at the end of her father's bed as the two men talked. She greeted the president, and as she walked around the end of the bed to take her chair on the far side, Lincoln extended his long arm to clasp her hand.

Lincoln said Stanton had told him that his first impression was that Seward would not survive. Then he spoke about his visit to Richmond. One of the last things he had done there, he said with evident satisfaction, was to pass through a hospital and shake hands with several thousand men, a task he had worked as hard at as sawing wood. He told of the escort of Admiral David Porter and a dozen armed sailors who had taken him into Richmond, and how, while in the South, he had met his son, Captain Robert Todd Lincoln, who was on General Grant's staff.

Lincoln stayed about an hour before rising from the bed and returning to the White House. It was the last time the Seward family saw him alive.

Later, Stanton visited once more, this time in high spirits, with the glorious news that the formidable General Robert E. Lee had surrendered his Army of Northern Virginia to Grant.

"God be praised!" said the delighted secretary of state as Stanton stayed to give more details of the historic event.

"Such news is unspeakably thrilling and momentous," Fanny wrote in her diary.[20]

Washingtonians awoke the following rainy Monday morning, April 10, to the echoing boom of guns saluting five hundred times in celebration of Lee's surrender.[21] The moment was so splendid that it had to be heralded with a crescendo. Officially, the fratricidal war was over, although pockets of resistance would fight on in ragged disarray for a month. Ulysses S. Grant had been honorable and magnanimous toward Lee's army, allowing the vanquished to return home with their horses and even their weapons.

The festive mood surged again as a carnival spirit took hold. Once more the bands led joyous people on a romp through the decorated streets. Government departments shut down, municipal offices closed, the courts adjourned, and shops were padlocked, freeing employees to join in the wildly disorganized jamboree. Groups formed randomly to sing "Rally Round the Flag" and the "Star Spangled Banner." Meandering workers from the Navy Yard added to the welcome sounds of victory by firing half a dozen howitzers.[22] By late morning several thousand celebrants in loose procession swaggered and pranced merrily down Pennsylvania Avenue, singing, laughing, and enjoying the tunes blared out by musicians from the Lincoln Hospital and by the marine band. A wagonload of young men displaying the Stars and Stripes melded into the ungainly mass, holding aloft a banner demanding, SHOOT THE FIRST MAN WHO DARES TO PULL DOWN THE AMERICAN FLAG.

The Seward family got a brief diversion from their private gloom when the women looked down on the carefree crowds from the secretary's third-floor window overlooking Lafayette Park. So many people had crushed onto the front grounds of the White House that the masses spilled across Pennsylvania Avenue into the park.

Lincoln was the hero of the hour. Treasury staff had serenaded him outside the White House while he ate breakfast.[23] At midday the vast assembly hollered and yelled for him to come out and speak. When they caught sight of Tad at the familiar center window above the front door, they called even louder for his father. Finally he appeared in a black suit, and the people responded with three cheers while a band struck up "Hail to the Chief."

They cheered again when he said he was glad that something so happy had taken hold of them that they could not restrain themselves. And they clapped and laughed when he said there would be some sort of formal demonstration in the evening or the following night, "and I shall have nothing to say if you dribble it all out of me before."

In the best of humor, Lincoln joined in the fun, requesting the musicians to play "Dixie," which he described as "one of the best tunes I have ever heard. Our adversaries over the way attempted to appropriate it," he teased, "but I insisted yesterday that we fairly captured it. I presented it to the attorney general, and he gave it as his legal opinion that it is our lawful prize. I now request the band to favor me with its performance." The crowd roared approvingly and laughed as one as the bands obliged, following up with the bouncy melody of "Yankee Doodle."

Finally the president called for three cheers for Grant and his troops, and three more for the gallant navy. Only then did the admired and beloved commander in chief withdraw from the window. Lawrence Gobright, the veteran Washington correspondent for the Associated Press, had seen Lincoln close up on countless occasions, but not until now had he observed the president "so quietly happy."[24]

That afternoon a musical composer, Henry Philips, was walking next to Willard's Hotel with some friends from the attorney general's office when he saw John Wilkes Booth and invited him to join them in a drink.

"Yes, anything to drive away the blues," Booth groaned.

"What is giving you the blues?" Philips asked his friend, whom he had known intimately since childhood.

"This news is enough to give anybody the blues," said Booth.

Philips decided to pass on. He was well aware of Booth's leanings, and it was neither the time nor the place to get involved in a political wrangle.[25]

On the same day Washington celebrated, Mrs. Surratt and John Lloyd, lessee of her tavern, recognized each other as their buggies approached from opposite directions at the village of Uniontown, close to the Navy Yard and the bridge of the same name over the Eastern Branch. She was on her way south, apparently to see him. Lloyd, en route to Washington, stepped out onto the muddy roadside and walked over to her vehicle. He did not understand when she asked cryptically about the articles at the tavern. Then she asked specifically whether he still had the "shooting irons." He told her the carbines, hidden by her son less than a month earlier, were still there and had been shoved far back for fear the tavern might be searched. She directed him to have them ready, as they would be called for soon.[26]

Within several miles David Herold walked by the side of James Walsh, the son of the Washington druggist for whom Herold had worked. Herold, still unemployed, announced his travel plans — to France or Idaho. When the two men had met a week earlier, Herold had suddenly flashed a stack of currency notes, totaling perhaps a hundred dollars. He never explained how he had come by the money.[27]

Meanwhile the celebrations over Lee's surrender continued unabated in Washington for three more days. Excess was overlooked and temperance ignored. The great majority would not be sated. But amid all the unrestrained jollity, there were poignant reminders of the toll of war and the necessary sacrifice for victory. Across the Potomac River, where Robert E. Lee had lived in the splendor of Arlington House, the ancestral mansion of his wife's Custis family, lay the graves of Union and even Confederate dead. When suitable cemetery space could no longer be found to bury the war's dead in Washington, graves had been dug on the sloping hills of the Custis-Lee plantation, confiscated by the Federal government during the war. Now, on April 11, 1865, under the light of incandescent fireworks, thousands of freed slaves gathered on the grounds of the former plantation where they lived in a sprawling new village. They raised their voices in a massed choir, singing "The Year of Jubilee."[28]

Inside the White House, Lincoln had written the speech he had promised the crowds the day before. At 7 PM he was going over the text in the quiet of his room when Elizabeth Keckly peeked in the open door. Mrs. Lincoln had invited the black dressmaker, who was now the first lady's most intimate friend, to be present that night for the president's historic speech. Keckly helped the president's wife dress. Then she watched Lincoln walk to the open window. As he stood there, Keckly whispered to someone by her side, "What an easy matter would it be to kill the president as he stands there. He could be shot down from the crowd, and no one be able to tell who fired the shot."[29]

The band had gone silent. The crowds stretched into the shadows, far beyond those in front who were illuminated by lights from the White House. Lincoln himself was visible from lamps held by his friend, journalist Noah Brooks, and his son Tad. Again the swollen ranks applauded, buoyed once more by the presence of the silhouetted, elongated figure by the window.

Dr. Charles Leale, twenty-three, was among those up front. Weary from work as a surgeon in charge of the Wounded Commissioned Officers' Ward at the Armory Square General Hospital about a mile southeast of the White House, he had stepped out for fresh air. Then he had followed the crowds streaming to the White House and had been fortunate in finding space near the front, where he now saw what he considered Lincoln's "divine appearance."[30]

Also within earshot of the president were John Wilkes Booth and two of his co-conspirators, David Herold and Lewis Payne. The president's speech had neither the rousing language nor the populist pull the crowds might have expected at the crowning moment of victory. Instead he spoke solemnly of the freed slaves and their future role in the body politic. "If universal amnesty is granted to the insurgents," he said, "I cannot see how I can avoid exacting in return universal suffrage, or at least suffrage on the basis of intelligence and military service."

It was the first time that Lincoln had called in public for blacks to be given the vote. Some two hundred thousand black men had served in the Union army and navy, and Lincoln believed this entitled them to cast their votes.

John Wilkes Booth turned to Herold and whispered, "That means nigger citizenship. Now, by God, I'll put him through!"[31]

Booth told Payne to shoot the president. Payne refused, saying it was too risky. As they walked around Lafayette Square, Booth uttered his chilling vow: "That is the last speech he will ever make."[32]

The next day Keckly passed on to Mrs. Lincoln her strange thoughts about the president being shot by the window.

"Yes, yes," Mrs. Lincoln replied with a sigh. "Mr. Lincoln's life is always exposed. No one knows what it is to live in constant dread of some fearful tragedy. The president has been warned so often that I tremble for him on every public occasion." Keckly would remember vividly Mrs. Lincoln's words. "I have a presentiment that he will meet with a sudden and violent end. I pray God to protect my beloved husband from the hands of the assassin."[33]

For three more days and nights the city wallowed in the blissful virtual end of war. An estimated one million candles twinkled in the windows at night, suggesting to one newspaper reporter that the city must have looked to a distant observer as if it was on fire.[34] The names of Lincoln and Grant were spelled out on tissue paper in decorated windows.[35] One clergyman sauntering outdoors was moved to record that "never in so great a throng anywhere have I known such good behavior."[36]

Seward, now suffering from gout and still periodically delirious, listened with apparent satisfaction when Fanny read him the text of Lincoln's remarks about voting rights for blacks.[37] Speech was more difficult for the bedridden secretary since physicians had run a wire between his teeth to secure the fractured jaw. But Fanny and her mother were cheered by the "beautiful" distraction of red, yellow, and green signal lights brightening the night sky over Lafayette Square. When the fireworks burst within full view of their third-floor window, the newly arrived male nurse, Private George Robinson, told them it looked like nocturnal skirmishes he had seen before his hospitalization with wounds.[38]

Robinson's arrival was greatly appreciated in the Seward household. The women were near exhaustion, and strong male help was more than welcome.

Lee's surrender accelerated Booth's need to strike soon or not at all. His original plan to force a trade-off of Southern prisoners for the release of the abducted president was moot. Confederate units under Lee had been disbanded, and the great bulk of soldiers were on their way home. Prisoners of war would soon join them. The remaining Southern fighting force had neither numbers nor credibility. They could never be winners, nor even expect to hold their ground. Booth's fury would become a personal vendetta. He would have to be the instrument of revenge.

While Washington savored the victory, Booth cavalierly barged into the back office of Grover's Theater on the afternoon of Thursday, April 13, interrupting a private discussion of a theatrical manuscript between Dwight Hess, the manager, and the official prompter. Though uninvited, Booth took a seat and oafishly cut into the conversation by asking Hess if he intended to illuminate the theater that night. Surprised by but tolerant of Booth's boorish behavior, Hess said the bright lights that evening would be no match for the sparkling splendor planned for the following night to celebrate the recapture of Fort Sumter, which had fallen to Confederate forces exactly four years earlier.

"Are you going to invite the president?" Booth asked.

"Yes. That reminds me," said Hess. "I must send that invitation."

For several days past he had been thinking about inviting the first couple for Friday, April 14. He made a mental note to get the invitation out to Mrs. Lincoln.

"John," Hess asked, "when are you going to Richmond again?"

"I shall never go to Richmond again," said Booth. And to emphasize his resolve, he repeated the words.[39]

The following day Booth went to a billiard saloon above Grover's Theater and asked the owner, John Deery, to reserve a box for that night's performance. He handed over the money, saying it should be in Deery's name because he did not want to be given a complimentary box, which he knew the management would grant immediately if he offered payment. Deery did as requested, assuring that Booth would be seated in the box adjoining the president's, if Lincoln came that night.[40]

Hess's sister-in-law Helen Palmes Moss happened to be in Grover's when Booth came to find out whether the White House had accepted the invitation to see *Aladdin or The Wonderful Lamp*. The impressionable woman would never forget her fleeting introduction to the handsome actor with riveting eyes and long, wavy black hair, who took her hand in his. Instantly she felt charmed by his "fascinating theatrical air of self-consciousness." But Booth did not linger, for word came that the White House had already accepted an invitation to attend rival Ford's Theatre.[41]

No evidence is available to chronicle the sequence of Booth's activities from Thursday evening until Friday morning, but at 2 AM on Good Friday his thoughts were centered on his mother. He wrote down the time on a brief, two-paragraph letter to her, regretting that the city's bright illumination could not have been "in a nobler cause. But so goes the world. Might makes right." Though the hour was late and the reveling over, Booth was not yet ready for bed. "Excuse brevity," he concluded. "Am in haste."[42]

It is likely that he had already begun orchestrating some of his co-conspirators for imminent action. Early on the morning of Friday, April 14, George Atzerodt, still without a job, registered under his own name at the Kirkwood House, the hotel at the northeast corner of Pennsylvania Avenue and 12th Street.[43] He was given room 126, a floor above the room occupied by Vice President Andrew Johnson. Their rooms were a mere 125 feet apart.[44]

At 10:30 AM a young messenger from the White House appeared at Ford's Theatre to pass the word that the president had accepted an invitation to attend that night's performance of the comedy *Our American Cousin* starring Laura Keene, and that he would be accompanied by Lieutenant General Ulysses S. Grant. It was a bonanza for the management. The presence of the two most popular men in the Union would guarantee a full house. James R. Ford, the business manager, hastened to draft the text for an advertisement in the *Evening Star,* boldly emphasizing the news that Lincoln and Grant would be present. Within a few hours the paper was on the streets and the city was agog with excitement. Ford himself took a copy of the text to a rival newspaper, the *National Republican.*[45]

The two-hour rehearsal began about 11 AM. This day it was scheduled to last longer because they would practice a new song, "All Honor to Our Soldiers," originally set to premiere the following night but now pushed forward because the president would be in the audience.[46] About midday Booth arrived at the theater, where he always picked up his mail. Harry Ford, the theater's treasurer and brother of James, told him there was a letter for him in the office. Booth sat down on the front steps, smiling often as he read the long letter.[47] Harry Ford heard someone tease Booth, saying, "Your friends

Lincoln and Grant are coming to the theater tonight, John, and we're fixing to have Lee sit with them."

"Lee would never do that," Booth replied lightheartedly. "He would never let himself be paraded, like conquered Romans."[48]

When he had finished reading his letter, he left the theater, intending to return after the rehearsal. Confirmation that Lincoln and Grant would be guests at the theater that night must have exhilarated Booth. They would be seated together in the presidential box, providing a unique opportunity to assassinate both men at one fell swoop. His celebrity status and familiarity with management and staff always gave him easy access to the theater,[49] where he would have to put in place the secret preparations he had thought over many times. But he could not move about the theater during the rehearsal. To do so would have raised suspicions. The high-stakes gamble that he could move about within the immediate area of the president's box, making holes in the vestibule wall and in an access door within gunshot range of Lincoln's chair, called for patience and a watchful wariness. It was not enough that he had an overabundance of self-confidence. Booth had to hope that the stairway up to the dress circle, and its passageway to the president's box, would be cleared of staff later that afternoon. If not, he could still go ahead with the assassination, but without putting in place a barrier to block theatergoers from seizing him in the presidential box.

Between 2 and 3 PM changes were made to the interior of the president's box, twelve feet above the stage, on the audience's right-hand side.[50] Harry Ford substituted for a supervisor who had a stiff neck,[51] sending staff to carry chairs from the reception room and the stage up into the president's box. A rocking chair, which Lincoln would use, was brought from Harry Ford's bedroom. He had kept it there for protection after noticing how ushers stained it with their greasy hair as they slouched in it when it was in the reception room. Harry Ford helped install a Treasury Department regimental flag in front of the center pillar of the box, flanking it above with two national flags. For the first time the decorations to the presidential box included a framed engraving of George Washington, positioned below the railing on the middle pillar, facing the audience.[52] James Gifford, chief carpenter, directed Edman Spangler to remove the slanted partition between boxes 7 and 8, providing the customary extra room for the presidential party. However, locks on the doors to both boxes remained broken, with screws loose in the woodwork since being forced open by theater staff weeks before.[53]

Booth had meanwhile hired the horse that would spirit him out of the city immediately after he had shot the president. At the livery stable, he pointedly instructed keeper James Pumphrey, "Don't give me any but a good one."

Pumphrey showed him a bay mare, about fourteen hands high, with black legs, mane, and tail and a distinctive white star on her forehead. At first Booth requested a tie-rein, but Pumphrey asked him not to hitch the mare because she was in the habit of breaking free. Eventually Booth said he did not need the tie-rein because he was going to write a letter at Grover's Theater, and he would keep her in the back alley stable. He arranged to pick up the mare at 4 or 4:30 PM that day, and when he eventually rode off, seated in the English saddle, it was the last Pumphrey ever saw of horse or rider.[54]

Mary Surratt would later tell law enforcement officials that she went down to Surrattsville that afternoon to retrieve money from a debtor who was absent, and that she left behind a demand in writing for immediate payment, failing which she would institute legal proceedings. But evidence from two independent sources would show that she was on an errand for Booth, not only to deliver his field glasses but specifically to have the carbines taken out of their hiding place and readied to hand over to Booth that night.[55]

At the boardinghouse shortly after 2 PM Booth had shaken hands with Weichmann, who like other government employees had been given much of the day off to attend Good Friday church services. However, Weichmann had agreed to Mrs. Surratt's request to drive her down on private business to the tavern she owned in Surrattsville, slightly more than two hours south by buggy. Weichmann disappeared to get a horse and buggy from a stable on the parallel street behind the boardinghouse. When he returned about fifteen minutes later, Booth and Mrs. Surratt were still talking together.[56]

Just as the widow was about to climb into the buggy, she paused. "Wait, Mr. Weichmann," she said, "I must get those things of Booth's."[57] When she came down the front steps, she was holding a package, about five or six inches in diameter, wrapped in brown paper and tied with string. The contents resembled opera glasses, but they were fitted with three sets of rare, small lenses, each of which could be turned by a screw to make them adaptable for use as opera, marine, or field glasses.[58] Mrs. Surratt said merely that it was glass, and put it on the floor of the buggy. During the journey south she was spirited and cheerful, stopping only to ask some pickets relaxing on the grass how long they would be there. When they told her until about 8 PM, she replied she was "glad to know of it."[59]

Booth made at least three stops at his hotel, the National, during an eventful day that had begun with his leaving his room so early that when three "shabbily dressed" strangers called for him at 8 AM, the office clerk, Henry Merrick, told them he was not in. When he passed by later that morning, Merrick thought he looked "unusually pale."

In midafternoon Booth walked up to the reception desk to ask if anyone had left him a letter; he seemed disappointed when Merrick had nothing for him. Then, apparently nervous, he asked for a sheet of paper and an envelope. As he handed them over, Merrick teasingly asked the celebrity actor, whom he knew well enough to address by first name, whether he had made a thousand dollars that day. Taken off guard, Booth replied in an undertone, "No, but I have worked hard enough to have made ten times that amount."

Booth was about to write when he seemed to have second thoughts about doing so in a public space, so he received permission to use the office. There he had written only a few words when he startled Merrick by asking, "Is this the year 1864 or '65?"

"You are surely joking, John," Merrick replied. "You certainly know what year it is."

"Sincerely, I do not," said Booth.

Merrick gave the correct date, and Booth resumed writing. Then he sealed the letter in the envelope, put it in his pocket, and left the hotel. Merrick had paid close attention to Booth after the disturbing question and concluded that he was "troubled and agitated." He would see the actor only one more time, about 6:30 PM, when Booth returned to the hotel for tea and dropped his key at the office before leaving.[60]

After Booth picked up his horse from Pumphrey, he was riding along Pennsylvania Avenue near Willard's Hotel when he stopped to greet John Mathews, a fellow actor who was appearing in *Our American Cousin.* Just moments before the two met up, Confederate prisoners had passed by. Mathews now asked, "John, have you seen the prisoners?"

"Yes, Johnny, I have," said Booth, demonstratively slapping his forehead in a gesture of despair. "Great God!" he blurted. "I no longer have a country!" He gripped the reins and added, "Johnny, I wish to ask you a favor. Will you do it for me?"

"Of course."

"I have a letter, which I wish you to deliver to the publishers of the *National Intelligencer* tomorrow morning, unless I see you in the meantime. I may leave town tonight, and it will not be much trouble for you to deliver that letter."

"Certainly, I will," Mathews obliged.

Booth reached down and slipped a sealed envelope into Mathews's hand. At that moment Grant and his wife, Julia, passed by in an open carriage.

"John! There goes General Grant! I understand he is coming to the theater tonight with the president," said Mathews.

Booth turned to look. He seemed nervous and excited as he squeezed Mathews's hand. "Good-bye," he said. "Perhaps I will see you again." Then he dug in his heels, spurring his horse in the direction of the Grants.[61] Booth rode twenty yards past the Grants before wheeling around and riding slowly toward them. Grant drew back as Booth bent over and, according to Julia Grant, "glared in a disagreeable manner" at her husband.

"General," remarked Mrs. Grant's female friend riding with them, "everyone wants to see you."

"Yes, but I do not care for such glances. These are not friendly," Grant replied.

The rider looked familiar to Mrs. Grant. She was sure he was the same "crazy" man who had unsettled her during lunch, when he kept staring at her while sitting with three other men opposite her hotel table.[62]

Later that afternoon, with the rehearsal over and the president's box readied for the evening performance, Booth returned to Ford's Theatre. John Morris, a stagehand who raised and lowered the curtains, was up on the rafters when he saw Booth coming up the alley from the stable. He entered the back door and crossed the stage before Morris lost sight of him.[63]

This may have been the moment when Booth climbed the staircase to the dress circle. There he would have walked along the narrow passageway between the curving back wall and the chairs farthest from the stage. The passageway led to a door, behind which was a cramped space only a few feet wide. Once inside with the door closed behind him, he could not be seen by anyone. To his left, another door opened directly into the private presidential box, overlooking the stage. If all went according to plan, Booth would open the second door and be within point-blank range of the back of the seated president. Booth knew the area well, having booked a partitioned half of the presidential box three or four times that season.[64] Now he used a knife to scrape away a section of plaster on the wall behind the first door. Then he positioned the three-foot-long sawn-off wooden shaft of a musician's stand between the scraped wall and the back of the door opening into the dress circle. If all worked well that night he hoped to jam this door so that no one in the dress circle would be able to open it immediately after he shot Lincoln, giving him time to jump onto the stage and escape out the back of the theater.[65]

Booth also used a gimlet to bore a peephole looking into the presidential box. He smoothed the rough edges of the hole with his knife. His preparations completed, Booth stooped to pick up the telltale wood shavings and chips from the carpet,[66] then walked circumspectly back through the dress circle and down to the lobby. No one noticed the chunk of wood Booth hid behind the door he hoped to jam later that night.

With a self-imposed deadline for assassination, Booth made multiple arrangements that day, crisscrossing the city to make stops at stables, hotels, saloons, and boardinghouses. There was little time for calm reflection and less for relaxation, but he knew so many residents that he had no choice but to pause for brief chats with friends and acquaintances at chance meetings.

James Ferguson said he was standing on the porch in front of his residence adjoining Ford's Theatre when Booth called out, "Ferguson, come here and see what a nice little horse I've got. She's mighty cute. See how she'll start off." With that, he kicked in a spur, and the bay mare took off down the street.[67]

On Pennsylvania Avenue he greeted a journalist on the *Daily Constitutional Union,* volunteering that a number of Canadian theatrical managers wanted to book him for a season. He also told the reporter that recent floods in Oil City, Pennsylvania, had cost him about six thousand dollars in oil investments. The observant writer, however, sensed that Booth was distracted, taking note of how his arms and body twitched, as if he was "anxiously thinking of something."[68]

Between 5 and 6 PM he went to the Kirkwood House Hotel, where Atzerodt had registered that morning. At the entrance Booth recognized John Deveny, an acquaintance of long standing whom he had last seen in Montreal when the actor professed to be "on a pleasure trip." Now, when Deveny asked if Booth would act again in Washington, he replied, "No, I am not going to play again. I am in the oil business." Deveny chuckled, as the very mention of speculation in oil had become something of a standing joke. The two men quickly parted.[69]

Booth went to the hotel office and handed over a card for Vice President Johnson on which he had penciled: "Don't wish to disturb you; are you at home? J. Wilkes Booth." It was an intentional ploy to compromise Andrew Johnson and implicate him in the assassination plot.[70] But Johnson and his secretary, William Browning, who was also staying at the hotel, had adjoining mailboxes, and the clerks often mistakenly placed messages for one in the other's box. Browning, who had met Booth several times when the actor performed in Nashville, was given the card when he returned to the hotel late in the afternoon ahead of the vice president. Thinking Booth had left the card because he might be performing in Washington, Browning innocently asked the clerk, "It is from Booth? Is he playing here?"[71]

Later Booth led his small bay mare into the stable behind Ford's Theatre, which he had used often since its construction several months earlier. He unstrapped and removed the saddle, but told Edman Spangler, the theater's scene shifter who occasionally looked after Booth's horses, not to remove the bridle. Then Booth went for a drink at the adjacent Star Saloon, accompanied by James Maddox, the man responsible for positioning furniture on the stage.[72]

John Lloyd was, in his own words, "right smart in liquor" toward evening on Friday, April 14, when he drove his buggy into the wood yard next to the tavern he rented from Mrs. Surratt. He had been to a trial in distant Marlboro and came back with fish and oysters. Mrs. Surratt, who had already arrived from Washington, strode up and bantered, "Talk about the devil, and his imps will appear."

"I was not aware that I was a devil before," he countered.

As he carried the fish and oysters into the tavern, she confided, "Mr. Lloyd, I want you to have those shooting irons ready. There will be parties here tonight who will call for them." She ordered him to have two bottles of whiskey ready for the unnamed persons, to whom he would also have to hand over the packaged field glasses she now gave him. Lloyd did not unwrap the package until he went upstairs.

According to Lloyd, his landlady did not stay more than ten minutes, including the time it took for him to fix the front spring bolts, which had become detached from her buggy's axle. After she left, he drank again before passing out in his bedroom sometime between eight and nine o'clock.[73]

Weichmann, who accompanied Mrs. Surratt back to the capital, got the impression she was anxious to return by 9 PM to meet a man at her boardinghouse. On his querying why Booth was in Washington when he was not booked to act, Mary Surratt said he had finished with acting and would soon go to New York, never to return. She asked Weichmann whether he knew that Booth was obsessed with only one subject, but did not elaborate.

They passed among the half dozen pickets they had seen earlier, and when they were a mile or two from the city, atop a hill with a commanding view of the buildings lit brightly to celebrate Lee's surrender, Weichmann remarked on the benefits of a return to peace.

"I am afraid that all this rejoicing will be turned into mourning, and all this glory into sadness," she said.

Puzzled, Weichmann asked what she meant, and she explained that the people were too proud and licentious, that God would punish them.

Their horse shied at the shimmering torchlight procession on Pennsylvania Avenue near the Capitol so they detoured up 2nd Street NW and pulled up in front of the boardinghouse before 9 PM.[74]

Just three streets away, Ford's Theatre was full to capacity. Like everyone else in the audience, the president was enjoying the comedy *Our American Cousin.*

CHAPTER 5

————— ✦ ✦ ✦ —————

"Like Banquo's Ghost, It Will Not Down"

Abraham Lincoln's day nearly always began early, when he read a few chapters of the Bible in the library until about 8 AM before joining his family for breakfast, which for him was nothing more than a single egg and a cup of coffee. Though he ate sparingly, with only a biscuit or fruit and a glass of milk for lunch, followed by one or two courses for dinner,[1] they were the breaks in the day that he savored most for the affection and closeness of his family.[2] Sometimes, however, he would go directly from his bedroom to his office to begin receiving citizens with special pleas, but after several hours he would excuse himself, pleading, "Won't you stay here till I get some breakfast?"[3]

He was unusually cheerful at breakfast on Friday, April 14, because Robert, twenty-two, his eldest son, was on leave from Grant's staff, where the president had posted him two months earlier with a captain's commission. Lincoln had postponed the cabinet meeting by two hours until 11 AM to spend time with his son, recently graduated from Harvard.[4] The privileged assignment had taken Robert to Appomattox Court House, Virginia, where five days earlier he had stood on the porch of a private home as Grant and Lee met inside for the historic surrender ceremony.[5] Now Robert showed his father a portrait of Lee. The president studied the gray-bearded face of the Virginian, who, in outwitting many of his Union counterparts, had added much to Lincoln's anxieties.

"It is a good face," said Lincoln. "It is the face of a noble, noble, brave man. I am glad that the war is over at last." He was filled with goodwill and forgiveness, telling his son that they would soon live in peace with "the brave men" of the South.[6]

portune moment for the president, a self-taught lawyer
his own education as "defective," to focus on his son's
rded patriarch told his firstborn that he wanted him
_vard to read law so that at the end of three years they
could decide whether he had it in him to be a lawyer.[7] A decade earlier
Lincoln had advised another aspiring young lawyer that it did not
matter whether he studied in a small or large town. "I read at New
Salem, [Illinois,] which never had three hundred people living in it. The
books, and your capacity for understanding them, are just the same
in all places." Most important, Lincoln emphasized, was the need for
determination. "Your own resolution to succeed is more important
than any other one thing."[8] Robert did not disappoint, but the father
would not live to savor his son's distinction as a lawyer, secretary of
war, US minister to Great Britain, and president and chairman of the
Pullman Company, manufacturer of railroad sleeping cars.

Close to 10 AM Lincoln opened his office to hordes of visitors,
most, according to the president's secretary, swarming in "like
Egyptian locusts,"[9] in search of jobs and favors, with many others
seeking pardons for relatives or friends. On Tuesdays and Fridays,
when the cabinet met, the masses were allowed in until noon, but
the stream seemed endless. Aspirants jostled at the doors long before
they opened, and when admitted, many senators and congressmen
pulled rank, pushing toward the front to be received ahead of the
pack.[10] Lincoln's devoted secretaries, John Nicolay and his assistant
John Hay, tried hard to stem the constant flow but were stymied
by the president himself, the man they affectionately nicknamed
"Tycoon."[11]

Lincoln seldom withheld the prerogative of mercy, which former
attorney general Edward Bates regarded as a flaw in an otherwise
perfect character because, he believed, the president's judgment was
always affected by a touching story.[12] Lincoln justified the pardons,
even when generals complained that they impaired military discipline, by telling one visitor, "It makes me rested after a day's hard
work if I can find some good excuse for saving a man's life."[13]

On the morning of Friday, April 14, Senator John Creswell of
Maryland rose early in Baltimore to be at the head of the line in the

White House. He had been a faithful and dependable Unionist in a border state that had teetered toward the South. Now he had come to plead with Lincoln to pardon a friend who had fought with the rebels and been captured, but wanted to take the oath of allegiance and be freed.

To Creswell's surprise, he was ushered in immediately. Lincoln was alone in his office, where a portrait of Andrew Jackson and a picture of signatories to the Declaration of Independence looked down on mostly shabby tables, chairs, desks, sofa, and carpet. Even the map stand and gas burner were only in fair condition.[14] The huge desk near the window was sometimes piled so high with papers that another recent visitor thought they enclosed Lincoln "like the walls of a confessional."[15]

The president bounded toward Creswell, thirty-six, in high spirits.

"Hello, Creswell! The war is over!" he said, shaking the senator's hand. "The war is over!" he repeated exuberantly, knowing that Lee's surrender would ensure imminent victory over remnants of Confederate forces. "But it has been an awful war. Creswell, it has been an awful war! But it's over!"

Then Lincoln asked mischievously, "But what are you after? You fellows don't come to see me unless you want something. It must be something big or you wouldn't be so early."

Creswell handed over a supporting affidavit on his imprisoned friend. The president was quick to counter, saying it reminded him of an Illinois story. For decades, Lincoln had enthralled and delighted friends and acquaintances with his uncanny talent for plucking stories from memory to relate them to conversations at hand.[16] Now he told the rapt senator of a time long past when a party of young men and women had crossed the Sangamon River in a scow to picnic on an island. When it came time to go back they discovered that the scow had broken free of its mooring and floated downstream. The women became frightened, until one of the boys suggested each male take off his shoes and stockings, pick up the girl he liked best, and carry her across the river. It was a great scheme and worked well until all had crossed to the other side with the exception of a short young man and a tall, dignified old maid. "Then there was trouble for one young man in dead earnest," said Lincoln. "Now do you see," he continued. "You fellows will get one man after another out of the business until Jefferson Davis and I will be the only ones left on the island, and I'm afraid he'll refuse to let me carry him over, and I'm afraid there are some people who will make trouble about my doing it if he consents."

Creswell laughed, thoroughly enjoying the deft way in which Lincoln had tied the pardon to the humorous tale.

"It is no laughing matter," said Lincoln. "It's more than likely to happen. There are worse men than Jefferson Davis, and I wish I could see some way by which he and the people would let us get him over. However, we will keep going on and getting them out of it, one at a time."

The president then wrote approval for the pardon, and Creswell left, well satisfied by the brief encounter.[17]

Lincoln's ebullient mood lasted well into the cabinet meeting, to which he had invited General Grant. Much of the discussion centered on the method and manner of reintroducing Federal authority into the subjugated rebel states. But everyone was anxiously awaiting word from General Sherman on the outcome of his push through North Carolina.

Grant's remark that he was expecting imminent word from Sherman prompted Lincoln to soliloquize about dreams. He told the cabinet that he expected favorable news from Sherman because the night before, he had had the dream that always seemed to precede great and important events. In the dream, he said, he appeared to be in some indescribable vessel, floating rapidly on a great expanse of water toward a vague shoreline. Though brief and murky, the dream had recurred just before major confrontations with the Confederates at Bull Run, Antietam, Gettysburg, Stone River, Vicksburg, and other locations.

When Grant noted that Stone River was not a victory, and that no great results had followed, the president looked at him curiously, then said that even though they might differ on that point, he had nevertheless had the dream.[18]

One cabinet member suggested the timing of the dream was merely coincidence. Another laughed, saying, "It cannot presage a victory nor a defeat this time, for the war is over."

Assistant Secretary of State Frederick Seward interjected. "Perhaps at each of these periods there were possibilities of great change or disaster, and the vague feeling of uncertainty may have led to the dim vision in sleep."

"Perhaps," said Lincoln, looking pensive. "Perhaps that is the explanation."[19]

Dreams, though nebulous and fleeting, often unsettled this thoughtful man with abundant common sense. Two years earlier he was so rattled that he had telegraphed his wife in Philadelphia: "Think you had better put Tad's pistol away. I had an ugly dream about him."[20]

A week or more before the cabinet meeting of April 14, Lincoln had a ghastly premonition of his own assassination. He dreamed that he was asleep in the White House when, hearing people weeping, he had gone downstairs to investigate, only to find no one there, even though the sobbing continued. Inquisitively, he had looked into the lighted rooms, where all the furnishings were familiar and in place, even though the cries of invisible mourners persisted. Bewildered and alarmed, Lincoln dreamed that he had continued to search until he came to the East Room, the largest of all the rooms in the executive mansion, where he had hosted so many joyous receptions. But now he halted, shocked by the sight of a catafalque upon which lay a corpse shrouded in burial clothes. An honor guard of men in military uniforms stood respectfully near the body, whose face was totally covered. Crowds of grieving mourners, now very visible, looked on.

"Who is dead in the White House?" Lincoln had asked one soldier.

"The president," came the reply. "He was killed by an assassin."

A collective cry of grief from those present woke Lincoln from his slumber, but the dream was so vivid that he was shaken and could not return to sleep. He was uneasy for days afterward, unable to erase the dream from memory.

Some days later the president and his wife were with two or three other people, including their close friend Ward Hill Lamon, when Mary Todd Lincoln remarked on her husband's gloom. Only then did Lincoln tell of the morbid dream that still troubled him. Lamon, who had spoken privately over the past two months of his fears the president would be assassinated,[21] was so overcome by the dream and the conversation immediately following that he wrote down as much as he could remember.

According to Lamon, Lincoln looked sad and reflective when he said, "It seems strange how much there is in the Bible about dreams. There are, I think, some sixteen chapters in the Old Testament and four or five in the New, in which dreams are mentioned. And there are many other passages scattered throughout the book which refer to visions. If we believe the Bible, we must accept the fact that in the old days God and his angels came to men in their sleep and made themselves known in dreams. Nowadays dreams are regarded as very foolish, and are seldom told, except by old women and by young men and maidens in love."

"You look dreadfully solemn," Mrs. Lincoln interjected. "Do you believe in dreams?"

"I can't say that I do," he replied. "But I had one the other night which has haunted me ever since. After it occurred, the first time I opened the Bible, strange as it may appear, it was at the twenty-eighth chapter of Genesis, which relates the wonderful dream Jacob had. I turned to other passages and seemed to encounter a dream or a vision wherever I looked. I kept on turning the leaves of the old Book, and everywhere my eye fell upon passages recording matters strangely in keeping with my own thoughts — supernatural visitations, dreams, visions, et cetera."

Perhaps regretting that she had provoked the macabre monologue, Mrs. Lincoln cried out, "You frighten me! What is the matter?"

Apologetically, Lincoln said he had been wrong to bring up the subject. "But somehow the thing has got possession of me and, like Banquo's ghost, it will not down."

Though plainly scared, his wife was even more curious and urged him to continue. Lincoln hesitated, but then calmly told the story of his wandering the rooms of the White House and finding the supine corpse in the East Room.

"I have been strangely annoyed by it ever since." he concluded.

"That is horrid!" exclaimed Mrs. Lincoln. "I wish you had not told it! I am glad I don't believe in dreams, or I should be in terror from this time forth."

"Well," said Lincoln. "It is only a dream, Mary. Let us say no more about it, and try to forget it."

But he could not rid himself of the nightmare and later made a feeble attempt to brush it aside when he told Lamon, "Don't you see how it will turn out? In this dream it was not me, but some other fellow that was killed. It seems that this ghostly assassin tried his hand on someone else."[22]

The unsettling dream seemed far from Lincoln's mind as he sat by the south window of the White House study, facing his cabinet and the victorious General Grant on Good Friday. When the president invited views on how to treat the rebels, everyone thought there should be minimal judicial proceedings. But Attorney General Speed thought they would have a more difficult time deciding what to do with the leaders of the rebellion.

"I suppose, Mr. President," said Postmaster General William Dennison, "you would not be sorry to have them escape out of the country."[23]

Lincoln, who would gladly have turned a blind eye to their crossing the country's borders, gave his answer with another lighthearted story. "The situation reminds me of an old Irishman in Illinois," he said, "who, having been a hard drinker, finally signed the pledge, and was living up to it until one day he went into a drug store and asked for a glass of soda-water. The clerk, knowing his propensities, said, 'Pat, shall I put a stick in it?' The Irishman replied, 'Well, if you please. I've signed the pledge, but if you do it *unbeknownst to me,* it will be alright.'"[24]

As most of the cabinet members dispersed, Frederick Seward asked Lincoln when it would be convenient to receive the credentials of the newly arrived British minister, Sir Frederick Bruce.

After a moment's thought Lincoln replied, "Tomorrow at two o'clock."

"In the Blue Room, I suppose?" Seward asked, referring to the oval stateroom in the White House where the president usually received dignitaries.

"Yes, in the Blue Room," said Lincoln with a smile. "Don't forget to send up the speeches beforehand. I would like to look them over."[25]

Frederick Seward would never forget this last brief exchange with the president.

Mrs. Lincoln had apparently botched an invitation to the Grants to be their guests that night, by sending word to the theater management of their impending joint appearance at Ford's Theatre without first notifying the general or his wife.[26]

Julia Grant recalled Mrs. Lincoln's courier coming to her hotel room at midday with a surprise directive to be ready at 8 PM, when the president and his wife would pick them up en route to the theater. Grant's wife had no intention of altering their plan to leave by train later that day for a long-awaited reunion with their children in Burlington, New Jersey.

"We will not, therefore, be here to accompany the president," she told the messenger.

"But Madam," he pleaded, "the papers announce that General Grant will be with the president tonight at the theater."

Unmoved, she commanded, "Deliver my message to Mrs. Lincoln as I have given it to you." She dismissed the man brusquely, ordering, "You may go now."

Then she sent a message to her husband saying she did not want to go to the theater and insisting he take her home. She reinforced this with verbal pleas to three members of Grant's staff to pressure him to take her out of Washington that night.[27]

Her stubborn refusal to accept the White House invitation more than likely sprang from an unfavorable opinion of Mary Todd Lincoln following a pair of embarrassing incidents a few weeks earlier near City Point, Virginia. She had suffered the first lady's jealous rage after Mrs. Lincoln suspected a general's wife of calling on the president, and then seeing another woman riding with her husband. On the second occasion, Mrs. Lincoln had even turned on Julia Grant, her host, who had tried to pacify her, and irrationally charged her with personal designs on the White House.[28]

Grant too welcomed the excuse to avoid contact with Mrs. Lincoln, telling his wife to pack their bags and have lunch. If he was able to finish his work in time, they would take the late-afternoon train to Philadelphia.[29] He did not want to socialize with the first lady so soon after discomforting incidents the evening before, when, at the urging of the president, he had accompanied Mrs. Lincoln on a carriage ride through the city to see the illuminations. As he stepped into the vehicle at the front door of the White House, a large crowd cheered and chanted his name. Upset that Grant was upstaging the president, Mary Todd Lincoln told the driver to let her out; but when the spectators then cheered for Lincoln, she reversed herself, ordering the coachman, "John, go on." However, other revelers repeated the scene throughout the drive as soon as they recognized the lieutenant general.[30]

By the time the president entered the military telegraph office later that day, Grant had already declined the invitation, and Lincoln now offered it to Secretary of War Stanton.[31] According to cipher operator David Homer Bates, Stanton implored Lincoln not to go to the theater. When Lincoln remained steadfast, Stanton suggested that he have "a competent guard." The president asked if he could invite Thomas Eckert, the physically strong head of the military telegraph office, whom Lincoln had once seen break five fireplace pokers over his arm. Stanton could not spare Eckert, saying he had important work set aside for him that evening.

"Well, I will ask the major myself, and he can do your work tomorrow," said Lincoln.

But Eckert, knowing Stanton's opinion, bowed out.

"Very well," Lincoln responded, "I shall take Major Rathbone along, because Stanton insists upon having someone to protect me. But I should much rather have you, major, since I know you can break a poker over your arm."[32] Henry Rathbone, twenty-seven, worked in the War Department's disbursement office and was engaged to be married to his stepsister Clara Harris, the daughter of Senator Ira Harris of New York, who lived a block north of the White House.

The virtual end of the horrendous war awakened in Lincoln a sense of levity and happiness that he had seldom felt during the years of unremitting carnage. The burden of the presidency had been so heavy during the long conflict that he doubted he would survive to the end. "This war is eating my life out," he told a former congress-man in 1864. "I have a strong impression that I shall not live to see the end."[33] The toll of the dead and the whiplash of critics impatient for peace and new leadership had left their mark on his prematurely aging face. A portrait painter, with the advantage of White House residency, painfully noted hollows in the cheeks of the lanky man who would turn fifty-six less than a month before his second inauguration. The complexion had become almost sallow, and the bluish gray eyes were "always in deep shadow from the upper lids." Lincoln's expression, though pensive and tender, was more often, to the artist's alert senses and keen eye, "inexpressibly sad, as if the reservoir of tears lay very near the surface."[34]

But the last three weeks had given proof that the end of the war was near, and Lincoln had been so exuberantly happy that even his wife thought he had become "almost boyish in his mirth," reminding her of the carefree days before they had come to Washington, when he had been surrounded by good and cherished friends.[35]

She thought he was even "playful" as they entered their carriage for an outing in midafternoon on April 14. When she asked if they should invite someone to join them, he very quickly said, "No, I prefer to ride by ourselves today." Recent events had so perked his spirits that she remarked, "Dear husband, you almost startle me by your great cheerfulness."

"And well I might feel so, Mary," he answered. "I consider this day, the war has come to a close." Then he added, "We must both be more cheerful in the future. Between the war and the loss of our darling Willie, we have both been very miserable."[36] It was a gentle reference to the saddest time of their White House residency, three years earlier, when their third-born son Willie, twelve, had died of an undiagnosed disease that may have been typhoid or malaria.[37]

During the carriage ride to the Navy Yard and back, he spoke long-ingly of the tranquil years to come, when they could return to their home in Springfield, Illinois, after the expiration of his second term.[38] But he made no mention of possibly moving to California, a prospect he had raised often with his friend, Noah Brooks, the Washington-based correspondent for a California newspaper. Lincoln had told him several times that California would probably offer more opportunities than any other state for his sons, Robert and Tad.

Brooks had arranged to see the president at the White House later that afternoon, and when they met Lincoln told him he "had had a notion" of sending for him to join them at the theater, but Mrs. Lincoln had already invited others to stand in for the Grants.[39]

After Brooks departed, Lincoln's enigmatic mood gave way once more to the dark and melancholic side, and he was noticeably depressed as he walked across to the military telegraph office.[40] For decades past, intimates and other observers had seen the mercurial change in his outward demeanor, signaling an inner plight pitifully beyond control. Years back, a young law student had often seen Lincoln's eyes sparkling with fun as he spun stories to clutches of lawyers entranced by the master storyteller. At the climax the crowd would rock with laughter, and no one seemed to enjoy the finale more than Lincoln. But an hour later the law student would see Lincoln sitting alone against a wall, feet drawn up, hands clasped around bent knees, eyes sad and downcast, hat tipped forward. Dejected and gloomy, Lincoln defied interruption even by his closest friends. "No one ever thought of breaking the spell by speech," the young man remembered, "for by his moody silence and abstraction he had thrown about him a barrier so dense and impenetrable, no one dared to break through."[41]

By early evening Lincoln was once more in fine fettle. Senator William Stewart of Nevada and his friend Judge Niles Searles entered the White House and gave their cards to an usher. A few minutes later the servant returned with a note signed A. Lincoln: "I am engaged to go to the theater with Mrs. Lincoln. It is the kind of engagement I never break. Come with your friend tomorrow at ten and I shall be glad to see you." Stewart, who had received many such notes from the president, did not think it was worth keeping and dropped it on the floor as he and his friend made their way out.[42]

Lincoln likewise had no time to socialize with two later visitors, George Ashmun and his friend, who called as the president was about to depart for the theater. Ashmun had chaired the 1860 Republican National Convention that nominated Lincoln as the party's candidate for president, but he had to make do with an impromptu invitation to call again, conveyed by a handwritten card bearing the president's last autograph: "Allow Mr. Ashmun and friend to come in at 9 AM tomorrow. A Lincoln. April 14, 1865."[43]

The president and his wife boarded the carriage and the burly coachman Francis Burke, seated beside footman-*cum*-messenger Charles Forbes, flicked the reins. They headed for the home of Senator Ira Harris to pick up the engaged couple Henry Rathbone and Clara Harris. It is not clear whether metropolitan police officer John Parker, recently detailed for unknown duties at the executive mansion, was on the carriage or had gone ahead. According to an account written thirty-seven years later by White House doorkeeper and messenger Thomas Pendel,[44] he asked Parker if he was prepared. "I meant by this to ask if he had his revolver and everything all ready to protect the president in case of an assault. Alphonse Dunn, my old companion at the door, spoke up and said, 'Oh, Tommy, there is no danger.' I said, 'Dunn, you don't know what might happen. Parker, now you start down to the theatre to be ready for the president when he reaches there. And you see him safe inside.'" Pendel wrote that Parker set off immediately.[45] William Crook, self-described body-guard to the president, wrote forty-five years after the assassination that Parker "accompanied the president to the theatre."[46]

Booth summoned the most fervent of his co-conspirators to Payne's room at the Herndon House about 8 PM for a portentous briefing. They met in the privacy of Payne's quarters diagonally opposite the Patent Office building where Lincoln had celebrated his second inaugural with an evening ball only six weeks earlier.[47] All but three of the original group from the kidnap plot were present. Surratt was in Elmira, New York, on an undercover assignment for the Confederacy; Arnold was employed at Old Point Comfort in Virginia; and O'Laughlin was into his second night of a drinking spree, having come down from Baltimore with friends to see the illuminations in the nation's capital. O'Laughlin had tried, for reasons unknown, to see Booth at his hotel in the morning and even after his arrival the evening before, only to be told the actor was out.[48]

Atzerodt and Payne claimed independently of each other that Booth never spoke of killing until this final huddle, when he announced that he would assassinate Lincoln and Grant that night.[49] Clearly relishing the prospect, he told them it "would be the greatest thing in the world" to kill the president.[50] He ordered Payne to slay Secretary of State Seward, and Atzerodt to murder Vice President Johnson. Instantly the alliance cracked when "Port Tobacco" refused to obey. Known for ducking scraps and suffering insults, he did not have the unwavering resolve of the others. He was only acting in character, but the depth of his fear emboldened Atzerodt to challenge Booth, the undisputed ringleader, and even to defy him. In the unexpected face-off Atzerodt said he had "gone into the thing to capture," not to kill, though the mystery remains why he checked into the same hotel as the vice president that day. Booth called him a fool, saying he would be hanged anyhow, and that it was "death for every man that backed out."[51]

But Atzerodt had no stomach for murder and left the room, walking alone back to the Oyster Bay bar for a drink. The liquor would not still his nerves, and he passed the long night in a state of restless fear and lonely panic.

Before riding over to Ford's Theatre, Booth made another stop at Mrs. Surratt's house. The boarders were having supper in the street-level dining room when they heard the booted thuds of someone climbing the outside steps. The doorbell rang, and Mrs. Surratt answered it. By the sound of the footsteps the residents knew she had taken the person into the parlor above the dining room. About five minutes later the diners heard the visitor leave. Only at breakfast would the man's identity be exposed, when, according to Weichmann, Anna Surratt declared, "Think of that man Booth having called at this house not more than an hour and a half before the assassination."[52]

Mrs. Surratt rejoined her boarders when they entered the parlor after dinner. She appeared to Weichmann to be ill at ease and fidgety, and paced up and down the room fingering her prayer beads. Weichmann heard her ask her daughter, Anna, and the female residents to "pray for my intentions." No longer able to endure the young women's chatter and giggles, she summarily ordered them to their rooms.[53]

Then she set off with a boarder, Eliza Holahan, for St. Patrick's Church, about a hundred yards north of Ford's Theatre. They had agreed that morning to attend the Good Friday evening service, which went on until at least 10 PM. It was only a short walk to the church, but they had no sooner passed by two adjoining houses when Eliza suggested they go back because it was "a heavy, disagreeable night." Mary Surratt agreed, and they returned home.[54]

Eliza went directly up to her room, but Mrs. Surratt lingered on the steps, still wearing her bonnet. As she entered the house Richard Smoot, the Port Tobacco area farmer from whom her son John had bought a boat to ferry Lincoln across the Potomac River, approached. He had visited her two days earlier, and when she had been tight-lipped and suspicious he'd disclosed his role in providing the boat for John. Then, he remembered, her attitude had changed, and she greeted him cordially, asking if the boat was in place and easily accessible, because, she confided, it might even be needed that night.

Now, in the darkness, Smoot had seen a woman in a bonnet entering the boardinghouse, but he could not make out the features.

"Who is it?" Mrs. Surratt asked from beyond the open door.

Smoot gave his name, was admitted, and saw she was in a state of "feverish excitement." She told the Charles County farmer and Confederate blockade-runner that "she was positive the boat would be used that night." Agitated and nervous, she implored Smoot to leave the city and not to come to her boardinghouse again.

Alarmed, Smoot hurried to the Long Bridge to get the stage out of Washington, but it had already left, so he walked south until he came to a hotel and checked in.[55]

Booth had meanwhile taken his mare out of the stable in the dark alley behind Ford's Theatre and summoned scene shifter Edman "Ned" Spangler, who was considered Booth's "good-natured drudge."[56] Booth was overheard saying, "Ned, you'll help me all you can, won't you?" "Oh, yes," Spangler replied.[57] Booth asked him to hold the horse for ten or fifteen minutes, insisting he not hitch the reins to anything. But as soon as Booth left, Spangler detailed the task to one of the theater's errand boys, Joseph Burroughs, nicknamed "Peanuts John" because he once peddled peanuts. Spangler told him to hold the horse until Booth came out. Peanuts John protested he was needed in the theater, but Spangler walked away, saying he would take the blame if there was trouble.[58] The simple boy sat down on a bench with no inkling he was holding the reins of a presidential assassin's getaway horse.[59]

Booth walked along the theater's basement side passage into a parallel alley toward 10th Street for a drink. He immediately turned left into Taltavul's Saloon, where he drank regularly. In a tone indicating he was in a hurry, he ordered a whiskey, but the saloon keeper forgot the water. "Give me some water," Booth ordered, again as if pressed for time.[60] He gulped it down and walked out the saloon's front door around 10 PM.

At about this time Atzerodt was also trying to steady himself with a whiskey at the nearby Union Hotel. Lonely and scared, having cut loose from men sworn to imminent murder, he had invited John Fletcher, the illiterate manager of Naylor's livery stable,[61] to join him for a drink. Atzerodt had called on Fletcher four times that day, stabling a bay mare there at midday, then reclaiming her six hours later, only to return with her after an hour with instructions not to remove the bridle or saddle. He reappeared around 10 PM to pick up his horse and buy Fletcher a beer.

Soon they were back at the stable, where a loose-tongued Atzerodt remarked, "If this thing happens tonight you will hear of a present." Fletcher shrugged it off as the odd comment of a man "half tight."

Fletcher seemed more focused on Atzerodt's friend Herold, who had also called on the stable manager that day about midday, paying five dollars for the hire of a roan horse. Fletcher gave him the horse but insisted it be returned no later than 9 PM,[62] and Herold was already an hour overdue.

Fletcher asked Atzerodt why his friend was late in returning his horse. "Your acquaintance is staying out very late with our horse," he complained.

"Oh, he'll be back after a while," said Atzerodt, adding as he settled into the saddle on his skittish horse that Herold had been delayed.[63]

But Fletcher was suspicious of both men. Only eleven days had passed since Atzerodt first visited the stables with another man, in "a suit of very fine clothes," whom Fletcher later identified from a photograph as Booth. They had come to stable a bay mare and a large brown common workhorse with thick fetlocks, a long bushy, wavy tail, and one blind eye who was strapped with a whitish leather saddle.[64] Fletcher knew little more about the men except that Atzerodt had written his own name on the back of a business card and said he lived in the distant Prince George's County village of TB. Perhaps Herold and Atzerodt were working together to swindle him out of a horse.[65]

He followed Atzerodt on foot, watched him enter the Kirkwood House Hotel, and a few minutes later, when he reappeared, continued the stalk for a few blocks. Desperate to recover his valuable horse, Fletcher turned around and searched the neighborhood in a frantic hunt for Herold. Suddenly he caught sight of his quarry opposite Willard's Hotel.

"You get off that horse now!" he screamed as he ran up. "You have had him long enough!"

But Herold galloped off, and the normally gentle light roan used most often as a lady's saddle horse sped toward the US Capitol and the Navy Yard Bridge beyond.[66]

CHAPTER 6

"The President Is Shot!"

Dr. Charles Leale was among more than sixteen hundred theatergoers inside Ford's Theatre on Good Friday, April 14, 1865. They had come to watch the comedy *Our American Cousin*. Unlike Europe, where the anniversary of Christ's death was commemorated piously and even austerely with churches filled and places of entertainment closed, the day passed much like any other in the United States. Critics who did not approve reserved their disgust for the privacy of their writings. The Reverend James Ward, parson of a Methodist church near Ford's Theatre, ranted in his diary that if every theater in Washington and the world were closed forever, "the whole human race would have cause to bless God for it."[1] In like censorious manner, the ascetic architect of the Capitol, Thomas Walter, wrote scornfully to his wife of the president "going to that low theater on the night consecrated to the death of our savior."[2] Condemnation also came from the Vatican, where Pope Pius IX told the American envoy that the president had outraged the common sense of Christendom by attending the theater on Good Friday. "Can you expect," the pope admonished, "that the blessing of God can follow such a want of all respect for religion in the ruler of a great nation?"[3]

Dr. Leale had no such qualms in going to Ford's Theatre that night. The young surgeon wanted to get another look at the president, whose "divine appearance" had so entranced him when he had seen Lincoln speak from the open window above the front door of the White House three days earlier. Leale could not find an empty chair in the packed orchestra level but found a seat up in the dress circle, about forty feet from Lincoln's private box.

When the president entered late, the actors briefly halted as every-one stood up and cheered the man who had led them to victory. Lincoln acknowledged the applause as the band struck up "Hail to the Chief."[4] Leale was only a few feet from his idol and saw Lincoln bow graciously during the ovation. The young man noted Lincoln's sad appearance as he walked slowly with bowed head and drooping shoulders to the private box. A man, most probably Charles Forbes, the president's footman and messenger, opened the door; the presidential party entered, and the door was closed. Harry Ford, treasurer of Ford's Theatre, said later that it was not customary to have a sentry by the door when the chief executive or any other distinguished person came to this box,[5] but Leale saw the man who had opened the door sit down "nearby."[6] Lincoln sat down in a cushioned rocking chair on the left, farthest from the stage. His wife took a seat beside him, to the left of a pillar, where a slanting partition would be if the enlarged box was again divided into two. Clara Harris took one of the chairs at the far right corner. Henry Rathbone sat to her left, at the edge of a small sofa behind.[7]

At some stage during the comedy, Charles Forbes left his chair to get a better view of the actors.[8] He also joined coachman Francis Burke and police officer John Parker in a drink of ale after the first act.[9]

Accounts differ substantially from eyewitnesses who saw Booth enter the door giving access to the tightly enclosed space before the president's box. In the second scene of the third act Dr. Leale turned toward a commotion outside the door through which he had seen the president enter. A man seemed to be arguing with "the reluctant usher to admit him." The intruder apparently prevailed because he entered, the door was closed, and the usher sat down again.[10]

Two junior army officers, A.M. Crawford and his friend Captain Theodore McGowan, had taken seats in the narrow passageway by the curving wall, behind the back seats of the second-floor dress circle and about six feet from the door through which the president had entered his private enclosure. McGowan was farther back against the wall, to the right of Crawford. During the comedy a State Department messenger carrying a large envelope brushed past McGowan and quietly spoke to the man nearest the door. He was allowed to pass inside, and McGowan saw him leave shortly afterward.

Booth approached from the left, wearing long boots he had ordered customized with a pocket inside the right leg to hold a pistol.[11] Crawford looked up at him several times, thinking the man was intoxicated. He seemed to have a glare in his eyes. Booth walked around Crawford, and McGowan had to push his own chair forward to enable Booth to squeeze between the chair and the wall. Booth then stood still between McGowan and the door, now plainly visible as he looked down toward the stage and imperturbably surveyed the audience. He stood for about a minute before taking a pack of visiting cards from his coat pocket, selecting one, and putting the others back. Then he walked down, pausing by the right shoulder of the uniden- tified man sitting beside the door, stooped, and presented his card. McGowan saw Booth enter the doorway to the cramped enclosure and close it behind him. Crawford was sufficiently troubled by the man's demeanor that he turned to McGowan to comment on it.[12]

According to Dr. George Todd, seated near the president's box, Booth was identified even as he made his way to the presidential box. Todd, who was surgeon aboard the monitor *Montauk* visited by Lincoln at the Navy Yard hours earlier, turned his head to look when he overheard a man remark, "There's Booth." The surgeon watched Booth walk slowly toward the door, stop to take a card from his pocket, then write on it before handing it to the unidentified man seated by the door. Todd saw the "usher" take the card inside, then return to admit Booth and close the door.[13]

James Ferguson remembered it differently. He lived in a building adjoining the theater, and early that afternoon had been tipped off by Harry Ford that his hero, General Ulysses S. Grant, who once lived in the same Ohio county where Ferguson spent his boyhood, would be attending the evening performance. Ferguson had promised a young lady that if ever Grant came to the theater he would take her to see him, so he booked seats 58 and 59, directly opposite the president's box in the dress circle. He took his opera glasses along and scoured any movement toward the president's box, thinking that

Grant had purposely delayed his arrival to avoid causing unseemly havoc among admirers.

Ferguson said he clearly saw Booth in the second scene of the third act. They had last spoken earlier that day, about 2 PM, when Ferguson was standing by his front door, and Booth rode by saying, "Ferguson, come here and see what a nice little horse I have got. She's mighty cute."

Ferguson watched Booth walk near the wall at the back of the dress circle. The actor paused about one or two steps from the door leading into Lincoln's enclosure, took off his black slouch hat, and held it in his left hand as he cast his eyes over the dress circle and the visible part of the orchestra level below. Then he eased open the door to the cramped enclosure with his knee, entered, and closed the door behind him. Ferguson wondered whether Booth was going in to see the president or Clara Harris.[14]

Once inside, Booth silently placed the bar of wood between the door and the wall so that it could not be opened from the outside, even by force. He peered through the peephole made earlier that afternoon in the other door leading directly into the presidential box, and saw the back of Lincoln's head only a few feet away. At that moment Mrs. Lincoln was touching her husband's right arm. Booth opened the door, leveled the lightweight Derringer, and fired the single shot behind Lincoln's left ear. Mrs. Lincoln would later recollect that her husband did not quiver when shot, but the sound of the pistol made her instinctively hold him tighter. When she turned toward her husband his head was already drooping upon his chest, his eyes closed, and his face calm, as if resigned to an act of providence.[15]

Harry Hawk, the lone actor on the stage, had just uttered the line, "You sockdologizing old man-trap,"[16] but many people heard the shot above the laughter. Instantly, with the gun smoke still clearing, Henry Rathbone leapt from the sofa and struggled with the assassin, who screamed "Freedom!" Booth dropped his pistol, slipped free, and grasped a large knife. As he lunged forward, Rathbone put up his left arm to deflect the blow.[17] The sharp blade sliced clean through the inner part of the arm, close to his armpit, penetrating the biceps muscle and grazing the bone. Henry would have bled to death within five minutes if the wound had not been off by a mere third of an inch from severing the brachial artery and deep basilic vein.[18]

Wincing from the deep slash, Rathbone loosened his grip and Booth sprang onto the railing in front of the box. But Rathbone made a desperate attempt to seize him and managed to grasp his clothing as he leapt to the stage twelve feet below, the knife glittering in the stage lights like a flashing diamond. Rathbone's lunge unbalanced Booth and the spur on his boot caught in the folds of a Treasury Guard's flag draped over the front of the box. Booth stumbled awkwardly onto the stage, cracking the small fibula bone three inches above his ankle joint.[19]

But once more he held center stage and stood up, knife in hand, to proclaim theatrically the Latin motto of Virginia: *"Sic Semper Tyrannis!"* — thus always to tyrants. Then, shouting "The South is avenged!"[20] he disappeared out the far left wing, apparently oblivious to the injured leg as the audience sat momentarily transfixed, many suspecting this might be a scripted part of the comedy.[21]

Harry Hawk, the actor, thinking he was targeted by the knife-wielding Booth, ran for cover up a flight of steps toward his dressing room.[22] One of the first people he saw was Henry Philips, composer of the new patriotic song to be sung that night.[23]

"That was Wilkes Booth who rushed past me!" said Hawk.

"Are you certain it was Wilkes Booth?"

"I could [illegible] it if I was on my death bed!" Hawk gasped.[24]

Above, in the presidential box, Rathbone cried out, "Stop that man!"

Clara frantically repeated, "Stop that man! Won't somebody stop that man!"

From below a voice asked, "What is the matter?"

"The president is shot!" Clara screamed.[25]

Mrs. Lincoln, not yet unhinged by hysteria, held her husband upright, preventing him from tumbling over. But his head was slumped to the right, and he was ominously inert.

From his seat in the third row from the front of the orchestra level, George Batchelder turned to his wife, Sarah Jane Hamlin — daughter of Hannibal Hamlin, Lincoln's vice president until six weeks back

— and said the man with the knife looked just like Wilkes Booth, who boarded at their hotel, the National. Sarah Jane was petrified. She would never forget "the chill passing over" her as the man with the knife leapt onto the stage so close by.[26]

One member of the audience, John Deveny, who had spoken with Booth hours earlier at the entrance to the Kirkwood House, saw Booth break his fall with one hand and one knee before running off stage. Instinctively he declared, "He is John Wilkes Booth, and he has shot the president!"[27]

Joseph Stewart, seated in the front row of the orchestra level, reacted quicker than anyone else. He had just turned to his left to whisper to his sister when the shot rang out. As Booth made for the wings, Stewart, a tall, stout man,[28] tried pushing through the orchestra but was stymied and lost valuable seconds as he skirted the curving banister and leapt on stage, roaring, "Stop that man!" He was closely followed by an army lieutenant who quickly got lost in the wings.[29]

In his dash to the rear door, Booth slashed wildly at anyone in his path, bumping into orchestra leader William Withers and cutting his coat and vest as the startled man was about to go under the stage to join the musicians.[30] Jacob Ritterspaugh, twenty-four, a French-born carpenter employed to shift wings on and off stage, ran to block Booth's escape but jumped back when the assassin struck out with his knife.[31]

As Booth raced out the back door he shouted at Peanuts John, "Boy! Give me my horse!"[32] He swung his arm as if to push Peanuts John out of the way but struck him with the knife handle, kicked him, and knocked him down. In a flash he had one foot in a stirrup and mounted the horse, grabbing the reins, which were on the saddle. Stewart followed blindly, repeatedly shouting "Stop that man!" Unaware of where he was until a door slammed, Stewart heard someone cry out, "He's getting on a horse!" Stewart had difficulty opening the door, and by the time he did Booth had already mounted his horse. Stewart was almost within reach when Booth crouched forward and spurred the horse onward. As he escaped out into F Street, residents aroused by the clatter and shouts opened the doors and windows of tenement buildings overlooking the darkened alley. Stewart hurried back to the theater, convinced the fugitive was John Wilkes Booth, the same actor he had applauded in earlier plays.[33]

Amid the commotion, Ritterspaugh saw Spangler looking helpless and frightened, as if he had been crying. "I know him! I know who it was! It was Booth!" said Ritterspaugh. The carpenter and the stage-hand had eaten supper together that night in their common board-inghouse, but now Spangler, the son of a former county sheriff in Pennsylvania,[34] slapped him in the mouth with the back of his hand and warned, "Don't say which way he went!" Stunned, Ritterspaugh asked why he had hit him. Without raising his voice Spangler snapped, "For God's sake, shut up!"[35]

The theater had by now become a scene of panic and terror as disbelief gave way to the horror of reality. Thinking that the assassin had been captured in the wings, voices rang out above the din. "Hang him!" "Kill the murderer!" "Shoot him!" "Lynch him!" Many trying to escape out the doors were shoved and crushed in the melee.

Dr. Leale crossed the aisle and clambered over chairs, pushing people aside as he hurried toward the presidential box. Rathbone had managed to lift the block of wood jamming the outer door, and Leale was the first person to enter. The fate of the head of state and commander in chief lay in the hands of a young man who had graduated with an MD only six weeks earlier from Bellevue Hospital Medical College in New York City.[36]

Rathbone, holding his bloodied arm with his other hand, begged Leale for help. The doctor put his hand under Rathbone's chin, looked into his eyes, and realized he was in no immediate danger. Then he turned his attention to Mrs. Lincoln and Clara, standing by the president's high-backed rocking chair.

"Oh, doctor, is he dead? Can he recover?" Mrs. Lincoln cried as she held the surgeon's hand. She was weeping as she held the president upright in the chair. "Will you take charge of him? Do what you can for him. Oh, my dear husband!"

Lincoln looked like a dead man. His eyes were closed and his head sagged. There was no pulse. Leale ordered two bystanders to get brandy and water. As they laid him flat on the floor, with Leale holding the head and shoulders, the doctor felt blood near the left shoulder. Thinking it was a stab wound from the knife-wielding assassin, Leale asked if anyone had a penknife. William Kent, a clerk in the paymaster general's office who had raced over from his seat almost opposite Lincoln's box, provided one and on the surgeon's instructions ripped open the patient's coat and shirt from the neck to the elbow.[37] But there were no visible wounds, not even when the president's body was turned over.

Only when Leale lifted the eyelids and saw a dilated pupil did he realize that Lincoln had suffered brain damage. Using the fingers of both hands to feel through the blood-matted hair, he quickly found the smooth opening of the puncture wound behind the left ear. With the little finger of his left hand he poked loose coagulating blood to relieve pressure on the brain. Even then, Leale knew the fatal consequences of a lead ball fired into the brain through the thickest and hardest part of the skull. As he studied the body, blood seeped from the wound, staining the white linen handkerchief he had placed behind the head.

Leale applied artificial respiration, kneeling on the floor and leaning forward. He inserted two fingers far into the mouth and pressed the base of the paralyzed tongue down and out, to open the larynx and create an open passage for air to reach the lungs. With the help of two men moving the president's arms downward, Leale pressed the diaphragm upward, drawing air in and forcing it out of the lungs. At intervals the surgeon stimulated the heart by sliding his thumb and fingers under and beneath the ribs. The heart began to react, and Lincoln started to breathe irregularly.

The doctor then drew deep breaths, exhaling directly into Lincoln's mouth and nostrils.[38] When he rested his ear over the president's thorax to listen to the heartbeat, it showed signs of feeble but definite improvement. Only then was the surgeon confident that his commander in chief would not die immediately. But he uttered the terrible words that would be flashed across the country: "His wound is mortal. It is impossible for him to recover."

Gently Leale let a small amount of brandy and water drip into the president's mouth. With relief, he saw all of it swallowed. At no time did Mrs. Lincoln interfere with the doctor's activities as she sat close by, but she watched intently, quivering and whimpering, "My husband! My husband! My God, he is dead!"[39]

At about this moment Dr. Charles Taft clambered over the railing and into the box. He had been sitting in the front row of the orchestra level, almost directly under Lincoln's box, when someone shrieked and cried out, "Water! Water! A surgeon!" Taft, dressed in military uniform after a shift at the Signal Camp of Instruction in neighboring Georgetown, vaulted over the railing in front, and as he landed on stage announced himself as an army surgeon. Two men, among many now milling about the stage,[40] bent over and made a bridge of their backs for Taft to stand on as he reached up and clawed his way into the box. A third physician, Albert King, had already come in through the passageway. Dr. Taft would later say that Lincoln would have died within ten minutes if Leale had not had the presence of mind to lay him flat on the floor.

Laura Keene, a British-born actress who had taken out citizenship five years earlier[41] and for whose benefit the play was being performed, had managed to push her way through the crowds and carried a glass of water into the box.[42] When Leale granted her request to cradle the president's head, she sat on the floor and gently caressed the sad face. William Kent looked on in horror as bloodied brain tissue appeared to ooze from the dying man's head wound onto her lap.[43]

Word arrived that the president's carriage was standing by to rush him to the White House, but Leale refused to use it, intimating Lincoln would not survive a six-block drive over bumpy roads. He insisted the president be taken to the safety and relative comfort of the nearest private home. He detailed Dr. Taft to hold the right shoulder, Dr. King to raise the left, and others to lift the legs. Leale, supporting Lincoln's head, went out first. But the passageway was filled with theatergoers, forcing Leale to shout for the military. "Guards, clear the passage! Guards, clear the passage!" Using swords, pistols, and bayonets, they created a hollow for safe but slow passage. When they reached the stairs leading down to the lobby, everyone wheeled around so that those holding Lincoln's legs and feet went down first.

As Leale helped carry the wounded man to a door leading into

10th Street, he again turned down suggestions to move the president to the White House. "No, the president would die on the way," he insisted, knowing there was only room enough in the carriage for the chief executive to ride in a mortally dangerous upright position.

By now hordes of disbelieving residents, bystanders, and pass-ersby, curious for confirmation and details of the shocking news, had swarmed into 10th Street in front of the theater. A gas lamp raised above a metal stand near the entrance revealed partially illu-minated, horror-stricken faces. Tumult had gripped a city readying for slumber.

The same officer who had cleared a path for Leale upstairs appeared again. "Surgeon," he addressed Leale, "give me your commands, and I will see that they are obeyed." When Leale asked for clear passage to the nearest house across the street, the officer unsheathed his sword and with others created a barrier between the throngs. They carried the president's body very slowly across the street, stopping several times so that Leale could keep the wound from closing up with clot-ted blood.

As some men came back to say the house directly opposite was closed, Leale saw Henry Safford holding a lighted candle on the steps leading up to a four-story, brick boardinghouse where he lodged diagonally across from the theater. "Bring him in here," Safford beck-oned. The owners, the Petersen family, were out of town. Safford, in charge of the Property Returns Division in the War Department, had been sitting in the front parlor reading when he heard the commotion outside and saw people streaming out of the theater and the provost guard running up and down the street as if giving chase. When he learned the president had been shot, he tried to barge into the theater, but had to retreat from crowds surging out the doorways.[44]

The men straining to carry Lincoln took extra care climbing the winding steps to the first-floor entrance. They passed two parlors on the left as they shuffled down a narrow corridor to a small bedroom at the back of the house. It was no bigger than a log cabin, the length of three tall men lying down head-to-toe, and much narrower.

The single walnut bed was much too short for Lincoln's six-foot-four frame, so his legs were bent at the knees. Leale, holding the president's face upward to prevent the head from rolling to either side, ordered the end of the bed removed or broken off. Neither could be done satisfactorily, so the surgeon and others laid the president diagonally across the bed, with extra pillows brought in to support the inclined head.

So many outsiders had crammed into the room, already cramped with a bureau, table, and eight or nine chairs on a very worn Brussels carpet,[45] that Leale ordered the window opened for fresh air. Military men were brought in to evict everyone but physicians. Leale personally pleaded with Mrs. Lincoln to leave because he wanted to examine the president for more wounds, and this meant stripping him of his clothing. She readily agreed and went into the front parlor, weeping on a sofa as Clara Harris tried to comfort her. The white lace scarf worn over her black silk dress had torn when it caught in the doorway on her way into the Petersen house. Safford would later free this prized trophy and snip it into tiny mementos for favored friends and relatives.[46]

Henry Rathbone, who had accompanied the first lady across the road, was bleeding profusely from his arm wound. Feeling weak and light-headed, he sat down in the hallway. His fiancée had partially stanched the flow of blood by tying a handkerchief tightly over the wound, but Rathbone fainted from loss of blood and was taken by carriage back to his residence five blocks west.[47]

Word of the assassination spread quickly. Two of the cipher clerks at the military telegraph office were in the audience when Booth opened fire. One ran to the home of the chief of the telegraph office, Major Eckert, on 13th Street near F Street. "The president is shot! J. Wilkes Booth shot him! Come at once!"[48] the clerk shouted without deference. Eckert, forty-six, who was shaving, hurriedly wiped the lather off his face and grabbed a coat. Quickly he told the clerk to rush to the military telegraph office and order the duty manager to call in all available cipher operators. Then Eckert ran to Stanton's home three blocks north.[49]

The other cipher clerk had already sped directly to the military telegraph office to spread the news in the War Department building. Word of the assassination had preceded him, but the office manager, David

Homer Bates, was desperate for detail. The clerk, who had witnessed the drama from his seat in the dress circle, said he understood what had happened only when a female shrieked from Lincoln's box, "The president is shot!" Even though this was followed by intense excitement there had been no rush for the doors, and only a few seats were broken when some theatergoers clambered over chairs. The clerk said he had remained in the theater until the president was carried down the stairs and Mrs. Lincoln, supported by two men, had exited the building. Fearing the worst, Bates exclaimed, "Oh! That good man ought not to die."[50] Later he would write that everyone in the room was "hushed into silence."[51]

CHAPTER 7

A Singular Night of Horrors

At about the same time John Wilkes Booth shot the president, Lewis Payne rode up to the front of the home of the secretary of state. He dismounted from the large workhorse with the conspicuously blind right eye that had been stabled with another horse by Booth and Atzerodt in the care of John Fletcher until two days earlier. Payne carried a small package that he hoped to pass off as medication prescribed by Seward's private physician, Italian-born Dr. Tullio Verdi.[1] He rang the bell, and the door was opened by William Bell, nineteen, a waiter and doorman.

"I am sent here by Dr. Verdi, Mr. Seward's family physician," said Payne.

He asked to see the secretary. Bell noticed that the package had a prescription label on it, but he told Payne he could not see Seward.

"I must see him. I am sent here by Dr. Verdi to let him know how to take this medicine, and I must see him."

"You cannot see him by any means at all," Bell replied. "He is asleep just about this time."

Payne insisted, but Bell was firm. He had orders not to let anyone upstairs. The face-off gave Bell time to get a good impression of the tall man with coarse, black hair, who spoke with a fine, thin voice, much like a tenor. He did not appear to be well mannered but rather like an excited, nervous, even vulgar person. The small and neatly tapered fingers seemed out of place for such a strong, broad-shouldered man dressed in black pants, a pinkish gray overcoat, and new boots. Bell noted the very flushed, roundish face with thin lips, and the way in which the top lip turned slightly upward when Payne talked.[2]

The impatient intruder would not be delayed and brushed past Bell, his right hand in his coat pocket and the left holding the package. As Payne started up the stairs, Bell apologized for being curt and somewhat rude.

"Oh, that's alright," said Payne, politely.

The young servant, in the employ of the Seward family for nine months, ran ahead of Payne, who was stomping up in heavy boots. The servant asked him not to go up so noisily. As they got to the top of the stairs, on the third floor, the conspirator confronted Frederick Seward, son of the secretary and himself assistant secretary of state. He had been drawn by the loud footsteps. They had the same exchange that had just passed between the intruder and the servant. Bell, standing beside Payne, interjected, "Don't speak so rough to that gentleman. That is Mr. Seward's son."

"I know that. That is alright," Payne answered.

Frederick peeked into his father's room and saw his sister Fanny sitting by the bedside with George Robinson, the male nurse who had served as a private with Maine volunteers until wounded, hospitalized in Washington, then detailed to look after the injured Seward.[3] The single gas light had been turned down low and a shade in front of it made it darker.[4]

"Father appears to be asleep," Frederick said to his sister. "I guess I won't have him disturbed at present."[5]

As soon as Frederick closed the door, the secretary opened his eyes, and he gave a smile of recognition when he saw Fanny. Seward lay on the far side of the bed, deliberately resting his broken arm over the edge to avoid painful contact with the blankets.

Frederick concluded that Payne was either dull or stupid. "Go back and tell the doctor that I refused to let you see him, if you think you cannot trust me with the medicine. I am Mr. Seward and in charge here," he said. "He will not blame you if you tell him I refused to let you see him."[6]

Fanny, thinking that her brother might have some good reason for seeing whether their father was awake, opened the door and saw Payne in a light slouch hat and overcoat next to her brother.

"Fred, father is awake now," she said.[7]

He gave her the impression he wished she hadn't said that. She turned to see her father apparently asleep again. But she was unsettled when Payne asked in too demanding a tone, "Is the secretary asleep?" She turned to look. "Almost," she replied.

Frederick quickly shut the door, and Fanny took her seat again by the bed, thinking the stranger was a messenger from the telegraph office. Payne made as if to go down the stairs, and Bell ran ahead of him. But the conspirator quickly wheeled around, revolver in hand. Frederick heard the click, but the weapon jammed. Payne grabbed Frederick by the collar and beat him so remorselessly over the head that the weapon came apart, the barrel, stock, cylinder, and spindle falling loose. Frederick tottered against the wall, put his hand to his head, and felt a hole in his skull.

Fanny heard a succession of sharp and heavy blows and thought they were chasing a rat down the hall as had happened some time ago. Robinson thought it sounded like someone being struck with a rattan cane.

They opened the door and saw Frederick's face smeared with blood. His eyes blazed intensely. In a flash Robinson realized that the tall man resembled a stranger who had come to the window of the dining room that morning and the day before, inquiring after the health of the secretary of state.[8] Payne charged in, grasping a knife in his right hand and the remains of the revolver in his left. He punched Fanny aside. Robinson saw the flash of the knife as it struck him on the forehead, knocking him off balance.

As the assassin leapt toward the bed, Fanny cried out, "Don't kill him!"[9] The secretary opened his eyes and later recalled how he thought Payne was coming toward the bed to sit down. The last thing he remembered was the piercing shriek of his daughter.[10] Payne pressed the secretary's chest down with one hand as he slashed maniacally, first tearing the bedclothes with two blows that missed their target, then mutilating the victim's face and stabbing both sides of his neck. The blade dug deep into the right cheek and down to the angle of the jaw, so that a chunk of flesh flipped over and dangled precariously.[11]

Fanny screamed "Murder!," swept out into the hall shouting that someone was trying to kill her father, then raced back to the room, shoved the slightly raised pane of a window all the way up, and again screamed for all the world to hear, "Murder!"[12] Robinson grabbed Payne's arms as he knelt, poised to slash again, but the powerful assailant wheeled and dug the blade as far down as Robinson's shoulder bone, quickly drawing it out to stab again. They grappled on the floor with Payne slamming the nurse at least twice under the ear with the shattered revolver. Then he dropped the gun and lunged with the knife at Robinson's abdomen as they wrestled face-to-face. Each reached for the other's throat. Robinson got his hand under Payne's jaw, hoping to haul him out into the hall where he could tip him over the banister.

Fanny's screams awakened her other brother, Major Augustus Seward, who had gone to sleep at 7:30 PM so that he could wake up refreshed for the late-night vigil beside his father, starting at 11 PM. Dressed only in his shirt and underwear, he saw a man trying to hold down another, whom he mistook for his father in a state of delirium. Only when he helped seize the man did he realize from the size and strength that it was perhaps the nurse gone berserk. During the melee Payne struck Augustus five or six times with the knife, wounding him on his head, forehead, and left hand as the intruder repeatedly shouted, "I'm mad! I'm mad!"[13] Robinson did not say anything, thinking the newcomer might be another assassin who, in the dimness, might accidentally wound the first assailant. But when all three stumbled into the brightness of the hall Robinson recognized Augustus.

"Major, for God's sake let go of me, and take the knife out of his hand and cut his throat!"

Augustus perhaps did not understand, so Robinson repeated himself, saying he had hold of Payne's right arm. But Payne released his grip around Robinson's neck and punched him to the floor. He broke away from Augustus, and as he raced down the stairs, he plunged the knife deep into the back of Emerick Hansell, a State Department messenger.[14] Payne pulled the knife free then fled out the front door. He dropped the knife in the street before mounting his horse and setting off at a curiously slow pace toward H Street.

"Where's father?" Fanny cried out. The bed was empty. She saw what looked like a pile of bedding near the bed, but as she got closer, slipping in streams of blood, she realized it was her father. "Oh my God! Father's dead!" she shrieked. So much blood had drained from his wounds that even in the pale light he looked ghastly. Robinson grabbed his wrist but could not feel a pulse. He tore off Seward's clothes and felt the heart. It was beating. The secretary of state struggled to open his eyes and whispered, "I am not dead. Send for a surgeon. Send for the police. Close the house."[15]

Robinson told him not to talk. He held his hand over the worst of the wounds as he explained to Fanny how to stanch the flow of blood with clothes and water.

Anna Seward saw her husband, Frederick, leaning against the door, his face and neck streaked with blood from open head wounds. She guided him into his room at the other end of the hall. Frederick staggered across the room and collapsed on the lounge, where he lay for most of the night.[16]

Terror-stricken, William Bell had meanwhile run from the house crying "Murder!" and turned left to sound the alarm at the neighboring building on the corner of Pennsylvania Avenue, where General Christopher Columbus Augur commanded the headquarters of the military department of Washington. He did not see any sentries on duty, but his cries alerted three soldiers who quickly followed him back. As Bell rounded the corner, he saw Payne mounting his horse. "There he is! Going on a horse!" he hollered.[17] The soldiers slowed as Bell went on ahead and followed Payne, getting within twenty feet until the rider crossed H Street into Vermont Avenue, the next block north, dug his heels into the bay mare, bent low over the mane, and escaped.

Moments earlier a gatekeeper had bellowed his nightly warning that he was about to lock the ornate gates of Lafayette Park, surrounded by a high metal fence. Alfred Cloughley, a British-born clerk in the second auditor's office at the Treasury Department,[18] was about to exit the gate with his female companion when they heard cries of "Murder!" "Stop thief!" The gas lights were not bright, but Cloughley saw a man on horseback bend forward, digging his heels into the horse. As the pursuers ran by, Cloughley took up the alarm, yelling, "Help! Murder! Stop thief!"

Cloughley followed Bell back to the Seward home and learned from him and others what had happened. Benjamin Ogle Tayloe and his wife, Julia, wealthy patricians living in the adjoining house, were among the first arrivals as strangers began filling the hallway.[19] Augustus, holding his pistol, stood stunned, bleeding from wounds to his head and left wrist. Cloughley heard him say that the secretary was dying.

Cloughley ran down toward the eastern gate of the White House, banged on the guard's door, and asked for help. The sentry said he had only two or three men but promised help. Cloughley quickly conferred with two other strangers who had heard the news, and one suggested the president should be informed of the attack. They weren't sure whether Lincoln was at Ford's or Grover's Theater, so Cloughley ran off toward Ford's, six blocks east.

When he reached the intersection of F and 13th Streets, he stopped two men rushing toward him. Cloughley asked if they had already told the president. In the dizzying rush of events, Cloughley thought they replied, "The president has been shot!" or "The president is dying!" Confused, Cloughley hailed them again, asking if they had told the president that Seward had been assassinated. To his horror, they told him that it was the president who had been shot.[20]

Cloughley was now beside the familiar residence of the famed abolitionist senator from Massachusetts, Charles Sumner. Instinctively he barged in. The tall, refined senator, fastidious in dress and a noted art collector, was sipping wine with Senator John Conness of California.

"Mr. Lincoln is assassinated in the theater!" Cloughley screamed. "Mr. Seward is murdered in his bed! There's murder in the street!"

Sumner did not believe it. "Young man," he cautioned, "be moderate in your statements. What has happened? Tell us."

"I have told you what has happened!" said Cloughley, as he repeated the sensational news.[21]

Sumner, whose manner was usually slow, simple, and cordial,[22] charged to the White House, where the sentry continued to pace quietly. The guard had twice alerted the doorkeeper, Thomas Pendel, telling him an attempt had been made on the life of the secretary of state. But Pendel had brushed it aside, thinking he was referring to Seward's accident the previous week, when he had been thrown from his carriage, broken his arm, and fractured his jaw.

When Sumner asked the sentry whether the president had arrived back at the White House, the man replied in the negative. The guards had heard nothing from the president. Sumner entered the White House, where Pendel gave the same reply.

"They say that the president has been assassinated," said Sumner.

Pendel ran upstairs to tell the president's oldest son, Robert, who rushed down and joined Sumner in a hackney coach that had suddenly appeared. Together they sped off to Ford's Theatre, hopeful that it was only rumor but fearful that it might be true.[23]

Stanton had returned home from his brief visit to Seward's bedside and cheerfully welcomed revelers still celebrating Lee's surrender. He made a short speech and the strangers departed. The servants were gone, and Stanton locked up his house. Before going to bed he always read Charles Dickens, whose books he knew so well that he could recite long passages from memory. As he began undressing in his bedroom he heard his wife talking downstairs.

"Mr. Seward is murdered!" she cried out.

"Humbug! I left him only an hour ago," Stanton replied.

But he went downstairs. "What's this story you're telling?" he demanded of the man she had let inside.

Simultaneously the room began to fill with others who spoke of assassination. Stanton was ready to set off for Seward's house when someone held him back, cautioning, "You mustn't go out! They have killed Seward and Lincoln, and they will kill you if you go out! They are waiting for you. As I came up to the house, I saw a man behind the tree box, but he ran away and I did not follow him."

Stanton said he would risk it. He jumped into a hack, fortuitously near his house, and drove directly to Seward's home, four blocks south. In the rooms upstairs he saw the horrific evidence of Payne's frenzied assault. Stanton, always precise and economical, later said of Seward, his son Frederick, and the nurse Robinson that each was "weltering in his own gore."[24] The doctors were on hand. There was nothing the secretary of war could do to help.

Gideon Welles, secretary of the navy, arrived at Seward's home about the same time as Stanton. Welles lived on the northern edge of Lafayette Square, directly facing the front of the White House at the other end of the park. He was already in bed, about to fall asleep, when his wife said someone was outside by their front door. Welles heard a voice below twice call out to their son, John, whose room was directly above the front door. The secretary raised his bedroom window. His messenger, James Smith, overcome by terror, said the president had been shot and Seward and his son Frederick assassinated. Welles told him his story was incoherent and improbable. Lincoln and Seward were not together and could not have been attacked simultaneously. He asked Smith where the president was when he was shot.

"At Ford's Theatre on 10th Street," came the reply.

"Well," said Welles, "Secretary Seward is an invalid in bed in his house, yonder on 15th Street."

The messenger was adamant. He said he had been there and checked inside before rushing over to tell Welles.

Against the pleas and appeals of his wife, Welles hurriedly dressed and set off with the messenger. They had less than two hundred yards to walk to Seward's home but as they crossed 16th Street, the secretary saw four or five men talking earnestly under the gas lamp by St. John's Episcopal Church. Suddenly Welles felt a jolt of fear as the flame went out and the men hurriedly scattered. Unknown to most Washingtonians, all the gas lights on the terrace of the west front of the Capitol also blacked out at about this moment, but were relit almost immediately when alert police saw what happened.[25] Welles pressed on in the darkness, thinking it was about time anyway for the lamps to be extinguished and the moon to rise. As he turned the corner into Seward's street, he was alarmed to see so many soldiers and citizens milling around the three gas lamps in front of the secretary's home.

Seward's hallway and office were packed with anxious people, among them diplomats trying to determine whether the terrible rumors were true. Two frightened servants tried to hold the crowd in check near the stairs and seemed relieved to see Welles's familiar face. To his horror, Welles quickly received confirmation from the staff that there had been an assassination, and that Frederick was gravely wounded. He passed Augustus who, though barely able to speak, told him to go up to his father's room.

Anna, on the third floor, was gallantly composed as she pointed to the secretary's room. Welles was not prepared for such a sickening scene. The bed was saturated with blood. Dr. Verdi was ministering to Seward, who looked feeble lying on his back, his eyes and head covered by a cloth, his mouth agape, and his lower jaw sagging.

Verdi, summoned by the servant William Bell, had arrived within twenty minutes of the attack and had to quell the hysteria of the uninjured even as he treated victims of Payne's indiscriminate violence. It would be another half an hour before his burden was somewhat relieved by the assistance of the surgeon general, Dr. Joseph Barnes.[26]

"Don't get excited! Don't get excited!" he kept repeating to Fanny. When this seemed to have little effect, he again urged, "Children! Children! Don't get excited!"[27]

He saw terror in every family member, but after his initial examination he had words of consolation. "I congratulate you all that the wounds are not mortal." Though weak and faint, Seward feebly reached out to comfort his family. No one had received fatal wounds, not even Hansell, the State Department messenger attacked on the stairway, whose three-inch-deep stab wound stretched from the spine over a rib.[28]

But the sight of so much blood nauseated Fanny. The women's dresses were drabbled with it. Blood was sprinkled on the stair carpet all the way down to the floor below. It had splashed over the white woodwork outside the secretary of state's bedroom. A distinct, bloody handprint stained the inner side of Seward's door. The floor was awash with blood.

Stanton and Welles withdrew to Frederick's room. His eyes were open but glazed, and he neither spoke nor moved. The attending physician told the secretaries that Frederick had sustained more dangerous wounds than his father.

Earlier, when Dr. Verdi arrived, Frederick had stammered, "It is, it is . . . ," then put his finger to the back of his head.

Verdi felt the skull and asked, "You want to know whether your skull is broken or not?"

"Yes."

It was cracked in two places. Eventually helped into bed, Frederick would sleep uninterrupted for sixty hours.[29]

As Stanton and Welles prepared to set off by carriage for Ford's Theatre, the secretary of war ordered General Montgomery Meigs, quartermaster general, to eject everyone who did not belong in the Seward house. Meigs, forty-eight, and others pleaded with Stanton not to go to 10th Street, but he was determined. As he and Welles stepped into the carriage, he invited Meigs and District of Columbia Supreme Court Chief Judge David Cartter to climb in. At that moment Major Thomas Eckert rode up on horseback, adding his concerns to others who had advised Stanton not to expose himself to unknown dangers in the open streets. Eckert said he had just come from 10th Street, which was crowded with thousands of people "of all sorts." But Stanton and Welles set off, with a mounted trooper on each side of the carriage.

The sidewalks and to some extent the carriageways were filled with people, most of them converging on 10th Street to see for themselves what they had learned piecemeal from others. The crowds parted to make way for the carriage, relieved to see Stanton and Welles, which squelched rumors the entire cabinet had been murdered.[30] The illustrious arrivals hurried up the steps of the boardinghouse to see yet another victim of this singular night of horrors.

CHAPTER 8

"They Have Killed Papa Dead!"

D r. Charles Leale had not found any other wounds, but the president's unclothed body was cold, particularly from his feet to a few inches above the knees, so the surgeon sent for blankets, bottles of hot water, and mustard plaster. They would warm the body and stimulate the nerves. Leale again freed the wound from clotting blood, and when he pushed forward a blocking fragment of bone from the shattered skull, blood oozed out onto the pillow.

Leale turned down Dr. Taft's request to give the president more brandy and water, fearing it would cut off his breathing, but Taft reappeared, saying others also thought it might help. "I will grant the request," Leale said reluctantly, "if you will please at first try by pouring only a very small quantity into the president's mouth." Leale was immediately vindicated when Lincoln began to choke as the diluted brandy almost blocked his larynx.[1]

The long and melancholic face that masked the gentlest of natures was now blotched around the eyelids and sockets, so flushed with blood that they looked bruised and battered. There was no symmetry in Lincoln's face. The left pupil was dilated and the right one contracted. Soon the bloodshot right eye would protrude in grotesque mockery of the man's true character.

Mrs. Lincoln had been invited to return and sat on a chair near the head of the bed, but she would not stay long, as the room once more filled with physicians, government authorities, and high-ranking officers. The first lady spent most of the night on a sofa in the front parlor, her pitiful anguish piercing the gloom of the quieter rooms. Leale sent messengers to summon the president's son Robert Todd

Lincoln; the surgeon general, Dr. Joseph Barnes; the president's private physician, Dr. Robert Stone; the Lincolns' pastor from the New York Avenue Presbyterian Church, Dr. Phineas Gurley; and the surgeon in command of Leale's Armory Square General Hospital, Dr. D. Willard Bliss.

Maunsell Field, assistant secretary of the treasury, was one of the first political appointees to arrive at the Petersen house. He had been in the reading room at Willard's Hotel when two men charged in, electrifying all with news that the president had been shot inside Ford's Theatre. Field ran four blocks down E Street and up 10th, where crowds had already formed. Bystanders thought the president had been wounded in the chest, but not seriously. Field talked his way past the guards and immediately saw Clara Harris in the long corridor.

"Oh, Mr. Field, the president is dying!" she exclaimed. "But for heaven's sake, do not tell Mrs. Lincoln."

Cautiously he entered the front parlor where Mary Todd Lincoln stood alone by a table, still wearing her bonnet and gloves.

"Why didn't he shoot me!" she wailed. "Why didn't he shoot me! Why didn't he shoot me!"

Field asked if there was anything he could do. She pleaded with him to bring Dr. Stone, who lived diagonally opposite Willard's Hotel on the corner of 14th and F streets. But as soon as he went out into the corridor he met Major Eckert, who said he himself was on his way to get Stone. Mrs. Lincoln then asked Field to summon another physician she knew well, Dr. James Hall, and the assistant secretary of the treasury disappeared into the milling throngs.[2]

Dr. Stone took charge as soon as he arrived, with Leale voluntarily yielding control. He quickly approved everything Leale had done and continued to keep the head wound open. He would forever remember gently pressing the scalp just below the wound, when "there would spring back from the aperture a coagulum of blood."[3] Stone skillfully inserted a delicate, thin silver probe about four inches into the wound, where it probably jabbed the lead ball, but when the instrument was withdrawn it did not have the telltale sign of lead markings on its white porcelain bulb. He tried again and when it once more touched what appeared to be the ball, they agreed there was nothing more to do other than monitor the pulse and respiration, and keep the wound from closing.

Blood and tissue continued to ooze from the wound throughout the night, and Lincoln's head was tilted to facilitate the discharge to prevent clotting. Whenever there was a pause in the seepage, breathing became more labored.[4]

As eyewitnesses murmured in subdued and respectful tones, one doctor took on the macabre role of recording the pulse rate and respiration. The clinical record peaked dramatically for both about three to four hours after the shot was fired, but from then on both pulse and respiration slumped, with two exceptions, in a steep and downward slope.[5]

The physicians were unanimous in their opinion that the president could not survive. He would probably not make it through the night. The humble room, wallpapered in brown with squiggly white designs, hung with copies of engraved rustic scenes of barnyards, a horse fair, and a blacksmith,[6] would soon be hallowed space. There was a compulsion among the exclusively male death watch to record the moment Lincoln died. Periodically, when the president's stertorous breathing gave hints of finally coming to an end, each looked intently at his pocket watch, ready to remember the very second that Lincoln breathed his last.[7]

Stanton and Cartter, the stuttering chief judge of the District of Columbia Supreme Court, occupied the back parlor, supervising evidence from a handful of eyewitnesses. The folding door separating their room from Mrs. Lincoln's front parlor did not muffle the sobs of the woman whose status would soon change from wife to widow. Yet Stanton remained focused and uncowed, ruthlessly determined to mobilize the massive resources he commanded to hunt down the assassins and choke off the conspiracy. He had never courted popularity and was personally disliked by the press, who nicknamed him "old bulldog."[8] Even his closest friends and admirers found it jarring to listen to his monotonous voice and rapid speech.[9] However, they overlooked his discourteous and overbearing manner as the inevitable consequence of the pressures of office during the long rebellion.[10] But the man whom Lincoln sometimes playfully called Mars,[11] after the Roman god of war, would now throw down the gauntlet to confront the shadowy enemy. Stout and stubby, but intimidating and aggressive, the formidable secretary of war had to impose discipline and order to counteract fear and tumult. No one knew the scope or depth of the conspiracy, nor the brains behind it. Where would they strike next? What was the ultimate aim? Whatever the answers, there could be no doubt that the assassins were highly professional. They had struck with speed and surprise, with deft coordination and fearlessness. Stanton's gruff and steely presence gave hope and reassurance in a time of doubt and despair. As Dr. Leale held the dying man's hand in the hush of the adjoining room, the physician listened with awe to Stanton dictating orders to the military and giving directives for the manhunt. Time and again Stanton demanded, "Guard the Potomac from the city down! He will try to get south!"[12]

With unflagging energy, Stanton issued a flurry of orders throughout the night, telegraphing detectives in New York and Chicago to come to Washington "at once"[13] and instructing the New York chief of police to send "three or four of your best detectives."[14] Even as he began assembling forces to track the killers, Stanton warned other prominent individuals to take extra precautions for their own safety. "I find evidence that an assassin is also on your track," he wired General William Tecumseh Sherman. "I beseech you to be more heedful than Mr. Lincoln was of such knowledge."[15] But Sherman was unruffled, replying to the War Department that the assassin "had better be in a hurry, or he will be too late."[16] Stanton pressed General Ulysses S. Grant, then en route to Burlington, New Jersey, to return to the capital immediately.[17] Within minutes another War Department message went out to Grant to "keep a close watch on all persons who come near you."[18] The last message suggested that an engine precede his train to be on the lookout for sabotaged tracks.

Grant and his wife, Julia, had stopped at a Philadelphia restaurant and ordered oysters before preparing to take the ferry across the Delaware River when a telegram was handed to him. Before he could open it, two more arrived. His wife, noticing that he had turned pale, asked, "Is there anything the matter? You look startled."

"Yes," he replied, "something *very* serious has happened. Do not exclaim. Be quiet and I will tell you. The president has been assassinated at the theater, and I must go back at once."[19]

Shock mixed with grief, for the army's only lieutenant general had also come under the spell of what he would describe as Lincoln's "goodness of heart, his generosity, his yielding disposition, and his desire to have everybody happy."[20] Grant was quick to sense that the violent passing of his commander in chief was an "overwhelming disaster."[21] Though it was midnight, he accompanied his wife to Burlington, knowing he could return to Philadelphia at about the same time his special train would be ready to take him through to Washington.

In the nation's capital, Stanton was commanding at his administrative best, exuding drive and authority, marshaling his forces, pulling the strings, devising strategy, and creating order in a time of turmoil. Within hours he would authorize a reward of ten thousand dollars, confident that it would stoke the self-interest of police and detectives in capturing the assassin and Seward's assailant.[22] Directives quickly went down the chain of command for armed guards to protect the Washington homes of other likely targets of assassins, including the vice president, cabinet members, the chief justice, and the quartermaster general.[23] The military blocked roads leading into and out of the capital and Baltimore, prevented steamboats from leaving, and halted train traffic in both cities. The first three early trains, which began leaving Washington at 6:15 AM, were allowed out only after being thoroughly searched and heavily guarded by detectives standing on the platform of each car. Further security delays halted them en route for several hours before they reached Baltimore.[24]

Mindful of the large number of Confederate prisoners of war, refugees, and deserters in Washington, Stanton authorized the arrest of anyone attempting to leave the city and the detention of "all suspicious persons" in Baltimore, Alexandria, and the upper reaches of the Potomac River.[25] Inevitably, innocents found themselves caught up in the wide dragnet. When Sergeant James Kane shouted three times for a man to halt at I and 18th streets, the suspect ran until seized by several other guards on patrol. When asked why he did not stop, the breathless man said it was none of their business. Only after he was escorted to his house did they confirm his identity as secretary of the Italian diplomatic legation, on his way to tell a doctor of the assassination.[26]

No measure seemed too drastic in the immediate aftermath of the president's assassination, and Stanton had no qualms in swinging the ax. "The recent murders show such astounding wickedness that too much precaution cannot be taken," he wrote a day later.[27] In the coming days and weeks he would issue more draconian orders for the swift arrest and incarceration of untold numbers of suspects, and his critics would multiply. But he never wavered, because he was convinced, as he wrote the US minister to Britain, that rebels had conspired in the "horrible crimes" to avenge the South.[28] Lincoln's secretary John Hay would later offer words of comfort, telling Stanton how much the fallen president had loved and trusted him, adding, "There were many meddlers whose knuckles you had rapped, many thieves whose hands you had tied, and many liars whose mouths you had shut for a time by your prompt punishments, who had occupied themselves in traducing you, so as to shake the faith of many decent people in you."[29]

Although overloaded with official duties that long night, Stanton managed to send word to relatives in Ohio and Pennsylvania that he and his family were "all well."[30] Though his own house was ringed by armed guards,[31] others feared he might also be on the assassins' list. Allan Pinkerton, the detective who had helped Lincoln evade possible assassination in Baltimore four years earlier, telegraphed under an alias from New Orleans, warning Stanton of "the necessity of great personal caution on your own part. At this time the nation cannot spare you."[32]

The secretary of war, Dr. Leale concluded, had become much more than "the master" by his performance in the Petersen house. He was, "in reality, acting president of the United States."[33]

Other physicians, including Dr. Hall, had already arrived at the Petersen house, and when Navy Secretary Gideon Welles asked Hall for a candid prognosis, he said the president was dead, to all intents. Lincoln might live three hours more, or perhaps even longer. Welles looked sadly at the man, who looked like a "giant sufferer." The president's long arms were exposed, but Welles was drawn to the rise and fall of the blankets with every long and labored breath. In this immediate aftermath of the shooting, Lincoln's face had never looked "to better advantage," according to the perceptive eye of former newspaperman Welles, even though the striking features were paradoxically awry and asymmetrical.[34]

Senator Sumner came face-to-face with Mary Todd Lincoln and Clara Harris when he entered the boardinghouse. He was one of Mrs. Lincoln's favorites, and she had always hoped the president would drop Seward and replace him with Sumner.[35] When she asked if her husband was dead, Sumner had to explain that he did not know, that he had only just arrived.

Sumner entered the dingy bedroom, sat on the edge of the bed, and held Lincoln's hand as he spoke a few words to the unconscious figure.

"It's no use, Mr. Sumner," said one of the surgeons. "He can't hear you. He is dead."

Sumner objected. "No, he isn't dead. Look at his face. He is breathing."

"It will never be anything more than this," said the surgeon.[36]

Sumner positioned himself during most of the long night behind the head of the bed. Robert Todd Lincoln stood beside him, occasionally resting his head on Sumner's shoulder as he sobbed childlike. They could not avoid seeing the pillows, saturated with blood that also spilled down to the floor.

Realizing that his mother was in dire need of the soothing presence of close friends, Robert sent for Elizabeth Dixon, wife of Senator James Dixon of Connecticut. She had gone to sleep at 9:30 PM, exhausted after a long visit to a hospital, but was awakened by the loud rattle of a carriage pulling up sharply outside her home and a man shouting to ask if it was the home of the senator. The stranger said he had a message for Mrs. Dixon from Captain Robert Lincoln. Instantly she expected that something ghastly had happened to her son who, like Robert, was on active service in the army. There could be no other explanation for this unusual late-night call. She opened the window, hesitating to ask what was the matter, because she did not want to hear his reply.

The messenger was brief. "Capt. Robert Lincoln has sent a carriage for Mrs. Dixon and wants her to come to his mother as quickly as possible. The president is dead."

Thinking Lincoln had died in the White House quite suddenly, of natural causes, she replied, "Certainly I will go, as soon as possible."

Only when she was ready to leave did she learn why they were headed for the Petersen house. Her all-night vigil beside a grieving friend would be so harrowing that she would later forbid artists from including her in deathbed scenes, convinced it would perpetuate memories she tried hard to erase.[37]

Stanton went back and forth between the back parlor and the bedroom, breaking from the burdens of state to sit near the foot of the bed and watch life ease out of the man he had come to love and admire. Stanton had strange and puzzling reactions to death. Even though he seemed to be forged from cast iron, with a personality just as inflexible, he had run like a crazed man into darkened woods two decades earlier on learning that his deranged brother had slashed his throat in an act of suicide.[38] And when his own daughter died he had exhumed the body after a year and kept her cremated ashes in his room. Stanton had buried his first wife in her wedding dress, then regularly went "to meet her" at her grave.[39] But he had also shown extraordinary courage while a student in Columbus, Ohio, in ignoring the risk to his own life during an outbreak of cholera to minister to the dying and walk among corpses.[40] Now, as he listened to the rise and fall of Lincoln's labored breathing, the sounds reminded him of an aeolian harp, similar to what he had heard when his own daughter died in his arms.[41]

Lincoln's youngest surviving son, Tad, was at Grover's Theater watching a performance of *Aladdin or The Wonderful Lamp* with one of the White House staff when a man rushed in and bellowed, "President Lincoln has been shot in Ford's Theatre!" Instantly many stood and looked around in confusion and shock, until someone cried out that it was a trick of the pickpockets. But just as people began to sit down again, another person appeared on stage and announced, "The sad news is too true. The audience will disperse."[42]

When Tad returned to the White House, he ran up to the assistant doorkeeper, Thomas Pendel, and cried out, "Oh, Tom Pen! Tom Pen! They have killed Papa dead! They've killed Papa dead!" Pendel, a former marine and metropolitan policeman, had the unenviable task of trying to comfort the twelve-year-old, sitting by his bedside until well after midnight before the weary boy finally fell asleep.[43]

A legless twenty-one-year-old corporal was also in the audience at Grover's Theater when the news broke. James Tanner, a clerk in the Ordnance Bureau of the War Department, could not rush from the theater as fast as others because he had artificial legs; both limbs had been amputated above the knees after a bursting shell mangled them three years earlier at the second battle of Bull Run. Tanner and his friend walked the half a block to Willard's Hotel, where they were stunned to hear that the secretary of state had also been murdered. Bewildered strangers were asking one another whether other government figures had been slain. "What news of Stanton? Have they got him, too?"[44]

Tanner went as fast as he was able to his boardinghouse adjoining the Petersen house. The bulging crowds were now quiet and expectant, anxiously pressing for news from anyone exiting the Petersen house, but always having their hopes crushed on hearing there was no hope of recovery. The double military guard stationed at the door and on the sidewalk now limited entry to a select few, but allowed Tanner to pass on to his building. He went up to the second-floor balcony, filled with residents peering down on the masses jamming 10th Street.

Testimony from some of the eyewitnesses was being taken down in slow, laborious longhand, so toward midnight, when Tanner had already gone indoors, General Augur came to the door of the Petersen house and asked loudly if anyone in the dimly lit crowd could write shorthand. A lone response came from a man standing on the balcony of Tanner's boardinghouse. He said his friend inside, James Tanner, knew shorthand. Augur told him to send the man over. Tanner, who had learned shorthand at Ames's Business College in

Syracuse, New York, walked in ungainly strides on his prosthetic legs and took a chair opposite the redoubtable secretary of war and beside Judge Cartter. The corporal was so awed and cowed at being among the most famous and redoubtable men in the land that his hand shook, and even though his writing was legible it did not resemble standard phonography. Within fifteen minutes the young amputee was convinced there was enough evidence to hang Booth "higher than ever Haman hung."[45]

About this time Lawrence Gobright, the longtime Washington correspondent for the Associated Press, had filed his last story and was sitting alone in his office browsing through an afternoon newspaper when a stranger burst in with news of the assassination. The intruder said he had been with a female companion in the audience at Ford's Theatre when the killer struck. Gobright was so convinced of the man's tale and the sincerity of his demeanor that even before confirming it he jumped into the tipster's carriage and sped to the telegraph office. At 12:30 AM the reporter dashed off his first "special," a single sentence datelined Washington, April 15: "The president was shot in a theatre tonight, and is perhaps mortally wounded."[46]

Only then did Gobright and the couple race off to the theater, where the men jumped out as the driver followed instructions to take the female back to her home. Gobright and his reliable source pushed through excited crowds, clambered up the stairs to the dress circle, and entered the unguarded presidential box overlooking the stage. By the dim glow of a few gas lights still burning, they saw blood spattered over the president's chair, the carpet, and the partition.

William Kent, who had earlier given Dr. Leale his knife to cut open the president's clothes in a frantic search for wounds, had returned to the box to look for his mislaid rooming house key. His foot brushed against Booth's Derringer pistol as Gobright walked in. "I have found the pistol!" the young man cried out. Kent, a lowly clerk in the office of the paymaster general, handed over the single-shot weapon to Gobright, forty-eight, a stern-looking man with a commanding presence, who instantly resisted the demand of a naval officer to give it to him. Later that night the reporter personally delivered the palm-size evidence of infamy to the superintendent of police.

En route to his first inauguration in the nation's capital, President-elect Abraham Lincoln raises the Stars and Stripes above Independence Hall, Philadelphia, February 22, 1861, to celebrate George Washington's birthday. (Courtesy of the Library of Congress.)

President Lincoln, flanked by Allan Pinkerton, left, and General John McClernand in an 1862 photograph. (Courtesy of the Library of Congress.) The year before, Detective Pinkerton learned of threats to Lincoln's life and outwitted potential assassins by smuggling the president-elect in special night trains from Harrisburg to Philadelphia, then through Baltimore into Washington, DC.

Cartoonists and other political opponents ridiculed President-elect Lincoln for dodging "imaginary" assassins in Baltimore and arriving undercover by train in Washington for his inauguration. Adalbert Johann Volck, signing himself V. Blada, sketched this cartoon before joining the Confederates as a blockade-running courier during the Civil War. (Original at Enoch Pratt Free Library, Baltimore. Courtesy of the Library of Congress.)

General Winfield Scott, in charge of military defenses in the nation's capital, feared secessionists would kill President-elect Lincoln before his inauguration on March 4, 1861. (Courtesy of the Library of Congress.)

Union troops march past Willard's, Washington's poshest hotel, where President-elect Lincoln stayed for almost two weeks until he moved into the White House after his inauguration in 1861. (Courtesy of the Willard Intercontinental Hotel, Washington, DC.)

THE INAUGURAL PROCESSION AT WASHINGTON PASSING THE GATE OF THE CAPITOL GROUNDS.—FROM A SKETCH BY OUR SPECIAL ARTIST.—[SEE PAGE 165.]

A sketch from *Harper's Weekly* shows crowds greeting President-elect Lincoln, seated beside President James Buchanan, raising his top hat, as they round the west front of the Capitol in an open carriage for Lincoln's first inauguration on the east front. (Courtesy of the Library of Congress.)

The dome of the US Capitol under construction as crowds gather at the east front for the inauguration. The gleaming beacon atop Capitol Hill was completed during his presidency. (Courtesy of the Library of Congress.)

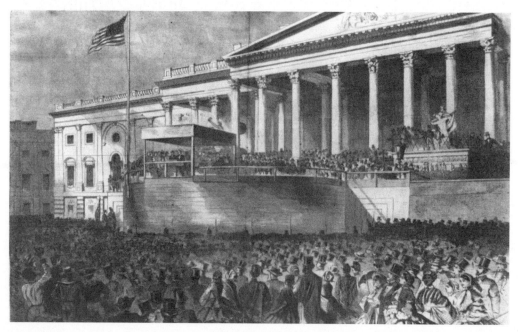

On March 4, 1861, Chief Justice Roger Taney administered the presidential oath of office to Abraham Lincoln, who swore to "preserve, protect and defend the Constitution of the United States." (Courtesy of the Library of Congress.)

Cattle graze near the incomplete Washington Monument in this 1862 sketch from *Frank Leslie's Illustrated Newspaper*. (Courtesy of the Library of Congress.)

The Long Bridge, which spanned the Potomac River from Washington to Virginia during the Lincoln administration, was described by a distinguished US admiral as "a disgrace to a civilized community." (Courtesy of the Library of Congress.)

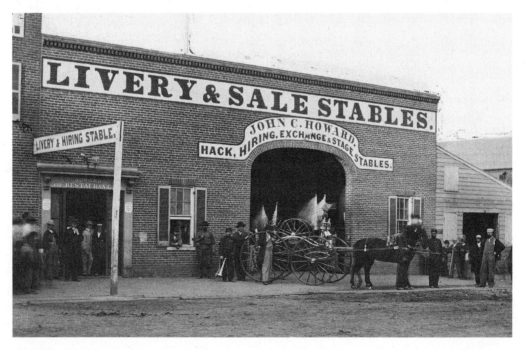

John Howard's stable, photographed in 1865 on G Street between Sixth and Seventh Streets behind Mary Surratt's boardinghouse. The manager, Brooke Stabler, was well acquainted with John Wilkes Booth and co-conspirators John Surratt and George Atzerodt from frequent visits. (Courtesy of the Library of Congress.)

During Lincoln's presidency the area around the Smithsonian Institutions's red-brick building, photographed by Andrew Russell in 1862, was a favorite stalking ground for predatory ruffians after sunset. (Courtesy of the Library of Congress.)

During the Civil War, Lincoln visited the War Department more than any other building. It housed the Military Telegraph Office, where he went at all hours of the day and night to keep abreast of breaking news. (Courtesy of the Library of Congress.)

Major Thomas Eckert, head of the Military Telegraph Office inside the War Department building, was admired by the president for his physical strength. (Courtesy of the Library of Congress.)

Washingtonians stroll in front of the White House during the Lincoln administration. (Courtesy of The White House Historical Association, White House Collection.)

ISOMETRICAL VIEW
OF THE
PRESIDENTS HOUSE
THE SURROUNDING
PUBLIC BUILDINGS
AND
PRIVATE RESIDENCES

A mid-nineteenth-century overview of the White House, center, flanked by the War and Navy Departments, upper left, and the State Department and Treasury buildings, lower right. Secretary of State William Seward was stabbed repeatedly by Lewis Payne in his home, far right center block, middle house facing open Lafayette Square. (Courtesy of the Library of Congress.)

Six weeks before the assassination, Benjamin Brown French, Commissioner of Public Buildings, forcibly restrained John Wilkes Booth from approaching Lincoln as the president walked through the Rotunda of the US Capitol to be sworn in for a second term. (Courtesy of the Library of Congress.)

LINCOLN TAKING THE OATH AT HIS SECOND INAUGURATION, MARCH 4, 1865.—PHOTOGRAPHED BY GARDNER, WASHINGTON.—[SE

Chief Justice Salmon Chase administers the presidential oath of office to Abraham Lincoln on the east front of the US Capitol, six weeks before the assassination in this illustration from *Harper's Weekly*. (Courtesy of the Library of Congress.)

Alexander Gardner's photograph of Abraham Lincoln, taken, according to most recent research, a week before his fifty-sixth birthday, and two months before the assassination, captures the heavy burden of leadership during the brutal Civil War. The image shows the crack from the original negative. (Courtesy of the Library of Congress.)

Gobright expertly pieced together a sequence of graphic moments from eyewitnesses still incredulous, making sure at the same time to keep a firm grip on the arm of the original source whom he feared might walk away. Military guards blocked entry to the boarding-house where Lincoln lay, so they took a hack to Seward's residence to check out rumors he had been slain. The skeptical Gobright expected they were off on a false alarm, prompted, perhaps, by people confusing Seward with Lincoln as the victim of a lethal attack.

They had no trouble getting by the front-door guard, but everyone inside Seward's house appeared too shocked and distraught to speak coherently. The servant who had tried to block Lewis Payne's entry could barely talk. Gobright, however, concluded he had heard enough to verify a murderous attack on the secretary of state. At 1 AM he filed a second bulletin to the Associated Press: "The president is not expected to live through the night. He was shot at a theatre. Secretary Seward was also assassinated. No arteries were cut."

When Gobright and his faithful source stopped by the White House, they learned from a military guard posted by the door that Lincoln had not returned home. The two men went back to 10th Street, now bulging with even more bystanders fixated on the house where the bleeding president had been carried. But the sentries would not budge and refused to admit the correspondent of the Associated Press. Gobright was no more successful in pinning down the identity of the assassin. Some people confidently identified him as John Wilkes Booth, but others would allow only that he resembled the well-known actor.

Though Gobright had reported for the Associated Press for almost twenty years, he could barely control his own excitement at breaking one of the most riveting stories in history. He could not steady his trembling fingers as he crafted a dispassionate, orderly flow from the jumble of frenzied eyewitness and hearsay accounts. He was interrupted several times when men burst into the office to volunteer what they had witnessed. One visitor, House Speaker Schuyler Colfax, told of the irony of the president not even wanting to go to the theater because Mrs. Lincoln had not felt well. But Lincoln felt obligated to go because, Colfax recounted, he could not disappoint the audience, who expected to see both the president and the general, and Grant had already left town.

At 1:30 AM Gobright filed a surprisingly stiff and dull dispatch, leaving out facts known exclusively to him and ignoring his own dramatic role in the accidental finding of the murder weapon. His first mention that the president had been shot came four paragraphs into the story.[47] In his zeal to rush transmission, Gobright relied on the uncorroborated and mistaken accounts of shaken and disoriented people with whom he had spoken inside the Seward home. As a result, readers of the New York Herald thought Lewis Payne had struck Frederick Seward with a billy club, then disabled two male nurses and a State Department messenger in the bedroom before knifing the secretary of state. They were minor inaccuracies, and Gobright was later surprised at how close he came to the facts, given the circumstances of what he called "those dark transactions."[48]

Harry Hawk, the lone actor on stage when the shot was fired, had been arrested in the immediate dragnet and taken before Mayor Richard Wallach, released on a thousand dollars' bail, and then picked up again by law enforcement officials, who brought him before Stanton and Cartter for questioning. Still shocked by the enormity of the crime, he could not bring himself to admit what he inwardly knew beyond doubt, that John Booth, as theater colleagues called him, was indeed the man who ran across the stage holding a knife.[49]

As James Tanner wrote shorthand records of the statements of a number of eyewitnesses and others with valuable leads, he was frequently distracted by the plaintive laments of Mrs. Lincoln beyond the folding door. About once an hour she would sit briefly beside her husband's bedside. Then, overcome with emotion, she would withdraw to the front parlor. Whenever she entered the bedroom, clean napkins were spread over the bloodstained pillow.[50] Once, as she passed by the door of the back parlor, Tanner heard her mutter, "Oh, my God, and have I given my husband to die."

Stanton too could not conceal his sorrow, even though he looked stolid and steady with his frizzly black beard, broad jaw, and long upper lip. Those who knew him well often saw him pinch his lower lip with his thumb and first finger, a habit especially notable when he seemed perplexed.[51] But now he was overcome by sadness. Once, when he returned from the bedroom, he could not suppress a choke in his throat as he announced, "There is no hope." At that moment he looked as if he might break down in convulsions.[52]

Vice President Andrew Johnson knew within minutes of the assassination what had happened because he was staying at the same Kirkwood House Hotel as one of the people in the audience, Leonard Farwell, a former governor of Wisconsin. Farwell had socialized with Johnson in the vice president's rooms, which overlooked 12th Street at the corner of Pennsylvania Avenue. When Farwell heard the shot and saw Booth escape off stage, he immediately suspected that Johnson's life was in danger because he had recently read a widely reprinted item from the December issue of the *Selma (Alabama) Dispatch* in which a Southerner had offered to kill the president, the vice president, and the secretary of state in return for a million dollars.[53]

Farwell ran two blocks to the Kirkwood House Hotel and shouted at the clerks to guard the entrance, the stairway, and Johnson's room because President Lincoln had been assassinated. Then he raced upstairs and pounded on the vice president's door.

"Governor Johnson," he roared, using Johnson's former title, "if you are in this room, I must see you!"

"Farwell, is that you?"

"Yes, let me in!"

Once inside, Farwell locked the door and recounted what he had seen and heard at Ford's Theatre. When he had finished, the two men clasped hands and embraced, as if, Farwell thought, "for mutual support." Soon some of the vice president's friends arrived, anxious for his safety, and passed on news of the attacks on Seward and his son. It confirmed everything Farwell suspected of a conspiracy against the government's political hierarchy.

Johnson ordered him to go out and obtain personal eyewitness proof of what was unfolding, and not to rely on rumors. Farwell, now inspector of inventions at the Patent Office in Washington, ran back up 10th Street, pushed through to the guards, and talked his way into the Petersen house and the bedroom at the end of the corridor. It did not take long to confirm the worst. Then he hurried six blocks west to Seward's house, where he learned of the bloodbath in the bedroom.

The vice president insisted on going to Lincoln's bedside, even though others argued against it because of the danger from at least two assassins still at large. He declined an escort of troops, offered by Provost Marshal Major James O'Beirne, whose men might normally be enforcing military regulations or on the lookout for military deserters. Johnson buttoned his coat, pulled his hat down low, and set off in tandem with Farwell while O'Beirne led the way.[54] Unrecognized in the dark, they shoved through the multitudes and into the boardinghouse, where Johnson joined the solemn clutch of red-eyed dignitaries. According to General Montgomery Meigs, guarding the bedroom door on Stanton's orders, the vice president "called and looked upon the dying man, and retired."[55]

Word of the assassination spread quickly beyond the nation's capital, even though a portion of the commercial lines between Washington and Baltimore were down for a few hours before dawn because wires had been crossed in the main batteries. It was never established who was responsible, but the cause was similar to throwing a ground wire over the main wires.[56] The downed lines did not affect traffic to New York City, where Leonard Grover, lessee of the Washington theater that carried his name, was asleep in his hotel on Broadway when a messenger pounded on his door.

"Mr. Grover, here's a telegram for you!"

Grover, thinking it was the usual message announcing receipts from another theater he managed in Philadelphia, answered, "Stick it under the door."

But the messenger banged again. "Mr. Grover! Mr. Grover! Please come to the door!"

Alarmed, Grover opened the door and saw a crowd in the corridor, anxiously awaiting proof of the contents. Grover knew from the phrasing that it was unmistakably from his manager, Dwight Hess. It read: "President Lincoln shot tonight at Ford's Theatre. Thank God it was not ours. C.D. Hess."[57]

In the early-morning hours, when it was still dark, Mrs. Lincoln went once more down the corridor, this time supported by the wife of Connecticut senator James Dixon. "Love," she pleaded, "live but for one moment to speak to me once, to speak to our children!"[58] She cried inconsolably, seated by the bed. She spoke to the unconscious man as if he could hear, recalling that she had not wanted to go to the theater that night, but he thought he had to go because it had been so widely advertised and people expected him to be there.[59] "Oh, that my little Taddy might see his father before he died!" she moaned. No one present thought this advisable.[60] When the president's breathing suddenly became loud and raspy, she stood up, cried out, and fainted.

Stanton rushed in from the adjoining parlor and, raising his arms, ordered in a loud voice, "Take that woman out and do not let her in again!"[61]

Mrs. Lincoln did not see her husband again, neither alive nor dead.

Dr. Leale held Lincoln's right hand for several hours. He knew the president was blind, judging by the paralysis, the dilated pupils, and the bulging and bloodshot eyes, which were now insensitive to light. But in perhaps the most poignant gesture toward the helpless leader, he thought Lincoln might still be able to hear or to feel, and if he could, he wanted him to know he had a friend, that he was in touch with humanity.[62]

Dr. Taft marveled at Lincoln's resilience. The surgeons agreed that most victims would have died within two hours of such injuries, yet the president appeared to be surviving the night. Lincoln held special memories for Taft, who had been in charge of the Church Street Hospital on H Street when the chief executive had visited numerous times to bring comfort and good cheer to the casualties of combat, while the first lady distributed flowers. Some of the less gravely wounded would stand by their cots as Lincoln offered kind words, asking where they came from and which units they belonged to. If the man was tall, Lincoln would mischievously suggest they stand back-to-back to see who was taller, but nobody ever "topped" the president.[63]

Few Washingtonians slept that night as mounted patrols criss-crossed the darkened city.[64] Sarah Jane Hamlin Batchelder, whose father had been vice president until the previous month, stayed up until dawn. Like many others she was too scared and haunted by the sequence of calamities. Even though exhausted, she could not sleep. "The scene of last night is in my eyes if I attempt to sleep or am awake. It has entirely unnerved me," she wrote her stepmother. Restless and nervous, the young woman could not shake off an "intense feeling of fear, and dread of more to come."[65]

Family in the home of Montgomery Meigs could not sleep even though their house was heavily guarded. Minerva Rodgers, mother-in-law of the quartermaster general, passed the night there in fearful suspense. "Every time the door was opened, I felt as if we might see the gleaming blade of an assassin, or hear the report of a pistol," she wrote her children. Meigs, who enjoyed catching snakes, even bringing them live to his office,[66] had quickly armed himself and hurried to the bedside of the president, where he remained throughout the night. His son, Montgomery, eighteen, held a pistol all night, frequently answering the doorbell when officers came looking for his father.[67]

Sound sleep came only to those who dismissed the late-night news as preposterous or were unaware of what had happened. Mathematics professor Simon Newcomb and his wife, Mary, had just gone to bed when they heard people running in the streets. Her mother burst in and announced, "The president has been shot!" But Newcomb convinced his trembling wife, the mother of their five-month-old baby, that the report could not possibly be true, and coaxed her back to sleep.[68]

Fear of vigilantes out to avenge the assassination of the president kept actors wide awake inside Ford's Theatre. Some of the cast had tried to go home but found their exit blocked by law enforcement officials, and word filtered back to the dressing rooms that everyone was under arrest. There was a chilling fear they might become victims of a crazed mob targeting anyone connected with the theater where Lincoln was felled. A rumor spread that men were assembling at Willard's Hotel to march on Ford's Theatre and raze it to the ground. One of the actors, John Mathews, talked himself into believing that the close proximity of Abraham Lincoln across the street would inhibit the mob from setting fire to the theater.

As Mathews took off his coat an envelope fell from a pocket. He had forgotten about the letter given him that afternoon by Booth for delivery to the *Daily National Intelligencer.* "Great God!" he said to himself, quaking from the realization that it could link him to the man some of his colleagues had already identified as the assassin. He tore open the sealed envelope and glanced rapidly over the script, which looked identical to handwriting he had seen on Booth's own photographs of himself. The text, written on both sides of a sheet of letter paper, appeared to offer patriotic justification for the assassination. Mathews, who was used to memorizing lengthy passages of manuscripts to recite on stage, would later recall some of the wording, especially that Booth claimed he had for a long time devoted his time, money, and energies to the accomplishment of an end; that until a short time ago he had been worth twenty or thirty thousand dollars, all of which had been spent in furthering this enterprise. So far as Mathews could remember, the text included the lines: "The moment has at length arrived when my plans must be changed. The world may censure me for what I am about to do, but I am sure that posterity will justify me." It was signed: "Men who love their country better than gold or life: J.W. Booth — Payne, — Atzerodt, and — Herold."

Mathews was afraid to handle the letter. He had to destroy it at once or risk being lynched if it was found in his possession. He could expect no mercy if found guilty by association. Without further delay he set fire to the incriminating evidence.[69]

As Washingtonians waited out the night in expectation of even more terror, authorities guarded against arson. But the dark and cloudy night made it difficult for government fire engines to move in safety. One vehicle, lit only on the sides, had almost crashed into a wagon when responding to an alarm. The chief engineer of the US Fire Brigade had just washed up after returning from a call when an officer from the War Department appeared, ordering him to ready the engines and equipment. But when the engineer called at the War Department, the guards refused to let him enter. He idled outside for three hours on Pennsylvania Avenue even as a squadron of cavalry galloped past in front of the White House.[70]

Up on Capitol Hill, Benjamin Brown French, commissioner of public buildings, awoke before sunrise as usual and was surprised to see the street lamps still burning. He was in charge of the lamplighters, who had orders to extinguish the gas lights at 3 AM. French lay in bed for about half an hour, then, seeing they were still alight and a sentry was pacing outside, hurriedly dressed and opened the front door.

"Are not the things of last night dreadful," the soldier remarked.

French was puzzled.

"Have you not heard?" asked the soldier. "The president has been shot at Ford's Theatre and Mr. Seward's throat cut in his bed at his own house."[71]

French was gripped with such nausea that he later described to a relative how he thought he would suffocate.[72] He loaded his revolver with five rounds and dashed to the Capitol, ordered it closed to the public, then went to the Petersen house and saw for himself that there was no hope.

French withdrew to the front parlor, where Mrs. Lincoln grasped his hand as she cried out. Robert too could not hold back his own pain when the two men clasped hands. The first lady asked him to take the presidential carriage and bring Mrs. Mary Jane Welles, wife of the navy secretary, to the parlor.

The secretary of the navy lived on the edge of Lafayette Square, a few hundred yards north of the front of the White House. When French arrived the housekeeper said Mrs. Welles was in bed, "too unwell to go." She had been ill for a week. As he turned to leave, someone called from an upper window that Mrs. Welles would come after all. She took nearly an hour to get dressed and have tea and toast while French waited downstairs, then was taken to the Petersen house. French made arrangements to keep the public out of the White House, then returned to his home for breakfast.[73]

Welles, whom Lincoln nicknamed Father Neptune,[74] had sat for several hours by the foot of the bed, listening to the heavy groans and reflecting on "this great and good man who was expiring before me." About 6 AM Welles, feeling faint, went outside for fresh air. He had been inside the cramped and stuffy room for seven hours. It was gloomy outside, and before he returned fifteen minutes later it had already begun to drizzle. The street was still blocked by large groups of cold and tired mourners, most of them black people who had come to pray for their liberator. When Welles told them the president could survive only a short time, they responded with wails.

Sleep had finally caught up with Interior Secretary John Palmer Usher, now lying on the bed in the back parlor. But others appeared even more alert now that the end seemed near. Surgeon General Joseph Barnes sat near the head of the bed, sometimes exposing the brawny chest as he placed his ear over Lincoln's heart.[75] He put his finger over the carotid artery to keep track of the pulse.[76] The beat flagged, at times registering no movement at all in the artery. Inhalations became long and guttural.

At 6:50 AM all respiration stopped and everyone looked at his own watch, only to be drawn back to the vigil when a long inhalation was followed by a loud expiration. Assistant Surgeon General Dr. Charles Crane gently held Lincoln's head while Dr. Leale continued to monitor the right wrist.

Lincoln's Presbyterian pastor and friend Dr. Phineas Gurley asked everyone in the room to pray, and they knelt as one.[77] Stanton was barely able to contain his sorrow. The muscles on his face began to twitch.[78] At 7 AM the town clocks struck the hour.[79]

The end came at 7:22 AM without a struggle or convulsion. As everyone knelt and Dr. Gurley began "Our Father and our God," Tanner reached into his pocket for his pencil and notebook to record the historic words for posterity — but in his haste the pencil caught in his pocket and the point broke off. Exasperated, he could only listen to the pastor invoke God's pity for the bereaved family and plead for help in preserving the stricken nation.[80] When the pastor intoned "Thy will be done, Amen," Stanton raised his hand as tears streamed down his face. Ten years earlier, when Stanton was already nationally renowned as a brilliant lawyer, he had glanced at Lincoln's ill-clad appearance and arrogantly derided the lanky midwesterner, then a junior colleague on the same patent-infringement defense team, as a "damned long-armed ape . . . [who] . . . does not know anything."[81] Now Stanton buried his head in the blankets and wept, as never before in public, for the man he had grown to respect and admire. When he had somewhat recovered he muttered the immortal words, "Now he belongs to the ages."[82]

Cabinet members filed out into the back parlor and put their signatures to a short letter, composed before death by Attorney General James Speed, notifying Andrew Johnson of Lincoln's death. Laconic and to the point, it advised: "The office of president has devolved under the Constitution upon you." The emergency demanded that he take the oath of office immediately. They requested his instructions.[83] The man who had appalled so many dignitaries with his apparent intoxication at the inauguration only six weeks earlier had now succeeded to the presidency. It was the first time in the history of the Republic that a man had become chief executive following the murder of his predecessor.

The assistant secretary of the Treasury had already closed the dead man's eyes. Leale, before leaving the bedroom, smoothed the contracted facial muscles and placed nickel coins over each eyelid, then changed his mind and replaced them with larger silver half dollars. When the jaw fell slightly, exposing the lower teeth, one physician bound it tightly with a handkerchief.[84] Leale, who since the shooting had ministered to the president longer than anyone present, finally covered Lincoln's face with a sheet.[85] Stanton came back to lower the window shades, and the mourners walked out wearily into the rain.

Dr. Charles Leale went out alone and deep in thought. It was cold and wet, but he was bareheaded because he had left his hat in Ford's Theatre. His clothes were stained with the president's blood as he walked the long blocks back to his hospital. He would never wash the blood off his cuffs. They would be his personal keepsake of a man he regarded as a martyr.[86]

Dr. Gurley prayed with Mrs. Lincoln and Robert in the front parlor before the widow and her eldest son prepared to go down to their carriage for the ride back to the White House. As they reached the front door of the Petersen house, she looked across at Ford's Theatre, now an object of scorn and loathing. "Oh, that dreadful house! That dreadful house!" she exclaimed.[87]

James Tanner hobbled back to his rooms in the adjoining boardinghouse. He had already transcribed his shorthand notes in time to witness the passing of the president. Conscious of the historic content of his writing, he decided to keep the original transcript for himself and make a copy for the secretary of war. As he wrote, he heard the familiar measured tread of the military in the street. He went to the window and saw the crowd parting to make way for a lieutenant and ten privates with arms reversed, surrounding the hearse carrying the body of Abraham Lincoln. Corporal Tanner raised his hand and saluted as the dismal cortege passed by. The modest procession turned left on F Street, quietly pacing toward the White House.[88]

Most of the weeping mourners in the street were black people. One of their community would later write that they had just lost their Moses.[89]

Major Thomas Eckert, the head of the military telegraph office, had been on duty at the Petersen house all night as Stanton's invaluable link to the outside. When he got back to his home, he opened his diary and grieved profoundly: "Our beloved President Abraham Lincoln breathed his last. My heart is *too* sad for expression."[90]

The unsuspecting journalist Noah Brooks had slept blissfully through the unfolding drama, having joked with his roommate before going to sleep that the sounds of passing cavalry must be a rebel attempt at carrying off the president. But early in the morning, the landlord cried out, "Wake, wake, Mr. Brooks! I have dreadful news!" He told of multiple murders that had taken the lives of the president and most of the heads of departments. Brooks fell back in bed, "cold and shivering with horror." Then he dressed and went out into the wet and cheerless streets. As he walked toward Ford's Theatre, past tearful men and women, he came upon the cortege escorting the corpse back to the White House. Bystanders uncovered their heads as the procession passed by in the rain.[91]

District of Columbia Supreme Court Chief Judge Cartter arrived home tired from monitoring the evidence of eyewitnesses. He had already felt the pain of war from the loss of his son in the Union army,[92] but now he would have to watch out for his own safety. A friend warned that the enemies of Lincoln might remember that the judge, as chairman of the Ohio delegation at the Republican National Convention in 1860, had given Lincoln the decisive votes that won him the party's presidential nomination.[93]

As many Washingtonians sat down to breakfast after the night's harrowing events, the tolling of church bells confirmed the worst. Abraham Lincoln was no more.[94] Cities as distant as Richmond soon reverberated with the loud bangs of artillery, fired in posthumous salute to the slain president.[95]

General Henry Halleck, army chief of staff, set off to advise Andrew Johnson not to leave the Kirkwood House Hotel without a guard. As Senator Sumner got into the general's carriage to be driven to the secretary of state's home, mourners in the street asked whether Lincoln was still alive. Sadly, Sumner shook his head.

Inside the home of the secretary of state, Mrs. Adeline Seward was seated halfway up the stairs, dressed in white, visibly devastated. Sumner arrived, and she grasped both of his hands. "Charles Sumner, they have murdered my husband! They have murdered my boy! Fred is dying! He will never speak to me again!"

Sumner offered feeble words of consolation. He asked the condition of her husband.

"Henry [his middle name] is doing better than I expected, but Fred will never speak to me again."

Rising from her chair, she threw up her hands, exclaiming, "I must fly," then disappeared.[96] He would never see her again. She died five weeks later; in her obituary a reporter would remember her telling him she seemed to have two hearts after that night, one throbbing for her husband and the other for her son.[97]

Stanton, Halleck, and Welles stood by Seward's bedside, the torn and jagged flesh now sewn up by attending physicians. Seward was a pathetic ghost of the man intimates often saw swinging in his hammock on the back porch, puffing on a long, strong cigar.[98] He was a crushed contrast with the image a visiting Frenchman had taken away some months earlier of "a lithe little man, nimble in spite of his age, with a bush of tousled white hair, . . . who looks at you with black eyes full of malicious good humor."[99] Gone, too, were the "mobile features often enlivened by a smile."[100] The secretary of state labored slowly to recollect what he remembered of the savage attack, painfully drawing breaths between each word. He sounded like a dying person gasping for air, and his daughter feared his efforts at breathing might drain his remaining strength.

Though brutal, the assault could not have been a total surprise to Seward. He had confided to a *New York Times* reporter several times over the past two years his expectations that he and others might be assassinated during the war. Assassinations, he prophesied, would be attempted either to serve the Confederacy or to avenge its defeat. He had even made what he called "personal arrangements" in the event he was assassinated.[101]

Mrs. Seward decided to tell her husband what she had just learned of Lincoln. "Henry, the president is gone." He remained calm but seemed to comprehend. Now unable to speak intelligibly, he tried to write on a white slate, holding a pencil with his uninjured arm, but it was barely decipherable.

Mrs. Seward turned to the secretary of war. "Are you safe, Mr. Stanton?"

"Not any more than anyone else," he replied.

Fanny, sickened by the odor of blood and petrified that the assassin might soon return to kill those he had only managed to wound, pleaded with Stanton for more protection. With kindly gestures and comforting words, he arranged immediately for the guard to be doubled around the home. Before leaving he took charge of Payne's shattered revolver and the brown hat that had fallen off during the struggle in Seward's bedroom.[102]

When Sumner arrived back at his home, haggard and spent, he had to pass through a protective cordon of guards stationed there on Stanton's orders. Many friends, worried by his absence, had gone looking for him. Others had entered his home and were anxiously awaiting his return. He assured them there was no fear of a second rebellion, reasoning, "Those who fought us are soldiers, not assassins."

"Our leaders are gone," said one.

"But the Republic remains," Sumner responded.[103]

At about this moment the body of Abraham Lincoln was carried up to the principal guest room in the White House, the same room in which the president's son Willie had died three years earlier. Overlooking Lafayette Park, this second-floor bedroom on the northwest corner was known as the Prince of Wales Room because Queen Victoria's son and heir had slept in it as a guest of President Buchanan in 1860. Dominating all the furniture was the rosewood bed, six feet wide and eight feet long, that Mary Todd Lincoln had bought shortly after moving into the White House; successive generations would come to know it as the Lincoln Bed.

Benjamin Brown French had driven his carriage through the White House gate and was on hand to accompany the temporary coffin upstairs into the Prince of Wales Room. He watched as the corpse, still "limp and warm," was lifted from the box and laid upon the floor, then stretched out upon a "cooling board" in preparation for the autopsy at midday.[104] Both eyes bulged from their sockets, the right one more so, with the skin below now vividly black and puffy.[105]

Mrs. Lincoln's equilibrium collapsed with the death of her husband. She had not yet overcome the loss of young Willie, for whom she grieved so deeply that she had never set foot in the ground-floor Green Room since his funeral service there in 1862. Now she cried so much that it seemed no one could lessen her burden nor lighten her suffering. It had been the same at Willie's death, when the president himself had led her gently to a window and pointed in the direction of the mental asylum, cautioning her to try to control her grief "or it will drive you mad, and we may have to send you there."[106]

With her world disintegrating, she sent for Elizabeth Keckly, the former slave. Perhaps no one knew the first lady as well, nor shared her trust and strictest confidences as much as the Virginia-born black woman. Keckly had been awakened less than an hour after Lincoln slumped forward in Ford's Theatre when a neighbor called with the horrendous news that the president had been wounded and the entire cabinet assassinated. "I felt as if the blood had been frozen in my veins and that my lungs must collapse for the want of air," Keckly recalled later.[107] Unknown to her, Mrs. Lincoln had already dispatched messengers to bring her to the White House, but all of them had failed to locate the residence.

Keckly hurried by foot to the White House, passing by armed guards surrounding Seward's house, only to be denied entry by other sentinels outside the executive mansion. Like others, she drifted in the streets, picking up rumors and snatches of information. When an old man walked by, Keckly asked, "Tell me whether Mr. Lincoln is dead or not."

"Not dead," he answered, "but dying. God help us."[108]

In the morning a White House carriage drew up before the dressmaker's residence. Keckly hastily put on her shawl and bonnet and was driven at great speed through the somber streets to the residence of the head of state, in front of which vast crowds, predominantly black, stood in silent homage, oblivious to the cold and the rain.[109]

Mrs. Welles was alone in the darkened room with Mrs. Lincoln.

"Why did you not come to me last night Elizabeth? I sent for you," Mrs. Lincoln said softly.

"I did try to come to you, but I could not find you," said Keckly as she laid her hand upon the widow's feverish forehead.[110]

When the two surviving Lincoln children entered, they tried hard to console their mother. Robert's affectionate impulses did little to stifle the anguish of his mother. But young Tad occasionally succeeded when he hugged her and cried out, "Don't cry so, Mama. Don't cry, or you will make me cry, too. You will break my heart." At moments like this Keckly saw the woman stifle her sobs and embrace the boy tightly.[111]

With permission, Keckly slipped into the room where the body of Abraham Lincoln lay. Cabinet secretaries and military officers made way for her as she lifted a white cloth and looked with reverence upon the stilled face. When she turned to leave, she had tears in her eyes and a choking sensation in her throat.[112]

Secretary of the Navy Welles spoke briefly in the White House library with his wife, who had also been trying to comfort Mrs. Lincoln. When Welles and Attorney General Speed went downstairs on their way out, Tad turned from a window and cried out tearfully, "Oh, Mr. Welles, who killed my father?" Welles and Speed could not give Tad any meaningful explanation. Neither could they hold back their own tears.[113]

Chief Justice Salmon Chase, meanwhile, prepared to administer the presidential oath of office to Vice President Andrew Johnson. Chase, a former secretary of the Treasury, had been asleep in the home he shared three blocks east of Ford's Theatre with his daughter and multimillionaire son-in-law when a Treasury Department employee rushed in to tell of Lincoln's assassination. When more people came to spread the news of the attack on Seward, Chase wanted to go and see for himself what he could not bring himself to believe, but he quickly changed his mind when he realized he would be of no help. Throughout the night he slept restlessly, kept awake by the noisy, rhythmic patrol of military guards sent by Stanton to protect him. In the morning Chase learned of the president's death when he walked near the Petersen house. Inside Seward's home, a surgeon told the chief justice that the secretary of state might live, but there was no hope for Frederick's survival.

When he called on Andrew Johnson at the Kirkwood House, Chase found him calm but grave. The arrival of Treasury Secretary McCulloch and Speed led to an arrangement to have the swearing-in ceremony at the hotel later that morning. Chase and the attorney general used the remaining time in Speed's office to brush up on legal precedents for the assumption of presidential power by vice presidents. It had happened only twice before, the first time when John Tyler was sworn into office in 1841 on the death of President William Henry Harrison after only a month in office, and then in 1850 when Millard Fillmore succeeded to the presidency following the death of Zachary Taylor.

When Chase arrived back at the hotel, Johnson and about a dozen dignitaries, including most of the cabinet, stood in a parlor. There, at 11 AM, Chase recited the brief, constitutionally prescribed oath, which Johnson repeated solemnly. Conscious of the perilous times, and wanting to convey an expression of personal solicitude, Chase volunteered, "May God guide, support, and bless you in your arduous duties."[114] Others came forward to express similar sentiments.

The new president made a brief speech, telling those present that he needed their support. Most memorably, he declared, "The duties of the office are mine. I will perform them. The consequences are with God."[115]

Johnson was quick to exert executive authority. At midday he chaired a cabinet meeting in the Treasury building, formally announcing that everyone would remain in office. He appointed William

Hunter as acting secretary of state, and pressed departmental heads to make arrangements for the funeral of his illustrious predecessor.[116]

The succession was now formally complete. The seventeenth president would not move into the White House until Mrs. Lincoln departed five weeks later. The delay was of little consequence. It would give people more time to accept the newcomer as head of state.

Abroad, observers mixed apprehension with disgust, remembering Johnson's drunken performance at his inauguration as vice president six weeks earlier. "The drunken madman Johnson is now President de facto," wrote Britain's top civil servant in the Foreign Office. "Whether his rule will be submitted to, and, if so, how he will rule is now the most vital question."[117]

CHAPTER 9

An Autopsy and Embalming in the White House

Some of the sleepless physicians and surgeons who had ministered to the dying president throughout the night had only several hours to rest before assembling in the White House for the autopsy. The postmortem had to be rushed before blood began to solidify and decomposition set in. Any delay in the postmortem would imperil the task of the embalmer, waiting his turn to cut the jugular and drain blood while it was still liquid.

There was not even time for the president's personal physician, Dr. Robert Stone, in a gesture of professional courtesy, to round up all the physicians who had attended Lincoln overnight. Dr. Charles Leale twice declined invitations to be present at the autopsy, fearing his absence from severely wounded patients would aggravate their shock over the assassination. One amputee had relapsed into deep depression and died shortly after declaring, "Doctor, all we have fought for is gone. Our country is destroyed and I want to die."[1]

The surgeon general had ordered two of his assistants, Dr. Edward Curtis and Dr. J. Janvier Woodward, to conduct the postmortem.[2] Both were proven and skillful anatomists, and each would become eminent in his field. Curtis and his wife, Augusta, had witnessed Payne's flight from Seward's house when he galloped past them as they sat on the stoop of their boardinghouse a few hundred yards north of the crime. Unaware that murderers were at large, the couple later strolled down Pennsylvania Avenue; they learned the president had been shot only after they had boarded a horse-drawn car carrying frightened passengers home. Curtis raced to the surgeon general's office to be available for emergency duty, but it was closed. Then he ran to the White House, where a cordon of sentries blocked entry. He hurried home, expecting to be summoned that night, but his orders came only the following morning.[3]

At the White House, Curtis was escorted to the second-floor northwest corner room, where a select few military officers and civilians, including Lincoln's friend Orville Hickman Browning, sat quietly or spoke in whispers. The oversize canopied bed bought by Mrs. Lincoln for this main guest room dwarfed the sofa, wardrobe, bureau, and chairs. Surgeon General Barnes, still awed by the president's "tenacity of life," stopped pacing up and down to brief his subordinate.

The autopsy began at noon with the arrival of Drs. Woodward, Stone, Taft, William Notson, and Assistant Surgeon General Charles Crane. Lincoln's cold and unclothed corpse, covered by sheets and towels, lay stretched out on rough boards brought into the Prince of Wales Room by the embalmers.[4] His eyelids and puffy facial flesh made him look like a battered boxer. The eye sockets were "gorged with blood," according to Woodward,[5] pushing the eyes forward, the right one even more so. The scalp around the head wound was thick from hemorrhaging.[6] Even though the autopsy was confined to the head, Curtis eyed Lincoln's nude body and was astonished to see well-rounded muscles and strong bones normal in a powerful athlete. He never expected the elongated, slightly stooping man to be so muscular. Now he had a better understanding of the stories told of Lincoln's youthful prowess as a wrestler.[7]

There were no qualms about defiling the body or affronting the dignity of the president as the surgeons prepared for the cranial autopsy. After removing the scalp from ear to ear, they saw clearly how the gunshot had pierced cleanly through the occipital bone at the base of the brain, less than two inches in back of the left ear. It had left a smooth, circular hole with beveled edges, "clean cut, as if done with a punch," according to Woodward and Stone.[8] To reach the brain, Curtis sawed off the calvarium, the hard, protective domed top of Lincoln's head. The gaping cranium was now wide enough for their hands to dip in and explore the brain. The anatomists sliced through layers of tissue until they saw the path of the ball, visible as a line of clotted blood all the way from the punctured skull across to the right hemisphere as far as the anterior lobe of the cerebrum, immediately behind the right eye socket. Splinters of bone lay along the route carved by the ball's velocity. Liquid smears of blood had hardened over the surface of the right hemisphere. Such was the momentum of the ball that it had slammed a plug of bone three inches into the lethal path. About an inch deeper into the brain the surgeons removed a small piece of the ball that had ripped off as it blasted into the skull.[9]

Curtis reached into the open skull to lift out the brain so they could get a better feel for the ball, hidden in spongy white cerebral tissue. As he raised it from the cavity the ball dropped free, slipped through his fingers, and fell with a clatter into an empty white china basin. Curtis looked down at "a little black mass" no bigger than the end of his finger.[10] The lead ball had been reshaped on its pulverizing course through the skull and become flattened and convex on both sides, with curled edges.[11]

As the surgeons probed the wrecked skull, a messenger arrived from Mrs. Lincoln, bedridden in her room across the corridor. She asked only for a lock of his hair, and Stone complied, snipping some strands close to the darkened wound. Taft signaled with his open hand that he too wanted a memento and was given a bloodstained lock. Each of the other surgeons received an identical personal keepsake.[12]

Stone used his penknife to mark the ball with the president's initials. Later in the office of the secretary of war he put it in an envelope, marked it with his seal, and wrote his name on the flap. Stanton sealed everything in a larger envelope and endorsed each end of the flap with the bold flourishes of his signature.[13] The ball had historic value, but it might also be used in evidence if the assassin was caught and brought to trial.

As the surgeons prepared to leave, Curtis got the surgeon general's permission to weigh the brain for a comparison with those of other men of great intellect. Oblivious to the embalmers, he moved to a corner and washed the soft, grayish white tissue of the brain's parallel, furrowed halves. Never before had he been so awed by the mystery of what he called "the vital spark." Without it, the brain was inert and ready to rot. But with it, he believed, the living brain had "the silent, subtle machinery" to rule the world. Lincoln's brain was normal, but Curtis made no record of the weight because it had already been lightened by the discharge of broken tissue, much of it sliding out when the president was carried to the Petersen house, where even more oozed onto the pillows.[14]

Inexplicably, the doctors did not agree on what they had seen at the autopsy when they wrote their official reports. Some said the fatal ball slowed to a halt in the left side, while others claimed it crossed far to the right. Woodward, reporting to the surgeon general the same day, said the ball passed through the left lateral ventricle and came to rest just above the anterior portion of the *left* corpus striatum.[15] Curtis merely said that the ball crossed the center of the brain,[16] while Taft noted that it ended up behind the *right* orbit.[17] Stone recalled that the same ball reached the posterior lobe of the brain's *left* hemisphere.[18] Browning, a lawyer, wrote contemporaneously in his diary that the ball had traveled toward the *right* eye, lodging in the brain about two-thirds of the way from where it entered to the front.[19]

When he was finished, Curtis crossed Lafayette Square to his boardinghouse. He was changing his clothes when he noticed splotches of blood on the shirt cuffs. The stains were clearly from the president's head. Mindful of the historic importance of the relic, his wife snipped the cuffs from the shirt and carefully put them in an envelope. Then her husband wrote on the outside:

SHIRT SLEEVES SOILED WITH THE BLOOD OF PRESIDENT ABRAHAM
LINCOLN AT THE AUTOPSY ON HIS BODY APRIL 15, 1865.
EDWARD CURTIS, ASST. SURG. U.S.A.

Soon after, Curtis was cleaning the surgical instruments used at the autopsy when he showed his wife a sliver of bone stuck to one of the implements. While she watched, he wrapped the tiny fragment of bone into a scrap of writing paper on which he carefully wrote:

SPLINTER OF BONE FROM SKULL OF ABRAHAM LINCOLN[20]

CHAPTER 10

⸻ ◆ ⸻

A Visceral Preference for Vengeance

aturday, April 15, 1865, was the glummest day Washington had ever known. A special edition of the *Daily Morning Chronicle* figuratively wept with moist type that began, "If tears had audible language, a shriek would go up from these States."[1] For nineteen days a rival newspaper, the *Daily National Intelligencer,* bordered the length of its columns with broad black stripes. And the *Daily National Republican* lamented, "The City is in the deepest gloom."[2]

Suddenly color drained from Washington as the outward signs of frivolity disappeared. Flags drooped at half-staff, and bunting vanished from roofs and windows. Fluttering cloth hailing the end of war came down swiftly to match the downcast mood. In their place came a show of black so emphatic, and heavy, and plentiful that the city seemed wrapped in a shroud. There was such a run on the shops that mourning material sold out. "I heard of several who, failing to get anything, tore up black dresses and skirts," a visitor, George Wheelock, wrote home to his wife.[3]

Stanton directed the headquarters of every department, post, and station to be similarly draped for thirty days.[4] At the State Department, the newly appointed acting head, William Hunter, ordered staff to use black-bordered writing paper and envelopes, and to seal all communications with black wax "for a reasonable time."[5]

On Easter Sunday the churches overflowed with residents seeking solace in the calm retreats of their sanctuaries. The sun shone brightly, but it was a dispirited and joyless city.[6] So many people packed the New York Avenue Presbyterian Church, where Lincoln occasionally worshipped as a nonmember in his rented pew, number 14,[7] that pious members had difficulty squeezing up the aisle to their accustomed pews. Many others who could not find seating left, hoping to find room elsewhere. Those who stayed sang a hymn for national humility.[8] Dr. Gurley tried hard to make sense of the martyrdom, but it fell short of honest conviction. It was the voice of a preacher made small by mysteries beyond his knowing. "In the midst of our rejoicings, we needed this stroke, this dealing, this discipline, and therefore He has sent it," said the pastor who had knelt by the president's bedside. But the man of God seemed to know this was a frail and wanting explanation. He sounded no surer of understanding than anyone seated before him. So again he appealed for their patience and summoned all to hold fast to their faith. "We will wait for this interpretation, and we will wait in faith," he concluded.[9] In another church, conspicuous black crepe fell in unsightly folds between the green fronds of palm branches, splayed above an altar decorated for Easter with red and white japonicas.[10]

When Lincoln's principal private secretary, John Nicolay, arrived back in Washington the following day after a visit to Charleston, it seemed as if he had set foot in a cemetery. "I cannot describe to you the air of gloom which seems to hang over this city," he wrote from the White House to the woman he would soon marry. "As I drove up here from the Navy Yard through the city, almost every house was draped and closed, and men stood idle and listless in groups on the street corners." The mood was no different at the White House, which Nicolay found "dark and still as almost the grave itself."[11]

Another observer likened the widespread sorrow to a biblical plague, "as though some Herod had robbed each home of its first-born."[12]

Just when it appeared that the Union had emerged triumphant, it seemed that the fate of the Republic once again dangled precariously. A diarist in Indiana wondered whether history was repeating itself, with America doomed to follow ancient Rome to ruin and dissolution now that it, too, "has begun a career of conspiracy and assassination."[13] But for some in far-flung states, the news was too calamitous, and they continued to hope it was a hoax.[14]

The Petersen house instantly became something of a shrine, with hundreds showing up daily to view the humble room where Lincoln died. But the resident occupant, William Clark, an infantryman from Massachusetts, kept a close watch on all who entered, fearing they might steal the contents because everyone wanted a keepsake. Clark, then working in the quartermaster general's department, spent nearly all of Easter Sunday with an artist from *Frank Leslie's Illustrated Newspaper* who came to sketch a picture of Lincoln's last moments.[15]

While many in the city felt numb, there were spirited howls for revenge. Rage quickly overtook grief. Targets were easy to find among Southern sympathizers, captive Confederates, and a few others who dared to show happiness that Lincoln was dead.

Early in the morning mobs began to gather across the street from the east front of the Capitol, outside the Old Capitol Prison, where Confederate troops and spies were detained. Penned in and defenseless, they would be the logical target of ruffians out for blood. Scores of Southern combatants were locked up in a second-floor room with tiered bunks and grated windows looking out on East Capitol Street. They had been captured a week earlier at the battle of Sayler's Creek, southwest of Petersburg, where Union forces pulverized the enemy in the last major conflict with the Army of Northern Virginia.[16] The first of the captives from Sayler's Creek to wake up alerted the others to a noisy stir of people on the street and the unusually loud voices of prison guards. They rushed to the windows and saw houses being draped in black cloth. Evidently someone of great distinction had died.

Only at breakfast, when they asked the sergeant of the guard what had happened, were they told, "Some damned rebel killed the president last night." Like others across the city, they were stunned. They ate in silence, worried about the possibility that they might be victimized in violent repercussions. The guards stood by sorrowful and silent. Only a few prisoners spoke, and then merely to denounce assassination.

Back in the large cell they spoke freely among themselves, and most said they disapproved of the murder, but no one was profoundly regretful. Beyond the barred windows the vengeful mob grew menacingly larger. Murmurs gave way to tumult until the agitated mass closed in, threatening to burn down the brick prison. Now frantic, the inmates braced for the worst until a sergeant appeared and said everything possible would be done to protect them. As if on cue an unflappable colonel sent out the guard of Veteran Reserve Corpsmen, who quickly dispersed the would-be vigilantes. The impromptu move to storm the prison prompted officials to surround it immediately with a large protective force that would shield it for days to come.[17]

Despite the ring of guards around the prison, Thomas Walter, architect of the Capitol, told his wife, "I should not be surprised if it were stormed by a mob and the traitors inside of it slaughtered." He was not at all shocked to see a suspected conspirator in police custody being stoned by a jeering crowd. Similar gangs roamed elsewhere in the city, and Walter, like many, hoped order would be restored soon. But he too quickly yielded to the visceral preference for vengeance, and the puritanical, churchgoing architect did not even try to mask these feelings from his wife when he admitted, "I heartily acquiesce in the spirit of revenge that now moves the loyal element of the entire nation."[18]

Just hours after the president's death, a Confederate general and lower-ranking captives were led into the city followed closely by a bellicose mob chanting, "Hang them! Hang them!" William Kent, who had rushed into Lincoln's theater box moments after the assassination, described to his mother, "It was with difficulty the guard could keep the crowd back."[19] Elsewhere in Washington an angry bunch swarmed over an itinerant preacher who foretold of the imminent assassination of Andrew Johnson if he dared pick up on Lincoln's policies. Lawmen probably saved his life when they dragged him off to jail.[20]

Even though police shut down all liquor outlets,[21] it had no effect on a city already heady with anger. The mood was so volatile that mere hints of activity out of the ordinary drew boisterous crowds coiled for violence.[22] Strong guards protecting suspects sometimes failed to hold back the raucous and mobile mobs.[23] The lawless scenes left a lasting impression upon Georgetown College undergraduate John Hamilton, twenty, heir to family farmlands accumulated over two centuries in southern Maryland. He followed a rabble pelting three men with stones as the victims, suspected of complicity in the attack on Seward, were led off in custody through the dangerous streets of the capital. "I never saw so much excitement in my life," he wrote home.[24]

Another eyewitness, corresponding with former president James Buchanan, told of streets and corners "thick with citizens and strangers expressing their wrath and vengeance upon the assassins."[25] Lincoln's immediate predecessor replied ominously, "God only knows what may be the direful consequences."[26]

George Wheelock had seen and heard enough to warn his wife, "The cry now is for vengeance. Thousands whom I have met feel not grief alone but indignation and desire for revenge."[27]

The army lieutenant who had gotten lost in the wings of Ford's Theatre as he ran after the fleeing assassin could not temper his rage when writing home to his father. "Let no man ever speak to me again of Southern chivalry, or balk in sympathy with traitors. While there is strength in my arm, I never will endure it."[28]

A compulsion to beat and brutalize the few who publicly rejoiced in Lincoln's death spread rapidly across distant state boundaries. In Cleveland, Ohio, a Democrat who stood on the steps of a building exclaiming "I'm damned glad of it!" was knocked down and almost stomped to death before policemen led him away.[29] In Florida the Union army court-martialed a soldier from Illinois for bragging, "That is good news and ought to have happened four years ago!" Found guilty of conduct prejudicial to good order and military discipline, he was sentenced to have a thirty-pound ball chained to his left leg during six months of hard labor.[30] Others were hauled off to prisons in New Jersey for "rejoicing and hurrahing" over the murder, but were freed when a grand jury refused to indict, even though a judge advocate labeled them "treasonable actings and doings." Similar gleeful outbursts were reported in Indiana.[31]

Passions were so roiled that primeval urges to kill or maim overcame even the better educated. A Clevelander admitted as much to his friend, the chief judge of the District of Columbia Supreme Court. "As much as I have always denounced the barbarity of the Spanish Inquisition, in this case I say, give us the rack and make them feel its terrible rending powers, until they shall be glad to reveal all they know of damnable conspiracy."[32]

Even Unionists who had cooled toward Lincoln since he had held high the banner of freedom for slaves were saddened by his loss.

From his base in Raleigh, North Carolina, Union soldier Henry Clay Weaver reflected how he and his unit were Lincoln men, but only for winding up the rebellion. "I am morally, religiously and politically opposed to protracting a gigantic struggle like this, attended as it is by such a vast loss of life and property, for no other purpose than the emancipation of the ignorant African," he wrote on hearing the news from Washington. But he was not nearly so brash and outspoken when he thought about what might come next. "We sadly regret the calamity to the land and his misfortune. We tremble for the consequences. A war of extermination would be terrible."[33]

Another Union soldier camped on Richmond's outskirts scribbled a field note back to his brother. A single line was all he needed to convey the extent of the loss: "When needed most he has been taken from us."[34] It was a refrain taken up across many parts of the grieving land. "All think that the South, in Mr. Lincoln, has lost the man, who of all others, was the most ready to forgive and forget and kill the fatted calf, if it would but return to its duty," wrote Philadelphian Samuel Meigs to his brother, the quartermaster general.[35]

The country buzzed with rumors that rioters were already running amok in New York City and elsewhere, and men and women everywhere yearned for more news from the capital. "Anxiously waiting for the wires to speak," one diarist noted while traveling in Sacramento.[36] Philadelphia seemed braced for lawlessness, with one resident sensing his city was about to become "a hunting ground for copperheads."[37]

The newly arrived British minister, who was scheduled to present his credentials the day Lincoln died, worried that opponents of the president's lenient policy toward the South would surge in influence as a result of "atrocious acts . . . hitherto unknown in the political history of the United States."[38]

Others fretted that Union soldiers in the South might take the law into their own hands. Armed and within easy reach of weaker victims, they were in a better position than anyone to take quick and deadly revenge. When the dramatic news arrived during the night at a military camp in Burkeville, Virginia, a brigadier general had a hard time restraining his Ohio volunteers, and even himself, from slaughtering the helpless prisoners of war. "I now feel like a demon," wrote General Joseph Keifer, twenty-nine. "I feel a remorse within my heart that I ever treated a rebel magnanimously."[39] A lowly private at the same encampment hoped rebel leaders would be hanged as fast as they were caught. Writing a female friend, he declared, "Mercy now would be a sin, almost."[40] The murder so enraged one major general that he wrote his chief of staff, "I advise that every officer of the rebel army within control of the Army of the Potomac be at once closely confined, with a view to retaliation upon their persons for so horrible an outrage."[41] General Sherman, "in the field" near Raleigh, North Carolina, immediately feared that his men would get out of hand and commit "excesses," but three days later he reported that feelings had "softened down and can easily be guided."[42] Union soldiers here and elsewhere may have held back from committing atrocities only because, as one chronicler suggested, events pointed to "the rapid decline of the Southern Confederacy, and the delightful idea of being permitted to return to happy homes, amid the wild shouts of a victorious peace."[43]

The president's death was a sobering jolt to Confederates, and many were quick to regret it. Sixteen captive generals signed on to a letter to Grant expressing their "unqualified abhorrence and indignation" at the killing of their foremost foe.[44] General Joseph Johnston, negotiating a cease-fire with Sherman, was even blunter in saying Southerners had begun to realize that Lincoln was "the best friend the South had."[45] In London the Confederates' unaccredited commissioner, James Mason, was quick to disavow the South's complicity. "Assassination for any cause has never been a vice of my countrymen, and none can regard it with more abhorrence than they do," he wrote the earl of Shaftesbury.[46]

Though Lincoln was only six weeks into his second term when assassinated he was already assured of a place in the pantheon of venerated leaders. The US minister to Britain, Charles Francis Adams, in a habitually candid aside to his chief secretary, remarked that Lincoln had died "at the proper time for his fame." Adams, himself the son and grandson of US presidents, observed that had he been in Lincoln's place, he "would not have desired anything better."[47]

A widespread belief swept across loyal states that the assassins were part of a rebel conspiracy rather than a handful of disgruntled Southerners or even a pair of maniacs. The synchronized timing of what appeared to be twin assassinations could only have come about by conspiratorial design. Bloodletting at the highest levels of government could not have been mere coincidence. The enormity of the crimes suggested a network of contacts, intricate planning, elaborate help, and much funding. It seemed beyond the scope of one or two desperadoes. Solo assassins could never have acted with such precision and boldness, managing to slip from sight into the unknown after striking down the most notable men in the land. Minerva Rodgers, mother-in-law of the quartermaster general, spoke for many Washingtonians when she wrote to her children insisting, "There must have been a conspiracy."[48] Associated Press correspondent Lawrence Gobright hinted at such in his first lengthy dispatch to the *New York Herald,* and later disclosed fears of "a wide-extended conspiracy."[49]

Early rumor and raw evidence pointed to more intended targets than the simultaneous assaults on Lincoln and Seward. Secretary of the Interior John Usher, forty-nine, wrote the day after Lincoln's death that the conspirators had also planned to eliminate the vice president and the entire cabinet. "A man was heard by [Attorney General] Speed walking on his back porch, and one was found at Stanton's hid behind a tree box who ran away. A person took cover at the Kirkwood House where the vice president was staying." In Usher's opinion, the conspiracy had probably been organized by Confederate leaders resident in Canada.[50]

The US consul general in Montreal, John Potter, was so convinced the conspiracy had been hatched in his city that he insisted his government demand expulsion of the Confederates, failing which America should sever all ties with Canada. Potter sent highly charged dispatches to the State Department denouncing Confederate agents in Montreal for reportedly celebrating the assassination with a champagne supper and drinking a toast to the health of the murderer on the very day Lincoln died. Potter noted the partying had been at St. Lawrence Hall, one of the leading hotels and a frequent rendezvous for Southern sympathizers beyond the reach of US authorities. In later, more specific finger-pointing, Potter reported, "A most respectable gentleman of this city informs me that a week before the death of President Lincoln it was asserted by some of these men in the office of the same hotel that 'Lincoln would not live a week longer.'"[51]

Filled with personal loathing for Confederate expatriates, whom he excoriated for being transformed by treason into brutes, Potter recalled Booth's presence in the city the previous October, followed probably, he claimed, by another visit later under an assumed name. "There are many facts which tend to prove that these persons were not only cognizant of the conspiracy," he wrote Seward, "but the conspiracy was planned and organized in this city."[52]

Others suspected the conspiracy to be the work of the Confederate leadership down south. On the day Lincoln died, Britton Hill, a top aide to Stanton, spoke at length with Seward's staff and then made calls at the coffeehouses in the neighborhood of Ford's Theatre. There was no doubt in his mind that Booth had taken the president's life, and he did not withhold from Stanton his finding that "you were to have been killed and the vice president." More significant, though, was his focus on a cabal that may have conceived the murders from a safe distance. "All the circumstances signify a plot laid at Richmond before the capture of that city," he reported to Stanton. "I regret to think so, but it must be so."[53]

Independently, Ulysses S. Grant also suspected a wide conspiracy, though he did not provide names nor give clues to its origin. In a reassuring letter to his wife about his own safety a day after returning to Washington, he declared, "There is but little doubt but that the plot contemplated the destruction of more than the president and secretary of state." To comfort his anxious wife, he said he was working out of a well-guarded office, staying indoors at night, and visiting his hotel only twice a day for meals.[54]

In the uncertain aftermath of the assassination, suspicion even fell on unidentified Union army soldiers, with the provost marshal's office in Washington warning military officials in Philadelphia to take precautions against "a large number of persons" plotting to torch that city.[55]

In distant Missouri, Lincoln's previous attorney general, Edward Bates, suspected "a great conspiracy" that might unravel from a clue given by the assassin on stage, when he had shouted, "I am avenged — Sic Semper Tyrannis!"[56]

CHAPTER 11

"I Am Right in the Justness of My Cause"

Asia Booth Clarke lay in bed, swollen and heavy with the weight of fetal twins, when her shriek broke the morning quiet in her West Philadelphia mansion. The newspaper brought first word of the assassination, as well as the searing news that her younger brother had fired the lethal shot. John Sleeper Clarke stopped shaving and ran to his wife's bedside. Hysterically, she pointed to the bold and unspeakable headlines.[1]

The horror was overwhelming, but they also had to cope with the instant shame and guilt of being tied by name and blood to a criminal of monstrous notoriety. Asia, then twenty-nine, would in time describe her feelings of listless desolation. But for now there was the loss of pride and dignity in being a Booth, the most acclaimed family of thespians the country had ever known. Laurels and luster brought to the family name by the late patriarch, Junius Brutus Booth the elder, were no longer of consequence to his descendants, who began to grapple with the stigma of public infamy and disgrace.

Edwin, an older and most famous of the Booth siblings, was in Boston when he learned of the assassination early in the morning from a newspaper. Though long accustomed to strutting the stage in dramatic roles before packed theaters, he now flailed childlike, as if struck by stage fright, uncertain what to do or where to go. "I am half crazy now," he wailed in a letter to a close friend.[2]

Ironically, the night before he had starred in the Boston Theater and uttered the lines, "Where is my honor now? Mountains of shame are piled upon me!"[3] It was a bravura performance, with the audience calling him back for repeated curtain calls. But Edwin was a

Booth, a name now spoken with revulsion throughout the Union. At 7 AM, while Abraham Lincoln still lived, a jittery Henry Jarrett shut his Boston Theater and canceled the show, fearful of public reaction, because, as he wrote Edwin, "Suspicion points to one nearly related to you as the perpetrator of this horrid deed."[4]

With no stomach to entertain or amuse, Edwin replied the same day, thanking Jarrett "for relieving me from my engagement with yourself and the public. The news of the morning has made me wretched indeed, not only because I have received the unhappy tidings of the suspicions of a brother's crime, but because a good man . . . has fallen."[5]

When tearful friends saw him arrive back at his New York home, he looked, according to one eyewitness, "as spectral as if the grave had given up its dead." Withdrawn and somber, Edwin stepped out of his carriage wrapped in a long coat, his hat lowered over much of his face.[6] On the advice of friends, he remained "cooped up" for weeks, stepping outside only occasionally to satisfy a craving for fresh air and exercise. But even then, he went among the public with great caution and only in the evenings.[7] Death threats and other hate mail arrived daily, warning that he would be shot and his house burned down.[8] Throughout the long ordeal, Edwin often sat mute and immobile. "[Here] I feel safe," he wrote with a measure of relief. "What I am in Philadelphia and elsewhere, I know not."[9]

Even though he was a Booth, he barely knew the much younger man who had murdered the president. John Wilkes was still a schoolboy in Maryland when Edwin was living in California, and as adults their professional acting engagements kept them geographically apart: The older man won plaudits in the East and North, while the younger gained experience mostly in the South.

Edwin remembered John Wilkes as a youngster charging on horseback through the woods, gripping a lance and "spouting" heroic speeches. The family looked on him as "a good-hearted, harmless, though wild-brained boy," and laughed at his "patriotic froth" whenever John Wilkes brought up the subject of secession with his Union-supporting family. Once, when Edwin asked his brother why he did not join the Confederacy, John Wilkes replied, "I promised Mother I keep out of the quarrel, if possible, and I am sorry that I said heir political views were so far apart that the younger Booth rarely visited Edwin's house, and then only to visit his mother.[10]

Scared, ashamed, wary, and reclusive, Edwin waited out the days and weeks secluded in his home, not knowing whether he would ever act again.[11] He could not decide whether to stay put in the safety of his home in New York or go down to Philadelphia, where he knew the family was in need of "someone stronger and calmer than they can be."[12] At length he decided to remain in New York.

Though he had twice voted for Lincoln and was a staunch Unionist, the general public would not know until decades later that Edwin had actually saved the life of the president's oldest son early in the war. Edwin never publicized the chance encounter to win sympathy or to erase the curse from his name. Only years later did Robert Todd Lincoln describe how he had been on a platform at a railroad station in New Jersey when a throng of passengers, swarming around a conductor to buy sleeping-car tickets, unwittingly pressed Robert against a carriage. As the train began to move out, Robert fell feet-first into the space between the carriage and the platform. Quickly Edwin seized the young man by the coat collar and pulled him up to safety. A grateful Robert, recognizing the celebrated actor, thanked him warmly, remarking, "That was a narrow escape, Mr. Booth."[13]

Mary Ann Booth, the matriarch, was in Edwin's New York home when friends visited within hours of Lincoln's death. John Wilkes had been her acknowledged favorite and now he was a fugitive, hunted like vermin and wanted by many dead rather than alive. There was little the friends could do to comfort the woman who had given birth to the killer.

Outside, flags were being lowered to half-staff and bunting replaced with black mourning material when the doorbell rang. A mailman handed over a letter for Mary Ann Booth. It was from her renegade son, the one she called "the fondest of all my boys."[14] Dated April 14, at 2 AM, John Wilkes had begun writing "Dear Mother" less than twenty-one hours before the assassination. After a passing reference to the illuminations in Washington signaling Lee's surrender, he noted almost wistfully that everything would have been more bright and splendid "if it had been a display in a nobler cause. But so goes the world. Might makes right." In this, his last letter to the mother he venerated, John Wilkes said he wanted her to know that he was well. "Excuse brevity; am in haste." Then he signed off, "Your affectionate son ever, John."[15]

Summoned to Asia's Philadelphia home, the distraught Mary Ann Booth arrived that Saturday afternoon to find the family equally desolate. But the day passed, and even the night, before Asia remembered the sealed packet John Wilkes had given her for safekeeping about a month earlier, when she told him she was four months' pregnant.[16] He had told her he might come back for it, "but if anything should happen to me, open the packet *alone* and send the letters as directed, and the money and papers give to their owners." Brother and sister had then carefully placed the packet of secret contents behind the inner iron door of a heavily barred and locked safe.

"God bless you, sister mine," he had said as he kissed her tenderly.[17]

Now, in fulfillment of her younger brother's command, Asia opened the packet alone. Without ever disclosing why, she burned one envelope written with the name of a man she never revealed, and blew the charred remains about the room to prevent identification. She kept for herself the long envelope John Wilkes had addressed to her, but its contents were forever withheld after confiscation by law enforcement officials. Asia handed over to her husband the rest of the packet's contents, including a separate envelope addressed to the actor Samuel Chester, bonds for Mary Ann Booth, and papers for the conveyance of oil wells to brother Junius Brutus and sister Rosalie.

A single envelope contained two compelling confessions by the obsessed assassin, evidently mulled over for a long time, because he altered the fluent script in only very few instances. Two undated pages were addressed to "Dearest beloved Mother." Three larger pages, dated 1864, were "to (sic) whom it may concern"

The letter to his mother was a wrenching valedictory in which his unsteady, asymmetrical script did not square with his immaculate dress and disciplined mind. Evidently torn by breaking his solemn oath to her not to link up with the Confederacy, he pleaded with God to watch over, comfort, and protect her, to soften "the blow of my departure." The favorite son described his motivation as a noble duty for liberty and humanity. He said he had lived like a slave in the North for four years, never daring to express his true thoughts and feelings, because they would have been denounced as treasonable. All the while he had cursed his own "wilful idleness," feeling like a coward while savage acts were committed against his countrymen. "For you alone, have I also struggled to fight off this desire to be gone, but it seems that uncontrollable fate, moving me for its ends, takes me from you, dear Mother, to do what work I can for a poor oppressed downtrodden people." Without specifying any criminal intent, he asked only, "May that same fate cause me to do that work well."

Though he might live through the war, he told her bluntly, "I cannot longer resist the inclination, to go and share the sufferings of my brave countrymen, holding an unequal strife . . . against the most ruthless enemy the world has ever known." Pointedly he referred to family, writing "none of you think with me." Nevertheless, he wanted her to proclaim that he had not acted out of any selfish motive, but rather from "a sacred duty" to the cause of the South, a cause of liberty and justice. "And should the last bolt strike your son, dear Mother, bear it patiently. And think at the best life is but short, and *not at all times happy.*" With a plea for her prayers and forgiveness, the wayward son concluded, "I feel that I am right in the justness of my cause, and that we shall, *ere long,* meet again. Heaven grant it."[18]

The longer letter, addressed to no one in particular, almost casually noted near the very end that he would attempt to kidnap Abraham Lincoln and deliver him captive to the South. "Nor do I deem it a dishonor," he asserted, "in attempting to make for her a prisoner of this man, to whom she owes so much of misery."

The litany of grievances that had brought him to the edge of treason was crafted by a man goaded by hate, rigidly sure of himself, and riveted on overturning the course of the war. "Right or wrong, God, judge me, not man," he began. "For be my motive good or bad, of one thing I am sure, the lasting condemnation of the North." For John Wilkes, all hope for peace was dead, and he now accepted, "God's will be done. I go to see, and share the bitter end."

Booth had always believed that Lincoln's election was confirmation that war would be waged against Southern rights and institutions. No longer could the impassioned young actor give allegiance to a Union that spurned justice. Railing at his enemies, he continued: "People of the North, to hate tyranny, to love liberty and justice, to strike at wrong and oppression, was the teaching of our fathers. The study of our early history will not let me forget it."

He unabashedly defended slavery and the subjugation of blacks, declaring, "This country was formed for the white not for the black man." He described slavery as "one of the greatest blessings" bestowed by God upon a favored nation. Blacks were happier and more enlightened in America than anywhere else. He had seen less harsh treatment between master and slave than he had witnessed between father and son in the North. "Heaven knows *no one* would be willing to do *more* for the negro race than I. Could I but see a way to still better their condition. But Lincoln's policy is only preparing the way for their total annihilation."

In a sneering attack on Lincoln's Republican Party, he accused it of hanging the abolitionist John Brown for a crime that had now become a virtue. "If Brown were living," Booth argued, "I doubt if he himself would set slavery against the Union." The South had no choice in Booth's mind. "It is either extermination or slavery for themselves (worse than death) to draw from. I would know my choice."

As a measure of his commitment to the South, Booth noted that he would have to abandon friends and the acting career that had given him fame and fortune in the North. By contrast, the only friends he knew in the South were dead and buried. Going South would mean he would have to become a private soldier or even a beggar. "To give up all of the *former* for the *latter,* besides my mother and sisters, whom I love so dearly, (although they so widely differ with me in opinion), seems insane. But God is my judge. I love *justice* more than I do a country that disowns it. More than fame and wealth. More (Heaven pardon me if wrong) more than a happy home. I have never been upon a battlefield, but, O, my countrymen, could you all but see the reality or effects of this horrid war, as I have seen them . . . I know you would think like me."

As he neared the end, Booth reminisced nostalgically about his love of the "Stars and Stripes, once so pure and spotless. But now it had become an *emblem* of *bloody deeds*. Her once bright red stripes look like *bloody gashes* on the face of Heaven," he lamented. "I now look upon my early admiration of her glories as a dream. My love (as things stand today) is for the South alone."

He signed off as "*A Confederate* (at present — deleted) doing duty *upon his own responsibility.*"

His signature, written J. Wilkes Booth, was apparently added at a later date and certainly in another pen with a much lighter ink and thinner point.[19]

John Sleeper Clarke, horrified that he was now very publicly linked by marriage to the most loathsome criminal on the run, held on to the letters until the following day, Monday, April 17, thinking, as he declared later, that law enforcement officials would shortly make a search of his house. When this did not happen, he voluntarily handed over the incriminating documents to William Millward, US marshal for the eastern district of Pennsylvania, with a special plea for publication of the letter to Booth's mother, expecting its contents to show that none of the family shared Booth's political views.[20]

But to Clarke's dismay, Wednesday's *Philadelphia Inquirer* carried only the letter "to whom it may concern," under the headline: "Letter of John Wilkes Booth. Proof That He Meditated His Crime Months Ago." Millward had purposely withheld the shorter letter to Mrs. Booth, convinced that publication would be "entirely inexpedient and improper" because "it might create undue and false sympathy" for the fugitive murderer. He had given a copy of the other letter to the *Philadelphia Inquirer* almost enthusiastically, believing it might do "good rather than evil, impressing the public mind . . . that he was not only the assassin, but that he had acted in concert with others as a member of an extended and diabolical conspiracy."[21]

The same day the *Philadelphia Inquirer* story spotlighted Booth's connections to relatives in that city, John Sleeper Clarke was shaken further by the uninvited arrival at his home of another Booth sibling, Junius Brutus Booth Jr. Fearing what outsiders might think of Junius's appearance so soon after the assassination, even while a dragnet was on for the murderer, Clarke told his brother-in-law it might lead to "talk." To forestall suspicion, he said he called on Marshal Millward, who was out. The following morning Millward came to the Clarke house, where he was introduced to Junius. Millward was quick to give a slightly different account, saying he first learned of Junius's presence when he saw him lying in bed while searching the Clarke house on Thursday.[22]

Junius had been acting on stage in Cincinnati, Ohio, the night of the assassination. At ten o'clock the next morning, he was in his hotel when word came of the shot fired at Ford's Theatre by his much younger brother. The furor in Cincinnati was so intense that Junius cowered in the hotel for three days before slipping out to take the late-night train for Philadelphia.

Junius had not seen John Wilkes for ten years until returning east from California in 1864. He said he had tried hard to keep his brother from joining the secessionists, arguing that the war was a family quarrel that would be patched up. According to Junius, the younger brother promised often not to join the South, for the sake of his mother and family.

With gratitude for Junius's concern, John Wilkes promised to make him a gift of some oil stock. But this largesse would bring only misery to Junius because John Wilkes's letter announcing the present, and advising him not to sell as it would soon be valuable, arrived in Cincinnati two days before the assassination. Worse still for the innocent Junius, the letter expressed hope that the two could meet up soon in New York. Junius's hurried reply, scribbled almost immediately and later published in the newspapers, also hoped they could see each other in New York. To some, this was sufficient evidence of possible fraternal collusion.

More than a week after the assassination, friends of Junius dissuaded him from traveling to Washington, arguing that it would be unsafe. An anxious Junius had wanted only to discuss with officials what he termed "a garbled and false account" of his letter to John Wilkes, now in the public domain through newspaper accounts. But two days later, on April 25, he was arrested at 2 AM in Clarke's Philadelphia home, even though a compassionate officer pocketed the handcuffs and allowed Junius to walk outside unmanacled. Junius would languish in the Old Capitol Prison in Washington for eight weeks, irritated by roaches and bugs, and enraged by conditions and injustices he equated with the infamous French Bastille. For three of those weeks he shared a dismal cell with Clarke, who had also been detained in the wide dragnet for anyone suspected of ties to the assassination, but who was imprisoned for the lesser term of a single month.[23]

The youngest of the Booth brothers, Joseph, twenty-five, had also been arrested and jailed in New York, suspected of complicity only because by a freakish coincidence he had sailed from San Francisco the day before the assassination. After disembarking in Panama, a steamer from New York brought word that a man named Booth had shot the president. Given how common his surname was, Joseph thought nothing of it. But his self-described history of "melancholy insanity" resurfaced after a later telegraph disclosed details of the assassination. Even though passengers reacted with horror and asked Joseph whether he was related, he never denied being the assassin's brother. However, military officials in San Francisco had already alerted the War Department of Joseph's departure by steamship, and orders went out for his arrest the moment he arrived in New York.[24] While in custody in New York, he told a military interrogator, "that news made me insane." He said two or three days passed aboard ship before he began to return to normal.[25]

Asia endured the glare of notoriety and what she called "a host of miseries" with wan resignation.[26] Neither the scorn of her husband, infuriated by the Booth connection, nor the temper of an unforgiving public, would ever weaken her stoic pride in the name of Booth. She protected and promoted it with biographies of her father and Edwin. And later, in self-imposed exile in England, far from the land she would return to only in a coffin, Asia completed a clandestine memoir with bittersweet recollections of John Wilkes, knowing it could only be published after the death of her husband and herself, when a new generation could read it free from the prejudices of the long war between the states.

But while the manhunt continued for her brother, she had to live with the cloying presence of male and female detectives, unable to evict them from her West Philadelphia home and helpless as they kept round-the-clock vigil outside. They searched her belongings and followed her through the house, denying her privacy and reading her mail. "Think no more of him as your brother," Edwin tried comforting in one letter. "He is dead to us now, as he soon must be to all the world, but imagine the boy you loved to be in that better part of his spirit, in another world."[27]

CHAPTER 12

---◆◆◆---

Escape in the Dead of Night

John Wilkes Booth rode his horse at breakneck speed to the Navy Yard Bridge spanning the Eastern Branch. It was the main military thoroughfare from Washington to the lower Maryland counties. Years of war had weighted it down with long lines of troops, wagons, horses, mules, and cattle, which together with accidental damage from passing vessels had brought it to a dilapidated condition.[1]

It had been a slow night for the duty sentinel, Sergeant Silas Cobb. From darkness to 1 AM only about ten government teams passed over. When he heard an approaching horse, Cobb challenged the rider. Booth reined in the bright bay with distinctive long tail and mane.

"Who are you, sir?"

"My name is Booth."

"Where are you from?"

"From the city."

"Where are you going?"

"I am going home, down in Charles."

The sergeant took this to mean Charles County.

"You must live in some town."

"I live close to Beantown, but do not live in the town," said Booth.

Cobb said he did not know that place.

"Good God!" said Booth. "Then you never were down there."

Cobb had asked why he was out at this late hour, and whether he knew that no one could cross over the bridge after 9 PM. With the practiced art of the consummate actor, Booth feigned shock, declaring it was news to him, and that even though it was dark he thought he could ride home by the light of the moon. It sounded plausible to Cobb. He noted the rider's high-keyed voice and well-trimmed black mustache. The stranger seemed polished in manner and gentlemanly in appearance. Cobb guessed he might be five foot eight tall and about twenty-five years old. His movements indicated muscular power. Thinking he must be the son of a rich man living in Charles County, Cobb waved him on, noticing that the small bright bay horse with shiny hide seemed much more restive and uneasy than the rider. Booth held the reins tightly as he walked the animal slowly across the elongated bridge until he was out of sight. Now he was across the Eastern Branch and heading down toward southern Maryland.[2]

Herold appeared about five or ten minutes later, riding at a much slower pace than Booth, with whom he had apparently agreed to link up at about this time at a rendezvous that was never disclosed. When challenged, Herold said he was "a friend" named Smith, on his way home to White Plains. Asked why he was out so late, Herold uttered a profanity and said he had been in bad company.

"You can't pass. It is after nine o'clock. It is against the rules," said Cobb.

"How long have these rules been out?"

"Some time. Ever since I have been here."

"I didn't know that before."

"Why weren't you out of the city before?"

"I couldn't very well. I stopped to see a woman on Capitol Hill and couldn't get off before."

Cobb tugged on the reins, bringing horse and rider under the light of the guardhouse for a better look. The medium-size roan horse carried his head downward. Herold's broad cheekbones were conspicuously wider than the lower part of his face. The rider looked a year or two older than the horseman who had passed through shortly before. Cobb ran his eyes over Herold's light coat and pants and snuff-colored felt hat. Nothing looked suspicious. He waved him on.[3]

Booth was about three miles south of Washington, riding at a furious pace near Good Hope Hill, when he tightened the reins immediately after passing two riders, Polk Gardiner and George Doyle, heading toward the capital. In a high-keyed, weak voice, Booth asked whether they had seen a horseman go by. When they said they had not, Booth spurred his horse on.

Gardiner, en route to see his dying father,[4] had already ridden up and over the hill when he saw Herold pull up and ask a group of men next to ten covered wagons by the roadside whether anyone had just galloped past. They told him someone had, and Herold pressed on, prompting Doyle to remark that the two strangers seemed to be riding their horses to death to overtake each other.[5] Not long after, the two conspirators linked up in a coordinated bid to charge through lower Maryland to the more southerly banks of the almost four-hundred-mile long Potomac River.

John Fletcher had meanwhile raced back to his stables, saddled and bridled one of his fastest rentals, and galloped off in pursuit of the horse thief he knew as Herold. Near the Capitol he pulled up to ask a stranger if any rider had passed by.

"Yes, two of them, and they were riding very fast."[6]

When Fletcher arrived at the Navy Yard Bridge, he gave Cobb a quick description of the horse and rider he was pursuing and asked if they had crossed over. Either he misunderstood Cobb's replies or the sentinel scrambled the sequence of riders and horses, for Fletcher would later recall their quick exchange with inaccuracies.

"Yes, he has gone across the bridge," Fletcher recalled Cobb replying.

"Did he stay long here?" asked Fletcher.

"He said he was waiting for an acquaintance of his that was coming on. He did not wait, and another man came riding a bay horse right *after* him."

"Did he tell you his name?"

"Yes, he said his name was 'Smith.'"

Fletcher asked if he could cross over.

"Yes, you can cross, but you cannot return."

"If that is so, I will not go," said Fletcher, puzzled that Cobb's description of one of the riders did not fit Atzerodt, because he knew the man he had drunk with that night had to cross the Navy Yard Bridge to reach the village of TB.[7]

Fletcher had been so focused on the theft of his own horse that he not only misunderstood the sentinel's reply but also missed an opportunity to identify Booth later that night to lawmen on the lookout for the assassin. In his haste to match the description of Atzerodt with one of the two men who had crossed the Navy Yard Bridge within minutes of each other, Fletcher had failed to ask for the name or description of the first rider — who had willingly identified himself as Booth.

Dejected, Fletcher rode slowly back to downtown Washington, stopping at a rival stable to ask the foreman whether his missing roan had by chance been brought in.

"No," said the foreman, "but you had better keep in, for President Lincoln is shot and Secretary Seward is almost dead."[8]

As Fletcher passed by crowds of disbelieving and jabbering townspeople, he overheard that the assassin had escaped on horseback. But he was obsessed by the loss of his own horse and the brazen manner in which it was stolen. It was as good as gone. He ambled back to his workplace, stabled his horse, and sat outside his office window, too wrapped up in his personal loss to be distracted by a national calamity.[9]

More than an hour passed before he sauntered around, randomly asking a cavalry sergeant whether any stray horses had been turned in that night. The sergeant thought some had been picked up and suggested he go to the police station. On the way he met up with an acquaintance, Charley Stowell, a special investigative officer working in the provost marshal's office, charged with tracking deserters and enforcing military regulations. Stowell too had heard of riderless horses being turned in, so when the two arrived at police headquarters they were directed to General Augur's office on Lafayette Square next to the White House.

There Augur grilled Fletcher down to detailed descriptions of Atzerodt and Herold, their horses, and even their equine equipment. Fletcher was describing how he followed Herold's trail as far as the Navy Yard Bridge when suddenly he spotted a bridle and worn whitish leather saddle on the floor. It was the same saddle that had been strapped to the horse with a blind eye, brought to his stable by

Atzerodt and Booth eleven days earlier. He had no doubt they were the same.

"They belonged to a man that kept a horse at the stable from 3 to 12 April," he told Augur.

He described the one-eyed horse but could not remember Atzerodt's name. However, he remembered that Atzerodt had signed his name on the back of a livery stable business card, and it was still in the office. Augur ordered Stowell to accompany Fletcher to find it and bring it to him.

Only about an hour had passed since Lieutenant John Toffey, riding to duty at Lincoln General Hospital, less than a mile east of the Capitol, had come across a sentinel holding a riderless horse with a blind eye. The guard had caught the dark bay by the hospital dispensary. It was strapped with a whitish, worn leather saddle and was sweating excessively, as if driven long and hard. There were no telltale signs that this was the same horse abandoned by Payne after he had galloped away from the mayhem at Seward's house, then hidden in the outskirts of Washington under a canopy of trees. An official in the picket office told the unsuspecting lieutenant who had taken possession of the one-eyed horse to take the animal to the Old Capitol Prison; from there he was directed to Augur's headquarters.[10]

When Fletcher and Stowell returned with Atzerodt's name on the business card, Augur again quizzed the stable manager, who more than made up for his illiteracy by a sharp eye for anything to do with horses and equine equipment. And he had a good memory for faces. Once more he told the general what Atzerodt and Herold looked like. Augur beamed.

"These are the men that done it!" he exulted.[11]

At 2:30 AM a telegraph from a divisional military headquarters in Washington arrived for Major George Worcester's brigade at Fort Baker, some two miles east of the Navy Yard Bridge. Having no idea that Booth had long since distanced himself from the Eastern Branch River, the telegraph mandated searches based upon inaccurate findings: "The horse and saddle of the supposed murderer have been found. Send a mounted patrol along the shore of the Eastern Branch to arrest anyone crossing the river in a boat. It is supposed that he will try and cross between the two bridges. Have searches made throughout the night and tomorrow."[12] Fort Baker stood only a few hundred yards from Booth's flight path, but the assassin was riding south and the troops had been ordered to hunt for him in the north. The area Worcester's men would now patrol covered about two and a half miles of Eastern Branch shoreline, between the Navy Yard Bridge and Bennings Bridge farther northeast.

At about this time Atzerodt was signing in for a room at his regular lodgings in Washington. He had learned of the murder hours earlier and was so scared that he later confessed, "I run [sic] about the city like a crazy man."[13] Confused, frightened, and irrational, he threw his knife in a gutter opposite the Patent Office on F Street, on the same block as the Herndon House, where earlier that night he had defied Booth's orders to kill the vice president. Then he rode up to the Pennsylvania House, where a servant took care of his horse while he went into the bar. The servant remembered that when Atzerodt came out again he asked for a switch or stick to spur on the horse. He was handed a piece of a hoop and rode off.[14] Later he returned the mare to Kelleher's livery stable[15] only a few hundred yards east of Ford's Theatre, and roamed aimlessly about the city, alone and restless.

Near the Navy Yard, he boarded a streetcar on 6th Street east. He did not appear to recognize a former Port Tobacco resident, Washington Briscoe, seated nearby, who knew him well. Briscoe thought it odd that Atzerodt would board a streetcar at such a "queer place" at that hour of the night. He disliked the uncouth, rough loafer with no fixed occupation, who wore the same double-breasted gray coat Briscoe had seen him in for the last three months. But he greeted Atzerodt out of a desperate need to engage anyone about Lincoln's murder.

Atzerodt appeared to be "a little excited," but when Briscoe asked if he had heard the news, the lonely man looked nervous and trembled. Meekly, he said he knew about it, but seemed more interested in remaining with Briscoe than in talking about the sensational murder. Three times he asked if he could stay with Briscoe, who had a home and store in the Navy Yard, but each time he was rebuffed. Briscoe did not care for Atzerodt's company and firmly resisted his pleas to sleep over. They had continued talking after stepping off the streetcar near the store, and Briscoe watched as Atzerodt boarded the next car about midnight.[16]

Between 2 and 3 AM Atzerodt arrived back at the Pennsylvania House, this time without his horse. He had stayed there for almost a month until checking out just two days earlier, then registering at the Kirkwood House Hotel. As he walked to his former room the manager called out, "Atzerodt, you have not registered."

"Do you want my name?"

"Certainly," said John Greenawalt.

Atzerodt paused, took a few steps, hesitated, then walked over to the registration desk. No one had ever signed in this late, and Greenawalt had never seen anyone balk at signing the register.[17] Atzerodt was something of an enigma. About two weeks earlier he had asked Greenawalt to join him for a drink and remarked, "I am pretty near broke, but I have always got friends enough to give me as much money as will see me through." Then he had bragged, "I am going away some of these days, but I will return with as much gold as will keep me all my lifetime."[18] The proprietor of the Pennsylvania House, mystified by the slovenly loner, had even asked around if Atzerodt might be a detective.[19]

With only a few hours left to daylight, Lieutenant W.R. Keim came into Atzerodt's room and lay down on the opposite bed. Atzerodt was still awake. The two men knew each other from sharing a room during Atzerodt's previous stay at the hotel. About a week earlier, when Atzerodt had stepped out of the room while they were drinking whiskey, the officer had picked up a knife from Atzerodt's bed and hidden it under his own pillow. When Atzerodt returned to the room and asked if Keim had seen the knife, the army officer handed it over. Atzerodt, who always had a revolver suspended from his waist, had then remarked, "I want that. If one fails, I want the other." Now the lieutenant asked Atzerodt if he had heard about the president's assassination. Atzerodt's only comment was that it was an awful affair.[20]

CHAPTER 13

"Betrayed into the Hands of the Government"

In the early hours of Saturday, April 15, armed detectives were tightening security for the new president in his temporary quarters at the Kirkwood House Hotel when Chief Detective John Lee of the provost marshal's office found a solid link between George Atzerodt and John Wilkes Booth. His early discovery opened a major break in the puzzling conspiracy. By chance, a hotel employee knew Lee well and told the detective there was "a very suspicious person" registered in room 126 under the name of G.A. Atzerodt. The hotel owner was even more suggestive, profiling Atzerodt as "a villainous-looking fellow" who could easily be identified.[1]

Atzerodt had checked into the Kirkwood House Hotel in the morning of Friday, April 14, according to a hotel clerk, and his third-floor room was one story above the vice president's. Anyone descending from Atzerodt's floor to the hotel office would have to pass by the single guard outside Andrew Johnson's room.[2] Lee and the hotelier went up to Atzerodt's room, but the door was locked and the occupant had taken the only key. With permission from the hotelier, Lee shoved the door open, burst inside, and quickly found a large loaded and capped revolver under the pillow and a dark coat hanging on the wall.

The detective reached inside the coat pocket and pulled out a bankbook in the name of John Wilkes Booth. It showed a credit balance of $455 at the Ontario Bank in Montreal. He ripped the bedclothes off and found a large, stained bowie knife on the mattress. His search turned up three packets of pistol cartridges, a pistol holster, a spur, a war map of the Southern states, a handkerchief marked MARY BOOTH, two leather belts, a pair of new leather gloves, a soiled collar, and a stick of licorice. Lee had no doubt that Atzerodt had taken the room to assassinate the vice president.[3]

Not far away William Eaton from the provost marshal's office was rummaging through Booth's personal possessions at the actor's room in the National Hotel. Investigators had gotten an early trace on Booth's lodgings when Colonel George Rutherford testified before Stanton and Judge Cartter in the house where Lincoln lay dying that he had seen the presumed assassin in the National Hotel at 7 PM. Eager to pass on personal knowledge of the suspect's whereabouts, he told of being in the hotel when a man passed by and threw his key on the front desk. Rutherford's companion that night recognized the celebrity actor, whom he knew well, and remarked, "There goes J. Wilkes Booth."[4] Booth had occupied room 228 for the past four days[5] and left behind embroidered slippers, black pants marked J. WILKES BOOTH on the fob pocket, a pair of unpolished boots, half a pound of tobacco, a broken comb, and a clothes brush.[6]

Eaton reached into a trunk marked with Booth's name and grabbed a stack of papers. But his disregard for a leather valise stuffed with clothing prevented investigators from stumbling on an immediate link between Booth and John Surratt. Booth had packed his black velvet vest into the leather bag and left a card with the name of J. HARRISON SURRATT in the pocket. The incriminating card went undetected for a year and a half until a curious hotel employee opened the unclaimed and forgotten valise in the baggage room.[7]

Still, the papers Eaton found in Booth's room were a bonanza for examiners in the provost marshal's office. Codes on a scrap of paper would match a secret cipher key taken later by Union officials from the abandoned Richmond office of the Confederate secretary of state. The codes in Booth's trunk were also identical to those used in Confederate dispatches intercepted en route from Canada to Richmond.[8]

A series of letters over the past four months from Booth's friend, business manager, and co-investor in land and oil fields in western Pennsylvania suggested that the actor had been secretive, hard-pressed for cash, and uncharacteristically aimless for many months.

The business manager, John Simonds, alone knew that Booth had never profited from his oil investments. But he knew nothing of the burgeoning conspiracy with which Booth was obsessed. He had accurately detected unfamiliar conduct that would horrify him when he learned the cause. "You must be blue not acting," John Simonds had written Booth in December 1864. "If you have nothing else to do and got hard up, just come out here and stop with us. We will guarantee to support you."[9] In another letter three weeks later the native Bostonian ached over the lassitude and financial straits of his thespian friend, expressing sorrow on learning that Booth was "not doing as well as usual." He had mistakenly thought that Booth had returned to the stage, "taking in greenbacks at the rate of $1,000 per week." Charitably, he enclosed a check for $500, describing it as "some assistance until you get to acting again."[10] By the end of February, Simonds was still puzzled. "I hardly know what to make of you this winter. So different from your usual self. Have you lost all your ambition or what is the matter? I cannot but think you are wasting your time spending the entire season in Washington doing nothing, where it must be expensive to live, and all for no other purpose beyond pleasure."[11]

The papers taken from Booth's trunk pronounced him something of a pack rat or disorderly by nature. His peripatetic lifestyle, forced upon him as an actor performing far and wide, may have accounted for the jumble of accumulated paperwork. It included a receipt more than three years old for room and board in Detroit.[12] Curiously, Booth had also saved six printed verses of a pro-Union poem, "Our Heroes" by Francis de Haes Janvier, who ironically had sent a complimentary copy to Abraham Lincoln the year before.[13]

> *Our Patriot Soldiers!*
> *When Treason arose*
> *And Freedom's own children*
> *Assailed her as foes;*
> *When Anarchy threatened*
> *And Order withdrew*
> *They rallied to rescue*
> *The red, white and blue!*[14]

Among other papers set aside and labeled "unimportant" by investigators was a letter retrieved from Booth's trunk mentioning the name of Surratt. The tightly squeezed handwriting by a professor, the Reverend John B. Menu, was dated St. Charles College, March 19, 1865, two days after the unsuccessful attempt to kidnap Lincoln. Both Weichmann and John Surratt had studied for three years at the Maryland Catholic institution, where Weichmann looked up to the priest as a "father confessor."[15] How the letter came into Booth's possession was never explained, and the identity of the addressee remains a matter of conjecture.

"Dear Friend," the guarded letter began, "Your last letter relieved me from great anxiety for I was not sure to have guessed well. Why do you not speak more fully? . . . You speak in a [sic] obscure way of Mr. Suratt [sic] as if [illegible] were a rebel. Could you not have said openly what is the perilous trip for which he is soon to depart? What is that *bad*! Between us there should no [sic] secret." After several paragraphs of irrelevant matter, the writer concluded, "My best regards to Mr. Suratt if he has not gone already on his trip."[16]

Another letter, which overshadowed all others and excited probers, was dated Hookstown, Baltimore County, March 27, 1865. Within hours, special editions of Washington's newspapers fed voracious readers with their insiders' details: it was written on notepaper in a small neat hand and bore the signature of "Sam."[17] It was Samuel Arnold's letter to the assassin, which Booth had pledged two weeks earlier at their final meeting in Washington to destroy once it arrived in the capital. Its discovery would doom the only conspirator who had threatened to shoot it out with Booth if the actor tried to kill him.

But officials in Baltimore were already on Arnold's trail. James McPhail, Maryland's provost marshal general, had been awakened at midnight with news of the assassination and quickly dispersed men to hunt down several of Booth's associates. The early breakthrough came from a devotee of the theater who knew many of the celebrated actors. Eagerly, the source said Booth was "on the most intimate terms" with two Baltimoreans, Samuel Arnold and Michael O'Laughlin. The informant also volunteered that the pair were invariably with Booth in Baltimore and that they had often gone to

Washington to see him. The invaluable tattler even gave the lawmen a photograph of Booth.[18]

Less than three hours after Lincoln died, McPhail telegraphed the War Department that Arnold and O'Laughlin were believed to be in Washington.[19] "Their arrest may prove advantageous. Both are well-known in Washington and were formerly in the rebel army."[20] Washington now had full names to fill in the blanks in the letter found in Booth's trunk. The signatory, "Sam," had to be Samuel Arnold. O'Laughlin was surely the person referred to when Arnold wrote Booth: "I called also to see Mike, but learned from his mother he had gone out with you."[21] Hookstown, Baltimore County, the letter's dateline, was about six miles northwest of Baltimore.[22] It did not take long for McPhail's men and city police to track down Arnold's father, who gave them a letter Samuel had sent two days before the assassination from his new place of employment in Virginia.

That same morning, Arnold was sitting in the counting room at his new job in Old Point Comfort when a telegraphic message arrived at noon in adjacent Fortress Monroe with a hazy rumor that the president had been assassinated while walking down Pennsylvania Avenue in Washington. Many in the isolated community doubted the vague and sensational report, which did not even name the assailant. But Arnold reeled the following day when word spread that John Wilkes Booth had fired the shot. He was under no illusions. His ties to the assassin could lead to his own arrest. Even to be suspected, he imagined, would be "almost equivalent to death." He had only just begun to feel secure, having turned a new leaf by severing connections with Booth and his associates and being, "to all intents and purposes, a law-abiding citizen." Yet rather than give himself up, he decided to ride it out, letting events take their course, even though he expected to be caught up in the dragnet.[23]

He was seated in the same room the following morning when Detectives Voltaire Randall and Eaton Horner arrived from Marshal McPhail's Baltimore office. They handed him a letter from his father that said Sam's apparently incriminating letter had been found in Booth's hotel room. The father advised his son to cooperate by telling all he knew. The detectives asked if he had written the letter.

Arnold balked. He would not make a blind admission to something they did not have with them. What did it say? Where and when was it mailed? Who signed it? When they gave him answers he already knew, there was no point in denying his authorship. But his surprise and alarm would in time give way to anger, evolving into flinty hostility toward Booth. Gradually it dawned on him that the duplicitous actor had almost certainly snared him in a trap. Booth had promised to destroy the letter when it arrived in Washington. He had given his word at their final meeting in the National Hotel. The broken promise was a sign of betrayal. The letter had not only been saved but left behind where investigators were sure to find it. However, Arnold was not immediately certain what to think. Charitably, he conceded that Booth might have been forgetful. But with the passage of time his opinion hardened into a certainty that Booth had acted with malice, and the duped victim raged against the "demented" ringleader for his "rancor, venom and revenge." Arnold believed it was payback for his outspoken challenge to Booth when they had all met at Gautier's before the kidnap plot went awry.[24] "I was basely betrayed into the hands of the US government," he charged, "forced to become a witness against myself."[25]

Arnold admitted writing the letter but denied any complicity in Lincoln's murder. He told Randall and Horner he knew nothing of the assassination. Nor was he at that time in any way connected with Booth or others. He admitted only limited involvement with the presumed assassin, being "at one period engaged with Booth in a scheme to attempt the abduction of Abraham Lincoln," whom they hoped to ransom for Confederate prisoners of war.[26]

Sly and guileful, the detectives tried to get him to divulge more, but much of what was said during the interrogation was forgotten because no one took notes.[27] When told, untruthfully, that O'Laughlin had given himself up, Arnold decided to be more open, as he recalled, "in justice not only to myself, but to those with whom I had been formerly connected."[28] But for the time being he withheld details, confirming only that Booth, O'Laughlin, John Surratt, and Atzerodt were involved in the abduction plot.

In the back room of the storehouse where Arnold slept, the

detectives found a pistol and a tin can of cartridges in his black traveling bag.[29] Arnold said he had another pistol and bowie knife, which they later recovered at his father's place near the Hookstown road.[30]

The detectives had done their job. Randall made for the telegraph office at Fortress Monroe to rush a coded telegram to the provost marshal in Baltimore: "I have arrested Samuel Arnold. You will arrest J.W. Booth and Michael O'Laughlin of Baltimore G.W. [sic] Atzerodt alias Port Tobacco of Charles County and John Surratt residence not known as all are implicated."[31]

Meanwhile the chief clerk at the War Department had arrived at the Fortress and, on learning that Arnold proposed making a written confession, alerted his superiors in Washington. The assistant secretary of war responded enthusiastically, even though it might delay the prisoner's transfer to Washington. "Let Arnold make the statement before he changes his mind," Charles Dana sanctioned.[32]

By the time the manacled clerk arrived by steamboat in Baltimore on Tuesday morning, Michael O'Laughlin had already been hunted down and hauled off by train to Washington in the personal custody of Provost Marshal James McPhail. McPhail had called three times during the weekend at the Baltimore home of O'Laughlin's mother, only to be told that her son was in the nation's capital. The break came on Monday after McPhail, in hiding, authorized his brother-in-law to bring the city police to arrest him in Baltimore.[33]

"I have Michael O'Laughlin, no doubt the Mike alluded to in the letter of Sam," McPhail notified the War Department. "I will hold him subject to order. He is not communicative."[34]

Dana instructed him to bring O'Laughlin to the capital by the evening train, where a carriage would be on hand to whisk him to secure confinement. "Have him in double irons and use every precaution against escape," Dana cautioned. But sensing how violent passengers might become if they linked O'Laughlin to the president's murder by spotting his leg irons and handcuffs, Dana warned, "As far as possible, avoid everything which can lead to suspicion on the part of the people on the train and give rise to an attempt to lynch the prisoner."[35]

Though Arnold was allowed to meet with his father, he would not be permitted to give him a duplicate copy of the statement about to be made.[36] It did not deter Arnold from confessing, and he was taken into the back room of the marshal's office.[37] At about this moment William McPhail, acting in his brother's absence, ejected an unidentified lawyer who demanded to be present to review the statement. "My brother properly refused him," the marshal later wrote Stanton.[38]

Arnold addressed the eight-page summary of his involvement "To Whom It May Concern." It was a stunning exposé that snipped the bonds of secrecy to uncover Booth's cohorts. Law enforcement officials got an insider's glance at Booth's cunning, his ruthless control over underlings, and the compulsion that pushed him over the edge. They also learned of the harebrained plot to seize the chief of state and carry him off in handcuffs to the Confederate stronghold of Richmond. Arnold bared more than the contours of the kidnapping. He re-created the fracas as Booth and he came close to a shootout in the charged face-off at Gautier's. He said it was at this conclave of conspirators that he had first met Payne, Herold, Atzerodt, and John Surratt. Arnold even divulged how Booth had assigned specific roles for the audacious strike to succeed. With his liberty gone and his life in peril, he disclosed how the wily Booth had recruited him and O'Laughlin eight months earlier, plying his childhood friends with wine and cigars, and seducing them with bonhomie, plausible logic, and a graceful assertiveness that painted the chances of success in "glowing colors." Under the spell of the polished actor they had willingly bound themselves by oath into a secret brotherhood. Arnold recounted Booth's reappearance in January with arms and ammunition and their visit to Ford's Theatre to check on exits and entrances. He confessed to seeing his mentor three or four times a week, although Booth had spent most of his time with John Surratt. He also revealed how he and O'Laughlin had rented a room in Washington for almost two months, passing the time at bars and amusement halls, while fooling friends and family into thinking they were living off trades in oil stocks. In the only reference to the notorious letter from "Sam," Arnold wrote, "The Richmond authorities, as far as I know, knew nothing of the conspiracy." He claimed to have "cut loose forever" from the conspiracy the moment he left his last meeting with Booth.

"He never to me said that he would kill him," Arnold stressed. "Further than this, I know nothing, and am innocent of having taken any active part in the dark deed committed."[39]

Arnold's cooperation earned him neither solace nor sympathy. He was not even the beneficiary of leniency. Instead, he was thrown into a "loathsome and filthy cell" in the same Fort McHenry immortalized by Francis Scott Key half a century earlier.[40] Word of his confession leaked to the press, even though the provost marshal had made a special plea to Baltimore newspapers the day before not to give publicity to anyone arrested in the city for the assassination.[41]

Stanton exploded with almost apoplectic rage. He fired off an inflammatory rebuke to McPhail, chastising him for being responsible for the leak. "Your conduct is highly disapproved. It will not be tolerated. In case of repetition, you will be dealt with as one who is endeavoring to defeat the ends of justice." He demanded an explanation.[42] Simultaneously, the secretary of war ordered the military commander of Baltimore to take custody of Arnold, place him in handcuffs and leg irons, and imprison him in Fort McHenry "until I send for him." Even though newspapers had stolen a march, Stanton fulminated, "Prohibit the publication of his examination, or any facts relating to him." He authorized the commanding general to arrest anyone violating orders.[43]

James McPhail bristled. His team of detectives had tracked Arnold with minimal input from Washington. He deplored Stanton's charges as "false and without the slightest foundation." He blamed the leak on the anonymous lawyer refused permission to be present while Arnold wrote his confession. "As regards the newspapers," McPhail countered, "they never get anything from my office or men, and it is a source of complaint from them. They often remark to me that other offices gas, and why don't you do so." McPhail would not be intimidated by Stanton's explosive temper. He insisted that no one had seen Arnold's statement until McPhail showed it to the military commander of Baltimore the same day it was written. This, he reminded Stanton, was shortly before the marshal left for Washington to deliver it personally to the secretary of war.[44]

Notwithstanding his denial of anything to do with the assassination,

Arnold now suffered as if already convicted. It was a quick slide into the rigors of degrading captivity. He was strip-searched, manacled hand and foot, and left in solitary confinement in a darkened dungeon, where he cowered under a tightly-wrapped blanket for protection against real or imagined rats and reptiles. In the dead of night, he was dragged up to the guardhouse and told to get dressed quickly. "I thought the days of the French revolution, with its hideous and barbarous murders, were going to be re-enacted in this Republic, and that I was thus taken out to be either shot or hung," he recalled.[45]

Before boarding the train with detectives for Washington, he was relieved of the chafing, heavy handcuffs that bit deeply into his wrists and fitted with lighter, less painful substitutes. Throughout the journey he kept silent. His voluntary confession had brought neither relief nor considerate handling. He was driven by hack to the Navy Yard, where a duty officer recorded his 2 AM arrival aboard the *Saugus*.[46] Once more he was bound tight with excruciatingly painful cuffs that lacerated his wrists and deformed his hands into blotched and swollen extremities.[47] He could not know that this suffering in cramped and stuffy quarters would be tame compared with the depravity to come.

CHAPTER 14

"Keep an Eye on Mrs. Surratt's House"

A chance brush with a bystander in the choked streets of Washington hours after the assassination led metropolitan police detectives to their first foray into the conspirators' lair. James McDevitt could never recall the identity of the man who hailed him by name and volunteered the crucial tip: "If you want to find out all about this desperate business, keep an eye on Mrs. Surratt's house on H Street."[1] The lead tied in with valuable information on Booth's frequent association with John Surratt, eagerly supplied to police by other sources.

Shortly after 2 AM McDevitt and his partner, Detective John Clarvoe, headed toward Mary Surratt's darkened lodgings four blocks east of Ford's Theatre, a building Andrew Johnson would later decry as "the nest where the egg was hatched." Before setting off with a supporting squad from the sixth police precinct, they spoke off the record with John Proctor, a respected reporter from the *Daily Morning Chronicle* still waiting around for late-breaking news. They told of a man named Surratt who, together with other unnamed suspects, was implicated in the assault on Seward. All resided at the H Street boardinghouse. They were so trusting in their sources that they predicted the arrest of every fugitive by noon if only they could get some cavalrymen to accompany them.[2] Desk-bound Police Superintendent A.C. Richards had authorized them to search the H Street premises, even though he would much later try to embellish his own role by dishonestly claiming to have led the raid himself.[3]

As some of the men took up positions on each corner and at the back of the house, a detective rang the bell and rapped on the door.[4] Eliza Holahan looked out the window from her third-floor bedroom overlooking the street. They demanded to be let in. Eliza shook her husband awake. "There are men rapping at the door! They want to get in the house! They look like policemen!"[5]

Louis Weichmann had just returned from the backyard outhouse and was still awake in his room on the same floor as the Holahans'. He pulled on a pair of pants, slipped into an unbuttoned shirt, and raced barefoot to the front door.

"Who is there?" he queried.

"Detectives, come to search the house for John Wilkes Booth and John Surratt."

"They are not here."

"Let us in anyhow. We want to search the house."[6]

As Weichmann backed away, Clarvoe pushed the door wide open.

Weichmann went ahead, saying he would rouse John Surratt's mother in the room she shared with Honora Fitzpatrick, separated by folding doors from the front parlor.[7] Weichmann knocked on the door.

"Mrs. Surratt, there are detectives in the parlor, to search the house! They would like to search your room."

Honora Fitzpatrick heard the landlady reply, "Ask them to wait a few moments, and I will open the door for them."[8]

Weichmann would later claim that Mrs. Surratt replied, "For God's sake! Let them come in. I expected the house to be searched." But Honora Fitzpatrick denied hearing this remark.[9]

When McDevitt asked the whereabouts of her son, Mrs. Surratt said he was not in the city and she had not seen him since the fall of Richmond. Turning to Weichmann, she asked, "How long has that been, Mr. Weichmann?"

"About two weeks," her boarder replied.

She told them she had received a letter the day before from her son in Canada, but when pressed to produce it she could not.[10]

On the floor above, John Holahan had scrambled into a pair of pants by the time the detectives appeared at his door. Clarvoe, a former plasterer, knew the tombstone cutter well and asked what he was doing in the house.[11]

"I am boarding here," replied Holahan, who had moved in two months earlier. "What's the matter?"

"Haven't you heard the news?"

"No, what is it?"

"The president has been assassinated."

"My God! Is that so!"

Clarvoe, a four-year veteran in the police force, held up a snippet of a bloodstained cravat he said he had picked up in Ford's Theatre. Briefly, he told his stupefied acquaintance about the assassination.[12]

While others looked in all the rooms, Clarvoe went up to Weichmann's bedroom.

"What is the matter? What does this searching of the house mean?" asked Weichmann.

"Do you pretend that you do not know what has happened?" Clarvoe tested.

Weichmann had no idea.

"Then I will tell you," said the detective. "John Wilkes Booth has shot the president, and John Surratt has assassinated the secretary of state."

Again he held up the bloodied black cravat, telling the horrified boarder, "Do you see the blood on that? That is the blood of Abraham Lincoln!"

"Great God! I see it all!" Weichmann exclaimed.[13]

Holahan preceded Clarvoe up more stairs to wake Anna Surratt and Olivia Jenkins, sharing a single bedroom. The detective apologized before pulling the covers from their faces, then, satisfied that they were not the men he was looking for, he returned to Mrs. Surratt downstairs.[14]

"I want to ask you a couple of questions," he said sternly. "Be very particular how you answer them for a great deal depends on them. When did you see John Wilkes Booth?"

She told him it was 2 PM, about twelve hours earlier.

"When did you see your son, John, last, and where is he?"

"I have told you, sir. I have not seen John for over two weeks." The last she heard from him he was in Canada. She asked the meaning of the police presence, almost lecturing Clarvoe that there were a great many mothers who did not know where their sons were.

Impatient to continue the search, Clarvoe turned to McDevitt. "Mac, you tell her."[15]

Down in the kitchen at street level, he saw two black women, one stout and thickset, the other slim. Clarvoe asked one of them, "Aunty, is John Surratt in this house?"

"I have not seen him for over two weeks," she replied.[16]

A search through all the rooms, closets, cupboards, and every nook and cranny failed to turn up the letter from Canada even though Mrs. Surratt had let Weichmann read it that night. He remembered it was written at St. Lawrence Hall, Montreal, dated April 12, and had arrived on the day of the assassination. So far as he could recall, John Surratt found Montreal so expensive that he would probably have to move into a boardinghouse because he could not afford $2.50 a day in gold for a room at St. Lawrence Hall. But he had splurged ten dollars in silver for a French pea jacket and even gone sightseeing at the impressive cathedral.[17]

Before leaving, McDevitt ordered Weichmann and Holahan to report to him at police headquarters at nine that morning.[18]

Shaken by the police raid, both men rose early. Sometime between 5 and 6 AM Weichmann read the *Daily Morning Chronicle*'s account of the twin murderous attacks, which left him relieved and even happy that the description of Seward's assailant did not match John Surratt's likeness. "Thank God! Thank God that is not John Surratt!" he exclaimed to himself.[19]

Before breakfast he walked down to Howard's livery stable, where he, Booth, Surratt, and Atzerodt were well known to the manager, Brooke Stabler, from frequent previous visits. His hand trembled as he greeted Stabler, and when the stable manager remarked on it, Weichmann talked of the assassination. He thought the newspaper description of Seward's attacker fit Atzerodt, better known to Stabler as Azworth, the round-shouldered out-of-towner with slicked, greasy hair set behind his ears. The stable manager remembered well how Surratt had once said of Atzerodt, "The son-of-a-bitch is crazy," a sentiment shared by Booth, who told Atzerodt, in the presence of

Stabler, "I have just told Stabler that I believed you were going crazy," to which the Prussian immigrant had replied, "I believe you told him the truth."

Rambling on in a disjointed state, Weichmann remarked, "It is said that Booth is charged with this, and Mrs. Surratt's house has been searched. This is a dreadful state of affairs. I don't know what is to be the consequence of this." He asked for some whiskey, but still unable to control his nerves he again said Booth was suspected of killing the president. And Weichmann pressed Stabler to keep mum about his acquaintance with Booth and Surratt. None of it should ever be made public.[20]

Illogically, Weichmann confided that Surratt had left America for Europe, then begged Stabler to keep it quiet.[21] Perhaps it was a slip of the tongue in a moment of panic, but it hinted at a deeper knowledge of John Surratt's private life. Though Weichmann and Mary Surratt spoke freely of John's frequent expectations of going to Europe,[22] it is not known whether either of them, or even Booth himself, knew how far John had secretly advanced that hope. Less than three months earlier, on January 24, John Surratt had deceived American and British colonial officials in Canada into granting him a passport in the name of John Watson. It was issued in Quebec in the name of the British colonial governor general, Lord Monck, and handed over in Montreal by authority of the provincial secretary, William McDougall. The US consul general in Montreal, John Potter, had been duped into issuing a visa. Surratt would later use the passport to escape across Europe to the Papal States.[23]

That same morning, according to Weichmann, he distinctly heard Anna Surratt declare at the communal breakfast that the death of Abraham Lincoln was no more than the death of a Negro in the army. Before setting off with John Holahan for police headquarters, Weichmann told the boarders that he intended to tell all he knew. Then he left with Holahan, who had updated himself on the assassination by reading an early edition of a newspaper.[24]

At the police station Weichmann was true to his word, giving the detectives their first insight into the nebulous figures who had conspired in secrecy, then flashed into public view. They had struck in the dead of night, felled a beloved father figure, and disappeared into the darkness. Weichmann was better positioned than anyone else to give substance to the mercurial bloodletters. For weeks, and in some cases months, he had seen them at close quarters. He was the only eyewitness when they had scampered back from the aborted kidnap attempt, and he had seen their fear and their frailties. His residency in the inconspicuous boardinghouse gave him special credence. It had enabled him to count the frequency of their visits and to note suspicious conduct. Intuitive, intelligent, nosy, and perceptive, the former seminarian had a prodigious memory and a critical eye for detail. He was a godsend to lawmen floundering for names and identities of anyone in league with Booth. Weichmann needed no prodding to be forthcoming about the men on the run. He would later justify collaboration with investigators as nothing more than "duty to my country."[25]

His enemies and detractors thought otherwise. They considered him a pariah and lonely outcast, a weakling so scared of being contaminated with guilt by close association with Booth's cabal that he would willingly fabricate and incriminate others to save himself from the gallows. None despised him more than John Surratt, whose mother's fate would be determined by crucial statements Weichmann attributed to her. "Give me a man who can strike his victim dead," John Surratt berated in the aftermath, "but save me from a man who, through perjury, will cause the death of an innocent person."[26] It was a charge that neither Surratt nor anyone else would ever be able to prove beyond reasonable doubt.

The detectives took Weichmann with them to the government stables, hopeful he could finger suspects they might run down during a search in the countryside on horseback. By chance Fletcher was at the stables, and he told Weichmann that Herold had taken off with his horse. Weichmann suggested they call at the home of Herold's family, but the lawmen decided to stop first at the boardinghouse, where Mary Surratt willingly handed over a photograph of her son. Weichmann beamed, knowing the likeness was so at odds with newspaper descriptions of Seward's assailant that it should immediately dispel suspicion of his friend's involvement. At the Herold family home, which stood opposite the nation's longest continuously manned marine sentry post in the Navy Yard, Herold's tearful mother said he had not been home since the evening before. But she too let them take away a photograph of her son. Within days the faces of the two undistinguished young men would look out from wanted posters published far and wide, becoming as familiar as the craggy features of the slain president.[27]

When they returned to police headquarters, McDevitt surprised the eager collaborator by telling him he would have to remain in custody.

"Are you going to hold me?" Weichmann asked incredulously.

"Certainly," the detective confirmed.[28]

That same Saturday evening one of Mrs. Surratt's servants, Susan Mahony, visited the home of her aunt's employer to unburden herself of news she could no longer keep to herself. She told her aunt, Mary Ann Griffin, also a house servant, that within an hour of the assassination three men had entered the boardinghouse and spoken guardedly about it while she lay on the floor feigning sleep. Susan Mahony claimed Mrs. Surratt was on the scene and one of the men told her that her son John was with Booth shortly before the murder.[29] The three men had apparently changed their clothing before leaving the boardinghouse. The following morning, the servant said, the Surratts burned and destroyed letters and other papers.[30]

The aunt waited until the evening of the following day before passing on the news to her employer, John Kimball.[31] He set off to alert authorities but, not knowing where to go, Kimball stopped at the office of an acquaintance. There a zealous amateur sleuth, P.M. Clark, intervened. Only the night before Clark had reported to the provost marshal's office his suspicions that two possible conspirators were at large in the National Hotel. Now he told Kimball to repeat what he had just related. Before even hearing him out, Clark clasped Kimball with both hands and ordered, "Come with me, quick!" En route the overbearing interloper extracted more information from the passive Kimball, so that by the time they reached the provost marshal's office Clark had siphoned off enough of what had been Kimball's exclusive intelligence to claim much of the credit for himself.

At the provost marshal's office they were halted and asked the purpose of their visit.

"Important information that I will communicate to Colonel Foster," replied Clark, referring to an acquaintance, Lieutenant Colonel John Foster, one of a trio of military officers appointed special commissioner and assigned by the War Department to investigate the assassination.

Throughout the interrogations Clark enhanced his own significance while minimizing Kimball's. At times he interrupted Kimball's statement to charge him with skipping over details, then embellished his own role.[32] Months would pass before Kimball found the courage to claim credit for himself and reject Clark's blatant "pretensions" in attempting to usurp kudos for the new lead.[33]

But for now another special commissioner, Colonel Henry H. Wells, had heard enough. Seventy-two hours had already elapsed since demonic phantoms had terrorized the city. By nature Wells was impatient, quick-tempered, and ruthless in the pursuit of criminals. Without delay, the former infantry officer and provost marshal dispatched detectives to the nondescript Surratt boardinghouse with orders to arrest everyone inside and to search for suspicious and incriminating items.[34]

The lead detective, Major Henry Warren Smith, quickly deployed one of the men in the backyard to block any escape. He posted another at the street-level door leading into the dining room. Smith climbed cautiously up the outside steps to the second-floor entrance and peeked through the blinds into the parlor. Anna Surratt lay on the sofa. Her mother, Honora Fitzpatrick, and Olivia Jenkins sat close by. Smith rang the doorbell. Mrs. Surratt came to the window and whispered, "Is that you Kirby?" — thinking it was her trusted friend Detective W.W. Kirby, who had visited several times since the assassination trying to get information on the whereabouts of her son.[35]

"No, it is not Kirby, but it is alright. Let me in."

She opened the door, and Smith stepped inside.

"Is this Mrs. Surratt's house?"

"Yes."

"Are you Mrs. Surratt?"

"I am the widow of John H. Surratt."

"And the mother of John H. Surratt Jr.?"

"Yes."

"Madam, I have come to arrest you and all in your house, and take you down to General Augur's headquarters for examination."

He told her to step into the parlor and identify each of the women.

"Ladies," said Smith, "You will have to get ready as soon as possible and go with me down to General Augur's for examination."

"'Oh, mother!'" Smith quoted Anna, who, he said, began to weep as she wrung her hands and cried out, "'To think of being taken down there for such a crime!'"

Smith said the mother wrapped her arms around Anna's neck and whispered something, which quieted the daughter. The detective told them he had ordered a carriage to take them away for interrogation.

"I will go upstairs and get the ladies' things," said Mrs. Surratt.

"I advise you to get warm wrappings as it is a damp, drizzly night," said Smith.

"I will go right upstairs," she replied.

"Excuse me, Madam," said Smith. "This house is suspected. I will accompany you upstairs."

He told Detective Ely Devoe to remain with the women, who were not to talk to one another, and to see that no papers were destroyed.[36]

The women were preparing to leave when two more investigators entered, Detective Thomas Sampson and his superior Richard Morgan, the right-hand man and chief assistant to Special Commissioner Henry Olcott of the War Department. Morgan considered himself in charge of everyone in the building.

According to Smith, they were waiting for the carriage to arrive when Mrs. Surratt asked permission to kneel down and pray, "to ask the blessing of God upon me, as I do upon all my actions." He did not object, and she knelt down in the parlor. Simultaneously there was a knock at the door.

Morgan, Smith, and Devoe all claimed to have opened the door and come face-to-face with Lewis Payne. None of them had any idea who the six-foot-two visitor might be as he stepped in shouldering a pickax. Over his head he wore a gray sleeve ripped from his woolen undershirt, and it dangled over his forehead like a nightcap. The tall man carried himself well, even though disheveled and obviously worn out. Beneath his gray coat, vest, and white linen shirt he wore black pantaloons, one leg of which was tucked into the top of a boot. The pants and boots were wet and muddied up to his knees, looking as if he had knelt in mud or waded through water.[37]

"I guess I am mistaken," said Payne.

"Whom do you want to see?" Morgan queried after shutting the door.

"Mrs. Surratt."

"You are right. Walk in."[38]

In the quick exchange between the detectives and their serendipitous catch, the unruffled Payne said he had come for last-minute instructions about digging a ditch in Mrs. Surratt's backyard the following morning. In fact he was famished, having abandoned his horse and hidden for three days in woods, even atop a cedar tree, past Fort Lincoln northeast of Washington. Mrs. Surratt was the only person he knew in Washington, and he hoped she would give him a meal.[39]

His noncommittal replies heightened investigators' suspicions. Payne said he had neither a home nor money nor even a permanent job, living on little more than a dollar a day that he earned from occasional jobs. But he could not name anyone he had worked for nor provide their addresses, and said he had slept at a railroad depot the night before. Mrs. Surratt had hired him that morning because, he said, she knew he was a poor man working in the neighborhood. He expected she would let him sleep in her house that night because he boarded wherever he found work. Under a barrage of questions, he claimed to be about twenty years old and said he had come to the District to avoid military service in Virginia. Payne showed them his oath of allegiance, signed a month earlier in Baltimore, which mandated him to stay north of Philadelphia during the war. He also told them he could write his name but was unable to read.[40]

Smith summoned Mrs. Surratt from the parlor.

"Do you know this man? Did you hire him to dig a ditch for you?"

She raised her right hand as if taking an oath. "Before God, sir, I do not know this man and have never seen him," she replied. "I did not hire him to dig a gutter for me."[41]

As Morgan ushered the women out the door to the waiting carriage, she turned to him with a parting remark. "I am so glad you officers came here tonight, for this man came here with a pickaxe to kill us."[42]

Discredited by Mrs. Surratt, Payne had no plausible reason to be there, especially in a strange garb and wielding a pickax close to midnight. He was told he was under arrest. When the carriage returned, he was escorted aboard and whisked under armed guard to General Augur's headquarters.[43]

While being searched, Payne had to exert himself to pry loose the squelching boots that held fast to his soggy stockings.[44] He was stripped to his shirt and drawers,[45] and it became clear that his make-shift nightcap was a sleeve he had torn from his undershirt. Though he told the arresting officers he had no money, they now found two new ten-dollar US Treasury notes, a five-dollar National Bank note, and a small amount of cash.[46] They also pulled out an unopened packet of Colt pistol cartridges, five bullets, a little pocketknife, and a small compass in a mahogany box. Though unkempt and unwashed, Payne had stuffed into his pockets a bottle of hair grease, a brush and comb, and two toothbrushes. Surprisingly, the search yielded a pocketbook with a newspaper excerpt of Lincoln's inaugural address and a clipping about Vice President Johnson. They also found pieces of chewing tobacco, a pocket dictionary, a postage stamp, a needle with thread, and a pincushion.[47]

He gave his name as Lewis Payne but revealed little else. His build and features appeared to resemble those already provided by Seward's servant, William Bell, the only uninjured eyewitness who had been with the assailant long enough to provide a valid description. His appearance at the Surratt house, now known through Weichmann to have been frequently visited by Booth, reinforced Wells's belief that he had to be Seward's assailant.

Wells sent a man to accompany State Department clerk E.D. Webster to Seward's adjacent home. Bell was irritable when told Webster was waiting to speak to him again. He was tired of being awakened in the middle of the night since the horrific events of Good Friday, but he had no option and went downstairs, where Webster escorted him to Wells. Though tired and groggy, the young servant, who guessed he was nineteen years old, went through yet another grilling by the intimidating Wells, whom Bell remembered by his large whiskers and mustache. Once more Bell answered that it was bright enough in the hallway to read and that he had taken note of the tall, broad-shouldered assailant's black hair, thin lip, and very fine voice. Wells invited him to scan the appearance of more than twenty men standing in the room to see if anyone looked like Seward's attacker, or even if they had matching hair, but Bell could not finger anyone.

"I will bring a man in here and show him to you," said Wells.

The young man crouched behind a desk to avoid being seen should the real assailant actually appear. A door opened and, Bell noticed, "a good many men walked in." Instantly he recognized Payne. Eagerly and unafraid, he sprang from his hiding place and walked boldly up to the stranger who had slashed and bloodied five men in the Seward household. Bell put his finger on the culprit's lips and exclaimed with triumphant certainty, "I know him! He is the man!"[48]

Weary officials were jubilant. Payne was the most wanted man after Booth. It would be a long, sleepless night for the hungry detainee, who was escorted by marine guard to the Navy Yard and at 5 AM taken by boat to board the ironclad *Saugus,* moored in a stream.[49]

Though the case against Payne seemed airtight, Wells was not yet finished with the remaining suspects. He clashed verbally with Mary Surratt over the veracity of her servant's disclosure that had led to her arrest. She denied that three or four men visited her house after the assassination, as reported by Susan Mahony.

"I assure you, on the honor of a lady, that I would not tell you an untruth," she told Wells.

"I assure you, on the honor of a gentleman, I shall get this information from you," he countered.

When he asked if she had met Payne earlier to arrange for his visit that night, she replied: "No sir. The ruffian that was in my door when I came away, he was a tremendous hard fellow with a skull cap on. And my daughter commenced crying and said 'those gentlemen came to save our lives.' I hope they arrested him."

But Wells persisted. "He tells me now that he met you in the street and you engaged him to come to your house."

"Oh! Oh!" she exclaimed. "It is not so, sir, for I believe he would have murdered us, everyone. I assure you."

"When did you see him first?" Wells inquired.

"Just as the carriage drew up. He rang the doorbell and my daughter said, 'Oh! There is a murderer!'"

"Did you ever engage a man to come and clean your yard?"

"No, sir. I engage a black man. I never have a white man."

Before he had done with her she told him that Atzerodt had stayed at the boardinghouse "part of a week." Then she had found liquor in his room. "No gentleman can board with me who keeps liquor in his rooms, and I told my son that that man could not stay."

She also noted that her son, John, had spoken several times in the fall of the preceding year of going to Europe. It was a significant clue that Wells failed to pick up on, allowing the elusive Confederate courier to slip abroad undetected.[50]

When nightfall came again, Wells boarded the *Saugus* carrying a bloodstained, mixed white-and-brown cloth overcoat he felt certain had been discarded by Payne as he hid. It had been picked up two days earlier by a private of the Third Massachusetts Heavy Artillery while on duty in woods about three miles northeast of Washington. A snail had fallen off the damp coat as the soldier lifted it up from the side of a grass-covered road between Forts Bunker Hill and Saratoga. Suspicious of the bloody marks on the sleeves and chest, he had turned it over to the provost marshal's office on the afternoon of Easter Sunday.[51]

Wells had Payne remove all his clothing, including a dark gray coat that he was wearing. Then, after describing to Payne how he must have been positioned when he slashed the bedridden Seward, Wells predicted he would find bloodstains on the inside sleeve of the dark gray coat, and he did.

"What do you think now?" he taunted.

The shackled man did not answer as he leaned back against the side of the ironclad. Weeks later he would confide to his court-appointed lawyer that the blood on his sleeve came from his own finger, cut when he assaulted Frederick Seward.[52]

Wells pointed to the stains on the overcoat found in the woods and asked, "How did that blood come there?"

"It is not blood," Payne answered.

"Look and see, and say if you can tell me it is not blood!" Wells thundered.

Payne looked again at the overcoat, then changed his mind. "I do not know how it came there."[53]

When Wells asked how Payne had come by the boots, one of which had a broad black ink stain on the inside, he said he had purchased them three months before in Baltimore.

"Liar!" Wells rebuked, noting the boots looked as if they hadn't been worn very often. Payne was silent.[54]

The colonel took the boots with him when he left the ironclad and handed the one with an inkstain to the head of the Treasury Department's Bureau of Engraving and Printing for expert analysis. Microscopic detection showed a layer of ink covering an earlier coating. When the outer coating was removed with oxalic acid, the initials J.W. appeared distinctly, but the name BOOTH was barely visible because, as the expert, Spencer Clark, later testified, he had left the acid on for too long. "But it left very little doubt upon my mind that the name was Booth," Clark declared.[55]

Although Wells had sufficient evidence for conviction, it was bolstered when Payne was brought up on the deck of the *Saugus* to face Augustus Seward. The secretary of state's son grabbed Payne the same way he had held him as he shoved the assailant out of his father's bedroom. Only now he looked closely at the prisoner. In every respect the man's size and smooth, hairless face matched those he remembered so vividly by the light in the hall. When Payne was told to repeat the words, "I'm mad! I'm mad!" Augustus instantly recognized the timbre of the voice, even though the volume was very much lower than the original piercing shriek.[56]

CHAPTER 15

———◆◇◆———

"We Know as Much of Your Operations as the Almighty"

As dawn broke over the city on Saturday, April 15, life ebbed from the unconscious president, and George Atzerodt prepared to leave his hotel.

"What brings you out so early this morning?" a servant asked Atzerodt.

"I have got business," said the unshaven, troubled guest, who left without paying his bill.[1]

He made his way across Rock Creek to neighboring Georgetown, where he called briefly on Lucinda Metz, who had shown no interest in his romantic advances.[2] He told her he was on his way to take the stagecoach north to Montgomery County, Maryland. When she spoke of the news on everyone's lips, she suspected, from his manner, that he knew more than he was letting on. He told her a man named Booth had killed the president and that only a quarter of an hour separated the attacks on Lincoln and the secretary of state.[3]

Still on Georgetown's main street, Atzerodt went into Matthews & Company store, where he made small talk with another acquaintance, John Caldwell. Atzerodt offered to sell his watch, but the storekeeper said he didn't need another. He asked for a ten-dollar loan, but Caldwell turned him down. Then the renegade took out his loaded revolver.

"Lend me ten dollars and take this as security," he said. "I will bring the money, or send it to you next week."

This time Caldwell agreed, and Atzerodt walked to the stagecoach terminal at Cunningham's Tavern and paid for a ride to Rockville, Maryland, about eighteen miles north.[4]

Unexpectedly, at about 11 AM military pickets halted the stage on the Rockville Pike in Maryland, and Atzerodt, the only passenger, was ordered off. There was a backup of about forty or fifty wagons waiting for permission to continue north. Orders had gone out in the early hours of the morning to close the roads and arrest anyone approaching the pickets or trying to get out of Washington. An exception was made for the stage on which Atzerodt had been riding, because it carried mail, so the driver was allowed to continue on his way alone. However, a verbal order came down soon after, allowing pickets to pass through anyone who did not look suspicious, so long as their names were recorded and the wagons and carts searched. It would be a long wait to clear the backup as the few pickets began their slow, methodical checks.

Atzerodt was unperturbed. He had recovered his nerve and mingled gregariously with the drivers and passengers, talking freely and comfortably as if he knew them all. He approached William Gaither, stalled in a two-horse spring wagon on the way back to his farm four miles north of Rockville. The two had never met before. Atzerodt asked if he could hitch a ride, explaining that he was from Germantown, Maryland, and had gone ahead of his father, who was delivering hay. Eager for companionship, Gaither said his wagon was empty and any company was better than none. Atzerodt treated him to several glasses of cider in the store beside the roadside. The animated hitchhiker was so flushed with self-confidence that he even drank with Sergeant Lewis Chubb, commander of the pickets, who had personally ordered him off the stage.

After four hours' delay, Gaither finally received approval to pass through. He jumped in the wagon and called out loudly for Atzerodt to join him. Atzerodt, who was talking with the picket commander, looked startled, but bowed politely to the sergeant and hurriedly took a seat beside the farmer. Then, as if to himself, he remarked, "It's all right so far."

As they traveled over the bumpy road, Atzerodt spoke freely of women, horses, dogs, and what Gaither called "trifling things." When Gaither, a slaveholder who sympathized with the South, asked what he knew of the assassination, Atzerodt gave the impression he didn't know, nor care much about it. He said only that a man named Booth was the suspect. He was remarkably composed for an almost penniless man on the run. When they reached Mulligan's Shop, two miles north of Rockville, Gaither reined in the horses and Atzerodt got out, saying he would wait for his father to catch up.[5]

That night he slept at the home of another acquaintance, Robert Kennell, about seven miles beyond Rockville on the road to Barnsville.[6] Most of the residents in this sparsely populated area of Montgomery County knew Atzerodt by his anglicized alias of Andrew Attwood, and it was this name that others used when he stopped over the next day for a Sunday midday meal at the home of Hezekiah Metz, whose daughter he had tried to woo. Before dinner, he was joshed by one of the guests, Somerset Leaman, who knew him from boyhood when Atzerodt's father had settled in the neighborhood. "Are you the man that killed Abe Lincoln?"

"Yes," Atzerodt replied with a laugh.

But Leaman, now serious, wanted to know whether the president had been assassinated. "Well, Andrew, I want to know the truth of it. Is it so?" he queried.

Atzerodt replied, "Yes, it is so. He died yesterday evening about three o'clock."

Leaman asked if it was true that Seward's throat was cut and two of his sons stabbed.

"Yes," said the runaway. "Mr. Seward was stabbed, or rather cut at the throat, but not killed, and two of his sons were stabbed."

Leaman pressed for news of General Ulysses S. Grant. Was it true that he too had been assassinated the same night?

"No," said Atzerodt. "I don't know whether that is so or not. I don't suppose it is so. If it had been, I should have heard it."[7]

Over dinner Leaman thought Atzerodt looked "confused," perhaps because of the rebuffs from the Metz daughter. But Leaman's brother, James, asked again whether General Grant had been killed.

Atzerodt said he did not think so, but foolishly let slip an opinion indicating that he knew much more than would be expected from an innocent observer. "If the man that was to follow him had followed him, it was likely to be so," Atzerodt replied.[8]

Later, when they were outside in the yard, Atzerodt groaned to James Leaman, "Oh, my! What a trouble I see!"

"Why?" asked Leaman. "What have you to trouble you?"

"More than I will ever get shut of," said Atzerodt.[9]

Within a short while he was at the home of his cousin Hartman Richter, who had immigrated eighteen years earlier from Thuringia, Prussia, where he had a reputation as an unprincipled scoundrel and thief.[10]

By now Federal authorities in Washington had targeted Atzerodt as a co-conspirator and launched a wide-scale manhunt for his capture. His name, accompanied by a faulty description, would be telegraphed far and wide by the War Department the same day Lincoln died.[11] Newspapers would publicize Atzerodt's identity to even wider numbers. There was overwhelming evidence of Atzerodt's ties to the conspiracy. Even though Payne had abandoned the one-eyed horse after fleeing from Seward's house, the animal was thought to have been ridden by Atzerodt because he had been identified by the stable manager, Fletcher, as the person who left it in his care until two days before Lincoln's murder.[12] Additionally, Booth's Canadian bank deposit record had been found in the room registered to Atzerodt at the Kirkwood House.

The arrest of the Prussian-born conspirator might have been accelerated if employees at Howard's livery stable had been as zealous as other residents in tipping off authorities to facts known only to them. One of the stable's employees, Francis Curran, was very familiar with the scowling Atzerodt, having seen him at the stable and at the Pennsylvania House on a number of occasions. By chance, as Curran drove the stable's carriage along the Rockville Pike in Montgomery County, Maryland, on the day the president died, he passed the wagon driven by William Gaither and clearly noticed Atzerodt seated beside the driver. Curran frequently talked to colleagues at the stable about people he met on his sixteen-mile route north from Georgetown into Maryland, and when he returned to Washington late that afternoon he told his manager, Brooke Stabler, that he had passed a two-horse market wagon about five miles south of Rockville in midafternoon and seen Atzerodt beside the driver, William Gaither, a reputed rebel.

Even though Atzerodt's name had been widely circulated, neither Curran nor Stabler rushed to report sighting him, nor to give the direction of his flight from Washington. It was all the more surprising because Curran and Stabler had wondered on a number of occasions how Atzerodt earned a living. When the owner of the Pennsylvania House suggested Atzerodt might be a detective, Stabler had replied, "There is no detective in him." He couldn't possibly be a government employee because he was "an arrant rebel."[13]

Meanwhile Atzerodt's careless comments on the assassination were finding a wider audience among the close-knit rural community in Montgomery County. Metz recounted the incident to a man called Page, who passed on the hearsay to a farmer, James Purdom, then doubling as a police informant. Much embellished, the story now had Atzerodt standing up at Metz's dinner table, throwing down his knife and fork, and exclaiming, "If the fellow that had promised to follow General Grant had done his duty, we would have gotten General Grant too."[14]

Even though three days had already passed since Atzerodt's loose talk at the dinner table, Purdom galloped off to alert law enforcement officials at Monocacy Junction. He had covered about five miles when he met up with a private in a cavalry company of Delaware volunteers based at Monocacy Junction. Purdom gave an exaggerated version of what he knew of the "suspicious character" believed to be staying with Hartman Richter, who might be implicated in the assassination. He told the private to rush the report to his superiors.[15]

Captain Solomon Townsend, whose cavalrymen had been on alert and scouting for suspects since the assassination, was hesitant. He told his superior Major E.R. Artman that the same informant had twice before given wrong information, and Richter's house was a long way off, about twenty miles. Artman thought it over for half an hour, then gave the go-ahead to make the arrest.[16] Sergeant Zachariah Gemmill, commanding a detail of six cavalrymen, rode out about 10 PM on Wednesday, April 19, with orders to bring back Atzerodt and arrest Richter if he appeared at all suspicious.[17] They stopped first at Purdom's farm, four miles short of Richter's residence, to get a description of Atzerodt, then wandered about lost in the dark, searching in vain for the house, even though Purdom was their guide.

A few hours before daylight they found their way and dismounted in front of the home. Purdom remained far back out of sight, so that Richter would not know he was the informant. Richter stalled in opening the door, then said his cousin had gone to Frederick. Only when Gemmill threatened to search the house did Richter confirm that his cousin was upstairs, an admission immediately contradicted by his wife, who said there were three men on the floor above. Gemmill found Atzerodt asleep in a single bed with two other men, who woke up. He ignored them and shook the man he knew only as Attwood. When he asked him his name, he thought the German-accented reply was fictitious, even though Atzerodt insisted it was his name. But the sergeant was confident he fit the description and ordered him to get up and dress. Silently, Atzerodt complied, neither questioning whether he was under arrest nor inquiring why he was being led away.

As a precaution, the cavalrymen rode with Atzerodt to the home of one of the Leaman brothers to authenticate his identity. One of the brothers, who stuck his head out the window and said he knew Atzerodt, came downstairs. Gemmill became even more suspicious of Atzerodt when he saw how he lowered his head as he shook Leaman's hand. To reassure himself, Gemmill asked the suspect if he had been in Washington recently. No, said Atzerodt. Then Gemmill asked directly whether he had anything to do with the assassination. Nothing at all, Atzerodt replied. But the cavalry sergeant would not be fooled. He knew he had his man. He ordered the unwashed detainee taken back to the Monocacy Junction camp while he returned to arrest Richter. Before parting, he asked Atzerodt if there was anything he wanted from his cousin's home. The only request was for tobacco and collars, which Gemmill brought back to the camp about noon.[18]

Atzerodt did not remain long in the cavalry base at Monocacy Junction. Artman had no doubt that Atzerodt was the man who had set off alarm bells with his imprudent remarks in the Metz home five days earlier. He was taken under heavy guard to the railroad junction at Relay House, near Baltimore, where the regional commander had already warned the resident general, Erastus Tyler, to make sure there was "no slip up in this matter."[19] Atzerodt dictated "a lengthy statement" while in Tyler's custody, but it was no sooner taken down than an unexpected telegram arrived from Washington. It was from Stanton himself, with the characteristic bluntness that instilled fear and enforced obedience. "Bring Atzerodt directly to Washington. Allow no examination or communication with him by any person. This order as to communication with him is peremptory."[20] Aware that his career was now on the line for taking an unauthorized statement, the general may well have destroyed the document — it was never published, and its fate remains unknown.

Tyler took personal charge of Atzerodt on the train to Washington. Such tight security greeted his arrival at the depot near the US Capitol that troops blocked the exits from every railroad car until Atzerodt had been led out of sight, to prevent a spontaneous riot and attempt on his life. A local newspaper reported that Atzerodt "maintained a sullen silence and endeavored to assume an air of indifference."[21]

Without delay he was transferred to the custody of Robert Murray, a gruff US marshal for the southern district of New York. When he clamped a new set of handcuffs on the prisoner's left wrist, Atzerodt cried out, "Don't pinch me!" Furious, Murray growled that he would pinch his neck before he was a week older.[22]

Flanked by a guard of mounted soldiers, the two men sat uncomfortably beside each other in one of Willard's commandeered stages for the horse-drawn ride southeast to the Navy Yard. When Murray asked where Atzerodt had slept on the night of the assassination, he replied truthfully that it was at the Pennsylvania House. But he said he had gone to bed at his usual hour of 10 or 11 PM. And although Atzerodt said he rose at 5 AM the next day, he would not reply when asked whether that was the usual time he woke up. They traveled in silence until Murray spoke.

"You made a great mistake in having your things in room 126 in the Kirkwood House."

Atzerodt denied having anything there.

"You lie!" said Murray. "You registered your name there."

"Yes, but simply to get a room for a friend."

"What is your friend's name?"

"It's of no consequence," Atzerodt answered.

After more silence, Murray asked, "Where is Booth?"

"I have not seen him since Friday night."

"At which hour?"

"About six o'clock on the steps of the theatre. I then told him I would have nothing more to do with this thing and backed out of it, and since that time have had nothing more to do with it."

Murray would have none of this cocky nonsense. His charge was as guilty as they come. No longer able to contain his personal feelings, the marshal said he did not believe that any man had ever been arrested and charged with a crime who was "fouler" than Atzerodt. He did not care for any of Atzerodt's alibis or lies. "We know as much of your operations during Friday night up to Saturday morning as the Almighty does. We know everyone you talked to, everyone you have seen, traced you to every place you have been, got your coat with the contents in the pocket, which have been identified by your brother as yours. We have got your pistol and the Bowie knife. There is not the slightest chance for you. The only chance would be by opening your mouth and revealing to us who the parties were in this conspiracy." But for now the prisoner held his tongue even though the marshal would later state that Atzerodt promised to comply.[23]

Just before midnight Atzerodt was rowed to the *Saugus,* moored in the stream off the Navy Yard. Earlier that month the ironclad had been in combat, firing some of the last shells from the James River before the fall of Richmond.[24] It had a narrow escape on arrival at the Washington Navy Yard when it collided with a steamer, losing its tripod, flagstaff, and six lifeline stanchions.[25] Now it held some of the most reviled men in the Union. Atzerodt, walking unsteadily in leg irons, joined Lewis Payne and Samuel Arnold in separated, solitary confinement.[26]

Three days later Atzerodt was transferred to another ironclad, the *Montauk,* moored close by, then shut in a windowless room and kept under guard by marines.[27] During that night his reserve wilted, and he asked the sentry to summon the supervisor.

Atzerodt was in a talkative mood, telling marine captain Frank

Munroe that he was not only innocent of any crime but that he had been instrumental in saving the life of the vice president. He told of meeting with John Surratt at Port Tobacco three weeks earlier and coming up to Washington to meet Booth, under the impression he was needed to help open a theater in Richmond and to run the blockade in a vessel obtained by Booth and Surratt. But Booth had instead ordered him to kill Andrew Johnson. When he refused, Booth had "threatened to blow his brains out unless he complied." Again he refused and returned to Port Tobacco. But Surratt had come for him once more, and when Atzerodt arrived in the capital he checked into the Kirkwood House Hotel. Again Booth told him to murder the vice president, but he would not give in. "Becoming frightened," Atzerodt locked his hotel room, leaving behind the revolver and knife that Herold had brought in earlier that day. He had walked down the street in the belief that they would not dare attempt the assassination. At daybreak, he told Munroe, he left the city and went north to his cousin's house in neighboring Montgomery County, Maryland.[28]

CHAPTER 16

A Funeral Surpassing All Others in Solemnity

On the night detectives raided the Surratt boardinghouse, Abraham Lincoln's body was placed in a six-foot-six walnut coffin and taken downstairs to lie in state in the executive mansion's spacious East Room. His hair was combed straight back[1] as he lay solid as marble in the fifteen-hundred-dollar lead-lined container, softened with fine white satin and silk and edged with fringes and tassels.[2] A solid silver-plate bullion fixed to the top cover bore the simple remembrance:

ABRAHAM LINCOLN
16TH PRESIDENT OF THE UNITED STATES
BORN FEBRUARY 12TH 1809
DIED APRIL 15TH 1865[3]

One of the privileged few to see the remains before the gates opened to the general public was Senator Solomon Foot of Vermont, a recent president pro tempore of the US Senate. "A good man struck down by the hands of an assassin for doing his duty," he lamented beside the body.[4]

The following day thousands of mourners swarmed toward the northwest gate leading into the circular drive of the front grounds of the White House. Most waited hours to enter as guards admitted only so many as exited at a nearby gate. "Myself and family tried for several hours to work our way through the immense crowd, that we might get a view, but not one of us had strength to succeed and we returned home much disappointed," wrote the Reverend James Ward, pastor of the Methodist Episcopal Church close by Ford's

Theatre.[5] Helen Varnum Hill McCalla pushed her way through the mass extending far down to the main leg of Pennsylvania Avenue. Most were grieving blacks. Women fainted and children screamed in the crush. A strong passing shower added to their discomfort. "We had to endure it, being, to say the truth, determined to enter the President's House," McCalla wrote in her journal. After two hours she joined the silent flow into the East Room, "but we were not permitted to wait a moment near the corpse, so that it was impossible to obtain a satisfactory view." Her eyes rested on the coffin, "studded with great numbers of silver nails," before she exited with a lasting impression of the abundance of black mourning cloth.[6] David Homer Bates, one of the cipher operators in the military telegraph office, also managed to pass through the gate into the mansion and was struck by the smallness of Lincoln's face, now shorn of the beard except for a tuft of hair left on the chin. "We shall never know his like again," he mused.[7] George Coffin, a student at Georgetown College, who would later become the political cartoonist at the *Washington Post,* arrived just as the gate was closed for the day, disappointing "tens of thousands."[8]

An estimated thirty thousand tried their luck the next morning, many streaming into Lafayette Square long before the scheduled 9:30 AM opening of the gate. Washington had never witnessed a funeral with so many wanting to be a part of it. Fully booked Willard's Hotel turned down four hundred telegraphed requests for rooms. Thick lines six or seven abreast stretched for blocks. But the multitudes gathered quietly, neither jostling nor ill tempered.[9] By midmorning they had to make way for those assembling on the road in front of the White House to accompany the coffin in a doleful procession to the US Capitol, where many more could pay their last respects.

But even as sedate dignitaries assembled inside the Treasury building, diplomats and US Supreme Court justices squabbled over rank and protocol, warring over which group should precede the other in the order of procession to the adjacent White House. The stand-off over protocol was not without precedent. Six decades earlier President Thomas Jefferson had flouted protocol by refusing to follow the custom of seating dinner guests according to rank and rejecting formal attire for the reception of diplomats presenting credentials. It was established etiquette the modern democrat neither cared for nor would uphold.[10] Now, as the status-conscious worthies prepared to exit in the reverse order of precedence, so that the new president would enter the White House last, Chief Justice Salmon Chase insisted that the diplomats, resplendent in court regalia, precede the black-robed justices. The foreign representatives demanded otherwise. As Assistant Secretary of the Treasury Maunsell Field shuttled between the camps in search of a breakthrough, the dean of the diplomatic corps abruptly gave way, without, however, yielding his right to future claims of higher rank.[11]

The great East Room had been transformed from the city's most glittering social venue into a silent and sepulchral chamber. Eight large mirrors that had reflected the sparkling whirl of animated receptions still hung from the gold-and-red wallpaper, but their flashy faces were now screened by wool and bordered with mourning cloth. A makeshift platform with layers of raised wooden steps covered in more black crepe had been constructed over much of the expansive floor. There was standing room only for the privileged attendees, each bearing a coveted white admission card bordered with black. They represented the most illustrious officials in the Union: governors, congressmen, military officers, diplomats, justices, pallbearers, and heads of government agencies.[12]

All stood respectfully before the four-foot-high catafalque positioned below a domed canopy, itself supported by four tall pillars. Twelve high-ranking army and naval officers, erect and motionless, formed a guard of honor around the coffin. A raised step all around gave mourners the opportunity to look down on Lincoln's face. Only the vivid colors of spring flowers relieved the pervasive gloom, with green sprigs and heather on the lid of the coffin, a cross of lilies at the head, and roses at the base.

Andrew Johnson and his cabinet adjourned their meeting in the Treasury building and arrived for the funeral service moments before the noon ceremony. The seventeenth president faced the middle of the coffin, his hands occasionally crossed over his chest. Beside him stood former vice president Hannibal Hamlin, who had been first in line to succeed Lincoln until Johnson was sworn in as his successor just six weeks earlier. Ulysses S. Grant, who had finally given Lincoln the victories lesser generals had sidestepped or botched, wore white gloves and sash and wept openly. The young captain on his staff, Robert Todd Lincoln, sat with other relatives near the coffin, stifling sobs with his handkerchief. Two of the preeminent journalists of their day gave conflicting reports of Tad Lincoln's presence, with George Alfred Townsend reporting that "Tad, his face red and heated, cried as if his heart would break," and Noah Brooks recording that Robert "was the only one of the family present."[13]

About sixty clergymen of different denominations had filed in by invitation, with Dr. Phineas Gurley, pastor of the New York Avenue Presbyterian Church, once more conducting a funeral service in the White House, where he had officiated only three years earlier on the death of young Willie Lincoln. Now, as in 1862, Mary Todd Lincoln was absent. Unable to mask her inconsolable grief, she remained in the dimness of her room upstairs. This time the pastor's thoughts were more of a fond remembrance of his friend than a standard homily. "We admired and loved him on many accounts," he intoned. "We admired his childlike simplicity, his freedom from guile and deceit, his staunch and sterling integrity, his kind and forgiving temper . . . his readiness to hear and consider the cause of the poor and the humble, the suffering and the oppressed; his charity toward those who questioned the correctness of his opinions and the wisdom of his policy . . . his true and enlarged philanthropy that knew no distinction of color or race, but regarded all men as brethren . . ." Yet the assassination was still beyond his understanding. "We will wait for His interpretation, and we will wait in faith, nothing doubting," he declared.[14]

It was the sixth East Room funeral attended by Benjamin Brown French, following those of young Willie, Presidents William Henry Harrison, Zachary Taylor, and John Tyler, and Secretary of State Abel Upshur. This one, he informed readers of a local newspaper, "surpassed any other in solemnity."[15]

So many notables and delegations from the states and territories formed the long and seemingly endless tribute down Pennsylvania Avenue to the Capitol that those in front reached their destination before others had even begun the mile-long march. With businesses closed and government departments shut down, it seemed like the entire city had turned out to witness the historic farewell. Even weak and wounded William Seward peered from his bedroom window to see the hearse leave the White House.[16] Spectators perched in unseasonably leafless trees and huddled on rooftops, balconies, and any overlook they could find. Mary Hassler Newcomb looked down for several hours from the bedroom window of a friend's house rising above "the largest procession ever known in Washington." Her own home displayed black silk flags over the front door, and miniature flags tied with red, white, and blue ribbons on black bows over each window.[17] Many women stood under open parasols in the broiling heat as straight columns of the military passed by shouldering reversed weapons, their left arms ringed with the black crepe that also wound around the hilts of their swords.[18] A mounted cavalry regiment led, followed by artillery batteries, marines, infantry regiments, dismounted and mounted military officers, and then a succession of civic organizations and the clergy.

The lead unit was overtaken along the avenue by the sudden arrival of members of the Twenty-second US Colored Infantry Regiment, who had been hastily assembled at City Point past midnight the day before to ensure the inclusion of black troops.[19] Stanton also demanded that black soldiers not be discriminated against in other cities preparing to honor the funeral train on its long ride back to Springfield, Illinois.[20]

The authorities had not overlooked Dr. Charles Leale, the first surgeon to reach the wounded president. Though only twenty-three, he was given a place of honor at the head of the coffin in the White House and now marched with the surgeon general immediately before the hearse.

About thirty bands passed by the silent onlookers, sounding dirges to the fallen commander in chief. "It was as still as Sunday," observed one bystander, "except the tolling of the bells and the playing of the bands. You could hear funeral dirges in every part of the town."[21] Elihu Washburne, the Illinois congressman who had been first to welcome the president-elect to Washington at the train depot four years earlier, was among the pallbearers, as was House Speaker Schuyler Colfax, who was unable to accept Lincoln's invitation to be his guest at Ford's Theatre on Good Friday.

Six light gray horses pulled the elaborate fourteen-foot-long hearse, constructed especially for this slow departure. A golden eagle, also draped with crepe, topped the elaborate canopy. Behind it came carriages two abreast carrying the family and relatives, the president, his cabinet, and other dignitaries. Bystanders could never even guess at the identity of so many thousands of strangers passing by in ceremonial homage. Many had come solely to be close to the remains of their emancipator. "There were no truer mourners, when all were sad, than the poor colored people who crowded the streets, joined the procession, and exhibited their woe," Gideon Welles reflected in his diary.[22]

Once more thousands passed through the Capitol's Rotunda for their final opportunity to be close to Lincoln's remains. Even here, paintings depicting glorious episodes in American history were draped, as if the images of other icons had joined in the nation's sorrow. Benjamin Brown French's son, Ben, an engineer, had personally built the pine catafalque to hold the coffin.[23] French's wife, Mary, had sewn and trimmed the black cloth cover. Quick to recognize the historic nature of these relics and the need to preserve them for future generations, French decided he would place the catafalque and cover in the empty space below the Capitol's crypt, which Congress had hoped to convert into a mausoleum for the remains of George Washington. There, French expected, they would rest as "a sacred memorial." His wish was fulfilled, and the catafalque, together with the black cloth that accompanied the body to Springfield, Illinois, for burial, were reunited within days of the funeral and have lain in the designated space ever since.[24]

Throughout the next day an unbroken line of mostly black viewers passed through the hushed rotunda.[25] Pvt. Jeremiah Lockwood. on leave from the Fourth New York Heavy Artillery, thought Lincoln "looked very well but rather dark."[26] The resourceful journalist Noah Brooks climbed the winding stairs almost to the eye of the great dome. From there he looked down on the casket, around which the double line of mourners appeared "like black atoms moving over a sheet of gray paper" as they filed by on either side of the coffin.[27]

Quartermaster General Montgomery Meigs, who had formerly supervised the architecture and beautification of parts of the Capitol, visited several times that day, impressed by the "well-preserved" corpse.[28] Thomas Walter, the Capitol's architect, sulked petulantly throughout the sad observances, untouched by the obsequies that had overcome other Washingtonians. The constant booming of the cannons "began to operate on my nerves," Walter wrote irritably to his wife. When he tried to walk down the avenue, he was blocked by the crowds. Frustrated by masses of people besieging the rotunda, he sneered, "I do not consider any of this nonsense as doing honor to our president, and I have not in any way participated in it, not even so much as to be a mere looker on." Unmoved by the public's banding together in a time of shared loss, Walter regretted only that "It stops work another day, which is wholly useless."[29] He was conspicuously the odd man out as almost forty thousand mourners filed by the casket during fourteen hours of public viewing on Thursday.[30]

Shortly after dawn on Friday, April 21, the president and cabinet were on hand to see the casket taken to the train depot for the final journey back to Springfield. Mary Todd Lincoln would not accompany it. She would stay closeted and reclusive in her room for another month before departing for Illinois. When a letter of condolence for "so terrible a calamity" arrived from Queen Victoria, another exalted widow, Mrs. Lincoln thanked her "for its expression of tender sympathy, coming as they do, from a heart which from its own sorrow, can appreciate the *intense grief* I now endure."[31] Charles Francis Adams, the top American diplomat in London, snickered on reading the maudlin letter for transmission to the monarch, telling his chief secretary it was "in bad taste."[32]

A week after the funeral train left Washington, Mary Todd Lincoln summoned Stanton to her room, ordering him to have her husband's remains buried in Springfield's Oak Ridge Cemetery. Under no circumstances would she agree to any other burial site under review, even if already purchased, and if the remains were placed elsewhere, she would demand their removal, knowing, she told Stanton, that

"Mr. Lincoln would himself have preferred to be placed in the Oak Ridge Cemetery."[33]

Yet even in her misery Mary Todd Lincoln was charitable toward those close to her. Elizabeth Keckly, her most intimate confidante, received the president's bloodstained cloak, the comb and brush that the seamstress had often used to tidy his hair, a glove worn at the first reception after the second inaugural, his overshoes, and Mrs. Lincoln's bonnet worn the night of the assassination.[34] The widow gave family friend and pastor Dr. Phineas Gurley the top hat worn by Lincoln for the first and only time at his second inauguration. "While its intrinsic value is trifling, you will prize it for the associations that cluster around it," she wrote when thanking him for his "Christian kindness" that "cast a ray of light across my dreary and blighted pathway."[35] She had always been kind to Gurley and his wife, but he still thought she was "queer," though her failings had perhaps been "somewhat exaggerated." Nevertheless, he had been taken aback by so many Springfield residents ferociously bad-mouthing her during his stay there for the funeral. "The ladies of Springfield say that Mr. Lincoln's death hurt her *ambition* more than her *affectations* — a hard speech, but many people *think* so who do not *say* so," he wrote a friend after returning to Washington. "Everybody in Springfield loved Mr. Lincoln, but as for Mrs. L I cannot say as much. Hard things are said of her by all classes of people, and when I got to know how she was regarded by her old neighbors and even by her relatives in S I did not wonder that she had decided to make her future home in Chicago."[36]

Though she remained sequestered in the dark gloom of her White House quarters during the funeral in Springfield, the isolated widow could not escape the sounds of public homage to her venerated husband. The loud blast of cannons carried across the city every half hour from noon until sunset in a farewell salute to the fallen leader.[37]

Weeks later, as she prepared to leave the White House forever, Benjamin Brown French went up to her room to say good-bye. He knew her better than did any other public official through frequent meetings with her over the years while overseeing expenditures for the executive mansion. He thought the assassination had "somewhat unhinged her mind, for at times she has exhibited all the symptoms of madness." Withholding all he knew about her because he thought it improper to mention it, even within the privacy of his own journal, French nevertheless wrote, "It is well for the nation that she is no longer in the White House."[38] He was more forthcoming in a letter to a family member, telling her Mrs. Lincoln was "crazier than she used to be" and that she had purchased about a thousand dollars' worth of mourning goods the month before the assassination. "What do you suppose possessed her to do it! Please keep that fact in your own house."[39]

Indeed, with her spirits at their lowest ebb, it would not be long before Mrs. Lincoln wrote Tad's White House tutor, "If it were not for my two remaining sons, I would pray the Father to take me too."[40]

With her exit French was free, as he informed the new president, to sell all the mourning material in the East Room at a public auction to help defray some of the thirty thousand dollars in funeral expenses.[41] The government was so slow in approving funds that two months after the funeral services in Washington, French made a frantic appeal to the secretary of the interior for remittance "as those to whom the money is due are hourly calling upon me for their pay."[42]

CHAPTER 17

Escape

At some point along their wild dash in the dark, John Wilkes Booth and David Herold lost valuable time and mobility when the actor's horse stumbled and fell in mud, throwing the rider hard against a rock and exacerbating the pain in his injured leg.[1] Thereafter they rode slowly until around midnight, when the horsemen arrived at the tavern in Surrattsville. John Lloyd had been drinking in the afternoon and evening and had flopped asleep in his bedroom about 8 PM. He had only just roused himself when Herold burst into the tavern.

"Lloyd, for God's sake make haste and get those things!"

Realizing he must be referring to the "shooting irons" that Mrs. Surratt had told him to have ready, Lloyd hurried up to his bedroom, where he had placed them within easy reach. Herold had taken a bottle of whiskey and was already back in his saddle swigging from it when Lloyd came out with the cartridges, field glasses, and one of the carbines. Booth, whom Lloyd had never met before, said he could not carry the other weapon because he had broken his leg and needed to find a doctor.

They were about to leave when Booth spoke.

"I will tell you some news, if you want to hear it."

"Use your own pleasure about telling it," Lloyd replied.

"We have killed President Lincoln and Secretary Seward."

Lloyd was too shaken to reply. He stood as if impaled at the moment of surprise. He could only look on as the horsemen disappeared into the darkness.[2]

But Booth was now distracted by a pang he could barely endure. He groaned from the sharp pain that was not only in his leg but now also in his back. He needed to have the leg set and dressed. Fortunately Dr. Samuel Mudd lived in the vicinity. Herold objected, trying hard to dissuade him from detouring so far off the quicker way south.[3] Mudd lived southeast of their escape route and east of the treacherous Zekiah Swamp. If they branched off to get medical help, it would mean rounding the northernmost tip of the unchartered swamp to get to the physician's farm. They dared not place the swampy obstacle between themselves and the easiest route south. It would not only delay their escape but possibly cost them their advantage of riding while darkness still held. Yet Booth was in no condition to yield nor in a mood for logic, and they pulled their reins sharply east.

They had covered about seventeen miles southeast of Lloyd's tavern when they arrived at Mudd's two-story farmhouse, set back a few hundred yards from the road. It was about 4 AM. Almost six hours had elapsed since the president was shot, and neither Booth nor Herold had slept or rested. Herold dismounted and banged on the front door facing the road. Mudd, thirty-one, and his wife, Sarah, twenty-nine, were asleep in their bedroom, beyond the front parlor at the rear of the house. The pounding awakened the physician, but he was hesitant and did not open the door immediately, even after Herold announced that they were two strangers on their way to Washington, and that one of them had been thrown from his horse and broken a leg.

When he gingerly opened the door, Mudd saw a man about twenty paces away holding the reins of a horse, with its rider still in the saddle. The riderless horse was hitched to a cedar tree.[4] Mudd helped the wincing man dismount and assisted him onto a sofa in the parlor. After a cursory examination, the physician helped Booth up the stairs into a room and gently laid him down on one of the two beds. Booth's clothes were damp from sweat and his pants splattered with mud, giving the impression he had been riding hard and fast, and had fallen.[5] His pale and haggard face was partially obscured by a thick shawl wrapped around his neck.[6]

The long boot gripped the slightly swollen part of the leg so tightly that the physician had to slit it lengthwise to peel it off. When he touched the bruised flesh tenderly to feel for bone damage, he picked up a distinctive cracking sound, pointing, in his mind, to a straight fracture of the tibia, about two inches above the ankle.[7] He did not think it was a serious injury. In Mudd's opinion there were no signs of a compound fracture. There was a wound, but it was not infected, and Mudd bandaged it, knowing that the dressing would have to be changed within two or three days, by which time it would be far more swollen. He would have preferred to have taken his time but Booth pressed him, in sounds muffled by the shawl, to hurry so he could get home. Only when Mudd had dressed the wound and set the splints did he notice a belted brace of revolvers under Booth's clothing.[8] Weak and tired, Booth moaned and shivered, breathing in short bursts. At times he dozed drowsily, as if to ease the sharp pain in his limb and back. Mudd improvised a splint by pasting together pieces of a broken box. Later, at Herold's request, he and his English gardener made a makeshift pair of wooden crutches.

Instead of returning to bed, Mudd set about managing his farm-hands, then invited Herold to breakfast while the patient upstairs slept. The doctor had never met Herold before and mistook him for a teenager who had yet to shave.[9] Though Herold had passed the night without sleep, he was demonstratively at ease and even garrulous as he boasted of his familiarity with many of the county's residents, whom Mudd knew well.[10]

Mudd would later insist he had no reason to suspect he was host-ing a man who had killed the president, and another who was an active accomplice. He would maintain that neither Booth nor Herold made any mention of the slaughter that night in Washington.[11] It would be many hours before word of the assassination reached the remote rural community of Bryantown, and even longer for horse-men to spread it among the scattered homesteads.

The doctor was about to return to his farmwork when Herold said Booth wanted a razor and soap and water to shave. "After dinner I went to see the patient," Mudd recollected, "and although he kept his face partly turned away from me, I noticed that he had lost his mustache."[12]

When Herold asked about the possibility of getting a buggy, Mudd rode with him toward the home of the doctor's father, but the only one in working order was unavailable. They rode off to Bryantown to look for a carriage, but, without recorded explanation, Herold changed his mind and turned around, saying he would ride back to the farm, get his colleague, and prepare to set off for the home of a mutual acquaintance, the Reverend Lemuel Wilmer, who lived about five miles west of the swamp.[13]

By the time Mudd, riding alone, reached the speck of a village on an errand for his wife to buy calico, soda, and matches,[14] the community was already in turmoil, overrun by detectives and cavalrymen. Lieutenant David Dana, brother of the assistant secretary of war, had arrived with his mounted force about midday, acting on guesses from rural informants that the fugitives must have taken the road south from Surrattsville to Bryantown. Guards ringed the tiny village, taking up positions on the roads leading in as Dana hauled in locals for questioning. He told them the president had been assassinated by a man named Booth. When they asked whether he was certain of the killer's identity, Dana replied, "Yes, as near as a person could know anything."[15] But some of the apparently German-born cavalrymen, unable to pronounce *Booth,* told inquisitive onlookers the assassin was a man named Boose.[16] Surprisingly, Dana told them another fugitive wanted for Seward's assassination was a man named Boyle, the same vigilante notorious throughout the county for murdering a political foe.[17]

The news jolted the torpid farming community, centered on a local tavern and less than a dozen scattered homes dependent on a general store and a lone blacksmith. Everyone was preoccupied with the astounding news out of Washington. Some living farther out rode home quickly to escape the dragnet. Others, afraid the military might hold them for hours, pleaded in vain to leave.[18] Throughout the afternoon soldiers strode in and out of the general store, where a single topic dominated all conversation. Mudd stepped in to purchase calico.

"Very bad news," the storeowner remarked.

"Yes," Mudd replied. "I am sorry to hear it."[19]

Mudd had to take a roundabout route back home to evade the soldiers blocking people from leaving the village.[20] He drew in his reins at the residence of Francis Farrell, about midway between Bryantown and his own home. Farrell's employer and neighbor Thomas Hardy came outdoors to greet him, thinking perhaps they would talk about the chestnut trees Mudd had ordered felled and cut into rails. But Mudd, unusually animated, had something else to convey. He said there was "terrible news." The president, Secretary Seward, and also his son had been assassinated in Washington during the night. The infamous Boyle, known countywide as a man who had already killed someone else, was believed to be Seward's assassin. Dumbfounded, Farrell asked who had slain Lincoln.

"A man by the name of Booth," replied Mudd.

Hardy asked if it was the same Booth he recalled seeing in the neighborhood in the fall. Mudd told them he did not know. He was not sure if it was the Booth who had visited their county or one of his brothers. Mudd looked genuinely earnest when he told his neighbors the assassination was a terrible calamity that would make things a great deal worse for the country.[21]

By the time Mudd rode up to the five-hundred-acre estate given him by his father, he had resolved a dilemma tormenting him since learning that Booth had assassinated the president. He had known Booth's identity all along, from the moment he treated him in the farmhouse,[22] but, he would maintain, neither of the two overnight visitors had spoken of the assassination.[23] He had no reason to question the tale that Booth had broken his leg when thrown from his horse. They had further misled him by saying they had crossed the Potomac River in the south, the opposite direction from Washington.[24] Mudd did not doubt them because he knew nothing of a conspiracy to kill. However, by stopping over at his house, they had placed him in a perilous position. How could he not be suspected of collusion? How could he dispel the assumption of being in a pact to harbor the fleeing criminals? With the cavalry only four miles from his farm, it would not be long before they might arrive. How long would it be before they learned of his earlier ties to Booth? Even his neighbor had instantly remembered Booth's appearance at the church. Mudd was in danger of imminent arrest as a co-conspirator or accessory after the fact.

Twelve long years would pass before Mudd described to a confidant what happened when he learned in Bryantown that Booth had shot the president. "His first impulse was to say, 'Come with me, and I will deliver him to you,'" recalled the confidant, Samuel Cox Jr., running in 1877 with Mudd on the Democratic ticket from Charles County to the Maryland state legislature. But instead, Mudd told Cox, he had ridden home determined to warn Booth and upbraid him "for his treachery and the danger he had placed him in." According to Cox, the doctor "felt outraged at the treatment he had received at the hands of Booth, and he did threaten to deliver him up." But, Cox recounted, "Booth, in a tragic manner, had appealed to him in the name of his mother not to do so, and he yielded to the appeal, but made them leave his premises forthwith."[25]

Mudd had given Booth and Herold directions to Parson Wilmer's house at Piney Church, suggesting they follow the shorter four-mile route directly west of his home by slipping through a fence. They mounted their horses and followed the slope up a hill toward the fence, too distant to be seen from the farmhouse.[26]

Faced with the likelihood of interrogation, Samuel and Sarah Mudd designed a scheme to deflect suspicion. They would have to portray the transients as strangers whom they neither knew nor recognized. They would emphasize that much of Booth's gaunt, pallid face was obscured by whiskers and a shawl wrapped high around his neck. They would also say the pair had been given food and shelter only because one of them had a painfully fractured leg.

The doctor wanted to preempt the expected arrival of the military by riding into Bryantown immediately and telling them about a pair of strangers who had come to his house, one with a broken leg who had raised their suspicions by shaving off his mustache. Sarah begged him not to go, pleading with him to wait at least until morning. A delay, she implored, would not prevent the search party from capturing Booth, because in his disabled condition he would not be able to get far. She also warned that a rush to Bryantown would provoke revenge by Boyle, who had reportedly killed the secretary of state. Far better, she counseled, to tell a third party so that it would give the appearance of others leading investigators to the Mudd farm. This way nobody could accuse them of betrayal.

Published for the first time, this letter from Samuel Arnold to Secretary of War Edwin Stanton pleads for a job three months *after* the co-conspirator signed on to Booth's plot to kidnap the president. (Photograph by the author. Courtesy of the National Archives.)

John Wilkes Booth, accomplished actor and fervent supporter of the Confederacy, wanted Lincoln removed by any means, including murder. During his frequent visits to Washington, Booth lodged at The National Hotel on Pennsylvania Avenue, in view of the US Capitol. (Courtesy of the Library of Congress.)

Portraits of "the conspirators" as published with the trial record, *The Assassination of President Lincoln and The Trial of the Conspirators,* compiled by Benn Pitman. Clockwise from top left: John Wilkes Booth, Lewis Payne, David Herold, Michael O'Laughlin, John Surratt, Edman Spangler, Samuel Arnold, George Atzerodt and, center, Mary Surratt. Dr. Samuel Mudd was not included. (Courtesy of the Library of Congress.)

Mary Surratt's boardinghouse, which still stands at 604 H Street NW, Washington, DC (minus the steps leading up to the second floor), where Booth visited frequently and where co-conspirators John Surratt, Lewis Payne, and George Atzerodt stayed periodically. (Courtesy of the Library of Congress.)

John Wilkes Booth shoots President Lincoln in the back of the head. This sketch from *Harper's Weekly* inaccurately depicts Henry Rathbone springing to action as Booth squeezes the trigger. (Courtesy of the Library of Congress.)

The rocking chair in which Abraham Lincoln was sitting when the assassin shot him behind the left ear. The chair is now on public display in the Henry Ford Museum, Dearborn, Michigan. (Courtesy of the Library of Congress.)

The fate of the president and commander-in-chief lay initially in the hands of the first surgeon to reach him, Dr. Charles Leale, age twenty-three, who had graduated as a doctor only six weeks earlier. (Courtesy of the Library of Congress.)

An artist's impression, printed in *Frank Leslie's Illustrated Newspaper,* of the Petersen boarding-house, opposite Ford's Theatre, where the wounded president was carried, and where he died nine hours after being shot. (Courtesy of the Library of Congress.)

A rare, full-face photograph of Secretary of State William Seward, who survived Lewis Payne's knife attack that left his face disfigured. (Courtesy of Special Collections, Rush Rhees Library, University of Rochester.)

Assistant Secretary of State Frederick Seward survived an assassination attempt moments before the same assailant slashed his father in their home close to the White House. (Courtesy of the Library of Congress.)

The brick home in which Secretary of State William Seward was stabbed multiple times during the synchronized attempt to murder the Union government's top officials. (From *Frank Leslie's Illustrated Newspaper.* Courtesy of the Library of Congress.)

Ford's Theatre draped with black mourning cloth and guarded by armed troops after the assassination. One hundred years would pass before theatrical performances were resumed in the landmark building. (Courtesy of the Library of Congress.)

Secretary of War Edwin Stanton, who took charge of the manhunt immediately after the assassination, wept into the blankets on Lincoln's deathbed, then uttered the memorable words, "Now he belongs to the ages." (Courtesy of the Library of Congress.)

Andrew Johnson was sworn in as Lincoln's successor by Chief Justice Salmon Chase at the vice president's temporary hotel residence two blocks from Ford's Theatre. Secretary of War Stanton is second from left in this sketch that appeared in *Frank Leslie's Illustrated Newspaper.* (Courtesy of the Library of Congress.)

7. *He is supported by Mr. Seward, on all occasions.*

Johnson had appeared tipsy at his inauguration as vice president six weeks earlier, whether from fatigue, liquor, or the stuffy windowless senate chamber, and cartoonists were quick to portray him as a drunk, here being supported by Secretary of State William Seward. (Courtesy of the Library of Congress.)

Andrew Johnson memorably told the first meeting of his cabinet, an hour after being sworn in as the seventeenth president: "The duties of the office are mine. I will perform them. The consequences are with God." (Courtesy of the Library of Congress.)

Funeral services in the East room of the White House, attended by privileged dignitaries bearing black-bordered invitations. (Published in *Harper's Weekly*. Courtesy of the Library of Congress.)

Washingtonians shade themselves with umbrellas as others sit or stand by buildings draped with black mourning cloth during Lincoln's funeral procession from the White House to the Capitol, where forty thousand people paid their last respects before the casket. (Courtesy of the Library of Congress.)

The president's remains traveled by railcar, attached to a US military railroad locomotive, photographed here two months before the journey to Springfield. (Courtesy of the Library of Congress.)

The Reverend Dr. Phineas Gurley, a friend of the assassinated president, prayed by Lincoln's death bed then officiated at the funeral services in the White House and at Springfield, Illinois. (Courtesy of the Library of Congress.)

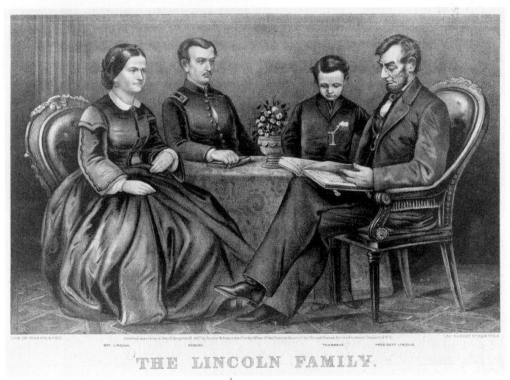

THE LINCOLN FAMILY.

A lithograph published by Currier & Ives about 1867 shows Abraham Lincoln with his wife, Mary, his oldest son, Robert, and his youngest surviving son, Tad, who ran into the White House after learning of the assassination while at another theater and cried out, "They have killed papa dead!" (Courtesy of the Library of Congress.)

A reward poster, illustrated with photographic prints of John Wilkes Booth, John Surratt, and David Herold, spawned dishonor among civilians and the military, many of whom lied about their roles in the manhunt to claim a share of the riches. (Courtesy of the Library of Congress.)

Persuaded by her logic and distress, Mudd decided to enlist the help of his trusted second cousin, Bryantown resident Dr. George Mudd, under whom he had studied medicine. The cousins were close even though Samuel was a Southern sympathizer and George a devoted Unionist.

The two spoke only briefly the following morning just before the Easter Sunday church service, when congregants buzzed earnestly and excitedly about nothing but the stunning news from Washington. Samuel decried the assassination as "a most damnable act."[27] After the service Samuel overtook the other on the road to Bryantown and invited him to his farm. There he asked for his help as an intermediary to tell the military authorities about the suspicious men who had called before dawn, and how one of them had a broken leg, which he had bandaged and set. He told of how the injured stranger had altered his appearance by shaving off his mustache and how they had searched in vain for a vehicle before the duo set off for Parson Wilmer's. George agreed, sympathizing with his cousin, who spoke tremulously of how this turning point could cost him his life from "guerillas," who might even then be in the neighborhood. Samuel would much prefer if George could arrange that authorities send for him. Then, he promised, he would tell all.[28] George Mudd waited until the following morning to call on Lieutenant Dana, but the officer, evidently overwhelmed with other demands, did not act until the next day.

Meanwhile an even more promising lead was developing about ten miles north at Surrattsville, where Detectives George Cottingham and Joshua Lloyd had arrived in search of John Lloyd, unrelated to the detective, who held the lease on Mrs. Surratt's tavern. The detectives had siphoned valuable gossip from Prince George's County residents willing to talk, one of whom, a hotelier in Piscataway, singled out John Lloyd for being "in the habit of entertaining blockade runners."[29] It was enough to send the detectives speeding south to the Prince George's tavern, but they learned Lloyd had gone down to a settlement called Allen's Fresh, only a few miles from the banks of the Potomac River. They placed a guard over the tavern, still unaware that Booth and Herold had picked up a carbine and whiskey at that very location. Then they summoned reinforcements from Washington, and the following morning, Tuesday, April 18, army lieutenant Alexander Lovett arrived with two special officers and nine mounted cavalrymen to take overall charge.

The tavern keeper was on his way back to Surrattsville after fetching his wife from his brother's home outside of Allen's Fresh when Lieutenant Lovett and his squad rode up and blocked the buggy near the village of TB, placed him under arrest, and left him in Cottingham's custody at Roby's post office near the leased tavern.[30]

Less than two weeks later Lovett claimed the frightened tavern keeper "made a partial confession to me in private of his implication in the crime, that he knew the whole party, and to save himself would 'come out' on all of them, and that though he supposed he might be hung, he would not hesitate to tell all he knew of the affair." According to Lovett, Lloyd was so overcome with fear that he cried during most of the confused and disjointed confession. Notwithstanding his physical breakdown, the tavern keeper told of Mrs. Surratt's visit hours before the assassination, when she advised the weapons would be picked up that night. And he revealed that Booth and Herold had called after midnight and taken only a single carbine, because Booth had a broken leg.[31]

However, the lieutenant told no one of this alleged spectacular breakthrough. If the tavern keeper had indeed confessed, Lovett would have pinpointed the path of escape and given the first unassailable account of where Booth had been. Instead, Lovett summoned George Mudd to the Bryantown tavern to follow up on the hearsay tale of two strangers staying overnight at his cousin Samuel's farm. But when George faltered, unable to answer every question because it had come to him secondhand, Lovett and his squad followed him out to his cousin's farm for a direct and personal confrontation.[32]

Samuel Mudd was shaken and unable to keep his composure when the lieutenant and about two dozen riders dismounted. His decision to dissemble took an awkward toll on his demeanor. Even though he tried to stick to fictitious details, his pallor betrayed his unease. Lovett thought he looked "very much excited and got as pale as a sheet of paper . . . and blue about the lips like a man that is frightened at something."[33] He was evasive and reserved, far from being the forth-coming agent he had pledged to be. He claimed he first learned of the assassination at church. And he would not budge in repeating that the uninvited visitors were "entire strangers."[34] Pressed once more to say whether he knew them, Mudd answered, "I think not."[35] The couple stumbled early into contradictions, with the doctor declar-ing the two men stayed "but a short time," and Sarah stating they departed the farm about three or four in the afternoon.[36] The doctor said they walked away from the farmstead, while his wife claimed one of them rode.[37] When Mudd said the two men had set off for Parson Wilmer's house, Lovett brushed it aside as "a blind to throw us off our track."[38]

For now there was more suspicion than certitude, and Lovett and his men left the farm. But his skepticism was such that he later recalled, "I had my mind made up to arrest him when the proper time should come."[39] During the next few days the lieutenant and his men poked among the farm's outbuildings and scoured the surround-ing area, even picking their way carefully through grim stretches of the foul swamp, where they picked up some promising tracks, only to abandon them later for want of compatability.[40] Lovett even conducted a fruitless search of the parson's home, an undertaking he found personally offensive because he already knew of the man's good standing.[41]

Though two days of relentless scouting yielded neither clues nor sightings, Lovett's hunch had solidified into certain belief that Booth was the stranger with a broken leg. On Thursday morning, six days after the assassination, he rode into Washington with his mind made up. He strode into General Augur's headquarters to announce that Booth had broken his leg and been treated by Mudd at Bryantown. Significantly, he still made no mention of the alleged confession by John Lloyd. Nevertheless, Colonel Wells hurried from his office in Augur's headquarters to the War Department, impatient to be the first to tell Stanton. The reaction was predictably decisive. The secre-tary of war sent Wells and Lovett hurrying down to Bryantown to seize the devious doctor.[42]

But Stanton was not focused solely on this freshest intelligence.

The morning newspapers carried an equally plausible story out of Pennsylvania where a manhunt was in progress after Booth was said to have boarded a train and conversed with another passenger, who claimed to have known him for years. A second train sent in pursuit had failed to catch up, and Booth had reportedly disappeared at one of the stops. A detective on the case confidently heralded, "The man is Booth."[43]

The search zigzagged in all directions over several states as officials floundered amid overlapping sightings. In Chicago the military charged into "a house of ill-fame" where Booth was said to be hiding disguised as a woman.[44] Down in Maryland's deep southeast St. Mary's County armed troops also went looking for Booth dressed up like a female.[45] Stanton himself cast a wide net, telegraphing Philadelphia's provost marshal to be on alert for Booth in arriving steamers[46] and informing detective Allan Pinkerton in New Orleans that "Booth may have made his way to the west with a view of getting to Texas or Mexico."[47]

Almost a week had drifted by since the president's murder, and the elusive assassin remained at large. The perpetrator of the most heinous crime in American history had apparently slipped through a thick cordon of troops and lawmen. The War and Navy departments had dislocated shipping and railroad schedules and held up wagons in the frantic quest. They had gunboats prowling the rivers and cavalrymen roaming the countryside, questioning the perplexed and sometimes seizing innocents at whim. Pickets stood watch at roadsides, and guards patrolled on heightened alert. Scouts and detectives formed skirmish lines only yards apart in slow and unrewarding sweeps through the marshes. In Washington the Old Capitol Prison bulged with the sudden influx of suspects. Yet the long claw of the military appeared to have reached out ineptly. The audacious gunman seemed to have outwitted them all as he held on to his precious freedom.

The general public had to be galvanized for a wider and more intensive manhunt. It was time to mobilize the masses and demand more of those already in the field. The same day Wells and Lovett rode out of Washington hoping to corner their prey, Stanton offered one hundred thousand dollars in reward money for the capture of Booth, Herold, and John Surratt. It was a chest of glittering treasure exciting the imagination of all. Even the best of contemporary incomes fell far short of such princely riches. A partnership of two accomplished Washington lawyers reported taking in fourteen thousand dollars in fees during the first five months of 1865, with the expectation that cash receipts would go slightly over thirty thousand dollars for the year. A pair of detectives who participated in Payne's arrest were on a modest annual pay scale of fourteen hundred dollars each, while the night watchman and doorkeeper at the White House were on lowly identical incomes of only seven hundred twenty dollars that year.[48]

Large printed posters offering rewards of fifty thousand dollars for Booth's capture and twenty-five thousand for each of the named accomplices quickly appeared in vast tracts of territory where the chase was under way. As an added inducement for citizens to come forward with confidences, the posters proclaimed an extra hundred thousand dollars in reward money from state and civic authorities.[49] The seductive scent of infinite luxuries overcame many. It quickly made a mockery of honor. Greed and the grasp for riches spawned lies, deceit, and a shameless melee among comrades. Exaggeration and fabrication became the norm, often at the expense of colleagues. The most frequent abuse involved individuals claiming credit due exclusively to others. Aware of the widespread mischief, one chief of detectives made all of his men dictate their performances as soon as they returned from assignments, wisely predicting they might later write contradictory narratives out of "cupidity or jealousy."[50]

Lovett too may have been corrupted by the lure of rewards with his dubious claim to have extracted a private confession from Lloyd. Whatever his motive, he became wholly focused on Samuel Mudd, who was absent from the farm when the lieutenant called on Friday, April 21. He sent the farmhand, Thomas Davis, to find him and bring him back. Mudd was lunching at his father's residence with John Hardy when the doctor's nephew ran in. "Uncle Sam," the child interrupted, unaware of the portentous summons, "Mr. Davis is out here in the yard and wishes to see you."[51] Davis told of many soldiers at the farm who wanted to speak with him.[52]

Mudd had not handled the previous encounter well, but this time he would be even less dignified. No sooner did he meet up with Lovett than his carefully rehearsed story began to crumble, and with it his protective mask. As soon as the lieutenant announced they were going to search the house, Mudd whispered to his wife, and she went upstairs.[53] When she came down she was holding Booth's slit leather boot and the razor with which he had allegedly shaved off his mustache. She told them she had found the boot under the bed while "dusting up" three days earlier.[54] Her husband said it was the same boot he had cut off the stranger's swollen leg. But when the lieutenant turned down the top of the long riding boot he found apparent proof of the doctor's duplicity. Clearly marked on the inside were the name and address of the boot maker: HENRY LUZ, 445 BROADWAY. Close by was the other, more significant name — J. WILKES.[55] Within three days a US marshal in New York City had the boot maker in custody, together with Booth's handwritten order for a custom-made pocket inside the right boot to conceal a pistol.[56]

The pretence was shattered. For more than five days the physician seemingly had withheld crucial evidence, and by so doing he had compounded his own complicity. The incriminating boot had unraveled his deceit, for there could be no mistaking the first initial and uncommon middle name of a killer now notorious throughout the land. Mudd appeared to have no option but to reverse himself. But still he clung stubbornly to the discredited alibi, insisting he had not recognized the strangers.

They put him under arrest and rode back to Bryantown, boxing him in with their horses in case he might impulsively flee.[57] When they showed him a photograph of Booth and asked if it resembled one of the strangers, he denied it, then corrected himself saying there was something of a resemblance "across the eyes."[58] Only then did Mudd speak of his introduction to Booth at a Bryantown church in the fall and confess to an acquaintanceship that had gone beyond a mere handshake. He also told of accompanying Booth to buy a horse from a neighbor. But he did not mention anything about their meetings seven and two days before Christmas.[59]

Mudd tried stonewalling, but the interrogator Henry Wells thought

nothing of threatening to hang obstinate victims by their wrists or
tying them up by their thumbs.[60] Wells quickly detected Mudd's
efforts to withhold important facts unless challenged by very direct
questions. Under the strain of a relentless inquisition, stretched over
three consecutive days, the doctor's reserve inevitably buckled, and
the colonel stood poised like a matador ready for the final thrust. As
Wells later recollected, "I said that it seemed to me he was concealing the facts, and that I did not know whether he understood that
that was the strongest evidence of his guilt." The colonel thought
Mudd looked "very much alarmed."[61] The doctor came as close as
he could to an open admission of knowing Booth all along. "He said
he did not recognize him at first, but on reflection he knew it was the
same person," Wells recalled.[62] Yet Mudd continued to insist that
Booth wore whiskers, even though he had shaved off his mustache.[63]
The inquisitor would not back off until he found out precisely when
Mudd realized he had treated Booth. Had he known in the house, or
only after the assassin rode away? The answer came at yet another
face-off on Sunday morning, when Mudd would normally have gone
to Mass. In a final act of submission, he admitted he knew it was
Booth, even as the actor lay bedridden in the doctor's house.[64]

That morning Wells and his browbeaten captive rode together to
the doctor's farm. Wells wanted to see the terrain for himself and
perhaps pick up clues to the route of escape. The colonel led the way,
following the prints of an easily identifiable horseshoe from the farmhouse up the hill, in the belief that no other horse had been on the
premises, even though Lovett's mounted squad had already covered
much the same ground. They followed the tracks for several miles
through the marsh, into a forest, and over some fields before losing
them near plowed land. Clearly the conspirators had turned abruptly
away from the direct route to Parson Wilmer's house because the
marsh there was, according to Wells, "full of holes and bad places."
The colonel concluded that Booth and Herold had got lost in the
forsaken landscape and found their way back to the main road.[65]

Mudd was escorted to Washington and locked up in the Old
Capitol Prison. Less than two weeks later his ordeal worsened when
he was transferred to the penitentiary on the grounds of the Arsenal,

almost two miles south of the Capitol, where arms were repaired and ammunition and gun carriages manufactured. Far from the familiarity of his open fields, within cell number 176,[66] he could only imagine how long he might have to endure solitary confinement in a space three and a half feet wide and seven feet long.

Sarah was allowed to remain behind with her four children, the oldest only seven years old.[67] Like her husband, she would not give up the ruse that Booth was disguised with a beard and unrecognizable when he arrived at their home.[68] She blamed herself for her husband's detention, howling that if it were not for her he would never have delayed going to the authorities. In desperation to win his release, she recited, under oath, a preposterous account of her husband returning from the excitement at Bryantown to seat himself by the fireside, where he read a book for the next hour and a half.[69] The depth of her loneliness was made worse by the miserable specter of poverty. "I only have a home to shelter me and my little babies," she wailed to the judge advocate general, "and under present circumstances I cannot tell how long I will have that."[70] Sarah's anguish gave way to despair at the absence of a man she had known since childhood. At times it seemed no amount of self-laceration would atone for her guilt at his jailing, and her grief took on tones of dementia. "Before doctor was taken from me I felt if one of our little children were to die, I would die too," she cried out to the man who would prosecute her husband. "Now, I pray the Almighty to take them all. I can better see them all die young than see them undergo the hardship they will have to undergo if they live to be grown."[71]

With Wells preoccupied in breaking down Mudd's defenses, it had fallen to Detective George Cottingham to do likewise with John Lloyd, the tavern keeper. For two days the troubled suspect denied all knowledge of the assassination or personal acquaintance with anyone involved. Cottingham had hoped that fear and confinement would break the hapless man's defenses, but Lloyd would stubbornly deny knowledge of the crime or any of its perpetrators. At length the detective told him his mind was made up and he was perfectly satisfied Lloyd was involved. "The sooner he got rid of it, the better," he recalled telling his prisoner.

"Oh my God!" Lloyd responded. "If I should make a confession, they would murder me!"

"Who would murder you?"

"These parties that are in this conspiracy."

"Well," said Cottingham, "if you are afraid to be murdered yourself, and let these fellows get out of it, that is your business, not mine."

The moment he held out for had arrived. There was no need to reason further, nor even to coax or cajole. Lloyd had become nervously excitable and blabbered under unmanageable stress. He implicated Mary Surratt, recounting her instruction to have the firearms ready for pickup that night. He also told Cottingham how Booth and Herold had taken the carbine, and how the killer had even boasted of the murder.[72]

Defenseless, forsaken, and terrified, Lloyd was ordered down to Bryantown, but no one cared to inquire about the carbine still on his property. On the night of Sunday, April 23, Lloyd was allowed to stop and say farewell to his wife at the tavern as cavalrymen escorted him to detention in Washington. Cottingham and six of the guards were present when Lloyd broke down, throwing his arms around his wife, crying out for his prayer book, and sobbing as he hollered out loudly, "Oh! Mrs. Surratt, that vile woman! She has ruined me! I am to be shot! I am to be shot!"

"Mr. Lloyd," Cottingham interjected, "remember you stated to me that there were two carbines, that Booth could not carry his carbine. Now, where is that carbine?"

Lloyd said it was upstairs in a small room, but Cottingham was unable to find it. He told Lloyd's wife it had to be located because it was definitely in the building. She directed a servant to bring an ax, and they went into an adjoining room to see the hired hand strike seven blows against the plastered wall. Cottingham came forward, pulled off the laths, reached through the shattered plaster, and grabbed a bag on the floor. Inside was the carbine.[73]

Justly proud of his singular find, Cottingham rode to Washington to deliver the weapon to his superior, Provost Marshal James O'Beirne. But he too would fall victim to the unmerited lunge of others for public kudos and cash. Wells was also heading back to the capital when the two met up. The colonel demanded the detective hand over the carbine. Outranked, Cottingham surrendered the proof of his zealous detective work, but asked if Wells would take note of his name. "He said it was not necessary," Cottingham later wrote Stanton. "I also told him I was a special officer on Maj. O'Beirne's force. He said it made no difference."[74]

Wells, in his own report to the War Department, singled out a number of individuals for "valuable services" rendered, but notably omitted Cottingham.[75]

CHAPTER 18

———— ◆ ◆ ◆ ————

"You Must Get Him Across"

John Wilkes Booth and David Herold had lost valuable time in distancing themselves from Washington by taking the detour to Samuel Mudd's house. Herold had warned against veering off course and was vindicated soon after they left the doctor's property, for the two men were now in unfamiliar territory. For all of Herold's vaunted knowledge of the sprawling county, he had never been in this specific sector, and because the sun had already set, he did not even know east from west. The luckless pair had lost the option of continuing through Bryantown after Mudd told them it was overrun by the military, with guards blocking entrances and exits.

Lost and bewildered, Herold found himself back among the cluster of farms near Samuel Mudd's home, hoping to get his bearings from any passing resident. By chance he came upon Electus Thomas, a black employee of Mudd's father, who stopped to talk with Herold while his wife and two other men walked on. In the fading light Thomas recognized Herold as the man he had seen twice that afternoon, when Herold rode toward Bryantown then returned along the same quiet country road. The fugitive had hitched his horse out of view and was on foot.

"Uncle, where am I at?" Herold asked.

Thomas told him he was on the property of Henry L. Mudd.

"Where does the sun rise and where does it set?" Herold inquired.

Thomas explained as best he could.

"I wonder, could I stay tonight?" Herold asked.

"I don't know. I think old master's gone over to the doctor's," the farmhand replied.

"I think I won't bother anyone tonight," Herold concluded. "Isn't there a large swamp near here?"

"Yes," said Thomas, pointing the way past the tobacco barn.

"Well, I will take the swamp," Herold replied ambivalently, either to mislead Thomas or to indicate an intention to continue south, with the swamp close by as a marker. Apparently satisfied that he had recovered his bearings, Herold walked away, remarking, "When I get to the Bryantown bridges, I know them."

By now it was dark, and Thomas lost sight of the stranger even before he reached the tobacco barn.[1]

Compelled by darkness to slow their pace in alien terrain, the conspirators skirted the treacherous swamp, keeping to the east of it as they plodded south. About 9 PM they came upon another black man, Oswald Swan, walking near his home about two and a half miles southeast of Bryantown.[2] Swan had already heard about the assassination but had no inkling the strangers might be connected. It was too dark to distinguish anyone's features. Only when they dismounted at Swan's home did he observe "a small man" and another with a lame left leg, supporting himself on a crutch. Swan gave them bread and whiskey, and they offered him two dollars to lead them to the home of another man two miles away, but they then changed their minds and upped the payment to five dollars if he would guide them more than double the distance, through the swamp, to the residence of Samuel Cox.[3]

It was easy money for a man who knew the land and the remotest of its isolated homesteads. There would be no difficulty in guiding them to Rich Hill, Cox's comfortable perch overlooking a domain of close to nine hundred acres. The double-story home was a splendid landmark, with gated piazzas in the front and back reflecting the prosperity of the slaveholding occupant.[4] Raised from infancy in a nearby foster home after the death of his mother, Cox, forty-five, attained wealth and prominence by shrewd assertiveness, backed by the force of his domineering personality. The honorary rank of captain had stuck even after the disbandment of his company of volunteer militiamen, which had drilled at Bryantown when Maryland teetered on the brink of secession.[5] On the night of the assassination, he owned, by his estimate, between forty and fifty slaves, accounting for his vehe-ment opposition to "the emancipation movement."[6] There could be no doubting his affinity for the South, of which Booth was already aware.

As the trio approached the estate in the early hours of Easter Sunday,[7] Herold warned the guide to keep his mouth shut, threatening, "Don't you say anything! If you tell that you saw anybody, you will not live long!"[8] Herold rapped the brass knocker on the front door forcefully, then stepped back in the unlit courtyard.[9] Swan watched Cox come out holding a candle. The stone-faced landowner had slipped on a pair of pants and a coat and peered leerily into the blackness. Booth dismounted and, satisfied with Cox's identity, hobbled out of Swan's hearing to say that he had shot President Lincoln in Washington. To prove his identity, he held up his wrist imprinted with the distinctive initials JWB. Booth said he would have reached the Potomac River the night before if only he had not been slowed by a broken leg. He pleaded for food and drink, a place to rest and hide, and help in crossing to Virginia.[10] Cox, who had learned of the assassination that night from slaves,[11] did not dither. From farther back in the darkness, Swan watched all three white men enter the house and close the door behind them.

They stayed indoors for three to four hours while Swan languished in the chill of the predawn darkness, presumably waiting for payment.[12] There is no written record of what transpired inside. Cox repeatedly told authorities he turned the strangers away without ever letting them in, "because I had the news that night of the tragedy in Washington."[13] Most likely he gave them food and shelter until it was light enough for them to hide out in the woods. When they left the house, Swan watched as Herold walked ahead until Booth snapped, "Don't you know I can't get on!" Herold went back to lift him into the saddle, then Swan heard one of them declare, "I thought Cox was a man of Southern feeling."[14] They had not expected to be ejected so soon, but Cox's motive was plain. He could not risk harboring men of such notoriety while Federal forces scoured the county in roughshod and vengeful pursuit. His own life and liberty would be in jeopardy if they caught the suspects in his house. Cox assured them he would give aid and comfort, and even help them escape across the river, so long as they agreed to hide out in a forest at a discreet distance from his home. Herold, perhaps, paid off the sleepless black guide before mounting his own horse. Swan never explained why he waited so long in the open.

With Swan on his way home, the outlaws followed Cox's overseer, Franklin Robey, to a dense thicket of pines a quarter mile off the main road and a mile west of Rich Hill. Robey told them to be quiet and stay put. He promised to send someone to help, then rode off.[15]

Before breakfast Cox sent his adopted son, Samuel Cox Jr., four miles southwest to Huckleberry, the home of Thomas Jones, forty-four, a neighboring farmer, fisherman, blockade-runner, and, above all, chief Confederate signal agent north of the Potomac River. Jones and Samuel Cox Sr. were foster brothers who had grown up in the same family after the death of Cox's mother. Jones immediately dismissed the subterfuge of being summoned to talk about seed corn, knowing the visit had to do with Cox Jr.'s whispered hint that "some strangers were at our house last night."[16]

It was still morning on Easter Sunday when Jones rode up to Rich Hill. Cox led his foster brother to an open space where no one could eavesdrop.

"Have you heard that Lincoln was killed Friday night?"

"Yes," said Jones, who had learned of it from passing soldiers the previous night.

Cox told of the visitors, one with a broken leg who identified himself as Booth, the assassin. They wanted help in crossing the Potomac River.

"Tom, you must get him across."

Jones hesitated. Since Robert E. Lee's surrender a week earlier, the war was all but over, aside from mopping-up operations. But aiding the assassin would put Jones's very life on the line at a moment when nothing could be gained in the cause.

Jones was a slim man of medium height, doleful looking but nimble, and proficient in smuggling over the sinewy river all manner of couriers, spies, businessmen, and agents of foreign bankers and governments. The month before he had even ferried the courier John Surratt to the

Virginia shore. Jones made the crossing so often, sometimes two or three times a night, that he could reach the opposite shore in less than an hour. The system had become so fine-tuned that he helped expedite the delivery of Northern newspapers to Richmond within twenty-four hours of publication. Since his arrest four years earlier for crossing clandestinely, he had become much more adept at avoiding detection. On the return trip he often waited until shortly before sunset, when pickets were not yet on duty and the setting sun made it difficult to detect small craft in the flickering glare on the water.[17] Four years of warfare had refined these skills and talents. He would need them in full measure to help Lincoln's assassin escape, because the area had never been infiltrated by so many armed Federal forces. But Jones's loyalty was equal to the challenge, and he gave the answer his foster brother expected.

"Sam, I will see what I can do, but the odds are against me. I must see these men. Where are they?"

Cox described the location and the coded whistle he would have to sound by way of identification.

"Take care how you approach them, Tom. They are fully armed and might shoot you through mistake."[18]

Jones approached with the wariness of a man experienced in skirting the law. When he saw Booth's unattended bay mare grazing in a clearing set aside for tobacco, he mistook it for a stray and tied her to a tree. Then he whistled. Herold stepped cautiously out of the thickets clutching a carbine.

"Who are you? What do you want?"

"I come from Cox. He told me I would find you here. I am a friend. You have nothing to fear from me."

Herold scanned the middle-aged intruder with high cheekbones and strong thick hair. "Follow me."

They brushed aside dense thickets for thirty yards before Jones saw Booth lying on the ground, his head resting on his hand and a pistol and knife within easy reach. His crutch was beside him. He did not look like he had shaved for several days, but Jones noted Booth's mustache, in significant contradiction to the Mudds' allegation that he had shaved it off.[19]

Jones told them he would do what he could to help but insisted they lie low during the tense hue and cry. He described how to reach a spring less than forty yards away, pledged to bring food every day, and promised to get them across the river as soon as security permitted. Booth held out his hand and politely thanked the willing new accomplice. He spoke proudly of shooting the president and with a look of defiance declared, "John Wilkes Booth will never be taken alive!"[20] He was especially impatient for newspapers to read how the world regarded him.[21]

Before Jones left, he suggested they kill the horses or risk discovery by their neighing. They did not try to hold off out of any affection for the animals. The ultimate goal was escape, and the horses had become expendable. Later, Cox told Jones that he was standing on a hill when he saw Herold lead the horses into the swamp. Soon, two shots reverberated through the quiet countryside. Days afterward Cox looked hard for the carcasses after the fugitives had moved on, but neither he nor anyone else found them. Jones imagined they were sucked below in quicksand.[22]

On the second day Jones stuffed his overcoat pockets with bread, butter, ham, and a flask of coffee, and approached with the telltale whistle. This time he found Booth hurting even more, but suddenly they turned mum and still as the hooves of Federal cavalry pounded by on the road.

"You see, my friend," Jones cautioned, "We must wait."

"Yes," Booth replied. "I leave it all with you."[23]

It was the first day of Jones's daily delivery of newspapers, which Booth craved as much as nourishment. He read them voraciously to follow the repercussions in Washington and gauge public opinion of himself. The earliest editions had little available detail and much of it was wrong, contradictory, or guesswork. Booth grew increasingly impatient for updated issues and asked Jones time and again what people thought of the killing. Initially Jones applauded the crime, declaring it "gratifying news to most men of Southern sympathies." But over time he changed his mind after weighing the detrimental consequences to the South.[24]

The more Booth read from the papers the closer he came to remorse for harming innocents he had not even targeted. With Herold his only companion during days of monotonous isolation, he began to reflect openly about what he had done. He regretted Seward had not been killed but said he was "sorry, from the bottom of my heart," that his sons Frederick and Augustus had been wounded.[25] And he told Herold he was "quite sorry" for the man who held his getaway horse at Ford's Theatre because "it might get him into difficulty."[26]

As he lay in the quiet of the pines, tormented by the crippled leg and weakened from living in the open, he took from his clothing a small, brown leather-bound pocket diary for the calendar year 1864. Like so many compulsive diarists of his time, he began to scribble down thoughts — jottings that were the equivalent of the confessional, that read like X-rays of the mind. As with other diarists, Booth had a need to chronicle, as if to make cerebral room for ever more private reflections. His sparse entries remain the only authentic evidence of his state of mind after the killing.

Striking a bold line through an arbitrarily chosen page dated Sunday, June 12, he backdated the entry to Good Friday, writing in his untidy right-sloping script, "April 13–14 Friday the Ides." Immediately he set the record straight by penciling in that the assassination had been a last-minute decision after months of planning an abduction: "Until today nothing was ever *thought* of sacrificing to our country's wrong. For six months we had worked to capture. But our cause being almost lost something decisive and great must be done." Booth bristled at charges he was cowardly by shooting a man from behind. To the contrary, he pictured himself as infinitely fearless and heroic, daring to cut down a tyrant in an enclosure packed with enemies. "I struck boldly, and not as the papers say. I walked with a firm step through a thousand of his friends, was stopped, but pushed on." He corrected eyewitness accounts by insisting, "I shouted sic semper *before* I fired." By his own estimation, he was even more valiant for pressing on though grievously injured. And with the purity of a messianic deliverer, he viewed himself as blessed by providence to rid the country of its errant leader. "In jumping broke my leg. I passed all his pickets, rode sixty miles that night, with the bone of my leg tearing the flesh at every jump. I can never repent it, though we hated to kill. Our country owed all her troubles

to him, and God simply made me the instrument of his punishment."
Though he had ridden only half the distance he claimed, in his own
mind he had overcome every obstacle and challenge of the night. By
way of a declarative valedictory, Booth wrote of himself as a noble
and unyielding patriot, putting country before personal consideration. "The country is not what it was. This forced union is not what
I have loved. I care not what becomes of me. I have no desire to out-
live my country."

In the final entry for that day, he referred to the letter to the
editor of a Washington newspaper that he had given to the actor
John Mathews the day of the assassination — though unknown to
him, the recipient had burned it for fear of being implicated in the
murder. "I wrote a long article and left it for one of the Editors of the
National Intelligencer, in which I fully set forth our reasons for our
proceedings." Booth did not finish the final sentence, which began,
"He or the Govmt . . ."[27]

While Booth and Herold marked time in the forested hideaway,
Jones readied one of his boats for the getaway. Until very recently,
he had lived two miles south of Huckleberry, on a five-hundred-acre
farm flanked on the west by the Potomac River and on the north by
Pope's Creek. His frame house rose above an eighty-foot-high bluff,
making it an ideal elevation from where he could signal Confederates
two miles over the water. Jones had developed the wary instincts of
animals, so that if ever he felt it unsafe to cross he would relay this
setback to Virginia by arranging to have black material hung in the
dormer window of the neighboring house.

He told his trusted help, Henry Woodland, to continue with the net
fishing but to take the boat at the end of every day to Dent's Meadow,
a remote and narrow valley opening on the river between steep and
heavily wooded cliffs. It lay behind Huckleberry, one and a half miles
north of Pope's Creek, and a mile from the public road, where there
were no houses at all. A small stream ran through the meadow but
widened as it neared the Potomac River. It was a perfectly isolated
inlet from where Jones would launch their escape.[28]

As Booth and Herold hunkered down for a third debilitating day
in the cheerless arboreal hideout, Jones rode into Port Tobacco. He

was drinking in the bar of Brawner's Hotel when a Federal officer made an open offer of a hundred thousand dollars "to anyone who will give me the information that will lead to Booth's capture."

"That is a large sum of money," said Jones, "and ought to get him if money can do it."[29]

But he did not take the bait and returned home, proud that he had resisted the temptation of easy money for betrayal. Almost a quarter century later the two men met again in Washington, when the officer, then a detective, said he had made the offer because he suspected Jones knew more than he was willing to confide.

Two more days passed as Booth's untended injury distended and festered, just as Dr. Mudd had foretold. He cried out pathetically, but there was no one qualified to tend it. For five nights and six days the devitalized pair shivered in the cold and damp of the underbrush. Treetops and clouds obscured any possibility of warmth. Throughout the hardship Jones remained faithful to his earlier promise, visiting daily with food, drinks and newspapers. These deliveries and the need to cross the river were the only things consuming Booth's thoughts.[30] He never tired of reading the newspapers, even though it was infuriating to read that he was not hailed as a liberating patriot. Racked by a fractured bone and the discomfort of idle immobility, Booth's mood soured and blackened. "His impatience to cross the river became insufferable," Jones recalled.[31]

On Friday, April 21, Jones rode three miles east of Huckleberry to the village of Allen's Fresh, where the Zekiah Swamp ended and the Wicomico River began. He was in Colton's Store when a cavalryman entered and told his subordinates, who were drinking, "Boys, I have news that they have been seen in St. Marys [County]." Instantly they mounted their horses and rode east to the neighboring county on a wild goose chase that would distance them even farther from their quarry.[32]

It was the break Jones had long awaited, and he rode at breakneck speed to relay the news to his charges. They would have to escape now or never. A fog rose over the marsh and skimmed the swamps as he neared the familiar hideout. It was already dark, and he moved with extra caution because he had never visited at night. Herold responded to the whistle and quickly led him to Booth.[33]

"The coast seems to be clear and the darkness favors us," said Jones. "Let us make the attempt."[34]

Their godsend was keenly alert now that they had broken cover and emerged into the open. He gave his own horse to Booth, who mounted with difficulty and told Herold to walk beside it. Jones went fifty to sixty yards ahead, paused, then whistled for them to catch up. If he did not whistle, they were to quietly get clear of the road and wait motionless until he made contact again.

They covered a mile and a half in fits and starts down a cart track before reaching the public road, then stealthily progressed another mile toward Huckleberry, where the trio grouped together under pear trees, fifty yards from the house.[35]

"Wait here, while I go in and get you some supper," Jones whispered. "You can eat here while I get something for myself."

"Can't I go in and get some of your hot coffee?" Booth pleaded.

"My friend," Jones answered, "it would not do. It would not be safe. There are servants in the house who would be sure to see you and then we would all be lost. Remember, this is your last chance to get away."[36]

Jones went inside and found Woodland eating in the kitchen.

"Henry, did you bring the boat back to Dent's meadow where I told you?" he asked the black man.

"Yes, master."

"How many shad did you catch, Henry?"

"I caught about seventy, master."[37]

Knowing the boat was in place, Jones gathered up food from the table and took it outside without any family member questioning him. It was wartime, and they were accustomed to his quiet and private ways.

The two fugitives pressed on across the fields, rigorously keeping to the slow and wary procedures demanded by their protector. They could not remove a fence blocking their path three hundred yards from the river, so Jones and Herold supported Booth in difficult maneuvers down the steep decline to the water. The flat-bottomed, twelve-foot long, lead-colored boat was exactly where Woodland had secured it to a large oak tree.

Booth sat in the stern with an oar for use as a rudder. Herold readied himself in the bow for a single-handed bout with the currents. The smallish man would be pushed to the limit to reach the other side. Jones lit a candle, shielding it with an oilcloth coat as he held it to Booth's indispensable compass.

"Keep to that," he demonstrated, "and it will bring you into Machodoc Creek. Mrs. Quesenberry lives near the mouth of this creek. If you tell her you come from me, I think she will take care of you."

After warning them to keep the light covered, he bid them goodbye and was about to give the boat a shove when Booth spoke.

"Wait a minute," he said.

He wanted to pay for the boat. Jones had paid eighteen dollars for it in Baltimore the year before. He knew he would never get it back, but he would not accept more than he had paid for it. Booth gave him what he had spent for the boat.

"God bless you, my dear friend, for all you have done for me. Goodbye," said Booth.[38]

Jones gave the boat a final push then stood still, listening to the sound of the oars slapping the water until all was quiet again. He had fulfilled his pledge to help them from the moment he heard "they are on our side."[39] For six days they had been dependent on his protection.[40] He had risked all for the sake of their common cause. Now, with his back to the disappearing boat, he returned up the hill and across the fields to resume the routines of lesser dangers.

Booth and Herold now embarked on the most hazardous leg of their staggered flight. Though the Potomac River narrowed to a relatively slim two miles wide near where they cast off, it was patrolled rigorously by a Union flotilla of steamships, gunboats, dispatch boats, schooners, tugboats, and small craft launched from mother vessels. These vessels plied the ancient waterway from the Washington Navy Yard in the north all along its hundred-mile winding descent southeast until it flowed into the mighty Chesapeake Bay. Supply vessels routinely restocked the flotilla with arms and ammunition, including eleven-inch shells and coal where necessary, so they did not have to sail all the way up to Washington to take on replenishments.[41] Though the ships were at times distant from one another, they communicated around the clock by firing colored signal flares. The flotilla had to be avoided at all costs by people trying to sneak over the river.

Anyone trying to circumvent the prowling flotilla might suddenly be startled by explosions shattering the riverine serenity. One day, while Booth and Herold hid out in the pine thickets, the flotilla's big guns banged every half hour in a synchronized salute to the murdered president, the blasts reverberating up and down the waterway and far into the hinterland.[42] At other times the decks, flying flags at half-mast, filled with sailors firing small arms to keep in the highest state of readiness.[43]

Night brought with it even greater perils for those daring to outwit the flotilla. It was impossible to predict what might lurk within the camouflage of darkness or thick fog. While anchored offshore at night, the ships often doused their lights and bobbed unseen, not even silhouetted in the opaque spectrum. Blockade-runners and others attempting to bridge the waterway without guiding lights might find themselves almost upon the looming shape of a larger enemy craft.

In the final hours of Friday, April 21, when only night predators and lonely sentinels were fully alert, Booth and Herold suddenly saw a steamer straight ahead. They had inadvertently rounded Mathias Point on the large chunk of land jutting out from Virginia into the river when they were startled by the hulking presence of the *Juniper*. It lay at anchor in cloudy weather, undisturbed by a light breeze from the south.[44] They must have been so alarmed by the Federal gunboat that they turned around and headed upriver, with a strong assist from the floodtide, about which Jones had neglected to caution them.[45] Herold's strenuous row over several miles had accomplished nothing. Now they had to distance themselves from the eighty-foot-long *Juniper*, which could blow them out of the water or slice their tiny boat in two.

Six miles later a weary Herold was finally able to release his grip on the oars and relax. He had rowed all the way across the river to Nanjemoy Creek, where the *Juniper* had anchored almost two weeks before, but they were back again in Maryland.[46] The attempt to reach Virginia had been a fiasco. They were now four miles upriver from where Jones had bade them Godspeed. Even worse, they were once more in Charles County, where Federal officials by the hundreds were narrowing their search and closing in on those who knew the whereabouts of the quarry. That night a message went out from Navy Secretary Gideon Welles to a steamer on the Potomac to hunt down and destroy all boats on both shores of the river. Patrols had to be made throughout the day and night. "Inform the people that more than $100,000 is offered for him."[47] From General Augur's headquarters came another order for "a rigid and active blockade of all the Potomac to prevent his escape into Virginia. Please communicate this to the tugs and other quartermasters' boats on duty guarding the river."[48]

Oswald Swan would soon tell where he had taken the pair. Not long after, Cox and Jones were hauled before Colonel Wells, the bullying dispenser of pain, who cared little for legal niceties when breaking down stubborn detainees. He gave Cox an ultimatum to tell all he knew by 4 AM or be tied up "by his thumbs." Under duress, they told more than they really wanted to. "He were a most bloodthirsty man," Jones remembered distastefully after being held for six weeks in Washington's Carroll Prison, where Cox was also held, but for a week longer.[49]

Fortunately Herold was familiar with the area and some of the residents, with whom he had stayed on annual fall retreats to shoot partridge. One of the estates where he often stayed at Nanjemoy Creek for the past five or six years was owned by Peregrine Davis, whose son-in-law, John Hughes, farmed Indianhead, the large property they now approached.[50] But once again sympathy was tempered by the fear of arrest for aiding and abetting, and Hughes offered nothing more than food. He would not allow them to stay over in his house. He was so agitated by their unwelcome call that he later rode eight miles to Port Tobacco to consult his lawyer, who thought it best to escort him to a Federal official to repeat his account and concerns.[51]

While Booth and Herold waited for nightfall to attempt another crossing, the crippled killer took out his pocket diary and again scribbled in the asymmetrical script so at variance with the fastidiously dapper man he had been. Stung by newspaper reports of widespread grief for Lincoln and revulsion and loathing for himself, Booth mixed melodramatic whimpering and self-pity with delusions of grandeur and continued to justify what he had done, even though the papers jolted him with the horrors of that terrible night.

After being hunted like a dog through swamps, woods, and last night being chased by gun boats till I was forced to return wet, cold and starving, with every man's hand against me, I am here in despair. And why? For doing what Brutus was honored for. What made Tell a hero. And yet I, for striking down a greater tyrant than they ever knew, am looked upon as a common cutthroat. My action was purer than either of theirs. One hoped to be great himself. The other had not only his country's but his own wrongs to avenge. I hoped for no gain. I knew no private wrong. I struck for my country and that alone. A country groaned beneath this tyranny and prayed for this end, and yet, now behold the cold hand they extend to me.

God *cannot* pardon me if I have done wrong. Yet I cannot see any wrong except in serving a degenerate people. The little, the very little I left behind to clear my name, the Govmt will not allow to be printed. So ends all. For my country I have given up all that makes life sweet and Holy, brought misery upon my family, and am sure there is no pardon in the Heaven for me since man condemns me so. I have only *heard* of what has been done (except what I did myself) and it fills me with horror. God try and forgive me, and bless my mother.

Tonight I will once more try the river with the intent to cross; though I have a greater desire and almost a mind to return to Washington and in a measure clear my name, which I feel I can do. I do not repent the blow I struck. I may before my God but not to man. I think I have done well, though I am abandoned, with the curse of Cain upon me, when if the world knew my heart, *that one* blow would have made me great, though I did desire no greatness.

Tonight I try to escape these blood hounds once more. Who, who can read his fate. God's will be done. I have too great a soul to die like a criminal. O may he, may he spare me that and let me die bravely.[52]

While they awaited nightfall they may have been recognized, but the Port Tobacco resident who told officials he had seen two men at

Nanjemoy Creek on the evening of Friday, April 21, "one answering the description of Booth," had let six days slip by before writing to the provost marshal.[53]

The second attempt to set foot in Virginia would be even more challenging for Herold, who claimed he had nothing more than a single paddle and a broken oar to propel the boat downriver.[54] Again they were dogged by the *Juniper,* which cruised from nightfall to midnight off Mathias Point before heading upriver.[55] It may have been the same gunboat Herold said came within three hundred yards of them before they passed Mathias Point.[56] It was a grueling effort for Herold, who rowed nine or ten miles before Booth steered the boat up Gambo Creek, a small stream about a mile from Mrs. Quesenberry's home and a little beyond Machodoc Creek, where there were too many boats for their liking.[57]

Though they had crossed a most formidable natural barrier and put the Potomac River behind them, Booth and Herold were still within the grasp of the hunters. However, luck had favored the duo when they were most in need. Had they crossed only a day or two later, they would have had to zigzag among many more vessels churning the waterway after a catastrophic collision downriver. Coincidentally, on the day the escapees landed in Virginia, the steamer *Black Diamond* sailed south of Washington, passing by Nanjemoy and Gambo creeks with a specific mission to look out for the pair of conspirators. Shortly after midnight, when the vessel was patrolling about fifteen miles south of Gambo Creek, it was accidentally rammed by the *Massachusetts,* an army transport side-wheel steamer carrying about six hundred Union troops. The 184-ton *Black Diamond* sank within seven minutes. Many aboard the *Massachusetts* jumped overboard and eighty-six men drowned, including a drummer boy so numbed by the frigid water that he could not clutch hold of a lifeline. Other flotilla craft changed course to join in the rescue, and even more came down from Washington to recover bodies.[58]

Only the foolhardy would have attempted a crossing at this moment of denser river traffic, but Booth and Herold had the good fortune to make landfall when all was still relatively quiet.

CHAPTER 19

———— ❖ ◆ ❖ ————

"I Don't Want to Know Anything About You"

About 1 PM, Sunday, April 23, David Herold appeared outside Elizabeth Quesenberry's house. She was not home, but one of the widow's daughters invited him to await her return.

"I suppose you ladies pleasure a good deal on the river," Herold remarked.

No, she replied, because they did not even own a boat. Herold told her he had crossed the Potomac River during the night and, perhaps hoping to offset its value for food or a horse, offered her the little boat on the riverbank. When Mrs. Quesenberry arrived, she later told law enforcement officials, Herold claimed he and "his brother" were escaped prisoners in need of some kind of conveyance to go "up the country." He had even offered to buy a horse if she had one to sell. His brother, he explained, could not walk because he had broken his leg in a fall from a horse. To Herold's astonishment, the woman refused to help at all and ordered him off her property. As Herold walked back across the field to the creek, the widow apparently had second thoughts and called out to him, telling him she would send him something to eat.

It is unknown whether she knew anything at all about the assassination or the roles of Booth or Herold. Like the statements of many others made voluntarily or under duress, hers may have been self-serving, evasive, or false. This woman of unquestionable attachment to the South said she ate dinner before giving food to one of her houseguests, Thomas Harbin, to take to the two men down by the creek. Disingenuously, she told Federal authorities she "supposed" Harbin and another guest, Joseph Baden, were soldiers who had been staying with her since the fall of Richmond, and that they had even been there before.[1] She withheld all information on Harbin's background as a top Confederate agent and of Baden's activities in the area's Confederate signal corps,[2] facts that she had to have known when agreeing to let them stay over.

Harbin remained less than half an hour with Booth and Herold. Four months earlier, when he had met Booth at the Bryantown tavern, he had pledged to help spirit the kidnapped president out of Maryland and into the embrace of Virginia. Now, despite the magnified risk, he would show himself impeccably trustworthy and a man whose word was his bond. Thomas Jones had been rightfully confident the runaways would be helped once they crossed the Potomac River, because he had married Harbin's sister. Better than most, he knew his brother-in-law's political convictions and stealth in smuggling mail and personnel over the watery divide. The hunted men were fortunate to have such a willing accomplice to provide sustenance and horses in one of the most deserted stretches of the state. Sparsely populated, it was all but virgin landscape.

Booth's fanaticism had made him impetuous and blind to danger, the results of which were beginning to tell. In the folly of deciding to assassinate mere hours before carrying it out, he had given only minimal thought to updating and refining his escape. Worse still, no one in the Maryland and Virginia counties south of Washington had been tipped off to the arbitrary switch from abduction to murder. He had no plans for relays of supporters waiting along the ride south with food, fresh horses, and shelter. It had been months since he had spoken directly with anyone in Prince George's or Charles County, Maryland. When he impulsively decided to strike in Ford's Theatre, he had surprised even his small coterie of conspirators in Washington. The invaluable help received so far from Dr. Mudd, Samuel Cox Sr., and Thomas Jones had been extended from bonds of political kinship rather than from any meticulous briefing beforehand. Mrs. Quesenberry had been eager to see him off, even if she knew his identity and the cause of his desperate flight. Even Harbin was quick to see Booth and Herold ride over the horizon. Nobody wanted to be contaminated by harboring Booth at close quarters. Distance would not only boost the runaways' chances of escape, but protect abettors from being caught in the company of an assassin.

Harbin and Baden took the stranded pair to the nearby farm of William Bryant, another in the tight circle of dependable Southerners, then left shortly before sundown having done their duty. But Bryant set limits to cooperation. He refused Herold's plea for a horse to take him and "his brother with a broken leg" to a doctor's country home eight miles away.

"Well," said Herold, "I'll give you ten dollars to carry me to Dr. Stuart's."

Bryant agreed and rode off to find Booth sitting in an open field about a quarter mile away. He lifted the injured man into the saddle, and the three rode off in silence. Curious about their destination, Bryant asked why they had to see Dr. Stuart when there were other doctors more conveniently located. As usual, the talkative Herold replied, explaining that Stuart had been recommended to treat his brother John's broken leg.[3]

Richard Stuart, reputedly the wealthiest man in King George County,[4] had just finished an evening meal with his wife, three daughters, a son-in-law, and a visitor at his country home, Cleydael, when Bryant rode up with Booth and Herold. It was already dark. Again Herold represented the two, telling the physician they were tired and hungry and needed somewhere to sleep. His brother had broken his leg.

Six days earlier Stuart had heard about the assassination, and he later claimed to be suspicious of both men, whom he did not know. After his arrest in a massive roundup of suspects, Stuart told prison authorities in Washington, "I did not know but that they might be some of the characters who had been connected with the vile acts of assassination." He noticed Herold was armed with a carbine and strapped with a satchel.

"Who are you?" Stuart said he asked Herold, who had dismounted.

"We are Marylanders in want of accommodations for the night."

"It is impossible. I have no accommodations for anybody." He said he had also turned away some soldiers from Maryland that day.[5]

Herold said Dr. Mudd had referred them to Stuart to treat his brother's leg and aid them on their journey.

Stuart was skeptical, because they did not offer a letter of introduction, a formality among men with connections. He told them he did not know Dr. Mudd, though he had heard of the Mudds of Maryland. And he bowed out because he was a physician and not a surgeon. But Herold continued to plead, begging for something to eat and drink.

"I don't want to know anything about you," the doctor remonstrated.

"If you will listen to the circumstances of the case, you will be able to do it," Herold urged.

The physician was adamant. "It is impossible." His house was full, the family was large, and he did not like the look of the men.

"Who are you? Where are you going?" he queried.

"We are Marylanders and want to go to Mosby," said Herold, referring to the daring commander of a Confederate cavalry unit.

"Mosby has surrendered," said Stuart.

Herold asked if he could help them get to Fredericksburg, but the doctor declined. He suggested they ask a black man living nearby who sometimes hired out his wagons. He might help if he was not busy.

But suddenly, without explanation, Stuart had a change of heart and invited them in to eat. It is doubtful the two ragged and smelly fugitives, famished, tired, and in no mood for small talk, sat down with the family and their guests.[6] They had been on the run for a week, living like escaped convicts chased by dogs. Most likely they ate and drank inelegantly in the kitchen while Stuart ran several hundred yards in the dark to recall Bryant so he could take them away.

Breathless from his run in the dark, Stuart told Bryant, "You must take these men away. I know nothing about the men. I cannot accommodate them. You will have to take them somewhere else." Bryant said he too knew nothing of the strangers. They had come to him out of the marshes and asked if he could bring them to Stuart's house.

The two returned to the doctor's house, and Stuart hurried Booth and Herold out the door. "The old man is waiting for you," he said, referring to Bryant. "He is anxious to be off. It is cold. He is not well and wants to get home," Stuart told the unwelcome pair. By Stuart's estimation they had not been in his house more than a quarter of an hour.[7] But Booth was enraged at being shown the door with such humiliating speed. Though limping and hurting physically, he would not forget this insult and slight to a man of his stature.

Later that Sunday night, William Lucas woke up in his humble log cabin when his dogs began to bark. He heard a neigh and thought someone was trying to steal his horses. A strange voice called out, "Lucas?" The free black man asked who was there. An anonymous person gave three names and asked if Lucas knew any of them. The old man did not recognize any and was too frightened to open the door. Only when the stranger asked if he knew a man called Bryant did Lucas open the door.

"We want to stay here tonight," a voice from the dark demanded.

"You cannot," said Lucas. "I am a colored man and have no right to take care of white people. I have only one room in the house, and my wife is sick."

Without identifying himself, the stranger continued, "We are Confederate soldiers. We have been in service three years. We have been knocking about all night and don't intend to any longer. We are going to stay."

Uninvited, Booth had already hobbled into the house. Lucas noted that he wore only one boot and a single shoe.

"Gentlemen," Lucas pleaded, "you have treated me very badly."

Booth was seated and pulled back his coat to reveal two revolvers and a bowie knife.[8] He held up the knife.

"Old man, how do you like that?"

Lucas had a particular fear of knives. "I do not like that at all."

"We were sent here, old man," said Booth. "We understand you have good teams."

Lucas said they could not have his team of horses. They would be needed in the morning for hired hands working on the corn fields. Suspecting that the intruders were out to steal his horses, Lucas said they were out to pasture.

"Well, Dave," said Booth, "we will not go on any further but stay here and make this old man get us this horse in the morning."

Too scared to fall asleep with armed men in their home, Lucas and his sick wife went outside and stayed on the step all night long.

In the morning Booth and Herold ordered them to hitch two of the scrawny[9] horses, then climbed into the wagon. Lucas asked whether they were going to take his horses without payment. He was asked how much he wanted for driving them ten miles to Port Conway on the bank of the Rappahannock River. The black man asked for ten dollars in gold or twenty in greenbacks, and he wanted his twenty-year-old son to accompany them. Booth refused, saying they might want to drive farther on. But Herold intervened, sensing the hardship that might befall the black man. "Yes, he can go, as you have a large family and a crop on hand. And you can have the team back again."

Unwisely, Lucas commented, "I thought you would be done pressing teams in the Northern Neck since the fall of Richmond."

Booth bristled. "Repeat that again!" he dared.[10]

Lucas kept quiet.

At dawn Booth was still smarting from being ejected by Stuart, and the reluctance with which the doctor had allowed them to eat their hurried meal. The cultured actor would not allow the snub to go unnoticed nor the indignity to be suffered without rebuke. He took out his pocket memorandum book and penciled a sarcastic note to the physician, offering five dollars as payment for the meal. But then he thought better of it, replacing the note in his book and writing essentially the same text, only this time reducing the payment by half. "Forgive me, but I have some little pride. I hate to blame you for your want of hospitality; you know your own affairs." Venting all his pent-up scorn, Booth wrote that he was "sick and tired, with a broken leg, in need of medical advice. I would not have turned a dog from my door in such a condition. However, you were kind enough to give me something to eat, for which I not only thank you, but on account of the reluctant manner in which it was bestowed, I feel bound to pay for it. It is not the substance, but the manner in which a kindness is extended, that makes one happy in the acceptance thereof." Of all the plays he had memorized, Booth selected a quotation from Shakespeare's *Macbeth* to return the stinging insult: "The sauce to meat is ceremony; meeting were bare without it."[11] With parting condescension, as if throwing change to a beggar, he concluded, "Be kind enough to accept the enclosed two dollars and a half (though hard to spare) for what we have received." He signed it "Stranger," dated it April 24, 1865, ripped the page from the book, and wrapped it around the money, fastening the little bundle with a pin. Then he told Lucas to deliver it to Stuart, which he did later that day.[12]

That same morning they paid Lucas's wife for the transport and set off for the ten-mile trip to Port Conway.[13]

Unknown to Booth and Herold, Federal forces had picked up a vital clue — they would add another a day later — that narrowed the geographic focus of their hunt and minimized the assassin's hopes of vanishing into the wild. John Lloyd, lessee of Mrs. Surratt's tavern in Surrattsville, was so cowed and submissive when taken into the custody of Wells that he even suggested where authorities should search. He pinpointed the home of Austin Adams, owner of a tavern in Newport, about six miles from the banks of the Potomac, as a place where Booth might stop before crossing the river.[14] One of Adams's employees, James Owens, tried stonewalling Colonel Wells until overcome by terror when told he would be hung by his handcuffed arms.[15] He babbled a stream of critical leads, outing a blockade-runner by the name of George Bateman, who had helped conceal the newly purchased getaway boat in the winter. Owens confessed that Bateman told him Jones had put Booth and Herold safely across the Potomac River in a boat taken out of hiding at Pope's Creek. But he gave no date for the crossing. Clearly within the loop of the county's network of Confederate secret agents, Owens told Wells that he himself had ferried three other men across the Potomac River from a point nearly opposite Mathias Point on the day the president died. The crossing more likely occurred the following day, Easter Sunday, when a farmer's son reported seeing men in a boat crossing over to Virginia.[16]

When roving detectives learned of this sighting, they incorrectly thought Booth and Herold may have been in the boat, even though the conspirators were then hiding in the dense thickets of pine near Cox's farm. They passed on their false assumption to Samuel Beckwith, a cipher operator from the military telegraph office in Washington, who had been rushed down to Port Tobacco to tap into telegraph lines and set up a quick link between lower Charles County and the War Department.[17] Beckwith flashed to Washington a coded dispatch asserting that the fugitives might still be in Charles County but that "other evidence leads to the belief that they crossed" to Virginia on Sunday morning, April 16. He reported correctly that the small boat used in the crossing had been captured by Major O'Beirne, even though, unknown to the pursuers, it had nothing to do with the targeted runaways.[18] When Beckwith eventually returned to Washington, the head of the military telegraph office, Major Thomas Eckert, was fulsome with praise, telling the cipher operator, "If Booth is caught it will be owing to the establishment of the station and the message received from it, sent by you."[19]

Colonel Lafayette Baker, head of the National Detective Police attached to the War Department, read Beckwith's telegram and rashly assumed that Booth and Herold had been positively sighted crossing the Potomac River. The fresh intelligence gave Baker, thirty-eight, a self-serving opportunity to highlight his own profile in the drama that had overshadowed all other national discourse. A former provost marshal of the War Department, Baker had distinguished himself at the outbreak of the war by crossing Confederate lines in Virginia and returning with information vital to the Union army. During another scouting foray into Virginia in 1863, in search of an elusive Confederate cavalry commander, Baker fainted from causes later linked by medical and military observers to the onset of meningitis, from which he died in 1868.[20] Stanton's confidence in him was such that he had telegraphed Baker in New York five hours after the assassination: "Come here immediately and see if you can find the murderers of the president."[21]

But the admiration Baker earned for daring enterprise would be offset by the rage of underlings he double-crossed. Practiced in the art of deceit, he applied it with equal measure toward subordinates. Within hours of arriving in Washington, Baker tricked two detectives into parting with exclusive information on the conspirators, then reneged on his promise of assistance even as he profited from their disclosures. They could only fume at his "duplicity . . . for his own gain and reputation."[22] It was vintage Baker, who later made preposterous claims that he was the first to be notified of reliable information that the runaways had crossed into Virginia, and that he had beaten everyone in distributing photographs of the wanted men.

Now that he was privy to the secret contents of Beckwith's telegraph, which he misconstrued, Baker requested the military to provide a squad of twenty-five cavalrymen under the command of "a reliable, discreet commissioned officer," whom he wanted to report to him forthwith.[23] Within an hour Baker had selected two of his "most reliable" detectives and was briefing them in his office to give chase. One detective, his cousin, Lieutenant Luther Baker, had served under him as a Secret Service detective before enlisting in the District of Columbia cavalry.[24] The other, Everton Conger, a wounded combat veteran who had enlisted at the outbreak of war, had risen to the rank of lieutenant colonel and was highly esteemed by his colleagues. Both Luther Baker and Conger had been mustered out shortly before the assassination when their cavalry unit had been consolidated with another in Maine.[25] "I want you to go to Virginia and get Booth," Colonel Baker instructed. "I have information that Booth crossed the river there" — he pointed with his pen on the map — "and that he landed about there."[26]

Half a mile away a bugler sounded "Boots and Saddles," and Canadian-born Lieutenant Edward Doherty, twenty-five, selected by the military as the "reliable, discreet commissioned officer" requested by Lafayette Baker, led his mounted horsemen from the Sixteenth New York Cavalry to join the detectives.

At the 6th Street wharf they boarded the steamer *Ide*. The officers showed photographs of Booth, Herold, and Surratt. Conger and Doherty told the cavalrymen that all would share in the reward money, now totaling almost two hundred thousand dollars from the War Department as well as state and civic authorities, if they captured the wanted men.[27] Instead of uniting all in spirited pursuit, it quickly incited avarice and soured relations within days between the detectives and the leader of the cavalry, as each contemptuously belittled the other's contribution. But at long last pursuers were on the right track.

They set sail down the Potomac River about sundown on Monday, April 24, and disembarked at Belle Plain, Virginia, four hours later.[28] Baker, sensing Conger's discomfort at being subordinate, especially as he had far outranked the lieutenant when they served together in the cavalry, now spontaeously ceded commmand. Conger, twenty-nine, was not only more experienced but also more familiar with Virginia. The year before he was gravely wounded in a skirmish when a ball passed through one hip and out the other, leaving the five-foot eight-inch, slightly built officer partially paralyzed, with a tendency to fall down if his right leg gave way. His left wrist bore the slash mark of an enemy sword, and he still carried a lead ball in his abdomen from an earlier engagement.[29] "Colonel Conger, you take charge of the cavalry," Baker declared. "You have been over the ground."[30] The gesture heartened the dark-complexioned Conger, forging a closer bond between the two.

About a mile and a half beyond the Potomac River the group parted at a fork in the road, with Doherty leading a team toward Fredericksburg and the detectives with five cavalrymen heading for the Rappahannock River. They waylaid anyone passing by and rode up to isolated homesteads, asking if anyone had recently sighted two men, one of whom had a lame leg.[31] Conger even pretended he and his men were rebels on the run who had lost sight of some of their companions — one of whom had an injured leg.[32] But they drew blanks, with nothing to buoy their spirits nor quicken the chase.

However, late in the morning of the eleventh day after the assassination they approached the banks of the Rappahannock River. The hunt was about to intensify dramatically.

CHAPTER 20

———— ◆ ◆ ◆ ————

"I Am Worth Just $175,000 to the Man Who Captures Me"

William Rollins was preparing his fishing nets in the backyard of his home at Port Conway by the banks of the Rappahannock River when Lucas's son drove up in the wagon with Booth and Herold about noon. Rollins came around to the front of the house and saw the trio, who had now traveled almost twenty miles southwest after crossing the Potomac River.

Herold had just exited the wagon and was now returning to it, carrying a tin dipper filled with water.

"It's too full. I'll drink some of it," said Herold.

"Bring it along here!" Booth snapped.

Herold turned to Rollins and asked if he knew where they could get transport to cross the river to the Virginia county seat of Orange Court House, about fifty-five miles west. Rollins did not know. Then Herold asked if Rollins could provide the conveyance. Again he said no, that he never went that far; but if they paid him ten dollars he would take them to Bowling Green, fifteen miles southwest, on the other side of the Rappahannock River.

They stepped closer to the wagon, where Herold introduced Booth as his brother, who had broken his leg at the siege of Petersburg and needed to rest somewhere for a day or two. Rollins suggested the hotel at Bowling Green, only two and a half miles from the Fredericksburg–Richmond railroad. He could take them across the half-mile-wide river for the usual ten-cent ferry charge, but only after he had finished with his fishing tasks.

"I don't want to be lying over here," said Booth, his slouch hat pulled low over his forehead. "We'll pay you more than the ferriage."

But Rollins could not oblige. The tide was rising, and he and his assistant urgently had to spread their nets. He promised to return shortly, then ferry them over.[1]

He left, and while he was gone three men dressed in Confederate uniforms rode up. Until recently Lieutenant Mortimer Ruggles, Absalom Bainbridge, and Willie Jett had fought with legendary John Mosby's elusive hit-and-run Confederate cavalry, but now that the war was all but over they were headed south to Caroline County, Virginia, across the river. Herold stepped from the wagon and approached them.

"If I am not inquisitive, can I ask where you are going?" he asked.

"That's a secret," Jett answered.[2]

Herold introduced himself as Boyd and said he and his brother, who had been wounded in the leg while escaping from prison, needed help crossing the river because their wagoneer would not take them farther.

Jett recalled that Herold walked with him to the wharf and said, "I suppose you are raising a command to go South?"

"I cannot go with any man that I don't know anything about," said Jett.

Herold could not hide his nervousness, and his voice quivered as he declared, "We are the assassinators of the president." He pointed toward Booth and said, "Yonder is J. Wilkes Booth, the man who killed Lincoln."

Jett was aghast. Booth struggled out of the wagon and limped over. Jett noticed the initials JWB marked on the back of his left hand.

According to Ruggles, Booth remarked, "I suppose you have been told who I am."

Yes, said Ruggles. But Booth suddenly drew his revolver and matter-of-factly declared, "Yes, I am John Wilkes Booth, the slayer of Abraham Lincoln, and I am worth just $175,000 to the man who captures me."[3]

The three newcomers were surprised and awed by his frankness and casual, easy manner. He was in obvious physical pain, and his dark and sunken eyes told of the hardships he had suffered on the run with a fractured and now infected leg. He looked haggard and wasted, with a dark beard, shapeless black hat, rumpled clothes, and a single dirty cavalry boot.

Ruggles assured him that none of them wanted any "blood money." He offered to take both of them across the river and beyond. Booth tucked the revolver back in his clothing. He told the trio he could not walk any farther. Ruggles dismounted and carefully eased the injured assassin into his own saddle. Close up, the untended wound looked ghastly behind the stained and filthy dressing with its crude pasteboard splint.

They moved over to the walkway where a black man, Peyton Washington, was plunging a pole into the water to propel the flat scow closer to them. By this time Lucas's son had departed with the wagon, and Rollins had finished with his nets. Herold picked up his blanket next to the house, and as he shouldered his carbine he told Rollins: "I have met with some friends out here, and they say it is not worthwhile to hire a wagon to go to Bowling Green, as we can all go together."[4] Rollins said it made no difference to him. He recognized Jett, who passed through frequently on his way to Bowling Green, where he was known to be courting a young woman.

With Booth and Herold now sharing the saddles of two of the three Confederates, the five men crossed the muddy-colored Rappahannock River in the unsteady scow, which was large enough to take on another four or five horses. After pulling up on the south bank, Jett rode ahead into Port Royal, one of the sprinkling of tiny riverine communities whose homes dotted the shoreline at this remote location along the almost four-hundred-mile-long river. He had hoped to arrange accommodation for Booth and Herold at a safe house, but the owner quickly refused. Jett walked across the street to another house, but the owner was out. They decided to ride ahead a few miles to Garrett's farm, on the road to Bowling Green.[5]

Richard Garrett came out to greet the three horsemen who rode onto his property in midafternoon that Monday, April 24. According to him, one of the strangers said he was Captain Ira Scott, who in turn introduced the others as Lieutenant Ruggles and a friend, Booth, whom he described as Mr. Boyd, a Confederate soldier wounded near

Petersburg. They asked Garrett if Boyd could remain over for two days while they went "on a little scout toward Richmond."[6]

John Garrett, Richard's oldest son, had only recently returned home from service in the Confederate army and was alerted to the strangers' arrival when the family's dogs barked. He raised the windowpane in his bedroom and saw Booth in the yard leaning on two crutches and wrapped loosely with a gray shawl. The other men were riding away.

After supper Booth sat on the steps of the porch, with its commanding view of the road from Port Royal to Bowling Green. He took out his pipe and asked for tobacco and a light. Later he and John walked up to the sons' bedroom, where Booth unbuttoned his belt, holding two pistols and a bowie knife, and hung it over the head of a bed. He sat in the chair and asked John to pull off his boot. When Booth took off his pants, John noticed the ugly wound wrapped in a stained and dirty bandage. Booth held to his story that he was a Confederate soldier from Maryland, wounded by shell fire during the evacuation of Petersburg. He said the injury was only painful when touched. He took one of the beds for himself, giving John and his younger brother, William, no option but to share the other.

The next morning after breakfast, while John Garrett was having his boots repaired at a neighboring shoemaker, he met a third party who said he had seen a Richmond newspaper announcing a reward of $140,000 for the arrest of the president's assassin. It was the first official confirmation John Garrett had of Lincoln's murder, which had first spread as a rumor through the countryside two or three days earlier.

During the early-afternoon dinner at the homestead, John Garrett mentioned the reward money.

"I wish he would come this way, so that I might catch him and get this reward," said William Garrett.

Booth instantly became the seasoned actor, in firm control of facial expressions and body language as he assumed the role of a dispassionate outsider. "If he were to come out, would you inform against him?" he asked William.

The Garrett son chuckled. If that much reward was offered, Booth had better not come their way . . . or he would be gobbled up, he replied. Booth asked how much reward money had been offered. John repeated the sum of $140,000.

"I would sooner suppose $500,000," said Booth without a hint of unease or self-awareness.[7]

According to Mrs. Garrett's sister, Lucinda Holloway, who was present at the dinner, the discussion turned to whether the assassin had been paid. One of Richard Garrett's daughters said she supposed the killer had been well paid.

"Do you think so, Miss?" Booth interjected. "By whom do you suppose he was paid?"

"Oh," she answered, "I suppose by the North and South."

"It is my opinion," said Booth, "he wasn't paid a cent, but did it for notoriety's sake."[8]

As they rose from the dinner table, Mrs. Garrett asked Booth if he would like to have his wound dressed. Incomprehensibly, he turned down the offer, thanked her, and said it did not give him "the slightest pain."[9]

While they sat on the porch, Booth looked at a large map and remarked that he wanted to reach Orange Court House, where he said he could probably obtain a horse from one of many Confederates gathered there from Maryland, then continue on to Mexico. He told them he did not want to return to his home state, because he would have to take the oath of allegiance to the Union, something he had sworn he would never do.

Booth reached inside his clothing, brought out the leather-bound memorandum book, and made a final wistful entry. "I bless the entire world. Have never hated or wronged anyone. This last was not a wrong, unless God deems it so. And it's with him to damn or bless me. And for this brave boy with me who often prays (yes, before and since) with a true and sincere heart. Was it crime in him. If so, why can he pray the same. I do not wish to shed a drop of blood, but I must fight the course. 'Tis all that's left me."[10]

At that moment some riders passed by on the road beyond the gate, heading toward Port Royal.

"There goes some of your party now," said John, referring to the men who had accompanied Booth to the Garrett farm the day before.

Booth rose. "Go up and get my pistols!"

When asked why he wanted his weapons, Booth replied that he always felt "safe when armed."[11]

By the time John got upstairs he could see that the riders had already passed by, so he came down without the firearms, telling Booth the horsemen had disappeared. Booth settled down again. But five minutes later Herold walked through the gate toward the house, apparently done with his scouting. Booth stood up and this time ordered William to run up and fetch his pistols. The boy came down with the belt and weapons, which Booth quickly buckled on as he hobbled over to meet Herold. The two huddled for a few minutes, then approached the house. Booth introduced Herold as his cousin, also named Boyd, and asked if he too could sleep over.

John Garrett did not trust the strangers. He was most suspicious of Booth, not only for being armed and apparently devious, but also because he had looked nervous when the horsemen passed by. Garrett did not want the two to stay overnight, but he could not bring himself to say so. He fudged, telling Booth and Herold that only his father could give permission, and he did not know when he would be back.

"Never mind," replied Herold, who said he would sit on the porch steps until the father returned.

About an hour before sunset Ruggles and Bainbridge rode up to the house. Herold and Booth stood to greet them. The horsemen brought word that about forty Federal cavalrymen were crossing the Rappahannock River by ferry. Instinctively, Booth and Herold set off by foot to the rear of the barn, in the direction of the woods.

Five minutes later Herold returned to the house and asked John what he thought of the report. The Garrett son did not think it was true, but even as they talked a former slave came by and confirmed that cavalrymen had gathered at Port Royal. Fearing that Booth and Herold were up to no good and would soon embroil the Garrett family in whatever trouble they were in, John asked, "If you have gotten into any difficulty, you must leave at once, for I do not want you to bring any trouble upon my aged father."

Booth said they had "gotten into a little brush" in Maryland, but it was all over.

Herold laughed. "There is no danger," he said. "Don't make yourselves alarmed about us. We will not get you into any trouble."

But when Herold asked for something to eat, John made it clear they were unwelcome. No food had been cooked, and none would be available before supper. If they wanted anything to eat, they would first have to promise they would leave. As he spoke, the cavalry rode by.

"There goes the cavalry now," said John Garrett.

"Well, that is all," said Herold.

Again, John asked him to leave, but Herold wanted to know whether they could buy a horse in the area. It was no use, said John. So many horses had been stolen by Union and Confederate soldiers passing through the county that there were none to spare. When Herold asked if he could hire transportation, John directed him to try a black man by the name of Freeman, living nearby, who sometimes hired out conveyances. He might charge six dollars in specie to go as far as Guinea Station, some thirteen miles west. Herold, unfortunately, did not have any specie, but he brought out one of the new ten-dollar US notes, named after Treasury Secretary Chase.

John Garrett decided to make the trip to Freeman's home, and he went alone, only to find the man was out. Freeman's wife said that the cavalry had stopped by and that they had asked if the couple were sheltering any white men.

John returned home. Realizing that the only way to get the nettlesome strangers off his farm would be by conveying them himself, he asked when they expected to leave. Both wanted to stay overnight and move out in the morning.

They ate supper together and then went out on the porch. Herold was talking such gibberish that John thought he had drunk too much liquor. At first Herold claimed to have been under Captain Robinson in the Thirtieth Virginia Regiment, but he modified his statement when John said he knew the regiment and there was no officer by that name.

"To tell the truth, I was there only one week," said Herold. "I was then on picket, and the first night I was wounded." He pulled up his sleeve to show a scar on his arm.

About eight or nine o'clock the troublesome visitors said they were ready for bed, until John asked where they intended sleeping.

"In the house," said Booth.

"No, gentlemen. You can't sleep in my house," said John.

"Well, we'll sleep under the house then," Herold replied.

Again, John dashed their hopes, saying the dogs would bite them.

"Well, what's in that barn?" Herold asked.

"Hay and fodder," said John.

"We'll sleep in there then."

Booth limped into the forty-eight-by-fifty-foot wooden tobacco house accompanied by Herold, who carried his rolled-up buffalo-colored blanket and the carbine slung over his shoulder.[12] The structure was fitted with tobacco-curing equipment and stuffed with bushels of hay, fodder, corn, sugar-corn seed, farm machinery, and beds, chairs, and other household furniture, which two old women had left for safekeeping after their Port Royal house had been shelled by Union army gunboats.[13]

But John Garrett remained uneasy, guessing they wanted to steal his horses and escape in the dark. While William quietly locked the barn door, John crept up to a slit in the wood and tried to make out what Booth and Herold were saying to each other as they lay on the plank floor. They were talking too softly, however, so the brothers went back in the house, said nightly prayers with their father, who had returned, and went up to bed.

John remained restless, so he and William took their blankets and lay down in the corn house between the barn and the stables, the younger one clutching a pistol. They would try to wait out the night, but they prepared themselves to take on two armed horse thieves.[14]

Meanwhile the cavalry had come tantalizingly close to the farm. They had reached Port Conway on the northern bank of the Rappahannock River at midday while Rollins sat on the steps of his house near the ferry. Lieutenant Luther Baker approached with a photograph of Booth, whom the fisherman said he recognized as the man who had crossed the river the day before, even though he was uncertain whether Booth had a mustache, because he had pulled his cap low over his forehead.[15] Rollins's wife told them that Willie Jett, one of the three Confederate soldiers who had accompanied Booth and Herold across the river, was courting a Miss Goldman, whose father kept a hotel at Bowling Green.[16]

Given the option of voluntarily accompanying the cavalry across the river or being compelled to do so, Rollins asked to be put under arrest to avoid the impression he had willingly collaborated. "There are a great many [Confederate] soldiers about," he told Baker.[17]

They crossed the Rappahannock on the rickety flat scows that could take on only seven horses at a time,[18] and at 9 PM dismounted outside The Trap, a roadside brothel, midway to Bowling Green. The presence of lawmen caused consternation among the young women until one detective said they were only on the lookout for a group of men who had sexually assaulted a girl. Pacified and now eager to help, the women described five men on three horses who had stopped by for drinks the day before. All had returned later except one, whom the detectives surmised might be the injured Booth, left behind at Bowling Green.[19]

Around midnight the exhausted detectives and almost a dozen cavalrymen dismounted half a mile from the little settlement of Bowling Green and walked quietly toward the hotel. Only Conger remained in his saddle, the remainder led their horses.[20] They separated silently to surround the rambling building, silhouetted in the still of the night. But even though the officers knocked and pounded on the doors, all the occupants slept on. Eventually a black man appeared on the road and led them to a shanty in the rear, where another black man said Willie Jett and a woman and her daughter were in the building. In a few moments a woman opened the door and took them to a room where Jett and her son were in bed.

Conger was brusque and forceful, cutting Jett short when he started to talk about why he was on his way to Richmond. The detective demanded only the whereabouts of the men he had helped cross the Rappahannock River.[21] With no possibility of escape, Jett agreed to lead the cavalry to the hideout on the Garrett farm, twelve to fifteen miles back along the same road they had just taken. Booth, he said, had never gone farther than the farm, and Herold had ridden back there.

Before riding off shortly after midnight, the officers warned Jett that they would kill him if he led them into an ambush. Along the way they called in mounted pickets posted along the roads. Jett had told them to look for a gate about four hundred yards from the road, leading to the farmhouse, but there was a momentary scare when Conger and Baker, riding ahead, could not locate it. They went back for Jett, who explained that he had mistaken its location.

As they reached the gate, Conger rode back to order the cavalrymen, "Show yourselves smart! We are going to surround a house."[22] Edward Doherty cautioned his men of the Sixteenth New York Calvary to be quiet until he gave the command.[23] "They are in that house, and we must take them. Shoot any person you see running away!"[24] Doherty ordered them to draw their pistols and check that they were loaded. Then he gave the command, "Open file to the right and left! Gallop!"[25]

CHAPTER 21

———— ◆◆◆ ————

"Tell My Mother I Die for My Country"

Richard Garrett, the father, woke up at the sound of his dogs barking. He went to the window, saw the cavalrymen, put on his pantaloons, and with a candle in one hand opened the door and went out onto the porch. Lieutenant Baker demanded to know where Booth and Herold were hiding out, but Garrett was slow and evasive, saying they had gone into the woods.

"What! A lame man go into the woods!" Baker roared.[1]

Conger turned to one of the cavalrymen. "Bring in a lariat rope here, and I will put that man up to the top of one of those locust trees."[2]

"Will you show me where they are?" Baker snarled, as if offering one last chance.

Garrett asked for his boots, and they were handed to him through a door to prevent him going inside again. As he dressed, his son John was brought from the back of the house wearing a Confederate uniform. He had just come out of the corn house and told a sergeant that he wanted to see the commanding officer to report on men hiding out in the tobacco house.

Doherty seized young Garrett by the collar and ordered the sergeant back to his post.[3] Then he pulled his captive down the steps, put a revolver to his head, and demanded to know where they were hiding.[4]

"In the barn," said John.

Hurriedly, they surrounded the wooden tobacco house. Then, as the officers stood near the front of the structure with its supports of heavy cedar posts, they took turns addressing the invisible runaways in the darkened hideout.

"You men had better come out of there," Baker insisted. "We know who you are."

"Who are you?" Booth asked.

"Never mind who we are," said Baker. "We know who you are, and you had better come out and deliver yourselves up."[5]

After William Garrett was ordered to bring the key for the tobacco house, Baker told the older brother to enter and tell the cornered men to surrender. John protested. They would surely shoot him. But Baker was in no mood for excuses. He gave an ultimatum to obey or be shot.[6]

With no choice, John Garrett stepped into the unlit tobacco house, not knowing where to turn, nor from which direction Booth and Herold might open fire. Suddenly Booth rose up and John reflexively announced that the building was surrounded. Resistance was useless. Booth had better come out and surrender.

"Get out of here, or I will shoot you, damn you! You have betrayed me!" Booth raged.

The instant Garrett saw Booth's hand go behind his back, as if to draw the revolver, he fled out the door and begged Conger not to order him back in.[7]

Baker relented and ordered the door locked again. Then, realizing he had made an easy target of himself by holding a candle in his hand, he walked about fifty feet and put it down.

To hasten the capture, the commanders decided to burn the building and force the conspirators out if they did not hand over their weapons and surrender immediately. Doherty alone argued against burning. He wanted to hold off until daylight, when, he suggested, they could storm the building from different directions. His senior sergeant, Boston Corbett, volunteered to go in immediately by himself, but Doherty would not allow it.[8]

The cavalrymen had meanwhile dismounted, only two at a time so that others in the saddle could still keep watch on the barn. They led their horses away from the building that would soon be a raging fire and dangerous to the animals. It is not clear whether they were under orders to hold their fire. Later that same day Conger told authorities that the cavalrymen "had no orders either to fire or not to fire."[9] But two years later Baker testified that Conger repeatedly ordered all the men not to shoot under any circumstances.[10]

Booth's reply came through audibly from the hollow interior. "Captain," he shouted. "That's rather rough. I am nothing but a cripple. I have but one leg, and you ought to give one a chance for a fair fight." With bravado and defiance, he suggested they stand in line fifty paces away and he would come out and take them on, even though he was lame.[11] Baker answered that they had not come to fight but to take him prisoner. Booth asked for five.minutes to think it over.

When the time elapsed, Booth called out, "Captain, there is a man here who wants very much to surrender."

Baker unlocked the door, taking care to keep the lock in the hasp. Then he overheard Booth cursing Herold, telling him to "go away from me," and calling him "a damned coward."[12] Booth raised his voice again, telling Baker there was someone with him who wished to surrender.

John Garrett, standing next to Baker, coaxed the officer to agree, saying they would have that much less to contend with. Surrender, he knew, might also save the family's barn.[13]

"Very well, let him hand out his arms," said Baker.

"I have no arms," said Herold.

"We know exactly what you've got," Baker replied.

"On the honor of a gentleman," said Booth, "he has no arms. I own all the arms."[14]

At that moment Baker would have valued the advice of his superior, but Conger was already on the far side of the tobacco house preparing to set it alight. He had told John Garrett to bring straw and pinecones, but as the farmer's son walked with an armful, Booth warned through a crack in the wall, "Young man, I advise you for your own good not to come here again."[15]

In the rough-and-tumble for portions of the reward money both Baker and Doherty claimed the central role in the dialogue with Booth. Doherty, backed solidly by his subordinates, said he opened the door and told Herold to put out one hand after the other. The cavalry lieutenant claimed, "I took hold of both of his wrists and pulled him out of the barn."[16] Baker refuted this, saying when Herold came to the door "I took hold both [sic] of his hands and drew him out."[17] Both narratives were at odds with the eyewitness accounts of John Garrett and Sergeant Boston Corbett, who said Herold came out with his arms raised.[18]

With Herold in captivity, Baker gave the lone holdout a final ultimatum: Exit within two minutes or the barn would go up in flames.

"Well, Captain," Booth taunted, "you may prepare a stretcher for me. Throw open your door; draw up your men in line, and let's have a fair fight."[19]

Conger's patience had run out. Clearly, Booth would not surrender. At the rear of the wooden building, Conger pulled out some hay, twisted the stalks, then set them alight and stuffed the burning bundle through one of the cracks. "It blazed almost like powder," he recalled.[20]

Baker distinctly heard Booth's last words from the barn: "One more stain on the old banner."[21]

Corbett, the senior cavalry sergeant, peered through a crack in a side wall and by the light of the flames saw Booth "stooping or springing" as if about to fire his weapons. The sergeant steadied his revolver, took aim, and fired. The bullet cut clean through Booth's neck, entering just behind the sterno-cleido muscle, two and a half inches above the clavicle. It crashed through the bony bridge of the fourth and fifth cervical vertebrae, sliced the spinal cord, and passed out the right side, three inches above the clavicle, leaving Booth instantly paralyzed.[22]

Just moments before Corbett fired, Baker had opened the door and seen Booth stoop in the direction of the blaze, then limp toward the door, a carbine in one hand. He had taken about five or six steps when Baker heard the shot and saw Booth fall.[23] Another eyewitness, John Garrett, watched Booth raise his arms and slump in a bending position.[24]

Conger also had watched Booth. He saw him frantically trying to look through the split walls, and realized that Booth had been blinded by the blaze. The lieutenant colonel had a clear view of Booth struggling toward the source of the flames. He had thrown down his crutch and was holding the carbine in a firing position. It looked to Conger as if Booth realized he could neither see outside nor stem the blaze. As the trapped man turned toward the door through which Herold had surrendered, Conger hurried in the same direction. At that moment Conger heard gunfire and thought Booth had shot himself.

Immediately after the shot Baker charged into the crackling building and found Booth. He turned him over and instantly recognized the wanted murderer from the well-publicized photo. Booth was clutching a pistol; the carbine had dropped between his legs.

When Conger entered the tobacco house, he saw Baker standing over Booth's body.

"Is he dead?" asked Conger. "Did he shoot himself?"

"No," Baker replied. "What on earth did you shoot him for?"

"I did not shoot him," said Conger.

The thought flashed through Baker's mind that if Conger had indeed fired the shot, it had better be kept secret. He turned to Conger and with a hint of fraternal understanding remarked, "All right."

But Conger repeated, "I did not shoot him."

"Well," said Baker, "The man who fired it should go back to Washington under arrest."

Conger lifted the limp body. "Where is he shot?" he asked. His answer came with a quick glance at blood on one side of the neck.[25]

Booth had grasped the pistol so tightly that Baker had to twist and pull to pry it free. Doherty, who said he rushed in dragging Herold as Booth fell, picked up the carbine and pulled a knife from the wounded man's belt. Booth's head was cradled in the arm of a cavalryman as Conger, aided by the two lieutenants using their free arms, hastily dragged the body from the brightening tobacco house.[26] They laid him on the ground about thirty feet beyond the door. Baker sat by him, resting the almost inanimate head on his knee.[27] They called for water, and Baker sparingly put some into the gaping mouth. Booth almost spat it out and opened his eyes. As he lay on the grass, his lips moved. Conger moved closer, tilting his head to put an ear next to Booth's mouth. With difficulty, he heard Booth whisper, "Tell mother . . ." Again he struggled to speak. "Tell my mother, I die for my country," he gasped. Conger repeated the words, asking Booth if that was what he had said. "He signified yes," Conger attested later.[28]

But as the heat intensified they called some cavalrymen to help carry the dying man onto the farmhouse porch, about two hundred feet from the burgeoning flames. When someone ordered a mattress brought out for him to lie on, Booth objected. "No, no. Let me lie here. Let me die here," he groaned.[29] Lucinda Holloway, a teacher and Mrs. Garrett's sister then boarding at the house, helped bring out a straw mattress, which was doubled up and used as a pillow to support Booth's head.[30] She alternated with the two officers in bathing his face and gunshot wound and moistening his lips and tongue with a wet handkerchief. Conger tore open the collar around the neck and removed a diamond pin from Booth's undershirt.[31]

As the detectives bent low to listen to Booth's barely audible whisper, they again heard him direct that they should tell his mother he died for his country, and that he had done what he thought was for the best.[32]

When Booth mumbled for water, Baker dipped a cloth into a cup of water and rinsed it in the dying man's mouth, repeating this every few minutes. It was still dark. The sun would not rise for about an hour after Booth was shot. As Booth seemed to revive, he strained to repeat, "Kill me . . . Kill me . . . Kill me."[33]

"No, Booth, we do not wish to kill you," Baker replied.[34]

Booth opened his eyes and looked surprised at the mention of his name.

Baker continued to dab his face, comforting him gently. When the detective left for a few minutes to wash the blood off his own hands, Lucinda Holloway took his place, moistening Booth's lips and tongue and stroking his forehead and temples. As she bent close over the stricken man, she too heard him gasp faintly, "Tell my mother I died for my country. I did what I thought to be best."[35]

Though immobile with a severed spinal cord, Booth was still alert to his surroundings and the passing conversations among the detectives. At the mention of Willie Jett, Booth opened his eyes, somewhat startled, and strained to ask, "Did Jett betray me?"

"Oh, never mind anything about Jett," Baker answered.[36]

At one point Booth made a feeble attempt to speak. Baker cocked his ear near Booth's mouth.

· "My hands," Booth mumbled.

They were by his side. Baker gently held up the deadened arms and bathed the crippled hands.

Exasperated by the paralysis, Booth despaired, "Useless! Useless!"

He asked Baker to turn him on his side, but when this was done, he begged to be turned on his back again, then immediately asked to be placed facedown. Baker refused, saying it would be too uncomfortable. As life faded from the twenty-six-year-old, he winced and grimaced especially during the spasms of sharp pain when his head was turned. Several more times he begged to be killed.

· Conger had briefly joined the cavalrymen in trying to stamp out the fire, once even futilely throwing a table over the flames.[37] He had also found Herold unbound, the result, according to Baker, of his being tied so tightly to a large locust tree that he had complained, and Doherty had removed the restraining rope. This so enraged Conger that he ordered the commander of the cavalry unit to tie him up again, with his hands behind his back. Conger stood by to make sure his order was executed, then he detailed a corporal to stand guard over Herold.[38]

Now Conger confronted Corbett, asking, "What in hell" he had shot for without orders. The sergeant stood ramrod-straight, saluted, then answered, "Colonel, Providence directed me." At a loss for words, Conger returned to Baker, who inquired, "Where is the man?" In a dismissive and almost jesting tone, Conger suggested Corbett was way beyond their control, saying, "I guess we had better let Providence and the secretary of war take care of him."[39]

Later, when Baker had a chance to take a closer look at the man who shot Booth, he did not notice anything startling or unusual. Corbett seemed to be a disciplined military man and even dignified and earnest in managing those under his charge. But he was quick to note the sergeant's "odd expression."[40] Corbett would never deny that he had shot Booth. Nor was he evasive. He had opened fire, he said, because he thought Booth might shoot someone, or even escape.[41]

Meanwhile, the prolonged death watch beside the unrepentant assassin angered an unidentified officer, who cussed within earshot of Lucinda Holloway, "The damn rebel is still living!"[42]

Like others tending Booth in his last moments, Lucinda could not resist the temptation to snatch a memento of his historic presence. She hid Booth's opera glasses with interchangeable lenses for use as high-powered binoculars, only to deliver them up to the military when later threatened with arrest.[43]

While Conger and Baker waited for a cavalryman to bring a surgeon from Port Royal, they assembled Booth's possessions, each detective reaching into the pocket closest to him. Baker retrieved a pocket compass stained with the congealed drippings of candle wax. He also pulled out forty-five dollars in greenbacks, a dirty handkerchief, a Meerschaum pipe, matches, and a handful of wood shavings that he thought had been whittled at leisure to keep ready for a fire. Conger already had Booth's twin revolvers, a bowie knife, and the loaded Spencer carbine. In pencil he wrote his own initials on Booth's three bills of exchange. Conger also removed from Booth's clothing the small pocket diary. The colonel glanced at it, then gave it to his colleague.

Though physically unable to object, Booth realized his pockets were being emptied and again rasped, "Oh . . . kill me."

Holding the memorandum book over Booth's body, Baker flipped the pages, noting that it was a diary, and that several leaves were missing. But neither he nor Conger made any effort to read the script or question Booth about the scribble. Conger made a bundle of all of the pockets' contents in his open handkerchief, then tied it up.

As dawn began to break Booth's mouth and lips turned purple. He wanted to cough and asked Conger to put his hand on the swollen throat. "Press hard!" Booth mumbled. Conger complied, but Booth was too feeble even to force a cough.[44] Barely able to talk, he gestured with his mouth for more water.

It was already daylight when the surgeon, Dr. Charles Urquhart of Port Royal, arrived by the flaming remains of the capsized barn.[45] The officers asked whether Booth would die within an hour and a half. If this was likely, they would wait. But if the doctor thought he might live longer, they would transport him back to Washington. Booth appeared to be unconscious while the physician probed the wound. Urquhart seemed unsure of his own findings, at first saying

Booth might live, then changing his mind to advise that he would not live an hour.[46]

Conger decided to leave at once for Washington. The long vigil had made him impatient to report back. Even if Booth lived, the manhunt was over, and the colonel could barely wait to spread the news. Twelve days had passed since the assassination, and the telegraph wires had heightened suspense. Throughout the country people eagerly awaited the outcome, braced for any word that would bring finality to the historic chase. Conger picked up the bundle of Booth's effects and rode off for Belle Plain, Virginia, on the Potomac, accompanied by a lone horseman, Sergeant Boston Corbett.

Only about fifteen minutes passed before Booth lay completely still, his head resting against the folded straw mattress. There was no longer any movement of the mouth nor painful twitches on the unshaven face. The surgeon announced that John Wilkes Booth was dead. The corpse was wrapped in an army blanket, but once again the lieutenants would quarrel, later disputing which of them had sewn it closed. Doherty, who claimed to have "administered to Booth until he died," said he carried out the task alone. Baker maintained that they shared in this final macabre detail.[47] Before them lay the man who had bowed to resounding applause of enthusiastic audiences from Richmond to Boston. Now all was quiet. His end came without ceremony in the cool dawn and quiet solitude of a remote tobacco farm in rural Virginia. Booth would begin the return to Washington like refuse, his body dumped among corn and fodder in a rickety wagon, drawn by an aged horse commandeered from a black man living nearby.[48]

It was not the last of the indignities inflicted on the cadaver. Booth's remains would suffer the consequences of the bitter rivalry for celebrity and rewards between the two lieutenants. At Port Royal, Baker pushed ahead with the wagon, driven by its owner, while Doherty and his cavalrymen lost time waiting turns to be ferried in the lone scow across the Rappahannock River. The cavalry's advance had been slow since leaving the farm because Herold and the captive Garrett brothers had been squeezed onto the back of a single horse that struggled to make headway with its overload.[49]

By late afternoon Baker realized he had overshot the Belle Plain landing by three miles. Desperately he hid Booth's body in the bushes, ordered the wagoneer to stand guard, then rode down to Belle Plain, where he requisitioned a boat from the steamboat *John S. Ide,* rowed upstream, placed the corpse in the craft, and headed back to the planned rendezvous with the cavalry.[50]

Doherty was about to send out a search party for Baker when he arrived with Booth's stiffening body.[51] As daylight receded they all boarded the steamer, together with Sergeant Corbett and the horse Conger had left in his care. The passage upriver to Washington would take seven hours. Once there, Baker and Conger would belittle Doherty as "the mere commander of soldiers" subordinate to them who "took no part in the communications with Booth."[52] They dismissed the cavalry as "dead-beats."[53] Doherty made out that he had taken the lead from the outset, and even reported that Baker "stole away with [Booth's] body."[54]

CHAPTER 22

A Secret Burial at Midnight

Everton Conger could not resist the temptation to filch a memento of the assassin he had hunted down. He took his chance on the *Keyport* as the steamer he had boarded at Belle Plain headed upriver to Washington. Alone now on his way to spread the electrifying news, and in sole possession of the assassin's diary, Conger untied the bundle of items pulled from Booth's pockets and opened the pages of the dead man's last handwritten jottings. The lawman read the final, intimate reminiscences of one of the most infamous murderers in history and decided to make a copy for himself. No one aboard could guess his intentions, and none had authority to stop him.

"I took this copy because of what seemed to me its peculiar character," he explained later. "I thought it was something I would like to keep."[1] But his conscience bothered him, and when he eventually asked Colonel Baker if he could keep the copy, a veto came down from the secretary of war, who demanded he hand it over forthwith.[2]

As soon as he arrived in Washington, Conger took the precious bundle directly to Colonel Baker's spacious, arched-ceiling office opposite Willard's Hotel. He gave a quick rundown of the manhunt that had ended with the fatal shot in a burning barn. It was about 5 PM on Wednesday, April 26, when the two men hurried to the War Department, but they were too late — Stanton had already gone home. They climbed in a buggy, with Baker holding the reins, and drove directly to Stanton's home about half a mile northeast.

The redoubtable secretary was lying on a sofa when the lawmen entered. Baker spoke first, declaring triumphantly that they had "got Booth."[3] Stanton sprang up to examine the proof, now spread out on the open handkerchief lying on the center table. He took the diary and moved to a side table, peering intently through his wire-rimmed spectacles to read every word Booth had written.[4]

More than half an hour later Stanton addressed the colonel. "Baker," he said, gesturing toward the rest of Booth's possessions on the table, "You take care of these things."[5] Pointedly, he withheld the diary, which was turned over to Major Thomas Eckert, who arrived shortly after the two detectives. Within the hour Eckert had sealed it closed and locked it securely in his office safe.[6]

Later, when Colonel Baker asked Stanton's permission to retain one of the items as a personal keepsake, the secretary refused, insisting that "not a thing should go out of the office." He would not even let Baker see the diary to reprint sections for his subsequent ghost-written memoirs.[7]

Once more Stanton orchestrated the movement of underlings as tension heightened in the ongoing national crisis. He ordered Colonel Baker to intercept the vessel, *Ide,* and accompany the corpse and prisoners for the remainder of the voyage to the Washington Navy Yard. Eckert was told to arrange for Booth's body and the captured suspects to be taken aboard the *Montauk,* which had survived intact when a hurricane roared through the previous month, inflicting severe damage on the city.[8]

At 1:45 AM on Thursday, April 27, the *Ide* pulled alongside the gray ironclad, anchored in waters just off the sprawling Navy Yard a few miles southeast of the US Capitol. Booth's decomposing body was carried aboard. Tired and fettered, Herold shuffled down to storage space in the ward room, where he was placed under a marine guard. Security was so tight that no one was allowed to board the monitor without a pass from the War Department.[9]

It was still dark when a dispatch arrived in the military telegraph office from the commandant of the Navy Yard: "The body of Booth is changing rapidly. What disposition shall be made of it?"[10] Stanton and Welles met before breakfast, then jointly ordered the commandant to allow the surgeon general and ten others identified by name to board the *Montauk* to view the body. "Immediately after [the] surgeon-general has made his autopsy," they continued, "you will have the body placed in a strong box, and deliver it to the charge of Col. Baker, the box being carefully sealed."[11]

Eckert hurried to round up the select few permitted to board with him: Surgeon General Joseph Barnes; Judge Advocate General Joseph Holt; Special Judge Advocate John Bingham; Colonel Baker; Lieutenant Baker; Conger; a clerk in the War Department, William Moore; the renowned photographer Alexander Gardner and his assistant, J.L. Smith; and a clerk at the National Hotel, Charles Dawson, who would be able to identify the body because he had frequently asked the actor to sign the registration book.

They boarded so rapidly at 11 AM that the commandant later charged them with snubbing and slighting his staff, showing neither respect nor proper etiquette to fellow officers, especially when the surgeon general began to cut loose the blanket around the corpse without submitting authorization. Eckert vigorously denied the accusations, while allowing, "the exigencies of the case required quick action."[12]

Colonel Baker hurried to summon and escort aboard the ironclad a twelfth person, Dr. John May, fifty-two, even though his name was not on the list authorized to view the autopsy. Sometime within the previous eighteen to twenty-four months, May had removed a large fibroid tumor from the left rear of Booth's neck, which the actor found "annoying" because it had begun to show above the collar of his theatrical costumes.

Before the procedure Booth had insisted that if ever anyone asked the surgeon why he had operated, he was to say that "it was for the removal of a bullet from his neck." May, a former professor of surgery and anatomy, reluctantly agreed, even though it clearly had no connection with a bullet. But May had pointedly warned Booth that if the wound tore open before it had healed, it would eventually leave an ugly scar. A week later Booth returned to the stage, and the wound reopened when an actress embraced him too forcefully. As predicted, it healed as an unsightly, corrugated scar.

When Dr. May came aboard about midday, Booth's body, completely covered by a tarpaulin, lay on a carpenter's workbench on the forward deck of the ironclad.[13] But when the surgeon general removed the cover, May was flabbergasted. There was no resemblance at all to the "remarkably handsome young man" on whom he had operated. Astonished and incredulous, he told Dr. Barnes, "There is no resemblance in that corpse to Booth, nor can I believe it to be that of him."

Again he looked long and hard at the stiff, drawn figure. The skin was yellow and discolored; the face sunken, with evidence of exposure and want of food. Once lustrous, wavy black hair was now dry, matted, and disheveled. The left leg was so contused, it had become perfectly black from the fracture. If it was Booth, the transformation was stunning. There was no trace of the vigorous young man who had made such a lasting impression on the able physician.

Then suddenly, as if inspired, May asked, "Is there a scar upon the back of the neck?"

"There is," replied the surgeon general.

"If that *is* the body of Booth, let me describe the scar before it is seen by me," said May.

He outlined minutely where the scar would be, its size, and its general appearance. May remembered the case well, particularly as Booth had refused to heed his warning to take a break from acting until the wound had healed.

"You have described the scar as well as if you were looking at it," said his fellow physician. "It looks as if you have described it, more like the cicatrix of a burn than that made by a surgical operation."

The cadaver was rolled over to expose the neck, and May instantly recognized the unmistakable mark of his scalpel. He had no doubt at all that he was looking at the body of his former patient, John Wilkes Booth. But he remained shocked by the changed appearance, and asked for the body to be placed in a sitting position. The rotting flesh was appalling, but as May looked down he finally began to make out some of the classic features that had so impressed him when he last saw Booth in 1863. Yet "never in a human being had a greater change taken place," he recorded later.[14]

There was other visible proof that the body was, indeed, that of Booth. Charles Collins, a signal officer and clerk to the ironclad's captain, had looked at the corpse when it was carried aboard and noticed the distinctive JWB initials indelibly written onto Booth's left wrist.[15] Collins told Judge Holt that he had known Booth personally for six weeks, and by sight for three years. He had last spoken very briefly with him in the office of Booth's hotel, the National, about four hours before the assassination, when he said the actor greeted him.[16]

During the autopsy Surgeon General Barnes held the dark, festering left leg while removing the soiled bandage and makeshift splint set by Dr. Mudd two weeks back. But surprisingly, the surgeon general reported a fracture of the fibula, three inches above the ankle joint. Dr. Mudd, five days earlier, had told lawmen that Booth had a fracture of the tibia about two inches above the ankle.[17] After tracing the path of the fatal bullet through Booth's neck, vertebrae, and spinal column, Barnes was certain not only that paralysis had been immediate, but that Booth had died sensitive to pain and aware of his imminent demise. "All the horrors of consciousness of suffering and death must have been present to the assassin during the two hours he lingered," the surgeon general wrote.[18]

Stanton had already arranged for the body to be taken away swiftly and secretly after the autopsy. It was to be smuggled to a secure place with tight security, out of the watchful probe of those who would mourn his death. Rumors were rife that Booth's admirers and Southern sympathizers might try to seize the corpse as a trophy. Other reports suggested enraged Unionists would attempt to board the craft to mutilate the cadaver.[19] Stanton decided that the Old Penitentiary at the Arsenal grounds would be the most fitting burial place, screened as it was from public view and tightly guarded by Federal forces. He was determined to deny Booth's followers any opportunity to glorify him as a martyr. By whisking the body to an inaccessible hiding place, Stanton hoped to frustrate any attempt to make a shrine of the murderer's grave. "I thought it would be a source of irritation to the loyal people of the country if his body was permitted to be made the instrument of rejoicing at the sacrifice of Mr. Lincoln," Stanton offered by way of justification much later.[20] Accordingly, he detailed Colonel Baker to bury the corpse at the Arsenal, "where it will not be disturbed until Gabriel blows his last trumpet."[21]

By 2:30 PM[22] the body was once more wrapped in the gray army blanket, but it was spirited away so abruptly that it was not even put into the plain coffin specially prepared in the joiner's shop on Stanton's orders. Caught off guard, an attending marine officer could not even report to the commandant of the Navy Yard until the body was long gone.[23]

It was ferried close to shore in a boat rowed by two sailors. Colonel Baker, his cousin Lieutenant Luther Baker, and Eckert were the only others aboard as they rounded the confluence of the Potomac River and the Eastern Branch before pulling up at the Arsenal's modest wharf. According to Luther Baker, they had deliberately tried to deceive onlookers by taking aboard the boat a heavy ball and chain as a "blind"[24] and may have thrown these overboard to simulate a watery burial for Booth. Word quickly spread, with gory embellishment, that Booth's mutilated and weighted body had been dumped in the Potomac River, so that it could never be found. "Booth is dead and his head having been cut off and his heart taken out, his devlish carcass has been sunk in the river," Benjamin Brown French wrote approvingly to his son.[25]

The widely read *Frank Leslie's Illustrated Newspaper* devoted the entire front page to a sketch of two oarsmen dumping a bound and blanketed form into the Potomac River at night. The publisher himself vouched for its truthfulness, informing his readers that the sketch was given by one of two officers who ditched the corpse in the middle of the river, and who wanted to remain anonymous.[26]

Eckert thought the rumors may have been triggered merely because the corpse had been ferried over water.[27] But Colonel Baker suggested otherwise. Under oath two years later, with his credibility already shredded after exposure of his own multiple exaggerations and fabrications of his role in the post-assassination events, Baker said it was "very likely" that he had told newspaper reporters that Booth's body had been tied with stones and sunk. "At the time the body was disposed of, I was beset by correspondents and others who wanted to ascertain where it was buried," he explained. "The secretary did not want anybody to know." But he resolutely denied that the corpse had been decapitated or tipped into the river.[28] Stanton also denied that he had engineered the stories, saying he was "disgusted" with the rumors. "That was a story gotten up for sensation," he said. "There was not a particle of truth in it."[29]

It was already dark when the boat pulled slowly alongside "the summer house," a small building at the end of a little pier marking the officers' landing on the military base. The commander of the Arsenal, Major James Benton, looked at the corpse and conferred quietly with Colonel Baker. Then the colonel took leave of the body as it was carried into the summer house with its idyllic view over the river. It was left there in a corner, looking like a nondescript bundle wrapped in a gunnysack. The pier was closed and river craft banned from approaching. A sentry stood guard with orders to open fire on anyone attempting to land.

Later that afternoon Dr. George Porter, an assistant army surgeon and medical officer at the Arsenal, was returning to the pier after a boat ride with his wife when a sentry ordered them away, threatening to open fire if they tried to land. Porter managed to disembark, but only after forcefully demanding that the officer of the guard come forward to clear his passage. As the surgeon walked through the summer house, he glanced at the unsightly, conspicuous bundle in the corner, yet gave it no further thought. But later that day he was selected to be part of the small unit detailed to bury Booth's corpse.

At midnight Porter went to the darkened summer house to join four enlisted men from the Ordnance Corps and E.M. Stebbins, military storekeeper of the Arsenal. All had been sworn to secrecy in what they were about to do. Two of the enlisted men lifted the deadweight into a horse-drawn cart. Then the sepulchral procession moved forward in silence, headed by Porter, the only commissioned officer, and one of the enlisted men carrying a lantern to light the way. Enlisted men walked on each side of the cart as Stebbins followed. They crunched over the gravel surface of the tree-lined avenue, past the ceremonial display of cannonballs and artillery on their right and the expansive lawn laid out all the way to the edge of the Potomac on their left.

Sentries ushered them through as they neared the western entrance to the penitentiary, between the outermost administration offices on their left and the beginning of the rows of tiered cells to their right. Stebbins unlocked the colossal door opening into a spacious store-room, holding ammunition and cases of other military supplies. Once the horse and cart were in, Stebbins locked the door. In a corner they could see by the flickering light of the lantern a pile of earth next to a shallow hole in the dirt floor. A pair of enlisted men lifted the rigid corpse, wound with an army blanket and wrapped in the gunnysack-ing, and laid it in the makeshift grave. They covered it, tamped it, and smoothed it over. Everyone went outside, Stebbins locked the door, and all returned to their quarters.[30] Over the years the tomb remained quiet and dark, giving off the musty odor of an airless burial vault.

In New York City, meanwhile, a telegram arrived at the home of Mary Ann Booth asking her to return to Philadelphia, where her pregnant daughter Asia lay ill. As she set off in the carriage to catch the ferry to Jersey City, she apparently did not hear a newsboy shout-ing out the day's headlines: "Death of John Wilkes Booth! Capture of his companion!" But when she was already seated in the southbound train, a friend brought her a newspaper, then offered pitiful words of comfort before parting. "You will need now all your courage," he said. "The paper in your hand will tell you what, unhappily, we must all wish to hear. John Wilkes is dead."[31]

It took eleven days longer for word to reach Britain, because the transatlantic cable would not startle the world with instant commu-nication until the following year.[32] Consequently, one week after the assassin's burial, a top official from Britain's Foreign Office appeared at the American diplomatic legation with word that Booth had arrived in London four days earlier and was under surveillance by detectives. Charles Francis Adams, chief of mission, was asked to sign an appli-cation for a warrant of arrest with a view to extradition. He rushed a separate letter by the same day's steamer asking Washington for evidence to support extradition. Two days later a ship arrived with the news that Booth had been shot "somewhere in Virginia, and that his body had been sent to Washington."

Benjamin Moran, the legation's chief secretary, took dry note of it in his daily diary: "This disposes of his having come to England."[33]

CHAPTER 23

---◆◆◆---

"What My Imagination Pictured the Inquisition to Have Been"

The military waited until well into the night before transferring the bedraggled remaining conspirators to the military prison. Both ironclads were still anchored in the stream away from the Navy Yard wharf when the steamer *Keyport* came alongside at 10 PM on Saturday, April 29. With synchronized timing the captives were led ironed and blindfolded out of the cramped holds of the *Montauk* and *Saugus* into the side-wheel steamer for the ride downriver to the cells in the penitentiary. None of the shackled men could see anything, nor even distinguish night from day. Canvas hoods, cut with a small hole to breathe, had been slipped over their heads days earlier and tied tightly around their necks. Guards, occasionally pushing and shoving, led them every step of the way in the slow and clanking maneuver. Escape was impossible as they inched forward with the tentativeness of the blind, their leg irons hampering movement of one foot beyond the other. Tightly clamped handcuffs prevented them from resisting with their hands or even flailing their arms.

Edman Spangler, the scene shifter who had held Booth's horse briefly outside Ford's Theatre before summoning "Peanuts John" to replace him, vividly remembered the sequence of suffering since his arrest at a downtown boardinghouse on suspicion of being implicated in the conspiracy.[1] A detective had roused Spangler late at night in the Old Capitol Prison and sarcastically declared he had some jewelry to put on him. He handcuffed the prisoner's hands behind his back and took him first to the *Saugus* and then almost immediately to the neighboring *Montauk,* where he was left trussed up with leg irons and handcuffs in the small sail room among old life preservers and filthy blankets between two water closets. A few nights later an officer came in.

"Spangler," he announced, "I am going to tell you something, but don't get scared. They are going to place a bag on your head. It is the orders of the secretary of war, and I must obey it."[2]

Stanton had ordered the canvas hoods placed over the heads of every prisoner aboard the ironclads "for better security against conversation." He also instructed they should not be able to see through the head covers.[3] Spangler recalled that it was only through the kindness of two guards who took pity on him that he was able to eat. One kept lookout while the other fed him because he could not maneuver his immobilized hands to the opening in the hood.

On the night of transfer to the penitentiary, guards awakened him and tied the bag so tightly he almost choked.

"Don't let him go to sleep," one man taunted. "We are going to take him out and hang him directly."

Spangler heard the chains rattling on deck before he was shoved onto the vessel.[4]

Arnold too remembered being manhandled and almost suffocating inside his canvas hood when hauled from the *Saugus* onto a bench in the side-wheel steamer. His hands had bloated and blackened from the squeeze of the cuffs, though the pain eased after an officer took pity on him and exchanged them for a looser-fitting pair.

Payne suffered most, with a ball and chain fastened to each ankle through the direct intervention of Stanton, who also demanded he "be secured to prevent self-destruction."[5]

Major James Benton, commandant of the Arsenal, was on hand to witness the arrival of his charges toward midnight. A talented artist, Benton later sketched the haunting scene from memory, portraying one of the hooded men in double irons being led in by guards guiding him by the arms. Grim-faced officials held lanterns in a scene evocative of condemned men being led off to execution. The soaring arched entrance under which they passed had so impressed visiting Frenchman Alexis de Tocqueville three decades earlier that he thought it "more fit for a palace than a prison."[6] The presence of those suspected of conspiring to kill the president would bring the

Arsenal morbidly to the forefront of public attention for the third
time in half a century. An accidental explosion of barrels of gunpowder had taken the lives of about thirty invading British troops during
their occupation of the city in 1814, and fifty years later overheating
flares from signal rockets touched off a firestorm in a wooden building, burning to death some twenty-one females making cartridges for
small arms.[7]

Arnold was groggy from lack of sleep during his confinement on
uneven hard board inside a narrow closet of the *Saugus*. But he was
clearheaded enough to sense they were being led a long distance
over muddy puddles as the leg irons bit deep into his flesh. After
struggling in sorry procession from the wharf to the penitentiary,
Arnold, Herold, Payne, Atzerodt, Spangler, and O'Laughlin went up
and down flights of stairs before each was locked in a separate cell,
secured by doors with heavy iron crossbars.[8]

The holding cells in the red-brick penitentiary had already been
swept clean and nails pulled from the walls. The only contents were
shuck mattresses and blankets, brought in that afternoon on Stanton's
orders.[9] But the tight cubicles were still damp, drab, and claustropho-
bic. Three decades earlier, architect Charles Bulfinch of Boston had
deliberately designed identical narrow cells only three and a half feet
wide by seven feet long to hold no more than a single prisoner. He
did not want to repeat the problems of other penal institutions he had
read about, where several inmates occupied a single room, leading to
what supervisors described as "the bad effects of associating in night
rooms, such numbers of depraved and unprincipled men." Bulfinch's
penitentiary on the grounds of the historic Arsenal was an elongated
structure with forty identical cells on each of four levels.[10] In keeping
with the aims of the prison reform movement of the early nineteenth
century, stressing redemption through discipline, work, and silence,[11]
Bulfinch had designed every alternating cell to open at the opposite
end of its neighbor, so that convicts could neither see nor speak to one
another.[12] But the Federal penitentiary built for District of Columbia
inmates had failed over the years through overcrowding, poor administration, and insufficient work opportunities. The new arrivals were
the first prisoners held in the gloomy penitentiary since 1862, when

Abraham Lincoln had ordered all the inmates sent to the state prison in Albany, New York, and supervision of the vacated structure transferred to the War Department for use by the military.[13]

During a search of each new arrival, $1.44 was confiscated from Atzerodt, and a gold ring and $15 from Herold.[14] When Mary Surratt arrived the following night from the Old Capitol Prison, she was neither shackled nor manacled, a special exemption in deference to her gender that would apply throughout her appearances in court.[15] Much more was taken from her, including a gold watch ring, two pocketknives, and a thimble and needles.[16]

She too was locked in solitary confinement, which Stanton hoped would eliminate any chance of communication among the captives. But his motives had as much to do with vengeance as with the need to prevent a jail break. The secretary of war held the prisoners under conditions so harsh and punitive that their guilt was presumed even before charges were filed, and two months before a military court was ready to announce its verdict.

Shunting aside most of their constitutional protections as trifling obstacles, Stanton issued broad outlines for "secure detention" just hours before the cells slammed shut. He would insulate the captives from nearly everything living and even from their inanimate surroundings, rarely allowing removal of the hoods or irons, and forbidding them to speak unless questioned. Contact would be so minimal that only the governor, attending doctor, and a few others specially authorized could talk to them. Their names were withheld from the physician, who knew them only by numbers.[17] No one else could enter the cells without Stanton's written approval. The aim was to isolate them in a manner both merciless and unforgiving.

The governor of the prison had special responsibility to prevent prisoners from possessing knives, spoons, or other items they might use to escape, or kill, or injure themselves. Stanton was so determined that the suspects be convicted and hanged that he allowed Major General Winfield Scott Hancock, commander of the Middle Military Division at Washington, to impose any other rules "to prevent the escape of the prisoners alive, or their cheating the gallows by self-destruction."[18] He knew he could rely on Hancock, whom he had praised effusively for leadership and courage after the general was thrown from his horse with a severe thigh wound during the battle of Gettysburg two years earlier.[19]

Within hours Hancock, forty-one, promulgated his own set of rules, forbidding the prisoners from speaking, even when being escorted to the latrine, unless compelled by necessity.

Although eventually the conditions were grudgingly modified for relief, the detainees' ordeal spread over six weeks. Hancock's charges suffered in cocoons of silence, the stillness broken only by the occasional crow of a cockerel, the chirping of passing birds, or guards making spot checks, delivering food, or walking them to the toilets. Weeks of deprivation in idle monotony began to affect their sanity. Though looked upon as caged wild animals, several could not even prowl the perimeters of their monastically quiet cells because of the drag of the heavy metal balls chained to their legs.

Security remained at the highest level of alert, with soldiers posted on each side of the ground floor just to watch over other sentinels on duty. Outside, a regimental guard stood ready to block any attempt to storm the fortified jail.[20] Within days of the prisoners' arrival more guards were brought in, raising the number inside the grim building to sixty-two.[21] Neither they nor any soldiers or employees were allowed into or out of the Arsenal grounds between sunset and sunrise.[22]

Hancock picked Major General John Frederick Hartranft of Pennsylvania for the demanding job of prison governor. But any honor attached to his selection was eclipsed by the onerous new responsibilities. A single misstep, security lapse, or suicide could bring his career to a standstill. Although only thirty-four, with a scant four years of military service, Hartranft was held in high esteem for battlefield heroism. He would receive the Medal of Honor after "rallying several regiments which had been thrown into confusion" at the first battle of Bull Run in 1861.[23] He had been promoted brevet major general for "conspicuous gallantry in recapturing Fort Stedman" outside Petersburg, Virginia, three weeks before Lincoln's assassination.[24] He had served in major clashes, including the first and second battles of Bull Run, Antietam, Fredricksburg, Vicksburg, the Wilderness, Spotsylvania, and Cold Harbor.[25]

But military success had ripped him from his young family, leaving Sallie, his wife of eleven years, pining for his return. He had been absent from Norristown, Pennsylvania, since the fall of 1864,[26] and just weeks before he took command of the penitentiary she wrote plaintively, "I wish that you could come home. I want to see you so bad. I will give you 100 kisses when you come."[27] But the general's sudden elevation had made him a captive of his own command. His daily presence was mandatory for inspection of the prisoners and their quarters. Sallie's pleas could only echo as the wistful yearnings of a lonely wife. He would have to remain in Washington under the inflexible discipline of his calling. Bearing ultimate responsibility for safe custody of his charges turned his own domestic strains into trifles. Sallie tried passing the time in needlework. "I am making you a very pretty handkerchief," she wrote. "It is a fine hem stitch, with your initials and one corner worked in white, and our glorious old flag on a small scale in the other, worked in the national colors."[28] But it was a futile distraction, and two weeks after he took command of the prison she traveled to Washington for a surprise and unauthorized reunion. It did not go unnoticed, and the military was quick to rebuke.

"The secretary of war learned from some source that Mrs. Hartranft was visiting you," Hancock reproached the governor. "He desires me to say that until your duties are ended at the prison, he does not wish anyone, man, woman, or child, to enter the prison building unless on duty."[29]

Though Sallie was contrite and apologetic, it did nothing to diminish her ache. "My Dear Jackie," she wrote, "I wish that I had not gone to Washington but I wanted to see you so bad. I am a perfect baby, but cannot help it. I love Jackie so much it was a relief that I could be with you a short time."[30]

The young general, however, was preoccupied with duties, even showing up to see the detainees given their first breakfast, noticeably without knives, forks, or spoons, when they were fed soft bread, salted meat, and bowls of coffee. Invariably, the diet was salted or boiled meat with soft bread and coffee for the 7 AM breakfast; boiled or cold meat with soft bread and water for the noon dinner; and soft bread and coffee for the final meal at 6 PM. Both he and Dr. George

Porter began their simultaneous twice-daily inspections of the prisoners and cells, after which each submitted written reports.

Initially Mrs. Surratt said she had no appetite and refused to eat anything. Porter, suspecting she was trying to make herself ill, told her he would have to force-feed her because he was responsible for her health. Only then did she yield, nibbling on toast and sipping tea. "There was no more trouble after that," Porter wrote later, noting that Mrs. Surratt thanked him for his "considerate treatment."[31]

Officials closely monitored the irregular attention given to the prisoners' personal hygiene. Only two cells were opened at the same time, with each inmate taken into respective adjoining vacant cells. Guards removed the irons and hoods, but the captives had to wash themselves in the presence of the governor or a field officer. Back in their bleak cubicles they were given clean underwear and bedding. On the fourth day of confinement Atzerodt washed and changed his underclothing but could not remove his drawers because of the weighty iron ball fastened to his leg.

That same day Lewis Payne spoke up as Hartranft was about to lock his cell door.

"General," said Payne, "I would like to talk to you if you would condescend to do so."

"I have no time," the governor replied.[32]

Later that night Mary Surratt also broke her silence, telling the governor, "I am a Catholic; I would like to see the priest."[33]

The next day Hancock quashed any hopes of spiritual comfort by banning clergymen from the penitentiary until the end of the trial. The general also forbade private correspondence, even with families. But in twin concessions made without explanation, Hancock said Dr. Mudd, who arrived on Thursday, May 4, need not be hooded, and he approved the prison doctor's recommendation for Mrs. Surratt to be fed a "less rigorous" diet.[34] Most of the detainees preferred to keep their boots and shoes on for warmth, but Payne and Surratt accepted slippers supplied by the physician.[35]

Atzerodt was the first in the penitentiary to volunteer details of the conspiracy. At 8:20 PM on Monday, May 1, the governor opened cell 161 and removed Atzerodt's hood. The scruffy young man, who had refused to go along with the assassination, stood up as Provost Marshal McPhail entered with an aide. For almost two hours the Prussian immigrant rambled, often in disjointed remarks and sometimes with a lucid chill, as when he spoke of his own terror. "After I heard of the murder, I run about the city like a crazy man." He had no doubt about Mudd's implication, telling the visitors, "I am certain Dr. Mudd knew all about it." But he left unclear the extent of Mudd's involvement. When Atzerodt claimed that Booth told him he had sent liquor and provisions to Mudd's farmhouse "for the trip with the president to Richmond, about two weeks before the murder," it was not clear whether the physician was savvy to the kidnap plot or to the assassination, or both.

With Atzerodt's disclosures, there was no doubting Mrs. Surratt's role in the conspiracy. Without knowing that the widow had already been implicated by Weichman and Lloyd, Atzerodt corroborated their most damning evidence against her when he volunteered, "Booth told me that Mrs. Surratt went to Surrattsville to get out the guns [two carbines], which had been taken to that place by Herold. This was Friday" — the day of the assassination.

Law enforcement officials also learned from him how Booth may have surreptitiously gathered intelligence on the home of Secretary of State William Seward. "I overheard Booth, when in conversation with Wood [alias Payne], say that he visited a chambermaid at Seward's house, and that she was pretty. He said he had a great mind to give her his diamond pin."

Cryptically, Atzerodt told of pressures on Booth to act quickly before other plotters killed the president. He recounted how Booth told him of a person he had met in New York "who would get the president certain." The intricate plot involved getting friends of the president to arrange a social event, during which they would infiltrate and somehow manage to detonate explosives at the White House. As the two law enforcement officials huddled uncomfortably with Atzerodt in the cell built for a single inmate, the prisoner told them: "Booth said if he did not get him [Lincoln] quick, the New York crowd would."[36]

The War Department made a sustained effort to woo Payne into divulging secrets of the conspiracy. Stanton designated Eckert, his trusted head of the military telegraph office, to be the link, passing word down to the prison governor that Eckert had his "unlimited confidence," with authority to enter any of the cells. Within days of Payne's arrival, Stanton authorized Eckert to give the muscular captive a small quantity of chewing tobacco and a "fine" cushion, small favors that ranked as luxuries in the austere penitentiary.[37] Eckert came at night to cell 195 and stayed alone with the enigmatic conspirator for almost an hour. Without explaining why, the governor deliberately left the door unlocked, telling the guard to distance himself and not let anyone within hearing range.[38]

Payne was not immediately forthcoming, claiming he knew little about the plot. He was not inquisitive, and Booth, he said, did not seem to want to confide in him. But in a rare aside about others, he spoke disparagingly of Herold, calling him "a little blab." He had such strong reservations about Herold that he said he had passed them on to Booth. Yet even though he implicated John Surratt, without providing details, he held his tongue about others, blocking Eckert's persistent questions with the tantalizing remark, "All I can say about that, is that you have not got the one-half of them."[39]

Secretary of State Seward was also hoping Eckert would pry from Payne the reason he had burst into his home and almost stabbed him to death. He asked Eckert to find out his motivations and to report anything the strongman said about him. The patient courting paid off when Payne himself requested a meeting, but Eckert stalled for four or five days. "Finally he became so distressed," Eckert remembered, "that I listened to him. But it was simply a statement of his own action the night of the assassination, of his feelings while in the room, and after he left the room, and where he went up to the time of his arrest."[40] Eckert, however, never took notes in Payne's presence, and several years passed before he spoke publicly of their dialogue. But he mislaid the notes he made later, and no one has ever located them.[41]

Intermittent visits by Eckert and others were welcomed by the prisoners, if only because the muffling hoods were pulled off, instantly restoring sight, sound, and the normality of easy breathing. Porter had been quick to suggest the hoods be padded, and Hancock agreed at once, telling the prison governor to supply sketches and even sizes.[42] The padding, it was hoped, would foil suicide if they bashed their heads against the walls.[43] But Hancock demanded secrecy, writing Hartranft a day later, "I send you a man to make the masks. He had better take his material to your place — and be cautious to keep his mouth silent."[44] The new hoods, which would not be ready until after the trial had begun a week later, were even more severe on the sensibilities of the detainees. They fit over their heads, but when the cords were tied tightly around their necks, the padded cotton pressed painfully hard against the eye sockets and ears. Only two slits at the nose and mouth enabled the prisoners to breathe and eat.[45]

Stanton had rashly expected the conspirators to be tried, convicted, and hanged before the president's funeral, but the graveside eulogies were over almost a week before the prisoners were first led into court.[46] The secretary of war wanted no more than a spartan courtroom, with only basic fixtures and fittings. "The rooms will not require carpets, but chairs, tables, and stationery," he instructed the provost marshal general on the same Saturday the suspects arrived at the penitentiary. A single weekend, he anticipated, would be time enough to prepare for the trial, which could then open by Monday, May 1.[47]

It was an uncharacteristic lapse in plain common sense, but with such minimum essentials to assemble, it did not take long to create the court in a third-floor room at the eastern edge of the penitentiary. The bare forty-by-fifty-foot room quickly became cluttered with unadorned pinewood furniture. Not a single picture or map relieved the blankness of the whitewashed walls. Gas lights were readied to illuminate the room if proceedings continued beyond nightfall. All four windows were already grated for security.[48] But Stanton's deadline was arbitrary and allowed to pass as workmen built a stairway from the second to the third floors, sparing outsiders from having to pass through the prison to reach the court. At Hartranft's suggestion, the laborers also laid thick, new coconut fiber matting over the staircase, floors, and adjoining rooms set aside for legal officials.[49] Then they positioned the spittoons, which, an observer noted during the trial, were "abundantly patronized."[50]

Even though many hoped for quick retribution to avenge the blood of the president, few expected such a clamor over the choice of a military trial. Stanton's decision to bring the suspects before a tribunal made up of senior army officers enraged advocates for a trial by jury. Much of the inflamed opposition came from influential newspapers in the populous mid-Atlantic states. One newspaper even intimated that "hanging will soon begin," a statement sharply denounced by the pro-government *Daily National Intelligencer* in Washington, which said the days of "hanging first and trial afterwards" were long gone.[51] Proponents of a military trial argued the futility of expecting to find an impartial jury in such a politically divided city. They could not imagine any jury in Washington ever being able to reach unanimity, essential for a verdict to convict.[52] A military tribunal, by contrast, required only a simple majority to convict, with two-thirds necessary to hang.[53]

Attorney General James Speed backed Stanton, arguing for the government that even though civil courts continued to hold sessions in Washington, the capital remained firmly under martial law. Moreover, the assassination had taken place in a time of civil war, with the city defended by fortifications and guarded by Federal troops. Speed's lengthy opinion, accepted by President Johnson, described Booth and his accomplices as "secret active public enemies." He reasoned that it would be as wrong for the military to hand them over to the civil courts as it would be for a civil court to convict a man of murder who had killed another in battle. "The civil courts have no more right to prevent the military, in time of war, from trying an offender against the laws of war, than they have a right to interfere with and prevent a battle," Speed concluded.[54]

The military tribunal drew scornful contempt from Speed's immediate predecessor, Edward Bates, whom Lincoln had chosen as his first attorney general. Bates suggested that Speed had been courted and caressed by Stanton. "If he be, in the lowest degree, qualified for his office, he must know better. Such a trial is not only unlawful, but it is a gross blunder in policy: It denies the great, fundamental principle, that ours is a government of law, and that the law is strong enough to rule the people wisely and well."[55]

Many lawyers and other critics shared Bates's fear that death sentences handed down by the military would turn the conspirators into martyrs. Opposition to the military tribunal focused sharply on the Fifth Amendment, which clearly mandated that "no person shall be held to answer for a capital, or otherwise infamous crime, unless on a presentment or indictment of a grand jury, except in cases arising in the land or naval forces, or in the militia, when in actual service in time of war or public danger." As none of the suspected conspirators were in the land or naval forces, nor even in the militia, many believed they had to face trial in a civilian court.

But Stanton would not budge, not even during a cabinet meeting when Navy Secretary Welles and Treasury Secretary McCulloch spoke up for trial by jury. "Stanton, who says the proof is clear and positive, was emphatic," Welles confided to his diary, "and Speed advised a military commission, though at first, I thought, otherwise inclined. It is now rumored the trial is to be secret, which is another objectionable feature, and will be likely to meet condemnation after the event and excitement have passed off."[56] But as opposition grew more shrill to the possibility of a secret trial, Stanton assured Welles that journalists would be admitted, even though some of the initial testimony had to be classified and taken behind closed doors.[57]

It did little to pacify Stanton's foes. Snap judgment by an imperfectly constituted court could do lasting damage to the ideals and reputation of the Union. Even the Union quartermaster general's father reminded his son that "to secure the triumph of the Republic, it is essential that it should act worthily. It will assuredly become an object of contempt and disgust," he wrote, "if it descends from its high state of triumph to revel and gorge on the bodies and blood of the insane mob it has quelled and conquered."[58]

A bewildered public faced contradictions in the highly charged partisan press as the start of the trial drew near. The *Daily National Intelligencer* reported that Stanton had apparently directed verbatim reports to be made of all the proceedings, which would be distributed daily to the Associated Press and local newspapers.[59] But the rival *Washington Evening Star* said reporters would be excluded, and testimony withheld from the public.[60]

Using Speed's opinion as a shield, President Johnson authorized the adjutant general's office to detail "nine competent military officers" ιο serve as a commission for the trial.[61] That same day the War Department announced a nine-man military commission to begin the trial on Monday, May 8. Major General David Hunter, who had commanded White House security during the perilous first six weeks of Lincoln's presidency, would preside over two major generals, four brigadiers, a colonel, and a lieutenant colonel.[62]

One of the most talented was Major General Lew Wallace, thirty-eight, a lawyer and former Indiana state senator. The previous summer he had probably saved Washington from capture — winning high praise from Grant in the process — by battling Confederate forces in a delaying action that bought time for the capital's reinforcement and left the invaders little choice but to withdraw.[63] Wallace would later write the best-selling novel *Ben Hur: A Tale of the Christ* and be honored posthumously with his statue in the US Capitol.

Brevet Brigadier General Cyrus Comstock was in Vicksburg as an aide-de-camp to Ulysses S. Grant when named to the military commission. He had been deeply affected by news of the assassination, writing in the privacy of his diary, "Death is too good for the murderers."[64] But when he arrived in Washington on May 8, he learned to his consternation that he had been appointed one of the judges. "Wish I could get off," he groaned in his diary. "They ought to be tried by civil courts. This commission is what is yet worse, a secret one I believe."[65]

The following day he looked on aghast as the prisoners were paraded into court, their anonymity secured by identical black linen hoods pulled down over each of their heads. Only their mouths and noses could be glimpsed through the punctured cloth. Arnold later recalled everything "as dark as Egypt."[66] All were shackled except Mary Surratt. They stepped clumsily into the courtroom, the metal chains jangling as guards led them in single file to their row. "It was a horrid sight," Comstock, thirty-four, wrote later.[67]

Another of the military judges, Brevet Major General August Kautz, blanched at the spectacle of eight masked figures before him "clad in black dominos" to shield their identities. Kautz, thirty-seven, had served in the bloody Antietam campaign and witnessed untold carnage on the battlefield, but now he flinched at the ghastly sight. It was, he shuddered in recollection, "so much of what my imagination pictured the Inquisition to have been, that I was quite impressed with its impropriety in this age."[68]

Unable to hold his tongue, Comstock questioned the chief military prosecutor, Judge Advocate General Joseph Holt, about the legitimacy of the court's jurisdiction. Swiftly Holt rebuffed him, saying the attorney general had already resolved the issue. But Comstock would not be silenced. The two clashed again when Holt wanted to limit counsel to five-minute arguments and when he called for a secret trial, assuming that evidence given in public would impede the arrest of others and deter some witnesses from testifying.[69]

Within twenty-four hours Comstock was dismissed as a judge, together with Brevet Colonel Horace Porter, twenty-eight, whose valor at the battle of Chickamauga, Georgia, in 1863, would earn him the Medal of Honor. Stanton told them they were removed only because they were aides to Grant, who had also been targeted by assassins. Whatever the reason, neither officer took offense. "We were both very much delighted," Comstock exulted in his diary.[70] They were replaced by Brevet Brigadier General James Ekin and Brevet Colonel Charles Tomkins, thirty-four; Tomkins would receive the Medal of Honor for having twice charged through enemy lines at Fairfax Court House, Virginia, two months earlier.

This "carefully selected" panel appealed to Attorney General Speed for its composition of men "taught by experience and habit to maintain coolness and equanimity in the midst of the most exciting scenes."[71]

Judge Advocate General Holt, a gruff Kentucky lawyer, had been secretary of war in the waning months of the Buchanan administration. Since his appointment three years earlier as the first judge advocate general of the army, Holt, fifty-eight, had worked on the evolution of military commissions to handle cases beyond the jurisdiction of courts-martial and the civil courts. Benjamin Perley Poore, a noted historian, newspaper reporter, and chronicler of life in the national capital who was now preparing to take down all of the proceedings in shorthand, was taken by Holt's "tall, imposing presence, gray hair, and a manner which not only imposes respect, but wins admiration."[72] It was not an opinion shared by Samuel Arnold, who would later watch Holt sitting "immovable . . . like some grim statue carved in stone, neither the face nor the eye emitting the slightest impression."[73]

The suspects' first court appearance had been brief. When asked whether they wanted to engage lawyers, all had replied affirmatively. Then they were led back to their cells.

Later that afternoon Hartranft was summoned by the judge advocate general to receive copies of detailed charges against each of the eight accused. He was told to serve them personally and without delay. Until then no reason had been given for their detention. Now they were charged with "maliciously, unlawfully, and traitorously" conspiring to kill Lincoln, Johnson, Seward, and Grant, "within the military department of Washington, and within the fortified and entrenched lines thereof."[74] If convicted, they would face the hangman, but none of them had as yet seen a lawyer.

Hartranft began the grim task in the evening after ordering all hoods removed. He entered each cell alone, holding a burning lantern to light his way. The glow was bright enough for prisoners to scan the charge sheets and learn the official reason for their detention. Occasionally the general recited the details, but only upon special request. It was a slow and monotonous procedure that took four hours to complete. The accused had to wade through circumlocutory legal language that was opaque to many laymen. Though they had permission to speak, only two apparently did so. Mudd asked to write to a friend whom he thought could hire a lawyer. O'Laughlin wanted to speak with Baltimore's Marshal James McPhail, who had known his family for thirty years.[75]

Far off in Pennsylvania, Sallie Hartranft waited out the days in unmitigated despair. She loathed the prison role assigned her husband and was still impatient for it to end. She thought it unbecoming of her beloved and sat down to write him so. "I cannot bear the idea of your having the hanging of those men," she scribbled in her untidy hand, "but as soon as you are relieved of the command I want you to come home."[76]

Her wait would last longer than expected, as her husband's role became ever more arduous. Even though still governor of the penitentiary, he was now also provost marshal general for the trial. It meant supervising security for the accused and being responsible for their appearance in court. They had to be shaved and brought in together, without the dreaded hoods. Hartranft alone had to decide whether he thought it safe to let them walk in without the unsightly leg irons. However, he was told never to remove the irons clamped to the wrists of the males. Hartranft also had to be present at open sessions and always in possession of the prison keys, having made sure that the doors were locked. Despite all these precautions, Hancock warned, "Now is the time to have all your intelligent officers on duty."[77]

An even tighter cordon was drawn around the Arsenal. Orders went out for no less than thirty horsemen to report daily to the prison governor a full hour before court resumed. The cavalry were to remain on duty until stood down personally by Hartranft.[78] And a detail of ten soldiers under the command of a noncommissioned officer was to be stationed daily at each of thirteen blocks leading north from the Arsenal grounds to the main thoroughfare of Pennsylvania Avenue.[79] There was no knowing how long the trial would last nor what dangers lurked ahead. Rage among Lincoln's admirers was still raw and unabated, even as rebel fanatics abounded. The likelihood of Hartranft's early reunion with Sallie seemed more remote than ever.

CHAPTER 24

Weeks of Deprivation and Solitude

The seven-week trial instantly took on the semblance of a freak show. Gossiping voyeurs delighted in being shocked or amused. Spectators came to be titillated, feeling like daredevils in their proximity to fiends. So eager were they to get close to the notorious eight that guards on occasion shoved them back from the dock, where they blocked the view of defense lawyers. Still, they stood on tiptoe to relish the moment and revel in their brush with infamy.[1] After newspapers noted that the accused always sat in the same order, spectators came armed with diagrams to pinpoint the individuals who excited most curiosity.[2] Many women, oblivious to court decorum, whispered animatedly or indulged in such noisy asides that others strained to follow the proceedings.[3] Spectators eventually showed up as late as midday to avoid having to listen to the dull recitation of the previous day's proceedings, mandated for an accurate transcript.[4] A few observers were so shameless in wanting souvenirs that they carried off chips of furniture.[5]

Those hopeful of gaining admittance used ingenious stratagems to procure seats, which were severely limited by space. Marian "Clover" Hooper, twenty-one, who would later marry historian Henry Adams, braved pouring rain to squeeze into the crowded courtroom, where she claimed a chair reserved for reporters. "Being a woman has its advantages on this occasion," she wrote gleefully to a cousin.[6]

"Clover" Hooper spoke for many when she observed, "The evidence is not very interesting, but it is to see the prisoners." Like other spectators, she saw little of Mrs. Surratt, who held a palm-leaf fan close to her face. All the men, with the exception of Payne, seemed to her to have weak, low faces. "Payne is handsome but utterly brutal," she relayed, "and sits there a head higher than all the others, his great gray eyes rolling about restlessly, not fixing on anything, looking like a wild animal at bay. It is a sad, impressive sight."[7]

Payne's glare similarly transfixed Lincoln's pastor, Dr. Phineas Gurley, who came away dazzled, by "a man never to be forgotten by anyone who has once seen him — large, muscular, and having eyes that are perfectly terrific."[8]

Compulsive diarists went home to capture impressions in ink. Benjamin Brown French, prominent Freemason and prolific poet, wilted in the sweltering heat of the densely packed courtroom but made a quick study of Herold's "meaningless face and low baboon-like forehead." Payne's tall, sinewy frame and smooth, brazen face indicated "a willingness to do any desperate act." French, the commissioner of public buildings, seemed disturbed by Atzerodt, "a bad-looking man" with "low, dark, round face." But with apparent relief he considered O'Laughlin "a handsome, genteel, plain-looking man, the last one, from his appearance, whom one would believe guilty of such a crime." Arnold too did not look to him like a criminal, and Mudd was "an ordinary-looking man with red hair and whiskers . . . but prematurely bald on the top of his head." He had no comment on Spangler, the scene shifter at Ford's Theatre, who leaned forward on the railing, entirely obscuring his face.[9]

Mathematics professor Simon Newcomb pushed his way through the crowds in the uncomfortably hot room to lean on the bar of the court. It was an ideal position to see everything, but marred by the crush of those pushing from behind. Newcomb, thirty, was disgusted by the miserable appearance of the prisoners, though they did not look as "villainous" as he expected. However, "except Dr. Mudd, they are about as dirty, unwashed, uncombed, unshaven set as I ever set eyes on," he wrote his wife. "They did not seem to have changed their clothes since they were arrested."[10] As if to underscore his revulsion, he too turned to his diary to vent his feelings: "The culprits are a miserable-looking set, except Dr. Mudd, who is probably innocent."[11]

Celebrities came regularly. John Hay, who had been Lincoln's assistant private secretary, was one of the first to show, soon followed by Augustus Seward; the historian George Bancroft; the three Ford brothers, recently discharged from custody on suspicion of being implicated in the conspiracy; and even Edwin Booth, who had been summoned as a witness though he was never called to testify.[12] A lone newsman reported sighting "Master Tad Lincoln" among the spectators.[13] The Union army's top general, Ulysses S. Grant, caused as much of a stir with his brief appearance for the prosecution as he did in pulling himself up sharply at a doorway, beyond which a balcony had been removed above a sheer drop of fifteen feet to the ground.[14]

Newspapermen made much of the gestures, antics, and countenances of those on trial for their lives. They did not shy from stoking public passions through snap impressions and prejudicial commentary. George Alfred Townsend, writing for *The World* in New York City, all but condemned Atzerodt for being "a disgusting little groveler."[15] The evidence was so eagerly awaited and compelling that the editor of Washington's *Daily National Intelligencer,* a staid broadsheet, removed all advertisements from the front page to fill it with columns of verbatim testimony.

The legal proceedings got off to an inauspicious start. A judge's acrimonious outburst against a defense lawyer coarsened the tone of the trial even before any dignified etiquette had been established. General Thomas Harris, the only physician on the panel of military judges, objected to Reverdy Johnson representing Mrs. Surratt. He implied that the sixty-eight-year-old lawyer sympathized with the rebels because of his stand over a disputed oath prescribed the year before, to test the loyalty of Marylanders.[16]

Johnson bristled, his face visibly flushed.[17] He was a distinguished member of the US Senate from Maryland and a former attorney general of the United States. He had even been an honorary pallbearer at the funeral of Abraham Lincoln. However, he replied in the calm and courteous manner customary to the ways of the Senate.[18] He explained that a convention called to frame a new constitution for Maryland had overreached its authority in demanding that anyone wanting to vote should first take an oath of loyalty to the Union. He had no objection to the oath itself, only to the violation of the US Constitution, which had no such precondition for voting.[19]

Then he silenced Brigadier General Harris with words of sulfurous irony. "Let me tell you that I have taken the oath you speak of before the Senate of the United States, of which I am a member, the body which creates armies and navies, *and makes major-generals!*"[20] The two foes glared at each other so provocatively that it seemed they might come to blows.[21]

General Kautz squirmed at the "absurdity" of a colleague challenging the right of a US senator to appear before them. Later he made a note in his diary that it must have been insulting to Johnson's dignity, and he hoped the senator would not think other members of the commission supported the "ill-advised objection."[22] But Harris was unrepentant, irrationally believing for decades that Johnson took on the defense of a female only to play on the sympathies of the court so that he could then denounce Lincoln's "tyrannical usurpations of power."[23]

The commission turned its back on Harris and admitted Johnson. But the senator refused to overlook the insult and after a few days declined to appear again in person for the defense. Later he would challenge the court's jurisdiction, leaving his opinion to be read by a colleague. His absence was not without damage, since it looked as if he had given up on the defense of Mrs. Surratt.[24]

Once, during the first week of the trial, the military judges escorted by a detachment of cavalrymen made an early-morning on-site inspection of Ford's Theatre to familiarize themselves with the layout and to examine every exit and entrance. Eerily, stage settings were still in place for the comedy that Lincoln had watched, with the conspicuous red-curtained recess in the center. But the green baize stage cloth had a foot-long tear, apparently where Booth had stumbled. Twelve feet above, the framed portrait of George Washington still hung in front of the presidential box, but the bloodstained rocking chair was gone.

The military had not taken effective control of the theater until two days after Lincoln's death, when guards were posted inside. But even their presence had not prevented theft. Two months after the assassination, James Ford, the theater's business manager, returned to his sleeping quarters on the upper floor of an adjoining building, accessed from the theater. He reported the disappearance, during his arbitrary detention on suspicion of being tied to the conspiracy, of more than six hundred dollars' worth of watch chains, as well as a ring and cluster pin set with diamonds.[25]

As the military judges and their escort walked from the narrow dress circle passageway through the doorway Booth had entered, they noticed where he had scraped a ledge in the wall, about three inches long and one inch wide, to support one end of the bar of wood he positioned to jam the door and block entry by the audience. A journalist reported that a squarish slip of wallpaper appeared to have been pasted over this gash before the assassination, to conceal the cut in the wall. Though missing, the piece of wallpaper had left a very visible paste-mark impression over and around the scraping.[26]

That night, after the court adjourned, trial judge Kautz went back to his rooming house to commune with his personal diary. He made a brief entry with a single, emphatic conclusion: "The court met informally at Ford's Theatre where we witnessed the scene of the president's assassination. An accomplice seemed to have been absolutely necessary to enable Booth to accomplish his purpose."[27]

Payne transfixed and fascinated all who came in to gape. A reporter for the *Washington Evening Star* wrote that Payne "directed a cool, impudent stare by turns upon every person in the room. His bold eye, prominent under jaw, and athletic figure gave all the marks of a bold, desperate villain." He sat with his head defiantly thrown back against the wall, his tall form towering above the others.[28] On another occasion, the same reporter related, "Payne is amusing himself by returning stare for stare of all given him so abundantly by the lady visitors."[29]

He was an enigma, a mysterious, elusive character who belied the first impression of being an amoral brute with muscles straining to rip open his collarless shirts. He had changed his name from Powell to Payne and even used the alias of Wood. He was vague and uncertain about his past, even when asked his age and place of birth. Public curiosity stirred when a former female slave tearfully swore she had been Payne's nurse in Washington, and that his real name was Daniel Murray Lee, nephew of Robert E. Lee, an identity confirmed by a military officer before an intimate of the Lee family emphatically dismissed it as bogus.[30]

Payne's conduct was not only erratic but decidedly irrational. When led from the court in the opening days of the trial, he turned to a guard, saying he was tired of life and wished they would make haste and hang him.[31] Now as he faced the ultimate penalty, he seemed almost carefree and even slightly amused.

His puzzling aloofness held steady even though his face flushed red when the wounded male nurse demonstrated how Payne had held the elevated knife with the blade pointed down as he repeatedly stabbed Secretary Seward. A reporter noted how the almost breathless spectators scanned Payne's body language for clues to his guilt or innocence. But the muscular man remained stoic, "his wild stare fixed upon the witness . . . his mouth closed tightly . . . and he stood up straight as a statue, with no sign of fear, trembling or trepidation."[32] When judge Lew Wallace asked for the hat that had fallen off the assailant's head the night of the attack to be placed once more on Payne's head, a court orderly reached up to put it in place. Again Payne evoked curiosity by smiling during the grave procedure.[33]

The public demeanor of the males gave little clue to their suffering. Few realized how the terrible strictures of confinement had begun to unbalance their minds, though one illustrated weekly publication reported they were "already undergoing a living death" and that they feared death by vigilantes who might storm the penitentiary.[34] The moment the court adjourned, either for lunch or at the end of the day, they were led back to their solitary cells and capped with the tormenting hoods. Arnold would later report that his guards, "imbued with deep hatred," replaced the dreaded hood even before he entered his cell. He was forever after mystified that he kept his sanity.[35] Payne and Atzerodt endured even harsher restrictions, with metal balls chained to their ankles. As the trial approached a fourth week, Payne showed signs of dementia. One afternoon a sentinel saw him strike his head with one of the metal balls. The prison governor hurried to prevent possible suicide and later reported, "I at once unfastened the balls from the shackles and removed them from the cell." Then he rushed to Atzerodt's cell to take identical preemptive action.[36] Ironically, Hartranft had asked permission only the day before to remove the weights from Atzerodt's legs so that he could change his underwear regularly.[37]

But the men remained trapped under hoods, helpless against the slow constriction of their senses. Arnold blamed Stanton for the torture, branding him "that mastermind of cruelty."[38] Within days of Hartranft's dash to the cells he was compelled to focus on the head covers. "The prisoners are suffering very much from the padded hoods," he wrote Hancock. He asked that they be removed, with the exception of Payne. "This prisoner does not suffer as much as the others, and there may be some necessity for his wearing it, but I do not think there is any for the others."[39] One guard marveled at Payne's "iron nerve," noting how he never complained, even when the heavy padded hood brought on a steady sweat that coursed down his forehead over his eyes and nose.[40] Four days passed before Hartranft received authorization, and on the night of June 10 the prison governor did the rounds of the cells, bringing instant relief to all but Payne.[41] Removal of the hood came coincidentally during the week of Herold's twenty-third birthday. But there was no relief from the leg irons, which remained fastened by day and by night.[42]

Even though the hoods were gone, the prisoners still sat alone in silence. Weeks of deprivation and solitude within the squashed area of numbered cells had taken a toll on their moods and sanity. Spangler, who was fond of riding horses, romping in the outdoors with dogs, and fishing and crabbing every summer, was most in need of mercy.[43] Remembered from childhood for his "good nature and simple-mindedness,"[44] he had not been able to withstand what he described as "the torture of the bag."[45] The prison governor did not elaborate when he said Spangler's mind was "wandering." He called in Porter, whose instantaneous remedy was to order the prisoner let out of the building, where he could wallow in the unaccustomed open and inhale abundant fresh air. For the next hour Spangler roamed outside in the enclosed yard, pried loose for the moment from the narrow limits of his cell. It was a luxury he had not known since his arrest two months earlier, and it restored some sense of equilibrium.[46]

Meanwhile Dr. John Gray, head of the Utica, New York, asylum, had been summoned by the secretary of war to advise, and he and Porter entered the cells, closely examining the other detainees. There was no doubt in their minds that all were in urgent need of the outdoors, at least for an hour of exercise daily. Gray was confident it would be "sufficient for the general health of the prisoners." Porter recoiled from each hood, which he described as a "sweating bath to the head." They had to come off forthwith, and exercise allowed in the open air, or, he warned, Stanton would have "a lot of lunatics on his hands."[47] Both physicians, however, judged the prisoners' diet "good and abundant," and the arrangements for bathing "ample."[48]

Authorities yielded swiftly to this and other recommendations: Each cell was immediately supplied with hair pillows and a box or small stool to sit on. Mrs. Surratt was more fortunate and got a rocking chair brought from her boardinghouse. From now on each man received a small piece of tobacco to chew on after meals. Stanton was even more generous toward Mrs. Surratt, allowing her to have any food she desired. But he modified Porter's plea for reading material by banning all books and papers published within the last thirty years.[49] Porter, given sole discretion to select the reading material, provided books by James Fenimore Cooper and even those written by Charles Dickens within the proscribed period of publication.[50] Out in the enclosed yard the detainees played with quoits, sometimes joined by a guard.[51]

Payne's apparent attempted suicide jolted the military and confirmed to his lawyer, William Doster, the need for a plea of insanity. He had learned little from their limited meetings since taking on the defense, which had been at the urging of the assistant judge advocate when no one else volunteered. But Doster, twenty-eight, had already concluded that his client had a mind "of the lowest order, very little above the brute, and his moral faculties equally low."[52] Payne had gradually confided how he had hidden atop a cedar tree for three days after stabbing the secretary of state. Only hunger had driven him down and into the arms of detectives when he called at Mrs. Surratt's boardinghouse in desperate expectation of a meal.[53] Even though he privately expressed remorse to Doster for harming Frederick Seward, saying he owed him an apology, the lawyer had no doubt his client was non compos mentis. "Either this," he thought, "or he played his part very well to the end."[54]

Surprisingly, doctors for both the defense and prosecution testified on Payne's mental state after only one or two examinations,
some lasting less than an hour, held just before the opening of court.
George Porter, the prison doctor who had observed Payne over the
longest period, saw nothing to suggest insanity. He testified that the
accused was neither restless nor sleepless and was the only one of
the prisoners "almost always . . . asleep" when the physician made
his evening rounds of the cells.[55] Surgeon General Joseph Barnes was
even more blunt, declaring, that there was "no evidence of insanity
— none whatsoever."[56] Knowing that Payne had been constipated
for a month, Doster drew an admission from the superintendent
of the Government Hospital for the Insane that "long continued
constipation frequently precedes insanity."[57] But any hope of gains
for the defense evaporated when a messenger brought word of
the imminent death of the witness's wife. Questioning halted and
the witness left, never to return. Doster was crestfallen.[58] Only he
knew how much supportive testimony had been lost. But it was no
longer of any consequence. It was apparent that the plea of insanity would fail. Not a single physician had testified that Lewis Payne
was insane.

On the same day that David Herold told his lawyer and the judge
advocate general that he wanted to write a confession,[59] a journalist
observed, "Herold is in the grinning mood this morning."[60] Three
weeks had already passed since Herold had boarded the *Montauk*
in handcuffs while Booth's corpse was laid out on the deck. He had
made a long voluntary statement that night before Judge Advocate
Bingham. But it was a fanciful denial of even being in the capital
during the assassination and a tall story of meeting Booth by chance
on a country road, when Herold said he had been browbeaten into
riding with the assassin through the swamps.[61]

As soon as Herold opted to confess, Hartranft appealed to
Hancock: "I would respectfully ask if permission can be granted to
take off his handcuffs and allow this privilege between the sessions
of court."[62] Permission came back the same day, but it was hedged
with suspicions about Herold's motives. He was to be searched well

beforehand to prevent self-inflicted injury from something that might have been smuggled in by visitors. The guards were told to be especially vigilant.[63]

The following morning Herold was led alone into the empty courtroom, where his handcuffs were unlocked and removed. He was given paper, a quill pen, and ink, and wrote steadily until midmorning. Then his wrists were again clamped with handcuffs as the military trial resumed.[64] His fluctuating feelings that day were caught by an observant journalist, who informed his readers, "Herold's mood is mercurial, sometimes exuberantly buoyant, and sometimes as much depressed."[65] For three days he wrote under guard in the quiet of the historic courtroom. But the contents would forever remain a mystery. It was never given out to the public, and its whereabouts remain unknown. The confession had no bearing on the trial, nor was he rewarded with relief from privations.

Herold appeared unmoved by the gravity of the charges. An attentive newspaper reporter was quick to take note "when a woman of unusual attractions enters the court, Herold is much more interested in her than in his acquittal."[66] His six sisters were allowed in to see him half a dozen times during incarceration, with visits in the vacated courtroom stretching as long as three hours. Within days of writing his confession, two of them brought him soda crackers, butter, and strawberries.[67]

There appeared to be little that his lawyer, Frederick Stone, could do to defend him, because Herold had been cornered with Booth. He had willingly linked up with the assassin not long after galloping out of Washington, and there were witnesses who had spotted them in tandem along the route of escape. Stone, forty-five, lived at Port Tobacco, the Charles County area of Maryland that sent his great-uncle to sign the Declaration of Independence and elected his grandfather to the first US Congress.[68] Though elevated to the State House of Delegates, he shared with his simple client an ardent feel for the countryside they both knew better than most. But it seemed doubtful that Herold would ever again ride free through the wilds of the county. The best hope of saving him from the rope would be to portray him as essentially naive and pliable, without any malice or guile. Stone appealed to the court's compassion by presenting the young man as a simpleton. He brought in a succession of witnesses, all of whom knew Herold well. All five described him as boyish and gullible, and a person easily led and influenced.[69] One of them, a doctor who had known him for years, said Herold had the mind of an eleven-year-old.[70]

When Stone compared Herold with his mentor, he described Booth as "a man of determined and resolute will, of pleasing, fascinating manners, and one who exercised great influence and control over the lower orders of men with whom he was brought in contact. In his search he met with Herold, then out of employment, and he at once marked him for his own. Such a boy was only wax in the hands of a man like Booth."[71]

At the end of his eloquent argument, Stone offered the contrasting personalities to explain how Herold could have willingly ridden off at night by the side of the president's assassin. Herold was not only cowardly but unfit for bloody deeds of violence. Though obviously weak and trifling, he could still be made useful to Booth. "He knew some of the roads through lower Maryland, and Booth persuaded him to act as guide, foot-boy and companion." This, said Stone, accounted for their companionship.

In a final plea to the judges, he suggested, "It by no means follows because he aided Booth to escape, that he aided him to kill the president. It is bad reasoning to conclude that because he was guilty of one crime, he was guilty of others."[72] Pointedly, he reminded them of what Booth was heard to shout just before Herold left the barn to surrender: "I declare before my Maker that this man here [Herold] is innocent of any crime whatever."[73] If true, it might sway the court in Herold's favor. But the uncorroborated testimony came from a single, suspect cavalryman, Sergeant Boston Corbett, who was already notorious for shooting Booth on his own initiative. The defense lawyer, however, made sure to repeat the testimony as proof of his client's innocence. Herold, said Stone, was neither an accessory before the fact to the murder nor an aider and abettor in the assassination. "That is what he [Booth] meant," he told the nine bearded and mustachioed officers.[74] But if the rigidly erect commission members were to concentrate instead on the twelve days of flight from lawmen, then it seemed more likely that Herold would die on the gallows.

Journalists were so focused on the trial that none learned of scandalous misconduct, mischief, and bumbling among forces assigned to protect the penitentiary and the courthouse. In one instance, a lieutenant and thirty infantrymen reported for duty instead of an equal number of cavalrymen. "I have no service for this infantry," an exasperated Hartranft wrote the delinquent colonel, "and have therefore ordered them back to camp."[75] On another occasion, when armed soldiers appeared without ammunition, Hartranft directed soldiers about to be relieved to remain at their posts, but his orders arrived too late to halt the departure, and a soldier sent to recall them lost sight of the men in the teeming city. Worse still, Hartranft learned that the Arsenal did not have ammunition to fit the weapons of the incoming shift.[76] Later the commanding officer of a unit detailed for duty beyond the Arsenal perimeter complained that others had relieved his men without his knowledge.[77] That same night a lieutenant colonel reporting at the penitentiary with his men was so intoxicated that Hartranft had him arrested.[78]

Drunks were a familiar sight in Washington, but two young inebriates were arrested half a mile from the military court when one of them shouted at a guard: "God damn the country. I would like to have the place burned up. You kiss my a— Abraham Lincoln, or anybody else." When the soldier told them to stop using such language, one of the drunks responded, "Go to hell."[79] They were taken into custody and brought before Hartranft, who received orders from Hancock to send them off to the Old Capitol Prison. "You were perfectly right in having the men arrested," Hancock wrote. "The sentries should arrest any stranger coming near the penitentiary without authority, and particularly in such cases."[80]

Even though Mrs. Surratt began to eat regularly after Porter's warning of forcible feeding, she appeared dispirited, tired, and withdrawn. Her black bonnet and clothes, veiled face, and listless presence were outward signs of flat and punctured spirits. She was without spark

or animation, passively accepting the dull monotony of every passing day. Sometimes she tottered toward her allotted seat at the end
of the prisoners' row. She supported her head on her right hand as
if devoid of hope.[81] At other times she leaned forward, resting her
hands and forearms on the railing but seldom raising her head.[82]
She seemed to suffer most from the stifling heat in the overcrowded
courtroom, where water was passed to thirsty prisoners in a large,
communal tin dish. Her only energetic motions came from cooling
herself with a palm-leaf fan, but even then she frequently sat with
eyes closed.[83] Only in the solitude of her cell did she seek relief from
pressing misery, passing many long hours looking at the open pages
of her prayer book.[84]

Word leaked out to the press how Mrs. Surratt had apparently
steeled herself against crying during an emotional reunion with
her daughter, shortly after Anna's release from six weeks of detention in Carroll prison, where she had been held with other suspects
caught up in the wide dragnet. Unable to restrain herself, the younger
woman ran to hold and embrace her mother in the empty courtroom, hugging and kissing possessively as she wept in the arms of
the accused. Guards who looked on sympathetically thought the
mother strained to suppress her feelings, perhaps to prove she would
not buckle under during the long imprisonment. They were allowed
several hours together under the watchful eyes of prison guards, but
when the precious time elapsed, the sentinels moved in to separate
the stoic mother and her wailing daughter.[85] Mrs. Surratt remained
demonstrably stiff until Anna had left the prison; then she dropped
down in a dead faint.[86]

Anna was allowed to visit twice within the next two weeks, once
for no more than a few minutes in the courtroom.[87] But Mrs. Surratt's
health deteriorated so visibly that by mid-June she came into court
leaning upon the arm of an attendant.[88] Concerned officials transferred her from the cell into a room at the rear of the court that until
then was assigned to the judge advocate general. Every precaution
was taken to prevent suicide. "The window sash must be taken out
if there is any in, and curtain or blind put on," Hancock ordered.
Anna was permitted to bring in any provisions approved by Porter,

but, warned Hancock, "great care must be used to prevent anything being carried to her which she should not have."[89]

Still, in her very next court appearance Mrs. Surratt became so ill that the court had to adjourn abruptly and she was returned to her room. When the trial resumed after lunch, she sat on a chair inside the door to her room, where the air was fresh and cooler, though she was still visible to members of the court. After Dr. Gray visited her that night, Hartranft reported that her unspecified illness appeared to be worsening. "I would suggest that her daughter be allowed to remain with and wait on her," he advised, "as her illness is evidently such as to require a female attendant."[90] Approval came quickly, and the following evening Anna moved in to care for her ailing mother.[91]

Interest in Mrs. Surratt's ultimate fate never slackened as trial testimony gripped the country. If convicted and sentenced to hang, she would be the first woman in America legally put to death by the Federal government. Capitalizing on the prospect of what would be a socially jarring and unspeakable precedent, anonymous sympathizers distributed handbills in Washington hotels and public venues extolling the good deeds of Mrs. Surratt, "a Christian lady, gifted with excellent qualities." She was praised as "a devoted wife and fond mother, pious, kind, and charitable to a fault." The flyers denounced the character of those testifying against her and the cruelties of confining a weak and defenseless woman.[92] Even in court her legal team coaxed a succession of dependable witnesses to attest to her kind and pious ways. One priest commended her as "a proper Christian matron."[93] A black woman who had been Mrs. Surratt's servant for six years said she had not only treated her servants "very well" but had even fed many Union soldiers at her house.[94]

The case against her rested manifestly on the damning testimony of John Lloyd, lessee of her Surrattsville tavern, and Louis Weichmann, a resident in her Washington boardinghouse. Even though Lloyd and others testified to his drunken state when Mrs. Surratt arrived at the tavern some five hours before the assassination, he was adamant that she had told him to get the "shooting irons" ready for pickup later that night. No one had been within earshot to contradict this crucial assertion, and Booth and Herold had indeed called for the carbines that night, telling Lloyd they had assassinated the president and secretary of state.

Not once during Weichmann's lengthy testimony did he implicate his landlady directly, but he volunteered so much circumstantial evidence of her complicity that the defense had to discredit him personally to offset the impression of her guilt. Weichmann, a clerk in the office of the commissary general of prisoners, was so precise in attaching dates to incidents long past that at first blush he came across as invulnerable. He outlined a series of suspicious comings and goings by Booth, John Surratt, Payne, and Atzerodt at the H Street boardinghouse. Sometimes, he recalled with inevitable innuendo, he had seen Booth and Mrs. Surratt leave the parlor and converse in the passage, though he never once overheard what was said.[95]

His revelations bore the implication of sinister and shady activities in a boardinghouse frequented by mysterious strangers, some of whom frightened the young women who lived there.[96] He told the court how Payne had initially used an alias and tried to pass himself off as a Baptist preacher when boarding at Mrs. Surratt's. He recounted in vivid detail the dramatic scenes of Booth, Payne, and John Surratt bursting into the building after the abduction plot went awry. Even the most dubious spectator could not help but believe the suggestion of mischievous and criminal intent when Weichmann told of the day he entered a bedroom and found John Surratt and Payne handling bowie knives and long-barreled navy revolvers.[97] By the time he stood down from the witness stand, Mrs. Surratt appeared as an active and willing co-conspirator. How else to describe the frequent presence in her boardinghouse of men known to have shot the president and stabbed the secretary of state, and the furtive appearance of others known to have been their associates? And what explanation could be offered for her reaction to Payne's arrest at her house, when she had denied knowing him or ever having seen him before, even though he had boarded with her on several occasions?

Though it was a military tribunal, with swifter procedures and administered by less experienced judges whose prospects of promotion lay within the same hands as those who had appointed them, defense counsel Frederick Aiken reminded them of bedrock principles behind criminal jurisprudence: Mrs. Surratt was entitled to the presumption of innocence and had to be acquitted if there were a reasonable doubt of guilt.[98] "All there is, is circumstantial," he summed up. "Nothing is proved against her, except some few detached facts and circumstances, lying around the outer circle of the alleged conspiracy, and by no means necessarily connected with guilty intent or guilty knowledge."[99]

The acquaintance with Booth, the message to Lloyd, the nonrecognition of Payne constituted the sum total of her receiving, entertaining, harboring, and concealing, aiding, and assisting those named as conspirators. "The acts she has done," said Aiken, "in and of themselves, are perfectly innocent. She received and entertained Booth, the assassin, and so did a hundred others. She may have delivered a message to Lloyd — so have a hundred others. She might have said she did not know Payne, and who within the sound of my voice can say that they know him now?"[100] Aiken easily explained her nonrecognition of Payne at the moment of his arrest by recalling that several witnesses had testified to Mrs. Surratt's poor eyesight. One of her boarders, Honora Fitzpatrick, had even testified that she herself did not recognize Payne the night of his arrest until his head cover was removed.[101]

But Aiken knew that her fate depended on the credibility of Weichmann and Lloyd. Her role as a conspirator could be proven, he suggested, *"solely"* by their testimony.[102] To save his client he would have to raise doubts about their truthfulness. Aiken portrayed Weichmann as a man who appeared to be everywhere at crucial moments, and so knowledgeable about the conspirators' aims and plans that, Aiken deduced, "all the facts point strongly to him as a co-conspirator . . . He knows too much for an innocent man."[103] He asked why Weichmann had not communicated his suspicions to Mrs. Surratt after he found the false mustache in Payne's room.[104] He noted Booth's telegram to Weichmann three weeks before the assassination, instructing him to direct John Surratt to telegraph Payne's address in Washington. "What additional proof of confidential relations between Weichmann and Booth could the Court desire?" Aiken asked.[105]

But the defense lawyer's insinuations failed to sway General Lew Wallace, who would later write of Weichmann: "There he stood, a young man only twenty-three years of age, strikingly handsome, intelligent, self-possessed, under the most searching cross-examination I have ever heard . . . and his testimony could not be confused or shaken in the slightest detail."[106]

Lloyd was an easier target for Aiken because of his heavy drinking the night of the assassination. Confidently the lawyer declared: "At a time when, as testified by his sister-in-law, he was more than ordinarily affected by intoxicating drink . . . and others corroborate the testimony as to his absolute inebriation, he attests that he positively remembers that Mrs. Surratt said to him, 'Mr. Lloyd, I want you to have those shooting irons ready.'" Aiken reminded the court that Lloyd had voluntarily helped conceal the carbines and that he was "in a state of maudlin terror when arrested . . . For two days he maintained denial of all knowledge that Booth and Herold had been at his house . . . and in a weak and common effort to exculpate himself by the accusation of another, he proceeded to place blame upon Mrs. Surratt."[107]

Confident that he had damaged the standing of Weichmann and Lloyd, Aiken urged the nine military judges to give Mrs. Surratt the benefit of all reasonable doubts. Just before concluding, he raised the specter of a woman being sentenced to death and appealed to their contemporary instincts as masculine protectors of a weaker sex: "Let not this first State tribunal in our country's history, which involves a woman's name, be blazoned before the world with the harsh tints of intolerance, which permits injustice."[108]

At least one judge was not impressed. When the court adjourned, Kautz took a ride to the Capitol grounds to listen to the marine band, then returned to his rooming house to enter in his diary, "Mrs. Surratt's counsel made his argument, which was flowery enough but neither legal or [sic] logical."[109]

Unknown to the court, Herold privately scoffed at the notion of Mrs. Surratt's innocence. "That old lady is as deep in as any of us," he remarked, according to William Doster, defense counsel for Payne and Atzerodt.[110]

George Atzerodt was doubly handicapped by unsavory looks and evidence of serial cowardice. Few would quibble with a newspaper reporter's observation that Atzerodt's "face is a terrible witness

Over Eastern Branch, Potomac,
1850-1865

The Navy Yard bridge spanning the Eastern Branch (now called the Anacostia River) over which John Wilkes Booth escaped on horseback after assassinating President Lincoln. (Courtesy of the Library of Congress.)

Top: Port Conway, Virginia, on the north bank of the Rappahannock River, sketched by journalist George Alfred Townsend while retracing Booth's escape route. Townsend described the settlement as "nothing but a group of five or six white washed houses on each side of a road descending the hill to the wharf and ferry." *Bottom:* Townsend also sketched Port Royal, Virginia, on the south bank of the Rappahannock River, through which Lincoln's assassin fled. The celebrated journalist wrote that the two-hundred-year-old settlement had "broad streets and abundant shade trees in the numerous gardens." (Photographs by the author. Courtesy of the Manuscripts Division, Library of Congress.)

Townsend's drawings of "the road Booth went up at Port Royal" (top) and the Garrett farmhouse, which Union cavalrymen surrounded shortly before seizing David Herold and shooting John Wilkes Booth inside a blazing barn. (Photographs by the author. Courtesy of the Manuscripts Division, Library of Congress.)

Top: An artist's impression in *Frank Leslie's Illustrated Newspaper* of John Wilkes Booth being dragged from a burning barn in Virginia after being shot through the neck by a Union cavalry-man. He died a few hours later. *Bottom:* Booth's corpse was brought on board the *Montauk,* an ironclad anchored in waters close to the Navy Yard in Washington, for an autopsy supervised by the surgeon general. (Courtesy of the Library of Congress.)

A contemporary photograph by Alexander Gardner of the Old Capitol Prison, opposite the US Capitol, where many of those rounded up as suspected co-conspirators were detained in the aftermath of Lincoln's assassination. The structure was originally built to house Congress after British troops burned the Capitol and seized Washington in 1814. (Courtesy of the Library of Congress.)

General Winfield Scott Hancock, to whom General John Hartranft, right, had to report daily as governor of the penitentiary where the conspirators were detained. Hartranft would later receive the Medal of Honor for battlefield bravery and be elected Governor of Pennsylvania. (Hancock photograph courtesy of the Library of Congress. Hartranft photograph courtesy of Ron and Helen Shireman.)

The military commission judges and prosecutorial team. Standing, left to right: Brigadier General Thomas Harris, Major General Lewis Wallace, Major General August Kautz, Assistant Judge Advocate Henry Burnett. Seated, left to right: Lieutenant Colonel David Clendenin, Colonel Charles Tomkins, Brigadier General Albion Howe, Brigadier General James Ekin, Major General David Hunter, Brigadier General Robert Foster, Assistant Judge Advocate John Bingham, and Judge Advocate General Joseph Holt. (Courtesy of the Library of Congress.)

One of the military judges, General Lewis Wallace, sketched six of the accused conspirators during the long trial. Clockwise from top left: Samuel Arnold, Edman Spangler, Dr. Samuel Mudd, George Atzerodt, David Herold, Lewis Payne. (Courtesy of the Indiana Historical Society.)

A view of the penitentiary where the eight conspirators were held for the duration of the trial. Gallows were erected for the hangings in the open courtyard. (Courtesy of the Library of Congress.)

Eyewitness Major James Benton, commander of the government Arsenal, later drew the scene of a hooded conspirator, manacled at the wrists and ankles, being led into the penitentiary by armed guards. All eight conspirators were held here in solitary confinement during the two-month-long trial. (Courtesy of Special Collections, National Defense University Library.)

An armed guard watches over Lewis Payne, fitted with the tormenting canvas hood cut with a single slit through which he was able to breathe and eat. (Courtesy of the Library of Congress.)

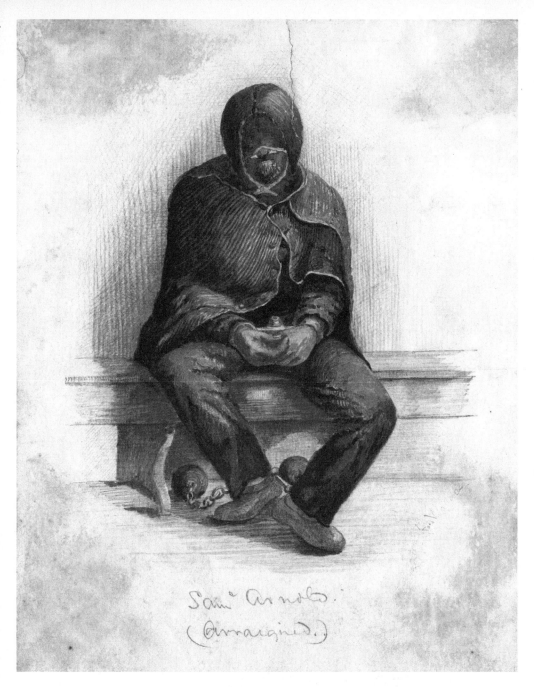

The appearance of hooded and shackled conspirators in court on the opening day of the trial provoked one of the judges, Major General Kautz, to write: "It was so much of what my imagination pictured the Inquisition to have been that I was impressed with its impropriety in this age." Sketch of Samuel Arnold by trial judge General Lewis Wallace. (Courtesy of the Indiana Historical Society.)

Security was exceptionally tight around the penitentiary and adjoining courthouse during the trial of the conspirators. (Pictured in *Frank Leslie's Illustrated Newspaper.* Courtesy of the Library of Congress.)

Celebrities and others packed the stiflingly hot courthouse during the long trial. Those charged with conspiracy to murder the president are seen at the far end of the room in this sketch for *Harper's Weekly.* (Courtesy of the Library of Congress.)

Mary Surratt, the first woman hanged by the Federal government in the United States. Until the moment officials tied her arms and legs, onlookers expected a last-minute commutation of her sentence, but none arrived from the White House. (Courtesy of Special Collections, National Defense University Library.)

Father Jacob Walter, who ministered to Mary Surratt until the moment she was hanged, was so convinced of her innocence that he later declared: "You cannot make me believe that a Catholic woman would go to communion on Holy Thursday and be guilty of murder on Good Friday." (Courtesy of the Library of Congress.)

John Surratt, son of co-conspirator Mary Surratt, dressed in the regimental uniform of a papal Zouave, which he was still wearing when captured in Egypt after fleeing Rome. (Courtesy of the Library of Congress.)

In the final moments before the hangings, George Atzerodt, right, waits his turn to be fitted with a noose and hood. Mary Surratt is extreme left, beside Lewis Payne, while an official in white coat and straw hat looks towards David Herold. (Courtesy of Special Collections, National Defense University Library.)

against him. A villainously low forehead, pinched-up features, mean chin, sallow complexion, snaky eyes of greenish-blue, nasty twisted moustache, head sunk into his shoulders and crouching figure make up the disagreeable presentment of George A. Atzerodt."[111] There was nothing in his looks or demeanor to mitigate unfavorable comment. Herold at least looked harmlessly boyish and even silly, while Payne, muscular and handsome, excited wonder for an apparent indifference to death. Atzerodt alone looked like a caricature of a felon who had slithered out of the shadows with darting eyes and furtive looks.

Doster called four men to the witness stand to show by repetitive emphasis that the Prussian-born immigrant "is a constitutional coward; that, if he had been assigned the duty of assassinating the vice president, he never could have done it."[112] One witness after the other testified to his reputation as a notorious coward who would quickly duck out of barroom and other scrapes instead of putting up a fight.[113] There was nothing to fear from such negative commentary. It could only reinforce Atzerodt's claim to have backed out of the plot when Booth substituted assassination for the original plan to abduct.

The court never learned why Atzerodt had checked into the Kirkwood House Hotel on the morning of the assassination, about twelve hours before, he said, Booth told him to kill the vice president. Neither the defense nor the prosecution addressed the question. But Atzerodt had apparently told the truth to Maryland's Marshal McPhail when he said that the loaded revolver, bowie knife, and coat with Booth's bankbook — all found in his room at the Kirkwood House Hotel — belonged not to him but to Herold. His own knife, thrown in a gutter near a shoe store on the night of the assassination, had been found and was produced by the prosecution.[114] Likewise, his revolver, pawned in Georgetown the morning after the assassination, was identified in court by the storeowner, who had kept it as security for the loan of ten dollars.[115]

But Atzerodt's participation in so many conspiratorial meetings in the months leading up to the assassination made his denials of agreeing to murder look hollow. The judges might well decide he had lost his nerve *after* the 8 PM meeting the night of the assassination, long *after* Booth ordered him to murder the vice president. But even this finding would not absolve Atzerodt from legal liability. He had conspired with others and had full knowledge of the criminal plot. Worse, he had taken no action to prevent it. The law was pellucid and unambiguous. It was no defense to conspiracy to claim remoteness from the scene of a crime performed by any one of the co-conspirators. Each was as guilty as the other in the settled precedent of the law. Atzerodt's absence from Ford's Theatre at the time of the assassination could never be raised as a defense.[116]

General Lew Wallace was ecstatic when defense lawyers began their arguments in the seventh week of the trial. "The everlasting Commission is just out," he exulted in a letter to his wife. "I feel like a boy out of school."[117]

Keen observers began to guess who would hang and which of the eight would be saved. Benjamin Brown French had read daily newspaper transcripts avidly and speculated that none but "the vindictive rascal" Payne would die. "Herold is too simple to be hung. Mrs. Surratt is a woman, and Atzerodt, however guilty at one time, backed out at the last moment, confessed, and put the detectives on the track of Booth," he wrote to the wife of his half brother. But, he cautioned, "Perhaps the president may think it best to make an example of one or two more. If he does, Mrs. Surratt and Herold will be in danger."[118]

Even the judges seemed close to a verdict. Wallace had sounded them out on the eve of the prosecution's argument and thought it would take no more than a few hours at most to agree on innocence or guilt. "Three, if not four of the eight will be acquitted," he wrote his wife. "That is, they would be, if we voted today."[119]

CHAPTER 25

---◆-◆-◆---

"The Trial Concluded at Last"

When Judge Advocate John Bingham made a passing reference to the fallen president as the trial neared its end, an observer noticed how "his lips would quiver with emotion, and his voice became as tender and reverent as if he were repeating 'The Lord's Prayer.'"[1] It was a fleeting moment of emotion during a marathon review of the trial testimony and defense of the military court's jurisdiction.

Bingham mixed law and logic with echoing reminders that the assassination was "a crime, the atrocity of which has sent a shudder through the civilized world."[2] Beginning on the afternoon of Tuesday, June 27, he took almost two days to complete his summation. August Kautz, already exasperated by the judge advocate's frequent objections based on law,[3] groaned into his diary that the argument "had for its principal defect the volume of words in which it is enveloped, although otherwise well prepared and very conclusive."[4]

Time and again, Bingham defended the military tribunal as a necessity for a beleaguered republic in time of war. He denounced defense attorney Reverdy Johnson's claim that anyone not in the military should still be tried by juries in civil courts during war. "The argument amounts to this," he mocked, "that as military courts and military trials of civilians in time of war are a usurpation and tyranny, and as soldiers are liable to such arrests and trial, Sergeant Corbett, who shot Booth, should be tried and executed by sentence of a military court; while Booth's co-conspirators and aiders should be saved from any such indignity as a military trial. I confess that I am too dull to comprehend the logic, the reason, or the sense of such a conclusion."[5]

A small man dressed in a long black frock coat reaching to his shoes,[6] Bingham scoffed at the notion that the court was unlawful, a proposition that, if accepted, would mean the court would have to deny its own existence.[7] He found no justification for "this clamor about a Spanish Inquisition."[8] Far from being secret, the trial was open, in the presence of the accused and their lawyers, with proceedings published worldwide. Repeatedly pillorying Reverdy Johnson for his "extraordinary speech"[9] in favor of civil jurisdiction, Bingham declared: "I have said this not by way of apology for anything the government has done or attempted to do in the progress of this trial, but to expose the animus of the argument, and to repel the accusation against my country sent out to the world by the counsel."[10]

Martial law and military tribunals were as essential to the successful prosecution of war as were men, arms and munitions. Asserting "facts in our history not open to question," Bingham claimed that powers entrusted by the Constitution exclusively to Congress and the president for the common defense were, in a time of civil war or foreign invasion, to be exercised without limitation or restraint, to the extent of public necessity, and without any intervention of the Federal judiciary or of state constitutions or state laws.[11] The people's remedy against presidential abuse would be through Congress, by withholding supplies or removal from office by impeachment.[12]

As Bingham read his final paragraphs, he reminded the panel of military officers: "In this treasonable conspiracy, to aid the existing armed rebellion, by murdering the executive officers of the United States and the commander of its armies, all the parties to it must be held as principals, and the act of one, in the prosecution of the common design, the act of all. I leave the decision of this dread issue with the court, to which it alone belongs. It is for you to say, upon your oaths, whether the accused are guilty."[13]

With relief the court adjourned to the following morning for the judges to deliberate in secret. The sensational trial had stretched into seven weeks, and observers impatiently awaited the outcome. A subheadline in the New York Times seemed to sum up the mood of many: "The Trial Concluded At Last."[14] Since April 14 the country had been traumatized and obsessed by the assassination. But the time had come to move on, and all that remained for closure were the verdicts and anticipated hangings. Even those wounded in the night of terror were reportedly back on their feet. Frederick Seward had recently walked out of his bedroom for the first time since Payne cracked open his skull, and was expected to ride in his carriage within days.[15] His father was already back at the State Department, having just returned from his wife's funeral in Auburn, New York.[16] More significantly, all remaining Confederate prisoners below the rank of colonel were set free even as the conspiracy trial judges considered verdicts.[17] And as a sure sign that time had again been a healer, the comedy *Our American Cousin,* suspended since Booth's leap onto the stage, reopened at the end of June, albeit with a new cast performing at rival Grover's Theater.[18]

On Thursday, June 29, the commissioners met in the courtroom at 10 AM. Summarily everyone was ordered out, leaving the commission members alone with the judge advocate general and his assistants.[19] According to Kautz, his colleagues "got along very amicably but did not finish," and adjourned until 10 AM the following day.[20]

Again they met in secret without the public or reporters and were quick to reach agreement before adjourning sine die.[21] Though commission members had taken an oath of secrecy not to divulge the findings or sentences until promulgated, rumors spread that all eight accused had been found guilty.[22] As Kautz and others prepared to leave Washington, he hurriedly collected autographs of Grant, Halleck, and other luminaries, regretting he had not thought of it earlier.[23] Meanwhile everyone prepared to celebrate the Fourth.

Two weeks earlier, Sallie Hartranft began to fret that she might have to spend the joyful national holiday alone again. "It will be to [sic] bad if you cannot come home," she wrote her husband. "This will be the fifth 4th that you have been away from home. It is very provoking to me when I think how you are penned up in that old Arsenal." But her long wail began to sound like a fading echo. Even she sensed that her wait would not end soon. "I do not believe that they will hang those prisoners for a long time," she conceded.[24] Sometimes her plaintive letters gave way to musings about the children's shenanigans. Linn, still ten days shy of his third birthday, had grabbed a five-year-old boy by the shirt and struck him with his free hand. "It is not Linn's first battle," she wrote the prison governor, "but you must make allowances for him. He was born in a bloody time."[25]

Chitchat, however, was no substitute for her husband's physical presence. Four days later she howled, "I want to see you so bad and have been thinking all the time how many hundred little things I will do to add to your pleasure and comfort. I am irritated all the time to think that you must be penned up in that hateful jail. The idea of making a hangman of you after all your 4 years labor, I cannot think of it in another light."[26]

He had not come home, and Sallie had passed "the most sorrowful 4th I ever spent."[27] She had tied a blue silk scarf on their oldest boy, Sam, nine, and over his head placed a cap with red, white, and blue stars. She had even fastened a sword to his belt and hung flags from the windows of their home. But the festive trappings did nothing to lighten her spirits. Before the day was over she wrote to her Jackie, "Last Friday night I could not sleep for thinking of you, but cried all night."[28]

Hartranft himself had passed the eighty-eighth anniversary of Independence no differently from every other rigidly disciplined workday. He observed the prisoners exercising within the yard in the morning and evening, and accompanied Dr. Porter on his rounds for medical checks. He had also made a request that an army private, who called irregularly to shave and cut the hair of the male prisoners, remain permanently inside the Arsenal to be instantly on hand when needed.[29]

Eighty days had passed since the assassination, and most Washingtonians had overcome their grief and returned to regular pastimes. In time they would even spread jokes about the trial. A reader of the *Philadelphia Press*, signing himself Veritas, humorously reported "suppressed testimony" in an exchange involving Judge Advocate General Holt:

Judge Holt: "Mr. Murphy, were you at Ford's Theatre on the night of the assassination?"
Mr. Murphy: "I was indeed your honor."
Judge Holt: "Did you see J. Wilkes Booth jump from the box after shooting the president?"

Mr. Murphy: "I did, your honor."

Judge Holt [knowing Booth had cried out, *Sic Semper Tyrannis*]: "Did you hear what he said, and if so, what was it?"

Mr. Murphy: "I heard what he said very well, your honor, and all he said was 'I'm sick, send for Maginnis.'"[30]

Gloom had receded by Independence Day. Even the marine band had commenced regular summer concerts on the Capitol grounds on Wednesdays, and south of the White House on Saturdays.[31] On July 4 artillery salutes thundered across Washington at dawn, and again at noon and at sunset. Several thousand former slaves gathered with public figures to pray by a decorated stand erected on grounds south of the White House. They listened to a reading of the Declaration of Independence and to rousing tunes from the Union Cornet Band, then cheered when Senator Henry Wilson of Massachusetts declared, "Slavery is dead and buried forever!"

Almost seven thousand residents took the ferry and other boats from Georgetown to Analostan Island in the Potomac River to picnic, stroll, and play games. Others sailed sixteen miles down to George Washington's estate, Mount Vernon, or dispersed to the cooler "suburban retreats." In the evening the city lit up with exploding fireworks and rockets, launched from grounds near the executive mansion and from the enclosures of private properties. Less than six dozen arrests were made for drunk and disorderly conduct.[32] But Benjamin Brown French recorded in his daily journal that the day "was observed in this city with uncommon noise." He used the occasion to fire off the five rounds he had defensively loaded into his revolver on learning of the president's assassination. At 8:30 PM he and his wife stood on the terrace of the Capitol to see "the magnificent display of rockets and bombs at the President's" before going to the roof of their Capitol Hill home for an even more panoramic view.[33]

Elsewhere in the city, Thomas Ewing, who had defended Mudd and Spangler, relaxed from the rigors of the trial with Lincoln's close friend Orville Hickman Browning by having, as Browning wrote, "some fireworks at night for the amusement of the children."[34]

Momentarily public attention shifted from the long-awaited verdicts to the varied delights of the holiday.

The next day the verdicts came down like thuds. Payne, Atzerodt, Herold, and Mrs. Surratt had been found guilty and sentenced to death. With only a simple majority required to convict, Mudd was found guilty by the narrowest margin of 5–4 of being involved in the conspiracy. Another single vote, 5–4, saved him from the gallows, with two-thirds being necessary to hang.[35] Mudd was sentenced to life imprisonment with hard labor. Ewing had served his client with distinction, which even Holt acknowledged. "Judge Holt told me the other day that I had saved Dr. Mudd's life and that if he lived a thousand years he never would make a narrower escape!" Thomas Ewing Jr. wrote to his father.[36] Ewing acknowledged as much in words of consolation to the doctor's wife. "You should seek comfort," he wrote Sarah, "in the reflection that the vindictive and energetic efforts to take his life failed."[37]

O'Laughlin was found not guilty of lying in wait to kill Grant, but he and Arnold drew sentences of life imprisonment with hard labor because of their guilt in the general conspiracy. The commission, voting 5–4, found Spangler guilty only of aiding and abetting Booth's escape, well knowing he had just murdered the president. For this he would have to serve six years of hard labor.[38]

In another dramatic 5–4 split among the judges, Hunter, Kautz, Foster, Ekin, and Tompkins later joined with Judge Advocates Bingham and Burnett in a written appeal to the president to commute Mrs. Surratt's sentence to life imprisonment "in consideration" of her sex and age.[39] "We who signed it," wrote Kautz, "did not deem it wise or expedient to hang her," foreseeing negative reaction from the public.[40] One of her defense attorneys, John Clampitt, would later claim, "from most credible authority," that it was first proposed to acquit Mrs. Surratt or to spare her life and that Holt had objected, successfully proposing instead that she be sentenced to death with the recommendation for commutation to life imprisonment.[41] It offered Andrew Johnson a way out of having to send a woman to the gallows. Only he had authority to spare her life.

CHAPTER 26

———— •◆• ————

"The *Posse Comitatus* of the Court Is Not Able to Overcome Armies"

On Wednesday, July 5, Judge Advocate General Holt carried a sheaf of documents into the White House, bypassing the public entry by walking through the private family entrance to the president's office. Andrew Johnson had not yet overcome an illness that had sidelined him for weeks from the rigors of his daily schedule.[1] But he could not decline to see Holt, who needed the presidential imprimatur for approval of the penalties. Johnson told his new military secretary, General Reuben Mussey, not to disturb him, while he and Holt reviewed the findings of the court.[2]

The president and the judge advocate general stepped into the White House library, where they remained closeted for several hours. What passed between them would be heatedly debated for decades and forever remain a mystery. One of them lied or was forgetful about whether Holt gave Johnson the written recommendation for a commutation of the woman's sentence of death. The president fiercely denied receiving it.[3] Holt vigorously proclaimed the opposite. The absence of an independent eyewitness embroiled each man's partisan supporters in a feud by print that lasted years beyond the president's term of office.

But it appeared to make no difference to the outcome, because both men shared a belief that gender could never be a mitigating factor. Johnson said they discussed the uniqueness of a woman facing the gallows, because the issue had already been aired in the press. He recalled Holt remarking "with peculiar force and solemnity" that if they discriminated in favor of Mrs. Surratt merely because of her sex, it would encourage women to be criminals, and even to take the lead in committing crimes. Holt, he remembered, said women had aided and abetted traitors since the beginning of the rebellion; execution in this clear-cut case would serve as a deterrent to others of her gender. According to the president, Holt favored execution as soon as practicable. When the president was ready to approve the sentences, Holt wrote out the brief order, which Johnson immediately endorsed with his signature. The hangings were set for Friday, July 7, between 10 AM and 2 PM.[4]

General Mussey looked up from his desk with surprise when the president appeared and announced that the conspirators would be hanged on Friday. Mussey, a resident in the White House since his appointment, asked whether the interval before the hangings was not too short, a reaction later shared by most other Washingtonians, according to newspaper reporters.[5] Johnson agreed, but said there had been time enough since the trial began for "preparations." The president told his secretary not to admit anyone who came to discuss the hangings. He had a disagreeable duty, and he knew attempts would be made for him to reverse his decision. Anyone with concerns about the scheduled executions should see Judge Holt.

Eight years later Mussey recalled Johnson telling him that Mrs. Surratt's gender made her no less guilty. The president told him there had not been "women enough hanged in this war." He recalled Johnson declaiming upon the illogicalness of a woman committing treason and then seeking to avoid its penalty only because she was a female.[6]

The following morning at eleven o'clock Hartranft began the solemn task of going from cell to cell to pass on the news to each of the four who would die. Hancock stood by as Hartranft recited the formal wording of the findings and sentences before giving copies to each of the condemned.[7] Payne, in cell 195 on the second floor,[8] accepted the news with the same "stolid indifference" he had shown throughout the trial.[9] When asked if he wanted to see anyone, he replied that his friends and relatives were too far away, but he did want to see the Reverend Striker of Baltimore and Major Eckert of the military telegraph office.[10]

The two generals walked along the same quiet corridor to cell 161. Atzerodt listened calmly, as if unaffected by the imminence of death. But word leaked to the press how shortly afterward he began to tremble, and the pallor of his face turned ashen.[11] He requested a Lutheran minister, and asked to see his brother John, a brother-in-law, Marshal McPhail, and his common-law wife, Rose Wheeler, and their small daughter, who lived in Port Tobacco.[12]

Herold, one floor above in cell 169,[13] was completely taken by surprise, expecting nothing worse than imprisonment.[14] When told he would be hanged the next day he reportedly looked "wholly unmanned"[15] and asked for his family to send him a clergyman.[16]

Mrs. Surratt, in cell 200 on the same third-floor level, was most affected by the judgment and the notion that she had a single day left to live. Though journalists were barred from the prison, the *Washington Evening Star* reported that she was "completely unstrung,"[17] and the *New York Times* recorded how she "sank under the dread announcement."[18] Anna was away at the time, and the mother pleaded for her to be brought back. She also asked to see her pastor, Father Jacob Walter, family friend Father Bernardine Wiget, and Professor John Brophy, who taught at Gonzaga Catholic College.[19]

Stanton telegraphed Robert Todd Lincoln in Illinois with each of the verdicts and sentences, and prepared him for the macabre finale: "Execution ordered tomorrow."[20]

No sooner had official announcement of the sentences and timing of the hangings flashed across Washington about noon than the press began reporting "an impression" that Mrs. Surratt's life would be saved.[21] Word of the court's recommendation to commute her sentence had leaked to journalists, with the *New York Times* incorrectly reporting that "all the members of the Commission" had called for her life imprisonment.[22]

The distinguished lawyer Orville Hickman Browning, though a close friend of the murdered president, was livid. "The execution of these persons will be murder," he scratched in his daily diary. "This commission was without authority and its proceedings void."[23]

John Clampitt was sitting in his office awaiting the findings of the commission, confident that he and his colleagues Frederick Aiken and the absent Reverdy Johnson, then in Baltimore, would win acquittal for their widowed client. Suddenly he was startled by newsboys crying out in the street, "The execution of Mrs. Surratt!" Clampitt's and Aiken's astonishment was compounded when they learned that she would be hanged the very next day. "So sudden was the shock, so unexpected the result, amazed beyond expression at the celerity of the order of execution, we hardly knew how to proceed," Clampitt reminisced.[24]

He hurried with Aiken to the White House, hoping the president might delay execution at least for a couple of days, but they were unceremoniously rebuffed. Johnson refused to see anyone. When they tried to enter through the main doors, they were blocked by former senator Preston King of New York, one of Johnson's private secretaries.[25] King motioned to guards armed with fixed bayonets stationed by the foot of the staircase and warned it was "useless to attempt an issue of that character."[26]

With less than twenty-four hours to the hangings, the defense lawyers tried unsuccessfully to win the backing of distinguished citizens. Clampitt hurried with Anna Surratt to plead with Holt for a stay of execution, but according to the defense lawyer, "his heart was chilled, his soul impassive as marble."[27] Anna begged Holt again, sobbing as she knelt down before him, pleading for a delay of just three days. His only concession was to tell them to meet him later that day at the White House. But when they arrived at the appointed time, Holt was already on his way out and had no words of comfort. "I can do nothing. The president is immovable," he told them. "He has carefully examined the findings of the commission and has no reason to change the date of execution." To underscore the futility of further appeals he told them, "You might as well attempt to overthrow this building as to alter his decision."[28]

The only outsider admitted to the president's office that evening was Adele Cutts Douglas, twenty-nine, the tall and elegant widow of former US senator Stephen Douglas, who had defeated Lincoln in their 1858 race in Illinois for the US Senate, then lost to him in the 1860 presidential election. A descendant of prominent Maryland Catholics, Adele was also a niece of the celebrated Confederate spy

Rose O'Neale Greenhow and a great-niece of Dolley Madison, in whose house she had been raised. Her pedigree and social standing as one of the most popular hostesses in the capital were license enough to push aside the soldiers' bayonets in a defiantly imperious entrance into the president's private quarters. But she too failed to persuade Andrew Johnson to spare Mrs. Surratt's life.[29]

Father Jacob Walter, pastor of St. Patrick's Church, three blocks from Mrs. Surratt's boardinghouse, was most vocal in trying to save her from the gallows. His denunciation of the verdict and sentence instantly entangled the Catholic hierarchy in an unwanted controversy, forcing Archbishop Martin Spalding of the Baltimore Archdiocese, which included metropolitan Washington, into delicate maneuvers to protect the church from embarrassment, public rage, and possible retribution by the government.

The ascetic, bespectacled Father Walter claimed he had not been allowed to visit Mrs. Surratt when she asked to see him shortly after her arrest. As soon as he learned the trial was over, and even before the verdicts were announced, he went to the War Department to ask Inspector General James Hardie for a pass to visit the penitentiary. Within hours the two were at loggerheads; the headstrong prelate, thirty-seven, up against an aggressively stubborn general, forty-two, who had converted to Catholicism but was overly protective of its public image. They were openly scornful of each other in impassioned explanations to their archbishop, but more restrained in accounts to the press.

According to Walter, the general said that even though the secretary of war was out, Hardie would let him have a pass within hours. The priest was lunching at home when a War Department orderly arrived with the pass, signed by Hardie. As they walked to the door, Father Walter told the messenger he had read reports of the trial and found "there was not evidence enough to hang a cat. Besides, you cannot make me believe that a Catholic woman would go to communion on Holy Thursday and be guilty of murder on Good Friday."[30]

After the orderly had left, the priest claimed he was visited by two men, one of them John Holahan, a boarder at Mrs. Surratt's house, who told him she had been sentenced to hang the next day. At that moment a "much excited" Hardie appeared and told Walter in the privacy of the parlor that he had brought a new pass, this one signed by the secretary of war, "but I want you to promise me that you will not say anything about the innocence of Mrs. Surratt."

The comment so enraged the priest that he threw aside any pretense of clerical restraint. "Do you know the relation existing between a pastor and his flock?" he scolded, according to his recollection years later. "Thank God I do not know what fear is. I fear neither man nor devil, but God alone. You wish to seal my lips. I wish you to understand that I was born a free man and will die one. I know where all this comes from. It comes from your secretary of war, whom a congressman in my breakfast room two weeks ago called a brute." Despite this outburst, Walter said, he submitted reluctantly to Hardie's demand because, as he told the general, "I cannot let Mrs. Surratt die without the sacraments, so if I must say yes, I say, yes."[31] Having secured the priest's promise not to speak about the innocence of Mrs. Surratt, Hardie handed over the pass. It was about 2:30 PM on the day before the scheduled hanging.

Hardie recalled the encounter otherwise. He denied that the offer of a pass to the penitentiary was conditional on Walter keeping quiet about his belief in Mrs. Surratt's innocence. Only seven weeks had passed since Hardie had urged a public display of mourning crepe on all church buildings to stave off the danger of bloody anti-Catholic riots.[32] Sensitive to the ugly mood in Washington and long-standing hostility toward Catholics, he warned the archbishop that "the impudent conduct of Father Walter and others is capable of producing great mischief." Hardie said he had encouraged the priest to be discreet and prudent.[33] He accused Father Walter of having a violent and excitable temper and of being inflammatory and even mischievous. Convinced that the secretary of war had to appoint a more suitable priest to attend to Mrs. Surratt, he had turned to leave when, he said, Father Walter promised to be more prudent, and the pass was handed over.[34]

The feuding had gone on for several weeks after the hangings when the pugnacious priest wrote the archbishop that Hardie should mind his own business and not interfere in church affairs. "He is, in my opinion, a weak, timorous man, almost afraid of his own shadow,"[35] Walter noted acerbically. But the archbishop had a wider audience to pacify and demanded an end to friction with the government.[36] Archbishop Spalding told him to hold his tongue "as any further discussion of the innocence of Mrs. Surratt can do no possible good, and may do harm, in the present excited condition."[37] The firebrand priest replied with meek but grudging subservience. "You require of me a very painful duty, not to assert the innocence of one who is considered here even by Protestants as a kind of martyr. I will do what I can."[38]

Twenty-six years passed before Walter reopened the public feud, convinced that enough time had elapsed for people to lay aside prejudices and calmly listen to reason. He now added more detail, writing how he used the pass to visit Mrs. Surratt in the penitentiary, then went with Anna to the White House. Upstairs they confronted Mussey in a room adjacent to the president's office. Twice the general went in to see Johnson, to no avail. Walter said he then urged Mussey to tell the president he was not asking for a pardon or commutation but only for ten days' reprieve "to prepare Mrs. Surratt for eternity." Again the president refused, with Mussey passing on his inflexible refrain that they should see Holt. "I went with Annie to see this man," Father Walter wrote, "but it was perfectly useless. He had no more feeling for the poor daughter than a piece of stone." When the "cold, heartless" judge advocate general told them to go back to the president, Walter said, he told Mrs. Surratt's daughter, "Come Annie, it is battledore and shuttlecock. The president sends you to Holt, and Holt sends you to the president."[39]

John Brophy, a teacher at Washington's Catholic Gonzaga College, accompanied Walter with his own controversial new evidence that he hoped would prevent Mrs. Surratt's execution. Brophy, an acquaintance of Louis Weichmann, had failed in the final week of the trial to get the court to admit his own accusations that Weichmann had perjured himself and might even have been linked to the conspiracy.[40] He claimed to have damning proof of Weichmann's lies, evidence that should compel a halt to the hanging. In an affidavit Brophy signed the next morning and delivered to the White House without effect, he said

Weichmann confessed to lying on the witness stand and believed in Mrs. Surratt's innocence. "Since the trial closed, he told me he would rather be hooted at as a spy and informer and do everything, rather than be tried as a conspirator," Brophy swore under oath. Weichmann, he claimed, had also confided to him since the trial that Mrs. Surratt had been suspicious about the presence in her home of men later identified as conspirators and was afraid of "something going on"; but when she demanded an explanation from her son, John, he "did not, and would not tell her why the men were there, or what they were about."[41] Brophy, however, made no more impression on Holt than had Walter or Anna, and his assertions were swiftly rejected.

Exhausted by hours of strain, Anna returned to the boardinghouse where hundreds of curious gawkers watched from across the road as she arrived about 8 PM by hackney carriage in an obvious state of distress. Many in the crowd wept at the sight of the weary daughter being helped up the steps and into the house, dimly lit by a single lamp.[42] Later she returned to the penitentiary, where mother and daughter were allowed to spend their last night together.[43]

Meanwhile Clampitt and Aiken telegraphed their lead counsel at his home in Baltimore, imploring Reverdy Johnson to come to their aid. But close to midnight the former attorney general telegraphed back, "It is very late. There are no trains to carry me to Washington." He urged them to apply for a writ of habeas corpus, which, if successful, would free Mrs. Surratt from the custody of military authorities. To encourage them in this last-ditch stand, he reminded them, "We are now in a state of peace, not war."[44] To bolster their chances, he telegraphed Thomas Ewing Jr., who had defended Mudd and Spangler, asking him to lend a hand.

Ewing helped draft the petitions on behalf of the condemned woman, then Clampitt and Aiken hurried off[45] to the residence of Andrew Wylie, a justice of the Supreme Court of the District of Columbia, who had been fearlessly public in support of Lincoln, even surviving an assassination attempt years earlier while living among secessionists in Alexandria, Virginia.[46] A clock struck 2 AM as the lawyers rang the front door bell at Wylie's residence. A window opened above.

"What do you want?" asked the fifty-one-year-old judge.

A voice answered, "Important business of a judicial character, upon which hangs life or death."

Wylie lowered the window and opened the door. Clad only in a dressing gown, he led them into his study, lit the gas light, and sat down, looking to Clampitt like an immovable statue as he listened raptly while one of them recited the petition.[47] It described the military commission as unlawful and argued that Mrs. Surratt should have been tried by a jury before a criminal tribunal. It required that General Hancock bring her before the judge.[48] A brief oral plea followed before Wylie gathered up his papers and courteously remarked, "Please excuse me, gentlemen," as he walked away to his chamber.

Clampitt and Aiken watched dejectedly as the judge closed the door behind him. They were certain he would reject the petition and had left only to get properly dressed. In a few moments he returned, clutching the documents. "Gentlemen, my mind is made up," he said. "I have always endeavored to perform my duty fearlessly, as I understand it." He told them the points in the petition were well taken, but, conscious of the gravity of the moment and the risks to himself, he declared, "I am about to perform an act which, before tomorrow's sun goes down, may consign me to the Old Capitol Prison. I believe it to be my duty as a judge to order this writ to issue, and I shall so order it." His endorsement ordered the writ to be returned before the court at ten o'clock that morning, meaning Hancock would have to bring Mrs. Surratt before the court, together with proof of his authority to hold her.[49]

Elated, Aiken and Clampitt hurried off to the clerk of the court, who made out the writ in compliance with Wylie's endorsement. At 4 AM the two lawyers handed it over to the US marshal for expedited service, and by 8:30 AM Hancock had the writ in his hand at Washington's Metropolitan Hotel.[50]

Less than twenty-four hours before the scheduled hangings, all four of the condemned were brought down to cells on the ground floor.[51] A small projection of the building running south of the penitentiary blocked their view of a portion of the yard where they would die.

The remaining convicted conspirators, Mudd, Spangler, Arnold, and O'Laughlin, were kept well away, still unaware of their own sentences and ignorant of the fate of their associates.[52]

All those requested by Atzerodt to visit him arrived, with the exception of his young daughter.[53] Scruffy-faced and whimpering, Atzerodt alternately prayed and cried. His female visitor, dressed in black and clutching a prayer book, left shortly after midnight racked by the finality of the farewell. The dismal man remained restless and fidgety, unable to fall asleep even when he closed his eyes.[54]

By early morning he was more composed and spoke earnestly with his minister, the Reverend J.S. Butler. Still partially immobilized by irons clamped to his wrists, Atzerodt sat on his bed in the corner of the cell, dressed in nothing but a white linen shirt and gray pants. When the minister left the cell momentarily, Atzerodt held on to the Bible and looked frantically toward the single barred window, below which troops had already assembled.[55]

Atzerodt told the minister he was part of a plot to kidnap Lincoln but denied agreeing to assassination. Booth, he said, had wanted Herold to kill the vice president, with Atzerodt only providing backup. Atzerodt confessed to hating blacks and thought they should be kept in ignorance. He told of once listening to a sermon in which the preacher explained that Negroes were black because the entire race had been cursed. He was committed to the South because of his belief in slavery. Though he had not received any money for conspiring to kidnap Lincoln, he said Booth had promised him they would all be rich and celebrated if they succeeded in abducting the president.[56]

Herold had asked his sisters to find a minister and the Reverend Dr. Olds, an Episcopalian, made his first visit the day before the execution.[57] On his last night Herold apparently slept well for several hours even though the following morning he was so overcome by fear that he trembled and twitched very visibly.

At no time did Payne lose his placid composure. He alone among the four ate breakfast, and with a hearty appetite.[58] He had turned down the prison governor's offer to send for friends or relatives, but he had asked to see Major Eckert, head of the military telegraph office, who had already secured a measure of trust and confidence from Payne. Additionally, Payne wanted to see the Reverend A.P. Striker, an Episcopalian, in whose Baltimore church he had worshipped occasionally. Until Striker's arrival much later, another clergyman, the Reverend Dr. Gillette, who had been introduced by Eckert, ministered to Payne.[59] The strongman was equally candid with Gillette, saying he bore no malice toward the secretary of state, "as between man and man." He confessed to stabbing Seward only because he had agreed to do his duty and mistakenly thought he could not back out. No reward was promised, and he had expected nothing but promotion and approval from the Confederate government.

Now somewhat forthcoming in speaking about the conspiracy, Payne volunteered that he had seen a number of men in Richmond who appeared to be intensely interested in the plot to abduct the president, but he thought Booth was the leading spirit. He regretted "more than anything else" having brought Mrs. Surratt "into trouble," insisting he had gone to her home on the night of their arrests only to borrow clothes before trying to escape into Virginia. But he was scornful of her son, John, for deserting his mother at this critical moment.[60]

The military cordoned off the Arsenal with armed troops, all carefully selected to meet Hancock's demand for "efficiency and reliability."[61] Primed for instant action, each man stood at the ready with a cartridge box of forty rounds of ammunition. In expectation of another day of scalding heat and wearying hours of unbroken foot patrols, every soldier carried a full water canteen and a day's supply of cooked rations in a haversack.[62]

At dawn, Hartranft deployed an entire regiment north of the Arsenal's main gate, positioning the men on every square for more than a mile as far as the city's main thoroughfare, Pennsylvania Avenue. Troops were on the alert to maintain "perfect order" and to stay put long after the executions.[63] No one could predict how the general public might react, nor whether bands of partisans might rally as mobs, either supportive of the Federal government or allied with its bitterest opponents. The four awaiting execution had now become prominent symbols. Loyalists prepared for the ultimate retribution as the outcome of a just and legal process. Fanatics among unbowed rebels excused the condemned as victims of a simmering cause.

Hartranft's lonely burden was to anticipate outbreaks of disorder and to forestall unwelcome surprises. He spread three regiments in a long line of sentinels to block access through the Arsenal's perimeter. No one approaching from the Potomac River or the canal could hope to crash through this formidable barrier. Anyone innocently trying to enter the Arsenal grounds would be diverted to the main gate, where tight security required passes signed by Stanton, Hancock, Hartranft, or others specified by the officer of the day. Mounted cavalrymen waited at the main gate to whisk to Hartranft the names and references of anyone arriving without the vital pass.[64] In all some three thousand armed troops were deployed within and without the Arsenal, including twenty-one cavalry companies. The prison governor also had on standby six ambulances — horse-drawn covered carts — for swift transportation in emergencies.[65]

But the army looked to more than defenses while planning for the doleful day. There had to be an orderly sequence to the ceremony in keeping with military discipline. A rigid protocol would be followed before soldiers enforced the sentence of the military tribunal. To highlight the gravity of the assignment, officers summoned a drum corps from each of the activated regiments. The drumroll had a way of eliciting a hush and holding undivided attention.[66]

When the Supreme Court of the District of Columbia opened at 10 AM neither Hancock nor Mrs. Surratt was present. Justice Wylie, alone on the bench, sounded slighted, if not ignored. It seemed as if his court had been brushed aside as inconsequential. "He has neglected to obey the order of the court," said Wylie. "The question now before us is, 'What is the court to do under the circumstances?'" Without inviting discussion, he decided to back down and avoid confrontation. It would be futile to find Hancock in contempt and precipitate a showdown with the military. "If it is their determination to treat the authority of this court with contempt," he reasoned, "they have the power and will to treat with equal contempt any other process which the court might order." Intimating that the court was lame and weak, he closed the proceedings with an uncharacteristic admission: "The court must submit to the supreme physical force, which now holds the custody of the petitioner."[67]

The lawyers hurried to Mrs. Surratt's cell, but just ninety minutes later, while they were still in the penitentiary, Hancock and Attorney General Speed made a surprise appearance in the courtroom, forcing Justice Wylie to suspend a sensational trial of a woman charged with murder in the Treasury building. Speed apologized to Wylie for their late appearance, explaining that even though Hancock had received the writ two hours earlier, he had many persons to see and important matters to attend to immediately. "No disrespect was intended," said the attorney general. Then he presented the president's written orders suspending the writ of habeas corpus and demanding that the hanging proceed.

Wylie did not object. "This court finds itself powerless to take any further action in the premises," he replied, "and therefore declines to make orders, which would be vain for any practical purpose." Without rebuke, he accepted the reasons given for their late appearance.

Speed tried to soften the blow to the judiciary, citing the harsh realities of war that permitted "human life to be taken without the judgment of the court, and without the process of the courts. It permits prisoners to be taken and prisoners to be held." Wylie acknowledged the limits of judicial enforcement, though he could not help but be rueful. "The writ was applied for, and I had no authority to refuse to grant it," he said. "It is a writ dear and sacred to every lover of liberty, indispensable to the protection of citizens, and can only be constitutionally set aside in times of war. I could not, I dared not, refuse to grant the writ."[68] But he had no choice other than to submit to the might of the ruling authority, concluding, "the *posse comitatus* of the court is not able to overcome the armies of the United States under the command of the president."[69]

The final maneuver to bring Mary Surratt before a civilian court had failed. It did not deter William Doster from immediately applying for writs on behalf of his own clients, Payne and Atzerodt, but the judge declined, citing the case just heard.

Ewing was so offended by the judge's timid submission that he privately denounced it as feeble.[70] Orville Hickman Browning, who had witnessed the proceedings at City Hall, excoriated the judge's behavior, writing in his diary, "He should have proceeded against him [Hancock] for contempt, and have seen whether the president would have taken him forcibly from the hands of the court."[71]

Attorney General Speed had no misgivings about the consequences for Mrs. Surratt. He knew Americans would recoil at the prospect of hanging a woman. But as he mused long afterward, "All the crimes in the calendar have at one time or another been perpetrated by females. It was Jezebel who stirred up Ahab and incited him to commit the foulest murders."[72]

Anna Surratt crisscrossed the city early in the morning in frantic quest of a reprieve. She could not sit still in the death cell, waiting passively for the final embrace. Only by facing the men who mattered could she beg for compassion and mercy. No one but she could reach out with such disarming sincerity. But when Anna found Hancock at the Metropolitan Hotel shortly before he received the writ, she gained nothing but sympathy. He said he had no authority to intervene. He too hoped the condemned woman would be spared by presidential pardon and suggested she "throw herself on her knees" before the president and beg for the life of her mother.[73]

At 8:30 AM, accompanied by Brophy, she entered the White House again, only to be blocked by a doorkeeper at the steps to the president's office. She asked to see Mussey; when he came down, she knelt like a childish supplicant, grasping his coat as she cried out to see Andrew Johnson. The whites of Mussey's eyes had yellowed since his wartime bout with malaria, and he suffered chronically from headaches and sleeplessness.[74] Until recently he had commanded black troops in Tennessee, but now he followed orders only from the president, and he told Anna what she dreaded to hear. He could not allow her to pass. There was nothing more to be said, so he turned and went back to his office.

She lay crumpled at the foot of the stairs, loudly proclaiming her mother's innocence. She cried out that her mother was too good and kind to be guilty, and that if she were put to death, she also wanted to die. Some of the military guards could no longer hold back their tears. Eventually, when Anna quieted, she was coaxed into a seat in the East Room where Lincoln's body had lain. Whenever a visitor entered, she rose in expectation of good news or to waylay the stranger for help.[75] But her fitful wait was in vain. Within days she would say she felt "spurned and treated with the utmost contempt by everyone at the White House."[76]

Two of Herold's sisters, dressed in black and heavily veiled, entered the White House after Anna on a similar mission. They too were barred from the president, and ushers refused to deliver their note to Eliza Johnson, the frail and ailing first lady. They would not even forward the card to Martha Patterson, the president's plain and unassuming daughter, who often substituted for her invalid mother as official White House hostess.[77] The Herold siblings had no more success in trying to win the support of influential Freemasons, who had respected their late father as a brother Mason.[78]

As the execution deadline neared, the cabinet convened for its regular Friday session even though President Johnson was ill, apparently with apoplexy.[79] No written record survives, but controversy lingers over the content of their secret discussions. Judge Advocate John Bingham insisted that Stanton and Seward told him the president and cabinet had considered the petition for commutation of Mrs. Surratt's death sentence and unanimously rejected it.[80] Attorney General Speed steadfastly refused to divulge anything said in the privacy of cabinet meetings.[81] Seven years after the assassination, Navy Secretary Gideon Welles said he had no recollection of any discussion of the conspirators during meetings of the cabinet from the trial to the date of the hangings.[82]

That morning Anna returned to her mother's cell and, in the presence of Father Walter, asked, "Mother, are you resigned?" — to which

Mrs. Surratt replied, "Yes, my child." Shortly afterward, according to the priest's recollection a quarter century later, Mrs. Surratt said, "Father, I wish to say something."

"What is it, my child?"

"That I am innocent."

"You may say so if you wish," he rejoined, "but it will do no good."[83]

Fifteen years after the incident Clampitt, who was also in the cell, remembered the dialogue somewhat differently, writing that Walter had just given the last rites when Mrs. Surratt asked, "Father, can I not tell these people before I die that I am innocent of the crime for which I have been condemned to death?"

"No, my child," Walter replied. "The world and all that in it has now receded forever. It would do no good, and it might disturb the serenity of your last moments."[84]

Attorneys Aiken and Clampitt were not permitted to stay long in Mary Surratt's cell.[85] Yet even though the writ of habeas corpus had been suspended they still held out hope for a reprieve. On their way to the penitentiary, they had driven past mounted couriers, waiting like relay runners to gallop from the White House with word of a pardon or reprieve.[86] Both men paced anxiously in the anteroom, whispering to each other out of earshot of inquisitive reporters.

Suddenly attention focused on an echoing rattle from the wooden scaffold, where three-hundred-pound weights had plunged to test the efficiency of the twin traps. Two bodies were to fall through each trap, six feet long and four feet wide, separated by the upright timber supporting the crossbeam. One trap worked perfectly, but the other needed adjusting with a saw and a hatchet. The lone hangman now waited confidently for his quartet to approach.[87] He had taken every precaution he could think of to ensure a satisfactory outcome. But hangmen had limited opportunities for experience. Another hangman, four years later, so bungled his job that the rope stretched until the victim's toes touched the ground, whereupon infuriated onlookers manually hoisted the rope to strangle the murderer to death.[88]

The Lincoln conspirators would have to climb thirteen steps at the rear of the scaffold up to the spectral platform, twenty feet long and fifteen feet wide. All of it rested about ten feet above ground.[89] Dangling below the twenty-foot-high crossbeam were the four elliptical nooses, readied with twists and knots to break the necks of their loads. Two days earlier, Major Eckert had told the hangman, Captain Christian Rath from the prison governor's staff,[90] to prepare to hang four people even though he did not think more than three nooses would be used. Rath inferred, like many others, that Mrs. Surratt would not hang with the rest, but now it appeared he was wrong. A handful of artists from illustrated publications sketched the spare and forbidding gallows, which would have a life not much longer than the ceremony they had come to witness. It had been put together in the south yard hurriedly but so noisily that from his cell Mudd correctly guessed what the workmen were assembling.[91]

Untold numbers of men and woman filled the horse-drawn "cars" heading toward the penitentiary.[92] All hoped to witness the hangings, but only a few were allowed in when the main gate opened at ten o'clock.[93]

Hancock had received more than one thousand applications for passes but limited entry to several hundred, with a quarter reserved for the press. He banned anyone overtly sympathetic to the South or drawn out of mere curiosity. Many who could not get in through the gate boarded boats passing by to Alexandria. But none of their maneuvers outwitted authorities, because the gallows were obscured by walls. The celebrated photographer Alexander Gardner positioned himself at a penitentiary window, preparing his lenses to record the prisoners' arrival, recitation of their death warrants, adjustment of the nooses, and suspension of the inert corpses. Voyeurs jostled at available windows while more spectators squeezed tightly for vantage points atop the only other building overlooking the scaffolding.[94]

A slight breeze brought temporary relief from the oppressive heat, hovering around a hundred degrees, when Hancock pulled up in his buggy about noon. He entered an anteroom near the heavily riveted door blocking a corridor to the prisoners' cells and conferred in low tones with Hartranft. As they parted, Hancock raised his voice. "Get ready, general," he ordered. "I want to have everything put in readiness as soon as possible."[95] It was the signal for clergymen, relatives, and friends to make haste for the executions.

Aiken stepped up to speak with Hancock, and the press noted the lawyer's crestfallen expression. In a voice quivering with emotion, Aiken told a reporter, "Mrs. Surratt will be hung."[96]

CHAPTER 27

"I Could Have Jumped upon the Shoulders of Each as They Hung"

About 12:30 PM Anna's shrieks and cries pierced the building when she was forced to part with her mother. Prison guards made no effort to hide their tears from ever-watchful reporters.[1] Herold's sisters followed shortly afterward, all of them crying out loudly.[2] John Clampitt pressed Mrs. Surratt's hand in a parting gesture of support as he bid her a final farewell.[3] William Doster, the last of the lawyers to depart, took leave of his client, Atzerodt. Then chairs were taken from the cells to make room for the prisoners' exits.

There was no shade for those who had scrambled for tickets to witness death under the midday sun. A delay in the prisoners' appearance sparked rumors and lively guessing. Perhaps there had been some reprieves or military obedience to a writ of habeas corpus. Maybe Hancock had been arrested for refusing to obey the court.[4]

Almost fifteen minutes passed before journalists were escorted into the yard, where the public with passes had gathered. The gallows dominated the enclosure, its crossbeams supporting the ropes. One spectator was so surprised to see four nooses instead of three that he exclaimed incredulously, "My God! They are not going to hang all four, are they!"[5] Then four armchairs were carried onto the scaffold, each positioned close to a suspended noose.

Even though the prisoners had yet to be hanged, their graves were open to receive them. They had been dug ten paces to the right of the scaffold and would be visible unless the prisoners walked with bowed heads up to the gallows. Beside the fresh mounds of red soil that soon would be shoveled back over the graves lay the four unplaned pinewood coffins, looking like packing boxes made for long-barreled weapons.[6]

Rows of guards formed a protective square around the scaffold, prepared for instant but unlikely intervention. A brick wall soared behind the scaffolding, its white stone top densely packed with armed troops.[7] No one could scale this wall without facing fire from above. Unrest in the courtyard below could be suppressed easily by deadly force overhead.

A lofty prison door creaked as Hancock came out for a hurried survey. Mrs. Surratt, accompanied by Fathers Walter and Wiget,[8] led the dismal procession at the pace of a funeral cortege. All four condemned were manacled at their wrists and ankles for the thirty-yard shuffle to death. Guards and prayerful clergy also flanked each male prisoner. The woman was clothed in black, from the bonnet and dark veil on her head to the hem of her alpaca dress. At first she glanced up at the gallows, then lowered her head and looked down. She faltered at the base of the steps and had to be assisted to the platform. One of the priests held a crucifix in front of her as if to encourage and sustain her faith.

She seemed to collapse into the chair at the extreme left as she faced the spectators. Then she leaned wearily on her right arm, her head inclined upward toward a priest. The other prelate clasped an umbrella to shield her from the blazing sun.

Atzerodt followed in the familiar drab, dark gray coat and pants, black vest, and white collarless shirt that he had worn throughout the trial. He still looked roguish and dirty, with a thin mustache and goatee. Woolen slippers without heels made him look even shorter, especially as he moved with rounded shoulders. Motioned to take the chair farthest from Mrs. Surratt, he crouched at an angle to look to his right. Atzerodt alone arrived bareheaded, but someone placed a white handkerchief on his head to protect him from the scorching heat. The cleric who stood by to console him also held an umbrella for shade.

None seemed as unnerved as Herold, who looked frightened from the moment he followed Atzerodt. He was haggard and even sloppy, with the rim of his black slouch hat pulled down. Herold too appeared in a collarless white shirt beneath the rumpled black cloth coat and light pants he had worn in court daily. When he took his seat on Atzerodt's right, he looked around wildly, like prey without hope of escape.

Though restrained by leg and wrist irons, Payne seemed cheerfully oblivious to the drama, walking straight and erect as if proud. He was even jauntily dressed, sporting a straw hat with ribbon on his head and a matching sailor-blue color for his shirt and long-legged pants. To one observer Payne looked "much like a clean-faced, well-developed Jack-tar."[9]

As a stillness fell over the courtyard, Hartranft recited the death warrants while an aide held up an open umbrella to shield the governor from the sun.[10] Atzerodt appeared to listen attentively, glancing only once at the crowd. But even though concentrating on the proceedings, he looked the epitome of misery. Mrs. Surratt leaned forward several times to kiss the crucifix. Herold could not suppress profound fear, which made his body tremble. But Payne remained blissfully serene, to the astonishment of all who looked on. When a sudden breeze blew off his straw hat, he looked around to see where it landed. A bystander picked it up and returned it, but he intimated that he no longer needed the hat, and it was put aside.

When the governor had completed his recitation, the clergymen spoke for their charges and offered prayers for the salvation of their souls. Father Walter prayed with Mrs. Surratt as Father Wiget held the cross to her lips. Dr. Gillette said Payne wanted to thank Hartranft and the prison staff "for their uniform and disinterested kindness" and for never giving him an unkind word, look, or gesture. Herold, speaking through Dr. Olds, asked forgiveness for "all the evil he had done" and said he died in charity with the world. Atzerodt's minister also thanked prison officials for their kindness, but when he concluded, "May the Lord God have mercy on you and grant you His peace," Mrs. Surratt could not stifle a very audible moan.

Then they were made to stand while bound with strips of tenting near their elbows, knees, and ankles. It would constrain them from flailing and kicking. For a moment Mrs. Surratt looked unsteady, and it was feared she might collapse in a faint. "Please, don't let me fall," she begged of those standing closest.[11] Then she turned her head slightly and muttered something inaudible. She may have said her elbows were pinioned too tightly, because officials adjusted the bonds. Atzerodt too spoke while his arms were being tied. "Gentlemen, take ware," he said indistinctly as his body shook with fright.[12] The bonnet, slouch hat, and handkerchief were removed and replaced by identical white hoods that slipped over their heads and fell down to their shoulders. The hangman, Captain Christian Rath, fearing he might see their tongues hanging out after execution, had made the head covers from the cloth of an army tent.[13]

Rath moved down the line, positioning the nooses around each neck. A spectator near the scaffold threw up his hands in disbelief. "Gentlemen," he exclaimed, "I tell you this is murder! Can you stand and see it done!" No one moved in to seize him, because he appeared to be a loner, but he was kept under intensely careful watch.[14] When the hangman adjusted Payne's noose, explaining that it would make death easier and quicker, the bound man replied, "All right, Captain Rath, you're the boss, and should know better."[15]

Accounts differ on who clapped hands or otherwise signaled the traps to be sprung at precisely 1:30 PM.[16] It was either Hartranft,[17] an army infantry captain,[18] or the hangman.[19] Instantly, four soldiers under the platform knocked away the poles supporting the drops, and the traps opened wide with a slam. The bodies plummeted into the void until the nooses yanked them short. Atzerodt was speaking audibly, saying, "Goodbye gentlemen who are before me now. May we all meet in the other world. God help me now! Oh! Oh! Oh!" when his body dropped into space.[20] Witnesses saw his stomach heave and a quiver pass through his legs, but he died abruptly.[21] Father Walter peered over the open trap to look at the woman he had prayed with, but she made no movement.[22] Others in front of the scaffold saw her hands twitch fleetingly before the corpse hung limp and heavy.[23] Herold jerked and shuddered for five fitful minutes, his pants soiling with urine during the extended death throes.[24] Payne suffered most in a reflexive resistance to death. Witnesses timing his seven minutes of exertion watched with awe as he tried to lift himself into a sitting position, to relieve the pressure on his neck.[25] But his strength was no match for the rope that gripped his windpipe.

A hush fell over the courtyard as no one moved or spoke. Spectators stood as if paralyzed. Minutes passed and still no one budged or said anything.[26] Hangings were rare and seldom witnessed by masses, but this spectacle had been multiplied fourfold. Twenty minutes elapsed before surgeons Otis, Woodward, and Porter moved up to examine the corpses and then to pronounce them dead.[27] Ten more minutes passed before the bodies were taken down. As a ladder was placed against the scaffolding, a corporal knelt upon the platform and cut the rope holding Atzerodt. His corpse fell to the ground with a thud, and the soldier was immediately called to order for a public reprimand.[28]

The remaining bodies were taken down with more fitting decorum and carefully examined by the surgeons. When the rope holding Mrs. Surratt was cut, her head fell limply toward her breast. "She makes a good bow," quipped one bystander. The comment drew an instant rebuke from an officer.[29] The rope had cut deeply into her neck, and as the hangman removed the noose pieces of flesh stuck to the strands. Rath would remember it with revulsion long into his old age.[30]

Herold's neck may also have broken, but the nooses on Payne and Atzerodt had apparently caught at the base of their skulls, leaving the bones intact.[31] Soldiers unclasped the metal manacles and cut loose the strips of binding.[32] But the white hoods were left in place as the corpses were laid in their coffins.[33] To guarantee their identities in the event of future exhumation, the name of each was written on paper, slipped into a bottle, and placed inside the appropriate coffin.[34]

Hancock telegraphed Stanton with confirmation of the hangings even before the surgeons certified all were dead. "The bodies will be interred near the scaffold," he added a full half hour before this was done.[35]

Father Walter took Anna back to her home on H Street. Now notorious, the boardinghouse had attracted hundreds of curious bystanders, some of whom expected to see the arrival of Mrs. Surratt's corpse. By evening souvenir hunters were hacking pieces from the front steps, until they were chased off by police. Hundreds more remained across the road to stare at the capital's newest landmark.[36]

Others rejoiced deliriously on receiving news of the executions. Benjamin Brown French metamorphosed from scholar, poet, eminent Freemason, and worthy Washingtonian into a gleefully vengeful killer, fantasizing in a letter to his son that he probably could have "jumped upon the shoulders of each as they hung, after the ancient manner of rendering death certain."[37]

Bereft and without hope of solace, Anna waited two days before writing a personal letter to Hartranft. She had learned that Hancock needed her consent to release from his custody some meager possessions of her mother. "Don't forget," she wrote pitifully, "to send the pillow upon which her head rested, and her prayer beads if you can find them — these are things dear to me."[38]

She expected to receive the remains of her mother, writing Stanton that "she lived a Christian life, died a Christian death, and now don't refuse her a Christian burial."[39] But the War Department responded icily, informing her two weeks later that the president and cabinet had discussed it, and Andrew Johnson had directed that "the bodies should continue interred where they now are, as the proper place for persons found guilty of the crime for which they suffered."[40] Anna, like relatives of the other dead, would wait almost four years before the president, in a parting gesture just weeks before leaving office, authorized release of all the remains.[41]

The passing years gave no peace of mind to aging Judge Advocate General Joseph Holt, who was tormented by the fate of Mrs. Surratt. Twenty years after the hangings Holt's shaky handwriting betrayed the frailty of a seventy-eight-year-old man when he wrote Hartranft asking whether Mrs. Surratt had confessed shortly before she died. "I have the impression, and still have it, that she died without making on the scaffold in any public way, any declaration of her guilt or innocence," he wrote. "Your presence, and your official relation to the case will enable you to say without hesitation whether this impression of mine is well or ill-founded."[42] But Hartranft could not comfort the old man's troubled conscience, because, as he wrote, he did not know.[43]

CHAPTER 28

"A Perfect Hell"

Samuel Arnold heard the rattle of chains along the corridor outside his cell and brushed it off as the jangle of fettered steps of new arrivals. He assumed the hammering on the unseen gallows had been workmen repairing the building. But within an hour of the executions, a colonel opened the cell door, sat down on a small box used as a table, and with gentle sensitivity told of the hangings and identified the four put to death. Arnold was "thunderstruck," not even knowing they had been convicted. He was flabbergasted by the inclusion of Mrs. Surratt, whom he firmly believed to be innocent.[1]

Shock turned to dread, for neither the colonel nor anyone else divulged the verdicts on the four still alive. Arnold imagined he and the others would be taken out and hanged at intervals.[2] Eight days passed, during which they exercised briefly in the morning and evening in the yard with the gallows and the graves. The four fresh mounds looked like offerings to a hungry scaffold, with Arnold imagining the graves as "its feast of death."[3]

He had prepared for execution or incarceration in a farewell letter to his mother, almost sobbing that he had been tempted "in an evil hour" into conspiring to abduct the president. But he assured her, "I know nothing of the act for which I suffer." Not knowing whether he would live or die, he saved his tenderest thoughts for his pet. "Keep my dog till he dies," he instructed his mother. "Erect a slab inscription, 'A true friend,' for he would never forsake me even should the whole world do so."[4]

On the ninth day following the hangings Hartranft sat at the far end of the yard and called each of the prisoners separately to listen to the findings of the court. All were to have been imprisoned at Albany, New York, but Hartranft, following orders, withheld a secret modification by President Johnson that banished them to Fort Jefferson, a military prison on one of the remote islands collectively labeled Dry Tortugas, ninety miles north of Cuba.[5]

A strong force of guards came at midnight, unlocked the cells, and led Arnold, Mudd, Spangler, and O'Laughlin in double irons to the Arsenal wharf. They boarded the steamer *State of Maine* and at 2 AM sailed down the Potomac to a destination known to only a few, and to none of the prisoners.[6]

Hartranft had completed his regimen without blemish. His long and trying vigil was over. The condemned had been hanged and buried, and the convicts shipped off to hard labor. Now he would boost the careers of those who had served him well, recommending promotions for the hangman, the doctor, and some officers.[7] His own performance won plaudits from Stanton, who wrote a personal letter of gratitude.[8] It was time to go home to Sallie.

The prisoners were manhandled as if inanimate cargo. At Fort Monroe, Virginia, they were hauled by tug to a gunboat, where leg irons tore into their flesh as they climbed down ladders with rungs spaced farther apart than the distance between their manacled limbs. Only when they were opposite the coast of South Carolina were they brought out of the sweltering lower hold and allowed on the open deck. During daylight, while freed of the handcuffs, they wrote letters to those left behind. But they were forbidden to engage the crew.[9] While anchored overnight at Hilton Head, South Carolina, women and musicians boarded for a night of revelry as the sleepless prisoners lay chained and debased below.[10] They were back at sea when told of their destination, and it struck them with dread for the future. Arnold had never forgotten a description of the prison as "a perfect hell."[11]

George Porter, the prison doctor accompanying them, reached out to Mudd, even loaning him Rudolf Virchon's classic book on pathology. But while Porter and the officers relaxed in the Atlantic breezes, playing card games, checkers, and chess, the prisoners were miserably quiet. "Spangler's goodness seems to have vanished," Porter observed in his diary.[12]

Spangler daydreamed wistfully of his favorite saloon, where companions were as plentiful as whiskey. "When joy shall swell your heart," he wrote nostalgically to his friend, the owner, "stop for a moment to cast a lingering but bright thought upon him who was life, all life, amidst you. Sometimes think of me."[13]

In his obsession with the circumstances of his plight, Mudd may even have spoken indiscreetly about everything he knew of the crime. One of the guards later claimed the doctor told him he knew the assassin's identity when setting Booth's broken leg, and that he also knew "of what crime he was guilty."[14]

But even as Mudd sailed farther south from Washington, those left behind remained tenaciously loyal. His trial lawyer, Thomas Ewing Jr., wrote a letter of encouragement to the doctor's wife. "I do not know where he has been sent but . . . if he is sent to the Tortugas, the place is better for his health than almost any other. The island is dry and the climate good. Rely on it, wherever he has gone, his sanguine temperament will busy him and preserve his health and strength."[15]

Yet Mudd, like the others, yearned for the presence of family, writing Sarah that life had become "a void."[16] He drew her a picture of their farmhouse and colored it green with sea moss, then mailed it with a sketch of the island. But it brought neither comfort nor relief. "I am gloomy, sad and disponding [sic]," Sarah wrote Ewing, who had become her substitute confessor. "I feel like soul and body has [sic] been separated." Blaming herself for all of her husband's woes, she reasoned that "Our Lord has caused him to suffer . . . to punish me for loving the creature more than the Creator."[17] She told Ewing that everything on the farm had been destroyed by soldiers on the lookout for Booth, and that nothing had been planted, because equipment and fencing had been wrecked, and the laborers carried off to prison.[18] Fervently she begged the lawyer, "Write him a friendly letter. Tell him enough to give him hope."[19]

But the castaway was beyond consolation. He would never adapt to servitude in the barren and lifeless confine, which he detested as a "God-forsaken isle."[20] Having risen from the ocean, the island had no natural fresh water and had to rely on whatever trickled down from the sky, lashed over with passing storms, or else was brought in on supply ships. The cracked forty-five-foot high red-brick walls reached over most of the island's sixteen acres, shutting off the inmates from the clear waters and corrugated coral reefs and boulders upon which the fort's foundations had been built twenty years earlier. When first viewed in 1513 by Spanish explorers, the seven islands were dubbed Las Tortugas for the proliferation of sea turtles, but others, struck more by the scarcity of vegetation, gave them the more fitting name of Dry Tortugas.

That summer the four newcomers mingled with almost four hundred prisoners, most of whom had been convicted of rape, murder, mutiny, larceny, manslaughter, desertion, and insubordination.[21] The food was often stale and tasteless, and inmates fell ill with diarrhea and scurvy.[22] Officers were frequently drunk from liquor brought in on vessels or from raiding supplies set aside for the sick.[23]

Mudd's brittle tolerance collapsed after only two months when he learned that the relatively benign regiment of white guards from New York would be replaced by what he called "ignorant and prejudiced negro troops" from the Eighty-second US Colored Infantry Regiment, which had marched in Lincoln's funeral procession in Washington. Guards scheduled for departure warned that many of his existing privileges would be withdrawn when the black troops assumed control. It was more than the former slaveholder could stomach, and he groaned to his lawyer in a letter, "Their representations had much to do towards inflaming my already prejudiced feelings."[24]

He conspired with a young quartermaster to hide him aboard a steamer but was discovered even before the ship set sail when an officer ran his sword into the coal bunker and jabbed at the luckless stowaway.[25] Retribution was swift and severe. Mudd, Arnold, Spangler, and O'Laughlin were instantly handcuffed, shackled, and taken down to the dungeon.[26] There the physician's misery was compounded by the presence of black sentinels, provoking him to fulminate to his lawyer, "It is goading and humiliating to be subjected to a negro guard."[27]

Until then supervision and discipline had been lax. Now this gave way to despotic control, coinciding with word of a plot to rescue the four convicted co-conspirators. All the prisoners were confined after dusk; heavy ten-inch guns were readied to quell any uprising; and a gunboat was sent for from the mainland.[28] Overseers turned ruthless and sadistic. Those whom the military had found guilty would now suffer the punitive sequel. For four months they were forbidden to talk to anyone and were closely watched over to enforce the restriction.[29] Heartless abuse persisted, even when white units returned to relieve blacks. "We had traded off the witch for the devil," Arnold concluded.[30]

No one had expected barbarity, much less that they would witness atrocities. But all the island's prisoners were at risk. One sickly prisoner was tortured even though a doctor had exempted him from work. He was made to carry a thirty-two-pound ball until he could no longer stand, then he was shoved off the wharf into the sea with his hands tied behind his back and his legs bound firmly together. Though pulled out alive but gasping, he was tossed back several times and ultimately sent off to work.[31] Another prisoner targeted for drunkenness was suspended from a window by his thumbs, then left to dangle by his wrists through the night.[32]

Many who survived the terror did not live through an epidemic of yellow fever. The disease struck the island garrison in the broiling summer two years after the quartet's arrival from Washington. By the fourth week a hundred men lay jaundiced and vomiting, with the post's physician among the first to die. Dr. Mudd took charge spontaneously, ministering with wearying devotion even before the replacement arrived.[33] But O'Laughlin ignored his advice to stay bedridden and died within thirty-six hours of being diagnosed. It was a blow felt deeply by Mudd, who had warmed to O'Laughlin's personality and intellect.[34] When Mudd himself fell ill, he attributed his own survival to Arnold and Spangler, who watched over him "as if their own brother."[35]

As Andrew Johnson's presidency neared the end in the winter of 1868–1869, he reviewed the trial record of the conspirators and their sentences.[36] Three years earlier he had dismissed the possibility of pardoning any of those convicted, in the belief that political enemies would use it as a pretext for renewed attacks on himself.[37] But with only weeks left in office he had no fear of political repercussions.

Besides, the Constitution gave him the exclusive prerogative of clemency, which he could exercise without explanation.

Mudd's selfless attention to the sick and dying during the epidemic weighed heavily with the outgoing president. A lieutenant and 299 noncommissioned officers and privates who had witnessed Mudd caring for the afflicted petitioned for a pardon in tribute to the many lives saved by the doctor.[38] Medical colleagues pleaded for "a lenient" interpretation of their fellow physician's decision to set Booth's broken leg, writing the president that it came "within the obligations of professional duty." Thirty-nine members of the US Congress also pressed for a pardon. At length, Andrew Johnson concluded there was "room for uncertainty as to the true measure and nature of the complicity in the attempted escape" of Booth and Herold, and signed the full and unconditional pardon on February 8, 1869.[39] In mid-March, Mudd left the island a free man in the schooner *Matchless*.[40]

Arnold's absence from Washington on the night of the murder gave the president more leeway when considering a petition from the Baltimore City Council and several hundred of the city's residents. The pardon came three weeks after the petition arrived, with the president noting that Arnold had "rendered no active assistance to Booth and his confederates in the actual execution of the abominable crime."[41]

Friends of Spangler's family cited the physically disabled condition of his octogenarian father, a former county sheriff, and his septuagenarian mother, both of whom needed his support after another son had been crippled in a fall from a building.[42] Spangler's pardon, also backed by the mayor and city council of Baltimore, was granted the same day as Arnold's, though signed without comment.[43]

The president had not overlooked the dead. He ordered the remains of David Herold delivered to the family's pastor,[44] who had written Johnson, "It seems unworthy of Christian civilization that the vengeance of human law, however righteous, should be carried into the grave, where it can punish none but survivors."[45]

Father Jacob Walter, who had given the last rites to Mrs. Surratt in the penitentiary, was allowed to receive her remains after Anna Surratt begged for permission to bury her mother in consecrated ground.[46]

After the lawyer representing George Atzerodt's family wrote scathingly that "the present enlightened age . . . will not permit the mediaeval and barbaric custom of seeking revenge on a handful of dust and ashes,"[47] the president authorized exhumation and delivery of the remains to a brother, John Atzerodt.[48]

A plea from Michael O'Laughlin's mother for the removal of her son's remains from the Dry Tortugas was granted the very next day.[49]

The oldest of the Booth siblings, Edwin, appealed on behalf of his "poor mother" for the return of her son's body to "lessen the weight of grief that is hurrying my mother to the grave." Aware of the controversy that might follow re-interment of Lincoln's assassin, Edwin promised "the strictest secrecy," pledging that the sexton of Christ Church, Baltimore, would keep the body in a vault "until such time as we can remove other members of our family to the Baltimore cemetery, and thus prevent any special notice of it."[50]

The man who had succeeded to the presidency responded with a rare show of the compassion that had come naturally to his predecessor: He ordered what was left of the assassin to be removed and "properly interred."[51]

CHAPTER 29

"Why This Flight, and Why This Concealment?"

Sheltered by Catholic clerics in a remote Canadian hideaway, John Surratt had no inkling that his mother's life was in danger until the noose was readied to hang her. Throughout the trial he had been protectively duped by friends in Montreal with misleading assurances that she would be found innocent, or at least be spared the gallows.

His lawyer later would state that John Surratt "was driven frantic with grief when at last, on the eve of the execution, he discovered that she had been convicted and was about to be executed, and was only prevented by force from returning to Washington to surrender himself."[1]

Surratt had slipped into Canada more than a week before Lincoln's assassination, registering on April 6 at Montreal's St. Lawrence Hall, a hotel favored by Booth and resident Confederate agents. In what would be his final assignment as a courier for the collapsing Confederate government, he handed over dispatches to General Edwin Lee, the newly appointed top Southern agent in Canada.

A week later Lee sent the venturesome young man on one of the last espionage missions of the war. Surratt filtered south of the border to scout out a prison at Elmira, New York, for a possible raid to free Confederate captives. Edwin Lee, cousin of Robert E. Lee — who had surrendered a few days earlier to Ulysses S. Grant — stood alone among his expatriate coterie in refusing to despair of the rebellion. "No one here pretends to believe now that there is a shadow of hope for our cause — except myself," he confided in a letter to his mother. "I scoff the idea [sic] of submission. Everybody thinks I am a fool."[2] He ordered Surratt to sketch guard posts and approaches to the prison, and report back on the number of sentinels, the quantity of stored weapons, and the condition and location of the imprisoned Southerners.[3]

Surratt registered under the alias of John Harrison at the Brainard House in Elmira on April 12, two days before Lincoln's murder.[4] Over the next three days the Confederate spy was mistaken for a Canadian because he wore a "Garibaldi" coat with pleated front and back and belted waist, a garment popular at the time only north of the border. The coat had been made in Montreal specifically for him by a tailor attached to the underground.[5] Surratt, under cover, immediately began sketching the prison, noting its approaches and assessing its forces.

On the morning of Saturday, April 15, with his mission accomplished, the secret agent with sunken eyes walked into an Elmira clothing store to buy shirts. The proprietor, having read of the assassination in the newspaper, then confirmed it by rushing across the road to the telegraph office, reported that he had some "some very bad news."

"What?" asked Surratt.

"The death of Abraham Lincoln."

Surratt muttered something disrespectful that made the clothier "feel rather incensed," but the shopkeeper quickly dismissed it as the thoughtless reaction of a Canadian opposed to Unionists.[6] On his way back to Montreal, Surratt stopped at Canandaigua, New York, registering at the Webster House as John Harrison from New York.[7] The following day he arrived in St. Albans, Vermont, not far from the Canadian border, and was breakfasting in a hotel when someone asked whether he knew Lincoln had been assassinated.

"I do not believe it, because the story is too good to be true," Surratt replied.

He was handed a newspaper that made him reel. An article pointedly named him as the assailant who had tried to kill Seward. He was so shaken that the paper slipped from his fingers, and he instantly left the room.[8]

He returned to Montreal, relieved to be once more among friends and allies in the relative safety of neutral Canada. Lee paid him a hundred dollars for the valuable intelligence and crude sketches and another forty for expenses.[9]

But Surratt quickly moved out of St. Lawrence Hall into hiding places known only to fellow agents and intimates. Bounty hunters and amateur sleuths might soon be on his trail, attracted by the twenty-five-thousand-dollar reward for his arrest. His face was already known to millions through photographic reproductions in newspapers and on wanted posters. News outlets throughout the country and in Canada had described him accurately as a slim man about five foot nine, weighing 145 to 150 pounds, with thin dark hair, a low broad forehead, prominent cheekbones, a narrow chin, square shoulders, and a slightly pale complexion.

Detectives accompanied by two of Mrs. Surratt's boarders, Louis Weichmann and John Holahan, were already en route to Canada in the hope of tracking him down. By the time they arrived in Montreal on April 20, however, their quarry had disappeared.[10]

Surratt hid out briefly in the Montreal home of an expatriate Tennessee banker before fleeing the city and arriving at the home of a Catholic priest, Father Charles Boucher, in the hamlet of St. Liboire, about forty-five miles northeast of Montreal.[11] The small band of Confederate agents who had colluded with sympathetic French-speaking Catholic clerics in smuggling Surratt this far would provide him with food and shelter, and maintain a secrecy as exacting as that in the confessional.

Father Boucher had been told that a "Charles Armstrong" was being sent into his care in the countryside because of the man's failing health and what was cryptically described as his "being compromised in the American war."[12] The priest provided peace, comfort, and privacy, keeping his thoughts to himself and betraying little if any curiosity. Almost two weeks passed before the cleric read in the papers that Surratt was accused of being one of the conspirators linked to Lincoln's murder. Only then did he suspect that Charles Armstrong, his English-speaking guest, might be the target of the American manhunt. But he never questioned his ward, and when Surratt voluntarily disclosed his identity, Father Boucher made no attempt to inform on him.[13]

For three months Surratt remained hidden in the village, sometimes falling so ill with fever that Boucher feared he might die.[14] But he was flushed from safe haven only weeks after his mother's execution when a suspicious female servant saw movement in his darkened bedroom and, mistaking Surratt's blurred figure for a female, tattled to villagers that their parish priest was harboring a mistress.[15]

To escape the uproar and prying eyes, Surratt was hustled more than two hundred miles north to Murray Bay on the St. Lawrence River. In mid-August he returned to Montreal,[16] where he lay low for a month at the home of the trusted father of another dependable Catholic priest, Father Larcille La Pierre.[17]

Exactly five months after Lincoln's death, Surratt set off on a perilous escape to England and Europe to distance himself from American lawmen. Now much thinner and looking run-down, Surratt disguised himself by wearing glasses, staining his face, and darkening his hair, eyebrows, and mustache with dye.[18] He took a mail steamer with Father La Pierre to Quebec City, then boarded the steamer *Peruvian* for Liverpool. Before parting from his charge, the priest furtively introduced Surratt to the ship's surgeon, Lewis McMillan, whose relationship with the clerics sheltering the fugitive remains baffling.[19] McMillan had once tussled with Father Boucher over their opposing views on abortion after the surgeon called the anti-abortion priest a "blackguard."[20]

The surgeon, a small man with florid complexion and bright eyes,[21] thought Surratt's behavior normal during the voyage, except for a nervous alertness, as though guarding against surprise capture. On the first day at sea Surratt pointed to one passenger, telling the surgeon that he thought the man was an American detective on the lookout for him.

"What have you done that you should be afraid of an American detective?" McMillan asked.

Surratt only hinted, saying he had done more things than the surgeon was aware of and that, very likely, if he knew, it would make him gape. McMillan told him not to fear, for he was aboard a British ship in British waters, and if a US detective had been pursuing him, the detective would have attempted the arrest before they left

Quebec. Surratt drew a small four-barreled revolver from his waist-coat pocket and swore that if the man did try to arrest him, "this will settle him."[22]

On another occasion, while talking of the possibility of being arrested in England, Surratt said he would shoot the first officer who laid a hand on him. McMillan countered that he would be shown little leniency in England, to which the American responded, "I know it, and for that very reason I would do it, because I would rather be hung by an English hangman than by a Yankee one, for I know very well if I go back to the United States, I shall swing."[23] Over the course of eight days, according to the surgeon, Surratt spoke of the aborted plot to kidnap Lincoln and acknowledged his role in the planning. He also traced his movements before, during, and after the assassination, placing himself far from Washington, DC, on the night of the murder.

Late on the night that they approached Londonderry, Ireland, the surgeon was surprised to see Surratt preparing to disembark. "Are you going ashore?" McMillan inquired. "I thought you were coming down to Liverpool."

"I have thought over the matter, and I believe it is better for me to get out here," the fugitive replied. "It is now dark and there is less chance of being seen."

"Will you please give me your own name?" the surgeon asked.

The wary man going into exile looked around, then whispered, "My name is Surratt."[24]

McMillan would later state that once he knew Surratt's identity he had a duty to report all he had heard to US authorities. Shortly after landing at Liverpool, he called on the US vice consul, Henry Wilding. Yet, eager to keep his identity and the name of his employer out of the public domain, McMillan described himself only as a passenger aboard the *Peruvian*. He asked the American diplomat to promise confidentiality in return for revealing "a secret of importance." He received the vice consul's assurance, then signed an affidavit disclosing all, linking Surratt by the fugitive's own admission to the conspiracy to kidnap the president. Wilding responded by telling the surgeon that he would be entitled to a "heavy reward" if Surratt were to be captured.[25]

Surratt left Londonderry, traveled on to Liverpool, and then three days later took a train to London.[26] There he may have called on the former Confederate brigadier general Roswell Ripley, who was notorious for having been in charge of the artillery battery that had fired on Fort Sumter in the opening barrage of the Civil War. Surratt and Ripley had met and conversed several times while crossing the Atlantic on the *Peruvian,* and the general had promised that he or his agent in London would provide a remittance if ever Surratt found himself "very hard up for money."[27]

McMillan and Surratt linked up several more times at the Canadian's boardinghouse near Liverpool, even though the surgeon had double-crossed the runaway and hoped he would soon be arrested. They met only at night, with Surratt burying his face in the folds of a long cloak for fear he might be recognized.[28]

While Surratt remained in England, the US vice consul had alerted Washington, sending the State Department a copy of McMillan's affidavit but doubting it was sufficient to press for Surratt's extradition.[29] Wilding later sent another dispatch pinpointing Surratt's lodgings as the Oratory of the Roman Catholic Church of the Holy Cross in Liverpool. Catholic clergy traveling to and from America frequently stayed there, and, he wrote, as "Mrs. Surratt was a very devout Roman Catholic . . . the fact of this young man going there somewhat favors the belief that he is really Surratt. If it be Surratt, such a wretch ought not to escape."[30]

But the State Department dictated to the perplexed vice consul that "upon consultation with the secretary of war and the judge advocate general, it is thought advisable that no action be taken in regard to the arrest of the supposed John Surratt at present."[31] Stanton thought Surratt should be "fully identified" before any attempt at arrest.[32] The State Department thought it "useless" to try to arrest him in any country controlled by the British, whose courts had so frustrated Americans, most recently by refusing on legal technicalities to extradite pirates who had fled from the Chesapeake Bay.[33]

Meanwhile the former seminarian, cultured, resourceful, and wily, had become a scrounging dependent, relying on others for food and shelter and concerned that his hosts at the Oratory seemed to have tired of him.[34] Yet somehow he found the wherewithal to leave the country and cross into France en route to his ultimate destination — Rome.

Once more he exploited his Catholic ties, entering the office of the papal nuncio in Paris, which had been authorized by the sympathetic papal government to issue visas to holders of Confederate passports.[35] He presented a Canadian passport in the name of John Watson, acquired under false pretenses in Montreal eleven months earlier,[36] and said he wanted to continue to Rome to enlist in the Zouaves Regiment of the papal military forces. The visa was issued without the usual demand for payment.[37]

Surratt arrived penniless at the port city of Civitavecchia but once again was rescued from destitution, this time by the rector of the English College in Rome, some fifty miles southeast. There in the ancient city, the sole survivor of Booth's cabal still at liberty enlisted in the Zouaves on December 9, 1865, using the alias of John Watson.[38] "It would appear that he slipped through this country with little official cognizance," the US minister to Britain reflected later in his diary, and "his Catholic sympathies carried him safely to Rome through the continent."[39]

Under the guise of a false name, Surratt was safely ensconced in the military guard among thousands of enlistees from far-flung countries. Nothing in his appearance made him stand out. All wore the identical uniform of tasseled cappa, gray jacket trimmed with red, and baggy trousers reaching down to the calf.

But his relief and fictitious identity would be short-lived. On March 24, 1866, a French Canadian, Henry St. Marie, enlisted in the Zouaves and was assigned to the Ninth Company.[40] About three weeks later, while at Sezze, sixty miles south of Rome, he recognized Surratt, then attached to the Third Company.[41] It has never been established whether this meeting was by chance or the result of a calculated design by St. Marie to hunt down Surratt for the reward. The two had met through a mutual acquaintance three years earlier when St. Marie was teaching at a school in the Maryland village of Ellen Gowan, so isolated that he was desperate to leave.[42] He had begged Surratt and another visitor, Louis Weichmann, to help him obtain a teaching position in Washington, and hinted that he might go to the South. Surratt had no success in finding him the job, but he offered to smuggle St. Marie through Union lines to the Confederate States. While St. Marie might have to bide his time in Washington for two or three weeks, Surratt offered warm hospitality, once writing to him: "We can easily make the time pass agreeably."[43]

Weichmann too was fascinated by the Canadian's sophistication, polished manners, charming conversation, and fluency in French, English, and Italian. But even though Weichmann arranged for St. Marie to be an assistant teacher at the school in Washington where he taught, they had a falling-out. Within weeks the Canadian had disappeared without any farewell.[44]

Weichmann's hand of friendship and Surratt's generous offer of the past were of no consequence to the new arrival, who now relished the prospect of riches for turning in the man on the run. He hailed the American by his real name, and during that momentous meeting, at an inaudible distance from their colleagues, St. Marie said Surratt admitted being part of the assassination plot and that Confederate president Jefferson Davis had incited it, or at least been aware of it.[45] He quoted Surratt telling him, "Damn the Yankees, they have killed my mother. But I have done them as much harm as I could. We have killed Lincoln." Accusing Weichmann of being responsible for his mother's death, Surratt vowed, according to St. Marie, "If I ever return to America, or meet him elsewhere, I shall kill him."[46] The Canadian found nothing implausible in Surratt's self-incrimination, even as the fugitive appealed for the virtual stranger to hold his tongue.

At the earliest opportunity, St. Marie sped to Rome's Palazzo Talviati to pass on his joyous discovery to Rufus King, US minister to the Papal States. The informant, thirty-three, begged for his own role to be kept secret, then pressed for quick action, worried that his company might be deployed deeper into the mountainous area, from where it would be even more difficult to communicate with Rome.[47]

Euphorically, St. Marie wrote to his brother in Montreal: "I believe that I have found an affair, which will make me rich and will bring me back soon to Canada, if I succeed."[48] Later he was more precise but no less avaricious. "I have discovered here in Italy, John Surratt, one of the assassins of Lincoln. You know there was a reward of $50,000 offered for him," he wrote, erroneously doubling the amount. "I think I will be well rewarded, if I live to get back."[49]

He would not learn for almost a year that the secretary of war had long since revoked the offer of a reward for Surratt's capture.[50] Stanton had decided the fugitive was not in the United States, and that if captured abroad the arrest would have to be made by a government official, who should not be allowed to profit for doing his duty. He also thought that withdrawing the offer of a handsome payout would deceive Surratt into thinking the hunt was over, thereby luring him back to America.[51]

King, fifty-two, an earnest emissary and former West Point graduate, newspaper owner and editor, and Union army combat general, did not doubt any of St. Marie's exposé.[52] But if he knew of the revocation of the reward, he never told his informant. Instead King passed on the startling disclosures to the State Department, writing Seward: "There seemed such entire absence of motive for any false statement."[53]

Washington, however, was cautious, demanding St. Marie provide more information about himself.[54] The Canadian complied, disclosing that he had moved to Washington about six months before the end of the war. After "difficulties" with Weichmann he had joined the Union army, been captured and released, then returned to his native Canada. Following Lincoln's assassination, he said, he had informed the US consul in Montreal that Weichmann and Surratt were "as guilty as the other" and that Weichmann had acted through fear "in selling his accomplice."[55]

Though serving in an army of Catholics to protect the pope and his realm, the enigmatic St. Marie went on to flay the clergy of his faith, convinced not only that they were protecting Surratt but that the hierarchy was implicated in the assassination as well. "The murder is the result of a deep laid plot, not only against the life of President Lincoln, but against the existence of the Republic, as we are aware that priesthood and royalty are, and always have been, opposed to liberty," he charged in a sworn affidavit.[56]

Confident of Surratt's real identity, King called on the papal secretary of state, Cardinal Giacomo Antonelli, who had expressed "horror" at the assassination and refused the Confederacy official recognition even though he had warmly received rebel emissaries.[57] Pope Pius IX had been similarly ambivalent in private meetings with Unionists and secessionists, welcoming both and offending neither. Now, Antonelli intimated, he would probably consent to hand over Surratt to US custody if requested.[58]

However, months elapsed without action as Seward lay ill in Washington and top officials were absent from the US capital.[59] King tried to placate the impatient St. Marie, promising he would be "amply recompensed."[60] Reinvigorated, St. Marie wrote to his brother: "Sooner or later I shall be a rich man."[61]

But more weeks slipped by, and St. Marie, despairing of progress, threatened to disclose all to newspapers in New York and Philadelphia to force the US government's hand. His claims had become ever more bloated, with assertions that the Confederate government had financed the assassination and that Surratt had confessed to departing Washington on the evening of the assassination after "all was prepared for the deed."[62] St. Marie's threats to go public reached Washington, where Seward read his letter at a meeting of the cabinet and authorized King to reward the Canadian with $250 in gold and to help him achieve his other goal of receiving a discharge from the papal army.[63]

On November 2, 1866, Rufus King arrived at the Vatican to seek custody of John Surratt. It was an opportune moment to ask for a favor from a politically weakened papal government sorely in need of allies. King was well aware of the pope's crumbling political power as armed opponents, battling to strip him of temporal authority and unify the multitude of independent states, moved closer to the papal heartland of Rome. Pius IX had earlier told the American diplomat, "The poor Pope will be left all alone in his little boat in the midst of the tempestuous ocean."[64] It would not be long before the pontiff, fearing his enemies would overrun the Papal States and take Rome, pointed to a crucifix on his table and told King, "This is all my artillery."[65] The American would soon tell the State Department that several officials in the papal government had confided to him that "if the Pope felt to abandon Rome he might seek a refuge in the United States."[66]

King was buoyed to find Cardinal Antonelli "alone and disengaged." The American carried with him Benn Pitman's book-length transcript of the trial: *The Assassination of President Lincoln and the Trial of the Conspirators*. He opened it to show Antonelli photographs of Booth and Surratt, the four who were hanged, and the quartet sent to prison. Antonelli thought it would not be in keeping with the spirit of the papal government to surrender a criminal who might be put to death. However, "in so grave and exceptional a case, and with the understanding that the US government, under parallel circumstances, would do as they desired to be done by," he thought the request would be granted.[67]

Within days authorities arrested Surratt at Veroli, about sixty miles southeast of Rome, and locked him overnight in a cell within a monastery built on the slope of a mountain overlooking a valley. The commander of the armed escort detailed to take Surratt to Rome saw him sipping coffee at four o'clock one morning with "a calmness and phlegm quite English." But as Surratt was being escorted near the prison gates, he bolted, leaping over a balustrade and falling to a rocky ledge thirty-five feet below. He fled in the darkness, eluding shots from above and an armed chase.[68] Years later a Dutch-born Zouave, Henry Lipman, derided the official account, disclosing that he and other guards connived with the American, enabling him to escape through a sewer several hours before they fired wildly in a make-believe attempt to stop the runaway.[69] Once more Surratt gave contradictory versions of his escapades, at first "laughing heartily" that he jumped down a high precipice, saying it was a lower embankment, but later confirming he did jump into a void, landing on the ledge about thirty-five feet below.[70]

The escapee turned himself in to police at Naples, beyond the boundaries of the Papal States, where he told authorities he was a penniless Englishman fleeing from a Roman regiment that had imprisoned him for insubordination. Three days later he was released at the British consulate after asserting he was a Canadian. A sympathetic

Englishman paid for his passage aboard the British steamer *Tripoli* sailing for Alexandria, Egypt.[71]

A series of bureaucratic and communications hurdles prevented US consuls at Naples and Malta from blocking Surratt's flight. However, a diplomatic dispatch reached the US consul at Alexandria in time to warn that Surratt would be arriving on the *Tripoli* dressed as a Zouave and using the alias John Agostino.[72]

When US consul Charles Hale boarded the *Tripoli* at Alexandria, only one of the seventy-eight passengers in third class was dressed in the uniform of a Zouave. Hale confronted Surratt, whose appearance matched the photograph he had studied in his own copy of Pitman's book on the conspirators' trial. Hale introduced himself as the resident US consul.

"You are the man I want. You are an American," he said.

"Yes, sir. I am," Surratt replied.

"You doubtless know why I want you. What is your name?"

"Walters," Surratt answered.

"I believe your true name is Surratt," Hale responded.

He put the fugitive under arrest, and they walked with an escort of armed soldiers to the quarantine quarters. There Hale cautioned Surratt that he need not speak, but anything he did say would be taken down in writing.

"I have nothing to say," Surratt replied.

He had neither passport nor baggage and only six francs. He was clothed in the same malodorous, rumpled uniform he had worn since leaping to freedom nineteen days earlier.[73] Two days later he was taken to the prison to await transport to the United States.

"But for the possibility that the wretch may throw some light upon the secret history of the great crime," wrote Consul Hale, "I should regard his capture as not worth the trouble it has cost."[74]

Surratt traveled back to the United States aboard a warship, the corvette *Swatara*. It became a floating prison for a man who had crossed continents and oceans to keep ahead of his pursuers. Surratt was handcuffed in a locked room and told that if he tried to flee he would be shot; if he became violent his legs would be shackled and his arms handcuffed behind his back. He was not allowed to talk to anyone, and precautions were taken to prevent suicide.[75] The prisoner promised "no trouble whatever."[76]

Rear Admiral Louis Goldsborough, commanding the European squadron, was taken aback by Surratt's manner and bearing after boarding the *Swatara* at Villefranche, France, where it anchored to take on coal. Hours earlier Goldsborough had written his wife he would "send the scamp direct to Washington."[77] Now the man who could "scarcely believe the stubborn fact" that he was about to turn sixty-two[78] was instantly impressed by the younger man's deportment — "modest and proper in every respect." Surratt had apparently bathed and had his clothes cleaned, for Goldsborough withheld none of his admiration in a glowing report to the navy secretary, who read it to his cabinet colleagues.[79] Surratt, the admiral observed, was "well clad, clean and composed. His countenance struck me as being mild and undisturbed, and he is evidently far from wanting in intelligence. His complexion is quite blond, and in person he is tall and slender. Indeed, he is certainly a handsome young man, and I should say from his appearance and bearing, prepossessing."[80]

The *Swatara* dropped anchor about fifty yards from the Navy Yard wharf in Washington on February 18, 1867.[81] Twenty-two months had passed since Surratt had fled from Elmira, New York, into the Canadian underground. His long odyssey in the shadows across Europe and the Mediterranean was over, and he was finally back in the land of his birth. Smoldering passions over Lincoln's assassination had long since subsided. Had he been caught in the dragnet that rounded up his mother and others, he would surely have joined them on the gallows. But now he was something of a curiosity as bystanders gathered on the wharf, speculating on his fate and hoping for a glimpse of the notorious outlaw from the past.

Armed with a warrant for Surratt's arrest, Marshal David Gooding appeared at the Navy Yard. A boat was lowered from the *Swatara* to bring Surratt ashore. Spectators cried out, "That's him!" "That's John Surratt!" Marshal Gooding approached the prisoner.

"Is your name John H. Surratt?"

"It is, sir."

"Then, sir, I arrest you by virtue of a bench warrant issued to me by the Criminal Court of the District of Columbia."

Surratt lowered his head. Still dressed in the gray Zouave uniform with white cotton leggings and the tasseled cappa on his head, he stepped into the backseat of the carriage beside the marshal. They drove quickly, passing by the Old Capitol Prison where his mother had been held before transfer to her cell near the gallows. Surratt said little, but observed that Washington looked very familiar. At the city jail he was transferred into the custody of the warden and led up to a recently renovated ironclad cell on the second floor.[82]

Nothing in his confinement resembled the brutalities suffered by his mother and the seven other prisoners two years earlier. Surratt was immediately allowed to roam the main corridor for daily exercise and licensed to smoke his pipe and read at will. A local newspaper reported that "the people of lower Maryland provide him with not only the substantials, but the delicacies of life."[83] Within days his sister Anna began visiting frequently, bringing choice items of food approved by the warden. His older brother Isaac, a former Confederate soldier, also visited to complete the reunion of the siblings. The prisoner spoke often of his travels, even laughing uproariously at false reports he had escaped from the Zouaves by leaping over a precipice as high as Washington's Patent Office building. It was nothing more than a low embankment, he told visitors, even though he cut his hand severely when landing.[84]

Authorities limited access to a few authorized visitors, to isolate Surratt from those who might manipulate him for political propaganda. The president's congressional enemies had already begun investigations that would lead to articles of impeachment, and Andrew Johnson worried they might entice Surratt to make false accusations to bolster their case. Under siege by ferocious antagonists, the president feared that a desperate and resentful Surratt, with his life at stake, might even agree to slander the head of state.[85]

When newspaper accounts of Surratt's flight and capture reached the US legation in Rome, Rufus King was flabbergasted to read he had been given no credit. Mustering a semblance of diplomatic reserve to complain of the slight, he wrote directly to Seward, accusing the papers of publishing "a variety of fictions" he needed to correct. "Yesterday I observed in a Boston paper of 19 April 1867 all the credit of his [Surratt's] arrest awarded to Dr. McMillan and a consul at Liverpool. They have no more to do with the capture than the man in the moon," he fumed.[86]

St. Marie faced similar shock and dejection on his return, complaining to the War Department that "much to my astonishment, one of the first things I learned on landing in the United States was there was no reward for the capture of Surratt. I think General King too much of a gentleman not to have informed me of the revocation of that order if he himself had been aware of its revocation. Surely the government of the United States cannot think that mileage and expenses from Italy here a sufficient remuneration for the dangers I have been and still am exposed to."[87]

As the date approached for yet another showcase trial stemming from the assassination, fears mounted that this one might be as controversial as the first. Many still believed Mary Surratt had gone to the gallows an innocent. The most seasoned lawyer on the prosecutorial team, former New York judge Edwards Pierrepont, warned: "If Surratt is now to be tried, and the evidence fails to convince the public that he is guilty, the hasty conclusion will be drawn that his mother was unjustly executed." Ominously, Pierrepont added: "The belief here is that which the [New York] Herald of today suggests, that this trial is also to be a farce."[88]

His colleague Albert Riddle despaired of any jury drawn from such a politically divided city being able to reach unanimity necessary for conviction. He lobbied Congress for legislation to allow for a change of trial venue and for authority to summon jurors from elsewhere. His bid, however, failed to win more than negligible support in the Senate.[89]

One potential juror after another was dismissed for political bias or opposition to capital punishment.[90] Five days dragged by before the twelfth and final juror was sworn in shortly before midnight in the city hall's Council Chamber, which, unlike the courtroom, was equipped with gas lights.[91] But expectations that the jurors might be fair and open-minded were never fulfilled. Even presiding judge

George Fisher, a former Republican congressman from Delaware and Lincoln devotee, concluded that he had "never known of a jury trial in which partisan feeling was so rampant."[92]

Unlike his co-conspirators who had been led into court hooded and manacled, John Surratt ambled from the nearby jail on a night so balmy that, after his handcuffs were removed, he cheerfully told his lawyers he wished it could be a regular stroll.[93] The four-count indictment charged that "not having the fear of God before his eyes, but being moved and seduced by the instigation of the devil," he shot to death, aided and abetted, and conspired to murder Lincoln.[94] After the prosecution's opening remarks a journalist noted the accused's "marked uneasiness."[95]

Rarely had the cramped, dingy forty-foot-square courtroom drawn such crowds. Surratt's presence excited the promise of so much sensation and distraction that every seat within the bar was taken before the daily proceedings. Propriety gave way to roughhouse impulse, with one woman clambering on a chair to glare at the accused.[96] Standing room was so packed that even jurors, court officials, and counsel suffered from the lack of ventilation. The trial so dominated newspapers that it was swept from the lead only when an enraged husband was arrested for shooting his wife's lover at the scene of the illicit tryst.[97]

Throughout the two-month-long trial, lawmen guarded the jurors without break. The deputy marshal removed a man edging suspiciously close to the jury box, and bailiffs forcibly hauled off another who approached as they entered sequestered living quarters.[98] The late president's oldest son, Robert, came to hear Louis Weichmann's testimony. Some days later his brother, Tad, took the stand for little more than a minute to describe how the accused "looked very much like" a man who boarded the steamboat at City Point weeks before the assassination, saying he wanted to see the president "real bad." Tad testified that officials would not let the man through.[99] Later the boy walked up to Louis Weichmann, seated in an anteroom, sat down on the man's knees, placed his arms around his neck, and kissed him on the cheek, declaring: "I desire to thank you, sir, for your testimony in behalf of my murdered father."

"Who are you, sonny?" Weichmann asked.

"My name is Tad Lincoln," said the fourteen-year-old.[100]

Surratt's guilt or innocence pivoted on his whereabouts on the night of the assassination. Some crucial prosecution witnesses took the stand to give questionable testimony that had the whiff of perjury and the odor of fabrication. Even though the reputations of a few were sullied by criminal records and breach of military discipline, they were allowed to testify. All swore that they had seen Surratt in Washington, when he claimed to be in Elmira, New York.

One of the most controversial was Joseph Dye, twenty-two, a recruiting sergeant in the regular army whose indictment for passing counterfeit money was dismissed after he testified against Surratt.[101] On the night of the assassination, Dye said, he had walked out of his encampment without permission and headed two miles to Ford's Theatre because he had heard Lincoln would be there and he wanted a glimpse of the president. As he sat down on the platform next to Lincoln's carriage, he continued, he saw John Wilkes Booth appear along with "a villainous-looking person" joined by a "neatly-dressed" individual whom he identified in court as Surratt. As theatergoers filed out during an intermission, the sergeant testified he heard Booth say "he would come out now, as I supposed, referring to the president. He did not come. They then hurriedly had a conversation together. One of them examined the carriage." Dye said Surratt, whom he had never seen before, called out the time to Booth three times. His suspicions aroused, the sergeant clasped his revolver inside his artillery jacket. Surratt, he swore under oath, finally announced it was ten minutes past ten o'clock and with "a countenance of great excitement, exceedingly nervous and very pale," hurried away as Booth went into the theater.[102]

Dye's testimony was the turning point for Judge Fisher, a former attorney general of Delaware. Until Dye took the stand, the judge later volunteered, he had been biased in Surratt's favor, because the accused had entered a theological seminary "and I could scarcely conceive how one so young, and trained under such influences, could at one bound descend to such a depth of infamy. But the testimony of Sgt. Dye impressed me very decidedly with the prisoner's guilt."[103]

Surratt's lawyers debunked other testimony with contemptuous ease.

Charles Ramsell, a private in the Third Massachusetts Heavy Artillery, claimed to have been walking back to his base northeast of Washington in the predawn hours the morning after the assassination when he passed a horse hitched to a fence. A quarter of an hour later a man rode up on the same horse and asked if there would be trouble getting through the pickets. Ramsell said he asked the man if he had heard the news of the assassination, and the man's response was "a sneering laugh . . . He appeared to be very uneasy, fidgety and nervous."

When the rider saw another horseman approaching from the capital, Ramsell testified, he announced he would try the pickets, and galloped off.

Surratt was told to stand with his back to the witness.

"Did you ever see that man before?" asked associate prosecuting counsel, Edwards Pierrepont, pointing toward Surratt's back.

"I think I have seen that back before," said Ramsell.

"Did you see it on that horse?"

"I think I did," Ramsell replied.[104]

Defense counsel Richard Merrick, "highly cultured" by the judge's reckoning,[105] delighted in the opportunity to discredit this sequence of evidence with ridicule.

"Gentlemen," he addressed the jury, "I could but fancy a private theatrical between my learned friend Judge Pierrepont and Ramsell.

"Pierrepont: 'Do you see yonder cloud that is almost in the shape of a camel?'

"Witness: 'By the mass, and 'tis like a camel, indeed.'

"Pierrepont: 'Methinks it is like a weasel?'

"Witness: 'It is backed like a weasel.'

"Pierrepont: 'Or like a whale?'

"Witness: 'Very like a whale.'"

Scornfully, Merrick told the jury, "It is a farce, unbecoming pranks before a dignified jury, to be introducing such evidence on which to risk the life of a man."[106]

In line with several other prosecution witnesses, a local barber,

Charles Wood, claimed phenomenal recall of a chance encounter with Surratt, whose appearance he was able to remember vividly more than two years after the lone sighting. He testified that about nine o'clock on the morning of the assassination the only other barber in the shop was out to breakfast and he was working alone under intense pressure to cater to "droves" of strangers coming in, especially soldiers from the adjacent paymaster's office. He told the court he trimmed Booth's hair immediately before John Surratt sat down and said, "Give me a nice shave, and clean me up nicely. I am going away in a day or two." He said Surratt looked "a little dusty, as though he had been traveling some little distance." The barber had not seen Surratt again until a week before his own testimony, when he said he recognized him as he came out of the court with the jailer.[107]

One of Mary Surratt's servants, Susan Mahony, since married and taking the name of Jackson, who had not testified in the conspiracy trial two years earlier, though she had been interrogated, now asserted for the first time that she had seen John Surratt in the boardinghouse about an hour before the assassination. Though she had never seen him during the three weeks she had been living in the H Street residence, she told the court that Mrs. Surratt was alone with him in the dining room, when "she told me that was her son. She asked me did he not look like his sister Annie?"[108] Not one of the other boarders corroborated her claim.

A lawyer, Benjamin Vanderpoel, who had been a lieutenant in the Fifty-ninth New York Volunteers in 1865, said he was walking along Pennsylvania Avenue on the afternoon of the assassination when he was attracted by music in a saloon, where scores of raucous patrons drank while a woman danced on stage. There he saw Booth with two or three others, one of whom he identified as Surratt, remembering him even though it was no more than a cursory, first-time glance, two years before his court appearance. "I have very seldom seen anyone who would remember faces so well as I do," he told the rapt court.[109]

By contrast, four credible residents of Elmira, New York, insisted Surratt was in their clothing stores on the critical dates before, during, and after the assassination. All clearly remembered his distinctive Garibaldi dress.[110] Clothing store proprietor John Cass could not erase the memory of the face of the man who had made a derogatory remark about Lincoln that initially incensed him. A bookkeeper, Frank Atkinson, and a cutter, Joseph Carroll, pinpointed Surratt's appearance in their store on April 13 and 14, specific dates noted in a cash book to show their employer who was then absent on a buying trip.[111] Similarly, a merchant tailor in another clothing store, Charles Stewart, was adamant that Surratt was the man he saw in both his stores on either April 13 or 14, when his partner was out of town.[112]

The defense suffered a double setback, however, when it was unable to produce the register of the Brainard House in Elmira, where Surratt had signed in under the alias of John Harrison two days before the assassination. The lessee could not explain its loss.[113] Then Judge Fisher refused to allow in evidence the hotel register for the Webster House in Canandaigua, showing Surratt had written the same alias on April 15. The defense listened with dismay as the judge ruled that the accused could have crossed the border a hundred times to make the entry to establish an alibi. "It is evidence made by himself, and although it might be put in evidence against him if in his handwriting, yet it cannot be used as evidence in his favor."[114]

Discord and friction between the judge and senior defense counsel, Joseph Bradley Sr. — strained by more than 150 exceptions to rulings from the bench[115] — erupted in public uproar during the fourth week of the trial. The visibly weak and sickly judge had not fully recovered from "walking typhoid." As he stepped down from the bench for a recess, Bradley, head of the city's criminal bar, approached and demanded to know why the judge had insulted him at the morning session. The distinguished lawyers traded insults and threatened to beat each other. Bradley, tall and bulky with a firm jaw, slit mouth, and balding head,[116] said that if the judge were not ill he would whip him. Fisher taunted that even though sick, his antagonist knew where to find him. The judge, forty-nine, proposed they put off the clash until he was well enough. The sexagenarian Bradley said his older age offset the younger man's infirmity. As Fisher continued down the hall, Bradley followed until he was physically restrained by bystanders. The judge let it be known among mutual friends that in the absence of an apology he would disbar Bradley.[117]

.Opening the summation for the defense, Merrick vilified government informants, singling out St. Marie for special condemnation. "The jingle of yellow earth has been the knell to many a man's honesty," he gibed. "If I had the power, I would take every informer in the United States, unite them as one man, and swing them as high as Haman. They suck the blood of the government. They have depleted its treasury."[118]

Anticipating imminent disbarment, Bradley announced, "This may be, and probably will be, the last time I shall ever address a Washington jury." But in his valedictory he wanted the twelve men to know that in his more than forty years of court appearances "no man at this bar has ever dared to assail a prisoner as this prisoner has been."[119] The assassination, he told jurors, had been committed when Surratt was four hundred miles away, when the plan had been changed without his knowledge. A new plan had been formed when it was physically impossible for Surratt to have assisted in its execution.[120] Aware that the verdict would hinge on whether Surratt was in Washington or Elmira on the night of the murder, he compared defense and prosecution witnesses, likening his to pure metal. "It has a clear ring. We give you Cass, Stewart, Carroll, Atkinson. They ring like a morning carol. They ring with a cheerful peal. They ring triumphantly. They ring victory — not guilty."[121] As for the government's array, he mocked them as rakings from hell, corrupt and debased. "What are those poor leaden things? You can get no sound out of them but a dead sound."[122]

Pierrepont, formidably stern with heavy mustache and long side whiskers, preferred biblical allusion, suggesting to the jury that Surratt "had that same stamp upon him which the Almighty put upon Cain, when he said that he should be a fugitive for the blood of his brother. Again I ask, why this flight, and why this concealment?"[123] He spoke for so long that by evening he was too hoarse to continue, and the court recessed until morning.[124]

With the case certain to go to the jury before the end of the day, every available space had been taken when the court met at 10 AM on

Wednesday August 7, 1867. Judge Fisher had no doubt of Surratt's guilt, and his charge to the jury sounded much like a command to concur. He all but rejected Surratt's presence in Elmira by discrediting alibis for being easily supported by perjury. And even if Surratt had not fired the fatal shot, Fisher reminded jurors that biblical King David had been found guilty of murder in the eyes of the Lord though he had not personally killed Uriah the Hittite, having ordered him to the forefront of battle to have him slain, so the monarch could claim the warrior's widow.[125] Flight from the scene of a crime, the judge added, was indicative of guilt. With Surratt's alleged confessions to St. Marie and McMillan in mind, Fisher lectured the jury that "a confession of crime, when freely and fairly made . . . is one of the surest proofs of guilt, because it is the testimony of the Omniscient speaking through the conscience of the culprit."[126] By the time he concluded it was clear the prosecution had his full and unqualified endorsement.

At 11:32 AM bailiffs escorted the jury to their room.[127] Fisher hovered in and around the courtroom, fully expecting a verdict before sunset, but no word came from the sequestered dozen. Candles flickered in the courtroom as crowds lingered inside and outdoors. But close to midnight the courthouse was dark and empty, with the exception of a light burning in the jury room.[128] The judge returned on Thursday and again on Friday, but each day the foreman came out alone to tell him they were deadlocked.[129]

At midday on Saturday, Surratt was led in from the jail and his handcuffs removed. He looked pale and fanned himself with his hat. A large contingent of police took up positions in the room to preserve order. At 1 PM the jury filed in.

The clerk of the court spoke. "Gentlemen of the jury, have you agreed on a verdict?"

"We are not able to agree," the foreman answered.[130]

Fisher began to read from a note signed by all the jurors. "The jury in the case of the *United States vs John H. Surratt* most respectfully state that they stand precisely now as when they first balloted upon entering the room, nearly equally divided, and they are firmly convinced that they cannot possibly make a verdict."

They asked to be dismissed to go home to their families and return to private life. Some reported that their health had suffered from the long confinement. Fisher remarked that it was the third note reporting deadlock.[131] He would later learn that eight voted for conviction and four for acquittal,[132] but one juror, William Birth, years later recalled the exact opposite, with eight voting to acquit and four to convict.[133] With no expectation of a breakthrough, the judge ordered them discharged. Surratt was remanded into the custody of the marshal.[134]

Instantly the feud between the judge and the lead defense counsel flared publicly when Fisher disbarred Bradley for unapologetic contempt of court the month before. Bradley stormed after the judge, who was stepping into a streetcar when the irate lawyer thrust him a note. It challenged Fisher to meet outside the boundaries of the District of Columbia, where duels were banned, "that we may arrange to our mutual satisfaction the points of difference between us, without the risk and odium which might accompany any controversy here or in public."[135] Fisher thought he was spared the possibility of a severe beating only because General Ulysses S. Grant happened to be in the streetcar, and other passengers demanded the driver move on. The judge ignored the note, preferring to let the matter rest.[136] A few days later Fisher received a letter from an admirer. "Bradley has been my lawyer for years," the stranger wrote, "but ever since the commencement of the rebellion, he has been growing more and more insolent until his assumptions and arrogance, especially towards loyal members of the court and bar, have rendered him perfectly obnoxious." He praised the judge for being "manly and dignified."[137] Fisher held on to the letter like a trophy for those who would inherit his estate.

The case against John Surratt sputtered to a close more than a year later after another judge, Andrew Wylie, ruled that the statute of limitations had run its course on a new indictment for "engaging in the rebellion," and a grand jury ignored yet another indictment.[138] Booth's most ardent recruit was finally free to go home.

EPILOGUE

———— ◆ ————

The Scramble for Rewards

So many rivals lunged for reward money that the War Department withheld all payouts on New Year's Day 1866, the deadline for filing claims, and set up a special commission to adjudicate.

Rank and profession mattered little as generals and privates elbowed lawmen and civilians in the stampede to snatch chunks of the riches. Even those with no chance of success scribbled bids. "My arm, while on this duty, was broken by the fall of my horse," wrote one cavalryman hopeful for a share, even though he had been far from the scene of Booth's capture.[1]

Another argued superior officers of the regiment "encouraged us to think that as we participated in searching for Booth, we should also come in for our share of said reward."[2]

Many had taken oaths before notaries to shore up the appearance of truthfulness. Others mailed in simple notes that read like appeals from children. Some were in elegant and tidy script. A few had been painstakingly penciled in broken English. "I worse told to rite to you to find out ef I could not draw my claims for carpthern Boot," wrote a German immigrant serving with the New York cavalry.[3]

The richest prize — seventy-five thousand dollars for the arrest of Booth and Herold — was the most contentious. Colonel Lafayette Baker and his cousin Lieutenant Luther Baker had no doubt that Everton Conger was in command of the entire force, including the twenty-six cavalrymen. But the commission disagreed, arguing that even though Conger had been a lieutenant colonel in the volunteer service, he had been formally mustered out, and at the time of the manhunt had no military rank that would validate his overall command. Noting that "the expedition was eminently of a military character," operating in hostile territory, the commission declared Lieutenant Doherty solely responsible for its discipline. Moreover it ruled that Doherty, not Luther Baker, had seized Herold as he exited the barn. Applying the same rule allowing ships' captains 10 percent of the prize value of captured enemy vessels, the commission awarded Doherty a tenth of the seventy-five-thousand-dollar reward. Conger and Baker, although recognized for their "great value," were to receive lesser amounts of four thousand dollars each.[4]

The report did not please outspoken congressmen who would legislate as final arbiters. The House of Representatives referred it to the Committee of Claims to consider "the fairness and propriety" of the distribution. Ten weeks later, with the trial of John Surratt well under way, the committee overturned the War Department's decisions.

Lafayette Baker and Conger were the most favored new beneficiaries, receiving $17,500 apiece, on the grounds that Baker had planned and directed the successful expedition, which the committee did not agree was purely a military operation. Luther Baker's share rose to five thousand. Doherty's portion was slashed to twenty-five hundred, the same amount proposed for each of the cavalrymen under his command.[5]

The committee apportioned smaller amounts to fearsome interrogator Colonel H.H. Wells and to George Cottingham, the detective he had kept out of the limelight by refusing to give him credit for finding Booth's carbine. Four more recipients were rewarded for the capture of Payne, notably Mrs. Surratt's servant, Susan Mahony Jackson, her aunt Mary Ann Griffin, the latter's employer John Kimball, and the rival who tried to steal all his credit, P.M. Clark.[6]

Outraged congressmen flayed the committee's report in a raucous debate marred by prejudice. "This man Baker is building a big hotel in my State with the money he has made off the government, and yet it is proposed to pay him $17,500," fumed Representative John Driggs of Michigan, one of the congressmen who had accompanied Lincoln's body to Springfield for burial.[7] Left unsaid was that the congressman was from the same state and party as Everett Conger's brother, who would soon be elected to the US House and Senate.[8]

Another congressman, incensed by Lafayette Baker's munificent handout, exclaimed: "That a man who did nothing should have $17,500 while those who did the work should only get $1,000 is too monstrous."[9]

Representative Giles Hotchkiss, the New York lawyer who had drawn up the committee's report, praised Conger as a "brave and gallant a soldier as any who fought in our army." By contrast, he lambasted Doherty as "a downright coward" who, he charged, had lain under a shed while Lieutenant Baker single-handedly took Herold prisoner. "That is the evidence," said Hotchkiss. "Yet in deference in part to popular clamor he must be allowed something. When you cannot do as you would, you must do as you must," he concluded, to justify a hefty award to Doherty.[10]

Final payments, agreed to by the House and Senate and signed into law by the president, awarded the following amounts:[11]

FOR THE CAPTURE OF BOOTH AND HEROLD

EVERTON CONGER	$15,000
EDWARD DOHERTY	5,250
LAFAYETTE BAKER	3,750
LUTHER B. BAKER	3,000
JAMES O'BIERNE	2,000
SGT. BOSTON CORBETT AND 25 CAVALRYMEN, EACH	1,653
H.H. WELLS	1,000
GEORGE COTTINGHAM	1,000
ALEXANDER LOVETT	1,000

FOR THE CAPTURE OF PAYNE

MAJ. H.W. SMITH	1,000
RICHARD MORGAN	500
ELI DEVORE	500
CHARLES ROSCH	500
THOMAS SAMPSON	500
WILLIAM WERMERSKIRCH	500
JOHN KIMBALL	500

P.M. Clark	500
Susan Mahony Jackson	250
Mary Ann Griffin	250

For the capture of Atzerodt	
Sgt. Zachariah Gemmill	3,598
Pvt. Christopher Ross	2,878
Pvt. David Barker	2,878
Pvt. Albert Bender	2,878
Pvt. Samuel Williams	2,878
Pvt. George Young	2,878
Pvt. James Longacre	2,878
James Purdum	2,878
Maj. E.R. Artman	1,250

The finality of disbursements by Congress muted hordes of hopeful claimants, most of whom returned to the obscurity from which they had come. But three who were left out refused to submit. For eight years Provost Marshal James McPhail and Detectives Voltaire Randall and Eaton Horner demanded rewards for the arrest of Arnold and O'Laughlin. But they too joined the long line of disappointed rejects when the House of Representatives ruled that no reward had ever been offered for Arnold and O'Laughlin.[12] Moreover, congressmen appeared to give them a backhanded slap, telling the last of the holdouts they "did no more than they were bound to do as officers of the government."[13]

No more was heard from any of those passed over until years later, during annual commemorations of Lincoln's birthday or on the anniversary of his death. Then aging and often forgetful men, some of whom had not even applied for reward money, would inflate their roles in the saga or spin fanciful tales of the past to gullible newspaper reporters and even occasionally to book publishers. The passing generation seized these opportunities to magnify themselves in a drama that would not fade, even after their deaths.[14]

ACKNOWLEDGMENTS

First and foremost I thank my wife, Marion, who had to compete with Abraham Lincoln for my time and attention during the nine years it took to research and write this book. The author's calling is decidedly selfish and lonely, too often demanding isolation and silent concentration that seals off the outside world. Only the disciplined can survive to the finish in this compulsive undertaking. My hope is that this volume will be somewhat worthy of her sacrifices through years of unfailing support.

My daughter, Nomi, offered persistent and persuasive reasons to continue with the book during bleak stretches of burnout when I all but gave up. She had been so moved by the unfinished manuscript that she wrote: "I spent the last half hour crying, reading through tear-filled eyes. You managed to touch me with American history! Can't wait to see the completed copy." If I could strike a chord in one so close, yet so disinterested in history, I had an obligation to press on. My son, Michael, frequently saved the emerging manuscript from being lost or erased, most notably when trapped in an aging computer that died close to my agent's deadline. Time and again I was also fortunate in being able to draw upon the invaluable computer skills of his gifted wife, Elaine, and her father and my friend, Ira Weiss. All three rescued me on countless occasions from this intimidating technology. As with some of my previous books, James Greenberg was always ready with technical assistance for recurring problems with my computer.

My agent, Charles Everitt, reacted like my daughter, telephoning to say he was so overcome with emotion after reading only a third of the manuscript that he had to down a stiff drink before taking a long walk alone. He too groaned when I told him I was thinking of abandoning the book, and coaxed me back into finishing it, for which I thank him profusely. I would also like to express appreciation to Chip Fleischer, publisher, Steerforth Press, for inviting my opinion on aspects not normally accorded authors, from the cover design to the texture of the paper. I was fortunate in having managing editor Kristin Sperber deftly guide me through to the final editing and selection of illustrations.

Most of my research was done at the Library of Congress, where specialists assisted in so many ways, even helping to decipher handwritten documents and advising on recent acquisitions. My most effusive thanks go to those in the Manuscript Division: Jeffrey Flannery, head of the reference and reader services section, and his assistants, Lia Apodaca, Frederick Bauman, Jennifer Brathovde, Ernest Emrich, Joe Jackson, Ahmed-Jamal Johnson, Patrick Kerwin, Bruce Kirby, and since deceased Mary Wolfskill.

During the long preparation of this book many experts assumed new positions but all acknowledgments refer to titles at the time I benefited from their expertise. I am grateful to others at the Library of Congress, including Lyle W. Minter, head of the reference section, Serial and Government Publications Division; Marilyn K. Parr, head of the Digital Reference Section and Public Service and Collections Access Officer; Leroy Bell, reference librarian, Humanities and Social Science Division; Clark Evans, Head of Reference Services, Rare Book and Special Collections Division; and Lewis Wyman, reference assistant, Jeff Bridgers, librarian, automated reference specialist, Marilyn Ibach, reference specialist, and Jan Grenci, reference specialist, posters, all at the Prints and Photographs Division. Edward J. Redmond, cartographic reference specialist, Geography & Map Division was very generous with his time.

Specialists at the National Archives in Washington, DC, and at College Park, Maryland, were always willing to guide me through the labyrinth of holdings. I have to thank archivist Trevor Plante for unwittingly leading me to the discovery of an unpublished letter from Samuel Arnold asking Secretary of War Stanton for a job three months *after* he had agreed to help Booth kidnap Lincoln. I had told Plante I was on the lookout for correspondence from prisoners on the island garrison of Dry Tortugas, off the coast of Florida, where four of the convicted conspirators were serving time. Plante suggested I look at records in the Office of the Quartermaster General and it was among those files that I stumbled upon Arnold's sensational letter. I also have to acknowledge much assistance over the years from others at the National Archives in Washington, including Cindi Fox, chief, Old Military & Civil Records; Richard Peuser, Jill Abraham, Robert Ellis, Jack House, Chris Killillay, George Briscoe, Brenda Kepley, and DeAnne Blanton; and Rod Ross, archivist, Center for Legislative Archives. Valuable assistance in obtaining the Samuel Mudd Pardon File from the vault at the National Archives in College Park was given by David Pfeiffer, Gene Morris, and Tim Nenninger. John Van Dereedt and Wayne DeCesar also gave advice at the same location over the years.

This book is richer through the generosity of Helen and Ron Shireman, of Pennsylvania, who readily granted me access to the private papers of Helen's great-grandfather, Major General John Hartranft, a Medal of Honor recipient and governor of the penitentiary during the detention of the conspirators. Their gracious consent to share copies of the plaintive letters written to the general by his young wife, Sallie, enhanced this narrative immeasurably, providing even more instances of heartbreak derived from the assassination.

Joan Chaconas, former president of the Surratt Society, sent me a copy of George Atzerodt's prison cell confession, which she located in 1977 in the possession of a descendant of the conspirator's lawyer. Laurie Verge, long-time director of the Surratt House Museum, was always forthcoming when I called with queries.

After C-Span filmed my tour of Lincoln assassination sites in Washington, I received from Virginia Brown, in Florida, a typescript copy of a letter written by her great-grandfather, William Kent, who had helped cut open Lincoln's clothes in Ford's Theatre moments after the shooting so a surgeon could look for wounds. Later that night Kent returned to the president's box to search for his mislaid keys when he stumbled upon Booth's Derringer pistol on the floor. Virginia Brown described the original letter, written by Kent to his mother the day Lincoln died, as "a cherished part of my childhood." However, it disappeared after the death of Brown's grandfather and subsequent sale of the family house and possessions in Jackson, Mississippi. Brown said she had given a typescript copy to Lincoln enthusiasts at Kennesaw Mountain National Park, Georgia, exactly half a century before contacting me — a statement verified by park officials who sent me a copy of her letter to them dated 1953. I have quoted from the typescript copy because I do not have any doubts about its authenticity, based upon her lineage and Kent's language, vivid descriptions, and the dateline, Washington, April 15, 1865.

Lydia S. Tederick, assistant curator at the White House, honored me by setting aside the beautiful China Room in which to research the photographic archives. I have been in the White House on countless occasions, even narrating inside for Tribune Broadcasting television, but I now savored the privilege of being seated alone among exquisite portraits and historic furnishings.

As with my previous book, *The Burning of Washington: The British Invasion of 1814,* I benefited in untold ways from the kindness of Greg Harness, since retired as US Senate librarian, whose knowledge of congressional history was time and again surpassed only by his skills in locating specific information.

Dr. Susan K. Lemke, head of the National Defense University special collections at Fort Lesley McNair, Washington, DC, and her colleague,

Scott Gower, technical information specialist, treated me as if I were royalty, volunteering archival documents and photographic material, some of it rare and unpublished, which was scanned especially for this book. Dr. Lemke also favored me with a private tour inside the neighboring, remodeled section of all that remains of the original courtroom where the conspirators were tried and convicted.

Exceptional service was provided at the History of Medicine Division, National Library of Medicine, in Bethesda, Maryland, by Dr. Stephen Greenberg, coordinator of public services, and Deshaun Williams, historical audiovisuals, who located obscure publications from centuries past. Additional research on artificial respiration applied to the wounded president was enhanced by the input of Dr. Quentin A. Fisher, professor of anesthesiology and pediatrics, Georgetown University Hospital and of the Department of Anesthesia, Washington Hospital Center, who canvassed opinions from colleagues far afield, and led me to the Wood Library, Museum of Anesthesiology, in Park Ridge, Illinois, whose librarian, Karen Bieterman, instantly forwarded the definitive study of the history of resuscitation by Paul Safar. Jan Schmidt, administrative assistant, Canadian Anesthesiologists Society, Toronto, Canada, supplied even more material.

For several decades I have had the good fortune to draw on the resources of the US Senate Historical Office. Dr. Richard Baker, veteran Senate historian, and Dr. Donald Ritchie, associate historian, gave unstintingly of their time and knowledge, offering wise guidance. I am also indebted to this invaluable archival resource for photographs offered by Heather Moore, photo historian, and, in her absence, by Beth Hahn, historical editor.

A very valuable find for corroboration of the plot to assassinate President-elect Lincoln came from the Samuel Morse Felton Family Papers at the Archives Center, National Museum of American History, Washington, DC, where I was given every assistance by Craig A. Orr, acquisitions archivist, and staff under the direction of Deborra Richardson, chief of reference and later chair of the Archives Center.

I would be remiss if I did not single out for special praise Tom Hyry, archivist, Manuscripts and Archives, Yale University Library, for going to extraordinary lengths to provide a distinct copy of a letter from Elizabeth Cogswell Dixon, who found the ordeal of comforting Mary Todd Lincoln so harrowing that she would prohibit artists from including her in deathbed scenes for fear it would perpetuate memories she tried to erase.

I wish to thank the following for making my research so much easier because of their shared devotion to the study of records from the past:

Jonathan Stayer, reference section supervisor, Pennsylvania State Archives, Harrisburg; Michael G. Rhode, chief archivist, Kathleen Stocker, assistant archivist, and Alan Hawk, historical collections manager, National Museum of Health and Medicine, Armed Forces Institute of Pathology, Walter Reed Army Medical Center, Washington; Tracy Elizabeth Robinson, reference archivist, Smithsonian Institution Archives, Washington, DC; Sarah Hartwell, reading room supervisor, Rauner Special Collections Library, Dartmouth College Library, Hanover, New Hampshire; Dr. Tricia T. Pyne, director, Associated Archives at St. Mary's Seminary & University, Baltimore; Professor Roberto Severino, retired from the Italian Department, School of Languages and Linguistics, Georgetown University, Washington, DC, who located the book in French disclosing the dates of service in the Papal Zouaves of John Surratt and Henry St. Marie; Teresa Roane, library manager, The Museum of the Confederacy, Richmond, Virginia; Michael Plunkett, director, special collections, University of Virginia Library, Charlottesville; Nicholas Graham, reference librarian and Megan Milford, assistant reference librarian, Massachusetts Historical Society, Boston; Betsy Caldwell, library assistant, Reference Services, Indiana Historical Society, Indianapolis; staff at the Archives of American Art, Smithsonian Institution, Washington, supervised by chief of reference services, Judy Throm, succeeded by Marisa Bourgoin; Patricia McGarry, coordinator, and Bonnie White, archives assistant, College of Southern Maryland, La Plata; Anne Marie F. Chase, circulation assistant, Chicago History Museum, Chicago; Dr. Wayne Temple, chief deputy director, Illinois State Archives, Springfield; Dr. William Seale, historian and author of the definitive history of the White House, for many years of enthusiastic support, during which he offered much material and leads to sources; Rae Emerson, site manager, Gloria Swift, curator, and, since deceased historian, Michael R. Maione, Ford's Theatre, for an abundance of hospitality, especially for providing space to research the theater's archives; Paul R. Tetreault, producing director, and Jeffrey Hale, associate director of development, annual giving, for permitting me to go into Lincoln's box and onto the stage at Ford's Theatre; Stephen Lohrmann, Rapp Funeral & Cremation Services, Silver Spring, Maryland, for sharing knowledge of embalming procedures; Scott Sheads, author and historian, historic weapons officer, Fort McHenry National Monument and Historic Shrine, Baltimore, for volunteering research material and microfilm over many years; Rob Schoeberlein, director, Special Collections, Maryland State Archives, Annapolis; A.T. Palmer, of Chicago, for facilitating contact with third parties in Rome; Juanita Rossignol, archives Canada coordinator,

Canadian Council of Archives, Ottawa; Lynn Conway, archivist, Special Collections, Georgetown University, Washington; Janie Morris, research services librarian, and David Strader, research services assistant, Rare Book, Manuscript, and Special Collections Library, Duke University, Durham, North Carolina; Stephen Budiansky, author, for providing material on George Sharpe; Wayne Wright, associate director, Research Library, New York State Historical Association, Cooperstown; Dr. Richard J. Sommers, chief of patron services, US Army Military History Institute, Carlisle, Pennsylvania; Leslie A. Morris, curator of manuscripts, Houghton Library, Harvard University, Cambridge, Massachusetts; Anita Carrico, special collections librarian, Enoch Pratt Free Library, Baltimore; Jennie A. Levine, assistant curator for historical manuscripts, Hornbake Library, University of Maryland, College Park; Jean Ashton, director, Bernard R. Crystal, curator of manuscripts, and Jennifer B. Lee, librarian for public services and programs, Rare Book and Manuscript Library, Butler Library, Columbia University, New York; Dr. David R. Curfman, neurological surgeon, Lincoln devotee, and a gentleman of singular charm, grace, and erudition, since deceased; William J. Moore, director, Greensboro Historical Museum, Greensboro, North Carolina; Lyle Slovick, assistant university archivist, The Gelman Library, George Washington University, Washington, DC; John Rhodehamel, Norris Foundation curator, American Historical Manuscripts, and Edward Rinderle, Photo Department, The Huntington Library, San Marino, California; Leslie Fields, associate curator for the Gilder Lehrman Collection, The Pierpont Morgan Library, New York; Sophia Lynn, project manager, President Lincoln and Soldiers' Home National Monument, Washington, DC, for a private tour of the site then being restored; John Y. Simon, executive director, Ulysses S. Grant Association, Morris Library, Southern Illinois University, Carbondale; Kim Bernard Holien, historian, Department of the Army, Fort Myer and Fort McNair, Virginia; Dwayne Cox, head of special collections and archives, John Varner, library assistant, Cindy Mitchell, manager, information specialist, and Brenda Ray, office manager, InfoQuest, Auburn University Libraries, Auburn University, Alabama; Geraldine Strey, reference archivist, Wisconsin Historical Society, Madison; Carolyn Smith, for passing on the location of the graves of men who drowned in a shipping accident while pursuing Booth; Barbara Bahny-David, director, public relations, Willard Intercontinental Hotel, Washington, DC, for the opportunity to publish a contemporary sketch of the hotel; and abroad, staff at the National Archives, Kew, England.

NOTES

Abbreviations

AAB, AASMSU Archives of the Catholic Archidiocese of Baltimore, and Associated Archives at St. Mary's Seminary & University, Baltimore, Maryland.

AJII Andrew Johnson Impeachment Investigation, House of Representatives Report 7, 40C 1S, serial 1314.

AJP Andrew Johnson Papers, Library of Congress.

AKP August Kautz Papers, Library of Congress.

ASP Archbishop Spalding Papers, Archives of the Archdiocese of Baltimore, Maryland, Associated Archives at St. Mary's Seminary & University, Baltimore, Maryland.

BBFFP Benjamin Brown French Family Papers, Library of Congress.

BBP Benjamin Butler Papers, Library of Congress.

CTPit Conspiracy Trial. *The Assassination of President Lincoln and the Trial of the Conspirators,* compiled and arranged by Benn Pitman. Cincinnati: Moore, Wilstach & Baldwin, 1865.

CTPoore Conspiracy Trial. *The Conspiracy Trial for the Murder of the President and the Attempt to Overthrow the Government by the Assassination of Its Principal Officers,* edited by Ben Perley Poore. 3 volumes. Boston: J.E. Tilton & Co., 1865.

ESP Edwin Stanton Papers, Library of Congress.

GWD Gideon Welles diary, volume 2. Boston and New York: Houghton Mifflin, 1911.

GWP Gideon Welles Papers, Library of Congress.

HP John Hartranft Papers, Pennsylvania State Archives, RG 393.

HR House of Representatives.

JHP Joseph Holt Papers, Library of Congress.

JNP John Nicolay Papers, Library of Congress.

JST John Surratt Trial.

LC Library of Congress.

MdHS Maryland Historical Society.

NA National Archives.

OR Official Records of the Union and Confederate Armies in the War of the Rebellion.

SC Shireman Collection, New Oxford, Pennsylvania.

TEFP Thomas Ewing Family Papers, Library of Congress.

TWP Thomas Walter Papers, Archives of American Art, Smithsonian Institution. Originals at Athenaeum, Philadelphia.

WSP William Seward Papers, Library of Congress. Originals at University of Rochester Library, Rochester, New York.

Microfilm Abbreviations

M89 Letters received by Secretary of Navy from commanding officers of squadrons. European Squadron 1841–1886, RG 45.

M90 Despatches from US Ministers to Italian States, Papal States, RG 59.

M149 Letters sent by Secretary of the Navy to Officers, 1798–1868, RG 45.

M179 Miscellaneous Letters of Department of State, 1789-1906, RG 59.

M221 Letters received by Secretary of War, main series, 1801–1870, RG 107.

M371 Records of District of Columbia Commissioners and of offices concerned with Public Buildings, 1791–1867, RG 42.

M473 Telegrams collected by Office of Secretary of War (bound), 1861–1882, RG 107.

M599 Investigation and Trial Papers relating to the assassination of President Lincoln, RG 153.

M619 Letters received by Office of Adjutant General (main series), 1861–1870, RG 94.

M745 Letters sent by Office of Quartermaster General (main series), 1818–1870, RG 92.

T222 Despatches from U.S Consuls in Montreal, 1850–1906, RG 59.

T967 Copies of Presidential Pardons and Remissions, 1794–1893, RG 59.

1. "Lincoln Shall Not Pass Through Baltimore Alive"

Chapter title: Pinkerton report, February 21, 1861, in Cuthbert, *Lincoln & Baltimore Plot,* 59.

1. Thomas Cadwallerder to Lincoln, December 31, 1860, series 1, #5479, Abraham Lincoln Papers, LC.

2. Peter Page to Abraham Lincoln, January 3, 1861, Abraham Lincoln Papers, folder 142, Chicago History Museum. Lincoln to Page, January 21, 1861, Abraham Lincoln Papers, folder 145, Chicago History Museum.

3. Undated manuscript, introduction by John Nicolay and John Hay, Herndon-Weik Collection, 14:1842–1843, LC.

4. B.B. French, *Journal,* February 27, 1861, reel 2, BBFFP. Sidney George Fisher, *A Philadelphia Perspective: The Diary of Sidney George Fisher,* edited by Nicholas B. Wainwright (Philadelphia: Historical Society of Pennsylvania, 1967), 379.

5. Winfield Scott to Joseph Holt, January 28, 1861, container 101, JHP.

6. Jacob Thompson testimony, Select Committee Report 79, HR 36C 2S, 87.

7. *Population of the US in 1860; Compiled from the Original Returns of the Eighth Census* (Washington: Government Printing Office, 1864), 588.

8. Thomas Hicks testimony, Select Committee Report 79, HR 36C 2S, 166.

9. Benjamin Berry testimony, Select Committee Report 79, HR 36C 2S, 93, 95.

10. Godard Bailey testimony, Select Committee Report 79, HR 36C 2S, 112. *Daily National Intelligencer,* November 13 and 16, 1860.

11. Horatio Taft diary, volume 1, January 20, 27, 1861, LC.

12. Susan Hill to John Hamilton, February 2, 1861, Hamilton Family Papers, series 1, box 1, Special Collections, University of Maryland Libraries.

13. Anna Maria Thornton diary, January–March 1861, reel 7, Anna Maria Thornton Papers, LC.

14. Horatio Taft diary, volume 1, February 2, 1861, LC.

15. Charles P. Stone. "Washington on the Eve of the War." *Century Magazine* (July 1883), 461.

16. Winfield Scott to Joseph Holt, January 29, 1861, Winfield Scott Papers, LC.

17. Winfield Scott to Joseph Holt, January 28, 1861, container 101, JHP.

18. Winfield Scott testimony, Select Committee Report 79, HR 36C 2S, 69, 70.

19. James Berret, Select Committee Report 79, HR 36C 2S, 5, 6. John Blake testimony, Select Committee Report 79, HR 36C 2S, 16, 24.

20. John Blake to Joseph Holt, January 30, 1861, M371, 7:238.

21. John Blake to Captain C.W.C. Dunnington, February 1, 1861, M371, 7:239.

22. Winfield Scott testimony, Select Committee Report 79, HR 36C 2S, 61, 69.

23. Winfield Scott to E.D. Morgan, January 17, 1861, Letters, Telegrams & Memoranda Sent by Headquarters, box 1, entry 9, RG 108.

24. Harrison Ritchie to John Andrew, February 6, 1861, reprinted in William Schouler, *A History of Massachusetts in the Civil War* (Boston: E.P. Dutton, 1868), 37–38.

25. Winfield Scott to Joseph Holt, January 24, 1861, Letters, Telegrams & Memoranda Sent by Headquarters, box 1, entry 9, RG 108.

26. Winfield Scott to L.P. Graham, February 4, 1861, Letters, Telegrams & Memoranda Sent by Headquarters, box 1, entry 9, RG 108.

27. Winfield Scott to Joseph Holt, February 12, 1861, typescript copy, container 101, JHP.

28. L. Thomas, general instructions of General Scott, February 12, 1861, Letters, Telegrams & Memoranda Sent by Headquarters, box 1, entry 9, RG 108.

29. Select Committee Report 79, HR 36C 2S, 2.

30. Thomas Hicks testimony, Select Committee Report 79, HR 36C 2S, 172.

31. Henry Winter Davis to William Turnbull, December 25, 1860, Turnbull Family Papers, Ms. 1719, MdHS. Thomas Hicks testimony, Select Committee Report 79, HR 36C 2S, 171.

32. Message of the Governor of Maryland to the General Assembly, December 4, 1861, Maryland State Archives, SC M3174.

33. Statement of Thomas Hicks, "To the People," broadside, January 3, 1861, Maryland State Archives, SC 295.

34. James Welling to Thomas Hicks, December 24, 1860, Thomas Hicks Papers, Ms. 1313, box 2, MdHS.

35. George Stearns to Thomas Hicks, February 7, 1861, Ms. 2104, Thomas Hicks Papers, MdHS. Samuel Morse Felton, *Extracts from an Autobiography Written for His Children in 1866,* box 1, folder 1, and *The Baltimore Plot* by Conway Felton, 1885, box 1, folder 8, Samuel Morse Felton Family Papers, #170, Archives Center, National Museum of American History, Smithsonian Institution.

36. Fisher, *A Philadelphia Perspective,* 378.

37. Felton, *Extracts from an Autobiography,* box 1, folder 1, Samuel Morse Felton Family Papers, #170, Archives Center, National Museum of American History, Smithsonian Institution.

38. *Population of the US in 1860,* 214.

39. T.W. to Pinkerton, February 19, 1861, in Cuthbert, *Lincoln and Baltimore Plot,* 45.

40. A.F.C. to Pinkerton, February 19, 1861, in Cuthbert, *Lincoln and Baltimore Plot,* 47.

41. Felton, *Extracts from an Autobiography,* box 1, folder 1, Samuel Morse Felton Family Papers, #170, Archives Center, National Museum of American History, Smithsonian Institution.

42. Allan Pinkerton, January 8, 1868, *History & Evidence of the Passage of Abraham Lincoln from Harrisburg, Pa. to Washington, D.C. 22–23 Februrary 1861,* 7, Pinkerton's National Detective Agency, box 23, LC.

43. Cypriano Ferrandini testimony, Select Committee Report 79, HR 36C 2S, 137.

44. Pinkerton report, February 15, 1861, in Cuthbert, *Lincoln and Baltimore Plot,* 36–37.

45. Pinkerton to Herndon, August 23, 1866, 3. Copy in Pinkerton's National Detective Agency Papers, box 23, LC.

46. Pinkerton report, February 21, 1861, in Cuthbert, *Lincoln and Baltimore Plot,* 53.

47. William Stearns to Pinkerton, December 4, 1867, in Pinkerton, *Passage of Lincoln,* 24.

48. "The Baltimore Plot to Assassinate Abraham Lincoln," *Harper's New Monthly Magazine* 37 (June 1868), 126. Pinkerton to Herndon, August 23, 1866, 6. Copy in Pinkerton's National Detective Agency Papers, box 23, LC.

49. *Philadelphia Inquirer,* February 22, 1861.

50. Dona Kight to Dave Joens, April 21, 2005, provided to this author by Wayne Temple. Kate Warn obituary, Pinkerton's National Detective Agency Papers, box 25, LC.

51. Pinkerton report, February 21, 1861, in Cuthbert, *Lincoln and Baltimore Plot,* 59–60.

52. *Philadelphia Inquirer,* February 22, 1861.

53. N.B. Judd to Allan Pinkerton, November 3, 1867, in Pinkerton, *Passage of Lincoln,* 18–19.

54. Pinkerton report, February 21, 1861, in Cuthbert, *Lincoln and Baltimore Plot,* 64–67.

55. N.B. Judd to Allan Pinkerton, November 3, 1867, in Pinkerton, *Passage of Lincoln,* 19.

56. *Ibid.*

57. Pinkerton report, February 21, 1861, in Cuthbert, *Lincoln and Baltimore Plot,* 67.

58. "The Baltimore Plot to Assassinate Abraham Lincoln," 127.

59. Lincoln oral interview with Benson Lossing, December 1864, *Pictorial History,* 280.

60. William Seward to Lincoln, February 21, 1861, microfilm 17, #7438, Abraham Lincoln Papers, LC.

61. Scott to William Seward, February 21, 1861, microfilm 17, #7427, Abraham Lincoln Papers, LC.

62. Lincoln oral interview with Benson Lossing, December 1864, *Pictorial History,* 280. Nicolay and Hay, *Abraham Lincoln,* 3:311–312.

63. Pinkerton report, February 22, 1861, in Cuthbert, *Lincoln and Baltimore Plot,* 69. G.C. Franciscus to Pinkerton, November 5, 1867, in Pinkerton, *Passage of Lincoln,* 29.

64. Pinkerton report, February 22, 1861, in Cuthbert, *Lincoln & Baltimore Plot,* 60–70. H. E. Thayer to Pinkerton, November 3, 1867, in Pinkerton, *Passage of Lincoln,* 39.

65. *Philadelphia Inquirer,* February 23, 1861.

66. *Ibid.*

67. Edwin Fowler to an unnamed uncle, February 22, 1861, Edwin Fowler Papers, LC.

68. N.B. Judd to Allan Pinkerton, November 3, 1867, in Pinkerton, *Passage of Lincoln,* 21.

69. Lamon, *Recollections,* 42.

70. Margaret Williams, *Reminiscenses,* typescript, January 4, 1921, Margaret Williams Papers, LC. *Philadelphia Inquirer,* February 23, 1861.

71. Governor A.G. Curtin to Pinkerton, December 8, 1867, in Pinkerton, *Passage of Lincoln,* 37.

72. N.B. Judd to Pinkerton, November 3, 1867, in Pinkerton, *Passage of Lincoln,* 22.

73. Andrew Wynne to Pinkerton, November 3, 1867, in Pinkerton, *Passage of Lincoln,* 41.

74. H.E. Thayer to Pinkerton, November 3, 1867, in Pinkerton, *Passage of Lincoln,* 40.

75. John Pitcairn Jr. to Pinkerton, November 23, 1867, in Pinkerton, *Passage of Lincoln,* 33.

76. H.F. Kenney to Pinkerton, December 23, 1867, in Pinkerton, *Passage of Lincoln,* 27–28. Pinkerton to Herndon, August 23, 1866, 17–18. Copy in Pinkerton's National Detective Agency Papers, box 23, LC.

77. Lamon, *Recollections,* 44.

78. *Harper's New Monthly Magazine* 37 (June 1868), 128. Pinkerton to Herndon, August 23, 1866, 17–18. Copy in Pinkerton's National Detective Agency Papers, box 23, LC. Lamon, *Recollections,* 44.

79. Pinkerton to Herndon, August 23, 1866, 17. Copy in Pinkerton's National Detective Agency Papers, box 23, LC.

80. William Stearns to Pinkerton, December 4, 1867, in Pinkerton, *Passage of Lincoln,* 26.

81. Hungerford, *Story of Baltimore & Ohio Railroad,* 355.

82. Pinkerton to Herndon, August 23, 1866, 19. Copy in Pinkerton's National Detective Agency Papers, box 23, LC. Lamon, *Recollections,* 45.

83. Told by Lincoln in 1844 to John Usher, later secretary of the interior, who recounted it to G.A. Townsend, Christmas 1878, George Alfred Townsend Papers, LC.

84. Lamon, *Recollections,* 46.

85. *Washington Evening Star,* February 23, 1861.

86. Lamon, *Recollections,* 46.

87. *Philadelphia Inquirer,* February 25, 1861.

88. *Ibid.*

89. Lamon, *Recollections,* 46. H.E. Thayer to Pinkerton, November 3, 1867, in Pinkerton, *Passage of Lincoln,* 40.

90. Nicolay and Hay, *Abraham Lincoln,* 315.

91. The artist of this most celebrated anti-Lincoln cartoon, Adalbert Johann Volck, a Bavarian immigrant and dentist, signed his works V. Blada and was a Confederate blockade-running courier during the Civil War. See Volck to *Baltimore Sun,* April 21, 1898, Ms. 2092, MdHS, and Volck Collection, Special Collections, Enoch Pratt Free Library, Baltimore.

92. Margaret Williams, *Reminiscenses,* typescript, January 4, 1921, Margaret Williams Papers, LC.

93. Charles Wilkes, *Autobiography,* 740–741.

94. Edwin Fowler to an unnamed uncle, March 6, 1861, Edwin Fowler Papers, LC.

95. William Pettit to Hannah Pettit, January 2, 1864, William Pettit correspondence, #177, Archives Center, National Museum of American History, Smithsonian Institution.

96. William Pettit to Hannah Pettit, March 19, 1864, William Pettit correspondence, #177, Archives Center, National Museum of American History, Smithsonian Institution.

97. Duvergier de Hauranne, *A Frenchman in Lincoln's America,* 2:350–351.

98. Undated manuscript, 14:1734–1735, Herndon-Weik Collection, LC.

99. As told by US Marshal Walden to George Alfred Townsend, July 1881, scrapbook, George Alfred Townsend Papers, LC.

100. *Daily National Intelligencer,* March 5, 1861.

101. Harrison Ritchie to John Andrew, February 6, 1861, reprinted in William Schouler, *A History of Massachusetts in the Civil War* (Boston: E.P. Dutton, 1868), 37.

102. Anonymous letter to Abraham Lincoln, February 21, 1865, container 92, JHP.

103. John Nicolay to Therena Bates, January 6, 1861, box 2, JNP.

104. John Nicolay to Therena Bates, February 24, 1861, box 2, JNP.

105. Luther Barnett Bruen to Augusta Bruen, March 3, 1861, Ms. 1891, MdHS.

106. Luther Barnett Bruen to Augusta Bruen, March 5, 1861, Ms. 1891, MdHS.

107. Thomas Walter diary, March 4, 1861, Archives of American Art, Smithsonian Institution.

108. Stone, *Washington on Eve of War,* 466.

109. B.B. French, *Journal,* March 6, 1861, reel 2, BBFFP.

110. *Daily National Intelligencer,* March 5, 1861.

111. B.B. French to Francis French, April 25, 1861, part 2, box 11, BBFFP.

112. *Daily National Intelligencer,* March 5, 1861.

113. Stone, *Washington on Eve of War,* 465.

114. Inaugural address, *Daily National Intelligencer,* March 5, 1861.

115. B.B. French, *Journal,* February 27, 1861, reel 2, BBFFP.

116. *Ibid.,* March 6, 1861.

117. *Ibid.*

118. Undated manuscript, introduction by John Nicolay and John Hay, Herndon-Weik Collection, 14:1842–1843, LC.

119. John Nicolay to Therena Bates, March 5, 1861, box 2, JNP.

120. Hunter, *Report of the Military Services,* 5–7.

121. Francis Sidney Low to an unnamed son, April 18, 1861, Francis Sidney Low Papers, LC. *Daily National Intelligencer,* April 19, 1861. *Washington Evening Star,* April 19, 1861.

122. Robert Stewart to James Stewart, September 18, 1861, Marian S. Carson Papers, LC.

2. A Presidential Envelope Marked "Assassination"

Chapter title: Charles Dana testimony, CTPoore, 3:491.

1. Carpenter, *Six Months,* 62.

2. Charles Dana testimony, CTPoore, 3:489–491.

3. Noah Brooks, "Lincoln's Re-election," *Century Magazine* (April 1895), 866.

4. Cole, *Memoirs,* 214.

5. Nicolay and Hay, *Abraham Lincoln,* 288.

6. Baker, *History of US Secret Service,* 475.

7. Noah Brooks, "Glimpses of Lincoln in War Time," *Century Magazine* (January 1895), 464.

8. *New York Daily Tribune,* March 19, 1864.

9. Pendel, *Thirty Six Years,* 13.

10. Nicolay and Hay, *Abraham Lincoln,* 288.

11. B.B. French to Charles Train, January 5, 1863; French to John Rice, March 7, 1864; French to Rice, June 16, 1864, M371, 7:392, 459, 490.

12. Duvergier de Hauranne, *A Frenchman in Lincoln's America,* 2:349.

13. B.B. French to John Rice, July 5, 1866, M371, 7:697.

14. Keckley, *Behind the Scenes,* 120–121.

15. Brooks, *Washington in Lincoln's Time,* 43.

16. Thomas Pendel, *Thirty Six Years,* 28.

17. Lamon, *Recollections,* 267–268.

18. Colfax, *Life and Principles,* 10.

19. From Lincoln's first inaugural speech, quoted in the *Daily National Intelligencer,* March 5, 1861.

20. James Mason to Judah Benjamin, July 14, 1864, James Mason Papers, volume 7, LC.

21. Abraham Lincoln personal memorandum, August 23, 1864, in *The Collected Works of Abraham Lincoln,* edited by Roy P. Basler, Marion Dolores Pratt, and Lloyd A. Dunlap (New Brunswick, N.J.: Rutgers University Press, 1953), 7:514–515.

22. *Chicago Tribune,* March 6, 1865.

23. French to Montgomery Meigs, September 30, 1861; French to John Rice, June 16, 1864, M371, 7:312–313, 489.

24. *Daily Morning Chronicle,* March 3, 1865.

25. Samuel Busey, *Personal Reminiscences,* 64.

26. Henry Blanchard to his parents, June 25, 1861, Ms. 417, Historical Society of Washington, DC. French to Solomon Foot, June 17, 1864, M371, 7:491. Thomas and Hyman, *Stanton,* 85.

27. Report of the Board of the Metropolitan Police, House of Representatives Executive Document 1, 37C 1S, 861.

28. George Walbridge to N. Colby, April 25, 1865, Records of Superintendent, Old Capitol Prison, Records of US Army, Continental Commands 1821–1920, Part IV, entry 2129, RG 393, NA.

29. B.B. French to Solomon Foot, February 23, 1863, M371, 7:398.

30. B.B. French to Robert Stone, May 21, 1862, M371, 7:364.

31. Duvergier de Hauranne, *A Frenchman in Lincoln's America*, 1:76.

32. John Nicolay to Therena Bates, March 26, 1865, box 3, JNP.

33. B.B. French to Thaddeus Stevens, January 12, 1865, M371, 7:529.

34. Duvergier de Hauranne, *A Frenchman in Lincoln's America*, 2:294.

35. August Kautz diary, June 25, 1865, box 1, AKP.

36. Louis Goldsborough to Elizabeth Goldsborough, February 24, 1867, Louis Goldsborough Papers, LC. *Daily National Intelligencer,* February 6, 1867.

37. *Daily National Intelligencer,* March 4, 1865.

38. *Ibid.,* March 20, 1865. William Pettit to Hannah Pettit, December 27, 1864, Letters #177, Archives Center, National Museum of American History, Smithsonian Institution.

39. B.B. French to John Rice, May 29, 1866, M371, 7:690.

40. *Daily National Intelligencer,* March 6, 1865.

41. Report of Board of Metropolitan Police, House of Representatives Executive Document 1, 37C 1S, 850. Archbishop Martin Spalding to John Francis Maguire, February 25, 1867, letterpress, 276, ASP.

42. Report of Board of Metropolitan Police, House of Representatives Executive Document 1, 37C 1S, 844.

43. Report of Warden of Jail in the District of Columbia, House of Representatives Executive Document 1, 37C 1S, 852.

44. *Ibid.*

45. Report of Board of Metropolitan Police, House of Representatives Executive Document, 1, 37C 1S, 850–851.

46. B.B. French to Thaddeus Stevens, May 18, 1866, M371, 7:686.

47. Timothy Vedder to parents, June 26, 1861, Timothy Vedder Letters, box 1, Gelman Library Special Collections, George Washington University.

48. Charles Bowers to Lydia Bowers, May 14, 1861, Civil War Papers, P-376, reel 15, Massachusetts Historical Society.

49. *Washington Post,* May 7, 1905, Records of the Old Washingtonians, LC.

50. London *Times,* March 20, 1865.

51. *Daily National Intelligencer,* March 6, 1865.

52. London *Times,* March 20, 1865.

53. *Chicago Tribune,* March 6, 1865.

54. *Ibid.*

55. *Daily Morning Chronicle,* March 4, 1865.

56. *Chicago Tribune,* March 6, 1865.

57. *Ibid.*

58. *New York Times,* March 6, 1865.

59. *Daily National Intelligencer,* March 6, 1865. *New York Times,* March 6, 1865. London *Times,* March 20, 1865.

60. William Pettit to Hannah Pettit, March 25, 1864, William Pettit

correspondence, #177, Archives Center, National Museum of American History, Smithsonian Institution.

61. Adolphe de Chambrun, *Impressions of Lincoln,* 37.
62. Brooks, *Washington in Lincoln's Time,* 210–211.
63. *Ibid.,* 211.
64. Isaac Bassett Papers, unpublished, US Senate Collection.
65. London *Times,* March 20, 1865.
66. Sue Wallace to Delia Wallace, March 10, 1865, Lew Wallace Collection, reel 3, Indiana Historical Society Library.
67. Isaac Bassett Papers, unpublished, US Senate Collection. Brooks, *Washington in Lincoln's Time,* 212.
68. Sue Wallace to Delia Wallace, March 10, 1865, Lew Wallace Collection, reel 3, Indiana Historical Society Library.
69. *New York Times,* March 6, 1865.
70. Thomas Walter to Amanda Walter, May 16, 1865, letterbook, roll 4142, TWP.
71. George Boutwell, quoted in Hamilton Fish diary, November 12, 1869, container 277, reel 1, Hamilton Fish Papers, LC. Judge Advocate Henry Burnett later wrote that Booth had been given a ticket of admission from a girlfriend, Lucy Hale, daughter of US Senator John Hale. See Burnett, *Some Incidents in the Trial,* 16. Also, Thomas Walter to Amanda Walter, May 20, 1865, letterbook, roll 4142, TWP. Samuel Chester said Booth told him a young lady "gave him a ticket to the stand on inauguratiion day." See Chester, April 28, 1865, M599, 4:143–170.
72. Oaths of Office, 1861–66, Records Public Buildings and Public Parks, National Capital, box 1, entry 58, RG 42.
73. *Daily National Intelligencer,* July 6, 1848.
74. B.B. French to Francis O. French, April 24 and 30, 1865, part 2, box 12, BBFFP.
75. de Chambrun, *Impressions of Lincoln,* 39.
76. Busey, *Personal Reminiscences,* 25.
77. B.B. French, *Journal,* September 4, 1866.
78. Brooks, *Washington in Lincoln's Time,* 213. Brooks, in "Glimpses of Lincoln in War Time," *Century Magazine* (January 1895), 466, says it happened when Lincoln took the oath of office.
79. Richtmyer Hubbell in *Potomac Diary,* 121.
80. *Chicago Tribune,* March 6, 1865. *New York Times,* March 6, 1865. London *Times,* March 20, 1865.
81. Brooks, *Washington in Lincoln's Time,* 214.

3. "An Excellent Chance to Kill the President!"

Chapter title: Samuel Chester testimony, CTPit, 45.

1. "His Schooldays." by a classmate, December 3, 1878, in Clarke, *Unlocked Book,* 155.
2. Clarke, *Sister's Memoir,* 76.
3. Henry "Harry" Clay Ford statement, April 20, 1865, M599, 5:459–488.

4. *Ibid.*

5. Clarke, *Sister's Memoir,* 75, 81.

6. Samuel Chester statement, April 28, 1865, M599, 4:143–170.

7. Clarke, *Sister's Memoir,* 13.

8. *Ibid.,* 84.

9. *Ibid.,* 67.

10. Edwin Booth to Nahum Capen, July 28, 1881, reproduced in Grossmann, *Edwin Booth,* 227.

11. Townsend, *The Life,* 23.

12. Thomas Ewing Jr. to his father, August 8, 1865, box 71, TEFP.

13. Clarke, *Sister's Memoir,* 76.

14. John Ford testimony, JST, 1:547.

15. Clarke, *Sister's Memoir,* 45.

16. M. Helen Palmes Moss, "Lincoln and Wilkes Booth as Seen on the Day of the Assassination," *Century Magazine* (April 1909)), 951.

17. Clarke, *Sister's Memoir,* 43, 44, 45, 54.

18. *Ibid.,* 44, 45. Samuel Arnold statement, April 18, 1865, M619, reel 458.

19. Arnold, *Defence and Prison Experiences,* 36–37.

20. Arnold interrogation by W.H. Gleason, December 3, 1867, box 175, BBP.

21. Arnold, *Defence and Prison Experiences,* 37.

22. James McPhail testimony, CTPit, 222.

23. Samuel Arnold statement, April 18, 1865, M619, reel 458.

24. Arnold interrogation by W.H. Gleason, December 3, 1867, box 175, BBP.

25. Samuel Arnold statement, April 18, 1865, M619, reel 458.

26. Arnold, *Defence and Prison Experiences,* 39.

27. Littleton Newman testimony, CTPoore, 1:423.

28. Samuel Arnold to Quartermaster General, November 18, 1864, Letters Received, volume 61, entry 19, RG 92. C.W. Thomas to Samuel Arnold, November 1864, M745, 48:463.

29. Samuel Arnold to Stanton, November 23, 1864, Consolidated Correspondence File, Records of the Office of the Quartermaster General, box 57, entry 225, RG 92, NA.

30. M.C. Meigs to Samuel Arnold, November 24, 1864, M745, 48:514.

31. Samuel Chester testimony, CTPit, 44.

32. John Ford testimony, AJII, 535.

33. John Simonds to Booth, December 7 and 31, 1864, M599, 2:314, 2:328, and February 21, 1865, M599, 2:318. Arnold, *Defence and Prison Experiences,* 49.

34. Samuel Chester statement, April 28, 1865, M599, 4:143–170.

35. A month before his death Booth gave his sister Asia an envelope to be given to Chester "should anything happen to me." Shortly after his death she gave it to her husband, but its contents or whereabouts are unknown. See Clarke, *Unlocked Book,* 126–127.

36. Samuel Chester statement, April 28, 1865, M599, 4:143–170.

37. John Deveny testimony, CTPit, 39.

38. Eaton Horner testimony, CTPit, 235. John C. Thompson testimony, CTPit, 178. Atzerodt confession, *Washington Evening Star,* July 10, 1865.

39. Samuel Mudd statement, April 22, 1865, M599, reel 5. John C. Thompson testimony, CTPit, 178. Steers, *Blood on the Moon,* 74–79.

40. "The Eccentricities of Booth," by Gath alias George Alfred Townsend, *Cincinnati Enquirer,* April 18, 1892. List of Bryantown postmasters by F.I. Ferrall, Ford's Theater collection. Jones, *J. Wilkes Booth,* 28.

41. Milo Simms testimony, CTPit, 172.

42. Sarah Mudd affidavit, July 6, 1865, Samuel Mudd Pardon Case File B-596, folder 1, NA.

43. William Gleason statement, December 19, 1867, box 175, BBP.

44. Thomas Gardiner testimony, CTPoore 1:361–365. Samuel Mudd statement, April 22, 1865, M599, 5:213–225.

45. John C. Thompson testimony, CTPit, 178.

46. B.B. French, *Journal,* June 18, 1865, BBFFP.

47. Sarah Mudd to Joseph Holt, September 4, 1865, JHP.

48. Mary Simms and Elzee Eglent testimony, CTPit, 170–171.

49. Milo Simms and Daniel Thomas testimony, CTPit, 172–173.

50. Louis Weichmann testimony, CTPit, 116. John Atzerodt statement, April 18, 1865, M599, 3:558–567.

51. Mary Simms testimony, CTPit, 170.

52. *Ibid.*

53. Weichmann, *True History,* 13.

54. John Surratt lecture, Rockville, Maryland, December 6, 1870, in *Washington Evening Star,* December 7, 1870.

55. E.L. Smoot testimony, JST, 1:190.

56. Sue Wallace to Delia, March 10, 1865, Lew Wallace Collection, reel 3, Indiana Historical Society Library.

57. Louis Weichmann, CTPit 114, 117. William Gleason statement, December 19, 1867, box 175, BBP. Samuel Mudd statement, August 28, 1865, in Laughlin, *Death of Lincoln,* 216.

58. John Surratt lecture, Rockville, Maryland, December 6, 1870, in *Washington Evening Star,* December 7, 1870.

59. Weichmann, *True History,* 28–29.

60. *Ibid.,* 20. Louis Weichmann testimony, CTPit, 114.

61. John Dempsey testimony, CTPit, 124. Anna Surratt testimony, CTPit, 131.

62. *Washington Evening Star,* July 10, 1865. Nicholas Crangle undated statement, entry 38, Correspondence and Reports Relating to Disloyal and Suspect Persons, RG 110, NA.

63. Nicholas Crangle undated statement, entry 38, Correspondence and Reports Relating to Disloyal and Suspect Persons, RG 110, NA.

64. David Herold statement, April 27, 1865, M599, reel 4.

65. Louis Weichmann statement, May 5, 1865, M599, reel 6.

66. John Atzerodt statement, April 18, 1865, M599, 3:558.

67. Alexander Brawner and Louis Harkins testimony, CTPit, 153.

68. Nicholas Crangle undated statement, entry 38, Correspondence and Reports Relating to Disloyal and Suspect Persons, RG 110, NA.

69. Eddy Martin testimony, JST, 215.

70. George Atzerodt statement, April 25, 1865, M599, reel 3.

71. Anna Surratt testimony, CTPit, 130.
72. Eliza Holahan testimony, CTPit, 133.
73. *Washington Evening Star*, November 3, 1863.
74. David Herold statement, April 27, 1865, M599, reel 4.
75. *Ibid.*
76. S.P. Currick statement, undated, M599, reel 4.
77. James Steel affidavit, April 25, 1865, M599, reel 4.
78. James Walsh statement, April 27, 1865, M599, reel 6.
79. *Ibid.*
80. Jane Herold statement, M599, reel 4.
81. David Herold statement, April 27, 1865, M599, reel 4.
82. George C. Powell to William Doster, September 30, 1865, in Doster, *Episodes of Civil War*, 272.
83. Ely Devoe statement, April 19, 1865, M599, reel 2.
84. William Doster summation, CTPit, 308.
85. George Powell to the Reverend A.D. Gillette, November 7, 1865, George C. Powell Papers, LC.
86. William Doster summation, CTPit, 314.
87. Thomas Eckert testimony, AJII, 674.
88. Lucy Grant and John Grant testimony, CTPit, 166–167.
89. Margaret Branson testimony, CTPit, 160–161. Margaret Branson statement, May 1, 1865, M599, reel 3.
90. Margaret Kaighn testimony, CTPit, 161.
91. Smoot, *Unwritten History*, 2–3. *Biographical Directory of Congress, 1892–1893*. Frederick Stone to Charles Lanman, January 20, 1867, Charles Lanman Collection, box 1, Hornbake Library Special Collections, University of Maryland Libraries.
92. M.E. Martin statement, May 6, 1865, M599, 5:331–533.
93. John Atzerodt statement, April 18, 1865, M599, 3:558–567.
94. Clay Ford statement, April 20, 1865, M599, 5:459–488.
95. Andrew White to William Seward, May 17 1865, Miscellaneous Letters, State Department, M179, reel 224, RG 59, NA.
96. John Surratt lecture, Rockville, Maryland, December 6, 1870, in *Washington Evening Star*, December 7, 1870.
97. Arnold interrogation by W.H. Gleason, December 3, 1867, box 175, BBP.
98. Samuel Arnold statement, April 18, 1865, M619, reel 458.
99. Mary Van Tine testimony, CTPit, 222.
100. Samuel Arnold statement, April 18, 1865, M619, reel 458. Weichmann, *True History*, 382.
101. Louis Weichmann testimony, CTPit, 115.
102. *Ibid*, 114–5.
103. Anna Surratt statement, April 28, 1865, M599, reel 6.
104. Eliza Holahan testimony, CTPit, 132.
105. John Hapman testimony, CTPit, 223.
106. Louis Weichmann testimony, CTPit, 116.
107. *Ibid*, 115.
108. *Ibid.*
109. Weichmann, *True History*, 98.

110. *Ibid.,* 28.
111. Honora Fitzpatrick testimony, CTPit, 121. Honora Fitzpatrick testimony, JST, 1:234.
112. Eaton Horner testimony, CTPoore, 1:434.
113. Samuel Arnold statement, April 18, 1865, M619, reel 458: 305–312.
114. Arnold, *Defence and Prison Experiences,* 46.
115. John Surratt lecture, Rockville, Maryland, December 6, 1870, in *Washington Evening Star,* December 7, 1870.
116. Samuel Arnold statement to William Gleason, December 3, 1867, box 175, BBP.
117. *Daily National Intelligencer,* March 18, 1865.
118. John Surratt lecture, Rockville, Maryland, December 6, 1870, in *Washington Evening Star,* December 7, 1870. Arnold confession, April 18, 1865, M619, reel 458, NA.
119. *Daily National Intelligencer, Constitutional Union,* and *National Republican,* March 18, 1865.
120. John Surratt lecture, Rockville, Maryland, December 6, 1870, in *Washington Evening Star,* December 7, 1870. Samuel Arnold obituary, *Baltimore American,* September 22, 1906.
121. Louis Weichmann, CTPit, 118. Weichmann, JST, 1:399.
122. Undated report by William Wood, superintendent of Old Capitol Prison, HR 39A-H2.3, Petitions & Memorials, Committee on Appropriations, House of Representatives, RG 233, NA. Though Wood reports Lloyd saying that this took place in late February or early March, it more likely occurred at the time of the aborted kidnap attempt. John Lloyd testimony, CTPit, 85.
123. Louis Weichmann testimony, CTPit, 115. Weichmann testimony, JST, 1:380. Mary Van Tine testimony, CTPit, 222.
124. Louis Weichmann testimony, CTPit, 118.
125. Payne oath of allegiance, Office of Provost Marshal, March 14, 1865, M599, reel 4.
126. Louis Weichmann testimony, CTPit, 113.
127. Louis Weichmann testimony, JST, 1:385–386.
128. John McOmber undated statement, M619, 458:333.
129. Samuel Arnold statement, December 3, 1867, box 175, BBP. Arnold, *Defence and Prison Experiences,* 49.
130. Arnold to Booth, March 27, 1865, reprinted in CTPit, 236.
131. Arnold statement, December 3, 1867, box 175, BBP.
132. *Ibid.*
133. *New York Daily Tribune,* March 19, 1864.
134. Louis Weichmann testimony, CTPit, 119–120.
135. Samuel Chester testimony, CTPit, 45. Samuel Chester statement, April 28, 1865, M599, 4:143–170.

4. "The Last Speech He Will Ever Make"
Chapter title: Thomas Eckert testimony, AJII, 674.
1. Thomas and Hyman, *Stanton,* 351–352. Brooks, *Washington in Lincoln's Time,* 220–221. Frederick Seward, *Reminiscences,* 251.
2. Thomas and Hyman, *Stanton,* 352.

3. Gordon Arthur Willett to Mary Willett, April 6, 1865, Ms. 308, Historical Society of Washington, DC.

4. *Ibid.*

5. *Ibid.*

6. Brooks, *Washington in Lincoln's Time,* 221.

7. *Daily Express,* Petersburg, Virginia, March 31, 1865.

8. Louis Weichmann testimony, JST, 1:387.

9. John Surratt lecture, Rockville, Maryland, December 6, 1870, in *Washington Evening Star,* December 7, 1870.

10. Pendel, *Thirty Six Years,* 33–34.

11. Edmund Poole to his family, April 5, 1865, Edmund Poole Papers, LC.

12. James Knox to his father, April 10, 1865, James Knox Papers, LC. *Daily National Intelligencer,* April 5, 1865.

13. Marsena Patrick, *Journal,* March 27, 1865, April 5, 1865, LC.

14. Porter, *Incidents and Anecdotes,* 295. B.B. French to Francis French, April 15, 1865, part 11, box 12, BBFFP.

15. Porter, *Incidents and Anecdotes,* 297–299.

16. Duvergier de Hauranne, *A Frenchman in Lincoln's America,* 2:324.

17. Fanny Seward diary, April 5, 1865, reel 198, #6666, WSP.

18. *Ibid,* April 9, 1865.

19. Frederick Seward, *Reminiscences,* 253.

20. Fanny Seward diary, April 9, 1865, reel 198, #6666, WSP.

21. Brooks, *Washington in Lincoln's Time,* 223.

22. *Ibid.,* 223–224. *Daily National Intelligencer,* April 11, 1865. Fanny Seward diary, April 10, 1865, reel 198, #6666, WSP.

23. Brooks, *Washington in Lincoln's Time,* 224.

24. *Ibid.,* 225. *Daily National Intelligencer,* April 11, 1865. Gobright, *Recollections,* 345. Fanny Seward diary, April 10, 1865, reel 198, #6666, WSP.

25. Henry Philips statement, April 14, 1865, M599, reel 7.

26. Undated report by William Wood, superintendent Old Capitol Prison, HR 39A-H2.3, Petitions & Memorials, Committee on Appropriations, House of Representatives, RG 233, NA. John Lloyd testimony, CTPit, 85–86.

27. James Walsh statement, April 27, 1865, M599, 6:405–406.

28. Brooks, *Washington in Lincoln's Time,* 225.

29. Keckley, *Behind the Scenes,* 178. Keckly's name is spelled throughout this volume as she herself signed her name, see Elizabeth Keckly to Jesse Weik, April 2, 1891, Herndon-Weik Collection, Group V 13:582–583, LC. The incorrect spelling in the bibliography has been retained as it appears in her book, *Behind the Scenes; or, Thirty Years a Slave and Four Years in the White House* (New York: G.W. Carleton, 1868, reprinted New York: Arno Press and the New York Times, 1968).

30. Leale, *Lincoln's Last Hours,* 2.

31. Townsend, *Katy of Catoctin,* 489 and footnote. Herold to Frederick Stone, quoted in Gath, alias George Alfred Townsend, "Booth Was Greatly Enraged," *Cincinnati Enquirer,* April 21, 1892.

32. Thomas Eckert testimony, AJII, 674.

33. Keckley, *Behind the Scenes,* 178.

34. *Daily Morning Chronicle,* April 14, 1865.

35. Gordon Arthur Willett to Mary Willett, April 13, 1865, Ms. 308, Historical Society of Washington, DC.

36. James Ward diary, April 13, 1865, James Ward Papers, LC.

37. Fanny Seward to Abraham Lincoln, April 12, 1865, Abraham Lincoln Papers, LC.

38. Fanny Seward diary, April 12, 13, 1865, reel 198, #6666, WSP. George Robinson testimony, JST 1:261.

39. C.D. Hess, CTPit, 99. George Wren statement, April 19, 1865, M599, reel 6.

40. Leonard Grover, "Lincoln's Interest in the Theater," *Century Magazine* (April 1909), 949.

41. M. Helen Palmes Moss, "Lincoln and Wilkes Booth," *Century Magazine* (April 1909), 951.

42. John Wilkes Booth to Mary Ann Booth, April 14, 1865, reproduced in Rhodehamel and Taper, *Right or Wrong,* 144.

43. Robert Jones testimony, CTPit, 144.

44. Lyman Sprague testimony, JST, 1:324.

45. James Ford testimony, CTPit, 100–101.

46. Thomas Raybold testimony, JST, 1:612–613. Louis Carland testimony, JST, 1:570.

47. Harry Clay Ford testimony, CTPit, 99.

48. Harry Clay Ford to Clara Laughlin, in Laughlin, *Death of Lincoln,* 63.

49. John Sleichmann testimony, CTPit, 73.

50. Harry Clay Ford testimony, JST, 1:553–554.

51. James Gifford testimony, CTPit, 77.

52. Harry Clay Ford testimony, CTPit, 99. Harry Clay Ford testimony, JST, 1:554.

53. Thomas Raybold testimony, JST, 1:612–614. John Ford undated manuscript, Ms. 371, John Ford Papers, MdHS. Undated report by William Wood, superintendent Old Capitol Prison, HR 39A-H 2.2–2.3, Petitions to Memorials, Committee on Appropriations, House of Representatives, RG 233, NA. Abram Olin testimony, JST, 1:520.

54. James Pumphrey testimony, CTPit, 72. Pumphrey testimony, JST, 1:225–226.

55. Notes of Atzerodt confession, May 1, 1865, discovered in 1977 by historian Joan Chaconas, past president of the Surratt Society, among papers of a descendant of Atzerodt's lawyer, William Doster, copy provided to this author by Chaconas. John Lloyd testimony, CTPit, 86.

56. Louis Weichmann testimony, CTPit, 113.

57. Louis Weichmann testimony, JST, 1:391.

58. L.B. Baker testimony, AJII, 489.

59. Louis Weichmann affidavit, August 11, 1865, in CTPit, 420.

60. *New York Tribune,* April 17, 1865.

61. John Mathews testimony, AJII, 782–783.

62. Julia Grant, *Personal Memoirs,* 156.

63. John Morris statement, April 18, 1865, M599, reel 5.

64. Harry Clay Ford testimony, CTPit, 100.

65. John Ford testimony, JST, 1:547. James Gifford testimony, CTPit, 77.

66. Abram Olin testimony, JST, 1:519.

67. James Ferguson statement, April 18, 1865, M599, 5:387–399.

68. "John Wilkes Booth," *Daily Constitutional Union,* April 15, 1865.

69. John Deveny testimony, CTPit, 39.

70. Ingraham, "Pursuit and Death of John Wilkes Booth," 445.

71. William Browning testimony, CTPit, 70.

72. James Maddox testimony, CTPit, 76. Edman Spangler statement, April 15, 1865, M599, 6:202–204.

73. John Lloyd testimony, CTPit, 85–87. William Wood report on Lloyd, undated, HR 39A-H2.3, RG 233.

74. Louis Weichmann affidavit, August 11, 1865, in CTPit, 420. Weichmann testimony, JST, 1:392–393. Weichmann, *True History,* 172.

5. "Like Banquo's Ghost, It Will Not Down"

Chapter title: Lamon, *Recollections,* 115.

1. John Hay Papers, undated manuscript, reel 22, LC.

2. Crook, *Memories of the White House,* 15–16.

3. Colfax, *Life and Principles,* 19.

4. Julia Grant, *Personal Memoirs,* 154. Lincoln to Frederick Seward, April 14, 1865, reel 88, WSP.

5. Randall, *Lincoln's Sons,* 160.

6. Keckley, *Behind the Scenes,* 137–138.

7. *Ibid.,* 138.

8. Lincoln to Isham Reavis, November 5, 1855, in Angle and Miers, *The Living Lincoln,* 192.

9. John Nicolay to Therena Bates, March 5, 1865, box 7, JNP.

10. John Hay Papers, undated manuscript, reel 22, LC.

11. John Hay to John Nicolay, August 7, 1863, in *Century Magazine* (February 1909).

12. Carpenter, *Six Months,* 68.

13. Colfax, *Life and Principles,* 17–18.

14. Inventory of President's House, May 26, 1865, M371, 27:307, NA.

15. Duvergier de Hauranne, *A Frenchman in Lincoln's America,* 2:350.

16. Brooks, *Washington in Lincoln's Time,* 258.

17. A.S. Draper, "Lincoln's Parable," *Harper's Weekly* (October 26, 1907), 1567.

18. GWD, April 14, 1865, 283 and footnote 1.

19. Seward, *Reminiscences,* 255.

20. Bates, *Lincoln in Telegraph Office,* 215.

21. Browning, *Diary,* April 14, 1865.

22. Lamon, *Recollections,* 114–118.

23. Seward, *Reminiscences,* 254–255.

24. James Speed to Merrill Watson, summer 1885, in David Homer Bates Papers, container 2, reel 1, LC.

25. Seward, *Reminiscences,* 257.

26. It is not clear whether Lincoln invited Grant before, during, or after the cabinet meeting. Julia Grant suggested *before* in *Personal Memoirs,* 155. Grant intimated *during* in *Personal Memoirs,* 508. Frederick Seward declared *after* in *Reminiscences,* 257.

27. Julia Grant, *Personal Memoirs,* 155.

28. Sandburg and Angle, *Mary Lincoln,* 106–108.

29. Julia Grant, *Personal Memoirs,* 155.

30. U.S. Grant, quoted in Hamilton Fish diary, November 12, 1869, container 277, reel 1, Hamilton Fish Papers, LC.

31. In Howe, *Portrait of an Independent,* 64, Stanton recalled his wife coming to the War Department that afternoon, saying Lincoln had invited them to the theater and that he had told her to send regrets, because he thought the president should not go as "it was too great an exposure."

32. Bates, *Lincoln in Telegraph Office,* 367–368.

33. Carpenter, *Six Months,* 17.

34. *Ibid.,* 218.

35. Mary Todd Lincoln to Francis Bicknell Carpenter, November 15, 1865, in Turner and Turner, *Mary Todd Lincoln,* 284.

36. *Ibid.,* 284–285.

37. Randall, *Lincoln's Sons,* 99.

38. Crook, *Through Five Administrations,* 65.

39. Brooks, *Washington in Lincoln's Time,* 229.

40. Crook, *Through Five Administrations,* 65.

41. Jesse Weik, "A Law Student's Recollection," undated, Herndon-Weik Collection, 14:1522–1528, LC.

42. Stewart, *Reminiscences,* 190.

43. *Daily National Republican,* April 15, 1865.

44. B.B. French to President Johnson, May 6, 1865, M371, 7:546–547.

45. Pendel, *Thirty Six Years,* 40–41. Pendel's memory was clearly faulty: He wrote that John Nicolay, Lincoln's secretary, was inside the White House that night when in fact he was indisputably in Charleston, South Carolina. See Nicolay and Hay, *Abraham Lincoln: A History,* 10:301.

46. Crook, *Through Five Administrations,* 72.

47. Notes of Atzerodt confession, May 1, 1865, discovered in 1977 by historian Joan Chaconas, past president of the Surratt Society, among papers of a descendant of Atzerodt's lawyer, William Doster, copy provided to this author by Chaconas.

48. Bernard Early testimony, CTPit, 228. Edward Murphy testimony, CTPit, 229. James Henderson testimony, CTPit, 230.

49. Doster, *Episodes of Civil War,* 269. George Atzerodt statement, April 25, 1865, M599 reel 3. George Atzerodt undated statement read by Doster, CTPit, 307.

50. George Atzerodt statement, April 25, 1865, M599, reel 3.

51. George Atzerodt undated statement read by Doster, CTPit, 307.

52. Louis Weichmann undated statement, M599, reel 3.

53. Louis Weichmann testimony, JST, 1:390–394. Weichmann affidavit, August 11, 1865, in CTPit, 421. Weichmann undated statement, M599, reel 3.

54. Eliza Holahan testimony, JST, 1:689.
55. Smoot, *Unwritten History*, 2–5.
56. John T. Ford undated manuscript, John Ford Papers, Ms. 371, MdHS.
57. John Sleichmann testimony, CTPit, 73.
58. Edman Spangler statement, April 15, 1865, M599, reel 6. Joseph "Peanuts John" Burroughs statement, April 24, 1865, M599, reel 4.
59. Joseph "Peanut" Burroughs testimony, CTPit, 74.
60. Peter Taltavul statement, April 22, 1865, M599, reel 6.
61. Fletcher to Stanton, September 23, 1865, M619, 456:307, has Fletcher's mark in lieu of a signature.
62. John Fletcher statement, May 17, 1866, LC collection, box 166, RG 233, NA.
63. John Fletcher testimony, CTPit, 145. Fletcher statement, April 23, 1865, M599, 5:415–421.
64. Fletcher statement, April 23, 1865, M599, 5:415–421. Fletcher statement, May 17, 1866, LC collection, box 166, RG 233, NA.
65. Fletcher to Stanton, September 23, 1865, M619, 456:306–307.
66. Fletcher testimony, CTPit, 84. Fletcher statement, May 17, 1866, LC collection, box 166, RG 233, NA.

6. "The President Is Shot!"

Chapter title: Clara Harris affidavit, April 17, 1865, reprinted in Baker, *History of US Secret Service*, 473.
1. James Ward diary, April 21, 1865, James Ward Papers, LC.
2. Thomas Walter to Amanda Walter, April 15, 1865, letterbook, reel 4142, TWP.
3. *Boston Pilot*, June 24, 1865, quoting *London Tablet*.
4. Henry Rathbone testimony, CTPit, 78.
5. Harry Clay Ford statement, April 20, 1865, M599, 5:459–488. Self-described presidential bodyguard William Crook wrote forty-five years later in *Through Five Administrations*, 72, that "it was the custom for the guard who accompanied the president to the theatre to remain in the little passageway outside the box." And he added on the same page that police officer John Parker "confessed to me the next day that he went to a seat at the front of the first gallery so that he could see the play." For a meticulously reasoned case for Charles Forbes being the man who sat outside Lincoln's box, see James O. Hall, "The Mystery of Lincoln's Guard," reprinted from the May 1982 edition of *The Surratt Society News* in Surratt Society, *In Pursuit Of*, 233–238. Parker was later charged by the police superintendent with "neglect of duty" after having been "detailed to attend and protect the president, Mr. Lincoln," but had "allowed a man to enter the president's private box and shoot the president." However, the case was dismissed a month later. The trial records have never been found, and Parker continued in the police department until his dismissal for "gross neglect of duty" three years later. See the photocopy of the charge sheet, May 1, 1865, in *Washington Sunday Star*, February 9, 1936, and Records of Government of District of Columbia, Register of Appointments to the Force 1861–1930, entry 117, RG 351, NA.

6. Leale's observations in this chapter are from his account in "Lincoln's Last Hours" and in Charles Leale to Benjamin Butler, July 20, 1867, Leale Papers, LC.

7. Henry Rathbone affidavit, April 17, 1865, M599, reel 6.

8. Britton Hill to Stanton, April 15, 1865, 9:221–223, ESP. Elizabeth Keckley, *Behind the Scenes*, 195.

9. Francis Burke testimony, JST, 2:792. Francis Burke statement, April 25, 1865, M599, 4:83–84.

10. Leale, *Lincoln's Last Hours*, 3.

11. Robert Murray to Henry Burnett, April 24, 1865, entry 38, Correspondence and Reports Relating to Disloyal and Suspect Persons, RG 110, NA.

12. A.M. Crawford statement, April 14, 1865, M599, reel 7. Theodore McGowan statement, April 15, 1865, M599, 5:318–322, and McGowan testimony, CTPit, 78.

13. George Todd to his brother, April 15, 1865, Abraham Lincoln Papers, folder 263, Chicago History Museum.

14. James Ferguson statements, April 14, 1865, M599, 7:487–489; April 15, 1865, M599, 4:340–343; April 18, 1865, M599, 5:387–399.

15. Elizabeth Blair Lee to Phil Lee, April 22, 1865, in *Letters of Elizabeth Blair*, 499.

16. Harry Hawk interview, *Washington Post*, March 10, 1894.

17. Henry Rathbone affidavit, April 17, 1865, M599, reel 6.

18. G.W. Pope, *Washington Post*, November 13, 1896.

19. Joseph Barnes to Edwin Stanton, April 27, 1865, Ford's Theatre collection. While escaping through southern Maryland, Booth wrote, "In jumping [from Lincoln's box] broke my leg." See Booth diary photocopies and transcription, Ford's Theatre collection.

20. Joseph Stewart statement, April 15, 1865, M599, 4:59–63. William Kent to his mother, April 15, 1865, typescript of lost original letter provided to the author by Kent's great-grandaughter Virginia Brown.

21. Skeptics who state that Booth could not have run with a fractured bone ignore countless heroics performed by wounded troops on the field of battle.

22. Harry Hawk interview, *Washington Post*, March 10, 1894.

23. Louis Carland testimony, JST 1:570.

24. Henry Philips statement, April 14, 1865, M599, reel 7.

25. Clara Harris affidavit, April 17, 1865, reprinted in Baker, *History of US Secret Service*, 473.

26. Sarah Batchelder to Ellen Hamlin, April 15, 1865, reel 1, Hannibal Hamlin Papers, LC.

27. John Deveny testimony, CTPit, 39.

28. Jacob Ritterspaugh testimony, CTPit, 97.

29. James Knox to his father, April 15, 1865, Abraham Lincoln Papers, folder 262, Chicago History Museum.

30. William Withers undated statement, M599, 6:469–470.

31. H.P. Wood undated statement on Jacob Ritterspaugh, M599, 6:48–49, and Ritterspaugh testimony, CTPit, 97.

32. Joseph Burroughs statement, April 24, 1865, M599, 4:65–70.

33. Joseph Stewart statement, April 15, 1865, M599, 4:59–63, and testimony, CTPit, 79–80.

34. George Ziegler to Andrew Johnson, February 15, 1869, Pardon Case Files, record B, page 585, box 36, case B612, RG 204, NA.

35. Jacob Ritterspaugh testimony, CTPit, 97–98.

36. Charles Leale Papers, LC.

37. Charles Leale to Benjamin Butler, July 20, 1867, Leale Papers, LC, said he asked a bystander to cut the coat and shirt. William Kent testimony, JST, 1:123, said a surgeon cut the clothes.

38. Exhaling into the mouth and nostrils to resuscitate a patient had been recommended for more than a century by medical experts. See Jackson, *A Physical Dissertation on Drowning,* 59, 69–70, 79; *Directions for Recovering Persons Who Are Supposed to Be Dead,* microfilm reel 61-4, item 5, p. 2, National Library of Medicine. See also Peter Safar, "On the History of Resuscitation," in *The History of Anaesthesia,* edited by Jochen Schulte am Esch and Michael Goerig, *Proceedings of the Fourth International Symposium on the History of Anaesthesia,* Hamburg, 1997 (Lubeck: Drager, 1998), 287–310.

39. Typescript copy of letter, William Kent to his mother, April 15, 1865, typescript of lost original letter, provided to the author by Kent's great-granddaughter Virginia Brown.

40. Julia Shepard to her father, April 16, 1865, *Century Magazine* (April 1909), 917.

41. Miscellaneous documents 1856–1877, Laura Keene Papers, LC.

42. Typescript copy of letter, William Kent to his mother, April 15, 1865, typescript of lost original letter, provided to the author by Kent's great-granddaughter Virginia Brown.

43. *Ibid.*

44. Henry Safford account, *Boston Globe,* February 12, 1909.

45. *Frank Leslie's Illustrated Newspaper,* April 29, 1865, 83.

46. Henry Safford account, *Boston Globe,* February 12, 1909. Keckley, *Behind the Scenes,* 310.

47. G.W. Pope, *Washington Post,* November 13, 1896.

48. Thomas Eckert diary, April 14, 1865, Auburn University Special Collections and Archives, RG 158.

49. Eckert to David Homer Bates, October 1909, recounted in typescript, 9, "Booth, the Assassin," Bates Papers, container 2, reel 1, LC.

50. George Maynard, *New York Herald,* April 11, 1915.

51. Bates, *Lincoln in Telegraph Office,* 371–372.

7. A Singular Night of Horrors

1. Doster, *Episodes of Civil War,* 268–269.

2. Britton Hill to Edwin Stanton, April 16, 1865, reel 9, ESP. William Bell testimony, CTPit, 154–155.

3. George Robinson testimony, JST, 1:261.

4. Anna Seward testimony, JST, 1:253.

5. George Robinson testimony, JST, 1:262.

6. Frederick Seward testimony, JST, 1:251.

7. Fanny Seward diary, April 14, 1865, written weeks after the event, reel 198, #6666, WSP.

8. Augustus Seward to H.H. Wells, April 21, 1865, M599, 6:95–96.

9. Fanny Seward diary, April 14, 1865, written weeks after the event, reel 198, #6666, WSP.

10. Gobright, *Recollections*, 382.

11. George Robinson testimony, JST, 1:265. Joseph Barnes testimony, CTPit, 157.

12. George Robinson testimony, JST, 1:262.

13. Augustus Seward testimony, CTPit, 156.

14. Register of Officers and Agents, 2. Tullio Verdi testimony, CTPit, 157. George Robinson testimony, JST, 1:263.

15. George Robinson testimony, JST, 1:264.

16. Anna Seward testimony, JST, 1:253.

17. William Bell testimony, CTPit, 154.

18. Register of Officers and Agents, 27. This publication spells his name Cloughly, but his transcribed verbal examination by Chief Justice Cartter on April 14, 1865, when he would likely have spelled out his own name, records Cloughley: see M599, 7:475.

19. Watson, *In Memoriam,* 79.

20. Alfred Cloughley statement, April 14, 1865, M599, 7:475–480.

21. Howe, *Portrait of an Independent,* 62.

22. Duvergier de Hauranne, *A Frenchman in Lincoln's America,* 1:63.

23. Howe, *Portrait of an Independent,* 63.

24. *Ibid.,* 65. Dolby, *Charles Dickens As I Knew Him,* 231–232.

25. B.B. French, *Journal,* April 15, 1865, reel 2, BBFFP.

26. Joseph Barnes testimony, CTPit, 157.

27. Fanny Seward diary, April 14, 1865, written weeks after the event, reel 198, #6666, WSP.

28. Tullio Verdi testimony, CTPit, 157.

29. *Ibid.*

30. Typescript copy of letter, William Kent to his mother, April 15, 1865, typescript of lost original letter, provided to the author by Kent's great-granddaughter Virginia Brown.

8. "They Have Killed Papa Dead!"

Chapter title: Pendel, *Thirty Six Years,* 44.

1. Leale, *Lincoln's Last Hours,* 9.

2. Field, *Memories,* 321–323. Field undated statement in Baker, *History of US Secret Service,* 468–470.

3. Robert Stone address to the DC Medical Society, May 3, 1865, in Milton Shutes, *Lincoln and the Doctors,* 1933, 142, Ford's Theatre collection.

4. Taft, "Last Hours of Abraham Lincoln," 453.

5. Clinical Record, April 14 and 15, 1865, Abraham Lincoln Papers, series 4, container 4, LC.

6. *Frank Leslie's Illustrated Newspaper,* April 29, 1865, 83.

7. Taft, "Lincoln's Last Hours," 635.

8. Brooks, *Washington in Lincoln's Time,* 36. Louis Koerth interview, *New York Commercial Advertiser,* March 24, 1903.

9. Johnston, *Life and Public Services of Stanton,* 6.

10. Proofed galleys of J.M. Carlisle memorial address to the Supreme Court, January 17, 1870, in Records of the Attorney General's Office, Miscellaneous Records, Unidentified Papers 1795–1870, box 3, entry 23, RG 60, NA.

11. Bates, *Lincoln in Telegraph Office,* 400.

12. James Tanner to James Frear, May 7, 1926, *Congressional Record,* 69C 1S, June 1, 1926, 10420.

13. John Young to Edwin Stanton, undated, M619, reel 456.

14. Edwin Stanton to Chief of Police, New York, April 15, 1865, M473, reel 88.

15. Edwin Stanton to William T. Sherman, April 15, 1865, M473, reel 88.

16. Sherman to Halleck, April 18, 1865, reel 9, ESP.

17. Thomas Eckert to Ulysses S. Grant, April 14, 1865, in *Papers of Ulysses S. Grant,* 14:390.

18. Charles Dana to Ulysses S. Grant, April 15, 1865, in *Papers of Ulysses S. Grant,* 14:390.

19. Julia Grant, *Personal Memoirs,* 156.

20. Ulysses S. Grant, *Personal Memoirs,* 508–509.

21. Grant to Charles Ford, April 17, 1865, Ulysses S. Grant Papers, series 10, box 3, LC.

22. I.W. Taylor to General Morris, April 15, 1865, Letters Received, Provost Marshal 8th Army and Middle Department, entry 2380, box 1, Part 1, RG 393.

23. Elizabeth Blair to Phil Blair, April 14, 1865, in Lucas, *Civil War Letters of Elizabeth Blair,* 494.

24. Elizabeth Blair to Phil Blair, April 17, 1865, in Lucas, editor, *Civil War Letters,* 496. *Daily Morning Chronicle,* April 15, 1865. George Koontz testimony, JST 1:524. Madge Preston diary, April 15, 1865, Preston Family Papers, box 6, Hornbake Library, University of Maryland Libraries.

25. Edwin Stanton to Ulysses S. Grant, April 15, 1865, in *Papers of Ulysses S. Grant,* 14:390. C.C. Augur to Gen. Michaels, April 14, 1865, M599, reel 7.

26. James Kane and Samuel Brown statements, May 4, 1865, M179, reel 224.

27. Edwin Stanton to General Hancock, April 16, 1865, M473, reel 88.

28. Edwin Stanton to Charles Francis Adams, April 15, 1865, reel 9, ESP.

29. John Hay to Edwin Stanton, July 26, 1865, reel 10, ESP.

30. Stanton to Mrs. Christopher Wolcott, Nancy Stanton, and Lewis Hutchison, April 15, 1865, M473, reel 88.

31. Louis Koerth, *New York Commercial Advertiser,* March 24, 1903.

32. E.J. Allen (alias Pinkerton) to Edwin Stanton, April 19, 1865, Pinkerton's National Detective Agency, box 24, LC.

33. Leale, *Lincoln's Last Hours,* 11.

34. GWD, April 15, 1865, reel 3, GWP.

35. Brooks, *Washington in Lincoln's Time,* 36.

36. Howe, *Portrait of an Independent,* 63.

37. Elizabeth Dixon to Othaniel Marsh, April 14, 1866, O.C. Marsh Papers, box

40, folder 106, Manuscripts and Archives, Yale University Library.

38. Thomas and Hyman, *Stanton, Life and Times,* 40–41.

39. Sandburg, *Prairie Years,* 281.

40. Johnston, *Life and Public Services of Stanton,* 7.

41. Howe, *Portrait of an Independent,* 66.

42. James Tanner to James Frear, May 7, 1926, *Congressional Record,* 69C 1S, June 1, 1926, 10419.

43. Pendel, *Thirty Six Years,* 10, 44.

44. James Tanner to James Frear, May 7, 1926, *Congressional Record,* 69C 1S, June 1, 1926, 10419.

45. James Tanner to Henry Walch, April 17, 1865, in *American Historical Review* 29, no. 3 (April 1924), 516.

46. *New York Herald,* April 15, 1865.

47. Gobright, *Recollections,* 351.

48. Gobright, *Recollections,* 348–350. *New York Herald,* April 15, 1865. William Kent testimony, CTPit, 82. William Kent statement, April 15, 1865, M599, 5:130–131. William Kent testimony, JST, 1:123. William Kent to his mother, April 15, 1865, typescript of lost original letter, provided to the author by Kent's great-granddaughter Virginia Brown.

49. Harry Hawk interview, *Washington Post,* March 10, 1894. Hawk statement, April 14, 1865, M599, 7:485–486.

50. Taft, "Lincoln's Last Hours," 635.

51. Lew Wallace, *An Autobiography,* 672.

52. James Tanner to James Frear, May 7, 1926, *Congressional Record,* 69C 1S, June 1, 1926, 10420.

53. Thomas Eckert to E.S. Allen, May 14, 1865, M473, 89:400.

54. Leonard Farwell to James Doolittle, February 8, 1866, series 15, reel 54, AJP.

55. Montgomery Meigs diary, April 15, 1865, Montgomery Meigs Papers, LC.

56. Thomas Eckert testimony, AJII, 673.

57. Leonard Grover, "Lincoln's Interest in the Theater," *Century Magazine* (April 1909), 949.

58. Taft, "Lincoln's Last Hours," 635.

59. Typescript, John Usher to Margaret Usher, April 16, 1865, Usher Papers, LC.

60. Leale, *Lincoln's Last Hours,* 11.

61. *Ibid.*

62. *Ibid.,* 12.

63. Taft, "Lincoln's Last Hours," 636.

64. Gobright, *Recollections,* 354.

65. Sarah Batchelder to Ellen Hamlin, April 15, 1865, Hannibal Hamlin Papers, reel 1, LC.

66. Wolf, *Shorthand Journals of Montgomery Meigs,* 267.

67. Minerva Rodgers to her children, April 17, 1865, Rodgers Family Papers, box 23, LC.

68. Mary Hassler Newcomb diary, April 14, 1865, Simon Newcomb Papers, box 2, LC.

69. John Mathews testimony, AJII, 782–784.

70. William Dixon testimony, JST, 1:584.

71. B.B. French, *Journal,* 386, 399, April 15, 1865, reel 2, BBFFP. B.B. French to Pamela French, May 21, 1865, reel 6, BBFFP.

72. B.B. French to Pamela French, May 21, 1865, reel 6, BBFFP.

73. B.B. French, *Journal,* April 15, 1865, reel 2, BBFFP. B.B. French to Francis French, April 15, 1865, part 2, box 12, BBFFP. GWD, April 15, 1865, reel 3, GWP.

74. Thomas and Hyman, *Stanton, Life and Times,* 150.

75. James Tanner to James Frear, May 7, 1926, *Congressional Record,* 69C 1S, June 1, 1926, 10420.

76. Leale, *Lincoln's Last Hours,* 11.

77. Charles Leale to Benjamin Butler, July 20, 1867, Charles Leale Papers, LC.

78. James Tanner to James Frear, May 7, 1926, *Congressional Record,* 69C 1S, June 1, 1926, 10420.

79. Field, *Memories,* 325.

80. James Tanner to James Frear, May 7, 1926, *Congressional Record,* 69C 1S, June 1, 1926, 10420. Leale, *Lincoln's Last Hours,* 12.

81. William Herndon to Jesse Weik, January 6, 1887, Herndon-Weik Collection, 10: 1–2, LC.

82. James Tanner to James Frear, May 7, 1926, *Congressional Record,* 69C 1S, June 1, 1926, 10420. Nicolay and Hay, *Lincoln: A History,* 10:302. Taft, "Lincoln's Last Hours," 635.

83. Secretaries of Treasury, War, Navy, Postmaster General, Interior, and Attorney General to Andrew Johnson, April 15, 1865, M179, reel 223.

84. Taft, "Lincoln's Last Hours," 635–636. Maunsell Field statement, in Baker, *History of US Secret Service,* 470. Leale, *Lincoln's Last Hours,* 12.

85. Leale, *Lincoln's Last Hours,* 12.

86. *Ibid.,* 14.

87. Taft, "Lincoln's Last Hours," 636.

88. James Tanner to James Frear, May 7, 1926, *Congressional Record,* 69C 1S, June 1, 1926, 10420. The *Washington Daily Constitutional Union* reported on April 15, 1865, that a cavalry escort followed by General Augur and six officers accompanied the president in a temporary coffin, and that they turned into G Street en route to the White House.

89. Keckley, *Behind the Scenes,* 190.

90. Thomas Eckert diary, April 15, 1865, Auburn University Special Collections and Archives, RG 158.

91. Brooks, *Washington in Lincoln's Time,* 230–231.

92. Mrs. David Cartter diary, September 7, 1862, Cartter Family Papers, box 3, LC.

93. Collins French to David Cartter, April 16, 1865, Cartter Family Papers, box 3, LC.

94. Julia Shepard to her father, April 16, 1865, in *Century Magazine* (April 1909), 918.

95. Charles Morrell to Isaac Morrell, April 17, 1865, Charles Morrell Papers, LC.

96. Howe, *Portrait of an Independent,* 63–64.

97. *Daily National Intelligencer,* June 24, 1865.

98. Field, *Memories,* 263.

99. Duvergier de Hauranne, *A Frenchman in Lincoln's America,* 1:71–72.

100. *Ibid.,* 2:324.

101. *New York Times,* May 12, 1865.

102. Fanny Seward diary, April 14, 1865, written weeks after the event, reel 198, #6666, WSP.

103. Arnold Johnson, "Recollections of Charles Sumner," *Scribner's Monthly* (June 1875), 224.

104. B.B. French, *Journal,* April 15, 1866, reel 4, BBFFP.

105. Orville Hickman Browning, diary, April 15, 1865.

106. Keckley, *Behind the Scenes,* 104–105.

107. *Ibid.,* 184.

108. *Ibid.,* 186.

109. George Wheelock to Winnie Wheelock, April 15, 1865, box 71, TEFP.

110. Keckley, *Behind the Scenes,* 188.

111. *Ibid.,* 192.

112. *Ibid.,* 190–191.

113. GWD, April 15, 1865, reel 3, GWP.

114. Salmon Chase journal, April 14 and 15, 1865, Salmon P. Chase Papers, 1:528–530, edited by John Niven, et al. (Kent, Ohio: Kent State University Press, 1993).

115. *Daily Constitutional Union,* April 15, 1865.

116. Edwin Stanton to John Dix, April 15, 1865, M473, 88:1020–1021.

117. Edmund Hammond to Lord Cowley, April 26, 1865, Cowley Papers, private correspondence, FO 519/192, National Archives, Kew, England.

9. An Autopsy and Embalming in the White House

1. Charles Leale, *Lincoln's Last Hours,* 14.

2. Edward Curtis, "Was at Lincoln Autopsy," *New York Sun,* April 22, 1903.

3. *Ibid.*

4. *Ibid.*

5. J.J. Woodward, undated draft report of the autopsy of President Lincoln, library, New York State Historical Association.

6. J.J. Woodward to Joseph Barnes, April 15, 1865, special file P117, entry 286, items 12–15, box 2, adjutant general's office, RG 94. Hickman, *Diary,* 2:20, April 15, 1865.

7. Curtis, "Was at Lincoln Autopsy."

8. J.J. Woodward to Joseph Barnes, April 15, 1865, special file P117, entry 286, items 12–15, box 2, adjutant general's office, RG 94. Hickman, *Diary,* 2:20, April 15, 1865. Robert Stone notes on Lincoln autopsy, April 14 (sic), 1865, library, New York State Historical Association.

9. Taft, "Last Hours of Abraham Lincoln," 454.

10. Curtis, "Was at Lincoln Autopsy."

11. Taft, "Last Hours of Abraham Lincoln," 454.

12. Taft, "Lincoln's Last Hours," 636.

13. Robert Stone testimony, CTPit, 82. M599, 7:664–666.

14. Curtis, "Was at Lincoln Autopsy."
15. J.J. Woodward to Joseph Barnes, April 15, 1865, special file P117, entry 286, items 12–15, box 2, adjutant general's office, RG 94.
16. Curtis, "Was at Lincoln Autopsy."
17. Taft, "Last Hours of Abraham Lincoln," 454.
18. Robert Stone testimony, CTPit, 82.
19. Hickman, *Diary*, 2:20, April 15, 1865.
20. Augusta Curtis affidavit, May 11, 1926, accession file 29719, Armed Forces Institute of Pathology, National Museum of Health and Medicine, Washington, DC.

10. A Visceral Preference for Vengeance

1. *Daily Morning Chronicle*, April 15, 1865.
2. *Daily National Republican*, April 15, 1865.
3. George Wheelock to Winnie Wheelock, April 16, 1865, typescript, box 71, TEFP.
4. Facsimile of Stanton order, April 16, 1865, in Bates, *Lincoln in Telegraph Office*, 374–375.
5. William Hunter to George Whiting, April 17, 1865, Domestic Letters of Department of State, M40, reel 59, RG 59, NA.
6. Elizabeth Blair to Phil Lee, April 17, 1865, reproduced in Lucas, editor, *Civil War Letters*, 496.
7. Edgington, *A History*, 242, 254.
8. Mary Newcomb diary, April 16, 1865, box 2, Mary Hassler Newcomb Papers, LC.
9. *Daily Morning Chronicle*, April 17, 1865.
10. Helen Varnum Hill McCalla diary, April 16, 1865, McCalla Papers, LC.
11. John Nicolay to Therena Bates, April 18, 1865, box 3, JNP.
12. Burnett, *Some Incidents in the Trial*, 4.
13. Margaret Ramsey diary, April 15, 1865, Margaret Ramsay Papers, LC.
14. Hannah Pettit to William Pettit, April 17, 1865, William Pettit Correspondence, #177, Archives Center, National Museum of American History, Smithsonian Institution.
15. William Clark to his sister Ida, April 19, 1865, reprinted in Laughlin, *The Death of Lincoln*, 298–299.
16. Roll of Prisoners of War Committed to Old Capitol Prison 5 Days Ending 15 Apr. 1865, box 262, Prison Records 1862–1865, RG 109, NA.
17. Westwood A. Todd, *Reminiscences of the War Between the States*, typescript, 249–250, #3626, M559, Alderman Library, University of Virginia. Thomas Walter to Amanda Walter, April 17, 1865, letterbook, reel 4142, TWP.
18. Thomas Walter to Amanda Walter, April 17, 1865, letterbook, reel 4142, TWP.
19. William Kent to his mother, April 15, 1865. Typescript of lost original letter, provided to the author by Kent's great-granddaughter Virginia Brown.
20. *New York Times*, April 17, 1865.
21. *Daily National Intelligencer*, April 15, 1865.
22. Simon Newcomb diary, April 15, 1865, box 1, Simon Newcomb Papers, LC.

23. Joseph Goldsborough Bruff Journal, April 17, 1865, Ms. 381, Joseph Goldsborough Bruff Papers, Historical Society of Washington, DC.

24. John Hamilton to his father, April 22, 1865, Hamilton Family Papers, series 1, box 1, Hornbake Library, University of Maryland.

25. William Flinn to James Buchanan, April 15, 1865, James Buchanan Papers, Historical Society of Pennsylvania, reel 43, LC.

26. James Buchanan to William Flinn, April 18, 1865, James Buchanan Papers, Historical Society of Pennsylvania, reel 51, LC.

27. George Wheelock to Winnie Wheelock, April 15, 1865, typescript, box 71, TEFP.

28. James Knox to his father, April 15, 1865, Abraham Lincoln Papers, folder 262, Chicago History Museum.

29. Collins French to David Cartter, April 16, 1865, Cartter Family Papers, David Kellogg Cartter Family General Correspondence 1850–1869, box 3, LC.

30. S.A. Saint John, House of Representatives Report 559, 50C 1S, February 21, 1888.

31. L.C. Turner to Joseph Holt, May 11, 1865, Letterbook of Judge Advocate Turner, volume 4, Records of Office of Advocate General, RG 94, NA.

32. Collins French to David Cartter, April 16, 1865, Cartter Family Papers, David Kellogg Cartter Family General Correspondence 1850–1869, box 3, LC.

33. Henry Clay Weaver to Cornelia Wiley, April 19, 1865, Henry Clay Weaver Papers, LC.

34. Charles Morrell to Isaac Morrell, April 17, 1865, Charles Morrell Papers, LC.

35. Samuel Meigs to Montgomery Meigs, April 15, 1865, Montgomery Meigs Papers, container 27, reel 9, LC.

36. John Russell Young diary, April 17, 1865, reel 1, John Russell Young Papers, LC.

37. Samuel Meigs to Montgomery Meigs, April 15, 1865, Montgomery Meigs Papers, container 27, reel 9, LC.

38. Sir Frederick Bruce to Earl Russell, April 17, 1865, Great Britain Foreign Policy Program, Embassy and Consular Archives, PRO FO 115, volume 437, #241, reel 83, LC.

39. Joseph Warren Keifer to Eliza Keifer, April 15, 1865, Joseph Warren Keifer Papers, LC.

40. Charles Field to Hattie Burleigh, April 28, 1865, Hattie Burleigh Papers, box 1, US Army Military History Institute, Carlisle, Pennsylvania.

41. H.G. Wright to General Webb, April 15, 1865, OR, series 1, volume 46, part 3, 759.

42. William Sherman to Henry Hallek, April 18, 1865, reel 9, ESP.

43. Henry Clay Weaver to Cornelia Wiley, April 22, 1865, Henry Clay Weaver Papers, LC.

44. R.S. Ewell to Ulysses S. Grant, April 16, 1865, OR, series 1, volume 46, part 3, 787.

45. William Sherman to Henry Hallek, April 18, 1865, reel 9, ESP.

46. James Mason to Earl of Shaftesbury, April 28, 1865, James Mason Papers, volume 8, LC.

47. Benjamin Moran diary, volume 14, April 26, 1865, Benjamin Moran Papers, LC.

48. Minerva Rodgers to her children, April 17, 1865, Rodgers Family Papers, box 23, LC.

49. Gobright, *Recollections*, 354.

50. John Palmer Usher to Margaret Usher, April 16, 1865, John Palmer Usher Papers, LC.

51. John Potter to William Seward, April 27, 1865, Dispatches from US Consul, Montreal, 1850–1906, T222, reel 6, Department of State, RG 59, NA.

52. John Potter to William Seward, April 24, 1865, Dispatches from US Consul, Montreal, 1850–1906, T222, reel 6, Department of State, RG 59, NA.

53. Britton Hill to Stanton, April 16, 1865, reel 9, ESP.

54. Ulysses S. Grant to Julia Grant, April 16, 1865, in Simon, *Papers of U.S. Grant,* 14:396.

55. Timothy Ingraham to Major General Cadwallader, April 30, 1865, M473, 89:215.

56. Edward Bates diary, April 15, 1865, reel 2, Edward Bates Papers, LC.

11. "I Am Right in the Justness of My Cause"

Chapter title: John Wilkes Booth to Mary Ann Booth, undated, Records of the Attorney General's Office, Letters Received 1809–1870, box 7, General Records of the Department of Justice, RG 60, NA.

1. McClure, *Recollections*, 247.

2. Edwin Booth to Adam Badeau, April 16, 1865, reprinted in *Century Magazine* (April 1909), 919–920.

3. *Ibid.* Theater bill, Boston Theater, Boston, April 14, 1865, container 2, John Russell Young Papers, LC.

4. Henry Jarrett to Edwin Booth, April 15, 1865, reprinted in Clarke, *Unlocked Book,* 200–201.

5. Edwin Booth to Henry Jarrett, April 15, 1865, reprinted in *ibid.,* 201.

6. Aldrich, *Crowding Memories,* 73.

7. Edwin Booth to Emma Cary, May 6, 1865, reprinted in Grossmann, *Edwin Booth,* 172.

8. Aldrich, *Crowding Memories,* 74.

9. Edwin Booth to Emma Cary, May 6, 1865, reprinted in Grossmann, *Edwin Booth,* 172.

10. Edwin Booth to Nahum Capen, July 28, 1881, reprinted in *Unlocked Book,* 202–203.

11. Edwin Booth to Emma Cary, July 31, 1865, reprinted in Grossmann, *Edwin Booth,* 173.

12. Edwin Booth to Mrs. John Murray, April 27, 1865, reprinted in Clarke, *A Sister's Memoir,* 114.

13. Robert Lincoln interview with *Century Magazine* (April 1909), 920.

14. Mary Ann Booth to John Wilkes Booth, March 23, 1865, Ms. 2125, MdHS.

15. John Wilkes Booth to Mary Ann Booth, April 14, 1865, reprinted in Rhodehamel and Taper, *Right or Wrong,* 144.

16. Clarke, *Unlocked Book,* 126. Alford, editor, A *Sister's Memoir,* 15, 89–90, says the twins were born August 20, 1865.

17. Clarke, *Unlocked Book,* 126–127.

18. John Wilkes Booth to Mary Ann Booth, undated, Records of the Attorney General's Office, Letters Received 1809–1870, box 7, General Records of the Department of Justice, RG 60, NA.

19. John Wilkes Booth "To Whom It May Concern," 1864, Records of the Attorney General's Office, Letters Received 1809–1870, box 7, General Records of the Department of Justice, RG 60, NA.

20. John S. Clarke affidavit, May 6, 1865, M599 7:411.

21. William Millward to James Speed, April 25, 1865, Records of the Attorney General's Office, Letters Received 1809–1870, box 7, General Records of the Department of Justice, RG 60, NA.

22. William Millward to James Speed, June 3, 1865, Records of the Attorney General's Office, Letters Received 1809–1870, box 7, General Records of the Department of Justice, RG 60, NA.

23. Junius Brutus Booth statement, May 5, 1865, M599 2:261–268, Junius Brutus Booth diary, April–June 1865, quoted in Clarke, A *Sister's Memoir,* 124–126. Clarke, *Unlocked Book,* 128. Stanton to the adjutant general, June 22, 1865, 14:513, ESP.

24. Irwin McDowell to Stanton, April 22, 1865, M473, 89:83. Stanton to Dix, April 23, 1864 (sic; an inadvertent mistake in Stanton's handwriting), M473, 89:82.

25. Union Provost Marshal's File of One-Name Papers Relating to Citizens, M345, RG 109, NA, reprinted in Alford, editor, A *Sister's Memoir,* 132–140. Clarke, *Unlocked Book,* 128.

26. Clarke, *Unlocked Book,* 128.

27. *Ibid.,* 130.

12. Escape in the Dead of Night

1. B.B. French to Thaddeus Stevens, February 5 and 12, 1864. B.B. French to Stanton, May 18, 1865, M371, reel 7.

2. Silas Cobb testimony, CTPit, 84. Silas Cobb undated statement, M599, 4:172–178.

3. *Ibid.*

4. Baker, *History of US Secret Service,* 530.

5. Polk Gardiner testimony, CTPit, 85. Polk Gardiner undated statement, M599, 4:345–347.

6. Fletcher statement, May 17, 1866, LC collection, box 166, RG 233, NA.

7. John Fletcher testimony, CTPit, 84. Fletcher statement, May 17, 1866, LC collection, box 166, RG 233, NA.

8. John Fletcher testimony, CTPit, 84.

9. *Ibid.*

10. John Toffey to L. Thomas, December 5, 1865, M619, reel 456. John Toffey testimony, CTPit, 159–160.

11. Fletcher statement, May 17, 1866, LC collection, box 166, RG 233, NA.

12. Hardin's divisional headquarters to George Worcester, April 15, 1865, part 2, volume 186, entry 6714, RG 393, NA.

13. Notes of Atzerodt confession, May 1, 1865, discovered in 1977 by historian Joan Chaconas, past president of the Surratt Society, among papers of a descendant of Atzerodt's lawyer, William Doster, copy provided to this author by Chaconas.

14. James Walker testimony, CTPit, 147.

15. James Kelleher and Samuel Smith testimony, CTPit, 151.

16. Washington Briscoe statement, April 22, 1865, M599, reel 2. CTPoore, 1:402–404.

17. John Greenawalt testimony, CTPoore, 1:342, 349.

18. *Ibid.*, 1:342.

19. Brooke Stabler undated statement, M599, reel 6.

20. W.R. Keim testimony, CTPoore, 1:400–402.

13. "Betrayed into the Hands of the Government"

Chapter title: Arnold, *Defence and Prison Experiences*, 49.

1. John Lee statement, April 16, 1865, M619, 456:473–476.

2. Robert Jones testimony, CTPit, 144. John Lee testimony, CTPit, 144. Lyman Sprague testimony, JST, 1:323–324. Jones testified that according to the register Atzerodt checked in on April 14. Lee testified he was told by another employee that Atzerodt had checked in the day before.

3. John Lee statement, April 16, 1865, M619, 456:473–476. John Lee to President Johnson, August 15, 1865, M619, 456:478–480.

4. George Rutherford statement, April 14, 1865, M599, 7:484.

5. G.W. Bunker testimony, CTPit, 46.

6. *Baltimore Sun,* April 18, 1865.

7. Charles Dawson testimony, JST 1:337–338.

8. C.A. Dana testimony, CTPit, 41. Thomas Eckert testimony, CTPit, 41–42.

9. John Simonds to Booth, December 7, 1864, M599, 2:328.

10. John Simonds to Booth, December 31, 1864, M599, 2:314.

11. John Simonds to Booth, February 21, 1865, M599, 2:318.

12. Receipt for room and board, $21.88, from Russell House, Detroit, November 20, 1861, M599, 2:366.

13. Francis de Haes Janvier to Abraham Lincoln, May 20, 1864, series 1, AL Papers, LC.

14. *Our Heroes,* M599, 2:361.

15. Weichmann, *True History,* 377.

16. J.B. Menu to "Dear Friend," M599, 2:381–382.

17. *Daily Constitutional Union,* April 15, 1865.

18. James McPhail statement, July 19, 1865, M619, 456:316–323. James McPhail to Stanton, April 19, 1865, M619, 458:247–252. James McPhail to Stanton, July 21, 1865, M619, 456:319–322.

19. James McPhail to Stanton, April 19, 1865, M619, 458:247–252.

20. James McPhail to C.A. Dana, April 15, 1865, M619, reel 280.

21. Arnold to Booth, March 27, 1865, reprinted in CTPit, 236.

22. William Arnold testimony, CTPit, 240.

23. Arnold, *Defence and Prison Experiences,* 51.

24. *Ibid.,* 15.

25. *Ibid.,* 49.

26. *Ibid.,* 52.

27. Eaton Horner testimony, CTPoore 1:430–432.

28. Arnold, *Defence and Prison Experiences,* 52.

29. Memo of property found on Arnold at Fortress Monroe, April 17, 1865, M619, 458:326.

30. Memo of property found on Arnold in Baltimore, April 19, 1865, M619, 458:324. Eaton Horner testimony, CTPoore 1:424.

31. Voltaire Randall to James McPhail, April 17, 1865, M619, 458:291.

32. James McPhail to Stanton, April 19, 1865, M619, 458:247–252.

33. P.H. Maulsby testimony, CTPit, 232–233. Thomas Carmichael to James McPhail, July 14, 1865, M619, 458:263.

34. James McPhail to C.A. Dana, April 17, 1865, M619, 458:267.

35. C.A. Dana to James McPhail, April 17, 1865, M619, 458:267.

36. Arnold, *Defence and Prison Experiences,* 52.

37. William McPhail testimony, CTPoore 1:422.

38. James McPhail to Stanton, April 19, 1865, M619, 458:247–252.

39. Samuel Arnold statement, April 18, 1865, M619, 458:305–312.

40. Arnold, *Defence and Prison Experiences,* 54.

41. James McPhail to the publishers of *American, Baltimore Sun, Gazette,* and *Clipper,* April 17, 1865, M619, 458:254.

42. Stanton to James McPhail, April 18, 1865, ESP 14:469.

43. Stanton to General Wallace, April 18, 1865, M473, 88:1058.

44. James McPhail to Stanton, April 19, 1865, M619, 458:247–252.

45. Arnold, *Defence and Prison Experiences,* 55.

46. Logs of US steamer *Saugus,* April 19, 1865, RG 24, NA.

47. Arnold, *Defence and Prison Experiences,* 56.

14. "Keep an Eye on Mrs. Surratt's House"

Chapter title: "Tragic Memories," *Washington Evening Star,* April 14, 1894.

1. *Ibid.*

2. John Proctor affidavit, May 13, 1865, notarized July 6, 1865, M619, 456:579.

3. A.C. Richards to Louis Weichmann, April 29, 1898, reproduced in Weichmann, *True History,* 411.

4. John Clarvoe testimony, JST, 1:696.

5. John Holahan testimony, JST, 1:672. James McDevitt testimony, CTPit, 140 and JST, 1:707.

6. Weichmann, *True History,* 175.

7. Honora Fitzpatrick testimony, JST, 1:713.

8. *Ibid.,* 1:717.

9. Weichmann, *True History,* 175.

10. James McDevitt testimony, CTPit, 140.

11. John Clarvoe obituary, *Washington Evening Star,* February 6, 1879. Clarvoe testimony, JST, 1:706.
12. John Holahan testimony, JST, 1:669, 672.
13. Weichmann, *True History,* 176. John Clarvoe testimony, JST, 1:697.
14. John Clarvoe testimony, JST, 1:699.
15. *Ibid.,* 1:698.
16. *Ibid.,* 1:699.
17. Louis Weichmann testimony, CTPoore, 1:92.
18. James McDevitt testimony, JST, 1:709.
19. Weichmann, *True History,* 179.
20. Brooke Stabler undated statement, M599, 6:122–142.
21. *Ibid.*
22. Mary Surratt admission during interrogation by H.H. Wells, April 17, 1865, M599, 6:238.
23. Benjamin Moran diary, May 8, 1867, volume 18. Benjamin Moran Papers, LC. Charles Francis Adams diary, May 9, 1867, reel 80, Adams Family Papers, LC.
24. Louis Weichmann testimony, JST, 1:454.
25. Weichmann, *True History,* 179.
26. John Surratt lecture, Rockville, Maryland, December 6, 1870, in *Washington Evening Star,* December 7, 1870.
27. Weichmann, *True History,* 218–219.
28. James McDevitt testimony, JST, 1:709.
29. John Foster statement, August 19, 1865, M619, 456:182–184.
30. John Kimball statement, August 1, 1865, M619, reel 458.
31. A congressional committee would later overlook the slowness of both female servants, explaining, "These colored women were somewhat tardy in their movements, but it should be borne in mind that they were under the restraints incident to their life-long position of servitude and assumed inferiority; and fears for their personal safety, with a certain prospect of loss of place and employment, to say nothing of persecution in case they should be suspected of being informers against their employers." See HR Report 99. July 24, 1866, 39C 1S.
32. P.M. Clark to Stanton, June 15, 1865, M619, 456:167–170. P.M. Clark to Stanton, August 24, 1865, M619, 456:176–180.
33. John Kimball to Joseph Holt, January 9, 1866, M619, reel 458.
34. H.H. Wells to I.H. Taylor, May 5, 1865, M619, 458:575.
35. W.W. Kirby statement, April 18, 1865, M599, 6:318–320.
36. Henry Smith testimony, CTPit, 121–22, and JST, 1:331–332.
37. Henry Smith testimony, CTPit, 122, and JST, 1:334–335. Richard Morgan testimony, CTPit, 122. W.M. Wermerskirch testimony, CTPit, 123. H.H. Wells testimony, CTPit, 158. Thomas Sampson statement, April 19, 1865, M599, reel 2.
38. Richard Morgan testimony, CTPit, 122.
39. Doster, *Episodes of Civil War,* 269.
40. Oath of Allegiance, March 14, 1865, M599, 4:397. Richard Morgan

testimony, JST 1:341 and CTPit, 122–123. Henry Smith testimony, CTPit, 121, and JST, 1:332–333. Thomas Sampson statement, April 19, 1865, M599, reel 2.

41. Henry Smith testimony, CTPit, 121–122, and JST, 1:333. W.M. Wermerskirch testimony, CTPit, 123.

42. Richard Morgan testimony, JST, 1:341.

43. Ely Devoe, a fourteen-hundred-dollar-a-year detective in the raiding party, was later fired after claiming a share of the reward money on the grounds that he, and not his superiors, had been the first to enter the boardinghouse, where he said he had quizzed Mary Surratt and Payne and placed everyone under arrest. See Olcott to Holt, August 21, 1865, M619, 455:903–908.

44. Thomas Sampson statement, April 19, 1865, M599, 2:1078–1084.

45. Ely Devoe affidavit, December 21, 1865, M619, 456:341–347.

46. Thomas Sampson statement, April 19, 1865, M599, reel 2.

47. *Ibid.* Sampson was the only one to say that they also found a loaded revolver. "Articles Found on Payne," M599, reel 2.

48. William Bell testimony, CTPoore, 1:477–478.

49. Logs of US steamer *Saugus,* April 18, 1865.

50. H.H. Wells interrogation of Mary Surratt, April 17, 1865, M599, reel 6.

51. Thomas Price statement, April 18, 1865, M599, reel 6, and testimony, CTPit, 158.

52. Doster, *Episodes of Civil War,* 269.

53. H.H. Wells testimony, CTPoore, 2:45–46.

54. *Ibid.* 2:46

55. Spencer Clark testimony, CTPit, 159.

56. Augustus Seward testimony, CTPoore, 2:9.

15. "We Know as Much of Your Operations as the Almighty"

Chapter title: Robert Murray statement, April 29, 1865, M599, reel 5.

1. John Greenawalt and W.R. Keim testimony, CTPit, 146–147.

2. Somerset Leaman testimony, CTPit, 152.

3. Lucinda Metz statement, April 24, 1865, M599, 3:580.

4. John Caldwell testimony, CTPit, 148.

5. William Gaither statement, April 20, 1865, M599, 3:549–553, and testimony in Lewis Chubb court-martial, May 18, 1865, court-martial case files, MM 2513, RG 153, NA.

6. James Purdom statement, April 26, 1865, M599, 2:227–229.

7. Somerset Leaman testimony, CTPit, 152.

8. Hezekiah Metz testimony, CTPit, 149. Somerset Leaman and James Leaman testimony, CTPit, 152.

9. James Leaman testimony, CTPit, 152.

10. Consul General William Murphy to William Hunter, May 17, 1865, container 92, JHP.

11. C.A. Dana to E.G. Spaulding, April 15, 1865, and C.A. Dana to Chief of Police, Baltimore, April 15, 1865, both in OR series 1, volume 46, part 3, 782–783.

12. John Fletcher statement, May 17, 1866, Library of Congress collection, LC box 166, RG 233, NA.
13. Brooke Stabler undated statement, M599, 6:137–142
14. James Purdom statement, April 26, 1865, M599, 2:227–229.
15. *Ibid.* Frank O'Daniel affidavit, December 7, 1865, M619, 455:835–836.
16. E.R. Artman statement, April 29, 1865, M619, 456:146–148.
17. Solomon Townsend statement, May 10, 1865, M619, 455:565–566.
18. Zachariah Gimmell statement, April 21, 1865, M599, 2:1015–1019, and Gimmell testimony, CTPit, 149.
19. Lew Wallace to Erastus Tyler, April 20, 1865, Letters Sent, Middle Department, entry 2328, volume 5, part 1, RG 393.
20. Stanton to Tyler, April 20, 1865, M473, 88:1106.
21. *Washington Evening Star,* April 21, 1865.
22. Robert Murray statement, April 29, 1865, M599, 5:263–265.
23. *Ibid.*
24. Logs of US steamer *Saugus,* April 2, 1865, RG 24, NA.
25. *Ibid.,* April 9, 1865.
26. *Ibid.,* April 18–20, 1865.
27. Logs of USS *Montauk,* April 23, 1865, RG 24, NA.
28. Frank Munroe affidavit, April 23, 1865, M599, 2:46–47.

16. A Funeral Surpassing All Others in Solemnity

Chapter title: "A Narrative of the President's Murder," *National Republican,* April 25, 1865.
1. Private viewing for reporter for *Daily Constitutional Union,* April 17, 1865.
2. Some incorrect public references are to a mahogany coffin. The official invoice refers to a walnut casket: Account Book, Lincoln Funeral, 85, Records of the Financial Division, Office of Secretary of the Interior, RG 48, NA.
3. *Daily National Intelligencer,* April 16, 1865.
4. B.B. French journal, April 15, 1866, in *Witness to Young Republic,* 507–508.
5. James Ward diary, April 18, 1865, James Ward Papers, LC.
6. Helen Varnum Hill McCalla diary, April 18, 1865, McCalla Papers, LC.
7. David Homer Bates diary, April 18, 1865, David Homer Bates Papers, LC. Townsend, *The Life,* 14.
8. George Coffin diary, April 18, 1865, George Coffin Papers, box 14, Gelman Library, special collections, George Washington University.
9. *Frank Leslie's Illustrated Newspaper,* May 6, 1865.
10. Anthony Merry to Lord Hawkesbury, December 6, 1803, and January 30, 1804, FO 115/12, 1803–1805, National Archives, Kew, England.
11. Field, *Memories of Many Men,* 329.
12. Funeral service admission card, box 11, JNP.
13. Townsend, *The Life,* 17. Brooks, *Washington in Lincoln's Time,* 233.
14. Edgington, *A History,* 247, 249–250.
15. "A Narrative of the President's Murder," *National Republican,* April 25, 1865.

16. GWD, April 19, 1865, reel 3, GWP.

17. Mary Hassler Newcomb diary, April 19, 1865, box 2, Simon Newcomb Papers, LC.

18. W.A. Nichols, Adjutant General's Office, April 17, 1865, OR, series 1, volume 46, part 3, 808.

19. G. Weitzel to E.W. Smith, April 17, 1865, OR, series 1, volume 46, part 3, 816. Brooks, *Washington in Lincoln's Time,* 235.

20. Charles Dana to Dix, April 24, 1865, M473, 89:105.

21. Unidentified letter from Fairfax Court House, Virginia, to sister, April 21, 1865, Abraham Lincoln Papers, folder 283, Chicago History Museum.

22. GWD, April 19, 1865, reel 3, GWP.

23. B.B. French to Francis French, April 24, 1865, part 2, box 12, and B.B. French to Katy Wells, August 13, 1865, part 2, box 8, BBFFP.

24. B.B. French to Montgomery Meigs, April 21, 1865, M371, 7:542, and French to Meigs, May 2, 1865, M371, reel 27, RG 42, NA.

25. Thomas Walter to Amanda Walter, April 20, 1865, letterbook roll 4142, TWP.

26. Jeremiah Lockwood diary, April 20, 1865, Jeremiah Lockwood Papers, LC.

27. Brooks, *Washington in Lincoln's Time,* 235–236.

28. Montgomery Meigs diary, April 20, 1865, Montgomery Meigs Papers, LC.

29. Thomas Walter to Amanda Walter, April 20, 1865, letterbook roll 4142, TWP.

30. "A Narrative of the President's Murder," *National Republican,* April 25, 1865.

31. Queen Victoria to Mary Todd Lincoln, April 29, 1865, reel 88, WSP. Mary Todd Lincoln to Queen Victoria, May 21, 1865, Turner and Turner, editors, *Mary Todd Lincoln,* 230–231.

32. Benjamin Moran diary, August 16, 1865, volume 15, Benjamin Moran Papers, LC.

33. Stanton to John Stuart, April 28, 1865, M473, 89:190–191.

34. Keckley, *Behind the Scenes,* 202–203.

35. Mary Todd Lincoln to Phineas Gurley, May 22, 1865, quoted in Edgington, *A History,* 252.

36. Phineas Gurley to E. Darwin Brooks, May 22, 1865, Phineas Gurley Papers, LC.

37. Gideon Welles to J.B. Montgomery, May 4, 1865, M149, 80:463.

38. B.B. French journal, April 24, 1865, reel 2, BBFFP.

39. B.B. French to Pamela French, May 21, 1865, reel 6, BBFFP. The only reference this author has found of any such purchase was 193 yards of black cambric worth $96.50, bought January 16, 1865, and signed for by Mrs. Lincoln, invoice from John Alexander, March 21, 1865, box 480, account #157178, Records of Accounting Officers of Department of the Treasury, Office of the First Auditor, Settled Miscellaneous Treasury Accounts, RG 217, NA.

40. Mary Todd Lincoln to Alexander Williamson, June 15, 1865, Abraham Lincoln Papers, folder 276, Chicago History Museum.

41. B.B. French to Andrew Johnson, May 6, 1865, M371, 7:546–547. Account Book for Lincoln Funeral, Records of the Financial Division, Records Office of the Secretary of the Interior, July 27, 1866, 95. RG 48, NA.

42. B.B. French to James Harlan, June 23, 1865, M371, 7:588.

17. Escape

1. Sarah Mudd affidavit, July 6, 1865, Pardon Case Files, Samuel Mudd Case File B-596, RG 204, in vault at NA, College Park, Maryland.

2. John Lloyd testimony, CTPit, 85–87. John Lloyd statement, April 22, 1865, container 92, JHP. William Wood undated report on Lloyd, HR 39A-H2.3, Records of House of Representatives, Petitions & Memorials, Committee on Appropriations, RG 233.

3. Thomas Ewing Jr. to President Johnson, July 10, 1865, Pardon Case Files, Samuel Mudd Case File B-596, RG 204, in vault at NA, College Park, Maryland.

4. H.H. Wells testimony, CTPoore, 1:291.

5. Samuel Mudd undated statement, M599, 5:227–239.

6. Samuel Mudd statement, April 22, 1865, M599, 5:213–225.

7. Dr. Joseph Barnes, after carrying out a postmortem examination of Booth's body, reported a fractured fibula three inches above the ankle joint; see Barnes to Stanton, April 27, 1865, Ford's Theatre collection.

8. Samuel Mudd statement, April 22, 1865, M599, 5:213–225. Samuel Mudd undated statement, M599, 5:227–239.

9. Alexander Lovett testimony, CTPoore, 1:258.

10. Samuel Mudd statement, April 22, 1865, M599, 5:213–225.

11. Thomas Ewing Jr. to President Johnson, July 10, 1865, Pardon Case Files, Samuel Mudd Case File B-596, RG 204, in vault at NA, College Park, Maryland. However, W.J. Keeler, writing to his congressman, Representative Burton (R-IL), January 21, 1869, said he was aboard the vessel taking Mudd to the Dry Tortugas when Mudd "admitted . . . that he knew who Booth was when he set his leg, and of what crime he was guilty." See Pardon Case Files, Samuel Mudd Case File B-596, folder 4, RG 204, in vault at NA, College Park, Maryland.

12. Samuel Mudd statement, April 22, 1865, M599, 5:213–225.

13. *Ibid.* Samuel Mudd undated statement, M599, 5:227–239.

14. Sarah Mudd affidavit, July 6, 1865, Pardon Case Files, Samuel Mudd Case File B-596, RG 204, in vault at NA, College Park, Maryland.

15. David Dana testimony, CTPoore, 2:68.

16. John Ward testimony, CTPoore, 2:64–65.

17. George Mudd testimony, CTPoore, 2:394.

18. John Ward testimony, CTPoore, 2:62–63.

19. E.D.R. Bean testimony, CTPit, 203.

20. William Gleason statement, December 19, 1867, box 175, BBP.

21. John Hardy testimony, CTPoore, 3:432, and CTPit, 218. Francis Farrell testimony, CTPit, 218–219.

22. Alexander Lovett to James O'Beirne, April 29, 1865, M619, 456:487–490. H.H. Wells testimony, CTPoore, 1:290, 292.

23. Thomas Ewing Jr. to President Johnson, July 10, 1865, Pardon Case Files, Samuel Mudd Case File B-596, RG 204, in vault at NA, College Park, Maryland.

24. Osborn Oldroyd interview with Samuel Cox Jr., May 1901, in Oldroyd, *Assassination of Lincoln,* 268.

25. *Ibid.,* 268–269.

26. Samuel Mudd statement, April 22, 1865, M599, 5:213–225.

27. George Mudd testimony, CTPit, 211. Benjamin Gardiner testimony, CTPoore 3:485–486.

28. George Mudd testimony, CTPit, 211.

29. George Cottingham statement, May 4, 1866, House Committee on Claims for Rewards, RG 233, LC Collection, box 50 for LC, box 166 for NA, NA.

30. John Lloyd statement, December 19, 1865, House Committee on Claims for Rewards, RG 233, LC Collection, box 50 for LC, box 166 for NA, NA. Alexander Lovett to James O'Beirne, April 29, 1865, M619, 456:487–490.

31. Alexander Lovett to James O'Beirne, April 29, 1865, M619, 456:487–490.

32. George Mudd testimony, CTPoore, 2:392.

33. Alexander Lovett testimony, CTPoore, 1:266–268.

34. *Ibid.,* 1:259.

35. Joshua Lloyd to James O'Beirne, April 30, 1865, M619, 456:492–494.

36. Alexander Lovett testimony, CTPoore, 1:263.

37. Joshua Lloyd to James O'Beirne, April 30, 1865, M619, 456:492–494. Simon Gavacan to James O'Beirne, May 1, 1865, M619, 456:497–499.

38. Alexander Lovett testimony, CTPoore, 1:264.

39. *Ibid.,* 1:260.

40. *Ibid.,* 1:270. Joshua Lloyd to James O'Beirne, April 30, 1865, M619, 456:492–494.

41. Alexander Lovett testimony, CTPoore, 1:269.

42. H.H. Wells statement, December 29, 1865, M619, 458:203.

43. *Daily Constitutional Union,* April 20, 1865.

44. Henry Burnett to B.J. Sweet, April 22, 1865, M599, 1:67.

45. Jonathan Waite to J.H. Taylor, April 23, 1865, OR, series 1, volume 46, part 3, 910–911.

46. Stanton to Provost Marshal, Philadelphia, April 21, 1865, M473 89:37.

47. Stanton to Allen Pinkerton, April 24, 1865, M473, 89:92.

48. Thomas Ewing Jr. to father, August 8, 1865, box 71, TEFP. Henry Olcott to Joseph Holt, August 21, 1865, M619, 455:903–908. B.B. French to President Johnson, May 6, 1865, reel 14, AJP.

49. Stanton proclamation, April 20, 1865, OR, series 1, volume 46, part 3, 847–848.

50. Henry Olcott to Joseph Holt, August 21, 1865, M619, 455:903–908.

51. John Hardy testimony, CTPoore, 2:436.

52. Thomas Davis testimony, CTPit, 200.

53. Alexander Lovett testimony, CTPoore, 1:263.

54. Sarah Mudd affidavit, July 6, 1865, Pardon Case Files, Samuel Mudd Case File B-596, RG 204, in vault at NA, College Park, MD. John Hardy testimony, CTPoore, 2:435.

55. Samuel Mudd statement, April 22, 1865, M599, 5:213–225. Alexander Lovett testimony, CTPoore, 1:261.

56. Robert Murray to Henry Burnett, April 24, 1865, entry 38, Correspondence & Reports Relating to Disloyal and Suspect Persons, RG 110, NA.

57. Joshua Lloyd testimony, CTPoore, 1:281.

58. Alexander Lovett testimony, CTPoore, 1:261.

59. Joshua Lloyd testimony, CTPoore, 1:275. Alexander Lovett testimony, CTPoore, 1:261. William Williams to James O'Beirne, May 1, 1865, M619, 456:501–503.

60. H.H. Wells to J.H. Taylor, April 28, 1865, M619, 458:407–410. H.H. Wells statement, May 8, 1865, M599, 4:207.

61. H.H. Wells testimony, CTPoore, 1:287.

62. H.H. Wells testimony, CTPoore, 1:286.

63. Samuel Mudd statement, April 22, 1865, M599, 5:213–225.

64. H.H. Wells testimony, CTPoore, 1:290, 292.

65. H.H. Wells testimony, CTPoore, 1:288. Wells statement, April 24, 1866, House Committee on Claims for Rewards, RG 233, LC Collection, box 50 for LC, box 166 for NA, NA.

66. Hartranft to Hancock, May 5, 1865, letterbook 9, SC.

67. Sarah Mudd to Joseph Holt, September 4, 1865, container 49, JHP.

68. Sarah Mudd statements, June 16, 1865, box 248, TEFP; July 6, 1865, Pardon Case Files, Samuel Mudd Case File B-596, RG 204, in vault at NA, College Park, MD. Sarah Mudd to Joseph Holt, September 4, 1865, JHP.

69. Sarah Mudd affidavit, July 6, 1865, Pardon Case Files, Samuel Mudd Case File B-596, RG 204, in vault at NA, College Park, MD.

70. Sarah Mudd to Joseph Holt, September 4, 1865, container 49, JHP.

71. Ibid.

72. George Cottingham testimony, CTPoore, 2:193.

73. George Cottingham testimony, CTPoore, 2:193–196. Cottingham to Stanton, July 19, 1865, M619 reel 458. James Owner statement, May 13, 1866, House Committee on Claims for Rewards, RG 233, LC Collection, box 50 for LC, box 166 for NA, NA.

74. George Cottingham to Stanton, July 19, 1865, M619, reel 458.

75. H.H. Wells to J.H. Taylor, May 5, 1865, M619, 458:430–441.

18. "You Must Get Him Across"

Chapter title: Jones, *J. Wilkes Booth*, 72.

1. Electus Thomas statement, April 21, 1865, M599, 6:377–379.

2. Swan's later undated, transcribed statement gives his first name as Oscar (Ausy), see M599, 6:228. But a statement of May 13, 1865, by an acquaintance, Joseph Padget, gives the first name as Oswald, see M599, 6:15.

3. Oswald Swan undated statement, M599, 6:228–229. Joseph Padget statement, May 13, 1865, M599, 6:15.

4. Townsend, "How Wilkes Booth Crossed," 827.

5. Ibid., 822–823.

6. Henry Olcott to Henry Burnett, April 28, 1865, M599, 5:493–494.

7. Samuel Cox Sr. said it was about 4 AM, quoted in Jones, *J. Wilkes Booth*, 71. Swan claimed it was near midnight in an undated statement, M599, 6:228–629.

8. Oswald Swan undated statement, M599, 6:228–229.

9. Osborn Oldroyd interview with Samuel Cox Jr., quoted in Oldroyd, *Assassination of Lincoln*, 266.

10. Samuel Cox Sr. to Thomas Jones, quoted in Jones, *J. Wilkes Booth*, 71–72. Samuel Cox Sr. to Thomas Jones, quoted in Townsend, "How Wilkes Booth Crossed," 828.

11. Samuel Cox Sr. statement, April 28, 1865, container 92, JHP.

12. Oswald Swan undated statement, M599, 6:228–229.

13. Samuel Cox Sr. statement, April 28, 1865, container 92, JHP.

14. Oswald Swan undated statement, M599, 6:228–229.

15. Jones, *J. Wilkes Booth*, 73.

16. *Ibid.*, 66.

17. Townsend, "How Wilkes Booth Crossed," 823–826. Jones, *J. Wilkes Booth*, 26.

18. Jones, *J. Wilkes Booth*, 72–74.

19. *Ibid.*, 77–78.

20. *Ibid.*, 80.

21. Townsend, "How Wilkes Booth Crossed," 829.

22. Jones, *J. Wilkes Booth*, 81–82. Townsend, "How Wilkes Booth Crossed," 829.

23. Jones, *J. Wilkes Booth*, 89.

24. Townsend, "How Wilkes Booth Crossed," 828.

25. David Herold statement, April 27, 1865, M599, 4:484.

26. *Ibid.*, 4:479–480. Herold could not remember whether Booth named "Peanuts" Burroughs or Edman Spangler.

27. Diary photocopies and transcription from Ford's Theatre collection.

28. Jones, *J. Wilkes Booth*, 85.

29. *Ibid.*, 90.

30. Townsend, "How Wilkes Booth Crossed," 829.

31. Jones, *J. Wilkes Booth*, 96.

32. *Ibid.*, 98–99.

33. Jones to Oldroyd, quoted in Oldroyd, *Assassination of Lincoln*, 106.

34. Jones, *J. Wilkes Booth*, 101.

35. Townsend, "How Wilkes Booth Crossed," 830.

36. Jones, *J. Wilkes Booth*, 105–106.

37. Townsend, "How Wilkes Booth Crossed," 830.

38. Jones, *J. Wilkes Booth*, 109–110.

39. Cox to Jones, quoted in Oldroyd, *Assassination of Lincoln*, 102.

40. Jones, *J. Wilkes Booth*, 111.

41. Ship's logs, *Ella*, April 21, 1865, RG 24.

42. Ship's logs, *Heliotrope, Juniper, Resolute*, April 18, 1865, RG 24.

43. Ship's logs, *Ella*, April 22, 1865, RG 24.

44. Ship's logs, *Juniper*, April 21, 1865, RG 24.

45. Jones, *J. Wilkes Booth*, 111.

46. Ship's logs, *Juniper*, April 9, 1865, RG 24.

47. Gideon Welles to Lieutenant Commander Eastman, April 22, 1865, OR series 1, volume 46, part 3, 902.

48. C.C. Augur to Commander Parker, April 22, 1865, OR series 1, volume 46, part 3, 903.

49. Townsend, "How Wilkes Booth Crossed," 832. Samuel Cox Sr. statement, April 28, 1865, container 92, JHP. H.H. Wells statement, May 8, 1865, M599, 4:207. Jones, *J. Wilkes Booth*, 126.

50. David Herold statement, April 27, 1865, M599, 4:444, 447.

51. Townsend, "How Wilkes Booth Crossed," 831.

52. Diary photocopies and transcription from Ford's Theatre collection. Joseph Holt testimony, AJII, 286–287.

53. William Wilmer to James O'Beirne, April 27, 1865, entry 38, Correspondence and Reports Relating to Disloyal and Suspect Persons, RG 110, NA.

54. David Herold statement, April 27, 1865, M599, 4:464.

55. Ship's logs, *Juniper*, April 22, 1865, RG 24.

56. David Herold statement, April 27, 1865, M599, 4:464.

57. Oldroyd, *Assassination of Lincoln*, 281.

58. Joseph Husted statement, May 20, 1874, Joseph Weiss to Secretary of War, January 28, 1878, Secretary of War to Louisa Miller, June 28, 1886, Adjutant General to L.D. Carman, October 16, 1925, and illegible to Chief Quartermaster's Office, April 25, 1865, all in Water Transportation 1834–1900, Office of Quartermaster General, box 29, RG 92, NA. Ship's logs, *Ella*, April 24, 1865, RG 24.

19. "I Don't Want to Know Anything About You"

Chapter title: Richard Stuart statement, May 6, 1865, M599, 6:206–211.

1. Elizabeth Quesenberry deposition, May 16, 1865, M599, 5:557–559.

2. Tidwell, Hall, Gaddy, *Come Retribution*, 431–432.

3. William Bryant statement, May 6, 1865, M599, 4:95–97.

4. Townsend, "How Wilkes Booth Crossed," 831.

5. William Bryant statement, May 6, 1865, M599, 4:95–97.

6. There is supporting evidence that it would have been absurd for the unshaven, odorous, and irritable Booth and/or Herold to have been invited to join the table guests. After the war one of that night's guests at Cleydael, Major Robert Hunter, said Booth told him the original plan had been to abduct Lincoln and that the killing had been planned in a night. But Hunter said Booth told him this in neighboring Caroline or Essex Counties, while the assassin was still on the run, so the discussion could not have taken place at the dinner table or anywhere else in Stuart's King George County home. See Grinnan Family Papers, Mss. 1, G8855a, 179, Virginia Historical Society.

7. Richard Stuart statement, May 6, 1865, M599, 6:206–211.

8. L.B. Baker testimony, AJII, 484.

9. Ruggles narrative, in "Pursuit and Death of John Wilkes Booth," *Century Magazine* (January 1890), 443.

10. William Lucas statement, May 6, 1865, M599, 5:145–147.

11. Lady Macbeth, act 3, scene 4.

12. Thomas Eckert testimony, AJII, 676–677. Richard Stuart statement, May 6, 1865, M599, 6:206–211. L.B. Baker testimony, AJII, 484.

13. William Lucas statement, May 6, 1865, M599, 5:145–147.

14. John Lloyd statement, April 22, 1865, container 92, JHP.

15. H.H. Wells to J.H. Taylor, April 28, 1865, M619, 458:408.

16. James Owens statement, April 28, 1865, M619, 458:412–415. Lieutenant P.S. Currier to John Foster, undated, M599, 4:229–230.

17. Samuel Beckwith to Joseph Holt, December 18, 1865, M619, 458:458–461.

18. Samuel Beckwith to Thomas Eckert, April 24, 1865, OR series 1, volume 46, part 3, 937.

19. James McPhail statement, April 25, 1866, and Samuel Beckwith affidavit, June 30, 1866, both in House Committee on Claims for Rewards, RG 233, LC Collection, box 50 for LC, box 166 for NA, NA.

20. Dr. E. Bezelton Jackson affidavits, July 14, 1870, and February 9, 1871; Dr. Basil Norris statement, July 12, 1870; Lieutenant Charles Schmidt affidavit, November 10, 1870, all in Lafayette Baker Pension File, application #174870, certificate #150246, NA.

21. Stanton to Lafayette Baker, April 15, 1865, M473, 88:1018.

22. Aquilla Allen to William Wood, July 10, 1865, HR 39A-H 2.3, Petitions & Memorials, Committee on Appropriations, House of Representatives, RG 233.

23. Lafayette Baker to Stanton, May 26, 1865, M619, 455:713–717.

24. Luther Baker testimony, AJII, 479.

25. Lafayette Baker to Stanton, May 26, 1865, M619, 455:713–717.

26. Everton Conger statement, April 27, 1865, M619, 455:725–729.

27. Boston Corbett statement, April 29, 1865, M619, 456:254–262. Stanton proclamation, April 20, 1865, OR 847–848.

28. Everton Conger and Luther Baker to Stanton, December 24, 1865, M619, 455:691–703.

29. Everton Conger pension file, application 145098, certificate 104277, NA.

30. Luther Baker testimony, AJII, 489–490. Everton Conger and Luther Baker to Stanton, December 24, 1865, M619, 455:691–703.

31. Boston Corbett statement, April 29, 1865, M619, 456:254–262.

32. Everton Conger and Luther Baker to Stanton, December 24, 1865, M619, 455:691–703.

20. "I Am Worth Just $175,000 to the Man Who Captures Me"

Chapter title: Ingraham, "Pursuit and Death of John Wilkes Booth," 443.

1. William Rollins statements, May 20, 1865, M619, 457:551–561, and May 6, 1865, M599, 6:79–82.

2. Willie Jett testimony, CTPit, 90.

3. Ingraham, "Pursuit and Death of John Wilkes Booth," 443.

4. William Rollins statement, May 20, 1865, M619, 457:551–561.

5. Willie Jett testimony, CTPit, 91.

6. Richard Garrett letter to *New York Herald,* April 2, 1872, reprinted in Report of Committee on War Claims, HR 743, 43C 1S, 5.
7. John Garrett affidavit, May 20, 1865, M619, 457:500–525.
8. Lucinda Holloway, "An Account of the Capture and Death of John Wilkes Booth: An Eyewitness," Eleanor S. Brockenbrough Library, Museum of the Confederacy, 5.
9. *Ibid.*
10. Diary transcription from Ford's Theatre collection.
11. Holloway, *An Account of the Capture,* 6.
12. John Garrett affidavit, May 20, 1865, M619, 457:500–525. Richard Garrett letter to *New York Herald,* April 2, 1872, reprinted in Report of Committee on War Claims, HR 743, 43C 1S, 5.
13. Richard Garrett statement of claim, June 28, 1865, reprinted in Report of Committee on War Claims, HR 743, 43C 1S, 3–4.
14. John Garrett affidavit, May 20, 1865, M619, 457:500–525.
15. Everton Conger and Luther Baker to Stanton, December 24, 1865, M619, 455:691–703. William Rollins affidavit, May 20, 1865, M619, 457:551–561. Edward Doherty to J.H. Taylor, April 29, 1865, M619, 274–284.
16. Edward Doherty to J.H. Taylor, April 29, 1865, M619, 456:274–284.
17. William Rollins affidavit, May 20, 1865, M619, 457:551–561.
18. Everton Conger statement, April 27, 1865, M619, 455:725–729. Boston Corbett statement, April 29, 1865, M619, 456:254–262.
19. Everton Conger and Luther Baker to Stanton, December 24, 1865, M619, 455:691–703.
20. Luther Baker statement, April 27, 1865, M619, 455:666–689. Edward Doherty to J.H. Taylor, April 29, 1865, M619, 456:274–284, claims both he and Rollins were also mounted.
21. Luther Baker statement, April 27, 1865, M619, 455:666–689. Everton Conger and Luther Baker to Stanton, December 24, 1865, M619, 455:691–703.
22. John Winter statement, May 29, 1865, M619, 456:229–233.
23. William McQuade statement, May 29, 1865, M619, 456:237–239.
24. David Barker statement, May 30, 1865, M619, 456:244–251.
25. Andrew Wardell statement, May 30, 1865, M619, 456:248–251. David Barker statement, May 30, 1865, M619, 456:244–251.

21. "Tell My Mother I Die for My Country"
Chapter title: Everton Conger statement, April 27, 1865, M619, 455:725–729.
1. Luther Baker statement, April 27, 1865, M619, 455:666–689.
2. Everton Conger testimony, CTPit, 91.
3. Oliver Lonkey affidavit, May 29, 1865, M619, 456:222–223.
4. Edward Doherty statement, April 29, 1865, M619, 456:274–284.
5. John Garrett affidavit, May 20, 1865, M619, 457:500–525.
6. Luther Baker statement, April 27, 1865, M619, 455:666–689.
7. Everton Conger and Luther Baker to Stanton, December 24, 1865, M619, 455:691–703. John Garrett affidavit, May 20, 1865, M619, 457:500–525.

8. Edward Doherty statement, April 29, 1865, M619, 456:274–284.

9. Everton Conger statement, April 27, 1865, M619, 455:725–729.

10. Luther Baker testimony, AJII, 480–481.

11. Edward Doherty statement, April 29, 1865, M619, 456:274–284.

12. Luther Baker testimony, AJII, 480. Luther Baker statement, April 27, 1865, M619, reel 455:666–689.

13. John Garrett affidavit, May 20, 1865, M619, 457:500–525.

14. Andrew Wardell statement, May 30, 1865, M619, 456:248–251.

15. John Garrett affidavit, May 20, 1865, M619, 457:500–525.

16. Edward Doherty statement, April 29, 1865, M619, 456:274–284.

17. Luther Baker statement, April 27, 1865, M619, 455:666–689.

18. John Garrett affidavit, May 20, 1865, M619, 457:500–525. Boston Corbett statement, April 29, 1865, M619, 456:254–262.

19. Luther Baker statement, April 27, 1865, M619, 455:666–689.

20. Everton Conger statement, April 27, 1865, M619, 455:725–729.

21. Luther Baker testimony, AJII, 481.

22. Joseph Barnes autopsy report to Stanton, April 27, 1865, Ford's Theatre collection. Boston Corbett statement, April 29, 1865, M619, 456:254–262.

23. Luther Baker statement, April 27, 1865, M619, 455:666–689.

24. John Garrett affidavit, May 20, 1865, M619, 457:500–525.

25. Luther Baker statement, April 27, 1865, M619, 455:666–689. Everton Conger and Luther Baker to Stanton, December 24, 1865, M619, 455:691–703. Everton Conger statement, April 27, 1865, M619, 455:725–729. Luther Baker testimony, AJII, 481.

26. Edward Doherty to Andrew Johnson, December 23, 1865, M619, 455:769–775. Herman Newgarten affidavit, May 29, 1865, M619, 456:226–228.

27. Luther Baker testimony, AJII, 482. Luther Baker statement, April 27, 1865, M619, 455:666–689.

28. Everton Conger statement, April 27, 1865, M619, 455:725–729.

29. Holloway, *An Account of the Capture*, 12.

30. Luther Baker testimony, AJII, 483. Luther Baker statement, April 27, 1865, M619, 455:666–689.

31. Luther Baker testimony, AJII, 482. Luther Baker statement, April 27, 1865, M619, reel 455:666–689. Osborn Oldroyd interview with Lucinda Holloway, in Oldroyd, *The Assassination*, 300.

32. Luther Baker testimony, AJII, 483.

33. Luther Baker statement, April 27, 1865, M619, 455:666–689.

34. Luther Baker testimony, AJII, 482.

35. Holloway, *An Account of the Capture*, 13.

36. Luther Baker testimony, AJII, 482.

37. John Garrett affidavit, May 20, 1865, M619, 457:500–525.

38. Luther Baker testimony, AJII, 487.

39. *Ibid.*

40. *Ibid.*

41. Everton Conger statement, April 27, 1865, M619, 455:725–729.

42. Holloway, *An Account of the Capture*, 12.

43. Luther Baker testimony, AJII, 489. Osborn Oldroyd interview with Lucinda Holloway, in Oldroyd, *The Assassination,* 301.

44. Luther Baker statement, April 27, 1865, M619, 455:666–689.

45. John Garrett affidavit, May 20, 1865, M619, 457:500–525.

46. Luther Baker statement, April 27, 1865, M619, 455:666–689. Luther Baker testimony, AJII, 485.

47. Luther Baker testimony, AJII, 485. Edward Doherty statement, April 29, 1865, M619, 456:274–284. Edward Doherty to Andrew Johnson, December 23, 1865, M619, 455:769–775.

48. John Garrett affidavit, May 20, 1865, M619, 457:500–525. Andrew Wardell statement, May 30, 1865, M619, reel 456:248–251. Luther Baker statement, April 27, 1865, M619, 455:666–689.

49. Edward Doherty statement, April 29, 1865, M619, 456:274–284.

50. Luther Baker testimony, AJII, 485.

51. Edward Doherty statement, April 29, 1865, M619, 456:274–284.

52. Everton Conger and Luther Baker to Stanton, December 24, 1865, M619, 455:691–703.

53. Luther Baker testimony, AJII, 488.

54. Edward Doherty to Andrew Johnson, December 23, 1865, M619, 455:769–775.

22. A Secret Burial at Midnight

1. Everton Conger testimony, AJII, 331.

2. *Ibid.,* 332.

3. Lafayette Baker testimony, AJII, 451.

4. Stanton testimony, AJII, 408.

5. Everton Conger testimony, AJII, 333.

6. Thomas Eckert testimony, AJII, 672.

7. Lafayette Baker testimony, AJII, 452.

8. Thomas Eckert statement, April 2, 1867, 11:593–594, ESP. *Daily National Intelligencer,* March 24, 1865.

9. Logs of USS *Montauk,* April 23 and 27, 1865, RG 24, NA.

10. Eckert to David Homer Bates, October 1909, recounted in typescript, 12, "Booth, the Assassin," Bates Papers, container 2, reel 1, LC.

11. Stanton and Welles to the commandant of the Navy Yard, April 27, 1865, reel 14, ESP.

12. Eckert to David Homer Bates, October 1909, recounted in typescript, 13, "Booth, the Assassin," Bates Papers, container 2, reel 1, LC.

13. Porter, "Booth's Body," 66.

14. May, *Mark of the Scalpel,* John Frederick May Papers, LC. May statement, April 28, 1865, M599 reel 4.

15. Porter, who was *not* present, reported that Charles Dawson identified intials on the *right* hand, between the thumb and forefinger, Porter, "Booth's Body," 69.

16. Charles Collins statement, April 28, 1865, M599, 4:350–352.

17. Joseph Barnes to Stanton, April 27, 1865, Ford's Theatre collection. Samuel Mudd statement, April 22, 1865, M599, reel 5.

18. Joseph Barnes to Stanton, April 27, 1865, Ford's Theatre collection.
19. Eckert to David Homer Bates, October 1909, recounted in typescript, 14, "Booth, the Assassin," Bates Papers, container 2, reel 1, LC.
20. Stanton testimony, AJII, 409.
21. Luther Baker undated statement, 14:1535–1536, Herndon-Weik Collection, LC. Luther Baker testimony, AJII, 486.
22. Logs of USS *Montauk,* April 27, 1865, RG 24, NA.
23. Porter, "Booth's Body," 70. *Washington Evening Star,* April 28, 1865.
24. Luther Baker undated statement, 14:1535–1536, Herndon-Weik Collection, LC.
25. B.B. French to Francis French, April 30, 1865, part 2, box 12, BBFFP.
26. *Frank Leslie's Illustrated Newspaper,* May 20, 1865.
27. Eckert to David Homer Bates, October 1909, recounted in typescript, 13–14, "Booth, the Assassin," Bates Papers, container 2, reel 1, LC.
28. Lafayette Baker testimony, AJII, 453–454.
29. Stanton testimony, AJII, 409.
30. Porter, "Booth's Body," 65, 71–72.
31. Aldrich, *Crowding Memories,* 75–76. Edwin Booth to Mrs. Murray, April 27, 1865, reprinted in Clarke, *A Sister's Memoir,* 114.
32. Benjamin Moran diary, August 1, 1866, volume 17, Benjamin Moran Papers, LC.
33. Charles Francis Adams diary, May 6 and 8, 1865, Adams Family Papers, reel 78, LC. Benjamin Moran diary, May 6 and 8, 1865, volume 14, Benjamin Moran Papers, LC. C.F. Adams to Earl Russell, May 6, 1865, FO5/1035, Domestic, May–December 1865, National Archives, Kew, England.

23. "What My Imagination Pictured the Inquisition to Have Been"

Chapter title: August Kautz, unpublished memoirs, 2:20, box 4, AKP.
1. William Eaton testimony, CTPit, 98.
2. Spangler undated statement, John Ford Papers, Ms. 371, MdHS. Ships' logs, USS *Saugus* and *Montauk,* April 23, 1865, RG 24, NA.
3. G.V. Fox to J.B. Montgomery, April 24, 1865, M149, 80:385.
4. Spangler undated statement, John Ford Papers, Ms. 371, MdHS. Ships' logs, USS *Saugus* and *Montauk,* April 23 and 29, 1865, RG 24, NA.
5. G.V. Fox to J.B. Montgomery, April 23 and 24, 1865, M149, 80:385.
6. de Beaumont and de Toqueville, *Penitentiary System in US,* 75.
7. Pitch, *Burning of Washington,* 138. *Daily National Intelligencer,* June 18 and 20, 1864. *Washington Evening Star,* June 17 and 20, 1864.
8. Porter, *Tragedy of the Nation,* 19.
9. Stanton to Joseph Barnes, April 29, 1865, reel 14, ESP.
10. Bulfinch, *Subject of Penitentiaries,* 5, 8.
11. Sullivan, *Behind Prison Walls,* 246–247.
12. Julian Raymond to George Chandler, January 5, 1944, typescript, special collections, National Defense University.
13. Sullivan, *Behind Prison Walls,* 261–262.
14. Hartranft to Hancock, May 1, 1865, Hartranft letterbook, 2, SC, and Hartranft to Hancock, July 8, 1865, Hartranft letterbook, 90, SC.

15. Hartranft to Holt, September 4, 1873, SC. Frederick Aiken to Editor, *Washington Chronicle*, September 17, 1873, reprinted in Porter, *Surgeon in Charge*, 26.

16. Hartranft to Hancock, July 8, 1865, Hartranft letterbook, 90, SC.

17. Hancock to Hartranft, May 1, 1865, HP.

18. Stanton to Hancock, April 29, 1865, container 43, reel 14, ESP.

19. Stanton to Hancock, August 5, 1863, in *Hancock Oration at National Cemetery*, 19, W.S. Hancock Papers, US Army Military History Institute, Carlisle, Pennsylvania.

20. Hancock orders, April 29, 1865, HP.

21. Hartranft to C.C. Augur, May 2, 1865, Hartranft leterbook, 7, SC.

22. James Benton to Hartranft, May 3, 1865, HP.

23. Gambone, *Hartranft,* 33.

24. George Ruggles to John Parker, March 27, 1865, Records of the Adjutant General's Office, General Papers, box 23, RG 94, NA.

25. Hartranft to C.C. Augur, July 14, 1865, SC.

26. Sallie Hartranft to John Hartranft, June 1865, SC.

27. Sallie Hartranft to John Hartranft, March 23, 1865, SC.

28. *Ibid.*

29. Hancock to Hartranft, May 9, 1865, SC.

30. Sallie Hartranft to John Hartranft, May 11, 1865, SC.

31. Hartranft to Hancock, May 3 and 5, 1865, Hartranft letterbook, 8–9, HP. Porter, "Booth's Body," 74. Porter, *Tragedy of the Nation,* 20.

32. Hartranft to Hancock, May 4, 1865, Hartranft letterbook, 11, SC.

33. *Ibid.*, 12.

34. Hancock to Hartranft, May 5, 1865, SC. Hartranft to Hancock, May 5, 1865, Hartranft letterbook, 13, SC.

35. Hartranft to Hancock, May 3, 1865, Hartranft letterbook, 8, SC.

36. Notes of Atzerodt confession, May 1, 1865, discovered in 1977 by historian Joan Chaconas, past president of the Surratt Society, among papers of a descendant of Atzerodt's lawyer, William Doster, copy provided to this author by Chaconas.

37. Hancock to Hartranft, May 1, 1865, SC.

38. Hartranft to Hancock, May 2, 1865, Hartranft letterbook, 4, SC.

39. Thomas Eckert testimony, AJII, 674.

40. *Ibid.*, 673–674.

41. *Ibid.*, 673.

42. Porter to Hartranft, May 1, 1865, reprinted in *Surgeon in Charge,* 9. Hancock to Hartranft, May 2, 1865, SC.

43. Christian Rath interview, *New York Press*, September 4, 1898.

44. Hancock to Hartranft, May 3, 1865, SC.

45. Arnold, *Defence and Prison Experiences,* 59–60.

46. GWD, May 9, 1865.

47. Stanton to James Fry, April 29 1865, reel 14, ESP.

48. *Washington Evening Star,* May 15, 1865.

49. Hartranft to Benton, May 2, 1865, Hartranft letterbook, 6, SC. Hartranft to Hancock, May 5, 1865, Hartranft letterbook, 9, SC. CTPoore, 1:9.

50. *Washington Evening Star,* May 15, 1865.

51. *Daily National Intelligencer,* May 2, 1865.

52. Harris, *Assassination of Lincoln,* 82.

53. Thomas Ewing Jr. to his father, August 22, 1865, box 71, TEFP.

54. James Speed, *Opinion on Constitutional Power of the Military to Try and Execute the Assassins,* reprinted in CTPit, 403–409.

55. Edward Bates diary, May 25, 1865.

56. GWD, May 9, 1865.

57. GWD, May 12, 1865.

58. Charles Meigs to Montgomery Meigs, May 28, 1865, container 24, reel 6, Montgomery Meigs Papers, LC.

59. *Daily National Intelligencer,* May 6, 1865.

60. *Washington Evening Star,* May 9, 1865.

61. Andrew Johnson to the Adjutant General's Office, May 6, 1865, reel 9, ESP.

62. Hunter, *Report of the Military Service,* 7, War Department Special Orders 211, May 6, 1865, SC.

63. Grant, *Memoirs* and *Selected Letters 1839–1865,* (New York: The Library of America, 1990), 2:305–306. 2:305–306.

64. Cyrus Comstock diary, April 19, 1865, reel 1, Cyrus Comstock Papers, LC.

65. *Ibid.,* May 8, 1865.

66. Arnold, *Defence and Prison Experiences,* 10.

67. Cyrus Comstock diary, May 9, 1865, reel 1, Cyrus Comstock Papers, LC.

68. August Kautz, unpublished memoirs, 2:20, box 4, AKP.

69. Cyrus Comstock diary, May 9, 1865, reel 1, Cyrus Comstock Papers, LC.

70. *Ibid.,* May 10, 1865.

71. Speed, "The Assassins of Lincoln," *North American Review* 147, no. 3 (September 1888), 317.

72. CTPoore, 1:6.

73. Arnold, *Defence and Prison Experiences,* 10.

74. CTPit, 18.

75. Hartranft to Hancock, May 9, 1865, Hartranft letterbook, 16, SC. James McPhail testimony, CTPit, 222.

76. Sallie Hartranft to John Hartranft, May 11, 1865, SC.

77. Hancock to Hartranft, May 7, 1865, SC.

78. H.M. Brewster to N.B. Sweitzer, May 11, 1865, HP.

79. Hartranft Special Orders 2, May 10, 1865, Hartranft order book, 73, HP.

24. Weeks of Deprivation and Solitude

1. *Washington Evening Star,* May 22, 1865. Doster, *Episodes of Civil War,* 265.

2. *Washington Evening Star,* May 27, 1865.

3. *Ibid.,* May 25, 1865.

4. *Ibid.,* May 15, 1865.

5. *Ibid.,* May 29, 1865.

6. Marian Hooper to Mary Louisa Shaw, June 2, 1865, in Thoron, editor, *Letters of Mrs. Henry Adams,* 10.

7. *Ibid.*

8. Phineas Gurley to E. Darwin Brooks, May 22, 1865, Phineas Gurley Papers, LC.

9. B.B. French, *Journal,* June 18, 1865, reel 2, BBFFP.

10. Simon Newcomb to Mary Newcomb, June 3, 1865, box 8, Simon Newcomb Papers, LC.

11. Simon Newcomb diary, June 3, 1865, box 1, Simon Newcomb Papers, LC.

12. *Washington Evening Star,* May 17, 19, 22, 29, and 31, 1865.

13. Randall, *Lincoln's Sons,* 172.

14. Richard Watts reminiscences in *Adrian (Michigan) Daily Telegram,* April 17, 1914, reprinted in Surratt Society, *In Pursuit Of,* 203.

15. *The World,* June 2, 1865.

16. Court proceedings, CTPit, 22.

17. August Kautz, unpublished memoirs, May 13, 1865, 2:21, box 4, AKP.

18. *Ibid.*

19. CTPit, 22.

20. Doster, *Episodes of Civil War,* 264.

21. Richard Watts reminiscences in *Adrian (Michigan) Daily Telegram,* April 17, 1914, reprinted in Surratt Society, *In Pursuit Of,* 202.

22. August Kautz, unpublished memoirs, May 13, 1865, 2:21, box 4, AKP.

23. Harris, *Assassination of Lincoln,* 111.

24. Doster, *Episodes of Civil War,* 264.

25. James Ford to Stanton, June 10, 1865, M221, 281:4–5. George Bell to Stanton, June 9, 1865, M221, 281:6–10.

26. *Washington Evening Star,* May 16, 1865.

27. August Kautz, diary, May 16, 1865, box 1, AKP.

28. *Washington Evening Star,* May 15, 1865.

29. *Ibid.,* May 31, 1865.

30. *Ibid.,* June 5, 1865.

31. John Hubbard testimony, CTPit, 166.

32. *Philadelphia Inquirer,* July 7, 1865.

33. CTPoore, 2:5.

34. *Frank Leslie's Illustrated Newspaper,* May 27, 1865.

35. Arnold, *Defence and Prison Experiences,* 16.

36. Hartranft to Hancock, June 2, 1865, letterbook, 49, SC.

37. Hartranft to Hancock, June 1, 1865, letterbook, 48, SC.

38. Arnold, *Defence and Prison Experiences,* 12.

39. Hartranft to Hancock, June 6, 1865, letterbook, 53, SC.

40. Christian Rath interview, *New York Press,* September 4, 1898.

41. Hartranft to Hancock, June 11, 1865, letterbook, 62, SC.

42. Arnold to Thomas Ewing Jr., December 23, 1902, box 248, TEFP.

43. John Ford undated manuscript, Ms. 371, John Ford Papers, MdHS.

44. Henry Welsh to Andrew Johnson, February 3, 1869, Pardon Case Files, box 36, case B612, RG 204, NA.

45. Spangler undated statement, John Ford Papers, Ms. 371, MdHS.

46. Hartranft to Hancock, June 18, 1865, letterbook, 68, SC.

47. Porter, *Tragedy of the Nation,* 19.

48. John Gray to office of military telegraph, June 20, 1865, 10:238–239, ESP.

49. *Ibid.* Hancock to Hartranft, June 18 and 19, 1865, HP. Stanton to Hancock, June 19, 1865, reel 10, ESP. Porter, "Booth's Body," 74.

50. Porter, *Tragedy of the Nation,* 20.

51. Christian Rath interview, *New York Press,* September 4, 1898.

52. Doster, *Episodes of Civil War,* 265.

53. *Ibid.,* 269.

54. *Ibid.,* 265–267.

55. George Porter testimony, CTPit, 168.

56. Joseph Barnes testimony, CTPit, 167.

57. Charles Nichols testimony, CTPit, 163.

58. Doster, *Episodes of Civil War,* 266.

59. Hartranft to Hancock, May 19, 1865, letterbook, 32, SC.

60. *Washington Evening Star,* May 18, 1865.

61. Herold statement, April 27, 1865, M599, 4:444–485.

62. Hartranft to Hancock, May 19, 1865, letterbook, 32, SC.

63. Hancock to Hartranft, May 19, 1865, HP.

64. Hartranft to Hancock, May 20, 1865, letterbook, 33, SC.

65. *Washington Evening Star,* May 20, 1865.

66. G.A. Townsend, in *The World,* June 2, 1865.

67. Hartranft to Hancock, May 29, 1865, letterbook, 44, SC.

68. *Biographical Directory US Congress,* 1892–1893.

69. Francis Walsh, James Nokes, William Keilotz, and Charles Davis testimony, CTPit, 96–97.

70. Samuel McKim, CTPit, 97.

71. Frederick Stone summation, CTPit, 274.

72. *Ibid.*

73. *Ibid.* Boston Corbett testimony, CTPit, 94.

74. Frederick Stone summation, CTPit, 274.

75. Hartranft to Taylor, May 11, 1865, letterbook, 22–23, SC.

76. Hartranft to Hancock, June 7, 1865, letterbook, 55, 57, SC.

77. G. Marrik to Hartranft, June 8, 1865, HP.

78. Hartranft to Wilcox, June 8, 1865, letterbook 59, SC.

79. Hartranft to Hancock, May 12, 1865, letterbook 24, SC.

80. Hancock to Hartranft, May 12, 1865, HP.

81. *Washington Evening Star,* May 15, 1865.

82. *Ibid.,* May 16, 1865.

83. *Ibid.,* May 17, 19, and 27, 1865.

84. *Ibid.,* May 20, 1865.

85. Hartranft to Hancock, June 5, 1865, letterbook, 52, SC. *Washington Evening Star,* June 2 and 5, 1865.

86. Christian Rath interview, *New York Press,* September 4, 1898.

87. Hancock to Hartranft, June 7, 1865, HP.

88. *Washington Evening Star,* June 12, 1865.

89. Hancock to Hartranft, June 19, 1865, HP.

90. Hartranft to Hancock, June 20, 1865, letterbook, 70, SC.

91. Hartranft to Hancock, June 21, 1865, letterbook, 71, SC.

92. *Washington Evening Star,* June 17, 1865.

93. Charles Stonestreet testimony, CTPit, 136.

94. Rachel Semus testimony, CTPit, 137.

95. Weichmann testimony, CTPit, 117.

96. *Ibid.,* 116.

97. *Ibid.,* 115.

98. Frederick Aiken summation, CTPit, 290.

99. *Ibid.,* 292.

100. *Ibid.,* 293.

101. Honora Fitzpatrick testimony, CTPit, 132.

102. Frederick Aiken summation, CTPit, 293.

103. *Ibid.,* 295.

104. *Ibid.,* 294.

105. *Ibid.,* 296.

106. Wallace, *An Autobiography,* 848.

107. Frederick Aiken summation, CTPit, 296.

108. *Ibid.,* 299.

109. August Kautz, diary, 21 June 1865, box 1, AKP.

110. Doster, *Episodes of Civil War,* 277.

111. *Washington Evening Star,* May 19, 1865.

112. William Doster, CTPit, 153.

113. Samuel McAllister, Alexander Brawner, Louis Harkins, and Washington Briscoe testimony, CTPit, 153.

114. William Clendenin testimony, CTPit, 148.

115. John Caldwell testimony, CTPit, 148.

116. John Bingham summation, CTPit, 402.

117. Lew Wallace to Sue Wallace, June 21, 1865, reel 4, Lew Wallace Collection, Indiana Historical Society.

118. B.B. French to Pamela French, June 25, 1865, reel 6, BBFFP.

119. Lew Wallace to Sue Wallace, June 26, 1865, reel 4, Lew Wallace Collection, Indiana Historical Society.

25. "The Trial Concluded at Last"

Chapter title: *New York Times,* June 29, 1865.

1. Richard Watts reminiscences in *Adrian (Michigan) Daily Telegram,* April 17, 1914, reprinted in Surratt Society, *In Pursuit Of,* 205.

2. Bingham argument, CTPit, 351.

3. August Kautz, diary, May 26, 1865, box 1, AKP.

4. *Ibid.,* June 27, 1865, box 1, AKP.

5. Bingham argument, CTPit, 361.

6. Richard Watts reminiscences in *Adrian (Michigan) Daily Telegram,* April 17, 1914, reprinted in Surratt Society, *In Pursuit Of,* 205.

7. Bingham argument, CTPit, 354.

8. *Ibid.,* 356.

9. *Ibid.,* 359.

10. *Ibid.,* 356.

11. *Ibid.,* 363.

12. *Ibid.,* 364.

13. *Ibid.,* 402.

14. *New York Times,* June 29, 1865.

15. *Washington Evening Star,* June 26, 1865.

16. *New York Times,* July 2, 1865.

17. *New York Times,* July 3, 1865.

18. *Washington Evening Star,* June 30, 1865.

19. CTPit, 247.

20. August Kautz diary, June 29, 1865, box 1, AKP.

21. *Ibid.,* June 30, 1865, box 1, AKP.

22. *New York Times,* July 4, 1865.

23. August Kautz diary, July 1, 1865, box 1, AKP.

24. Sallie Hartranft to John Hartranft, June 18, 1865, SC.

25. *Ibid.*

26. Sallie Hartranft to John Hartranft, June 22, 1865, SC.

27. Sallie Hartranft to John Hartranft, July 4, 1865, SC.

28. *Ibid.*

29. Hartranft to Hancock, July 5, 1865, letterbook, 83, SC.

30. Undated *Philadelphia Press* clipping in diary of Lincoln's first attorney general, Edward Bates, reel 2, Edward Bates Papers, LC.

31. B.B. French to Jacob Zeilin, May 29, 1865, M371, 7:552. B.B. French to Jacob Zeilin, October 2, 1865, M371, 7:611.

32. *Washington Evening Star,* July 5, 1865. *Daily National Intelligencer,* July 6, 1865.

33. B.B. French, *Journal,* July 5, 1865, BBFFP.

34. Browning diary, July 4, 1865.

35. Thomas Ewing Jr. to his father, August 22, 1865, box 71, TEFP.

36. *Ibid.*

37. Thomas Ewing Jr. to Sarah Mudd, July 30, 1865, box 165, TEFP.

38. Verdicts and Sentences, container 92, JHP. E.D. Townsend to Hancock, July 5, 1865, HP.

39. Hunter, et al., to Andrew Johnson, container 92, JHP.

40. August Kautz, unpublished memoirs, 2:26, box 4, AKP.

41. Clampitt, "The Trial," 239–240.

26. "The *Posse Comitatus* of the Court Is Not Able to Overcome Armies"
Chapter title: Clampitt, "The Trial," 238.

1. GWD, June 24, 27, 30, and July 8, 1865.

2. Mussey to Holt, August 19, 1873, container 67, JHP.

3. Andrew Johnson to Editor, *Washington Chronicle,* November 11, 1873, reprinted in Bergeron, *Papers of Andrew Johnson,* 16:484–485.

4. *Ibid.,* 16:485.

5. *New York Times,* July 7, 1865. *Philadelphia Inquirer,* July 7, 1865.

6. Mussey to Holt, August 19, 1873, container 67, JHP.

7. Hartranft to Hancock, July 8, 1865, letterbook, 87, SC.

8. *Daily National Intelligencer,* July 8, 1865.

9. *Ibid.,* July 7, 1865.

10. Hartranft to Hancock, July 8, 1865, letterbook, 87, SC.

11. *Washington Evening Star,* July 6, 1865.

12. Hartranft to Hancock, July 8, 1865, letterbook, 87, SC.

13. *Daily National Intelligencer,* July 8, 1865.

14. *Ibid.,* July 7, 1865.

15. *Washington Evening Star,* July 6, 1865.

16. Hartranft to Hancock, July 8, 1865, letterbook, 87, SC.

17. *Washington Evening Star,* July 6, 1865.

18. *New York Times,* July 7, 1865.

19. Hartranft to Hancock, July 8, 1865, letterbook, 87, SC.

20. Stanton to Robert Todd Lincoln, July 6, 1865, M473, 89:848.

21. *Philadelphia Inquirer,* July 7, 1865.

22. *New York Times,* July 7, 1865.

23. Browning diary, July 6, 1865.

24. Clampitt, "The Trial," 234–235.

25. *Dictionary of American Biography,* 397.

26. Clampitt, "The Trial," 235.

27. *Ibid.*

28. *Ibid.*

29. *Ibid.* Brophy speech, *Washington Post,* January 7, 1908, *American National Biography,* 6:790–791.

30. Walter, *Surratt Case,* 2.

31. *Ibid.,* 3.

32. Hardie to Spalding, April 16, 1865, 34-D-10, ASP, AAB, AASMSU.

33. Hardie to Spalding, July 22, 1865, 34-D-14, ASP, AAB, AASMSU.

34. Hardie to *New York Tribune,* July 1865, James Hardie Papers, LC.

35. Walter to Spalding, July 22, 1865, 36-K-8, ASP, AAB, AASMSU.

36. Hancock to Stanton, July 21, 1865, reel 10, ESP.

37. Spalding to Walter, July 21, 1865, letterpress 1865, 141, ASP, AAB, AASMSU.

38. Walter to Spalding, July 22, 1865, 36-K-8, ASP, AAB, AASMSU.

39. Walter, *Surratt Case,* 4.

40. John Brophy, "An Explanation," *Catholic Mirror,* July 22, 1865.

41. Brophy affidavit, July 7, 1865, in Charles Mason to Andrew Johnson, July 7, 1865, series 1, reel 16, AJP.

42. *Washington Evening Star,* July 7, 1865.

43. *Philadelphia Inquirer,* July 8, 1865.

44. Clampitt, "The Trial," 236.

45. Thomas Ewing Jr. to his father, July 7, 1865, box 248, TEFP.

46. Barnard, "Early Days Supreme Court," 4.

47. Clampitt, "The Trial," 236.

48. *Philadelphia Inquirer,* July 8, 1865.

49. *Ibid.*

50. Clampitt, "The Trial," 237. *Philadelphia Inquirer,* July 8, 1865.

51. *Daily National Intelligencer,* July 8, 1865.

52. *Philadelphia Inquirer,* July 8, 1865.

53. Thomas Eckert to J.S. McPhail, July 6, 1865, M473, 89:846. Hartranft, letterbook, 87, SC. Nicholas Crangle, undated statement, entry 38, Correspondence and Reports Relating to Disloyal and Suspect Persons, RG 110, NA.

54. *Philadelphia Inquirer,* July 8, 1865.

55. *Ibid.*

56. *Ibid.*

57. Hartranft, letterbook, 88, SC.

58. *Philadelphia Inquirer,* July 8, 1865.

59. Hartranft, letterbook, 88, SC.

60. *Daily Morning Chronicle,* July 8, 1865.

61. Adam King to C.C. Augur, July 6, 1865, HP.

62. C. Chryter to C.H. Morgan, July 6, 1865, HP.

63. R. Watts to unnamed colonel commanding regiment near Arsenal gate, July 6, 1865, Hartranft letterbook, 85, SC.

64. Hartranft to C.H. Morgan, July 7, 1865, Hartranft letterbook, 86, SC.

65. Hartranft to Taylor, July 6, 1865, Hartranft letterbook, 84, SC.

66. C. Chryter to C.H. Morgan, July 6, 1865, HP.

67. *Philadelphia Inquirer,* July 8, 1865.

68. *Ibid.*

69. Clampitt, "The Trial," 238.

70. Thomas Ewing Jr. to his father, July 7, 1865, box 248, TEFP.

71. Browning diary, July 7, 1865.

72. Speed, "The Assassins of Lincoln," *North American Review* 147, no. 3 (September 1888), 319.

73. Clampitt to T.W. Bartley, July 22, 1880, reprinted in Goodrich, *Life and Public Services,* 226–227.

74. Affidavits: Carlos Syman, December 15, 1892; John Eaton, May 3, 1893; and Basil Norris statement, April 27, 1893, in pension file, application #552322, certificate #349334, T-288, reel 343, general index to pension files 1861–1934, NA.

75. *Washington Evening Star,* July 7, 1865.

76. Anna Surratt to Hartranft, July 9, 1865, SC.

77. *Washington Evening Star,* July 7, 1865. B.B. French, January 12, 1866, in *Witness to Young Republic,* 497.

78. B.B. French to Francis French, April 30, 1865 and July 9, 1865, part 2, box 12, BBFFP.

79. GWD, July 8, 1865. *Philadelphia Inquirer,* July 8, 1865.

80. Bingham to Holt, February 17, 1873, quoted in "The Controversy Between President Johnson and Judge Holt," by Henry Burnett, read April 3, 1889, published in *Some Incidents in the Trial of President Lincoln's Assassins* (New York: Appleton & Co., 1891).

81. Speed to Holt, March 30, 1873, container 100, JHP.

82. Welles to Andrew Johnson, November 5, 1873, in Bergeron, *Papers of Andrew Johnson,* 16:472.

83. Walter, *Surratt Case,* 4–5.
84. Clampitt, "The Trial," 239.
85. Hartranft to Hancock, July 8, 1865, Hartranft letterbook, 88, SC.
86. Clampitt, "The Trial," 238.
87. *Philadelphia Inquirer,* July 8, 1865.
88. *Daily Morning Chronicle,* December 30, 1869.
89. *Daily National Intelligencer,* July 8, 1865.
90. Hartranft to Hancock, July 8, 1865, Hartranft letterbook, 88, SC.
91. *Daily National Intelligencer,* July 8, 1865. *Washington Evening Star,* July 10, 1865.
92. George Coffin diary, July 7, 1865, box 14, George Coffin Papers, Gelman Library, Special Collections, George Washington University.
93. *New York Herald,* July 8, 1865.
94. *Philadelphia Inquirer,* July 8, 1865. *Daily National Intelligencer,* July 8 and 10, 1865.
95. *Philadelphia Inquirer,* July 8, 1865.
96. *Ibid.*

27. "I Could Have Jumped upon the Shoulders of Each as They Hung"

Chapter title: B.B. French to Francis French, July 9, 1865, part 2, box 12, BBFFP.

1. *Washington Evening Star,* July 7, 1865.
2. *Philadelphia Inquirer,* July 8, 1865.
3. Clampitt to T.W. Bartley, July 22, 1880, reprinted in Goodrich, *Life and Public Services,* 224.
4. *Washington Evening Star,* July 7, 1865.
5. *Philadelphia Inquirer,* July 8, 1865.
6. *Ibid. Daily National Intelligencer,* July 8, 1865. *Washington Evening Star,* July 7, 1865.
7. *Philadelphia Inquirer,* July 8, 1865.
8. Hartranft to Hancock, July 8, 1865, letterbook, 88, SC.
9. *Washington Evening Star,* July 7, 1865.
10. Richard Watts reminiscences in *Adrian (Michigan) Daily Telegram,* April 17, 1914, reprinted in Surratt Society, *In Pursuit Of,* 207.
11. *Daily National Intelligencer,* July 8, 1865.
12. *Ibid. Harper's Weekly,* July 22, 1865.
13. Christian Rath interview, *New York Press,* September 4, 1898.
14. *Philadelphia Inquirer,* March 22, 1896.
15. Christian Rath interview, *New York Press,* September 4, 1898.
16. Hartranft to Hancock, July 8, 1865, letterbook, 88, SC.
17. *Philadelphia Inquirer,* July 8, 1865.
18. *Daily National Intelligencer,* July 8, 1865.
19. *New York Press,* September 4, 1898.
20. *Washington Evening Star,* July 7, 1865.
21. *Ibid. Philadelphia Inquirer,* July 8, 1865.
22. Walter, *The Surratt Case,* 5.

23. *Daily National Intelligencer,* July 8, 1865.

24. *Washington Evening Star,* July 7, 1865. *Daily National Intelligencer,* July 8, 1865.

25. *Ibid. Harper's Weekly,* July 22, 1865.

26. *Washington Evening Star,* July 7, 1865.

27. Porter, "Booth's Body," 79.

28. *Washington Evening Star,* July 7, 1865. *Daily National Intelligencer,* July 8, 1865.

29. *Daily National Intelligencer,* July 8, 1865.

30. Christian Rath interview, *New York Press,* September 4, 1898.

31. *Washington Evening Star,* July 7, 1865.

32. *Daily National Intelligencer,* July 8, 1865.

33. *Ibid.*

34. Richard Watts reminiscences in *Adrian (Michigan) Daily Telegram,* April 17, 1914, reprinted in Surratt Society, *In Pursuit Of,* 207. Christian Rath interview, *New York Press,* September 4, 1898. *Washington Evening Star,* July 7, 1865.

35. Hancock to Stanton, July 7, 1865, reel 10, ESP.

36. *Washington Evening Star,* July 8, 1865. *Philadelphia Inquirer,* July 8, 1865.

37. B.B. French to Francis French, July 9, 1865, part 2, box 12, BBFFP.

38. Anna Surratt to Hartranft, July 9, 1865, SC.

39. Anna Surratt to Stanton, July 8, 1865, 10:284, ESP.

40. E.D. Townsend to Anna Surratt, July 20, 1865, 14:538, ESP.

41. Andrew Johnson to Secretary of War, February 5, 1869, M619, 746:77.

42. Holt to Hartranft, August 8, 1885, SC.

43. Hartranft to Holt, August 14, 1885, box 78, JHP.

28. "A Perfect Hell"

Chapter title: Arnold, *Defence and Prison Experiences,* 65.

1. *Ibid.,* 62–63.

2. *Ibid.,* 17.

3. *Ibid.,* 63.

4. Samuel Arnold to his mother, reprinted in *Doylestown (Pennsylvania) Democrat,* July 27, 1867, pasted in *Lincoln Obsequies,* 115, LC.

5. Hartranft notation on orders from Hancock, July 16, 1865, reel 10, ESP. E.D. Townsend to Hancock, July 15, 1865, reel 10, ESP. Arnold, *Defence and Prison Experiences,* 63.

6. Hartranft to Hancock, July 17, 1865, Hartranft letterbook, 105, SC.

7. Hartranft to Hancock, July 8, 1865, Hartranft letterbook, 92–93, SC.

8. Stanton to Hartranft, July 17, 1865, SC.

9. Edman Spangler undated statement, John T. Ford Papers, Ms. 371, MdHS. Arnold, *Defence and Prison Experiences,* 65.

10. George Porter diary, July 20, 1865, in Mary Porter, *Surgeon in Charge,* 36.

11. Arnold, *Defence and Prison Experiences,* 65.

12. George Porter diary, July 23, 1865, in Mary Porter, *Surgeon in Charge,* 37.

13. Edman Spangler to "A Gentleman," undated, *Lincoln Obsequies,* 111, LC.

14. W.J. Keeler to B.C. Cook, January 21, 1869, Samuel Mudd Pardon Case File #B-596, folder 4, NA.

15. Thomas Ewing Jr. to Sarah Mudd, July 1865 [sic], box 165, TEFP.
16. Samuel Mudd to Sarah Mudd, August 24, 1865, reprinted in *The Life of Dr. Samuel Mudd,* edited by Nettie Mudd, 115.
17. Sarah Mudd to Thomas Ewing Jr., August 27, 1865, box 249, TEFP.
18. Sarah Mudd to Thomas Ewing Jr., November 17, 1865, box 248, TEFP.
19. Sarah Mudd to Thomas Ewing Jr., August 27, 1865, box 249, TEFP.
20. Samuel Mudd to Sarah Mudd, September 13, 1867, reprinted in *The Life of Dr. Samuel Mudd,* edited by Nettie Mudd, 259.
21. Supplementary roll of prisoners confined at Fort Jefferson, October 21, 1865, Provost Marshal Records Relating to Prisoners, entry 56, RG 393, NA.
22. G.S. Carpenter to E.D. Townsend, September 16, 1865, Provost Marshal Records Relating to Prisoners, entry 56, box 1, RG 393. Arnold, *Defence and Prison Experiences,* 68–69.
23. Arnold, *Defence and Prison Experiences,* 89.
24. Samuel Mudd to Thomas Ewing Jr., October 11, 1865, box 71, TEFP.
25. Correspondent for *New York Tribune,* September 25, 1865, in *Lincoln Obsequies,* 102, LC.
26. Arnold, *Defence and Prison Experiences,* 69.
27. Samuel Mudd to Thomas Ewing Jr., October 11, 1865, box 71, TEFP.
28. H.R. Prentice to E.D. Townsend, September 1, 1865, Letters Received, Fort Jefferson, entry 4, box 1, part 5, RG 393.
29. Edman Spangler undated statement, John T. Ford Papers, Ms. 371, MdHS.
30. Arnold, *Defence and Prison Experiences,* 77.
31. Edman Spangler undated statement, John T. Ford Papers, Ms. 371, MdHS.
32. *Ibid.*
33. D.W. Whitehurst to C. Crane, December 31, 1867, and George Andrews to Samuel Mudd, February 29, 1868, Samuel Mudd Pardon Case File #B-596, folder 2, NA. George Andrews to Joseph Barnes, September 8, 1867, letterbook, headquarters Fort Jefferson, entry 1, volume 1, RG 393.
34. Paul Roemer to Adjutant General, September 23, 1867, Fort Jefferson Letters Sent Relating to Prisoners, entry 2, part 5, RG 393. Samuel Mudd commentary, reprinted in *The Life of Dr. Samuel Mudd,* edited by Nettie Mudd, 295.
35. Samuel Mudd commentary, reprinted in *The Life of Dr. Samuel Mudd,* edited by Nettie Mudd, 293.
36. William Moore to Joseph Holt, January 29, 1869, reel 43, series 3A, AJP.
37. Jere Mudd to Sarah Mudd, February 18, 1866, reprinted in *The Life of Dr. Samuel Mudd,* edited by Nettie Mudd, 165.
38. Undated petition by Edmund Zabrinski, Pardon Case File #B-596, folder 2, NA.
39. Presidential Pardons and Remissions, February 8, 1869, T967, 4:395–401, NA.
40. Henry Hunt to Adjutant General, March 15, 1869, letterbook, headquarters Fort Jefferson, entry 1, part 5, volume 1, 178, RG 393.
41. Presidential Pardons and Remissions, T967, 4:469–474, NA.
42. Henry Welsh to Andrew Johnson, February 3, 1869, and George Ziegler to Andrew Johnson, February 15, 1869, Pardon Case File #B-612, box 36, RG 204, NA.

43. Presidential Pardons and Remissions, March 1, 1869, T967, 4:474–477, NA.

44. Andrew Johnson to Secretary of War, M619, 746:91.

45. John Vaughan Lewis to Andrew Johnson, February 12, 1869, series 1, reel 36, AJP.

46. Adjutant General's Office to G.D. Ramsay, February 8, 1869, M619, 746:78–79. Anna Surratt to Andrew Johnson, undated, M619, 746:80–81.

47. Louis Schade to Andrew Johnson, February 11, 1869, series 1, reel 36, AJP.

48. Charles Ramsay to E. Townsend, February 16, 1869, M619, 746:82.

49. M.A. O'Laughlin to Andrew Johnson, February 12, 1869, M619, 746:90. Andrew Johnson decree, February 13, 1869, M619, 746:89.

50. Edwin Booth to Andrew Johnson, February 10, 1869, M619, 746:86–87.

51. War Department to G. Ramsay, February 15, 1869, M619, 746:96. Andrew Johnson to Secretary of War, February 15, 1869, M619, 746:97.

29. "Why This Flight, and Why This Concealment?"

Chapter title: Edwards Pierrepont summation, JST 2:1349.

1. Joseph H. Bradley Jr., JST 1:542.

2. Edwin Gray Lee to his mother, April 11, 1865, Edmund Jennings Lee II Papers, special collections, Duke University.

3. Affidavit of Proof, *US v J.H. Surratt,* July 15, 1867, Case 4731, box 1, RG 21, NA.

4. John Surratt lecture, Rockville, Maryland, December 6, 1870, transcript in *Washington Evening Star,* December 7, 1870. Affidavit of Proof, *US v J.H. Surratt,* July 15, 1867, Case 4731, box 1, RG 21, NA.

5. Charles Stewart testimony, JST 1:723. John Cass testimony, JST 1:725. John Reeves testimony, JST 2:840–842.

6. John Cass testimony, JST 1:725–726.

7. William Failing testimony, JST 2:761. Joseph Bradley Jr. testimony, JST 2:766.

8. Lewis McMillan affidavit, September 26, 1865, reprinted in House of Representatives Executive Document 9, 39C 2S, 3. John Surratt lecture, Rockville, Maryland, December 6, 1870, transcript in *Washington Evening Star,* December 7, 1870.

9. Edwin Gray Lee's Canadian diary, April 19, 1865, Edmund Jennings Lee II Papers, special collections, Duke University.

10. Weichmann, *True History,* 221.

11. Lewis McMillan testimony, JST 1:472–473. Charles Boucher testimony, JST 2:903.

12. Charles Boucher testimony, JST 2:903.

13. *Ibid.,* JST 2:903, 914.

14. *Ibid.,* JST 2:896.

15. Lewis McMillan testimony, JST 1:473.

16. Edwin Gray Lee's Canadian diary, August 11, 12, 15, and 18, 1865, Edmund Jennings Lee II Papers, special collections, Duke University.

17. Charles Boucher testimony, JST 2:908–909.

18. Lewis McMillan testimony, JST 1:462–463. John Potter to William Seward,

October 27, 1865, reprinted in House of Representatives Executive Document 9, 39C 2S, 6.

19. Lewis McMillan testimony, JST 1:462.

20. Charles Boucher testimony, JST 2:897–898, 901.

21. Weichmann, *True History*, 362.

22. Lewis McMillan testimony, JST 1:463–464, 466, 474.

23. *Ibid.*, JST 1:469.

24. *Ibid.*, JST 1:474.

25. Lewis McMillan testimony, JST 1:481–83. Henry Wilding to William Seward, September 27, 1865, reprinted in House of Representatives Executive Document 9, 39C 2S, 3.

26. George Sharpe to William Seward, July 1867 [sic], reprinted in House of Representatives Executive Document 68, 40C 2S, 2.

27. Lewis McMillan testimony, February 5, 1867, reprinted in House Committee on Judiciary Report 33, 39C 2S, 14.

28. *Ibid.*

29. Henry Wilding to William Seward, September 27, 1865, reprinted in House of Representatives Executive Document 9, 39C 2S, 3.

30. Henry Wilding to William Seward, September 30, 1865, reprinted in House of Representatives Executive Document 9, 39C 2S, 4.

31. Acting Secretary of State William Hunter to Henry Wilding, October 13, 1865, reprinted in House of Representatives Executive Document 9, 39C 2S, 5.

32. Edwin Stanton testimony, January 10, 1867, House Committee on Judiciary Report 33, 39C 2S, 3.

33. William Hunter testimony, February 4–5, 1867, House Committee on Judiciary Report 33, 39C 2S, 10.

34. Lewis McMillan testimony, JST 1:484.

35. Dudley Mann to Judah Benjamin, November 21, 1863, Official Records of the Union and Confederate Navies in the War of the Rebellion, series 2, 3:963.

36. Benjamin Moran diary, May 8, 1867, volume 18, Benjamin Moran Papers, LC. Charles Francis Adams diary, May 9, 1867, reel 80, Adams Family Papers, LC.

37. George Sharpe to William Seward, July 1867 (sic), reprinted in House of Representatives Executive Document 68, 40C 2S, 3.

38. Rufus King to William Seward, November 25, 1866, M90, reel 10. *Régiment des Zouaves Pontificaux. Liste des Zouaves ayant fait partie du Régiment du 1er Janvier 1861 au 20 Septembre 1870*, volume 1 (Lille: Victor Ducolombier, 1910), 155.

39. Charles Francis Adams diary, May 9, 1867, reel 80, LC.

40. *Régiment des Zouaves Pontificaux. Liste des Zouaves ayant fait partie du Régiment*, 213. Henry St. Marie to his brother Oriel, October 1, 1866, T222, reel 8.

41. Rufus King to William Seward, April 23, 1866, reprinted in House of Representatives Executive Document 9, 39C 2S, 7. A year later St. Marie said they met at Velletri, JST 1:492.

42. Louis Weichmann to Henry St. Marie, April 23, 1863, M599, 3:228–230.

43. John Surratt to Henry St. Marie, April 24, 1863, M599, 7:96–97.

44. Weichmann, *True History,* 24.

45. Rufus King to William Seward, April 23, 1866, reprinted in House of Representatives Executive Document 9, 39C 2S, 7.

46. Henry St. Marie affidavit, July 10, 1866, reprinted in House of Representatives Executive Document 9, 39C 2S, 14–15.

47. Henry St. Marie to Rufus King, April 23, 1866, reprinted in House of Representatives Executive Document 9, 39C 2S, 8

48. Henry St. Marie to his brother Oriel, April 23, 1866, T222, reel 8. William Averell to William Seward, April 1, 1867, T222, reel 8.

49. Henry St. Marie to his brother Oriel, July 25, 1866, T222, reel 8.

50. E.D. Townsend, General Orders 164, November 24, 1865, reprinted in House Committee on Judiciary Report 33, 39C 2S, 3. Henry St. Marie to Ulysses S. Grant, October 11, 1867, reprinted in House of Representatives Executive Document 36, 40C 2S, 3–4.

51. Edwin Stanton testimony, January 10, 1867, reprinted in House Committee on Judiciary Report 33, 39C 2S, 3.

52. John A. Garraty and Mark C. Carnes, eds. *American National Biography* (New York: Oxford University Press, 1999), 12:713.

53. Rufus King to William Seward, April 23, 1866, reprinted in House of Representatives Executive Document 9, 39C 2S, 7.

54. Joseph Holt to William Seward, May 22, 1866. William Seward to Rufus King, May 24, 1866, reprinted in House of Representatives Executive Document 9, 39C 2S, 10–11.

55. Henry St. Marie statement to Rufus King, June 21, 1866, reprinted in House of Representatives Executive Document 9, 39C 2S, 13.

56. Henry St. Marie affidavit, July 10, 1866, reprinted in House of Representatives Executive Document 9, 39C 2S, 15.

57. Rufus King to William Hunter, May 6, 1865, M90 reel 10.

58. Rufus King to William Seward, August 8, 1866, reprinted in House of Representatives Executive Document 9, 39C 2S, 17.

59. William Seward testimony, January 21, 1867, reprinted in House Committee on Judiciary Report 33, 39C 2S, 7.

60. Henry St. Marie to his brother Oriel, October 1, 1866, T222, reel 8.

61. *Ibid.*

62. Henry St. Marie to J.C. Hooker, September 12, 1866, M90 reel 10.

63. Orville Hickman Browning diary, volume 2, October 15, 1866.

64. Rufus King to William Seward, March 2, 1866, M90, reel 10.

65. Rufus King to William Seward, January 14, 1867, M90, reel 10.

66. Rufus King to William Seward, November 20, 1866, M90, reel 10.

67. Rufus King to William Seward, November 2, 1866, M90, reel 10.

68. Captain De Lambilly to Lieutenant Colonel Allet, November 8, 1866, M90, reel 10. Lieutenant Colonel Allet to Minister of War Kauzler, November 9, 1866, M90, reel 10. *Washington Post,* April 3, 1898, Hanson Hiss article, reprinted in Weichmann, *True History*, 447.

69. Henry Lipman, *New York Tribune,* February 21, 1881.
70. *Daily National Intelligencer,* March 25, 1867. *Washington Post,* April 3, 1898, Hanson Hiss article, reprinted in Weichmann, *True History,* 447.
71. Frank Swan to Rufus King, November 21, 1866, M90 reel 10.
72. R.C. Legh to William Winthrop, November 20, 1866, reprinted in House of Representatives Executive Document 25, 39C 2S, 6.
73. Charles Hale to William Seward, November 27, 1866, reprinted in House of Representatives Executive Document 25, 39C 2S, 14.
74. Charles Hale to Charles Francis Adams, December 24, 1866, Records of US Legation, Great Britain, Miscellaneous Letters Sent, second series, volume 11, RG 84.
75. William Jeffers Orders relative to the State Prisoner, for Executive and Watch Officers, M89, 228:443, RG 45.
76. Louis Goldsborough to Gideon Welles, January 8, 1867, M89, 228:439.
77. Louis Goldsborough to Elizabeth Goldsborough, January 5, 1867, Louis Goldsborough Papers, volume 17, LC.
78. *Ibid.*
79. Orville Hickman Browning diary, volume 2, January 25, 1867.
80. Louis Goldsborough to Gideon Welles, January 8, 1867, M89, 228:439.
81. *Swatara* logs, February 17–18, 1867, Logs of US Naval Ships 1801–1915, RG 24. *Daily National Intelligencer,* February 20, 1867.
82. *Daily National Intelligencer,* February 20, 1867.
83. *Ibid.,* March 25, 1867.
84. *Ibid.*
85. GWD, January 31, 1867.
86. Rufus King to William Seward, May 7, 1867, M90, reel 10.
87. Henry St. Marie to Ulysses S. Grant, October 11, 1867, reprinted in House of Representatives Executive Document 36, 40C 2S, 3.
88. Edwards Pierrepont to William Seward, May 20, 1867, Records of Attorney General's Office, Letters Received 1809–1870, box 7, MLR-A-1, entry 9-B, RG 60.
89. Albert Riddle to William Seward, September 26, 1868, Records of Attorney General's Office, Letters Received 1809–1870, box 7, MLR-A-1, entry 9-B, RG 60.
90. George Fisher, *The Trial of John H. Surratt for the Assassination of President Lincoln, by the Judge Who Presided at the Trial,* 7, typescript, box 2, George P. Fisher Papers, LC. William Birth, undated *Reminiscences of the Surratt Jury,* 2, William Birth Papers, LC.
91. *Washington Evening Star,* June 17, 1867.
92. George Fisher, *Trial of Surratt,* typescript, 9, box 2, George P. Fisher Papers, LC.
93. *Washington Evening Star,* June 17, 1867.
94. Indictment, JST 2:1380–1383.
95. *Chicago Tribune,* June 18, 1867.
96. *Washington Evening Star,* June 17, 1867.
97. *Ibid.,* June 21, 1867.

98. William Birth, undated *Reminiscences of the Surratt Jury*, 3, William Birth Papers, LC.

99. Tad Lincoln testimony, JST, 1:525–526.

100. Weichmann, *True History*, 378.

101. Richard Merrick argument, JST, 2:1180.

102. Joseph Dye testimony, JST, 1:132, 134–135.

103. George Fisher, *Trial of Surratt*, typescript, 5–6, 8, box 2, George P. Fisher Papers, LC.

104. Charles Ramsell testimony, JST, 1:498–500.

105. George Fisher, *Trial of Surratt*, typescript, 5, box 2, George P. Fisher Papers, LC.

106. Richard Merrick argument, JST, 2:1187–1188.

107. Charles Wood testimony, JST, 1:494–498.

108. Susan Jackson testimony, JST, 1:162–163.

109. Benjamin Vanderpoel testimony, JST, 1:240–245.

110. Frank Atkinson testimony, JST, 2:730. John Cass testimony, JST, 2:725, 729. Joseph Carroll testimony, JST, 2:733. Charles Stewart testimony, JST, 2:723.

111. Frank Atkinson testimony, JST, 2:730. Joseph Carroll testimony, JST, 2:742.

112. Charles Stewart testimony, JST, 1:723–724.

113. John Surratt lecture, Rockville, Maryland, December 6, 1870, transcript in *Washington Evening Star*, December 7, 1870, reprinted in Weichmann, *True History*, 434. Affidavit of Proof, *US v J.H. Surratt*, July 15, 1867, Case 4731, box 1, RG 21, NA. Almeson Field testimony, JST 2:952–954.

114. Judge Fisher, JST, 2:768–769.

115. Judge Fisher charge to jury, JST, 2:1376.

116. *Chicago Tribune*, June 24, 1867.

117. George Fisher, *Trial of Surratt*, handwritten version, 2–4, box 2, George P. Fisher Papers, LC. *Washington Evening Star*, July 2, 1867, August 14, 1867, and September 28, 1874.

118. Richard Merrick summation, JST, 2:1193.

119. Joseph Bradley Sr. summation, JST, 2:1213.

120. *Ibid.*, 2:1231.

121. *Ibid.*, 2:1237.

122. *Ibid.*, 2:1231, 2:1237.

123. Edwards Pierrepont summation, JST, 2:1349.

124. *Washington Evening Star*, August 5, 1867.

125. Judge Fisher, JST, 2:1374.

126. Judge Fisher, JST, 2:1377.

127. JST, 2:1379.

128. *Washington Evening Star*, August 8, 1867.

129. George Fisher, *Trial of Surratt*, typescript, 16, box 2, George P. Fisher Papers, LC.

130. JST, 2:1379. *Washington Evening Star*, August 10, 1867.

131. JST, 2:1379.

132. George Fisher, *Trial of Surratt*, typescript, 16, box 2, George P. Fisher Papers, LC.

133. William Birth, undated *Reminiscences of the Surratt Jury,* 4, William Birth Papers, LC.
134. JST, 2:1379.
135. Joseph Bradley Sr. to Editors, *Daily National Intelligencer,* reprinted in *Washington Evening Star,* August 14, 1867.
136. George Fisher, *Trial of Surratt,* handwritten version, 4, box 2, George P. Fisher Papers, LC. *Washington Evening Star,* September 28, 1874.
137. S.J. Bowen to Judge Fisher, August 15, 1867, box 1, George Fisher Papers, LC.
138. Criminal Minutes Supreme Court, District of Columbia, case 4731, 7:211–213, case 6594, 6:286, RG 21, NA.

Epilogue: The Scramble for Rewards

1. Bernard Lyons to Adjutant General, December 8, 1865, M619, 455:322.
2. Stephen Merrell to Adjutant General, November 30, 1865, M619, 455:359.
3. George Roder to Adjutant General, December 6, 1865, M619, 455:426.
4. Awards for the Capture of Booth and Others, House of Representatives Executive Document 90, 39C 1S, 8–10.
5. Reward for the Capture of Booth, House of Representatives Report 99, 39C 1S, 3.
6. *Ibid.,* 1–3.
7. John Driggs, *Congressional Globe,* 39C 1S, July 26, 1866, 4186.
8. Omar Conger, *Biographical Directory of Congress,* 727. Undated *Chicago Tribune* feature, "End of J. Wilkes Booth," Herndon-Weik Collection, 14:1537–1538.
9. Thaddeus Stevens, *Congressional Globe,* 39C 1S, July 26, 1866, 4189.
10. Giles Hotchkiss, *Congressional Globe,* 39C 1S, July 26, 1866, 4187–4188.
11. July 28, 1866, 14 Stat. 341.
12. House of Representatives Report 742, 43C 1S, 2.
13. House of Representatives Report 325, 43C 1S, 1.
14. See especially, "First to Aid Lincoln Breaks Long Silence," William Flood interview in *New York Times,* February 28, 1909. Also *Reminiscences of Senator William M. Stewart,* edited by George Rothwell Brown (New York: Neale Publishing, 1908), 191–200. Field, *Memories,* 326

SELECTED BIBLIOGRAPHY

Manuscripts

Archives Center, National Museum of American History, Smithsonian Institution
  Samuel Morse Felton Family Papers #170
  William Pettit Correspondence 1864–1865 #177

Archives of American Art, Smithsonian Institution
  Walter (Thomas Ustick) Papers (original papers at the Athenaeum, Philadelphia)

Associated Archives at St. Mary's Seminary & University, Baltimore, Maryland
  Archbishop Martin John Spalding Correspondence and Letterpress

Auburn University, Auburn, Alabama
  Eckert (Thomas Thompson) Civil War Diary, RG 158

Chicago History Museum
  Abraham Lincoln Papers

Duke University, Special Collections, Durham, North Carolina
  Edmund Jennings Lee II Papers (Edwin Gray Lee Canadian diary 1865)

Ford's Theatre Collection
  John Wilkes Booth diary photocopy and transcription
  Joseph Barnes to Edwin Stanton letter, April 27, 1865
  Robert Stone address to DC Medical Society, May 3, 1865, in Milton Shutes,
    Lincoln and the Doctors, *1933.*

Gelman Library, Special Collections, George Washington University
  Coffin (George Y.) Papers
  Vedder (Timothy) Letters

Georgetown University Library, Special Collections
  Bearden (Margaret K.) Papers
  Maryland Province Society of Jesus Archives

Historical Society of Washington, DC
  Blanchard (Henry) Papers
  Bruff (Joseph Goldsborough) Papers
  Willett (Gordon Arthur) Papers

Houghton Library, Harvard University
  Dix (Dorothea Lynde) Papers

Indiana Historical Society Library
  Lew Wallace Collection

Library of Congress, Manuscripts Division, Washington, DC
  Abbott (Asa Townsend) Papers
  Adams (Charles Francis) Papers (originals at Massachusetts Historical Society)

Bates (David Homer) Papers
Bates (Edward) Papers
Birth (William W.) Papers
Buchanan (James) Papers (Historical Society of Pennsylvania Collection)
Butler (Benjamin) Papers
Carson (Marian) Papers
Cartter Family Papers
Comstock (Cyrus) Papers
Dana (Charles) Papers
Ewing (Thomas) and Family Papers
Fish (Hamilton) Papers
Fisher (George P.) Papers
Ford (John Thompson) Papers
Fowler (Edwin) Papers
French (Benjamin Brown) and Family Papers
Goldsborough (Louis M.) Papers
Grant (Ulysses S.) Papers
Great Britain Foreign Copying Program, Embassy and Consular Archives
Gurley (Phineas) Papers
Hamlin (Hannibal) Papers
Hardie (James A.) Papers
Harrison (James O.) Papers
Hay (John) Papers
Herndon (William Henry) Papers
Holt (Joseph) Papers
Johnson (Andrew) Papers
Kautz (August) Papers
Keene (Laura) Papers
Keifer (Joseph Warren) Papers
Knox (James) Papers
Leale (Charles A.) Papers
Lincoln (Abraham) Papers
Lockwood (Jeremiah) Papers
Low (Francis Sidney) Papers
Mason (James M.) Papers
May (John Frederick) Papers
McCalla (Helen Varnum Hill) Papers
Meigs (Montgomery C.) Papers
Moran (Benjamin) Papers
Morrell (Charles) Papers
Newcomb (Simon) Papers
Nicolay (John George) Papers
Patrick (Marsena R.) Journal
Pickett (John T.) Papers
Pinkerton's National Detective Agency Papers
Poole (Edmund Leicester) Papers

Powell (George) Papers
Ramsey (Margaret) Papers
Rodgers Family Papers
Scott (Winfield) Papers
Seward (William) Papers (Originals at University of Rochester, Rochester, New York)
Stanton (Edwin McMasters) Papers
Stern (Alfred Whital) Collection of Lincolniana
Townsend (George Alfred) Papers
Usher (John Palmer) Papers
Ward (James T.) Papers
Weaver (Henry Clay) Papers
Welles (Gideon) Papers
Wilkes (Charles) Papers
Williams (Margaret D.) Papers
Young (John Russell) Papers

Records of the Confederate States of America, LC

Maryland Historical Society (H. Furlong Baldwin Library)
Booth Papers Ms. 2125
Bruen (Luther Barnett) Papers
Civil War Papers Ms. 1860
Ford (John T.) Papers Ms. 371
Frick (Charles) Family Papers Ms. 2703
Hicks (Thomas) Papers Mss. 1313, 2104
Marine (William M.) Papers Ms. 1016
Mason (Louisa G.) Diary
Patterson (Mary) Correspondence Ms. 1865
Philpot-Randall Family Papers Ms. 2816
Turnbull Family Papers

Maryland State Archives
Thomas Hicks message "To the People," January 3, 1861, MSA SC 295
George Alfred Townsend Collection MSA SC 684

Massachusetts Historical Society
Charles Bowers to Lydia Bowers, May 14, 1861, Civil War Correspondence, Diaries, and Journals at the Massachusetts Historical Society, *microfilm edition, 29 reels (Boston: Massachusetts Historical Society, 1985), reel 15.*
Charles Frances Adams, diary, June 5 and August 5, 1865, Adams Papers, 1639–1889, microfilm edition, 608 reels (Boston: Massachusetts Historical Society, 1954–1959), reels 78, 80.

Museum of the Confederacy, Richmond, Virginia (Eleanor S. Brockenbrough Library)
An Account of the Capture and Death of John Wilkes Booth: An Eyewitness by Miss L.K.B. Holloway

National Archives and Records Administration, Washington, DC; and the National Archives, College Park, MD

House of Representatives Committee on Judiciary Papers, HR 40A-F13.4

Record Group 21, Records of District Courts of the United States

Record Group 24, Records of the Bureau of Naval Personnel

Record Group 42, Records of the Office of Public Buildings and Public Parks of the National Capital

Record Group 45, Naval Records Collection of the Office of Naval Records and Library

Record Group 48, Office of the Secretary of the Interior

Record Group 59, General Records of the Department of State

Record Group 60, General Records of the Department of Justice,

Record Group 84, Records of Foreign Service Posts of the Department of State

Record Group 92, Records of the Office of the Quartermaster General

Record Group 94, Records of Adjutant General's Office, 1780s–1917

Record Group 107, Records of the Office of the Secretary of War

Record Group 108, Records of Headquarters of the Army

Record Group 109 War Department Collection of Confederate Records

Record Group 110, Records of the Provost Marshal General's Bureau (Civil War)

Record Group 153, Records of the Office of the Judge Advocate General (Army)

Record Group 204, Records of the Office of the Pardon Attorney

Record Group 217, Records of the Accounting Officers of the Department of the Treasury

Record Group 233, Records of the US House of Representatives

Record Group 351, Records of the Government of the District of Columbia

Record Group 393, Records of the US Army Continental Commands, 1821–1890

National Archives, Kew, England

Foreign Office 115/12, 1803–1805

Foreign Office, Domestic, May–December 1865, Fo5/1035

Lord Henry Cowley Papers, FO 519/192

New York State Historical Association

Dr. Robert Stone Notes on Lincoln Autopsy

Dr. J.J. Woodward Draft Report on Lincoln Autopsy

Pennsylvania State Archives

Fenn (George Washington) Papers MG 333

Hartranft (John Frederick) Papers RG 393 (originals on deposit, though owned by National Archives)

Shireman Collection

General John Hartranft letterbook 1865 (original at Pennsylvania State Archives)

Sallie Hartranft letters to John F. Hartranft

Anna Surratt letter to John F. Hartranft, July 9, 1865

Miscellaneous correspondence with General Winfield S. Hancock

University of Maryland Libraries (Special Collections)
Hamilton Family Papers
Lanman (Charles) Collection
Keay (Edwin) Diary, Ms. 5433
Preston Family Papers

University of Virginia, Alderman Library (Special Collections)
Westwood A. Todd, "Reminiscences of the War Between the States" unpublished typescript, MSS 3626 (M559)

US Army Military History Institute, Carlisle, Pennsylvania
Burleigh (Hattie) Papers
Hancock (Winfield Scott) Papers

Virginia Historical Society
Grinnan Family Papers Mss1 G8855a

Yale University Library, Manuscripts and Archives
O.C. Marsh Papers

Maps

Geography & Map Division, Library of Congress
Arnold, E.G. *Topographical Map of the District of Columbia, 1862. G3851. S51862.A7 Vault CW674.*
Author unknown. Isometrical view of the President's House, Surrounding Buildings and Private Residences. Washington, DC, circa 1852. 63852-W46A3 1857.
Benjamin, Marcus. *Map Showing Civil War Hospitals, District of Columbia, 1902. G3851.E58 1865.B4.*
Boschke, A. *Topographical Map of the District of Columbia, 1861. G3850 1861 B6 Vault CW678.*

Books, Articles, and Dissertations

Aldrich, (Lilian) Mrs. Thomas Bailey. *Crowding Memories.* Boston: Houghton Mifflin, 1920.
Allen, William C. *History of the United States Capitol.* Washington, DC: US Government Printing Office, 2001
American Historical Review 29, no. 3 (April 1924).
Angle, Paul, editor. *The Lincoln Reader.* New Brunswick, N.J.: Rutgers University Press, 1947.
Angle, Paul M., and Earl Schenck Miers, editors. *The Living Lincoln: The Man, His Mind, His Times, and the War He Fought, Reconstructed from His Own Writings.* New Brunswick N.J.: Rutgers University Press, 1955.
Arnold, Samuel Bland. *Defence and Prison Experiences of a Lincoln Conspirator: Statements and Autobiographical Notes.* Hattiesburg, Miss.: The Book Farm, (Charles F. Heartman), 1943.
———. *Memoirs of a Lincoln Conspirator.* Edited by Michael W. Kauffman. Bowie, Md.: Heritage Books, 1995.

Author unknown. "The Baltimore Plot to Assassinate Abraham Lincoln." *Harper's New Monthly Magazine* 37, no. 217 (June 1868), 123–128.

Author unknown. *The Diary of a Public Man*. Reprints from *The North American Review*, 1879. New Brunswick, N.J.: Rutgers University Press, 1946.

Bak, Richard. *The Day Lincoln Was Shot: An Illustrated Chronicle*. Dallas: Taylor Publishing, 1998.

Baker, Lafayette C. *History of The United States Secret Service*. Philadelphia: King & Baird, 1868, reprinted New York: AMS Press, 1973.

Barnard, Job. "Early Days of the Supreme Court of the District of Columbia." Records of the Columbia Historical Society, edited by John B. Larner, volume 22. Washington, DC: Columbia Historical Society, 1919.

Bates, David Homer. *Lincoln in the Telegraph Office: Recollections of the US Military Telegraph Corps During the Civil War*. New York: Century Co., 1907.

Bates, Edward. *Diary 1859–1866*, edited by Howard K. Beale. In the annual report of the American Historical Association, volume 4, 1930. Washington, DC: US Government Printing Office, 1933.

Biographical Directory of the American Congress 1774–1996. Alexandria, Va.: CQ Staff Directories, 1997.

Boyd's Washington & Georgetown Directory. Washington, DC: Hudson & Taylor, 1865.

Brooks, Noah. "Glimpses of Lincoln in War Time." *Century Magazine* 49, no. 58 (January 1895).

———. *Washington in Lincoln's Time*, edited by Herbert Mitgang. New York: Rinehart & Co., 1958.

Browning, Orville Hickman. *The Diary of Orville Hickman Browning*, edited by James G. Randall. Volume 2, 1865–1881. Springfield: Illinois State Historical Library, 1933.

Buckingham, John E. Sr. *Reminiscences and Souvenirs of the Assassination of Abraham Lincoln*. Washington, DC: Rufus H. Darby, 1894.

Budiansky, Stephen. "America's Unknown Intelligence Czar." *American Heritage Magazine* 55, no. 5 (October 2004).

Bulfinch, Charles. *Report on the Subject of Penitentiaries*. Washington, DC: Gales & Seaton, 1827.

———. *The Life and Letters of Charles Bulfinch, Architect*, edited by Ellen Susan Bulfinch. Boston: Houghton Mifflin & Co., 1896. Reprinted 1973, New York: B. Franklin.

Burlingame, Michael, editor. *Lincoln Observed: Civil War Dispatches of Noah Brooks*. Baltimore: Johns Hopkins University Press, 1998.

Burnett, Henry. *Some Incidents in the Trial of President Lincoln's Assassins*. New York: Appleton & Co., 1891.

Busey, Samuel. *Personal Reminiscences & Recollections of Forty Six Years in the Medical Society of the District of Columbia & Residence in This City, with biographical sketches of many of the deceased members*. Philadelphia and Washington, DC: Dornan (printer), 1895.

Carpenter, F.B. *Six Months at the White House with Abraham Lincoln: The Story of a Picture*. New York: Hurd & Houghton, 1867.

Cavendish, W.H., and Edward Hertslet, compilers. *The Foreign Office List: Diplomatic and Consular Handbook.* London: Harrison, 1861.

Chamlee, Roy Z. Jr. *Lincoln's Assassins: A Complete Account of Their Capture, Trial and Punishment.* Jefferson, N.C.: McFarland & Co., 1990.

Clampitt, John W. "The Trial of Mrs. Surratt." *North American Review* 286 (September 1880). New York: D. Appleton & Co., 1880.

Clarke, Asia Booth. *John Wilkes Booth: A Sister's Memoir,* edited by Terry Alford. Jackson: University Press of Mississippi, 1996.

———. *The Unlocked Book: A Memoir of John Wilkes Booth by His Sister Asia Booth Clarke.* New York: Benjamin Blom, 1938. Reprint, New York: Arno Press, 1977.

Cocke, M. Ritchie Harrison. *Tales My Grandmother Told Me.* Richmond: Dietz Press, 1953.

Cole, Cornelius. *Memoirs.* New York: McLoughlin Brothers, 1908.

Colfax, Schyler. *Life and Principles of Abraham Lincoln.* Address delivered in the Court House Square, South Bend, Indiana, April 24, 1865. Philadelphia: James Rodgers, 1865.

Crook, W.H. *Memories of the White House.* Boston: Little, Brown, 1911.

Crook, William H. *Through Five Administrations,* compiled and edited by Margarita Spalding Gerry. New York: Harper & Brothers, 1910.

Curfman, David R. *"The Medical History of Abraham Lincoln."* *Loyal Legion Historical Journal* 54, no. 3 (1997).

Cuthbert, Norma B. *Lincoln and the Baltimore Plot.* San Marino, Calif.: Huntington Library, 1949.

de Beaumont, Gustave & de Toqueville [sic] Alexis. *On the Penitentiary System in the United States and Its Application in France,* translated from French by Francis Lieber. Philadelphia: Carey, Lea & Blanchard, 1833.

de Chambrun, Marquis Adolphe. *Impressions of Lincoln and the Civil War: A Foreigner's Account,* translated from the French by General Aldebert de Chambrun. New York: Random House, 1952.

Dewitt, David Miller. *The Assassination of Abraham Lincoln and Its Expiation.* New York: Macmillan Co., 1909.

Dictionary of American Biography, edited by Dumas Malone. New York: Charles Scribner's Sons, 1933.

Directions for Recovering Persons Who Are Supposed to Be Dead, from Drowning. Philadelphia: Humane Society of Philadelphia, 1805.

Dolby, George. *Charles Dickens As I Knew Him.* New York: Charles Scribner's Sons, 1912.

Donald, David Herbert. *Lincoln.* New York: Simon & Schuster, 1995.

———. *"We Are Lincoln Men": Abraham Lincoln and His Friends.* New York: Simon & Schuster, 2003.

Doster, William E. *Lincoln and Episodes of the Civil War.* New York: G.P. Putnam's Sons, 1915.

Draper, A.S. "Lincoln's Parable." *Harper's Weekly* (October 26, 1907).

Duvergier de Hauranne, Ernest. *Huit Mois en Amérique: Lettres et Notes de Voyage, 1864–1865,* translated and edited by Ralph H. Bowen as *A Frenchman in Lincoln's America,* 2 volumes. Chicago: Lakeside Press, 1974 and 1975.

Edgington, Frank E. *A History of the New York Avenue Presbyterian Church.* Washington, DC: New York Avenue Presbyterian Church, 1961.

"Edwin Booth and Lincoln." *Century Magazine* 77, no. 6 (April 1909).

Evans, Eli N. *Judah P. Benjamin: The Jewish Confederate.* New York: Free Press, 1988.

Field, Maunsell B. *Memories of Many Men and of Some Women.* New York: Harper & Brothers, 1874.

Fleischner, Jennifer. *Mrs. Lincoln and Mrs. Keckly.* New York: Broadway Books, 2003.

Forney, John W. *Anecdotes of Public Men.* New York: Harper & Brothers, 1873.

From the Letters & Papers of William H. Herndon, edited and compiled by Emanuel Hertz. New York: Viking Press, 1938.

Gambone, Al. *Major-General John Frederick Hartranft: Citizen, Soldier and Pennsylvania Statesman.* Baltimore: Butternut and Blue, 1995.

Garraty, John A., and Mark C. Carnes, editors, *American National Biography,* volume 6. New York: Oxford University Press, 1999.

Gibson, Charles Dana, and E. Kay, compilers. *Dictionary of Transports and Combatant Vessels, Union Army, 1861–68.* Camden, Me.: Ensign Press, 1995.

Gobright, L.A. *Recollections of Men and Things at Washington During the Third of a Century.* 2nd edition. Philadelphia: Claxton, Remsen & Haffelfinger, 1869.

Goodrich, Frederick E. *The Life and Public Services of Winfield Scott Hancock.* Boston: Lee & Shepard, 1880.

Goodwin, Doris Kearns. *Team of Rivals: The Political Genius of Abraham Lincoln.* New York: Simon & Schuster, 2005.

Grant, Julia Dent. *The Personal Memoirs of Julia Dent Grant,* edited by John Y. Simon. New York: G.P. Putnam's Sons, 1975.

Grant, Ulysses S. *Personal Memoirs,* volume 2. New York: Charles Webster & Co., 1886.

Grossmann, Edwina Booth. *Edwin Booth. Recollections by His Daughter, and Letters to Her and His Friends.* New York: Benjamin Blom, 1894, reprinted 1969.

Grover, Leonard. "Lincoln's Interest in the Theater." *Century Magazine* 77, no. 6 (April 1909).

Hanchett, William. *The Lincoln Murder Conspiracies.* Urbana: University of Illinois Press, 1983.

Harris, Thomas M. *Assassination of Lincoln: A History of the Great Conspiracy.* Boston: American Citizen Co., 1892.

———. *Rome's Responsibility for the Assassination of Abraham Lincoln.* Pittsburgh: Williams Publishing, 1897.

Headley, John W. *Confederate Operations in Canada and New York.* New York: Neale Publishing, 1906.

Hendrick, Burton J. *Lincoln's War Cabinet.* Boston: Little, Brown, 1946.

Hertz, Emanuel. *Abraham Lincoln: A New Portrait,* volume 2. New York: Horace Liveright, 1931.

Howe, M.A. DeWolfe. *Portrait of an Independent: Moorfield Storey.* Boston: Houghton Mifflin, 1932.

Hubbell, Richtmyer. *Potomac Diary: A Soldier's Account of the Capital in Crisis, 1864–1865,* edited by Marc Newman. Charleston, S.C.: Arcadia Publishing, 2000.

Hungerford, Edward. *The Story of the Baltimore and Ohio Railroad 1827–1927,* volume 1. New York: G.P. Putnam's Sons, 1928. Reprint, New York: Arno Press, 1973.

Hunter, David. *Report of the Military Services of Gen. David Hunter, USA During the War of the Rebellion, Made to the US War Department 1873.* New York: D. Van Nostrand, 1873.

Hyson, John M. Jr., and Gardner P.H. Foley. "Thomas Brian Gunning and His Splint for Jaw Fractures." *Maryland State Dental Association Journal* 40, no. 1 (winter 1997).

Ingraham, Prentiss. "Pursuit and Death of John Wilkes Booth." *Century Magazine* (January 1890).

Isacsson, Alfred. "A Biography of John Surratt." MA dissertation, Saint Bonaventure University, 1957.

Jackson, Rowland. *A Physical Dissertation on Drowning.* London: printed for Jacob Robinson, 1746.

Johnson, Andrew. *The Papers of Andrew Johnson,* volume 16: May 1869–July 1875, edited by Paul H. Bergeron. Knoxville: University of Tennessee Press, 2000.

Johnson, Arnold Burges. "Recollections of Charles Sumner." *Scribner's Monthly* (November 1874 and June 1875).

Johnston, William. Memorial Address, *Life and Public Services of Edwin M. Stanton.* Cincinnati: R.W. Carroll, 1870.

Jones, Thomas A. *J. Wilkes Booth: An Account of His Sojourn in Southern Maryland After the Assassination of Abraham Lincoln, His Passage Across the Potomac, and His Death in Virginia.* Chicago: Laird & Lee, 1893.

Kauffman, Michael W. *American Brutus.* New York: Random House, 2004.

Keckley, Elizabeth. *Behind the Scenes; or, Thirty Years a Slave and Four Years in the White House.* New York: G.W. Carleton, 1868, reprinted New York: Arno Press and New York Times, 1968.

Kennedy, Joseph C.G. *Population of U.S. in 1860. Compiled from the original returns of the Eighth Census.* Washington, DC: US Government Printing Office, 1864.

Kimmel, Stanley. *The Mad Booths of Maryland.* New York: Dover Publications, 1940.

Kincaid, Arthur. "Redefining 'Mediocrity' and 'Genius.'" *Surratt Courier* 26, no. 1. Clinton, Md.: Surratt Society, January 2001.

Kunhardt, Philip B. Jr., Philip B. Kunhardt III, and Peter W. Kunhardt. *Lincoln: An Illustrated Biography.* New York: Alfred A. Knopf, 1992.

Lambert, William H. *Maj.-Gen. Winfield Scott Hancock: Oration at the National Cemetery, Gettysburg 29 May 1886.* Privately printed, Philadelphia: H.C. Pennypacker, 1886.

Lamon, Ward Hill. *Recollections of Abraham Lincoln 1847–1865,* edited by Dorothy Lamon Teillard. Lincoln: University of Nebraska Press, 1994. Reprinted from the expanded second edition of 1911.

Lattimer, John K. "The Stabbing of Lincoln's Secretary of State on the Night the President Was Shot." *Journal of the American Medical Association* 192, no. 2 (April 1965).

Laughlin, Clara Elizabeth. *The Death of Lincoln: The Story of Booth's Plot, His Deed and the Penalty*. New York: Doubleday, Page & Co., 1909.

Leale, Charles A. *Lincoln's Last Hours*. Estate of Charles A. Leale, New York. Address delivered in New York City, February 1909.

Leech, Margaret. *Reveille in Washington 1860–1865*. New York: Harper & Brothers, 1941.

"Lincoln at the Helm as Described at the Time by John Hay." *Century Magazine* 77, no. 4 (February 1909).

Lindsley, Maggie. *"Maggie!"* Southbury, Conn.: Muriel Davies Mackenzie, 1977.

Longmore, T. "Note on Some of the Injuries Sustained by the Late President of the United States." *Lancet* (June 1865).

Lossing, Benson J. *The Pictorial History of the Civil War*, volume 1. Philadelphia: George Childs, 1866.

———. *The Pictorial History of the Civil War*, volume 2. Hartford, Conn.: T. Belknap, 1868.

Lucas, Virginia Jeans, editor. *Wartime Washington: The Civil War Letters of Elizabeth Blair Lee*. Urbana and Chicago: University of Illinois Press, 1991.

Macrae, David. *The Americans at Home*. Edinburgh: Edmonston and Douglas, 1870. Reprinted New York: E.P. Dutton & Co., 1952.

Maione, Michael, and James O. Hall. "Why Seward? The Attack on the Night of April 14, 1865." *Lincoln Herald* 29 (spring 1998).

May, John Frederick. *The Mark of the Scalpel*. Unpublished manuscript, 1887.

McClure, Alexander K. *Recollections of Half a Century*. Salem, Mass.: Salem Press, 1902, reprinted New York: AMS Press, 1976.

Meigs, Montgomery C. *Capitol Builder: The Shorthand Journals of Montgomery C. Meigs 1853–59, 1861*, edited by Wendy Wolf. Senate document 106-20. Washington, DC: Government Printing Office, 2001.

Moss, M. Helen Palmer. "Lincoln and Wilkes Booth as Seen on the Day of the Assassination." *Century Magazine* 77, no. 6 (April 1909).

Mudd, Nettie, editor. *The Life of Dr. Samuel A. Mudd*. Linden, Tenn.: Continental Book, 1975.

Nicolay, John G., and John Hay. *Abraham Lincoln: A History*, volume 10. New York: Century Co., 1917.

Oates, Stephen B. *With Malice Toward None: The Life of Abraham Lincoln*. New York: New American Library, 1978.

Oldroyd, Osborn H. *The Assassination of Abraham Lincoln: Flight, Pursuit, Capture, and Punishment of the Conspirators*. Washington, DC: O.H. Oldroyd, 1901.

Pendel, Thomas F. *Thirty Six Years in the White House*. Washington, DC: Neale Publishing, 1902.

Pierce, Edward L. *Memoir and Letters of Charles Sumner*, volume 4. Boston: Roberts Brothers, 1893.

Pinkerton, Allan. *History and Evidence of the Passage of Abraham Lincoln from Harrisburg, Pa. to Washington, D.C. on 22nd & 23rd Feb. 1861*. Chicago: Self-published, 1868.

Pitch, Anthony S. *The Burning of Washington: The British Invasion of 1814.* Annapolis, Md.: Naval Institute Press, 1998.

Pitman, Benn, compiler, *The Assassination of President Lincoln and the Trial of the Conspirators.* New York: Funk & Wagnalls, 1954.

Poore, Ben Perley, editor. *The Conspiracy Trial for the Murder of the President and the Attempt to Overthrow the Government by the Assassination of its Principal Officers.* 3 volumes. Boston: J.E. Tilton & Co., 1865.

Porter, David Dixon. *Incidents and Anecdotes of the Civil War.* New York: D. Appleton & Co., 1885.

Porter, George L. "How Booth's Body Was Hidden." *Columbian Magazine* 4 (April 1911).

———. *The Tragedy of the Nation.* Unpublished typescript, undated, Library of Congress.

Porter, Mary W. *The Surgeon in Charge.* Concord, N.H.: Rumford Press, 1949.

Purtle, Helen R. "Lincoln Memorabilia in the Medical Museum of the Armed Forces Institute of Pathology." Bulletin of the History of Medicine 32, no. 1 (January–February 1958), Baltimore, Md.: The Johns Hopkins Press, 1958, 68–74.

Randall, Ruth Painter. *Lincoln's Sons.* Boston: Little, Brown, 1955.

Reck, Emerson W. *A. Lincoln: His Last 24 Hours.* Columbia: University of South Carolina Press, 1994.

Register of Officers and Agents, Civil, Military, and Naval, in the Service of the US on 30 Sept. 1865. Washington, DC: Government Printing Office, 1866.

Rhodehamel, John, and Louise Taper, editors. *Right or Wrong, God Judge Me: The Writings of John Wilkes Booth.* Chicago: University of Illinois Press, 1997.

Ritchie, Donald A. *American Journalists: Getting the Story.* New York: Oxford University Press, 1997.

Salmon P. Chase Papers, The, volume 1: Journal 1829–1872. Kent, Ohio: Kent State University Press, 1993.

———. *Abraham Lincoln: The War Years,* volume 4. New York: Harcourt, Brace & World, 1939.

Sandburg, Carl. *Abraham Lincoln: The Prairie Years and The War Years.* New York: Harcourt, Brace & World, 1954.

Sandburg, Carl, and Paul M. Angle. *Mary Lincoln: Wife and Widow.* New York: Harcourt, Brace, 1932.

Schouler, William. *A History of Massachusetts in the Civil War.* Boston: E.P. Dutton & Co., 1868.

Seale, William. *The President's House: A History,* volume 1. New York: White House Historical Association, National Geographic Society, and Harry Abrams, 1986.

Seward, Frederick W. *Reminiscences of a War-Time Statesman and Diplomat 1830–1915.* New York: G.P. Putnam's Sons, 1916.

Sheads, Scott S., and Daniel C. Toomey. *Baltimore During the Civil War.* Linthicum, Md.: Toomey Press, 1997.

Simon, John Y., editor. *The Papers of Ulysses S. Grant,* volume 14. Carbondale: Southern Illinois University Press, 1985.

Smith, Margaret Bayard. *The First Forty Years of Washington Society.* New York: Charles Scribner's Sons, 1906.

Smith, Michael Thomas. "The Meanest Man in Lincoln's Cabinet: A Reappraisal of Montgomery Blair." Maryland Historical Magazine (summer 2000).

Smoot, Richard M. *The Unwritten History of the Assassination of Abraham Lincoln.* Baltimore: John Murphy Co., 1904.

Speed, Joshua. *Reminiscences of Abraham Lincoln and Notes of a Visit to California.* Louisville, Ken.: John P. Morton & Co., 1884.

Steers, Edward Jr. *Blood on the Moon.* Lexington: University Press of Kentucky, 2001.

———. *The Escape & Capture of John Wilkes Booth.* Gettysburg, Penn.: Thomas Publications, 1992.

Stewart, William M. *Reminiscences of Senator William M. Stewart,* edited by George Rothwell Brown. New York: Neale Publishing Co., 1908.

Stoddard, William O. *Abraham Lincoln: The True Story of a Great Life.* New York: Fords, Howard & Hulbert, 1884.

Sucquet, Dr. J.P. *De L'Embaumement Chez les Anciens et Chez les Modernes et des Conservations pour L'etude de L'anatomie.* Paris: Adrien De La Haye, 1872.

Sullivan, David K. "Behind Prison Walls: The Operation of the District Penitentiary, 1831–1862." Records of the Columbia Historical Society, edited by Francis Colman Rosenberger, volume 48. Washington, DC: Columbia Historical Society, 1973.

Surratt Society. *In Pursuit Of . . . : Continuing Research in the Field of the Lincoln Assassination* (compilation of newsletters). Clinton, Md.: Surratt Society, 1990.

Swanson, James L., and Daniel R. Weinberg. *Lincoln's Assassins: Their Trial and Execution, An Illustrated History.* Chicago: Arena Editions, 2001.

Taft, Charles S. "Abraham Lincoln's Last Hours." *Century Magazine* 45, no. 4 (February 1893), 634–636.

———. "Last Hours of Abraham Lincoln." *Medical and Surgical Reporter.* 12, (April 22, 1865). Philadelphia: Alfred Martin, 1865, 452–454.

Teevan, W.F. "How Were the Fractures of the Orbital Plates of the Frontal Bone of the Late President Lincoln Produced?" *Lancet* 2, no. 105 (fall 1865).

Temple, Wayne C. *Abraham Lincoln: From Skeptic to Prophet.* Mahomet, Ill.: Mayhaven Publishing, 1995.

———. *Lincoln's Travels on the River Queen.* Mahomet, Ill.: Mayhaven Publishing, 2007.

Thomas, Benjamin P., Harold Hyman, and M. Stanton. *The Life and Times of Lincoln's Secretary of War.* New York: Alfred A. Knopf, 1962.

Thoron, Ward, editor. *The Letters of Mrs. Henry Adams 1865–1883.* Boston: Little, Brown, 1936.

Tidwell, William, James Hall, and Winfred Gaddy. *Come Retribution: The Confederate Secret Service and the Assassination of Lincoln.* Jackson: University Press of Mississippi, 1988.

Townsend, George Alfred. "How Wilkes Booth Crossed the Potomac." *Century Magazine* 27, no. 6 (April 1884).

———. *Katy of Catoctin; or, The Chain-Breakers.* New York: D. Appleton & Co., 1887.

———. *The Life, Crime and Capture of John Wilkes Booth.* New York: Dick & Fitzgerald, 1865.

Trial of John H. Surratt in the Criminal Court for the District of Columbia.
2 volumes. Washington, DC: Government Printing Office, 1867.

Trindal, Elizabeth Steger. *Mary Surratt: An American Tragedy.* Gretna, La.: Pelican
Publishing, 1996.

Turner, Justin, and Linda Turner, editors. *Mary Todd Lincoln: Her Life and
Letters.* New York: Fromm International Publishing, 1987.

Wallace, Lewis. *An Autobiography.* New York: Harper & Brothers, 1906.

Walter, Jacob A. *The Surratt Case: A True Statement of Fact Concerning This
Notable Case.* Read before the US Catholic Historical Society, May 25, 1891,
Rare Books, LC.

Warner, Ezra J. *Generals in Blue: Lives of the Union Commanders.* Baton Rouge:
Louisiana State University Press, 1964.

Watson, Winslow M. *In Memoriam: Benjamin Ogle Tayloe.* Washington, DC:
Privately published, 1872.

Weichmann, Louis J. *A True History of the Assassination of Abraham Lincoln and
of the Conspiracy of 1865,* edited by Floyd E. Risvold. New York: Alfred A.
Knopf, 1975.

Welles, Gideon. *Diary,* volume 2. Boston and New York: Houghton Mifflin, 1911.

White, Ronald C. Jr. *Lincoln's Greatest Speech: The Second Inaugural.* New York:
Simon & Schuster, 2002.

Wilkes, Charles. *Autobiography of Rear Admiral Charles Wilkes, US Navy,* edited
by William James Morgan, et al. Washington, DC: Naval History Division,
Department of the Navy, 1978.

Wolanin, Barbara. *Constantino Brumidi: Artist of the Capitol.* Washington, DC:
Government Printing Office, 1998.

Government Documents

An Act authorizing payment of rewards for the capture of the assassins of
Abraham Lincoln and William Seward, 28 July 1866, 14 Stat. 341

Congressional Reports and Documents:

*War of the Rebellion: A Compilation of the Official Records of the Union and
Confederate Armies.* Series 1, vol. 46, part 3.Washington, DC: Government
Printing Office, 1894.

House of Representatives, Report of Select Committee on Alleged Hostile
Organization Against the Government Within the District of Columbia, Report
79, 36th Congress 2nd Session.

House Committee on Appropriations, Petitions & Memorials, 39A-H.2.2 to
HR39A-2.4 and H14.10.

Report of the Board of Metropolitan Police 1865, House of Representatives
Executive Document 1, 39th Congress 1st Session.

Report on Distribution of Rewards, House of Representatives Executive Document
63, 39th Congress 1st Session.

Report on Distribution of Awards for Capture of Booth and Others, House of
Representatives Executive Document 90, 39th Congress 1st Session.

Report of Committee of Claims, House of Representatives Report 99, 39th Congress
1st Session.

Report on Assassination of Lincoln, House of Representatives Report 104, 39th Congress 1st Session.

Report on Discovery and Arrest of John H. Surratt. House Executive Document 9, 39th Congress 2nd Session.

Report on Discovery and Arrest of John H. Surratt. House Executive Document 25, 39th Congress 2nd Session.

Report on Discovery and Arrest of John H. Surratt, House of Representatives Report 33, 39th Congress 2nd Session.

Report on H.B. Sainte-Marie, House of Representatives Executive Document 36, 40th Congress 2nd Session.

Report on Impeachment of the President, House of Representatives Report 7, 40th Congress 1st Session.

Report of George Sharpe, House of Representatives Executive Document 68, 40th Congress 2nd Session.

Report of Committee on War Claims, Report 325, 43rd Congress 1st Session.

Report of Committee on War Claims, Report 742, 43rd Congress 1st Session.

Report of Committee on War Claims, Report 743, 43rd Congress 1st Session.

Report of Committee on Military Affairs, House of Representatives Report 559, 50th Congress 1st Session.

Magazines and Newspapers

Boston Globe
Boston Pilot
Catholic Mirror, Baltimore
Chicago Tribune
Cincinnati Enquirer
Commercial Advertiser, New York
Daily Constitutional Union, Washington, DC
Daily National Republican, Washington, DC
Daily Morning Chronicle, Washington, DC
Daily National Intelligencer, Washington, DC
Evening Star, Washington, DC
Frank Leslie's Illustrated Newspaper
Harper's New Monthly Magazine
Harper's Weekly
London Times
National Republican
New York Herald
New York Press
New York Times
New York Tribune
New York World
Philadelphia Inquirer
Philadelphia Press
Scotsman
Sunday Star, Washington, DC
Washington Post

INDEX

NOTE: Page numbers with letters A, B, and C indicate picture plates.